In Search of the *Way*

Legal Philosophy of the Classic Chinese Thinkers

Wejen Chang 張偉仁

EDINBURGH
University Press

To Yinne Wang 汪瑩
my beloved wife,
sharpest critic
and
best friend

Edinburgh University Press is one of the leading university presses in the UK. We publish academic books and journals in our selected subject areas across the humanities and social sciences, combining cutting-edge scholarship with high editorial and production values to produce academic works of lasting importance. For more information visit our website: www.edinburghuniversitypress.com

Edinburgh University Press Ltd
The Tun – Holyrood Road
12 (2f) Jackson's Entry
Edinburgh EH8 8PJ

Typeset in 10/12 Goudy Old Style by
Servis Filmsetting Ltd, Stockport, Cheshire,
and printed and bound in Great Britain by
CPI Group (UK) Ltd, Croydon CR0 4YY

A CIP record for this book is available from the British Library

ISBN 978 0 7486 6956 1 (hardback)
ISBN 978 0 7486 6957 8 (webready PDF)
ISBN 978 1 4744 1297 1 (epub)

Published with the support of the Edinburgh University Scholarly Publishing Initiatives Fund.

Contents

Periods, Dynasties and Important Persons

Legendary period (*c.* 22nd century BCE)
Huangdi 黄帝 (mid-27th century)
Yao 堯 (24th century)
Shun 舜 (24th century)
Xia 夏 Dynasty (493 years [2205–1767])
Yu 禹, the first sovereign (2205–2198)
Qi 啟, the second sovereign (2197–2188)
Jie 桀, the last sovereign (1818–1767)
Shang 商 (Yin 殷) Dynasty (633 years [1766–1123])
Tang 湯, the first sovereign (1766–1754)
Pangeng 盤庚, who moved the capital and changed the dynastic title to Yin, (1401–1374)
Shou 紂, the last sovereign (1154–1122)
Zhou 周 Dynasty (899 years [1122–221])
Western Zhou 西周 (351 years [1122–771])
King Wen 文王 (–1124)
King Wu 武王, the first sovereign who established the capital in the West (1122–1114)
Duke Zhou 周公, regent before King Cheng 成王 assumed actual government power
King Cheng (1115–1153)
Eastern Zhou 東周 (548 years [770–256])
King Ping 平王, who moved the capital to the East (770–720)
Chunqiu 春秋 Period (242 years [722–481])
Guan Zhong 管仲, chief minister of Duke Huan of Qi 齊桓公 (–645)
Shuxiang 叔向, a minister of Jin 晉 (–528)
Zichan 子產, a chief minister of Zheng 鄭 (–522)
Yan Ying 晏嬰, chief minister of Qi under three dukes (–500)
Confucius 孔子 (551–479)
Laozi 老子, a contemporary of Confucius

Warring States 戰國 Period (246 years [467–221])
Mozi 墨子 (480–390)
Gongsun Yang 公孫鞅, Lord Shang 商君 of Qin 秦 (390–338)
Mencius 孟子 (390–305)
Zhuangzi 莊子 (365–290)
Xunzi 荀子 (340–245)
Han Fei 韓非 (280–233)
Li Si 李斯 (280–208)
Qin 秦 Dynasty (15 years [221–206])
Ying Zheng 嬴政, as king of Qin (25 years [246–221]), as the First Emperor (11 years [221–210])
Han 漢 Dynasty (427 years [206 BCE–220 CE])
Western Han 西漢 (231 years [206–24])
Liu Bang 劉邦, the first emperor (206–196)
Wu-di 武帝, the fifth emperor (140–87)
Xuan-di 宣帝, the seventh emperor (73–49)
Yuan-di 元帝, the eighth emperor (48–33)
Dong Zhongshu 董仲舒 (170–10)
Eastern Han 東漢 (169 years [25–198 CE])
Three-kingdoms 三國 Period (45 years [220–264])
China was divided into three kingdoms fighting one another
Jin 晉 Dynasty (155 years [265–219])
The Western Jin 西晉 (52 years [265–316]
The Eastern Jin 東晉 (103 years [317–219])
South and North dynasties 南北朝 (168 years [420–588])
In the South: Song 宋, Qi 齊, Liang 梁, Chen 陳 dynasties
In the North: North Wei 北魏, Western Wei 西魏 and Eastern Weu 東魏, North Qi 北齊 and North Zhou 北周 dynasties
Sui 隋 Dynasty (29 years [589–618])
Tang 唐 Dynasty (289 years [618–907])
Tai-zhong 太宗, the second emperor (627–649)
Han Yu 韓愈 (768–824)
Five Dynasties 五代 (53 years [907–959])
In the South: Liang 梁, Tang 唐, Jin 晉, Han 漢, Zhou 周 dynasties
In the North: Liao 遼, Western Liao 西遼, and Jin 金 dynasties
Song 宋 Dynasty (320 years [960–1279])
Northern Song 北宋 (167 years [960–1126])
Southern Song 南宋 (153 years [1127–1279])
Yuan 元 Dynasty (88 years [1280–1368])
Ming 明 Dynasty (276 years [1368–1643])
Qing 清 Dynasty (268 years [1644–1910])

Foreword

That Professor Chang Wejen of the Academia Sinica has produced a work for the ages that captures wonderfully the reflections of eight of China's most important and enduring pre-imperial thinkers about the role of legal institutions in a well-ordered (or non-ordered) society should come as no surprise to anyone familiar with this scholar or with his scholarship. Raised on the Chinese classics (major portions of which, as a boy in wartime Suzhou, he committed to memory) and later educated at National Taiwan University, South Methodist University, Yale and Harvard (where he obtained his doctorate), Professor Chang, it is no exaggeration to say, embodies the very best of the different intellectual traditions in which he has been immersed. Not only has his prior work evidenced extraordinary learning, deep analytic acuity, and a thoroughgoing humaneness but he has been a generous, inspiring and ever-patient teacher to those fortunate to have learned from him (as I have been from the time he took me in as a wayward graduate student to the present day).

In *In Search of the* Way, Professor Chang has set himself a most ambitious task. To show the breadth of thinking about the nature and role of law in pre-imperial China, Professor Chang engages eight foundational thinkers – Kongzi, Laozi,* Mozi, Zhuangzi, Mengzi, Shang Yang (Lord Shang), Xunzi and Han Fei. The book commences with a prologue that sets the stage for each that powerfully conveys a sense of the very difficult times in which they lived and that were clearly instrumental in leading them to search for "the Way" in order to move beyond the disorder of their day. With this as background, Professor Chang then treats each individually at length, first offering his own fresh translation of those parts of their *oeuvre* most germane to law and then providing his own detailed analysis of each thinker's vision of proper social ordering (appreciating that some, such as Zhuangzi, scarcely believed in what we would term society) and of the

* Professor Chang acknowledges that the text we know as *Laozi* is "quite probably . . . not a work by a single person but a compilation of short statements by wise old people of ancient times".

place of law therein. The book concludes with an extended essay, in the form of an epilogue, that first considers the political, social, economic, institutional and other implications of these bodies of thought for pre-imperial and imperial Chinese law before ending in a more suggestive manner by raising questions about twentieth- and twenty-first-century efforts at law reform in China and sounding a heartfelt plea for a greater attention to the richness of the Chinese past in any further such undertakings.

The very richness, over several hundred dense pages, that makes this such an impressive volume also belies any attempt to summarise what it has to say about this array of thinkers and the world in which they lived and that they influenced. Suffice it here, in an effort to offer illustrations of that richness, briefly to mention three of its more telling areas of insight. First, whereas many scholars have addressed the sociopolitical background against which the major pre-imperial Chinese thinkers wrote, and an even greater number, of course, have examined the work of these thinkers, Professor Chang enlists the former in a singularly effective manner to illuminate how these thinkers understood legal institutions and their role relative to other institutions. This is particularly so in Professor Chang's treatment of the *Analects* – which itself offers a second example of *In Search of the* Way's power. While the book's portrayal of all eight thinkers is highly nuanced, it is evident, at least to this reader, that Professor Chang's foremost sympathies lie with Confucius, not only relative to the other seven but even compared to latter-day Confucianists (or, as he would term it, Ruists), including such luminaries as Dong Zhongshu, Zhu Xi or Wang Yangming. Be that as it may, Professor Chang adroitly captures Kongzi's view of the advantages of ritual and morality as internalised, contextual, and affirmative relative to law which the Master sees as external, general and negative, and hence, ultimately more a default norm pertinent chiefly to those impervious to more desirable societal norms. And third, drawing on this unparalleled expertise in imperial Chinese law itself, Professor Chang is able in his Epilogue to depict how particular concrete institutions and practices from the Tang onward bear the imprint of the eight early thinkers he considers.

As Professor Chang observes, the very best teachers in the Ruist tradition were more concerned that their students pursue true learning than that they simply reiterate what they heard from their instructors. It is in that spirit in which I conclude this foreword by, as Professor Chang would say, noting that the search for the way itself must recognise that learning itself is a continuous, never-ending process and so suggesting as perhaps worthy of consideration two illustrative questions (of several) prompted for me by Professor Chang's tour de force.

First, while Professor Chang is surely correct in his characterisation of the highly authoritarian view of the world advanced by the *Laozi* (for example, its advice to rulers that they should empty their people's minds and fill their bellies), perhaps there is a stronger case than Professor Chang makes for what might be described as the libertarian vision that Laozi also espouses. Laozi's attack on Confucianism specifically targets that philosophy's reliance on an elaborate hierarchy of human relationships (for example, the five cardinal relationships) and its abiding confidence in wisdom, morality and the capacity of human beings constantly and consistently over time to improve themselves, in important part through education. In their place, Laozi would seem to be arguing for viewing human beings as equals, each endowed with the capacity and need individually to seek the way which, to be sure, he doubts any will attain (with perhaps the journey or process itself, rather than any preordained endpoint, the point). Some may wonder how two such seemingly divergent views could coexist in a single belief system but, even apart from the possibility noted by Professor Chang that the text may represent the work of more than a single person, I see a coherence in the shared disdain of these viewpoints for faith in the idea that humans have the capacity through ritual, morality or even law to tame an inherently unruly world.

Second, while I share Professor Chang's belief that Chinese law reformers would do well to look more concertedly at their millennia-long heritage, both because of the rich intellectual resources it contains and for tactical reasons (so that reforms can more fully be described as indigenously rooted rather than transplanted from abroad), I longed for a more direct treatment of the tensions between modern ideals (such as judicial independence) and historic values (such as the valuing of ethics over legal formality) and with that, more of the wisdom borne of Professor Chang's experience as to how to navigate these tensions. To be sure, these are, at least in broad outline, age-old dilemmas found, to some degree, in multitudinous human societies and, as such, not amenable to full resolution – and yet, I would dearly have relished exposure to more of Professor Chang's thinking about them.

That I might have these and other questions hardly detracts from this massive culmination of a life's worth of thinking by Professor Chang about the Chinese classics (soon, I would note, to be accompanied by his comparable magnum opus about imperial Chinese law). Indeed, he is not only to be lauded – but also to be showered with profound thanks – for going to such lengths to share with the world his singular knowledge and insight – borne from immersion in both China and the West – of pre-imperial Chinese thinking about the nature of law and its place among norms designed to order a disordered world.

William P. Alford
Cambridge
July 2015

Preface

In my youth I had a traditional Chinese education in a small village school with a single tutor teaching nothing but Chinese classics. I memorised many parts of the great canons, including those attributed to the eight thinkers we are to study here. My understanding of them was superficial but, later, after reading more annotations by scholars and doing much cross-referencing in my mind, the meaning became clearer. That made me quite happy. While in college and graduate school studying social sciences and law, I found that what was called "modern" was basically Western and was puzzled that, though many of the topics were also discussed by ancient Chinese thinkers, few of their ideas were mentioned. The reason was not difficult to know: China was defeated by Western powers in the late nineteenth century and had lost confidence in its own culture. But I thought it was regrettable, and often argued, that there is a lot of wisdom in traditional Chinese philosophy that can help all people establish a more balanced view of the world. After decades studying and deliberating this subject, I now venture to present my arguments in print and hope that they may invite people to rethink some of the conventional ideas.

My venture is rather small. I shall study only eight Chinese thinkers of the sixth and the third centuries BCE – Confucius, Laozi, Mozi, Zhuangzi, Mencius, Xunzi, Lord Shang and Han Fei. I choose them because, while there were others who helped the Chinese people solve the problems they encountered in the physical environment and still others who contemplated metaphysical problems, these eight were the foremost among those who tried mainly to address the problems arising from society – which were numerous and serious at their times when the long-established order was crumbling and the world, in Han Fei's words, was in a great strife. This fact interests me as a student of social sciences and law.

Since starting my study I have been thinking about a series of questions. Do humans have to live in society? When they interact, are there norms they have to follow? What are the norms: are they determined by nature, made by a superbeing, some men or inherent in human beings? If there are different kinds of norms, are they equal in value? If they are artificial, who are the norm-makers? Whence their authority? What are their qualifications? What are the bases on which norms should be made? What objectives are norms to pursue? What procedures are the norm-makers to follow? If they do not have appropriate qualifications or if they do not follow the established procedures, can what they make still be norms? How are people to know the norms? If the grounds and objectives are not self-evident, how are they to be understood? What makes a norm something that deserves or compels people's obedience? Can a norm justify itself? If not, is there anything above it by which it is to be judged as good or bad? Can a norm be independent and self-contained? If not, what is there to supplement and support it? What if a norm is illogical or in contradiction to common sense or shared human feelings and experience? What if one norm conflicts with another? Can a norm automatically take effect as a law of nature does? If not, who are to apply and enforce norms? What are their qualifications? How and from where do they obtain the authority? What objectives do they pursue? Justice is often considered as one but what does it mean? Is it the ultimate objective or can there be others? Can long-term harmonious coexistence through sympathy, compromise and tolerance be an alternative? How should they apply norms? Should they apply a norm uniformly in all cases or should they take into consideration particular circumstances in each case? If a norm is vague, what principle should be followed in construing it? What happens to a norm when its *raison d'être* has disappears? What happens if there is not a clear, specific norm to apply? How are norms to be enforced? Would the use of inducements and coercion be enough? Or should education precede it? Or could indoctrination be effective? How malleable are people's mind and behaviour? If, ultimately, punishment is necessary, should it match the offence? Or should heavy punishments be inflicted following minor offences to intimidate and deter serious offenders? Is there a limit on what punishments can accomplish? What if the judicial and law enforcement powers are misused or abused? What if a norm they apply and enforce is itself unacceptable? How should the damage of a wrong application or enforcement of a norm be redressed? What recourse can the victim have? What responsibility should the maker of the wrong application or enforcement have?

Of course, these are some of the widely recognised jurisprudential questions. Among them perhaps the most difficult one is about the objectives of the norms. It is connected with the philosophical question about the meaning of life. What are the objectives of a human being, and of humankind? What is more important in life: the uncertain future or the ephemeral present?

In college and graduate school I learned that thinkers of the West had studied these questions. Because of my early education I was aware that the ancient Chinese also did. What answers did they give? I wanted to know and, for years, I tried to learn and understand their ideas and how they came to have these ideas. I studied the relevant materials in three major categories. First were those that formed the historical background for understanding these thinkers, including inscriptions on oracle bones and bronzes, *Shang-shu* (尚書 *The Book of Historical Documents*, a collection of proclamations of government authorities of the Xia, the Yin and the Western Zhou Dynasties), *Shi-jing* (詩經 *The Book of Odes*, a compilation of folk songs and lyrics for ceremonial music of the same periods), *Chun-qiu Zuo-zhuan* (春秋左傳 *Zuo's Annotations of Chun-qiu*, an annotation to *Chun-qiu*, the annals of the state of Lu from 722 to 481), *Shi-ji* (史記 *The Book of History*, a work about ancient Chinese history from the time of the legendary Yellow Emperor to Emperor Wu [r 140–87] of the Han Dynasty), and several compilations of anecdotes of the Chunqiu and the Warring State periods by scholars of the Early Han Dynasty (206 BCE–AD 24).

In the second category are the works of the eight thinkers themselves, namely, *Lun-yu* 論語, *Laozi* 老子, *Mozi* 墨子, *Zhuangzi* 莊子, *Mengzi* 孟子, *Xunzi* 荀子, *Shang-jun-shu* 商君書 and *Han-fei-zi* 韓非子. Though, by their time, written language was widely used, these works were not entirely written by the presumed authors. *Lun-yu* was a collection of Confucius's words and acts noted down by his disciples. *Laozi* was compiled long after Laozi's time. The other works, with perhaps *Mengzi* as an exception, all included contributions of unknown writers. This, together with the fact that they were hand copied innumerable times over the past two millennia or so, have introduced into these works many inconsistencies. All these works have been edited and annotated by numerous scholars of later times. This is well recorded in the chapters in the official histories of most dynasties on important books existent or known at the time, and attested to by recent archaeological discoveries of several editions of the Classics, such as *Laozi*. Though some newly rediscovered editions contain certain features different from the traditional editions, the differences do not affect the overall themes and, therefore, the meaning and influence of the traditional editions are not challenged.

The third group of materials used for this study are the annotations, especially those by scholars of the eighteenth and nineteenth centuries who, as experts in philology and exegesis perused immense numbers of works relevant to those we discuss here and made amazingly detailed etymological study of crucial words and textual analysis of esoteric statements, thus reducing many misunderstandings and making the works more comprehensible.

Finally in the fourth group are secondary materials. They are countless and I have consulted a large number of them. But, to avoid unnecessarily burdening my readers, I have listed in the bibliography only a few that contain some primary materials not seen elsewhere or some particularly insightful and inspiring views on certain important points in Chinese legal history.

Among the eight thinkers, Mozi stood alone but the others were conventionally grouped in one "school" or another – Confucius, Mencius and Xunzi as "the Ruists" 儒家;[1] Laozi and Zhuangzi as "the Daoists" 道家;[2] and Gongsun Yang and Han Fei as "the Legalists" 法家.[3] Indeed, the theories of those in a school have common threads and emphases, and therefore to study them together or in succession would have an obvious advantage. But I decided to study the individual thinkers more or less in chronological order because each one was significantly influenced by the one ahead of him in time.

Each chapter of this study will appear in two parts, first a translation of the text of a thinker's work relevant to my topic. In doing the translation, I have, of course, consulted the work of others. The better ones are all similar because there are only so many ways in which to translate a text. But I must mention a few outstanding ones here. They are *The Chinese Classics*, *The Tao Te Ching* and *The Writing of Chuang-Tzu* by James Legge; *The Analects*, *Tao Te Ching* and *Mencius* by D. C. Lau; *Tao Teh Ching* by John C. H. Wu; *The Works of Motze* by Yi-pao Mei; *The Complete Works of Chuang Tzu* and *Han Fei Tzu, Basic Writings* by Burton Watson; *The Works of Hsuntze* by Homer H. Dubs; and *The Book of Lord Shang* by J. J. L. Duyvendak. They provide immense help to those who are interested in the eight thinkers but have not read the Chinese original of their works. They also make my translation so much easier and I am grateful. I only tried to make some improvements, and this was possible thanks to the vast number of works of textual analysis and annotations (many of them manuscripts and rare editions) available for me to peruse at the fabulous Fu Sinian Library of the Institute of History and Philology, Academia Sinica, and the invaluable help my colleagues at the institute, especially Professors Chen Pan 陳槃, Wang Shumin 王叔岷, Qu Wanli 屈萬里 and Shi Zhangru 石璋如, generously provided me with for over thirty years.[4] To let my readers see and verify my improvements I have given the page number of the original text after each paragraph of my translation for easy checking.

The second part is my interpretation. Again numerous others have made similar endeavours. What makes mine different is my effort to look at the works in the light of some fundamental jurisprudential principles.

The work attributed to a thinker is often a mixture of many parts, some forming a dominant theme, others not quite relevant or even inconsistent with it. I shall, in my translation and interpretation, present only the main theme and avoid being distracted by side issues. After perusing each work in its entirety to identify its main theme, I shall: explore its background and objectives; examine its presumptions, postulates, propositions, reasoning, implications and ramifications; and then check its conclusions against logic and widely recognised human experience. Though many points discussed by the eight thinkers have also been addressed by thinkers from other cultures, I have refrained from making comparisons because such attempts will inevitably be controversial and most likely not very fruitful.

After my study of the eight thinkers, I shall in the Epilogue quickly go over the theories of the eight thinkers to explore whether they addressed the various questions I raised above, how they influenced one another and people of their time. I shall then present a bird's-eye view of the development of the Chinese legal system thereafter to see how their theories affected it. Finally, because China is now in a period of rapid change, in some ways not unlike the time of the eight thinkers, and the Chinese people are searching for a right way for the future, I think it may be helpful to venture an assessment of the classic theories, their developments and their influences on the traditional Chinese legal system. In my interpretation of the those theories, I shall have already made some critical comments but, being keenly aware that though my focus is on the jurisprudential aspects of those theories, they are closely tied with political philosophy, and political wisdom is circumstantial, therefore, I tried not to make judgements according to values of our times. But the assessment I make in the Epilogue is different. Here I evaluate the legacy of the past in order to help find a course for the future and, thus, I do so in view of the situation of the present. Following the assessment I shall make some suggestions which are, of course, crude and cursory, only to invite deeper thought on the problems China now faces.

The gestation of this book has been very long. Drafts of translations and interpretations have been used as teaching materials for the course on early Chinese legal thought at the University of California at Los Angeles, at Harvard and at New York University. Parts of them were used in my lectures given at other universities in America, the Institute for Advanced Study, College de France and the Catholic University of Leuven, Belgium. I want to thank my students who raised questions and my friends who critiqued my ideas. I am particularly grateful to Professor William P. Alford who co-taught the course with me at Harvard Law School. His questions and comments made me think more carefully and rewrite my presentations many times. This book cannot appear as it is without his precious contributions but, of course, I am solely responsible for errors and shortcomings that remain. Professor Alison Conner of University of Hawai'i and Dr Mary Buck Young edited my drafts and made numerous suggestions for improvements. Professor Anthony Black of the University of Dundee, in Scotland, reviewed my draft and recommended its publication. They deserve my deep gratitude. I am pleased that Mr John Watson of Edinburgh University Press persuaded me to include in this volume not just my interpretations in the form of lectures but also my translations so as to do justice to the thinkers and allow my readers judge my views more accurately. He also suggested that I provide the Chinese characters of some of the key terms to help those who read Chinese determine what the thinkers thought in their own language. I readily agreed and double-checked the original texts and my translations, and corrected the Pinyin of Chinese characters with the help of Dr Li Yan 李燕 to whom I am much obliged. I also want to thank Mr Neil Curtis who tirelessly edited my typescript, making it more succinct and readable, and Mr Eddie Clark at Edinburgh University Press. Finally, I must express my eternal gratitude to Professor Hsu Cho-yun 許倬雲, a Fellow of Academia Sinica, who helped installing me at the Institute of History and Philology of the academy, a scholar's paradise where I did the research and writing of this book.

Wejen Chang 張偉仁
June 2016

Notes

1. In the West this school is generally called "the Confucians". But it is a misnomer. The principles hailed by them were popular long before Confucius's time. He said that he merely restated and explained, not created them. See Liu Baonan, Chapter 7 "Shu-er 述而", Section 1, p. 134. In many paragraphs of *Lun-yu*, he indicated that they were

the products of thinking men of the past. He particularly admired Lord Zhou 周公, one of the founding fathers of the Zhou Dynasty, giving him much credit for those principles. Those who followed them were known as *ru* 儒. Indeed, Lord Zhou himself was later known as a *da-ru* (大儒 great *ru*) and Confucius was known to his contemporaries as a *ru*. It would be ludicrous to call him a "Confucian". Therefore, in this study, he and those who followed the *ru* principles are referred to as "the Ruists". The name should be "rectified" as Confucius would say.

2. Practically all ancient Chinese thinkers discussed *dao* (道 the Way) but Laozi and Zhuangzi did put more emphasis on it as the paramount norm in a specific sense that it actually governs human beings as well as all other things. They thus denied human ability to create a uniquely human life different from that of other things and, mainly for this reason, they were reasonably called "the Daoists".
3. A common dogma of this group is that the ordinary people, being stupid and incapable of caring for their own long-term interests, need a ruler. To govern the people the ruler has to keep a special *shi* (勢 superior position) above them and use various *shu* (術 tactics of control) and *fa* (法 human-made law). Different members of this group placed different emphasis on these three means. They were known in ancient China by different monikers but became generally labelled as "the Legalists" in later times.
4. Inaccuracies in some of the existing translations could have been caused by the following facts: first, in ancient China, a word could be written in different forms and have different meaning in different texts. Moreover, different words could appear in the same form but have the same, or similar, meaning in the same text. Needless to say, this produced confusion. Second, in the time of the Zhou and Han dynasties people usually wrote on wood or bamboo slips and stringed them together, unnumbered. After some time the strings would rot, the slips fall apart, and the order lost. Even if every piece of the slips was preserved, reassembling them could be difficult. Third, most of the works attributed to the eight thinkers were delivered orally first and noted down by listeners later, each according to his own memory and understanding, using the forms of words he was accustomed to. As time passed, the meaning of the words became less clear, different interpretations became more numerous. Scholars of the early Han Dynasty in the first century BCE already had difficulty in reaching a common understanding of many parts of those copies, and they spent much of their effort in making the texts readable. The effort was continued through the later centuries. Remarkable success was achieved by scholars of the Qing Dynasty in the eighteenth century but many of them still had conflicting views. Recent archaeological discoveries of some ancient copies and other related documents have shed more light but provided no conclusions. The work to find the original meaning of the texts is still going on.

Prologue

In times of difficulty most people suffer silently; many complain; a few try to find a way out of the bad situation. The eight thinkers to be discussed in this book are in the last category, each in search of a *Way* that was *the* proper one.

What was their time? Why was it difficult? Was there an earlier period that was better? If there was, what changed it for the worse? What solutions had the thinkers suggested? How should we, more than two-and-a-half millennia thereafter, look at their suggestions? Can we find relevance of their theories to our time and learn anything from them?

To help answer the first four questions, I shall present in this prologue a sketch of the social, economic, political and ideological evolution in ancient China, particularly certain aspects that seem to have specially impressed the eight thinkers, obviously influenced their thinking and were clearly reflected in their works. The next eight chapters are to address the fifth question. An attempt to answer the last two questions will be made in the Epilogue.

(A) China prior to the time of the eight thinkers

At a time in the past when human population was small, what was life like? The eight thinkers had different imaginations in which it appeared either idyllic or harsh. But they agreed that, gradually, the initial "state of nature" began to change because some tribes invented fire, built shelters, domesticated animals, developed agriculture and tackled various problems arising from the people as well as from their environment. According to legends generally accepted by the eight thinkers, one tribe, later known as the Hans 漢族, became dominant because of its many wise leaders, including Huangdi (黃帝 the Yellow Emperor) who established its control of large areas along the Yellow River, and two of his descendants, Yao 堯 and Shun 舜, who governed well and, in old age, each abdicated his position – Yao in favour of Shun, Shun in favour of Yu 禹. Yu was a hero who led people to tame the great floods of the Yellow River and other waterways along which most people lived. The task was colossal and extremely difficult. It was said that he worked so hard that not a single piece of hair was left on his legs and, in seventeen years, he passed by his home three times but did not stop to see his family. The people worshipped him. He became their *gong-zhu* (共主 common ruler or hegemon), and his authority and power greatly increased. When he called a meeting in south-eastern China, leaders of "ten thousand *guo* (國 chiefdoms, later known as states)" came and one of them, arriving late, was executed. After his death his position was taken by his son Qi 啟, a historical figure, who established the Xia Dynasty 夏代 and the hereditary system of transmission of government power.[1]

The Xia was the largest and most powerful among many *guo*. Its hegemony lasted for more than four centuries (*c*.2205–1767 BCE) during which many generations of rulers took Yu as their role model and were attentive to government work although there were no tasks similar to his in scale and difficulty for them to tackle, and the numerous smaller *guo* were largely left alone to mind their own affairs. But, in the end, its last ruler Jie 桀, a tyrant, was defeated in a war initiated by Tang 湯, the ruler of the state of Shang 商, who then became the hegemon and established the Shang Dynasty (1766–1402). Some 335 years later, a descendant of his changed its name to Yin 殷, and it continued for another 279 years (1402–1123). In this long period, most rulers seemed to have kept the lesson of the fall of the Xia and were careful about the welfare of the people. The most notable events were again floods along the Yellow River which forced the Shang/Yin rulers to move the capital repeatedly, each time causing conflicts between them and powerful leaders of tribes and clans who had vested interests in the already cultivated land. But, in each case, the ruler prevailed and the moves brought new order and prosperity. Population grew and agricultural output increased. More people became involved in other activities, among which two were of particular importance. First, it was mining and metallurgy that ushered in the Bronze Age. The new material was used for tools and weapons that further improved the productivity of goods and enhanced the power of armed conflicts. The second, but more important, activity was the improvement of the Chinese written language. Initially, it was carved on animal bones and cast in bronzes to record important events. When writing became more popular, it was used in communication, enabling knowledge and ideas to be spread more efficiently and create a common civilisation. Generally, life became easier, particularly for those in power and those ivolved in trading goods which were now available in much greater variety and quantity. Thus, it was probably not a coincidence that merchants were known as *shang-ren* (商人 the *Shang* people),[2] and those who were well off were characterised as *yin* (殷 rich) and, quite likely, it was during this period the people living along the Yellow River developed a sense of being in the centre of the world, and this sense eventually made them call their abode *zhong-guo* (中國 the Central Country), vis-à-vis the less developed areas on its borders. They called those areas *man-huang* (蠻荒 uncultivated wasteland) and the residents there *yi-di* (夷狄 barbarians).

But *zhong-guo* was not a unified state. Besides the Shang/Yin hegemony there were many smaller *guo* or states which were often at war with one another. In each state, there was a small ruling class and a large number of peasants, labourers and slaves (people of vanquished states and victims of cruel criminal laws). When the economy developed, two new classes – merchants and craftsmen – emerged. They generally sided with the rulers in exploiting the masses and made wealth distribution more inequitable and social unrest more common. The situation was worsened by frequent conflicts on the borders with the "barbarians". Victories won by the *zhong-guo* concentrated more power in the hands of its hegemon, the ruler of the Shang/Yin Dynasty, and corrupted him. The outrageous behaviour of Shou 紂, the last king of Yin, induced an exodus of able officials and a general rebellion led by Ji Fa 姬發, the ruler of Zhou 周, a tributary state. Shou the despot was executed and Ji Fa established the Zhou Dynasty 周代. It was later known as the Western Zhou for its first 351 years (1122–771) when its capital was in western China. For another 548 years (770–222) it was known as Eastern Zhou because its capital was moved to the east. A span of 241 years (722–481) was later referred to as *Chunqiu shi-qi* (春秋時期 "the Spring and Autumn Period") because its major events were chronicled in *Lu Chun-qiu* (魯春秋 the annals of the state Lu). Another span of 245 years (467–222) was known as *Zanguo shi-qi* (戰國時期 Warring States Period) because of incessant interstate wars.

The Western Zhou was largely peaceful and orderly because of a number of measures, including: 1. the establishment of a new sociopolitical system; 2. a series of successful military pacification campaigns; 3. the creation of a new ideology; and 4. the improvement of a two-tier norms system.

First, after vanquishing the Yin, the Zhou ruler, Ji Fa, took a dramatic action known as *feng-jian* (封建 bestowing titles and establishing fiefdoms) by distributing the territory and people of Yin and its allies to the victors, giving the lion's share to himself and smaller portions to his relatives by blood or marriage.[3] He ascended the throne as *wang* (王 the king) and made those who received his largesse semi-autonomous rulers and they, in turn, gave some land and people to their relatives. Thus, unlike the Yin, which let many smaller states stand as independent political entities with the obligation only to pay tributes to it as the hegemon, the Zhou created a special feudal system. It was special because its members were connected by blood or by marriage. For this system, a set of rules known as *zong-fa* (宗法 lineage law) was established that prescribed a special type of primogeniture making the first son born to the patriarch's formal wife the inheritor of his status as the head of the family. In the case of the Zhou Dynasty, such a son in every generation was made the king and they formed the trunk of the founding father Ji Fa's family tree. His other sons were made feudal lords, each to head a branch. In the following generations, the same law would be observed to create more and more smaller branches, all of them submissive to the "trunk".[4]

In addition, some states not allied with the Yin were allowed to exist outside this feudal system, and a few of the aristocrats of the Yin who were opposed to the rule of the despot Shou were also given land and people to form states. In both cases the states were made tributaries of the Zhou.

This new political structure was to ensure, in theory, that everyone in it would be loyal to the king. But it was not readily accepted by everyone. Before it was firmly established, Ji Fa, now King Wu 武王, died, leaving an infant son. His younger brother Ji Dan 姬旦, the Duke of Zhou 周公, became regent but was the de facto king. Two other brothers and the remaining forces of the late Yin revolted. It took years of bloody military campaigns for the duke to pacify and stabilise the situation. To strengthen the feudal system and *zong-fa* rules, he and the later kings recruited senior relatives of the Zhou Dynasty to staff the central government and sent trusted agents to serve as ministers and military commanders in the feudal states. These measures helped keep the king informed of events in the kingdom and the feudal states, and enabled him to suppress unrest and fight foreign wars using the local militias under the command of officers appointed by him. The kingdom was thus made cohesive with an authoritative central government and many submissive feudal and tributary states. Power was concentrated and order prevailed.[5]

The third measure taken by the Zhou was ideological to justify the concentration of power. It was done through religion. Chinese religion was polytheistic. People believed in various deities, spirits and ghosts. During the Shang/Yin period, spirits of deceased ancestors were piously worshiped and their orders strictly obeyed.[6] Then, as a mirror image of the order in the human world, a supernatural one appeared, headed by *shang-di* (上帝 the supreme lord) or, more abstractly, *tian* (天 Heaven), that ruled all superbeings in a hierarchy. After creating this numinous order, the supporters of the human order invented the idea that the hegemon of *zhonggu* was *tian-zi* (天子 Son of Heaven), Heaven's agent on earth. Since the power and authority of Heaven were absolute, so were those of the Son of Heaven. He had *tian-ming* (天命 mandate from Heaven) to rule not only those in the Central Country but everyone in the then known world. This assertion was made by Shou, the last ruler of the Yin Dynasty. When told that the state of Zhou was starting a rebellion, he was surprised and demanded: "Wasn't I born with a mandate from Heaven [to govern the world]?"[7]

Apparently, a "mandate from Heaven" was not enough. But the leaders of the new Zhou Dynasty did not deny its importance. Instead, they added a new veneer to it, alleging that Heaven did not give its mandate haphazardly but only to one who was able to carry out its wishes – one who had *de* (德 virtue), by which they meant the trait of a man who was upright and benevolent to his fellow men. Who was such a man? The Zhou rulers pointed to Yao, Shun, Yu, Tang and certainly King Wu and his father Ji Chang 姬昌who was the ruler of the state of Zhou and now honoured as King Wen 文王. By this allegation, the idea of the ruler of Zhou as the Son of Heaven, with the authority to govern *tian-xia* (天下 all under the Heaven), was reinvented.[8]

More practically, the Zhou rulers improved on the two-tier system of norms – *li* (禮 rites) and *xing* (刑 punishments) – which had been in existence from time immemorial. According to Confucius, all societies in all times have both norms. He thought rites were particularly important and believed that he could know what rites of the Xia and the Yin were like because they all had similar reasons behind them but, because of the passage of time, he could not tell the details of those rites; he was familiar with rites of the Zhou and found them particularly appealing.[9]

In a broad sense, *li* referred to all kinds of rules that were to prescribe how social institutions, including the government, were to be organised and to function, and how individuals were, in different situations, to behave. In a narrower sense, rites were rules of refined, formal conduct observed by those living a privileged, well-off, leisurely life. Such rules prescribed in minute detail how these people were to conduct themselves at specific moments, under specific circumstances, in specific manners that would show their attitudes and feelings properly and elegantly. When they acted in accordance with these rules, their interactions would be smooth and their relationships orderly and harmonious.

How did such rules come about? The ancient Chinese did not see a supernatural origin. Instead, they recognised that, initially, a large number of rites were invented by religious priests to worship deities and ghosts. Then other rules were created for human interactions. While some of these rules were arbitrary, many had bases in custom and most were pragmatic and rational. A great number of them were recorded in *Zhou-li* (周禮 *The Rites of Zhou Offices*) and *Yi-li* (儀禮 *The Etiquettical Rites*) – the former concerning government organisation and operation, the latter individual behaviour. Both works appeared long after the period we are studying; it is therefore difficult to determine how accurate the recordings were but it is safe to say that some of the rules were observed. In the Western Zhou, when members of the feudal system were keenly aware of their close relationship in blood or marriage, and genuinely shared mutual affection and respect, the *zong-fa* rules worked well, problems between states and among individuals, especially the aristocrats, were normally resolved quite amicably before becoming serious threats to public order, by the king or his agents who would enforce the rules and discipline the violators. Thus, along with the feudal system, the *zong-fa* rules contributed significantly to peace and order then. In *Zuo-zhuan* 左傳 we find numerous instances where a significant statement or act of an individual or a government which produced serious consequences was commended by the people of the time as *zhi-li* (知禮 knowing and observing the rites) or censured as *wu-li* (無禮 violating the rites),[10] an indication that the rules were still largely recognised though less uniformly observed in the *Chunqiu* period.

The common people did not have the leisure and means to observe the rites. They were kept in order by a second tier of norms which prescribed prohibitions and punishments. Conceivably, it had existed since great antiquity but, according to *Shang-shu* 尚書, it was Chiyou 蚩尤, a contemporary of Huangdi and a leader of the Miao tribe (苗族 a smaller ethnic group), who created *fa* 法 that imposed five cruel punishments, including cutting off the nose and the ear, tattooing the face, castration and decapitation, to suppress his people who revolted against his egregious rule.[11] The situation of the Han tribe was different. Many generations after Huangdi, his descendant Yao 堯 found no need of punishments. Instead, he ruled by setting himself up as an example of *jun-de* (俊德 great virtue) that help him foster harmonious relationships first between his clan members and then among all peoples and the thousands of tribal states. Criminal provisions were first announced by Shun舜 but he adopted many rules against their wrongful application.[12] During the Xia and Shang Dynasties more punishments were prescribed against crimes committed by the aristocrats and by the commoners.[13] In the early Zhou, because of the special feudal system and the *zong-fa* rules, punishments were again largely reserved for the commoners. But, by the middle of the Western Zhou in the time of king Mu 穆王 (101–946 BCE), the need for criminal law became clearer and the king ordered Marquis Lü 呂侯 to compile a code of punishments. The code was lost but the order survived. It was a remarkable document that discussed many points which, as we shall see, influenced the development of traditional Chinese legal thought, institutions and practices; most importantly, it distinguished *li* from *fa* and placed the former above the latter as the norm for government as well as individual behaviour.[14]

Through most years of the Western Zhou the two tiers of norm seemed to have functioned reasonably well. But there were inherent problems in both of them. The *li* was effective only when the *zong-fa* principles and the feudal structure were properly maintained; and the *fa*, being made by political authorities and devoid of a transcendental or metaphysical justification, and often lacking moral support, had to be enforced by physical power held by the genuine or de facto head of *zhong-guo*.

Starting from the later part of the Western Zhou, the social and political situations began to change. First, the authority of the king waned because of an inherent defect in the feudal system based on the *zong-fa* principle which presupposed that relatives by blood or marriage would always have common interests and feelings of mutual respect and affection. This might be true in the very beginning when the Zhou Dynasty was established but, soon thereafter, this presumption became a fiction as relatives developed divergent or even conflicting interests and because of the simple fact that the king as the head of the trunk lineage could be of an age or a generation junior to feudal lords heading the branch lineages. This fact inevitably made it difficult for the king to demand their submission. Second, the king's power relative to that of some feudal lords declined because, although being initially the largest in size, the royal state was surrounded by feudal states guarding it, leaving little room for expansion, while some feudal states were able to go outwards to open up empty land beyond their borders and thus become larger and more powerful. Some such states even encroached upon the royal territory, and the king was unable to repel the aggression. Third, but most importantly, the supremacy of the throne was undermined by the later kings themselves. They, unlike the founding fathers of the dynasty who cared for the people and restrained from exercising power, lost such good virtues and became arrogant, reckless, inept and decadent, leading the way in ignoring or violating the rites and the principles of *zong-fa*.[15] Thus, gradually, they eroded their own power base by alienating their relatives, the feudal lords and the common people in general. Their claim to the mandate of Heaven became tenuous.

Then a horde of barbarians from the north-west invaded, forcing the king to move the royal capital to the east and begin the Eastern Zhou. The situation deteriorated further. The king became less and less capable of keeping even a semblance of political order in the kingdom. A similar condition emerged in the feudal states where the power and authority of the rulers were gradually usurped by their ministers. Small armed conflicts among the states and the aristocrats within a state became frequent. In the beginning they were often caused by personal grudges of wilful feudal lords or trivial disputes among them. For instance, in 656 Duke Huan of Qi 齊桓公 invaded the state of Cai 蔡 because he was angered by it for arranging a second marriage for Lady Cai, a concubine of his, who was sent home by him temporarily after rocking a boat he was in with her.[16] Such conflicts often involved small forces of a few scores of chariots led by rulers or aristocrats who fought like gentlemen playing martial arts games lasting only a day or two. The purpose was to defeat the other side and teach it a lesson. There could be casualties, even fatalities, but they were to be avoided if at all possible. Thus, in a war between the states of Song 宋 and Chu 楚 in 638, Duke Xiang of Song 宋襄公 refused to attack the Chu troops while they were still crossing a river. Later, after a "proper" fight, his army was defeated and he was fatally wounded, but he still argued that, according to established rites, one should not attack the enemy before its troops had completed their battle formation, nor ambush them in a narrow passage, harm the already injured and capture those with grey hair.[17] In 575 when the states of Jin 晉 and Chu were at war, a Jin general encountered the king of Chu three times on the battlefield and three times he alighted from his chariot, took off his helmet and ran along by the king's carriage to pay his respects. His courtesy was duly reciprocated – the king sent a messenger to him bearing gifts that same evening. In the same year another Jin general, in a battle against the state of Zheng 鄭, told his driver not to chase the Zheng ruler in retreat and humiliate him further.[18]

Another type of war was fought against enemies from outside *zhong-guo* or against feudal lords seriously disrupting order within it. During the Spring and Autumn Period, five feudal lords initiated such wars in the name of the king to uphold his authority and defend the political, economic and social systems of *zhong-guo*. They assembled armies from many feudal states and personally led the campaigns. Because the allied forces were so overwhelming, the battles were not fierce and prolonged, and the victorious leaders were hailed as heroes and became hegemons; among them Duke Huan of Qi 齊桓公 and Duke Wen of Jin 晉文公 were the most famous and much admired by people of their time and thereafter.[19]

Along with these developments some changes in people's behaviour occurred. First, many began to ignore the rites and violate the laws. More importantly, the fact that many evidently virtuous deeds were not rewarded and flagrant transgressions not punished generated in people's minds doubts about Heaven's fairness. Such doubts, expressed in popular folk songs, were later collected in *The Book of Odes*. If Heaven was doubted, how much trust could people have in its agents, the king and the feudal lords, and the norms created by them?[20]

(B) China in the time of the eight thinkers

The time of the eight thinkers (from the birth of Confucius in 551 BCE to the death of Han Fei in 233 BCE) spanned more than three centuries. It appeared to be noticeably different from the previous period because of more political, economic, social and ideological changes.

Politically, the feudal system broke down further. Inside a state, aristocrats intensified their struggle for dominance. They formed partisan cliques and resorted to intrigues, betrayals, assassinations and open armed conflicts. Strife was particularly fierce and brutal between the ruler and the powerful aristocratic families, the heads of which inherited important government offices and their private militias were often stronger than the ruler's army. When the ruler was weak, they usurped his power, controlled him with deceit and intimidation, or replaced him through court coups, murder or rebellion. Many regicides, even patricides, were recorded.[21] A strong ruler, on the other hand, could simply and effectively eliminate the aristocrats. For instance, during his reign (676–651) Duke Xian of Jin 晉獻公 executed the head of every branch lineage of his clan and even exiled several of his own sons. Similar actions were taken by rulers of other states, ruthlessly depriving the aristocrats of their titles, fiefdoms and inherited positions in the government, giving their offices to others, many of them commoners unrelated to the ruler by blood or marriage and therefore easier for him to control. This practice was possible mainly because the mutual respect and affection between the ruler and the aristocrats which gave rise to the *zong-fa* rules were lost.

The economic changes were less dramatic but more profound. The primary cause was population growth. As Han Fei pointed out, it was not uncommon for a man to have five sons who would each have five sons and thus, during his lifetime, a man could have over thirty male offspring. This Malthusian multiplication created above all a pressing need for food and arable land.[22] In the beginning of the Zhou, a feudal state would have a few hundred thousand people living in a small number of walled cities, towns and villages within a territory of several hundred square *li* (里 approximately one third of a mile) separated from the next feudal state by a large amount of waste land. Now it was necessary for every state to make the land it already had more productive and acquire more space beyond its borders.

This expansion took place in a time when the concept of private ownership of land had not yet emerged. Land was generally under the control of those in power – the king, the feudal lords and the lesser aristocrats. They divided what they possessed into many pieces, each with a large lot in the centre and several smaller ones around it. Upon coming of age a commoner man would be assigned a small lot to provide for his family. Together the tillers of the small lots would cultivate the large lot for its aristocratic owner. At certain old age a tiller would return his lot to be reassigned to a younger man.[23] In 594 the state of Lu started taxing arable land regardless of who was tilling it.[24] The new system regulated land use and gave the farmer encouragement for dedicated and intensive farming. It was soon adopted by all other states. In addition, every state began to encourage its people to explore barren land inside and outside its borders. The newly opened-up land was no longer distributed to aristocrats but was placed under the direct control of the state to be managed by magistrates appointed by the ruler, and these farmers were relieved of the burden of paying rents to the aristocrats. The common people responded enthusiastically. As a result, the wealth and power of the ruler were greatly augmented and those of the aristocrats further diminished.

Agricultural productivity was dramatically increased by the use of domestic farm animals, new cultivation techniques and, above all, iron tools which became more common during the Warring States Period. A surplus was produced, commerce and crafts became more widespread, cities with large populations and great concentration of wealth sprang up in many states,[25] and rural areas became less destitute.

But the economic developments also had many negative effects. One of them was the inequitable distribution of wealth. While wealth was created primarily by peasants, labourers and slaves, they were not the actual beneficiaries. A large proportion of their products was taken by the government in taxes; and merchants would buy another portion when it was abundant and cheap, sell it when it was scarce and expensive, thereby making huge profits. As Mencius pointed out, the peasants would toil day and night in a good year barely to get by and would, in a bad one, suffer starvation.[26] Often they needed loans and suffered usury. After the government stopped reassigning land, leaving it to remain with the peasant who could use it profitably, he could still lose it if he defaulted on taxes or loans. Often he had to use the land as collateral for more loans or transfer it outright, at a price, to someone else. Soon the notion of private ownership emerged from such practices, and some people, usually the merchants and those in power, became owners of large tracts of land farmed by hired labourers. The poor became more deprived, and many of them "did not have enough land to stand an awl on its sharp end".[27]

Another downside of the economic development was the increase in frequency and scale of armed conflicts. As some of the feudal states became richer, their rulers launched more aggressive wars to seize loot. During the Spring and Autumn Period of 242 years, 125 wars were fought among the twelve major feudal states, of which thirteen were between the states of Song and Zheng in ten years, all of them due wholly or partly to territorial disputes.[28] Consequently, the number of major feudal states was reduced to six in the Warring States Period. Then, in this period of 246 years, the frequency of war increased further and finally, at the end, the state of Qin eliminated all its rivals and unified China. Over the years the scale of the wars escalated exponentially. The size of the armies was greatly expanded. In the past, a big state of "a thousand chariots" would have about thirty thousand *guo-ren* (國人 men from the cities, towns and nearby farms) as warriors. After the land reforms *ye-ren* (野人 peasants from the outlying countryside, especially the pioneers of new lands) were conscripted as foot soldiers and sent to battles in large hordes. For instance, in 251 BCE, the state of Yan 燕 dispatched six hundred thousand men to attack the state of Zhao 趙; in 223 the Qin 秦 invaded the Chu 楚 with an army of more than eight hundred thousand soldiers. The fighting often lasted for months, even years. Beginning in 300, the capital of a minor state Zhongshan 中山 was under siege by the army of the Zhao for more than five years before being destroyed.[29] The gentlemanly rules of battlefield engagement were abandoned. The immediate aim became completely to eliminate the enemy and grab its land. The human cost was horrendous. Mencius observed that, in a battle to seize a field, the killed would cover the entire field; and, in a fight over a city, the slaughtered would fill the whole city.[30] Indeed, in 292, 242,000 soldiers of the allied armies of the Han 韓 and the Wei 魏 were annihilated by the invading forces of the Qin. Thirty-two years later, in 260, the Qin forces buried alive some four hundred thousand soldiers of the Zhao.[31] To the rulers such wars were necessary. Like beasts trapped in a pit with no food, they had to fight one another or be eaten by their rivals. Such need also made them more draconian and dictatorial in domestic politics so that they could prepare effectively for the fight-to-the-death interstate wars.

Inevitably the political and economic developments brought social changes. Most noticeably, it was the rise of two classes of people. First it was the craftsmen and merchants. After many peasants were freed from their bondage to land owned by aristocrats, and a considerable number of slaves emancipated for having participated in victorious military campaigns, they began to engage in different activities. Crafts and commerce were the popular choices. There were those who invented or improved agricultural and other tools and produced useful wares, and those who created devices for warfare. They were much welcomed and honoured.[32] There were those who made fine art objects or wonderful gadgets, perhaps only to demonstrate their ingenuity but more likely to cater for the idle rich and earn great profits.[33] Then there were hoaxers, such as a fraudster reported in *Han-fei-zi*, who, claiming to have the skill of carving a monkey on the tip of a thorn, won free food and lodging for many months from a gullible ruler of the state of Yan.[34]

Commerce became necessary and more popular. Even Zigong 子貢, a prominent disciple of Confucius, engaged in it and became a successful merchant. Some businessmen conducted themselves admirably. For example, in 627 a travelling trader, named Xian Gao 弦高, by chance encountered an army from the state of Qin on its way to invade Zheng 鄭, his home state. On his own initiative, he offered four cowhides and ten oxen as gifts from the Zheng ruler to the army's commander, leading him to believe that Zheng was prepared and therefore to cancel his plan for a surprise attack.[35] Fan Li 范蠡, a minister of the state of Yue 越 who, after helping vanquish its enemy the state of Wu 吳 in 473, resigned from office and, within nineteen years, three times made fortunes worth over a thousand *taels* of gold and three times gave them away to the poor.[36] A few merchants were directly involved in politics. The most notorious example was Lü Buwei 呂不韋 (*c*.290–235) who was made the chief minister of the state of Qin partly because his schemes and financial contributions had helped put a minor prince of that state on its throne in 249.[37]

On the other hand, ordinary businessmen, shrewd seekers of gain at the expense of the needy, were despised by the people and oppressed by the government, especially one in the hands of the Legalists, because it perceived them, particularly those travelling traders, as being without roots. In Lord Shang's words, they "had their capital carried on their body"[38] and constantly moved around chasing profits. It was difficult for the authorities to track them and hold them responsible for their actions. Quite likely, this view prompted Guan Zhong 管仲, a chief minister of the state of Qi around 685 to 645 and a forerunner of the Legalists, to order people to have fixed domiciles and engage in fixed trades generation after generation.[39] This policy was less applicable to merchants but their activities were strictly restricted by the government of Lord Shang and many others of his and later times.

Another class of people, known as *shi* 士, became prominent by this time. Originally they were probably men who made minor contributions to the establishment of the Zhou Dynasty and were therefore brought into the feudal system at its lowest level to provide it with some basic government services. They were neither producers of any material goods, as peasants, labourers and craftsmen were, nor traders who move such goods as merchandise. They were just employees of the feudal system. But they enjoyed few of the system's privileges except a special kind of education which taught the aristocrats *liu-yi* (六藝 the six arts), namely, *li* (禮 rites), *yue* (樂 music), *shu* (書 reading and writing), *yu* (御 charioteering), *she* (射 archery) and *shu* (數 mathematics). Those who learned well could be chosen for a better post in the government. But, as time passed, their chances became slimmer because they were joined by more and more descendants of those at higher levels of the system who, not being in the trunk lineage, received fewer and fewer benefits and fell into poverty. Such disenfranchised aristocrats became *shi* and had to find work. A few *shi* were successful but many were left unemployed. Among them, some, known as *xia-shi* 俠士, were strong-willed men of action. They often challenged the authorities and rules of the feudal system, ridiculed conventional wisdom and norms, hailed a brand of honour and justice popular among the oppressed common people, and, in some cases, led them to rob the rich. An interesting portrait of such a character appeared in *Zhuangzi* as Dao Zhi (盜跖 Robber Zhi), at whose hands Confucius suffered great humiliation.[40]

Another group was known as *ru-shi* 儒士. Though the term *ru* was later used to denote Confucians, it originally referred to men of thought and learning and mild temperament. Practically all of them wanted to serve in the government but, when there were few opportunities, many took up teaching as a profession to educate mostly the commoners and lived on the meagre tuition fees they were paid. The best among them constructed elaborate theories and were honoured as founders of various schools of thought, including the Ruists 儒家, the Daoists道家, the Mohists 墨家, the Legalists 法家, the Military Strategists 兵家, the Agriculturists 農家, the Logicians 名家, the Diplomatists 縱橫家, the Astrologers 陰陽家, and so on. They can simply be called the intellectuals.[41]

The authorities generally disliked *xia-shi* for obvious reasons, though some aristocrats employed them to attack or assassinate their enemies. The intellectuals were treated differently. Many people in power befriended them because of their learning and refined manners. High ministers often had them as guests, advisers or assistants. In the second half of the fourth century, King Wei of Qi 齊威王 (r 356–320) built a large campus outside the Ji Gate 稷門 of the capital city for hundreds of the intellectuals. Known as "masters of the Ji Academy", they lived there in comfort and leisurely spent their time studying, lecturing and discussing myriad social, philosophical and scientific subjects.[42] After a sojourn there, many of them entered government service, and some were appointed ministers immediately after a few interviews with state rulers. Why at this time was their fortune so dramatically changed for the better? It was because the struggles between the state rulers and ambitious aristocrats had become fiercer, and they both needed help from the intellectuals who were by then more sophisticated in analysing the situation and designing tactics and strategies. These facts gave the intellectuals high expectations and exalted self-esteem. They regarded themselves not merely as teachers of the people but more as tutors of the aristocrats and administrators of government affairs.

It has been pointed out that, before the period we are studying, people already had doubts about the authority of Heaven, deities and spirits. In this period, the common people expressed these doubts and protested against Heaven's injustice more frequently and vociferously. In many folk songs collected in *The Book of Odes*, the hard-pressed working people asked why the aristocrats, who never toiled in the fields, were entitled to so much of the produce and, referring to them as *shuo-shu* (碩鼠 big rats), audaciously told them not to devour the harvests.[43] Many in the ruling class stated that *tian-dao* (天道 the way of Heaven) was remote and inscrutable but *ren-dao* (人道 the way of man) was comprehensible and easy to follow, and therefore emphasised that there were no doors leading to good or bad fortune, and a person's success or failure depended entirely on his own efforts. Following this logic, some enlightened aristocrats went as far as maintaining that actually the people were the masters of the gods.[44]

Such thoughts diminished the reverence people had in their minds for the supernatural forces that were supposed to guide and judge people's behaviour. Then people naturally began to question the meaning and utility of the primary norm, the rites, which were created initially to pay respect to gods and spirits and to pray for their blessings. Not getting a satisfactory answer, some people simplified such rites or made them mere formalities. The *zong-fa* rules for the feudal system naturally lost significance when the lineage network frayed. As mentioned earlier, the decline started with inappropriate conduct among those in high stations: for instance, some kings of the Eastern Zhou began to ask for petty gifts from the feudal lords and fought them over small tracts of land.[45] Such events belittled the king and emboldened some aristocrats to act with insolence and audacity. As an example, a minister of the state of Lu 魯 staged in his residence pantomimes of eight rows of dancers, prompting Confucius to condemn it as intolerable because, according to rites, such performance was allowed only in the royal court of the Zhou king.[46] In interstate relations, rites were once of great importance but, by this time, many rulers and officials did not know how to behave properly on diplomatic occasions. And in wars, the elaborate rites mentioned earlier were gone: when the objective was simply to win and loot, the armed conflict became barbaric and brutal. In the everyday life of the ordinary people rites did not mean much to begin with and now, to Confucius's consternation, they were regarded just as rituals involving the use of some ornamental objects of jade and silk.[47] Thus, people of different status either did not know, or disregarded or abused, rites. In any case, when rites, as rules of proper and refined conduct, were lost, people in general became rudderless and behaved wildly and unscrupulously in pursuit of nothing but personal gratification and aggrandisement.

Thus, in a little over three centuries from Confucius's birth to Han Fei's death, the vestige of the state created by the Zhou founders, which was supported by the *feng-jian* system and governed by the *zong-fa* principles, fell into great disorder where mutual respect and affection among the feudal aristocrats were completely lost. The world entered into what Han Fei called *da-zheng zhi shi* (大爭之世 a situation of great struggles).

(C) Practical responses from the authorities to the ideas of the thinkers

This situation especially alarmed those with government responsibilities. They all wanted to change it for the better, and they needed rules in addition to power. Their first reaction was to revive the primary norm, the rites. By this means a few powerful feudal lords rose to impose order on their own states and on the interstate relations. Among them the most successful was Duke Huan of Qi 齊桓公 (r 685–645). First, he and his chief minister Guan Zhong initiated measures to make the state of Qi socially and militarily better organised and disciplined, turning it into a powerful machine[48] with which the duke was able to launch campaigns against barbarians invading *zhong-guo*, arbitrate disputes among the feudal states, stop their armed conflicts, and sanction against those who disobeyed. Nine times he, as the hegemon, summoned the rulers of major feudal states to sign treaties guaranteeing peace and order in the feudal system.[49] In the 651 Treaty of Kui-qiu 葵邱 the parties swore to good relationship and, according to Mencius, agreed: 1. to punish those who violated filial piety, and not to repudiate a lawful heir nor make a concubine a wife; 2. to honour the worthy, to nourish the talented and to give public recognition to the virtuous; 3. to respect the old, to be kind to the young, and not to neglect guests and travellers; 4. not to let a government post be kept by a family as its inheritance, not to allow an official to keep more than one job but to choose a right person for every post, and not to execute officials without authorisation from the king; and 5. not to construct dams to impede water flowing through neighbouring states, not to prevent the export of foodstuffs to states in need, and not to endow fiefs on anyone without reporting to the king.[50] Many of these agreements were obviously to uphold the rites supporting the *zong-fa* and the feudal system. In a ceremony to celebrate the treaty, the king bestowed great honour on the duke and told him not to perform the rite of kowtow in response. But the duke did it nevertheless with grave humility.[51] It was a good performance – a senior, powerful feudal lord submitting to a junior, weak king to maintain an elaborate, antiquated etiquette. Performances similar to this were staged by other hegemons of later times but, in reality, all were just mockeries as these actors actually committed the most serious offences against the *zong-fa* rules and the feudal system by actually usurping the authority of the king and swallowing up many smaller feudal states – Duke Huan vanquished more than thirty of them while other hegemons eliminated more. Thus, the hegemons' apparent observance of rites only whitewashed their egregious deeds. Under them, the disintegration of order accelerated.

Others in power attempted to restore order by use of the secondary norm – law. They tried, first of all, to make it more publicised and better known and trusted. In 536 Zichan 子產, chief minister of the state of Zheng, cast a bronze vessel with the state's *xing-shu* (刑書 criminal code) inscribed on it and put it on public display. That was an innovation. In the past, while special government orders were announced and disseminated by word of mouth, general laws governing people's everyday activities were not spelled out. Shuxiang 叔向, a senior statesman of the state of Jin 晉, was disappointed by the unprecedented act of Zichan and lectured him, saying that, in the past, a good ruler, who feared that people might dispute a law, would not publicise it. He would apply it strictly but would keep its basic principles in mind, consider all relevant factors in each individual case and make an appropriate decision. And to make sure that people would accept his decisions, he would teach them righteousness and other virtues, guide them with government measures and his own behaviour, treat them according to rites, care for them kindly, govern them with respect, win their trust with his faithfulness, reward them for their obedience, punish them for their misconduct, employ them gently, and resolve their problems definitively. Moreover, he would seek wise and upright ministers, loyal and trustworthy officials and beneficent and able instructors to assist him in getting people settled and out of trouble. If, instead, a law is put before the ordinary people, they would no longer respect their superiors and follow rites but would become disputatious. They would look only at the letter of the law, try to find loopholes, argue every tiny point, and hope that, with luck, they could achieve what they wanted, even if it were in violation of the real objective and true spirit of a law, and, if unlucky, they would resort to bribery to corrupt the judiciary. Such practices, warned Shuxiang, would surely ruin Zichan's government and eventually cause the downfall of the state of Zheng. Zichan humbly accepted Shuxiang's admonition but pleaded that he lacked the ability to do what the great rulers of the past did and was unable to make plans for the future generations. Instead, he was trying only to "save the contemporary world".[52]

We have seen some of the troubles of the world in the sixth century BCE but what made Zichan feel a particular urgency to solve them by publicising the law? In particular, it was the fact that his state was small and its powerful neighbours were about to dismember it. The more general and fundamental reason was that the great principle of *zong-fa* was lost and the rites to implement it had become meaningless. Society needed rules and, in the case of the state of Zheng in Zichan's time, the need was extremely pressing. There was no social authority to create a new set of moral rules that people could readily agree to and accept. Zichan had to act quickly in issuing laws and enforce them with government power. It could not be done in the old way. To win the people's trust and ensure the law's implementation, he could not just issue laws but had to demonstrate to the people that those laws would be definitive and observed by everyone including those in the government. That was why the bronze was cast and put on display for people to see and check whenever they had questions. The new approach apparently worked. Fifty years later, in 513, the mighty state of Jin also had its law publicised in a similar manner. It displeased Confucius who, echoing Shuxiang, argued that people should not be allowed to take the law into their own hands; to maintain order it should be up to the authorities to find, interpret and apply law.[53] Obviously, Confucius was nostalgic for the good old days when the feudal system and its organising and guiding principle, *zong-fa*, worked and would like to rescue or reconstruct them in essence and restore order and harmony. But this view was not shared by many others. More people agreed with Zichan, and publicising laws of definitive contents became a practice followed by all other states engaging in cut-throat struggles against one another.

But making laws was easy. The more difficult questions, as mentioned earlier, were on what bases laws were to be made, how they were to be implemented and, above all, for what objectives. Zichan was apparently aware of these problems. His laws were based on people's feelings and were designed to improve their welfare. In implementing law he was resolute but careful and considerate, keeping the long-term interests of the state and the people in mind. It was reported that, in his first year as chief minister, his policies were criticised by many and he was personally vilified but he refused a suggestion to close the public places where people could gather and discuss his measures. When he passed away twenty-six years later, the people cried like children mourning the death of a loving parent. The reason is that, though he made law prominent, he was well versed in rites and the spirits behind them. Thus, in making political and legal decisions and diplomatic manoeuvres, he was able to choose the appropriate rule, apply it in every specific circumstance and make all concerned see the appropriateness of the rule and the good, long-term consequences it could conduce.[54]

The problem was that by Zichan's time not many had knowledge of rites and were willing to abide by them. As those in power became ill-informed, the ordinary people were totally lost. This fact challenged men of thought to find a way out of the chaos. They all realised that the most urgent thing was to rein in many people's wayward social, political and economic activities. There was an absolute need for norms. Should they be the rites or the law or something else? What should be their objectives? Who were to implement and enforce them, and how? The eight thinkers studied here proffered many ideas. Some argued for restoration of the rites, or rather their basic principles; others extolled orders issued by government leaders, ultimately backed by the "will of Heaven"; a third group advocated law simply made by political authorities; and a last group, which had doubts about human ability, argued for abandoning civilisation and returning to a state where, according to them, humans and everything else coexisted in peace and order according to the laws of nature. Then there were questions about implementation and enforcement of the norms. Some of the thinkers insisted on using education to have the norms internalised; others wanted people to believe norms were enforced by gods and spirits; a third group made clear that law was backed by government power; and the last group asserted that natural law was self-enforcing and any attempt to deviate from it was futile.

Now we know that some of the questions about the bases, objectives and usefulness of various norm can have answers different from those offered by the eight thinkers, and some of us may think their ideas misconceived, narrow, wrong or outdated. But a closer look and deeper reflection will show that they had deliberated on many of the most profound human problems and proffered some reasonable solutions that can be valuable alternatives to the ones now more familiar to us. In any case, we cannot but be impressed by the originality, breadth and depth of their theories, and enlightened and inspired by the wisdom emanating from them. They are like a lode of gold: let us now dig in, pan the gravel and find the nuggets.

Notes

1. The historical events referred to in this study were mostly first recorded in *Shang-shu* 尚書, *Shi-ji* 史記, *Zuo-zhuan* 左傳, *Zhan-guo ce* 戰國策, *Guo-yu* 國語. Recent archaeological discoveries shed some light on these events. Some efforts have been made to report on the tentative interpretations of these discoveries; see for instance, Guo Jingyun. The hereditary transmission was not necessarily from a father to a son; it could be from an uncle to a nephew or between brothers and cousins. It only terminated the *shan-rang* (禪讓 transferring the ruler's position to a stranger) practice followed by Yao and Shun. The stricter father–son transmission was an innovation of the Zhou Dynasty to be explained later.
2. This speculation was endorsed by several scholars but was refuted by some. See Xu Fuguang, vol. 1, pp. 80–4.

3. Soon after conquering Yin, King Wu of Zhou created fifty-five new feudal states and gave fifteen of them to his brothers and forty to other relatives with the same surname. More feudal states were created later, some given to relatives of the Zhou by marriage. See Yang Bojun, "Zhao-gong er-shi-ba nian" 昭公二十八年 pp. 1494–5.
4. In the past, succession to the status of the head of a state was irregular – sometimes the position was passed on to a son, but not necessarily a particular one, sometimes to a brother, and sometimes even to a cousin. The special primogeniture mentioned here was established by the Duke of Zhou 周公 who acted as king for a number of years after his brother King Wu's death but returned the throne to King Wu's son, King Cheng 成王.
5. For a thoughtful analysis of this special type of feudal system created by the Zhou see Xu Fuguang, vol. 1, pp. 13–32.
6. As an example when Pangeng 盤庚, the first ruler of the Yin who wanted to move the capital, declared that he was to appeal to his ancestors, asking them to command the ancestors of the recalcitrant chieftains to move with him. The threat worked. See Kong Yingda, Chapter 9 "Pangeng zhong" 盤庚中 p. 132.
7. See Kong Yingda, Chapter 16 "Xi-bo kan-li" 西伯戡黎 p. 145.
8. In ancient documents the word *de* could mean virtue but also more broadly refer to the character of a person or a thing, therefore a person or a government could have *jun-de* (俊德beautiful character) but also *hui-de* (穢德 dirty character). See, for instance, ibid., Chapter 1"Yao-dian" 堯典 p. 20; Chapter 11 "Tai-shi" 泰誓, p. 151. For the Zhou emphasis on *de*, virtue, as the basis of the mandate see ibid., Chapter 11 "Wu-cheng" 武成, pp. 159–63; Chapter 15 "Zhao-gao" 召誥, pp. 218–24; Chapter 16 "Jun-shi" 君奭, pp. 244–9; Chapter 17 "Cai-zhong zhi ming" 蔡仲之命, pp. 253–4; Chapter 18, "Jun-chen" 君陳, pp. 273–5; Chapter 19 "Bi-ming" 畢命, pp. 290–2; Chapter 19 "Jiong-ming" 冏命, pp. 294–5; Chapter 19, "Lü-xing" 呂刑, pp. 295–304. Many admonitions issued by Zhou rulers to feudal lords, officials and the common people, especially those of the vanquished small states, pointed out how the exaltation and decline of virtue of the previous dynasties caused their rise and fall. See ibid., Chapter 16 "Duo-shi" 多士, pp. 236–9; Chapter 16 "Wu-yi" 無逸, pp. 240–4; Chapter 17 "Duo-fang" 多方, pp. 255–9.
9. See Liu Baonan, Chapter 2 "Wei-zheng" 為政, p. 39; Chapter 3 "Ba-yi" 八佾, p. 49.
10. Here is an example of acts of *wu-li* and their consequences: when Xiaobai小白, a prince of the state of Qi, was in the state of Tan 譚 seeking shelter from his enemies, the ruler of Tan treated him not according to appropriate rites. After becoming the Duke Huan of Qi 齊桓公, Xiaobai invaded Tan and extinguished it in 684 BCE. See Yang Bojun, "Zhuang-gong shi nian" 莊公十年 pp. 184–5. In another instance, as the crown prince of the state of Zheng 鄭 visited the states of Jin 晉 and Chu 楚 and in both cases behaved in violation of rites. In 566 BCE after becoming Duke Xi of Zheng 鄭僖公 he visited Jin again and again acted incorrectly and killed his attendants who advised against his bad behaviour. Shortly he died of poison administered under the order of his chief minister to save the state from being attacked by Jin. See ibid. "Xiang-gong qi nian" 襄公七年 p. 953. On the other hand, examples of acts of *zhi-li* being richly awarded were also many. In 648 BCE, after defeating the invasion against the kingdom of Zhou by a barbarian tribe *rong* 戎, Xiaobai, the Duke of Qi, sent his chief minister Guan Zhong 管仲 to Zhou to oversee the signing of a peace treaty. The grateful king of Zhou bestowed on Guan Zhong the title of *shang-qing* (上卿 minister of the first rank in the feudal system) which would make him equal to the other two hereditary high ministers of the state of Qi already appointed by the early Zhou kings. He humbly declined the honour and instead accepted the title of *xia-qing* (下卿

minister of the lowest rank.) This act made him widely admired by all feudal lords and helped promote his master Duke Huan their hegemon. A more remarkable example was the preservation of the state of Zheng 鄭 by Zichan子產. Before his tenure as chief minister from 543 to 522 BCE the state had long since become small and weak, and been repeatedly encroached upon by bigger and stronger neighbours. But for over twenty-one years under his watch, because of his adroit diplomacy, profound knowledge of the rites and scrupulous adherence to them, the state was respected and saved from humiliation and invasions. See Gao Shiqi, vol. 44 "Zichan xiang Zheng" 子產相鄭 pp. 628–47.

11. See Kong Yingda, Chapter 29, "Lü-xing" 呂刑 pp. 295–301.
12. See Sima Qian, Chapter 1, "Wu-di ben-ji" 五帝本紀 pp. 1–48.
13. See Sima Qian, Chapter 2, "Xia ben-ji" 夏本紀 pp. 48–90, Chapter 3, "Yin Ben-ji" 殷本紀 pp. 91–110, and Chapter 4, "Zhou Ben-ji" 周本紀 pp. 111–71. According to some sources, the Xia had three thousand punishable offences, and the Zhou had 2,500. See Zhangsun Wuji, p. 2. These statements are figurative, meaning only that punishments were numerous, because in neither dynasty were there published criminal laws. As to harshness of the punishments, we shall see later when we discuss *Han-Fei-zi* 韓非子. It was reported in that work that one Yin Dynasty law prescribed amputation of a hand for the person who threw ash into the street and that, during the Spring and Autumn Period in the state of Qi, crutches cost more than shoes because so many people suffered amputation of feet as a punishment.
14. The points include: 1. a statement about the inception of the criminal law, alleging that it had no divine origin but was crafted by Chiyou, that it was initially very harsh and arbitrary but was later made more humane by Boyi 伯夷, a minister under the legendarily sagacious ruler Shun; 2. an assertion (repeated many times) that the correct objective of law was to find *zhong* (中, the proper middle, a concept similar to "justice" but, in this document, it refers to a position between *lun* [倫, the ethic principle], and *yao* [要, the legal rule]); 3. a prescription that the function of law was not to punish people but *yi-jiao zhi-de* (以教祗德 to teach them to cherish virtue) and thus to avoid doing wrong; 4. a principle that criminal law should be made and applied *shi-qing shi-zhong* (世輕世重 sometimes light, sometimes heavy, depending on the circumstances) so that it could be *wei-qi fei-qi* (惟齊非齊 for true equity but not mere equality); 5. a list of crimes and their punishments and a scale of *fa-huan* (罰鍰 fines) to be paid by offenders deserving clemency; 6. a set of procedural rules to guide careful investigation and impartial trial, such as *wu-ting* (五聽 five techniques of listening to the parties' arguments) and *ming-qing yu dan-ci* (明清于單詞 clearly examine uncorroborated statements); 7. permission for the judge, in a case where there was not a precisely applicable law, to compare it with cases of similar nature governed by existing laws and *shang-xia bi-zui* (上下比罪 to compare the case in hand with similar cases, some more serious, some less so, and decide an appropriate punishment); 8. an emphasis that, in applying a law, the judge should *ming-qi xing-shu xu-zhan xian-shu zhong-zheng* (明啟刑書胥占, 咸庶中正 not merely to look at the letter of the law but also to take a step further to deliberate on its spirit and to achieve what was proper and balanced); 9. a requirement that judicial appointments should be given only to those who were *liang* (良 virtuous), capable of being compassionate and benevolent, never to those who were *ning* (佞 shrewd), inclining to find fault in people; 10. a set of severe sanctions against judicial personnel who committed *wu-guo* (五過 five mistakes, namely, *wei-guan* [惟官 abusing official position], *wei-fan* [惟反 harbouring a grudge against someone], *wei-nei* [惟內 wishing to do a favour to someone], *wei-huo* [惟貨 taking a bribe] and *wei-lai* [惟來 soliciting a gain]); and 11.

a demand that all those in power, particularly the king's clansmen, obey the law, and those with judicial responsibilities *wu-wei wu-xiu* (勿畏勿休 fear no threats to their positions and enjoy no conviction of criminals) but *wei-jin wu-xing*, *yi-cheng san-de* (惟敬五刑, 以成三德 administer the punishments with care in order to help them improve the virtues of the people.) See kong Yingda, Chapter 29. The emphasis on the rites over the law is obvious.

15. The first person who most seriously violated the very basic principle of *zong-fa* was You-wang 幽王, the last king of the Western Zhou, who dismissed his queen and crown prince and made a concubine and her son take their places. This caused Marquis Shen 申侯, father of the former queen, to lead a rebellion, with the help of barbarians from the west, and killed the king. After the establishment of the Eastern Zhou by Ping-wang 平王, the former crown prince and grandson of the marquis, this kind of violation of the *zong-fa* principles was repeated, and members of the immediate royal family – especially brothers and half-brothers – fought against one another for the throne. Such violations and even more heinous crimes, including sons assassinating fathers, were committed by aristocrats of various ranks, and the feudal system collapsed – some of the states initially established in the early Western Zhou were divided into smaller ones and many were conquered by stronger neighbours – even the Eastern Zhou was split into two little kingdoms and fought each other, and were exterminated by the state of Qin: first the western unit in 255 BCE, then the eastern unit in 249 BCE. See Sima Qian, Chapter 4 "Zhou-ben-ji" 周本紀 pp. 144–89.
16. See Yang Bojun, "Xi-gong san nian, si nian" 僖公三, 四年, pp. 286–7.
17. See ibid., "Xi-gong er-shi-er nian" 僖公二十二年, pp. 397–8.
18. See ibid.. "Cheng-gong shi-liu nian" 成公十六年, pp. 887–8.
19. See Gao Shiqi, Chapter 18 "Qi Huan-gong zhi-ba" 齊桓公之伯, pp. 179–212; Chapter 25 "Jin Wen-gong zhi ba" 晉文公之伯, pp. 299–322.
20. For examples see Qu Wanli, "Yu wu zheng" 雨無正 p. 362; "Qiao-yan" 巧言 p. 376; "Xiao-pan" 小弁 p. 372; "Ban" 板 p. 506; "Yun-han" 雲漢 p. 527.
21. During the Chunqiu period thirty-six feudal lords were murdered, fifty-two feudal states extinguished and countless aristocrats lost their fiefdoms and were reduced to the status of labourers, or even became slaves. See Sima Qian, Chapter 130 "Tai-shi-gong zi-xu" 太史公自序 p. 3297; Yang Bojun, "Zhao-gong san-nian" 昭公三年 p. 1263.
22. See Wang Xianshen, Chapter 49, "Wu-du" 五蠹pp. 339–40.
23. This arrangement was known as *jing-tian* (井田 the # field system) because the nine lots as a unit was in the shape of the Chinese character 井. Supposedly it was invented in ancient times and used through the Xia, the Shang and the early Zhou dynasties. But, by the time of the Warring States, the system was obsolete and Mencius was unable to describe it in detail. See Jiao Xun and Jiao Hu, Chapter 5 "Teng-wen-gong shang" 滕文公上 pp. 205–14.
24. See Yang Bojun, "Xuan-gong shi-liu nian" 宣公十六年 p. 766.
25. As an example, according to an interesting though exaggerated account, Linzi 臨淄, a city of the state of Qi, during the reign of King Xuan 宣王 (c.350–301), had seventy thousand households. Its streets were jammed with vehicles and pedestrians. When people in this great bustle lifted their arms to greet one another, their sleeves formed curtains; when they wiped sweat from their foreheads, the beads fell like rain. All families were well off; everyone played music, sports and games and were high spirited and ambitious. See Liu Xiang, Chapter 8 "Qi-ce yi" 齊策一 p. 337.

26. See Jiao Xun and Jiao Hu, Chapter 1 "Liang Hui-wang shang" 梁惠王上 p. 57.
27. This idiom, *wu zhi-zui zhi di* 無置錐之地, appeared in many ancient texts. See, for instance, Guo Qingfan, Chapter 29 "Dao Zhi" 盜跖 p. 429.
28. See Sima Qian, Chapter 14 "Shi-er zhu-hou nian-biao" 十二諸侯年表 pp. 509–683; Chapter 15 "Liu-guo nian-biao" 六國年表 pp. 685–758.
29. See Liu Xiang, Chapter 20 "Zhao-ce san" 趙策三 p. 678.
30. See Jiao Xun and Jiao Hu, Chapter 7 "Li Lou shang" 離婁上 Section 14, pp. 302–4.
31. See Sima Qian, Chapter 5 "Qin ben-ji" 秦本紀 p. 213.
32. The Mohists became a prominent school partly because they developed new means and methods for warfare. See Sun Yirang, Chapter 49 "Lu-wen" 魯問 pp. 291–2; Chapter 50 "Gongshu" 公輸 pp. 292–6; Chapter 52 "Bei cheng-meng" 備城門 pp. 298–319.
33. Reportedly, Mozi once crafted a wooden bird capable of flying for days but, being ashamed of wasting his talent and time on such a useless thing, he abandoned it and turned to the more important task of designing defensive weapons. See Wang Xianshen, Chapter 32 "Wai-chu-shuo zuo-shang" 外儲說左上 p. 199.
34. See ibid., p. 200
35. See Yang Bojun, "Xi-gong san-shi-san nian" 僖公三十三年 pp. 495–6.
36. See Sima Qian, Chapter 41 "Yue-wang Goujian shi-jia" 越王勾踐世家 pp. 1351–3.
37. The prince happened to be the future First Emperor of Qin. See ibid., Chapter 85 "Lü Buwei lie-zhuan" 呂不韋列傳 pp. 2505–14.
38. See Yan Wanli, Chapter 6, "Suan-di" 算地 p. 14.
39. See Dai Wang, Chapter 8, Section 20 "Xiao-kuang" 小匡 pp. 121–2.
40. See Guo Qingfan, pp. 426–39.
41. For analyses of the origin and evolution of *shi* as a class, see Xu Fuguan, pp. 86–92; Guo Moruo, pp. 54–61.
42. See Zhang Binnan.
43. See Qu Wanli, p. 191.
44. See Yang Bojun, "Xiang-gong er-shi-san nian" 襄公二十三年 p. 1079; "Zhao-gong shi-ba nian" 昭公十八年 p. 1395; "Huan-gong liu nian" 桓公六年 p. 111.
45. For instance, in 697 BCE, King Huan of Zhou, in violation of rites, sent an envoy to the state of Lu to ask for carriages as gifts. See ibid., "Huan-gong shi-wu nian" 桓公十五年 pp. 142–3. In 712 BCE, Zhou seized some farmland from the state of Zheng. See ibid., "Yin-gong shi-yi nian" 隱公十一年 pp. 76–7.
46. See Liu Baonan, Chapter 3 "Ba-yi" 八佾 p. 41.
47. See ibid., Chapter 17 "Yang Huo" 陽貨 p. 375.
48. See Dai Wang, Chapter 8 "Xiao-kuang" 小匡 pp. 121–4. The book appeared much later than Guan Zhong's time but probably reflected some of his ideas and policies.
49. See *supra* note 11.
50. See Jiao Xun and Jiao Hu, Chapter 12 "Gao-zi xia" 告子下 p. 497.
51. See Yang Bojun, "Xi-gong jiu-nian" 僖公九年 pp. 326–7.
52. See Yang Bojun, "Zhao-gong liu nian" 昭公六年 pp. 1274–7. Such exchanges were common among aristocrats of different states during the Spring and Autumn Period when the *zong-fa* rules were still effective. Zichan, a junior member of the Zhou lineage, obviously felt the need to pay respect to Shuxiang, a senior member. In the Warring States Period, when the rules were largely ignored, such communications became rare.
53. See ibid., "Zhao-gong er-shi-jiu nian" 昭公二十九年 pp. 1504–5.
54. See Gao Shiqi, "Zichang xiang-Zheng" 子產相鄭 pp. 617–48, esp. pp. 628–9. Zichan's good government was widely known and praised by many, including Confucius who

characterised him as *jun-zi* (君子 noble man), *hui-ren* (惠人 benevolent man). Upon hearing of his death, Confucius cried, calling him *gu zhi yi-ai* (古之遺愛 a person who inherited from great rulers of the past their love of the people). See Liu Baonan, Chapter 5 "Gongye Chang" 公冶長, p. 101, Chapter 14 "Xian-wen" 憲問 p. 305; Gao Shiqi, *supra*, p. 643.

Lun-yu 論語

PART 1
TRANSLATION

(A) The need for social authority and norms

[1] Confucius said, "When the Way prevails in the world, the rites, music and punitive expeditions are initiated by the Son of Heaven; when the Way does not prevail in the world, they are initiated by the feudal lords." (Chapter 16 "Ji-shi" 季氏 Section 2)
[2] Duke Jing of Qi 齊景公 asked Confucius about government. Confucius answered, "Let the ruler be a ruler, the subject a subject, the father a father, the son a son." The duke responded, "Well said! If, indeed, the ruler be not a ruler, the subject not a subject, the father not a father, the son not a son, then though there be grain, would I get to eat it?" (Chapter 12 "Yan Yuan" 顏淵 Section 11)

(B) The authorities

(1) Tian, ming (天, 命 Heaven and Fate)

[3] The Master said, "What does Heaven ever say? Yet the four seasons go round and the hundred things come into being. What does Heaven ever say?" (Chapter 17 "Yang Huo" 陽貨 Section 19)
[4] [When visiting the state of Song 宋, Confucius and his disciples practised the rites under a tree. Huan Tui 桓魋, a minister of Song who wanted to expel Confucius, had the tree uprooted. The disciples urged a quick departure, but Confucius said, "Heaven has produced the virtue that is in me. What can Huan Tui do to me?" (Chapter 7 "Shu-er" 述而 Section 23)
[5] When under siege in Kuang 匡 [a district of the state of Wei], the Master said, "Since King Wen 文王 [father of King Wu 武王, the founder of the Zhou Dynasty] had passed away, was not the responsibility of continuing cultural development lodged here [in me]? If Heaven were to let this culture perish, those of us who are to die long after him should not have participated in its development. If Heaven

were not to let this culture perish, what can the people of Kuang do to me?" (Chapter 9 "Zi-han" 子罕 Section 5)

[6] When Boniu 伯牛 [a disciple] was ill Confucius went to ask for him. Holding Boniu's hand through the window, the Master said, "He is dying. It is alas the work of Fate that such a person should have such sickness! Such a person should have such sickness!" (Chapter 6 "Yong-ye" 雍也 Section 8)

[7] Gongbo Liao 公伯寮 [an official of the State of Lu] in the presence of Jisun 季孫 [the principal minister of that state] slandered Zilu 子路 [a disciple]. Zifu Jingbo 子服景伯 [also an official of that state] said to Confucius, "The minister [Jisun] is indeed confused and led astray by Gongbo Liao, but I still have enough power to have him [Gongbo Liao] executed and his corpse exposed in the market." The Master said, "It is Fate if the Way is to prevail; it is also Fate if the Way is to fail. What can Gongbo Liao do to Fate?" Chapter 14 "Xian-wen" 憲問 Section 38)

[8] The Master said, "When I turned fifty, I began to understand Heaven and Fate." (Chapter 2 "Wei-zheng" 為政 Section 4)

[9] Zigong 子貢 [a disciple] said, "One can hear the Master speaking of his views on culture, but one seldom hears him talking about human nature and the will of Heaven." (Chapter 5 "Gongye Chang" 公冶長 Section 13)

[10] The Master seldom initiated discussions about profit, fate and humanity. (Chapter 9 "Zi-han" Section 1)

(2) Shen, gui (神, 鬼 Gods and Spirits)

[11] Jilu 季路 [a disciple, aka Zilu 子路] asked about serving spirits and gods. The Master said, "While you are not yet able to serve man, how can you serve ghosts of the dead?" Jilu said, "May I venture to ask about death?" The Master said, "While you do not yet understand life, how can you understand death?" (Chapter 11 "Xian-jin" 先進 Section 12)

[12] Wangsun Jia 王孫賈 [a minister of the State of Wei 衛] asked, "What is the meaning of the saying, 'It is better to be fawning over the god of the kitchen stove than the god of the south-west corner of the house?'" The Master said, "That is not right. A person who has been found guilty by Heaven has none to whom he can pray." (Chapter 3 "Ba-yi" 八佾 Section 13)

[13] Fan Chi 樊遲 [a disciple] asked what constituted wisdom. The Master said, "Devote to doing what is right for the people. Respect ghosts and gods but keep aloof from them." (Chapter 6 "Yong-ye" Section 22)

(3) Ren (人 Men)

[14] Ji Kangzi 季康子 [a minister of the State of Lu] asked Confucius about government. Confucius said, "To govern is to correct. If you lead the people with correctness, who would dare to be incorrect?" (Chapter 12 "Yan Yuan" 顏淵 Section 17)

[15] The Master said, "Once a person has made himself correct, what difficulty will there be for him to take part in government? If one cannot correct himself,

what has he to do with correcting others?" (Chapter 13 "Zilu" 子路 Section 13)

[16] The Master said, "If a ruler is himself correct, his government will be effective without his explicit orders. If he is not correct, he may issue orders but people will not follow." (Chapter 13 "Zilu" Section 6)

[17] Zilu asked about government. The Master said, "Lead the people and work hard for them." Zilu asked for further instruction. The Master said, "Be not weary." (Chapter 13 "Zilu" Section 1)

[18] Zizhang 子張 [a disciple] asked about government. The Master said, "While in office, do not show weariness; while on a job, do it with devotion." (Chapter 12 "Yan Yuan" Section 14)

[19] The Master said, "In guiding a state of a thousand chariots, be reverent to the task and trustworthy in words, economical in expenditure and loving towards people, employing them at the right time." (Chapter 1 "Xue-er" 學而 Section 5)

[20] Ji Kangzi asked, "How can the people be made respectful, loyal and enthusiastic in doing their best? The Master said, "Rule over them with dignity and they will be respectful; be filial and kind and they will be loyal; elevate the good and educate the less able and they will become enthusiastic in doing their best." (Chapter 2 "Wei-zheng" 為政 Section 20)

[21] Fan Chi requested to be taught how to grow crops. The Master said, "I am not as good as an old farmer." Fan Chi then requested to be taught how to grow vegetables. The Master said, "I am not as good as an old gardener." After Fan Chi had left, the Master said, "A small man indeed Fan Chi is! Where the ruler loves the rites, none of the common people will dare to be irreverent; where the ruler loves righteousness, none of the common people will dare to be insubordinate; where the ruler loves trustworthiness, none of the common people will dare to be insincere. In this way the common people from the four quarters will come with their children strapped on their backs. What need is there to learn about growing crops?" (Chapter 13 "Zilu" Section 4)

[22] Zigong asked about government. The Master said, "Let there be enough food and enough arms, then the people will have trust in the government." Zigong said, "If it cannot be helped, and some of these requisites had to be dispensed with, which one among the three is to be the first?" The Master said, "Give up arms." Zigong said, "If it cannot be helped and more had to be dispensed with, which one of the remaining two is to go?" The Master said, "Let go food. Since antiquity all have to meet death; but when people have no trust in the government they will have nothing to stand on." (Chapter 12 "Yan Yuan" Section 7)

[23] When the Master went to Wei 衛, with Ran You 冉有 [a disciple] as his driver, he observed, "The people are so numerous!" Ran You said, "Since they are numerous, what shall be done for them?" The Master said, "Enrich them." "When they have been made rich, what more shall be done?" The Master said, "Educate them." (Chapter 13 "Zilu" Section 9)

[24] Duke Ding 定公 [of the State of Lu 魯] asked how a ruler should employ the services of his officials, and how officials should serve the ruler. Confucius replied,

"A ruler should employ the services of his officials according to the rites; officials should serve their ruler with loyalty." (Chapter 3 "Ba-yi" Section 19)
[25] Zizhang asked Confucius, saying, "'When is a person considered qualified to serve in government?" The Master replied, "When he has learned to respect the five good practices and to eschew the four bad ones, he is qualified to serve." Zizhang asked what the five good practices were. The Master said, "A person in government is to be generous without being wasteful, to use the people's labour without giving them cause for complaint, to pursue his desires without being covetous, to be dignified without being arrogant, and to be forceful without being overbearing" . . . Zizhang then asked what the four bad practices were. The Master said, "To punish people with death without having educated them – this is called cruelty; to demand results of people without having warned them of their responsibilities – this is called oppression; to issue orders as if there were no urgency at first, and then when the time comes, to insist with severity on their being punctually carried out – this is called tyrannical; to be parsimonious and uncompromising in matters of receipt and disbursement – this is called acting like petty bureaucrats." (Chapter 20 "Yao-yue" 堯曰 Section 2)
[26] Duke Ding asked, "It is said, 'A single statement can lead the state to prosperity.' Is it true?" Confucius replied, "The adage cannot be understood literally. But here is a popular saying: 'To be a ruler is difficult and to be an official is not easy.' Now if a ruler understands the difficulty of being a ruler, then is this not almost a case of a single remark leading the state to prosperity?" "It is said, 'A single statement can lead the state to ruin.' Is it true?" Confucius replied, "The adage cannot be understood literarily. But here is a statement a ruler might make: 'I find no pleasure in being a ruler, except for the fact that no one goes against what I say.' Now if what the ruler says is good, it is well that no one opposes it. But if what is said is not good, and no one opposes it, then is it not almost a case of a single remark leading the state to ruin?" (Chapter 13 "Zilu" Section 15)

(C) Norms

(1) Types and hierarchy

[27] Zixia 子夏 [a disciple] said, "If one does not overstep the bounds of major norms, one can be allowed some discretion in observing minor norms." (Chapter 19 "Zizhang" 子張 Section 11)
[28] Zigong asked, "What must a man be like before he can be called a cultivated man?" The Master said, "He who keeps a sense of shame in conducting himself and, when sent abroad, does not disgrace his lord's commission, deserves to be called a cultivated man." "May I ask about a man of a lower class?" "He is someone praised by his clansmen for being filial and by members of his local community for being brotherly." "And who is below that?" "A man who insists on keeping his words and carrying his actions to fruition is an obstinate small person, but can be in the next class." (Chapter 13 "Zilu" Section 20)

[29] The Master said, "Small indeed was the capacity of Guan Zhong 管仲 [a principal minister of the State of Qi 齊]." Someone asked, "Was Guan Zhong parsimonious?" The master replied, "The Guan family had three households and its staff members did not have double duties. How could he be considered parsimonious?" "Then did Guan Zhong know the rites?" "The residence of the ruler of a state has a screen wall outside of the main gate blocking the view from the street, Guan Zhong's family residence also had a screen wall . . . If Guan Zhong knew the rites, who else did not know the rites?" (Chapter 3 "Ba-yi" Section 22)
[30] Zilu said, "Duke Huan 桓公 [the ruler of the State of Qi] had Prince Jiu 公子糾 [the duke's brother] killed [in a fight to seize the throne]. Shao Hu 召忽 [an assistant of the prince] died with the prince but Guan Zhong [also an assistant of the prince] did not die. Was Guan Zhong not virtuous?" The Master said, "Nine times Duke Huan assembled the feudal lords [for the cause of peace] without resorting to arms. It was the result of Guan Zhong's efforts. Who was so virtuous? Who was so virtuous?" (Chapter 14 "Xian-wen" Section 16)
[31] Zigong said, "Guan Zhong was not a virtuous person, is it right? After Duke Huan had Prince Jiu killed, Guan Zhong was unable to die for his master, and instead he served Duke Huan as his principal minister." The Master said, "Guan Zhong served Duke Huan as his principal minister, made him the hegemon among the feudal lords and united and rectified the world. People down to the present day are blessed by his achievements. But for Guan Zhong we should now be wearing our hair loose and the lappets of our coats buttoned on the left side. Surely he was not like the common man and woman who holding fast to their petty loyalty to one master committed suicide by drowning themselves in ditches without anyone taking notice." (Chapter 14 "Xian-wen" Section 17)
[32] Gongshan Furao 公山弗擾 [a magistrate], holding Bi 費 [a district in the State of Lu] to stage a revolt, invited the Master, and the Master was inclined to go. Zilu was displeased and said, "We may have nowhere to go, but must we go to Gongshan?" The Master said, "Can the man who invites me be without a reason? If anyone employs me, can I not, perhaps, recreate the Eastern Zhou?" (Chapter 17 "Yang Huo" Section 5)
[33] Bi Xi 佛肸 [the magistrate of a district of the state of Jin 晉] invited the Master, and the Master was inclined to go. Zilu said, "Sir, once I heard you say, 'Where a person has personally done evil a noble man would not enter his door.' Now Bi Xi is holding the district of Zhongmu 中牟 to stage a revolt. How can you justify going to him?" The Master replied, "It is true, I did say that. But is it not also said that, 'Something really hard can withstand grinding?' Is it not said that, 'Something really white can withstand black dye?' Am I a bitter gourd? How can I be hung up as an ornament but not be good as food?" (Chapter 17 "Yang Huo" Section 7)

(2) Dao (道 the Way) as the supreme norm

[34] See [1]
[35] Zigong said, "The Master's discourse on the classics can be heard; his remarks

on human nature and the Way of Heaven cannot be heard." (Chapter 5 "Gongye Chang" Section 14)
[36] The Master said, "Zhou Dynasty had the advantage of viewing the previous two dynasties and its culture was so complete and magnificent. I follow [the way of] Zhou." (Chapter 3 "Ba-yi" Section 14)
[37] The Master said, "[The State of] Qi, by one good change can reach the condition of [the State of] Lu. Lu, by one good change can reach the condition of a state where the Way prevails." (Chapter 6 "Yong ye" Section 24)
[38] The Master said, "Seriously my health has declined. For long I have not seen Duke Zhou 周公 [a founder of the Zhou Dynasty] in my dream." (Chapter 7 "Shu-er" Section 5)
[39] Youzi 有子 [a disciple] said, "The noblest use of the rites is to achieve harmony. It is the beauty of the Way of the ancient kings and it is to be sought in most cases, big or small, although there might be exceptions. Knowing what results in harmony and pursuing it is fine but if not tempered by the rites, the pursuit cannot go on." (Chapter 1 "Xue-er" Section 12)
[40] Youzi said, "A noble man devotes his efforts to what is fundamental. When the fundamentals are established the Way will grow from there. Filial piety and brotherly love are the fundamentals of humanity." (Chapter 1 "Xue-er" Section 2)
[41] The Master said, "The term 'great minister' refers to those who serve their ruler according to the Way and relinquish office when this is no longer possible." (Chapter 11 "Xian-jin" Section 24)
[42] Liuxia Hui 柳下惠 [a virtuous person of the State of Lu] as a judge was thrice dismissed from office. Someone said, "Can you not leave?" He replied, "If I am to serve straight according to the Way, where can I go and not get dismissed repeatedly? Because I am not to bend the Way in doing my service, why is it necessary for me to leave the state of my parents?" (Chapter 18 "Weizi" Section 2)
[43] The Master said, "When the Way prevails in the world one should work for the public; when the Way is not prevailing one should retire." (Chapter 8 "Tai-bo" 泰伯 Section 13)
[44] The Master said, "A cultivated man's aspiration is to follow the Way." (Chapter 4 "Li-ren" 里仁 Section 9)
[45] The Master said, "Having heard the Way in the morning a person would feel all right if he were to die in the evening." (Chapter 4, "Li-ren" Section 8)
[46] The Master said, "Wealth and honours are what people desire, but if they are obtained not through the right way one should not keep them." (Chapter 4 "Li-ren" Section 5)
[47] The Master said, "A noble man seeks the Way, not material rewards . . . A noble man worries about the Way, not poverty." (Chapter 15 "Wei Ling-gong" 衛靈公 Section 32)
[48] Ziyou 子游 [a disciple] said, "The disciples of Zixia are capable to sweep the ground, respond to simple questions, advance and retreat in correct manners. But these are trivial details. If they do not learn the important fundamentals, what

is to happen to them?" Zixia heard this and said, "Alas, Yan You 言游 (Ziyou's full name) is mistaken. Which part of the noble man's way is to be taught first and which last? It is like the grass and the tree. A distinction should be made. The steps of a noble man's way should not be misarranged. To learn everything at once is a feat only a sage can accomplish." (Chapter 19 "Zizhang" Section 12)

(3) De (德 virtues) as the norm below dao

(A) *REN* (仁 HUMANITY)

[49] The Master said, "By nature, people are close; by practice, they become widely apart." (Chapter 17 "Yang Huo" Section 2)
[50] The Master said, "Only the very wise and the very stupid are not susceptible to change." (Chapter 17 "Yang Huo" Section 3)
[51] Zhonggong 仲弓 [a disciple, aka Ran Yong 冉雍] asked about humanity. The Master said, "When you go out of your house, you should behave as if you are to meet with a great guest. When you employ the people, you should act as if you are conducting a grand sacrifice. What you do not like, do not impose on others." (Chapter 12 "Yan Yuan" Section 2)
[52] Zigong said, "If there is a man who gives extensively to the people and brings help to the multitude, could he be called humane?" The Master said, "It is no longer a matter of humanity with such a man. If you must describe him, 'sage' is, perhaps, the right word. Even Yao 堯 and Shun 舜 would have found it difficult to accomplish as much. Now here is a humane man: While he wishes to establish his own standing he also helps others to establish theirs, while he wishes to reach his own objective he also helps others to reach theirs. Thus to draw an analogy from what is near at hand can be called the method to achieve humanity." (Chapter 6 "Yong-ye" Section 30)
[53] Confucius said, "If a man is not humane, what he is to do with the rites? If a man is not humane, what he is to do with music?" (Chapter 3 "Ba-yi" Section 3)
[54] Fan Chi asked about humanity. The Master said, "Love your fellow men." (Chapter 12 "Yan Yuan" Section 22)
[55] Fan Chi asked about humanity. The Master said, "The humane man goes ahead of others in overcoming difficulties but remains behind others in reaping the benefits. Such a man can be called humane." (Chapter 6 "Yong-ye" Section 22)
[56] Zizhang asked Confucius about humanity. Confucius said, "A person is humane if he can keep doing five things wherever he is in the world." The disciple begged for explanation. "They are", the Master said, "respectfulness, tolerance, sincerity, diligence and kindness. If a man is respectful, he will not be treated with insolence; if he is tolerant, he will win the masses; if he is sincere, people will have trust in him; if he is diligent, he will have accomplishments; if he is kind, he will be able to command others." (Chapter 17 "Yang Huo" Section 6)
[57] The Master said, "Is humanity too remote to reach? When I desire to be humane, humanity is here in my hand." (Chapter 7 "Shu-er" Section 30)

[58] Yan Yuan 顏淵 asked about humanity. The Master said, "To be humane is to exercise self-restraint and observe the rites. Once a person becomes self-restrained and observant of the rites, the world will recognise him as humane. Thus, to be humane a person depends on himself not on others." Yan Yuan asked for detailed rules. The Master said, "Do not look at what is contrary to the rites; do not listen to what is contrary to the rites; do not speak what is contrary to the rites; make no movement that is contrary to the rites." (Chapter 12 "Yan Yuan" Section 1)

(B) *XIAO* (孝 FILIAL PIETY)

[59] The Master said, "A young man, when at home, should be filial; when abroad, respectful to his elders." (Chapter 1 "Xue er" Section 6)
[60] Ziyou asked what filial piety was. The Master said, "Nowadays, for a man to be filial means that he is able to sustain his parents. But dogs and horses are also sustained by their masters. If it is done without respect, how is the one act distinguished from the other?" (Chapter 2 "Wei-zheng" Section 7)
[61] Zixia asked what filial piety was. The Master said, "The difficulty is in the expression. As for the young taking on the burden when there is work to be done, or letting the elders enjoy the wine and food when these are available, that hardly deserves to be called filial." (Chapter 2 "Wei-zheng" Section 8)
[62] The Master said, "In serving his parents, a son should try gently to dissuade them from doing wrong. If he finds his advice is not followed, he should act more reverently and never be disobedient. He may be dismayed but should never complain." (Chapter 4 "Li-ren" Section 18)
[63] Mengyizi 孟懿子 [a minister of the State of Lu] asked what filial piety was. The Master said, "Do not disobey." Afterwards, as Fan Chi was driving him in his carriage, the Master told him, saying, "Mengsun [Mengyizi's other name] asked me what filial piety was, and I answered, 'Do not disobey'." Fan Chi said, "What did you mean?" The Master replied, "I meant that while a person's parents are alive he should serve them in accordance with the rites, and after their death, bury them in accordance with the rites, and offer sacrifice to them in accordance with the rites." (Chapter 2 "Wei-zheng" Section 5)
[64] The Master said, "While a man's father is alive, look at his aspirations; when his father is dead, look at his conduct. If for three years after his father's death, he makes no changes to the way of his father, he may be called filial." (Chapter 1 "Xue-er" Section 11)
[65] Zengzi 曾子 [a disciple] said, "I have heard this from the Master: Regarding Meng Zhuangzi's 孟莊子 [a minister of the State of Lu] filial piety, some of his acts expressing it could be performed by others as well, but his not changing his father's assistants and policies [after his father's death] is difficult to emulate." (Chapter 19 "Zizhang" Section 18)
[66] Youzi said, "Few who are filial and brotherly are inclined to offend their superiors. None who are not inclined to offend their superiors has been found liking to cause disorder. A noble man devotes his efforts to what is fundamental. When

the fundamentals are established the Way will grow from there. Filial piety and brotherly love are the fundamentals of humanity." (Chapter 1 "Xue-er" Section 2)

(c) *Yi* (義 rectitude)

[67] The Master said, "Seeing what is right and failing to do it is being not brave." (Chapter 2 "Wei-zheng" Section 24)
[68] Zilu said, "Does the noble man emphasise bravery?" The Master said, "The noble man holds righteousness as a higher virtue. A man in a superior position who is brave but without a sense of righteousness will cause trouble; a small man who is brave but without a sense of righteousness will commit robbery." (Chapter 17 "Yang Huo" Section 23)
[69] The Master said, "One who thinks of righteousness in view of profit . . . can be called an accomplished man." (Chapter 14 "Xian-wen" Section 12)
[70] Zilu said, "The noble man takes government office to do what he thinks is right, although he knows that the Way has long been in disuse." (Chapter 18 "Weizi" 微子 Section 7)
[71] The Master said of Zichan 子產 [a principal minister of the State of Zheng 鄭] that he had the way of the noble man on four counts: in conducting himself he was humble; in serving his superiors he was respectful; in caring for the people he was kind; and in employing their services he was just. (Chapter 5 "Gongye Chang" Section 16)
[72] The Master said, "Wealth and honours acquired through unjust means are like floating clouds to me." (Chapter 7 "Shu-er" Section 16)

(d) *Zhi* (直 straightness)

[73] The Master said, "In the past crudeness showed itself in straightforwardness." (Chapter 17 "Yang Huo" Section 16)
[74] The Master said, "Straightforwardness not in accordance with the rites becomes rudeness." (Chapter 8 "Tai-bo" Section 2)
[75] Someone said, "How about requiting injury with kindness?" The Master commented, "With what then will one requite kindness? Requite injustice with justice, requite kindness with kindness." (Chapter 14 "Xian-wen", Section 34)
[76] Fan Chi asked about humanity. The Master said, "Love your fellow men." Fan Chi asked about wisdom. The Master said, "Know your fellow men." Fan Chi did not understand the answers. The Master said, "Impose the straight upon the crooked, and the crooked will be straightened." (Chapter 12 "Yan Yuan" Section 22)
[77] The Master said, "How straight Shi Yu 史魚 [an official of the State of Wei 衛] was! When the Way prevailed in his state, he was straight like an arrow; when the Way fell into disuse in his state, he was still straight like an arrow. What a noble man Qu Boyu 蘧伯玉 [another official of that state] was! When the Way prevailed in his state, he entered public service. When the Way fell into disuse, he rolled up his principles, and kept them to his breast." (Chapter 15 "Wei Ling-gong" Section 7)

[78] The Master said, "When the Way prevailed in his state, Ning Wuzi 寧武子 [an official of the State of Wei 衛] showed his intelligence; when the way fell into disuse in his state, he appeared stupid. Others may equal his intelligence, but few can match his act of stupidity." (Chapter 5 "Gongye Chang" Section 20)
[79] See [43].
[80] The Master said, "When the Way prevails in the state, speak and act straight; when the Way does not prevail, behave straight, but speak with diffidence." (Chapter 14 "Xian-wen" Section 3)
[81] Lord of She 葉公 [the magistrate of She, a district of the State of Chu] said to Confucius, "Among my people there was a person who was so upright that when his father stole a sheep, he gave evidence against him." Confucius said, "Our people who are upright are different. Fathers cover up for their sons, and sons cover up for their fathers. Uprightness is to be found in this." (Chapter 13 "Zilu" Section 18)
[82] Yang Huo 陽貨 [an assistant to a principal minister of the State of Lu] wanted to see Confucius, but Confucius did not want to see him. He sent Confucius a steamed piglet as a present. Confucius chose a time when Yang Huo was not at home and went to return the courtesy. (Chapter 17 "Yang Huo" Section 1)
[83] Rubei 孺悲 [an attendant of Duke Ai of the State of Lu 魯哀公] wished to see Confucius. Confucius declined, on the grounds of illness. As soon as the man conveying the message had stepped out of the room, Confucius took his zither, played it and sang, making sure that Rubei heard him. (Chapter 17 "Yang Huo" Section 20)

(4) Li (禮 the rites) as a practical norm

[84] The Master said, "A ceremonial linen cap is prescribed by the rites, but today one of black silk is popular. This is more economical, and I follow the majority. To bow below the ceremonial hall [before ascending the steps] is prescribed by the rites, but today people bow after having ascended up there. This is impolite, and though it is against the majority, I follow the practice of bowing below." (Chapter 9 "Zi-han" Section 3)
[85] Zizhang asked whether the rites of ten generations hence could be known. Confucius said, "The Yin 殷 based its rites on those of the Xia 夏, what was added and omitted can be known. The Zhou 周 based its rites on those of the Yin, what was added and omitted can be known. Should there be successors to the Zhou following the same practice; the rites even a hundred generations hence can be known." (Chapter 2 "Wei-zheng" Section 23)
[86] Zai Wo 宰我 [a disciple] asked about the three-year mourning period, saying, "Even a full year is too long. If for three years the noble man does not practise the rites, they are sure to be in ruins; if for three years he does not practise music, it is sure to be in disorder." The Master said, "Would you then feel at ease to eat fine rice and wear embroidered clothes [after a shorter period]?" "Yes, I would." "If you feel at ease, do what you suggested. The noble man in mourning finds no relish in good food, no pleasure in music, and no comfort in his own home [in a shorter

period], therefore he does not do what you propose. Now that you can feel at ease, then do it." After Zai Wo had left, the Master said, "Yu 予 [Zai Wo's courtesy name] is so want of human feelings! Only until a child is three years old can it leave its parents' bosom, thus the three-year mourning period for one's parents is universally observed throughout the world. Didn't Yu also enjoy the three years' love of his parents?" (Chapter 17 "Yang Huo" Section 21)

[87] Lin Fang 林放 [a man from the State of Lu] asked about the essence of the rites. The Master said, "A great question! In ceremony, rather than extravagant it is better to be frugal; in mourning, rather than formal it is better to be in genuine deep sorrow." (Chapter 3 "Ba-yi" Section 4)

[88] Zixia quoted the verse, "The coquettish smile showing lovely dimples, the pretty eyes making flirting glances, by the white paint all is made so colourful and lively", and asked, "What is the meaning of these lines?" The Master said, "In painting, white paint is applied after the picture is basically done." "Does the practice of the rites likewise come afterwards?" The Master said, "Shang 商 [Zixia's formal name] is able to bring out my meaning. Now I can talk about *The Poetry* with him." (Chapter 3 "Ba-yi" Section 8)

[89] The Master said, "The noble man regards righteousness as the essence of his being and observes the rites to implement it." (Chapter 15 "Wei Ling-gong" Section 18)

[90] The Master said, "The noble man extensively versed in culture and restrained under the rites is not likely to go against what is right." (Chapter 6 "Yong-ye" Section 27)

[91] The Master said, "Dedication without the rites leads to excessive labour; carefulness without the rites leads to timidity; boldness without the rites leads to disorder; straightforwardness without the rites leads to rudeness." (Chapter 8 "Tai-bo" Section 2)

[92] When Yan Yuan died, Yan Lu 顔路 [Yan Yuan's father, also a disciple] begged that Confucius sell his carriage to pay for an outer case for the coffin. The Master said, "Everyone speaks up for his own son whether he is talented or not. When Li 鯉 [Confucius's son] died, he had a coffin but no outer case. I did not [sell my carriage and] go on foot to provide him with an outer case, because following in the rear of the great officers I cannot [according to the rites] walk on foot." (Chapter 11 "Xian-jin" Section 8)

[93] See [65].

[94] Confucius said of the Ji family 季氏 [a principal minister of the State of Lu], who had eight rows of eight dancers each to perform in their court, "If this can be tolerated, what cannot be tolerated?" (Chapter 3 "Ba-yi" Section 1)

[95] The Master said, "When we say 'the rites, the rites', do we refer merely to giving presents of jade and silk? When we say 'music, music', do we merely refer to playing bells and drums?" (Chapter 17 "Yang Huo" Section 11)

[96] When offering sacrifice to the dead, one ought to act as if their ghosts were present; when offering sacrifice to the gods, one ought to act as if the gods were present. Confucius said, "If I am not wholeheartedly engaged in the ceremony

of the offering it is the same as if I am not doing the offering at all." (Chapter 3 "Ba-yi" Section 12)

(5) Zheng xing (政刑 political measures and punishments)

[97] The Master said, "Guide them by orders, keep them in line with punishments, and the people may be prevented from troubles but will have no sense of shame. Guide them by virtue, keep them in line with the rites, and they will, besides having a sense of shame, become rectified." (Chapter 2 "Wei-zheng" Section 3)

[98] The Master said, "When the rites and music do not flourish, punishment will not fit the crime." (Chapter 13 "Zilu" Section 3)

[99] The Master arrived in the city of Wu 武 [a town in the State of Lu] and heard the sound of stringed instruments and singing. He broke into a smile and said, "You don't need an ox-knife to kill a chicken." Ziyou [the magistrate] protested, "Some time ago I heard it from you, Master, that the noble man instructed in the Way loves his fellow men and that the small man instructed in the Way is easy to command." The Master said, "Disciples, what Yan 偃 [Ziyou's formal name] says is right. My previous remark was only made in jest." (Chapter 17 "Yang Huo" Section 4)

[100] The Master said, "When the ruler loves observing the rites, the common people will be easy to command." (Chapter 14 "Xian-wen" Section 41)

[101] Zilu said to Confucius, "If the ruler of the State of Wei 衛 waited for you to administer his state, what would you do first?" The Master said, "If that is really the case, I would start with rectification of names." Zilu said, "Is that so? You are indeed circuitous. Why must there be such rectification?" The Master said, "How rude you are, You 由 [Zilu's formal name]! A noble man, in regard to what he does not know, will show cautious reserve. When names are not correct, what is said will not be reasonable; when what is said is not reasonable, tasks cannot be carried out successfully; when tasks cannot be carried out successfully, the rites and music will not flourish; when the rites and music do not flourish, punishments will not fit the crimes; when punishments do not fit the crimes, people will not know where to put their hands and feet." (Chapter 13 "Zilu" Section 3)

[102] Duke Ai asked You Ruo 有若 [a disciple]: "The year has a poor harvest and I have not enough to spend. What should be done?" You Ruo replied: "What about levying the tithe on the people?" The Duke said, "I have not enough when I tax them two parts in ten. How could I tax them one part in ten?" Youruo replied, "When the people have enough how can the ruler be insufficient? When the people are insufficient how can the ruler have enough?" (Chapter 12 "Yan Yuan" Section 9)

[103] Confucius said, "For those in the government what is to worry about is not poverty but inequitable distribution, not scarcity of people but inability to have them settled in peace. When the distribution is equitable none will be particularly poor. When the government can have the people settled in peace it will find no scarcity. When people in far away areas are not obedient, the government

should improve culture and virtue to attract them, and when they have come, settle them in peace." (Chapter 16 "Ji-shi" Section 1)

(D) Implementation of norms

[104] Ran Qiu 冉求 [a disciple] said, "It is not that I am not pleased with your way, but rather that my strength is insufficient." The Master said, "One whose strength is insufficient falls down exhausted in mid course. But now you draw a line of limit before starting." (Chapter 6 "Yong-ye" Section 12)
[105] The Master said, "Is there a man who can devote for a day all his strength to humanity? I have not come across such a man whose strength proves insufficient for the task." (Chapter 4 "Li-ren" Section 6)
[106] The Master said, "When the noble man is earnest in treating his relatives properly, the people will be aroused to humanity. When he does not neglect old relationships, the people will not become mean." (Chapter 8 "Tai-bo" Section 2)
[107] Ji Kangzi, troubled by the prevalence of thieves, asked Confucius for advice. Confucius said, "If you were not covetous, no one would steal even if you rewarded theft." (Chapter 12 "Yan Yuan" Section 18)
[108] Ji Kangzi asked Confucius about government, saying, "What about killing those who do not follow the right way for the good of those who follow the way?" Confucius answered, "In administering your government, why do you need to kill? If you desire what is good, the people will be good. The virtue of the noble man is like wind; the virtue of the small man is like grass. The wind blowing over the grass is sure to bend the grass." (Chapter 12 "Yan Yuan" Section 19)
[109] Zilu inquired about what makes a person a noble man. The Master said, "He cultivates himself to achieve respectability." "Is that all?" "He cultivates himself so as to bring peace and security to the people." "Is that all?" "He cultivates himself so as to bring peace and security to the people is a task even Yao and Shun would have found taxing." (Chapter 14 "Xian-wen" Section 42)
[110] The Master said, "He who governs with virtue is like the North Star – It stays in its position, and the multitude of stars moves around it." (Chapter 2 "Wei-zheng" Section 1)
[111] The Master said, "If a ruler ever governed effectively without doing much, it was, perhaps, Shun. What was there for him to do? Just to hold himself in a respectful posture facing due south. That was all." (Chapter 15 "Wei Ling-gong" Section 5)

(E) Administration of justice

[112] Yan Yuan inquired how to govern a country. The Master said, "Banish the tunes of [the state of] Zheng 鄭 and keep specious people at a distance. The tunes of Zheng are lascivious, and specious people are dangerous." (Chapter 15 "Wei Ling-gong" Section 11)
[113] The Master said, "In hearing litigation, I am like any other person. But if a different approach is necessary, I would like to cause the people not to litigate." (Chapter 12 "Yan Yuan", Section 13)

[114] The Meng family 孟氏 [a minister of the State of Lu] appointed Yang Fu 陽膚 [possibly a disciple of Zengzi 曾子] the chief judge, and he sought advice from Zengzi [a disciple of Confucius]. Zengzi said, "Those in authority have lost the Way and the common people have for a long time been let loose. If you succeed in extracting the truth from them, be grieved and pity them and do not feel joy." (Chapter 19 "Zizhang" Section 19)
[115] Zhonggong 仲弓 [a disciple], being made the chief officer of the Chi family, asked about government. The Master said, "Lead those on your staff who have specific responsibilities; pardon those who committed minor offences; and promote men of talents." (Chapter 13 "Zilu" Section 2)

(F) Social relationships

[116] See [14], [16], [17]. [19], [20]. [21], [24], [25], and [26] (especially 24)
[117] Duke Ai asked, "What should be done so that the people will be obedient?" Confucius answered, "Promote the upright over the crooked, then the people will be obedient; promote the crooked over the upright, then the people will not be obedient." (Chapter 2 "Wei-zheng" Section 19)
[118] The Master said, "In the case of a person who while occupying a high position is not magnanimous, while performing ceremonies not reverential, while in mourning is not sorrowful, how should I regard him?" (Chapter 3 "Ba-yi" Section 26)
[119] The Master said, "The common people can be made to follow a path of action but not to understand it." (Chapter 8 "Tai-bo" Section 9)
[120] The Master said, "To send untrained people to battle is to throw them away." (Chapter 13 "Zilu" Section 30)
[121] The Duke of Zhou 周公 said to [his son] the Duke of Lu 魯公, "A superior ruler does not treat those closely related to him casually, nor does he give his high officials occasion to complain because their advice is not heeded. Unless there are grave reasons, he does not abandon officials of long standing. He does not look for all-round perfection in a single person." (Chapter 18 "Weizi" Section 10)
[122] The Master said, "In serving the ruler, one should do the job with dedication before considering the emolument." (Chapter 15 "Wei Ling-gong" Section 38)
[123] Confucius said, "Serving the ruler strictly in accordance with the rites is viewed by some as obsequious." (Chapter 3 "Ba-yi" Section 18)
[124] When the ruler was present, Confucius was diffident and respectful but composed. (Chapter 10 "Xiang-dang" 鄉黨 Section 2)
[125] When summoned by his prince, Confucius immediately went on foot without waiting for his carriage to be made ready. (Chapter 10 "Xiang-dang" Section 20)
[126] Chen Chengzi 陳成子 [a minister of the State of Qi 齊] murdered Duke Jing 景公 [of Qi]. Confucius took a ceremonial bath, went to the court and reported to Duke Ai [of Lu] saying, "Chen Heng 陳恆 [Chen Chengzi's formal

name] murdered his sovereign. I beg you to punish him." The duke said, "Report the matter to the three principal ministers." Confucius retired and said, "As an official following in the rear of the great ministers, I did not dare not to report the matter. But the ruler said 'Report the matter to the three principal ministers.'" He went to the three principal ministers and reported the matter to them, but they refused his request. Confucius said, "Being an official following in the rear of the great ministers, I did not dare not to report the matter." (Chapter 14 "Xian-wen" Section 21)

[127] Zilu asked how an official is to serve the ruler. The Master said, "Do not cheat him, but challenge him." (Chapter 14 "Xian-jin" Section 22)

[128] The head of the Ji family was going to attack Zhuanyu 顓臾 [a small vassal state of the state of Lu]. Ran You and Jilu went to see Confucius and said, "The Ji family is going to take action against Zhuanyu." Confucius said, " Qiu 求 [Ran You's formal name], is it not you who are in fault here?. . ." Ran You said, "It is what our master wishes. Neither of us, being his officers, wishes it." Confucius said, "Qiu, there is this statement of Zhou Ren 周任 [an official historian of ancient time]: 'When a man is able to apply his strength in doing government work he takes his place in the rank of officers; when he becomes unable to do so he retires from it.' Why would a person use an assistant if when the person is in danger the assistant does not support him and when the person is to fall the assistant does not uphold him? Moreover, what you said is wrong. Whose fault is it when a tiger or rhinoceros escapes from its cage, and a piece of tortoise shell or jade is destroyed in its casket?" (Chapter 16 "Ji-shi" Section 1)

[129] Ji Ziran 季子然 [a relative of Ji Sun a principal minister of the State of Lu] asked, "Can Zhongyou 仲由 [the formal name of Zilu] and Ran Qiu be called great officials?" The Master said, " . . . The term 'great official' refers to one who serves one's ruler according to the Way and relinquishes office when this is no longer possible. Now men like You and Qiu can be described only as capable officials." "Then they would be obedient?" Confucius said, "They will not commit regicide and patricide even if so ordered." (Chapter 11 "Xian-jin" Section 24)

(G) Relationship between the individual and the state

[130] Yang Huo said to Confucius, "Come, I will talk to you. Can a person be called humane who hoards treasure in his bosom and left his country in confusion?" "No." Confucius replied. "Can he be called wise who, while eager to engage in public affairs, constantly misses the opportunity?" "No." Confucius again replied. "The days and the months are slipping by; time is not always with us" said Yang Huo. "Right," Confucius said, "I shall go to serve in the government." (Chapter 17 "Yang Huo" Section 1)

[131] The Master said, "There were those who would not lower their ideals and thus tarnish themselves. Are Boyi 伯夷 and Shuqi 叔齊 [two brothers who refused to serve in the government of the new Zhou Dynasty] not such people?" He then said, "Liuxia Hui and Shao Lian 少連 [a person known for his filial piety] lowered their ideals and thus tarnished themselves but nevertheless kept their

words and behaviour correct." He further said, "Yu Zhong 虞仲 and Yi Yi 夷逸 [two recluses] retired and held their tongue and were thus able to keep themselves clean and their integrity intact. But I am different from all of them. I do not view a course of action as absolutely acceptable or unacceptable." (Chapter 18 "Weizi" Section 8)

[132] The Master said, "Devote to learning with absolute sincerity. Uphold the good way until death. Do not enter a tottering state and do not stay in a state in disorder. When the Way prevails in the world work in the government; when the Way is in disuse retire. It is a shame to be poor and lowly when the state has order; it is also a shame to have wealth and honours when the state does not have order." (Chapter 8 "Tai-bo" Section 13)

[133] The Master said, "Wealth and honours acquired through unjust means are like floating clouds to me." (Chapter 7 "Shu-er" Section 16)

[134] The people of Qi sent to Lu a present of female musicians and dancers. Ji Huanzi 季桓子 [the principal minister of the State of Lu] accepted it and for three days no court was held. Confucius left Lu. (Chapter 18 "Weizi" Section 4)

[135] When travelling with Confucius, Zilu fell behind and met an old man carrying a weeding tool on a staff across his shoulder. Zilu asked, "Sir, did you see my master?" The elderly man said, "It seems that you never worked hard with your four limbs and you apparently cannot distinguish the five types of grain. Who is your master?" With this he put aside the staff and started weeding. Zilu held his hands up against his chest and waited respectfully. The old man then invited Zilu to stay overnight. He killed a chicken and cooked some millet to feed Zilu and presented his two sons to him. The next day Zilu went to report this to Confucius. The Master said, "He is a recluse" and sent Zilu back to see him, but when Zilu arrived he was gone. Zilu commented, "There is no justification for not participating in public affairs. Since the rules regulating the relationship between the senior and the junior cannot be disregarded, how can the principles governing the relationship between the sovereign and the subject be ignored? Wishing to keep his personal integrity, a person who refuses to serve in the government confuses the important relationships. A noble man enters public service in order to do his duty. That the Way is not to prevail simply because of his effort is a fact he already knows well." (Chapter 18 "Weizi" Section 7)

[136] Zilu stayed overnight at Shimen 石門. In the morning the keeper of the city gate asked, "Where do you come from?" Zilu said, "From Mr Kong 孔氏 [Confucius]." The gatekeeper said, "Is he the one who knows what is not doable and yet insists on doing it?" (Chapter 14 "Xian-wen" Section 38)

[137] Jieyu 接輿, the "madman of Chu", passed by Confucius, singing, "Phoenix, oh phoenix, how your virtues have declined! What is past is beyond help; what is to come may still be properly addressed. Give up, give up! Perilous is the lot of all those who engage in politics today." Confucius alighted from his carriage wishing to speak with him, but he quickly walked away to avoid Confucius, who thus did not get the chance to have a conversation. (Chapter 18 "Weizi" Section 5)

[138] While Confucius was playing the stone chimes in the State of Wei, some-

one carrying a basket passed by the door and said, "His heart is full of worries, the person who is playing the stone chime." After a while the man said, "It sounds narrow minded, this persistent clinking! When one is not taken notice of one should just stop doing what one does. Where the water is deep, cross it with clothes on; where the water is shallow, cross it with clothes held up." The Master said, "How self-assured this person is! It is difficult to change his view." (Chapter 14 "Xian-wen" Section 39)

[139] The Master said to Yan Yuan, "When called to office, carry out a mission; when left unemployed, retire. Only I and you are ready to do so." (Chapter 7 "Shu-er" Section 11)

[140] Someone addressed Confucius, saying, "Sir, why don't you serve in the government?" The Master said, "It is said in *The Book of Historical Documents*, 'Sincerely be filial to parents and loving to brothers.' Using these principles to influence those in government is also doing a government service. Why must one actually be in the government?" (Chapter 2 "Wei-zheng" Section 21)

[141] Weisheng Mu 微生畝 [a recluse] said to Confucius, "Qiu 丘 [Confucius's name], why are you so restless? Do you just want to demonstrate your ability of making artful talks?" Confucius said, "I do not dare to do that, I am troubled by those who are obstinate." (Chapter 14 "Xian-wen" Section 32)

[142] Changju 長沮 and Jieni 桀溺 [two recluses] ploughed the land together. Confucius passed by them and sent Zilu to ask for the ford. Changju said, "Who is he that holds the rein in the carriage?" Zilu said, "It is Kong Qiu [Confucius]." "Is it Kong Qiu of Lu?" "Yes." "Then he knows the ford." Zilu asked Jieni. Jieni said, "Who are you?" "I am Zhongyou" "Are you a disciple of Kong Qiu of Lu?" Zilu responded, "Yes." Jieni said, "Chaos is prevailing in the world and who is able to make a change? Moreover, rather than following a man who withdraws from certain persons would it not be better to follow those who withdraw from the world?" Then he went on covering up the seeds without stopping. Zilu went back to report to Confucius. For a moment The Master seemed lost in his thoughts and then said, with a bit of disappointment, "One cannot associate with birds and beasts. Am I not a member of this human race? If I do not engage with my fellow men in this world, who am I to engage with? If the Way were prevailing in the world, I would not engage in the effort of changing the situation." (Chapter 18 "Weizi" Section 6)

Lun-yu 論語

PART 2
INTERPRETATION

The changes in the sociopolitical system in the later period of the Zhou Dynasty happened together with a change in people's perceptions and conceptions. Passages in *The Book of Historical Documents* and *The Book of Poetry* show that when, gross injustice became prevalent – too often the debauched thrived, the virtuous suffered; good deeds were left unrewarded, wrongdoings unpunished – people felt perplexed and dispirited. Most of them had little control of their lives; they hoped that Heaven would take care of them. Now that that hope seemed unrealistic, they began to see Heaven as inscrutable and unreliable and wondered what they were to do. Could they have better ways to divine Heaven's will? If so, what were the ways? Or should they disregard Heaven and try self-help? If so, how should they conduct themselves? Were there common rules for their behaviour? If so, what were the rules and how could they be learned and implemented? Could people following such rules free themselves from the will of Heaven? Or were they hopelessly to remain in its or something else's iron grip, no matter what they would do? If so, had life any meaning and purpose? Was it worth living at all? These difficult questions were beyond the ability of ordinary people to answer. It was up to the thinkers to find solutions.

One of the first great thinkers was Confucius (551–479 BCE). Thanks to intense interests in his life, detailed records are available[1] to show that he was a descendant of aristocrats of the Song 宋, a vassal state established by the Zhou Dynasty in its beginning for the people of the defeated state of Yin. Six generations before him, his family emigrated to the Lu 魯, another vassal state of the Zhou, after losing a political struggle in the Song, and became commoners. His great grandfather was appointed a district magistrate and so was his father. His mother was a commoner, and her marriage to his father was considered informal and, therefore, shortly after giving birth to him, she was expelled from the Kong family. She moved to another town with the baby and lived in abject poverty.

Since childhood, Kong Qiu 孔丘 (Confucius's formal name) worked on odd jobs but nevertheless managed to obtain elementary education in a village school. Starting from the age of fifteen he began a lifelong pursuit of knowledge, learning from whoever had anything to teach him. He famously said that, in a group of several persons, there must be someone who could teach him something.[2] But, for more specific and profound knowledge, he travelled in his twenties to the capital of the Zhou and visited many learned men, including several great historians, maestros, statesmen and Laozi, then a government archive keeper.

He was particularly interested in the rites performed on various important occasions in people's life and in the local community and served as an assistant in those ceremonies, asking about, and pondering on, the meaning of the rituals. By the time he was thirty, quite a few people came to him for instructions, and he became a teacher. Traditionally higher education was reserved for aristocrats, to teach them *liu-yi* (六藝 six arts) – *li* (禮 the rites), *yue* (樂 music), *she* (射 archery), *yu* (御 charioteering), *shu* (書 calligraphy), *shu* (數 mathematics). He taught commoners, as well as some aristocrats who also came to study with him, the rites and music but substituted archery and charioteering with the *Shi* (詩 poetry), the *Shu* (書 historical documents), the *Chun-qiu* (春秋 annals of the State of Lu) and the *Yi* (易 the principles of ceaseless change): basically, the humanities and metaphysics.

In his twenties he served as a minor functionary in the government of the Lu. In 501 BCE at the age of fifty-one, he was appointed a district magistrate. In the next two years he was promoted first to the position of vice minister of public works, then chief judge, and then acting principal minister. Two years later he resigned because of a policy disagreement with the Duke of Lu and the principal minister. For the next fourteen years, he and a group of his disciples travelled back and forth in four other states seeking opportunities to realise his ambitions but failed. In 484 they returned to the Lu. He devoted his remaining years to teaching and to editing *The Book of Poetry*, *The Book of Historical Documents*, and *The Chun-qiu*. He died in 479 at the age of seventy-three.

Confucius was moderate, insisting that he was not an innovator but only a narrator of tradition. That was an understatement. He was familiar with the ideas and beliefs of his time and acquiesced in many of them but often gave them some new meaning. He also had new ideas, some of which were not quite conventional. Nevertheless, to say that he founded a new school, called "Confucian" in the West, is a mistake. Long before his time there were many people who recognised the special potentials of human beings and wanted to have those better potentials developed further to create a distinctive form of life that is constructive and moral – a civilisation. Among such people he particularly admired Duke Zhou 周公, one of the founders of the Zhou Dynasty,[3] who formulated many rites, or rules of proper conduct, and institutions for their implementation. In more than five centuries, between the establishment of that dynasty and Confucius's birth, countless people who shared the duke's ideas and ideals and tried to bring them to reality were known as *ru* 儒. The duke was labelled as such and so were

Confucius and his followers. They were different from other thinking men who, like Laozi, denied the special human potentials and disparaged civilisation.

Throughout his life Confucius developed and disseminated the ideas and ideals of the Ruists but what came down to us as the most authentic record of his words and deeds, plus some comments by his disciples, is a book known as *Lun-yu* (論語 *The Analects*). It is a small volume but its coverage is astonishingly wide. From the point of view of students of law, we see that he touched upon many basic legal topics, including the need for social authority and norms, their bases and objectives, the characteristics and hierarchical positions of various norms, the methods of making and enforcing laws, and the relationship between the individual, the authorities and the state.

(A) The need for social authority and norms

Most ancient thinkers discussed why human beings had to live in society and society had to have leaders and norms. Confucius did not say much on these topics. Apparently, he took this need for granted when he remarked that the world would not be in order if there was not a single authority to initiate and enforce norms, nor would it be so if each person did not play his role – a ruler, a subject, a father, a son, and so on – according to the norms prescribing it. He spent more time probing the nature of authority and norms.

(B) The authorities

(1) Heaven and fate

For a very long time it was commonly believed that the basis of social authority was the will of Heaven though, in late Zhou, some people began to have doubts about this. Confucius apparently accepted Heaven as a powerful force that caused the four seasons to go around and the myriad things to come into being, but he was unsure whether it also determined events in human life. He obviously sided with those who believed that, if it did, its decision was capricious and inscrutable. He was saddened and dumbfounded when Boniu, a particularly virtuous disciple, was stricken by an incurable disease. The premature death of his favourite student, Yan Hui, undoubtedly shook him even more. Sometimes he seemed to be uncertain about what was to happen to himself and his cause. For instance, when he and his followers were in danger in the state of Song and in Kuang, a district of the state of Wei, although he remained calm and talked about Heaven having bestowed upon him an ability and a responsibility to continue the development of civilisation begun by King Wen of Zhou, he was not positive about Heaven really wanting this civilisation to survive.

In addition to Heaven, many people believed in fate, a predetermined course from which people were unable to escape. It did not appear to have a will and was not always consonant with reason and ordinary human intelligence, and therefore largely incomprehensible and unpredictable. Some thinkers characterised it as the law of nature. Hard pressed to explain the kind of events mentioned above, Confucius was also found resorting to the popular belief of fate. He said this explicitly when one of his most able disciples, Jilu (also known as Zilu) was slandered by a fellow official, Gongbo Liao, in the court of Lu. His seemingly resigned response was: "It is fate if the Way prevails; it is also fate if the Way falls into disuse. What can Gongbo Liao do in defiance of fate?" Moreover he once observed: "Life and death are determined by fate; wealth and honours depend on the will of Heaven." On another occasion he averred: "If wealth and honours can be gained simply through one's own effort, I would not mind being a carriage driver", implying that there was something beyond human control that influenced human events, either by the name of Heaven or that of fate.

Was Confucius a fatalist? A true fatalist denies the existence of human free will and the value of human efforts. He is like a fallen leaf drifting along in a current, with no volition or ability to change what happens to be its course. Confucius could not be such a person. Even a casual reading of *The Analects* makes it clear that Confucius believed the opposite. Despite his remarks, his equanimity in adverse circumstances betrayed his true faith. It must have been his conviction that human beings are free agents with the ability to improve themselves and their living conditions, making life more enjoyable and meaningful. To him what was enjoyable and meaningful was civilisation, the glorious achievement of humankind. Every person should be proud of it and responsible for its advancement. It must be this belief that made him eager to make his contribution, regardless of its result. And obviously for this reason, as we shall see, he was known as the person who knowingly worked against overwhelming odds.

But if this understanding of Confucius is correct, how are some of his apparently fatalistic remarks to be interpreted? What did he mean when he said that he came to know Heaven and fate when he was fifty, and why did his disciples say that he seldom talked about Heaven and fate?

No passage in *The Analects* gives direct help but careful reading of the work can lead us to imagine Confucius making the following argument about fate. A social event is the product of many factors. A person involved in the event may have control over some of them and, if he tries hard, he may increase their number. But there are always other factors beyond his ability to see, let alone control. For convenience, such uncontrolled factors may be collectively called "fate". But fate is not cast in stone; to some extent it can be changed by human efforts. Therefore, it is worthwhile for a person involved in an event to gain control over as many influencing factors as possible. All else being equal, he who has more such factors in hand will have greater influence over the event. He may still be unable completely to determine the outcome but his chances are better than those who control fewer factors. If, after having tried hard, a person still fails to get the result he wants, he knows that he has not gained control of enough factors, not because a superbeing is wilfully against him nor because he is in the trap in a predetermined course. This became clear to Confucius when he reached fifty, perhaps after resigning from high office in the state of Lu.

This line of thought is of crucial importance to Ruist philosophy. On the one hand, it affirms the freedom of the human will and emphasises human ability in determining events to a certain degree; on the other hand, it points out the limitations of both the freedom and the ability, discourages unrealistic expectations and saves a person from the depression of failure after making earnest efforts. It is a rational, scientific way of thinking. It offers no assurance, as most religions try to do, that a person will receive rewards for his good deeds and retribution for his bad ones – if not in this life then in the next; if not to himself then to those close to him and his descendants. It is not a comforting thought to the faint-hearted but to those with a strong will and high intelligence it provides justification for their efforts in trying to improve themselves and their environment. It gives civilisation a meaning, makes a reasonable person believe that life is worth living, despite all the vicissitudes and uncertainties, and enables him to try hard to achieve what he wants and to keep his peace of mind if he fails. Thus the Ruist attitude is far from fatalistic; it is, rather, realistic, positive, and even optimistic. It was this attitude that prompted his attempts to improve the world and his invitation to others to do the same.

This argument may sound unfamiliar to most students of Confucius's philosophy. But it was clear to Xunzi. We shall see later that he explored this line of thought in dramatic ways and made it abundantly clear and convincing.

It is in the light of this thought that Confucius's remarks on life and death, and on wealth and honours, should be understood. While it is quite obvious to most people that life and death are matters determined by too many factors beyond human control, so were wealth and honours to Confucius. He did not gain much wealth and many honours but not because he did not try – he was eager to enter public service in order to realise his ideas and ideals. It was the intervention of "fate" – the cluster of factors beyond his control – that failed him. It was this belief that freed him from bitter disappointments.

Confucius's statement about getting to know Heaven and fate when he turned fifty can also be interpreted along this line. He did not mean that by then he became privy to Heaven's secrets and prescient. As a believer in human free will, he could not have meant that. What did he mean then? Keeping in mind his philosophy as a whole, we can confidently assume this: at the mature age of fifty, he finally came to understand that Heaven was not a wilful superbeing and fate a predetermined course. They both meant the same thing: a collection of factors that could influence events and could be, in many instances, beyond human control. When this occurred to him, he was able to feel that being "defeated" by Heaven and fate was not something to be ashamed of or bitter about.

(2) Gods and spirits

Moreover, the same belief must have made Confucius agnostic about gods and spirits as agents of Heaven capable of influencing human events. He did not deny their existence but thought an attempt to get their help less worthwhile than an effort to work with other humans. When he was told that it was more effective to pray to one god than to another one, he said if a person had been condemned by Heaven, there was nowhere he could turn in his prayers. Interpretation: when one has failed to gain enough control of the influencing factors of an event, one has no chance of getting a desirable result by appealing to numinous powers. His advice was to respect them but keep them at a distance.

In short, Confucius found Heaven and fate formidable and, in many instances, dominating. But they do not determine everything. Denying Heaven and fate as the absolutely controlling factors of human events was a necessary step before Confucius could build his theory that norms could have a more concrete and intelligible basis.

(3) Men

If Heaven and fate are not omnipotent, they cannot determine what humans are to do. But, if humans with their free will were to be let loose, there will be chaos and conflicts. They need norms, and authorities to make and enforce norms. Some norms can be formed more or less spontaneously among people in small communities and enforced by them in the form of customs. But, in a large society, rules have to be made and enforced by particular people – initially those with physical and intellectual force and later those with acknowledged authority. At Confucius's time, many people in political power made rules with disastrous results. He thought that to have order rules had to be made by a single supreme authority which he called *tian-zi* (天子 Son of Heaven). The person with this title was supposed to be an agent of Heaven but, since Heaven had been discredited, he could only be a person with high qualities and widely recognised authority. At Confucius's time the designation was still used for the king of the Zhou Dynasty but he used it only twice in *The Analects*, in both cases referring to an idealised sovereign of the entire world. More often he used the term *jun-zi* (君子 literally, a prince's son) for a noble man of high virtue and superior ability or, often more specifically, a good ruler of a state.

What qualities should a good ruler have? Because, according to Confucius, the main responsibility of such a ruler was to enforce the norms issued by the Son of Heaven and to correct the people, and, in order to be able to correct the people, the ruler must correct himself first, the essential qualities of a good ruler were those necessary for a good person. A good person must be filial and compassionate, have self-restraint, and be observant of the rites. In addition, a good ruler must be able to lead, be dedicated to his job and work tirelessly. He did not need knowledge and skills in any practical field but must know and abide by the basic norms of humanity and demonstrate this knowledge and abidance in his actions. He must select the righteous as officials to educate the common people. He must know when and how to employ the people without causing undue hardship. He must be generous but not wasteful, forceful but not overbearing. He should never be cruel, oppressive, tyrannical and petty. He must be trustworthy or the people would not follow him. Above all, he must know that to be a ruler is not easy and avoid abusing his power and authority.

Traditionally there are two ways to check abuse of power and authority – by self-restraint or by outside control. Confucius, starting with the premise that authority should belong to particularly virtuous persons, could not advocate outside control; he had to emphasise self-restraint. As he saw it, the worst sin of a person with authority was being megalomaniacal, that is, being conceited, self-indulgent, and self-righteous. Thus, when he was asked whether there was such a thing as a single remark which could lead a state to ruin, he replied that, if a ruler says he finds no pleasure in being a ruler except for the fact that no one goes against his orders, the state is sure to be ruined.

(C) Norms

(1) Types and hierarchy

In ancient China there were many types of norms, including *dao* (道 "Way"), *de* (德 morality), *li* (禮 rites) *fa* (法 law) and *ling* (令 orders). People often found that, in a particular situation, there were several different and conflicting norms applicable. It was not always easy for them to make the right choice and they became befuddled and incapable of acting. Thinkers offered some guidance – often elevating one type of norm as paramount and characterising other types as secondary or dismissing them as misleading. The Ruists did more in helping people to choose. They arranged the various types of norms in a hierarchy consisting of several levels and sublevels. The idea was expressed by Confucius when he said that there were three classes of noble men: one who kept their personal behaviour above reproach and carried out government assignments successfully was in the first class; one who was praised by members of their clan and village for being filial and brotherly was in the second; one who kept their word and persisted in their deeds was petty and was in the third class. The implication was that the norms observed by men in these different classes were of different significance. This point was made clear by Zixia, a disciple of Confucius, when he said that there were *dade* (大德 major virtues) and *xiaode* (小德 minor virtues) and that where one followed strictly the norms for the pursuit of major virtues one could be allowed some discretion in observing norms for the pursuit of the minor virtues.

Several passages in *The Analects* provide illustrations of this point. One was Confucius's comments on the conduct of Guan Zhong 管仲. When Duke Xiang of the state of Qi 齊襄公 died, his two younger brothers engaged in a struggle to succeed him. The first younger brother, Prince Jiu 公子糾, failed and one of his aides, Shao Hu 召忽, died with him, but another aide, Guan Zhong, surrendered to the successful second younger brother, Prince Xiaobai 小白, who became Duke Huan 桓公. Later Guan Zhong became the prime minister and lived in a luxury inappropriate for his status. Many people thought he was disloyal to his former master Prince Jiu, and Confucius criticised him for transgression of the rites prescribing proper lifestyle. Nevertheless, Confucius affirmed Guan Zhong's contribution to the preservation of China's peace and civilisation by suppressing strife among the feudal lords and assembling them in defence against the barbarous nomads on the borders of the Zhou Empire. For these achievements

Confucius ignored Guan Zhong's violations of minor norms and enthusiastically hailed him as a humane man, praise that the Master seldom lavished on lesser characters.

The point was central to two of Confucius's own deeds. When asked first (in 502 BCE) by Gongshan Furao 公山弗擾, a magistrate of district Bi 費 of the state of Lu, 魯 and then (in 490 BCE) by Bi Xi 佛肸, a magistrate of district Zhongmu 中牟 of the state of Jin 晉, to assist their rebellious causes, Confucius was ready to go but, in both cases was stopped by his disciple Zilu 子路 who thought it was not what a noble man should do. But Confucius probably thought that, although by revolting against their rulers the two officials had violated the political hierarchy he supported in principle, yet they were not entirely beyond salvation because of the fact that they sought his service. It was an indication that they valued his ideas and accepted his deeds which were by then well known. In any case, assured by his own moral strength – like something tough enough to withstand grinding and white enough to repel black dye – he was confident that he would not be used by his employers but that, rather, he would do his job with his principles upheld and his integrity intact. And, more importantly, he thought he could use the opportunities to achieve something of great significance, such as recreating a sociopolitical system similar to that of *Dong Zhou* (東周 the Eastern Zhou established by Duke Zhou 周公 in Luoyang 洛陽). To him it would be a mission, a command of a higher norm. And to respond to this command and carry out the mission, he did not have to be overly concerned about the moral character of the person who gave him the opportunity.

(2) Dao as the supreme norm

Among the many norms, *dao* (道 the Way) was regarded by practically all ancient Chinese thinkers as the highest, though they had different ideas about what it was. Confucius said when *dao* prevails, orders come from the king; when it is not, they come from the feudal lords. But he did not spell out what is *dao*, and his disciples did not hear him talking much about it. He said that, after studying the ways of the various dynasties, however, he found the way of the Zhou most admirable and therefore he would follow it. He even alleged that, before his health declined, he used to see Lord Zhou, one of the founders of the Zhou, in dreams. Presumably they would discuss the Way of the Zhou which was, in his words, magnificently civilised. Thus, his Way was not an abstract concept. It was not, as we shall find later, "natural" as Laozi said about his Way; nor was it preordained by a supernatural force such as Heaven as the Way Mozi advocated. It was artificial. Its course and goal, established by Wen 文 and Wu 武, the first two kings of the Zhou, were on record, and it was still followed later, though not strictly, by the state of Lu. Confucius believed that, with some correct changes, that state could be brought back to the Way.

The idea that the Way was an artificial norm has the obvious advantage of being more intelligible. But this idea is also problematic. An artificial norm needs constant human effort to maintain its relevance. Thus, this Way can prevail or fall into disuse, depending on whether there are the right people caring for it and implementing it. Most people of Confucius's time did not know how to address this problem. Indeed, many did not even know what his Way was. That was why he said a noble man must have his mind set on learning and following the Way. According to him, having heard about the Way in the morning, a person should have no regrets if he were to die in the evening. That was why he devoted his life to learning the Way, explaining it to people with the hope that enough of them could take his advice and acquire the qualities of noble men and help make the Way prevail again.

Another problem with Confucius's Way is that it was mainly a guide for how society might reach for a lofty objective. This was pointed out by his disciple, Youzi, who said that the beauty of the Way of "the former kings" (the sage rulers including King Wen and King Wu of the Zhou) was to seek harmony in society as the ultimate goal of humankind. To most people this aim might seem too high and nebulous and the course too difficult to follow. But Confucius thought it was not. According to him the starting point of the Way was filial piety and brotherly love. His disciple, Zixia, expounded on this saying that to learn and implement the Way one should start with learning the correct manner in doing the small chores of everyday life. After this training, one will be able to distinguish right from wrong and know what ought or ought not be done: for instance, that one should enter government service to implement the right policies not simply to earn remuneration, and that wealth and honour obtained in a wrong way is not worthy. This point was further explained in *Da-xue* (大學 *The Great Learning*):[4] The learning of the Way is to enable one to have one's heart rectified, one's mind made sincere, one's personal behaviour correct and refined, one's family put in order, one's country better ruled, and the world pacified. Thus the Way is in essence the *right way* to do everything and therefore it is a supreme norm above all lesser norms as its ramifications.

(3) De as the primary norm below the Dao

(A) *Ren*

People in ancient China recognised many norms known as *de* (德 moral principles) that were not as lofty as *dao* but more practical because the values they pursue were more specific and concrete. Unlike *dao*, these norms were not a priori, why should they be obeyed? The explanation was provided by Confucius. He observed that humans have something in common. It was labelled by later thinkers as *renxing* (人性 human nature) and discussed in great detail. Confucius, with his characteristic dislike of speculation, did not say much on this subject except that people are similar in nature but become different through learning. He did not elaborate what was similar but it is reasonable to assume that he meant some common human feelings, needs and aspirations. Norms based on similar human nature ought to be obeyed because disobedience would damage those feelings and make fulfilment of those needs and realisation of those aspirations difficult or impossible. For this reason, he held that a human being ought to take another human being as *a* human being basically like himself. He called this principle *ren* (仁). This character, being a combination of two *ren* (人 person), meant how people were to be together, and was thus used by Confucius to mean the right, humane way people are to treat one another. Thus, to put it simply, *ren* means *a human being should treat another human being as a human being*. Confucius maintained that every human being should strive to follow this principle, or *qiu-ren* (求仁 to be humane or to achieve humanity). To him this was the primary moral principle from which other moral principles could be derived.

What is exactly the concrete way to be humane? How is a person to achieve humanity? In *The Analects* there are many passages addressing these problems because it was evidently unclear to most of Confucius's disciples. He gave different answers to them, depending on the occasion and each disciple's character and ability to comprehend. In one case, he simply said "To be *ren* is to love your fellow man". In other cases he said to be *ren* was to be respectful, tolerant, sincere, diligent and kind; to lead in overcoming difficulties and to stay behind others in reaping benefits; to practise self-restraint and observance of the rites – not to look, listen, speak and move in violation of the rites. More specifically, he suggested two commandments: first, "Do not impose on others what you do not like" and second, "While you wish to establish yourself, help others establish theirs; while you wish to reach your goal, help others reach theirs". These commandments are concrete because they are obviously based on common human feelings, needs and aspirations; they are easy to follow because one needs only to reflect on one's own feelings, and so on; and they are very significant because the first one provides the basis for right and wrong, and the second helps society improve.

How can one tell whether a particular act is right or wrong? The criterion used to be something external – the command of a superbeing or an abstract notion or a utilitarian result. Confucius gave people an internal criterion – their own feelings, needs and aspirations. Besides being easy to comprehend, this criterion has another merit – it is not arbitrary and dogmatic but can be tested and proved right or wrong by human experience.

The significance of Confucius's second positive commandment is even greater. Only when people are willing to help one another realise their respective aspirations can society progress. Many other cultures had similar commandments. Admittedly, Confucius's proposition can be problematic because, though people may have similar aspirations, it is not always easy for a person to identify and approve the particular aspirations of others. But, of course, in Confucius's mind, the aspirations of a person worthy of the help of others must be congruent with the Way and other norms.

(B) XIAO

Among the more concrete moral principles, Confucius particularly emphasised *xiao* (孝 to be filial) because it is based on the most natural emotion a human being has towards another, hence the most basic expression of *ren*. Many of

Confucius's disciples asked what filial piety meant and how "to be filial". He emphasised that one should respect the wishes and legacy of one's parents, and one should show this respect in one's manners, particularly in one's facial expression, while providing sustenance or other service to one's parents, otherwise the act would not be different from that done for domestic animals. He also stressed obedience but not in the sense of subservience, as many people mistakenly believed. When a parent is in the wrong, a child should courteously advise correction but never just complain. In practice he suggested following the rites in treating one's parents both during their lifetime and when carrying out their burial and offering sacrifice to them.

(c) *Yi*

Another norm, commanding people to pursue *yi* 義, also received special attention from Confucius. The word appeared twenty-four times in *The Analects*. It generally referred to rectitude, justice or simply right, correct. Thus, Confucius maintained that a person should be brave in doing what is right, and he praised Zichan for being just in employing the service of the people. In ancient times, people often mentioned *yi* and *li* (利 profit) together. Mencius, as we shall see, thought there was almost an inherent conflict between the two. Confucius only reminded people that, when one saw profit, one should think whether it was right to pursue it. To him wealth and status gained unjustly were like drifting clouds. Generally, he thought there was a right principle governing every relationship, and a right way for a person to follow in his dealings with the world. But he did not define what was right, correct, or just. As mentioned above, he apparently believed in some basic feelings and aspirations common to humans. It can therefore be argued that what was in agreement with common human feelings and aspirations was right, and people should know this innately. But since, as Confucius admitted, humans change according to experiences, this argument is not on firm ground. Another argument is that, by his time, there were already many norms defining right and wrong, and a person who accepted them would know what was right.

(d) *Zhi*

A more commonly recognised norm, *zhi* (直 straight), received more scrutiny from Confucius. It was because, as the antonym of *wang* (枉 crooked), *zhi* was used extensively to mean not only straightforwardness, honesty, truthfulness, uprightness, and justice but also crudeness, rudeness, rigidity, and stupidity. Confucius valued uprightness, believing that placing an upright person in government could help make the crooked straight. And he thought the appropriate response to injustice is justice not kindness. He did not endorse simple straightforwardness, maintaining that even a straightforward act should be done in accordance with the rites lest it would appear rude, crude or stupid. In any event, he did not think a person should be rigidly straightforward. He praised those who were always straight regardless of the circumstances but he admired more the wisdom of those who entered public life and contributed their talents when the circumstances were favourable and, when they were not, retired from it and kept their personal integrity. It seems to be his view that to act straightforwardly under some circumstances was unwise because it could bring harm not only to the actor but also to the public at large. This point was illustrated by a story in *The Analects* of a man who testified against his father who was accused of stealing a sheep. The son's action was praised by the local magistrate as *zhi*. Confucius disagreed, maintaining that what he considered to be *zhi* was for the son to conceal the crime of the father and vice versa.

A person who conceals a crime is certainly not straightforward, and to characterise the act as upright contradicts common usage of the word. Why did Confucius make such a strange statement? To understand it we have to imagine what would happen when the case in question was brought to court. If the father denied the charge and there was no corroborative evidence supporting the son's story, it would be just the word of the son against that of the father, creating a procedural conundrum. An unbiased judge might have to throw the case out because it would be very difficult for him to make a correct decision.

If such a case is considered acceptable for adjudication, the authorities may encourage people to testify against those who are close to them, or may even make a law demanding people to report the offences of others. Such a law might make the work of discovering crimes easier but the consequences will be disastrous. Fearing betrayal, people will cease to trust one another and, being pressed by the demand, they may make careless accusations. The necessary bond between people of even the closest relationship – spouses, parents and children, siblings, friends – will be destroyed, society will cease to function properly, its members will live in suspicion and fear, and civilisation will decline and perish. This is not an exaggeration, it happened in China and elsewhere when such a law was adopted and enforced. Such a law could be a product of evil minds but it could be made simply because of a wrong sense of justice which is narrow, superficial, mechanical and short-sighted. It was reflected in the magistrate's use of the term *zhi*. To Confucius true justice is not merely to address the immediate problem of a wrong but more importantly to ensure long-term equity and harmony in society and the progress of civilisation. For this reason, a son should not be allowed to testify against his father, let alone praised for doing so. Where people of close relations are permitted to conceal one another's wrongdoings, a few criminals might escape punishment but society as a whole would be saved from disintegration. The choice between the two evils is clear.

Nevertheless, to describe a man who covers up someone's offence – even though it was his father or son – as *zhi* still sounds strange. The word seems to be a misnomer here. Perhaps "in compliance with a higher virtue" is a more appropriate description. But wasn't Confucius who, as we shall see, insisted on "rectifying the names", supposed to be precise in his language? A reasonable explanation is that his use of the adjective *zhi* was a direct rebuff to the magistrate's self congratulatory remarks which used the word in a narrow sense reflecting a superficial view of justice. And it must be pointed out that, even in demonstrating his annoyance, Confucius did not say that concealing a crime was literally *zhi*, he used the word in a broader sense, saying *zhi* was *implicit* in the special case of a father concealing an offence of a son and vice versa.

There were instances where Confucius seemed not to be straightforward. In one of them, after declining a visit from Yang Huo, a powerful official of the state of Lu with subversive ambitions, and receiving from him a steamed piglet as a gift, Confucius timed a return visit when Yang Huo was away from home. In another instance when Rubei, a messenger from Duke Ai, came for a call Confucius refused to see him, on the grounds of illness. But before Rubei departed, Confucius played his zither and sang loudly, making sure that the visitor heard him. Why did Confucius act in such strange ways? It is easy to understand that he did not wish to be friendly with Yang Huo and yet wanted to observe the rites of being reciprocal in social interactions. It is not clear why Confucius lied to Rubei. Mencius later said that to refuse seeing a person was a way in which to educate him. (It would, supposedly, force him to reflect on his own behaviour.) Perhaps Rubei did something wrong, and Confucius intended teaching him a lesson, so that to tell a white lie was to drive home the lesson.

Thus, it is obvious that Confucius did not consider *zhi* as a high virtue. His interpretation of it was another example of the principle that it is more important for a person to follow the higher norms and, in order to do so, he can be excused for being flexible in observing the minor ones.

(4) Li as a practical norm

Li (禮 the rites), as rules of propriety, were generally recognised in ancient China. Their contents and the principles behind them were studied by practitioners as well as by thinkers. Confucius was renowned for his knowledge of the rites and served as a *xiang* (相 master of ceremony) from youth until late in life. He must have said and done a great deal about and for the rites but not much is left to us. What we have are works of Han Dynasty scholars who collected what were supposedly the rites of ancient times and the discussion of them between Confucius and his disciples.[5] To them these rules were of crucial importance. They argued that a man not observing *li* was no different from other animals. These rules were based on custom or created by social authorities and changed from time to time and place to place. But, according to Confucius, the changes were limited and predictable because the core rules had roots in human feelings – for instance, sorrow after the death of a parent. Natural feelings could be expressed in different ways. One of the functions of the rites was to regulate such expressions, making them more refined – like adding some white paint as a final touch to highlight certain places on a colourful picture and make it more attractive. But the rites were not simply decorative, they were, more importantly, to establish specific criteria for all conduct, requiring those below it to move up and those above it to move down, and thus making conducts standardised, easy for other people to recognise and accept. The criteria were to be reasonable and the ultimate objective of the rules was, as pointed out by Confucius's disciple, Youzi, to achieve harmony in society. Thus, Confucius advised that, while in mourning, it was more appropriate to feel sincere sorrow than to perform elaborate rituals. He declined the suggestion of selling his carriage to buy an outer coffin for a favourite disciple. He condemned Jisun and Guan Zhong, the prime ministers of the state of Lu and the state of Qi respectively, for usurping the rites prescribed for persons of status higher than theirs. He criticised his disciple Zai Wo for his suggestion of shortening the three-year mourning period for one's parents. In *Li-ji* 禮記 it was reported that he also criticised his son, Boyu 伯魚, and his another disciple, Zilu, for prolonged mourning.[6] He emphasised that, while offering sacrifices to gods and ancestors, one should act as if they were present. And he lamented that people of his time thought that rites only meant giving and accepting presents. According to him, the rites were to help an individual to implement *ren*, the primary norm; to make government of the people easy; to transform a crude society into a civilised one.

The Ruists were criticised for their overemphasis of the rites. But the criticism missed the point which is that there was a critical problem in implementation of norms. Generally, the moral principles were too broad, abstract and susceptible to widely different interpretations; and the law was too narrow, specific, and rigid, incapable of coping with changing circumstances. The rites were in the middle – they were more concrete than morality and more comprehensive than law. While they had high objectives, they were more in consonance with human feelings and habits; while they were not backed by the full force of the political and judicial system, they had the support of tradition. They were thus easier to implement. Indeed, because they were there for the small details of everyone's everyday life – for instance, what things not to look at, listen to and speak and what moves not to make – observing them could produce a subtle influence which would, in the end, make a person's behaviour more agreeable to others and thus reduce social friction and eliminate the need for moral preaching and law enforcement.

(5) Zheng xing

According to Confucius, to govern was to correct, to make people conform to norms. Apart from those discussed above, there were finally two other types of norms: *zheng* (政 government policies) and *xing* (刑 penal measures). Confucius recognised the need of them when he said that, in an orderly society, punishments were initiated by a single central authority. But he pointed out that correction could be accomplished through many means – morality, the rites, government policies and penal measures – and he clearly preferred the first two over the second two. He taught his disciples that, when the common people had learned the correct way, they would become easy to command, and that to learn the correct way was to learn the rites and music. More importantly, resorting to the second set of norms would not only make governing easy but also make the people good. In his words, "When the government guides the people with executive orders and keeps them in line with punishments they will avoid sanctions without feeling ashamed about the proscribed acts; when it guides the people with morality and keeps them in line with the rites they will not only shun such acts but also feel ashamed about them and become correct." Therefore he urged those in the government to correct themselves and become moral examples for the people.

Confucius once said that, given an opportunity to govern a state, he could have a good start within a year and significant accomplishments in three years.[7] The fact that, while in the government of the state of Lu, he was rapidly promoted from a magistrate to acting chief minister in just three years proved that he was not boasting. He must have had many good policies and measures, and some of them were reported elsewhere,[8] but, in *The Analects*, we find only some principles he suggested as guidelines. Two somewhat more specific ones are worth mentioning here. Both were about how to keep stability and harmony in the state. One was reflected in the answer You Ruo, a disciple of Confucius, gave to Duke Ai of Lu about taxation; the other in a lesson Confucius gave to Ran Qiu, another disciple. The first pointed out that the ruler should not overtax the people; the second emphasised equitable distribution of wealth and peaceful settlement of the people, especially those who were not obedient. The advocacy of a policy of attracting such people from afar by the government improving culture and virtue instead of subduing them by force was, as we shall see, much repeated by the Ruists of later times.

(D) Implementation of norms

To make norms effective, Confucius prescribed a procedure, starting with *zhengming* (正名 rectify the names). Why rectify the names? It seemed to Zilu, and perhaps to many others, to be a rather circuitous approach to an urgent problem. To understand Confucius's prescription it is necessary first to know its background. As we shall see later, Mozi pointed out that, at his time, there was no common political and ethical language. People used the same words to mean different things and, as a result, serious, fruitful dialogue was impossible. This situation apparently already existed during Confucius's time. It indicated that society lacked a common orientation, a shared value system, and a consensus on what was right or wrong. The result was chaos. To establish order, such orientation, value system and consensus must be rebuilt. "Rectification of the names" was the shorthand for such a task. In more concrete terms, it was to make a person, a thing or an event what it was supposed to be – a ruler as a proper ruler, a subject as a subject, a father as a father and a son as a son, and so on.

According to Confucius, only after the names were rectified could arguments be reasonable; only with the support of reasonable arguments could tasks affecting people's welfare be accomplished; only after such tasks were accomplished would the people be willing to observe the rites; only when the rules of propriety were followed could punishments be appropriately applied to those who committed egregious offences; only when punishments were so applied could the people know how to behave properly. The logic in this assertion may not be self-evident but it is obvious that, when people do not resort to the same nomenclature, do not have common values and a shared sense of right and wrong, they will not know how to act, government will be difficult if not impossible and society will be in chaos.

How are Confucius's prescriptions to be implemented? More specifically, how are the various norms he hailed to be enforced? Confucius did not suggest any special method or technique. His advice was very simple: Let the ruler lead the way. As mentioned earlier, he emphasised that, first of all, those in authority must correct themselves – to act as rulers ought to be – and we have seen in *The Analects* what special qualities a person should have to be a ruler and how he was to acquire them – in other words, how to correct himself. Basically, a ruler needed to restrain his own desires and observe the rites. It was not necessary for him to have knowledge about special tasks such as farming or gardening. To govern, he needed only to be dedicated and trustworthy; for, without trust in the government, the common people would not know how to behave. He should not be niggardly towards the common people, not use them in an untimely way and not make excessive demands of them. Instead, he should be kind to them and treat them according to the rites, and, above all, teach them to observe the rites and behave correctly. To employ them in difficult tasks, such fighting a war without giving them proper training, was like simply throwing them away. All these steps were not easy but a person in government who wanted to govern well must strive to take them and not to limit his own efforts. When he had corrected himself and made himself a model for the people, his influence would be irresistible. He did not even have to give explicit orders. The people would willingly follow his way and become correct. They would not only obey the norms but also know why and feel ashamed of violating them even if they were induced to do so. That was why, when asked by Minister Ji Kangzi 季康子 of the state of Lu 魯 how to prevent theft and robbery, Confucius replied: "If you are not greedy, people will not steal or rob even if they were to be rewarded for doing so". When this attitude was established, prohibitions and punishments became unnecessary. Thus, on another occasion, when the same minister asked whether it would be right to kill those deviating from the Way in order to honour those following it, Confucius said: "Being a ruler, why do you need to kill people? If you desire virtue, the people will be virtuous. The character of a ruler is like wind; the character of an ordinary person is like grass – when the wind blows over, the grass is sure to bend."

This wind and grass metaphor may sound a little exaggerated, but the opposite of it is definitely true: a leader cannot expect people to observe a norm that he consistently ignores or violates. Such an expectation will be an affront to the common human feeling that one should not impose upon others what one dislikes oneself.

When the ruler had succeeded in educating the people by his own example, the result could be astonishing. According to legend, the sage king Shun 舜

ruled without having much to do. "What was there for him to do?" Confucius asked rhetorically and said, "Just hold his person in a respectful posture facing due south. That was all." In other words, having taught the people by example, all Shun had to do was to continue being a model. As we shall see, this ideal of government without much to do was common to most ancient Chinese thinkers although they differed on how it could be realised. What Confucius suggested sounds simple but actually it requires a ruler to do a lot. It is not easy.

(E) Administration of justice

But the age of the sage kings was long gone. By Confucius's time people were in difficulties and the authorities were under crushing pressure to address many problems. When one was brought to them in the form of a lawsuit, a trial had to be conducted. Confucius said he was no better than others to carry it out. But, if he could have his way, he would oblige people not to litigate. Was he serious? Civil disputes are inevitable in any society. How could he force people not to litigate? Ideally, he could create a situation in which people were all so enlightened, compassionate, rational, sympathetic and tolerant that they had no frictions and no disputes. But he never claimed such ability. What he possibly could claim was that he could make litigation unnecessary. To understand this claim we have to realise that there are other ways in which disputes can be solved, such as conciliatory deals, mediation and arbitration. We should also know that, in closely knit communities like those of ancient China, there were persons other than judicial officials in whom people could trust as intermediaries in solving disputes. Compared with such measures, litigation could seem quite unattractive because it was not only more costly but also less likely to produce satisfactory results owing to the fact that a judge, being an outsider, could not be familiar with all factors relevant to the dispute. Even in a case where the immediate problem was clear, the judge could find it difficult to sort out its deep and widely tangled roots that had grown through many years, even generations back in time, involving numerous persons of many complicated connections and interactions. A judgment might produce a seemingly clear-cut solution but it could quite possibly be unacceptable to one or even both parties. In such a case, not only the problem remained, but the judicial process might leave a new wound in the relationship between the parties. In addition, there was another reason why a judgment could be difficult and unsatisfactory – there was insufficient law governing civil matters in ancient China. A judge had to apply local custom which was perhaps unknown to him, or appeal to his own perceptions and ideas which might seem prejudiced and alien to the parties involved. For all these reasons, it would be wise and practical for the government to encourage people to settle their disputes out of court. Having these points in mind, we can reasonably assume that Confucius did not mean he could completely eliminate disputes but he could make it unnecessary for people to resort to litigation as a particular method to solve them – he could advise the parties to be conciliatory, to use mediation or arbitration and, of course he would educate the people first and set himself up as a model of correct behaviour. It was possible that he could succeed in realising his wish.

But even if his wish could be realised, Confucius had to face another problem – people sometimes committed crimes – and he never intimated that he had an effective way to eliminate crime. Nevertheless, he would undoubtedly argue that education could reduce their frequency and, in addition, he suggested a negative measure against certain elements – for example, lascivious music and specious persons – that could corrupt the people, inducing them to deviant behaviour. It was probably because of this suggestion that people later thought Confucius had been responsible for the execution of Shaozheng Mao 少正卯, a potential troublemaker in the state of Lu when Confucius was the acting prime minister.[9] But that was a fabrication. Confucius suggested only that those elements be expelled or kept away. He was averse to punishments, let alone killing a person not proven guilty of abominable crime. He advocated that leniency should be shown to people who commit minor offences. Even in a case of serious crime, where the authorities uncovered the truth, he would urge compassion. This position was made clear in a passage in *The Analects* attributed to Zengzi 曾子, a favourite student of Confucius: "When a judge finds the truth about an offence he should feel sad and piteous, not joyful, because those in high positions had lost their way and the common people had been on the loose without direction very long." It is fair to think that this reflected Confucius's view. It did not question the usefulness of the judicial system and punishments but expressed a doubt about their effectiveness. What can they achieve if both the offender and the authorities are to blame for the offence?

More importantly, Confucius maintained that, in deciding a serious criminal case, law should not be applied as the only norm. And, when it was applied, its interpretation should not be mechanical. The first point should be quite obvious by now – people should be taught morality and the rules of propriety first, and these norms should be applied before the law. The second point needs some explanation here.

Unlike in other legal systems, law in China had a narrow meaning, referring only to man-made rules. Some laws made by ancient sage kings were basically expressions of moral principles, but laws made by later rulers, particularly those of Confucius's time, were in a different category. He evidently had serious reservations about those rulers because they were often ignorant, short-sighted and biased, and, as a result, the laws they made could not be comprehensive and completely correct but very possibly be arbitrary and thus not readily acceptable to ordinary people. That was why Confucius observed that, at best, the people would try to avoid violating those laws but would not feel a sense of shame when they failed to do so. For these reasons, applying the law should be kept to a minimum. Instead, a higher norm should be considered first. And, where application of law was inevitable, a judge should not just look at the letter of the law. Rather, he should be allowed room to interpret the relevant law, making it consonant with higher principles, and to reach a decision that was not only appropriate for the case at hand but also, more importantly, helpful in a piecemeal and incremental way to reach the ultimate goal of society, namely to enable people to live in harmony and prosperity and contribute to the advancement of civilisation. These ideas were evident in Confucius's disapproval of a son giving testimony against his father. The same were also reflected in his response to the event of an official of the state of Jin casting a bronze pot with the criminal law of the state inscribed on it.[10] In short, he reportedly said that, before this event, the state of Jin had general legal principles which were followed by the authorities who interpreted them in ways appropriate to individual cases. Now that the law was cast in bronze, the people would look only at the letter of the law, leaving the authorities no room to make decisions fitting the circumstance. The result would be more disputes and disorder leading to the fall of the state.

(F) Social relationships

Now let us consider another important topic of Confucius's legal thinking – the relationship among people, particularly between the individual and the authorities. We have to start with his view that humans are similar in nature. This premise implies that humans are essentially equal, and therefore in principle people should treat one another equally. To be more specific Confucius suggested that each individual should use himself as a standard; therefore a person should not do to others what he does not want others do to him, and while wishing to realise his aspirations, he should help others to realise theirs. In other words people should treat one another with understanding, sympathy, respect and mutual help.

The relationship between the ruler and the ruled is special. It is functionally asymmetrical – the former is to lead and command, the latter to follow and obey. Confucius recognised this and confirmed the need of a social hierarchy. Nevertheless, he insisted that the behaviour of one occupying a specific position in this hierarchy must be properly befitting the position. His famous statement on this was: "Let the ruler be a ruler, the subject be a subject; the father be a father, the son be a son." What he meant was that there was a correct way for each person to act and interact with the other in those paired relations. What was this correct way?

First, concerning the ruler's personal behaviour, Confucius emphasised that the ruler should be keenly conscious that with his exalted position and many privileges came great responsibilities. To meet the responsibilities, he should cultivate and rectify himself. In ordinary times he should establish himself as a model for the common people; in times of difficulty he should be the vanguard fighting the problems. Moreover, even in leading and giving commands to the people and demanding their obedience, a ruler had to act in accordance with the rites, and he had to be sympathetic and caring. In short, he had to show *noblesse oblige* and observe a higher standard of conduct than that of the common people.

How should a ruler and an official in government service treat each other? Confucius had a succinct answer: "The ruler should employ a subject according to rites and the subject should serve the ruler with loyalty." In specific situations specific rites should be applied but here Confucius referred generally to the rites that would demonstrate the ruler's understanding, sympathy and respect towards the official concerned. By 'loyalty', Confucius could not have meant blind obedience; a better interpretation would be 'in good conscience'. This point was made clear by his many other statements on the subject. First, about the attitudes of officials, he said that fundamentally they should serve for a cause, not just for emoluments, and they should be faithful to the state, not only to the ruler. They should never be subservient to him but challenge him when he was in the wrong and resist his orders that would harm the state and the people. To be able to do so they should be upright and honest and never cheat. In sincerity they should offer advice to him even though it might fall on deaf ears or be brushed aside, as in the case when Confucius reported a regicide in the state of Qi and advised the ruler of the state of Lu to dispatch a penal expedition against the perpetrator. He was told to report the case to the principal ministers. He did and was ignored. He knew that that would be the outcome but offered the advice anyway because he thought it was the duty of officials to keep the ruler in the right and, if they failed and bad consequences followed, they were to blame, as he blamed his disciples Ran You and Jilu for the consequences of their failing to prevent the chief minister of Lu from invading the small vassal state of Zhuanyu. But Confucius was realistic. He knew that, in many instances, officials had no power to stop a ruler from doing wrong. In such cases, they should resign or nonchalantly accept dismissal like the wise man Liuxia Hui did three times.

Confucius did not say anything about how a father was to be a proper father. His silence was probably due to his belief that a father was naturally disposed to love his children and therefore there was no need to spell out norms for him to follow. On the other hand, he said a great deal about how a son was to behave properly towards his father. The norm was to be filial. Filial piety was exulted as the basis of many other norms. To be filial to parents, however, was not merely to provide for their sustenance, as many people thought, but to treat them with care and respect, otherwise it would not be different from providing food and shelter for dogs or horses. The treatment must be done in sincerity and in a pleasant manner, and it must be in accordance with the rites, neither inadequate nor excessive. Confucius said a son should not disobey. Fearing that his remark could be interpreted to mean simple subservience, he hastened to add that by "not to disobey" he meant not to serve parents in life and in death in a manner deviating from the rites. More importantly, to be filial, a son was not to change the course his father took. But if he thought his father was taking a wrong course, he was not to follow blindly but gently to counsel correction and, if the advice was rejected, to be more reserved and respectful, and offer it again later.

In short, Confucius believed that, in their interaction, people should all observe the rites and the principles behind them and have mutual understanding, sympathy and respect. They may live in a hierarchical society but it does not have to be authoritarian in the sense that one in a commanding positions can force his decisions upon those below him in total disregard of their opinions. In our time, Confucius is often accused of advocating authoritarianism. This is unfair.

(G) Relationship between the individual and the state

Apart from the relationship between the individual and the authorities, there is another that is of great importance to Confucius's theory. It was that between the individual and the state, particularly between a *shi* (士 intellectual) and a *guo* 國. A *guo* was a politico-socio-economic entity ruled by a feudal lord immediately under the king of Zhou who was known as the Son of Heaven. Though the king was supposed to be the sovereign of *tian-xia* (天下 all under the heaven, or the entire world), the territory under his direct control was also a *guo*, known as the state of Zhou, with him as its effective ruler. We have seen in *The Analects* much discussion about the intellectuals' relationship with the ruler of a state but we find few explicit references to their relationship with the state independent of its ruler. Nevertheless, implicitly Confucius recognised a distinction between the person and the institution. Thus, in many instances, he talked about an intellectual's duty towards the state even if the ruler was unworthy.

To Confucius the paramount duty of an intellectual to the state was to help the Way prevail. For this purpose, it was necessary for him to serve in the government. Confucius agreed with Yang Huo that it was neither humane nor wise for him to refuse government office. Actually Confucius did not, as a principle, refuse. He did serve in his home state Lu and travelled to many other states seeking office. More to the point, he was even ready to serve such unsavoury characters as Gongshan Furao and Bi Xi, before and after being a high official of Lu.

Why did he leave his post in Lu? Why did he fail to secure any post of significance in other states? And why, after declining the invitation of Gongshan Furao, was he later ready to accept an offer from Bi Xi? It was baffling to Zilu and more so to others. They had different ideas about how one should act if one were in Confucius's shoes. Some believed the situation at the time was completely hopeless and advised Confucius and his disciples to "avoid the world". Some thought the efforts made by Confucius and his disciples, who were unfamiliar with the everyday problems people faced – working in the fields and knowing how to grow various crops – were doomed. A person who heard Confucius playing a stone instrument and thought the tune reflected the player's fixation on achieving his objectives, quoted an adage: "Cross a ford with clothes on when the water was deep; pull them up when it was shallow." The lesson was clear: act according to the circumstances. Another person, who sounded more sympathetic but no less critical, characterised Confucius as a person who insisted on doing what he knew to be impossible. Yet another who, believing that Confucius had harmed his own integrity by continuously seeking office and that all those who were in office at the time were bringing disasters upon themselves and society, suggested that he should stop regretting what had happened to him in the past and try to save his future by not making the same mistakes again.

The suggestion of acting simply according to circumstances was most repugnant to Confucius. He thought the unprincipled accommodation as cheap and unworthy. He understood why some people would "avoid the world" and praised a few of them who, in order to preserve not just personal integrity but a principle, gave up life when in overwhelmingly hostile circumstances. He was also sympathetic with two other types: those who lowered their ideals and sacrificed their reputation but kept their words and behaviour correct, and those who retired and became silent in order to keep themselves clean and independent. But he said, "I am different from all of them. I do not hold a course of action as absolutely acceptable or unacceptable." What did he mean and what course would he take? To understand the first part of this question, it is necessary to remember that he was optimistic, did not think the situation of his time hopeless, and that he had high self-esteem, believing that, if he had an opportunity to govern, he could carry out his mission without being tainted by those who gave him the chance. As to the second part of the question, the answer was in his endorsement of the course taken by those who entered public service when the circumstances were possible for the Way to prevail and withdrew when they were not, in order to preserve their personal integrity. He repeatedly expressed his admiration of such people as Ning Wuzi and Qu Boyu, and alleged that he and his favourite disciple, Yan Hui, would do the same under similar circumstances because, to them, the wealth and honours that came with government offices in which they were unable to realise their ideals would be like drifting clouds. And, indeed, when it was apparent that rulers of Lu had no intention to let him implement his plans for government, he left office.

But he was rather more positive than others in adverse circumstances. After failing to secure significant government positions, he did not simply retire. Instead, he continued busily teaching, insisting that education was also a way in which to participate in government by influencing those actually in it. In any case, he never relented in his effort to help the state in spite of it being under the control of a ruler far from desirable, because he saw a difference between the two, and he felt the common people needed his contribution to achieve peace, order and prosperity; he believed he had a mission to help them return to the Way. These points finally dawned on Zilu and became convictions of his own. This was evident when he commented on the behaviour of a recluse farmer saying,

> "There is no justification for not participating in public affairs. Since the rules regulating the relationship between the senior and the junior cannot be disregarded, how can the principles governing the relationship between the sovereign and the subject be ignored? Wishing to keep his personal integrity a person who refuses to serve in the government confuses the important relationships. A noble man enters public service in order to do his duty. That the Way is not to prevail simply because of his effort is a fact he already knows well."

What he meant was that, while one might want to escape the disorder caused by bad rulers, one still had to recognise the need for the political system and the correct principles governing it. In other words, one could repudiate a bad ruler but not deny one's obligations towards the state.

(H) The ideal state

As mentioned in the Preface, humans created norms, institutions and practices to help realise some social objectives. What objectives did Confucius think society should seek? What kind of society did he wish people to have? *The Analects* does not give us a clear picture of his ideal state although we can gather from the scattered passages that he had one in mind. There is, however, a paragraph in *Li-ji* that described a utopia and its decline.[11] It was written by his disciples but attributed to him and probably reflected some of his ideas. It is therefore added here in my translation:

> When the Great Way prevails, the world is for the public; the virtuous are elected and the talented given government responsibilities; sincerity is valued and harmony cultivated. People do not love only their own seniors and care for their own young; they make sure that the old have provision for their declining years, those in their prime have employment, the youth have means to grow up with, and the unfortunate – the widower, the widow, the orphan, the childless, the disabled and the sick – have maintenance. Men will have their work, women their homes. One hates to see goods being discarded but does not necessarily want to keep them for one's own possession; one hates to see one's strength not being put to good use but does not necessarily want it to be used for one's own benefit. That is why plots against others do not arise; robbery and theft, violence and mayhem do not occur; and outer doors of buildings are left unclosed. This is called *da-tong* (大同 the Great Harmony, Grand Union).

What a beautiful state! In it every person is apparently equal, entitled to have a share of the resources and a responsibility to use his ability in helping others. It is altruistic, compassionate, peaceful and harmonious. It is not made clear when this state existed but, anyway, at some later time it vanished. The paragraph continues:

> Now the Great Way is in hiding. Everyone in the world is for his family – loving only one's own relatives, caring only for one's own children and gathering goods and using strength only for one's own benefit. Great lords turn it into a practice to transmit their posts to their descendants. People build walls and moats to secure cities and towns; adopt rites and laws to regulate relationships between ruler and subjects, father and son, elder and younger brothers, husband and wife; establish institutions and create landownership; value the clever and the brave; and make efforts only for their own advancements. Thus, plots and schemes take place and armed conflicts arise. Yu, Tang, Wen, Wu, King Cheng and Duke Zhou were the best from this situation. These six noble men were careful about the rites. They demonstrated their own righteousness, proved their own sincerity, exposed their own mistakes, used the benevolent as their models, and

> stressed their modesty and humility, all to show the people the constant, correct course. They dispatched anyone who deviated from it, even one in a position of power, and the masses would regard him as an evil. This situation is called *xiao-kang* (小康, small welfare, moderate prosperity)

When did the Way go into hiding? A hint is in the sentence "Great lords turn it into a practice to transmit their posts to their descendants." In Chinese history the first hereditary political dynasty was established by Yu. So perhaps the writer of this paragraph thought the Way disappeared after Yu? After that, the ideal state was lost. In its place came a world of self-centred souls. Among them, six rulers, including Yu, were the best. They tried hard to make themselves worthy models for the people and to keep the state in order. They did not quite succeed, so they made rules and punished those who deviated. As long as there were these good rulers, the situation was relatively tolerable but, of course, the other rulers were far less qualified and hence the miserable situation since Confucius's time.

The crucial difference between the two states are *wei-gong* (為公 for the public) or *wei-jia* (為家 for the family). But is the kind of altruism described here possible? The Ruists would argue that, because human nature is malleable, by proper education people can be made less solipsistic and the world more tolerable. It will be especially effective if those in power could be less greedy and more willing to share with the people what they have. As Confucius said, it is not scarcity but inequitable distribution that one should worry about and, if what the people need is adequately met, how can those in the government feel inadequate?

To sum up, Confucius lived in a difficult time, faced a troublesome situation and took upon himself a Herculean task to try to change it. We have only scant record of his actual work and practical suggestions. *The Analects* shows mainly that he constructed a theory which could justify civilisation and, indeed, life itself. He was to find a new basis for social authority and norms. He shifted people's focus of attention from Heaven to the real world, from gods and spirits to humanity, from the unknowable to the more comprehensible. He insisted that humans were, to certain extent, capable of influencing the outcome of the events in which they were involved and should try to do so. He was aware that the outcome was often unpredictable and he had to tell people how to understand and endure the failure of their efforts. His position was quite scientific but, for that very reason, not easy for people intuitively to grasp.

His greatest contribution to jurisprudence was to make common human nature, experience and aspirations, instead of the will of a superbeing, the bases of social norms. He thus held *ren* – the right way for a human being to treat another human being – as the primary social norm. To make *ren* less general and abstract, he listed a set of more specific and concrete norms that were to implement this primary norm. According to their effectiveness for this purpose, these secondary norms formed a hierarchy with moral precepts at the top, followed by the rites and the law. He placed particular emphasis on the rites as rules of propriety because they were more concrete than morality and less rigid than law. More importantly, they could make people unconsciously form certain behaviour patterns that were in conformity with *ren*. But the rites were necessarily formalistic and would change from time to time and place to place, making it difficult for universal observance. And, besides, there were always those who, incidentally or intentionally, violated the higher norms and caused civil disputes or committed crimes. Therefore, he did not dismiss the usefulness of law and the judicial system; he just stressed that, with proper education for the people, such outcomes could be minimised. But when law had to be applied, he reminded the people that it was the lowest of the norms which expressly regulated only certain types of behaviour, and its rules were imperfect. Therefore, he would argue that it should not be interpreted literally and applied mechanically, disregarding higher, broader and more important norms. In his view, literal interpretation and rigid application of the law would at best achieve superficial justice in an individual case but would certainly jeopardise the order and harmony of society as a whole. This view may not be widely accepted but there is an undeniable truth in it.

He was keenly aware that, to implement social norms, there was a need for social authority. By his time, China already had a long-established tradition of being under the control of hereditary political elites. Though deeply dissatisfied by it, Confucius never imagined any other form of government. What he wanted was to reform the ruling class. He preached the high norms to rulers and officials, urging them to restrain their desires and observe the rites and set themselves up as models for the people. His efforts failed dismally. His comments on their conduct and policy were largely ignored. The best of the elites wanted an instant fix for the contemporary problems; the worst craved immediate gratification of their personal desires for power and wealth. Though he stressed that the high officials should not be subservient to the ruler but he taught them only to be insistent on advising that ruler to change course and, when the advice was rejected or ignored, officials should resign. He did not invent any other method or mechanism to bring about change and detested any drastic action to force them. That was why he never succeeded in preventing the authorities of his time from becoming drunk with power and corrupt, and bringing about their own decline and destruction, dragging society along with them.

On the relationship between an individual and his superiors and inferiors, and between him and society and the state, Confucius's view was unconventional. By his time, in addition to the authoritarian hereditary ruling clique and the largely illiterate and ignorant masses, a new class of intellectual, consisting of disinherited aristocrats and their plebeian disciples, had risen. They were educated and had knowledge and skills to tackle problems faced by the states, were eager to serve in government, and were needed by the rulers. Those who succeeded would share in, or compete for, power with the old ruling class; those who failed would criticise it. The relationship was tenuous. Confucius suggested a relationship of mutual respect or tolerance at least. The rulers never quite accepted his view but it did encourage intellectuals of his time, and in the future, to stand up for their principles against arbitrary power. It was his concern for the Way that led him to make the important distinction between the ruler and the state and, when he talked about loyalty, he meant loyalty to the state, and he thought a loyal subject, as well as the ruler, had a moral obligation to help the Way prevail in the state. But, unfortunately, he did not make this power clear enough and used the term *jun* 君 to refer to both the ruler actually in power and the ideal ruler representing the state.

His view on the relationship between family seniors and juniors was more one-sided but he never preached unconditional submission of a child to his parents. Instead, he advised the junior to treat the senior according to the rites and to counsel returning to the correct way when the senior strayed on to a wrong path. This point was also ignored, unfortunately.

Thus his theory was not perfect and its legacy is mixed. It took centuries and continuous efforts by his disciples to substantiate his ideas and address their shortcomings, particularly how to change the course of a state when its ruler failed his responsibilities and betrayed the people's trust. But, in the process, impurities were introduced and, in many ways, his theory was distorted and adulterated by superficial and mistaken interpretations, of which the most regrettable was that he supported and justified authoritarianism. This particular misrepresentation was deliberately made by the government of the Han and all later dynasties. Efforts were even made to turn his teachings into a religion, producing pernicious and sometimes comical effects. In the nearly two centuries of the recent past, Chinese intellectuals in revolutionary mood blamed everything bad in China on Ruist ideology. They were blindly followed by the masses, among whom few had actually read *The Analects*. It is most unfortunate for Confucius and for China.

Nevertheless, his influence on Chinese thought is indelible and his contribution to world civilisation should not be underestimated. The vision of *da-tong* is superior to the utopia of most religious leaders who created dogmas on the basis of narrow ethnic or sectarian experiences and promised personal salvation to believers. His theory is also better, more reasonable, than doctrines some modern thinkers have invented on the basis of limited social, political and economic experiences and yet have claimed universal and eternal validity despite inevitable changes in human society and its environment. These dogmas and doctrines are largely irrational, exclusive and self-righteous and thus capable of inflicting cruelty on heretics and non-adherents. Confucius was different from these narrow-minded ideologues. He had the whole of humankind at heart, emphasised reciprocity in human relations and aimed at building a world society for all humans with mutual respect and compassion. More importantly, he pointed out that humans can be educated to work together for a better society, and his reasonable optimism has been a singularly crucial support for people who struggle against seemingly insurmountable odds to do their best in reaching a better world. It was these ideas that attracted most Chinese who seriously considered ways for the improvement of society and human life. When his ideas become widely accepted mankind will have a brighter future.

Notes

1. See Sima Qian 史馬遷, *Shi-ji* 史記 Chapter 17 "Kongzi shi-jia" 孔子世家 pp. 484–94; Zhang Bingnan 張秉楠, *Kong zi zhuan* 孔子傳.
2. In his words, *san-ren xing bi-you wu-shi-yan* 三人行必有吾師焉. See Liu Baonan 劉寶楠, *Lun-yu Zheng-yi* 論語正義 Chapter 7 "Shu-er" 述而 p. 164.
3. Near the end of his life, Confucius realised that death was approaching and lamented only that he no longer saw Duke Zhou in his dreams. See Liu Baonan, *supra*, p. 137.
4. *Da-xue* was initially a chapter of *Li-Ji* (禮記 *Book of the Rites*). The short text (205 words) was supposedly a statement of Confucius recorded by Zengzi 曾子, a disciple. In the Song Dynasty, Zhu Xi 朱熹 (1130–1200), a Ruist scholar, selected it and *Zhong-yong* (中庸 *The Golden Mean*), another chapter of the same book, and grouped them with *The Analects* and *Mencius* into a collection known as *Si-shu* (四書 *The Four Books*). Since his time, this collection has been held as the most important of Ruist canons.
5. The most commonly available among such collections are *Yi-li* 儀禮 and *Li-ji* 禮記. The former describes some of the rites observed by aristocrats; the latter has more explanation of the rites.
6. *Li-ji* "Tan-gong shang" 禮記 '檀弓上'.
7. See *The Analects*, Chapter 13 "Zilu" Section 10.
8. For instance, *Xunzi*荀子 reported that, before Confucius was about to assume the post of chief judge of the state of Lu, sheep butchers and cattle herders stopped cheating, an indulging husband divorced his adulterous wife, and a local bully escaped to a neighbouring state. See *Xunzi* 荀子 Chapter 8 "Ru-xiao".
9. This story first appeared in *Xunzi* 荀子 in Chapter 28 "You-zuo".
10. See *Zuo-zhuan* 左傳 p. 1504
11. See *Li-ji* Chapter 9 "Li-yun" pp. 413–14.

Lao-zi 老子

PART 1
TRANSLATION

(A) The *Way*

(1) Its nature and description

[1] Something was chaotically formed, coming into being before heaven and earth. It is silent and undefined. It stands alone, undergoing no change; and moves about, never getting tired. It may have been the mother of all things . . . Not knowing its name I give it a label – the *Way*. (*Laozi* Chapter 25)
[2] The *Way* takes nature as its model. (Chapter 25)
[3] The way that can be spoken is not the constant *Way*; the name that can be named is not the constant *Name*. (Chapter 1)
[4] What we may look at but cannot see is named "formless"; what we may listen to but cannot hear is named "soundless"; what we may try to grasp but cannot hold on to is named "incorporeal". These three cannot be probed separately, so we mix them together . . . This is something we may call "the formless form" and "an imageless image". It is nebulous and elusive. (Chapter 14)
[5] As a thing the *Way* is nebulous and elusive. Being nebulous and elusive it nevertheless has an image; being elusive and nebulous it nevertheless has a substance. It is shadowy and imperceptible and yet within it there is an essence. This essence is quite real and within it there is something that can be verified. (Chapter 21)
[6] The *Way* produces one; one produces two; two produces three; three produces the myriad things. (Chapter 42)
[7] The *Way* is hidden and without a name, and yet it is this *Way* that is good at investing and enabling success. (Chapter 41)
[8] The *Way* brings all things into being . . . It gives them life but does not possess them; it does everything for them but takes no credit; it facilitates their growth but does not determine the outcome. This is called the most mystic virtue. (Chapter 51)

(2) Its attributes and lessons

(A) MODERATION AND MODESTY

[9] A gusty wind does not last all morning. A sudden downpour does not continue all day. What causes these? It is heaven and earth. (Chapter 23)
[10] To hold a vessel and fill it to the brim is not as safe as to let it stand less full. One can grind an object to make it sharp but cannot keep it so for long. A hall can be filled with gold and jade but no one can safeguard them. One who is wealthy and holds high position and is arrogant will bring disaster upon himself. Having accomplished a task, retire. This is the Heaven's *Way*. (Chapter 9)
[11] One who is on tiptoe cannot stand for long, one who strides cannot walk far, one who displays himself does not make himself shine, one who is self-assured will not be popular, one who boasts his own ability will not have many achievements, one who has self-conceit is not to endure. In the view of the *Way*, such behaviour and attitude are "left-over food and superfluous action" loathed by all and therefore not cared for by those who have the *Way* at heart." (Chapter 24)
[12] The five colours make a man's eyes blind; the five tunes make his ears deaf; the five flavours injure his palate; galloping and hunting make his mind go wild with excitement. (Chapter 12)
[13] Excessive desire comes at great cost; large hoards results in deep loss. One who knows contentment suffers no humiliation; one who knows where to stop does not end in disaster, and instead will last long. (Chapter 44)
[14] Is not the *Way* of Heaven comparable to the way of drawing a bow? The upper end of the bow is bent down and the lower end of it is raised up – what is overabundant is reduced, what is insufficient is compensated. While the *Way* of Heaven reduces the surplus and compensates the deficit, the way of man was not so – it takes from the insufficient to enrich the overabundant. (Chapter 77)
[15] No disaster is greater than not knowing what is enough, no curse is greater than having excessive desire. Therefore one who is content with what one has is the one who will always have enough. (Chapter 46)
[16] The highest form of excellence is like that of water. Water is good at benefiting the myriad things and does not contend with them. It stays in the low places disliked by all men and thus comes near the *Way* . . . Because it does not contend it is free from blame. (Chapter 8)
[17] The reason why the river and the sea are able to be king of the hundred valleys is that they are good at taking a position lower than theirs. (Chapter 66)
[18] Nothing in the world is softer and more yielding than water, and yet nothing is more effective than it in attacking something strong and rigid. (Chapter 78)
[19] In their interaction, the female in the world always prevails over the male by being quiescent and lying low. (Chapter 61)
[20] The *Way* of Heaven does not strive and yet is good at winning. (Chapter 73)

(B) Selfless and devoid of emotion

[21] Heaven and earth are long lasting. The reason why they can last long is that they do not live for themselves. (Chapter 7)
[22] When everyone in the world recognises something as beautiful, then there is ugliness; when everyone knows something as good, then there is evil . . . The haves and the have-nots are coexistent; the difficult and the easy are complementary; the long and the short are relative; the high and the low are comparative; the music and the voice of a song are harmonious; what is ahead is followed by what is behind. (Chapter 2)
[23] How much difference is there between an approval and a reproach? How much difference is there between "good" and "evil"? (Chapter 20)
[24] Heaven and earth are not benevolent. They treat the myriad creatures as straw dogs. (Chapter 5)

(C) Inactive and covert action

[25] The *Way* normally does nothing and yet nothing it does not do. (Chapter 37)
[26] Shape a lump of clay into a vessel; it is the empty space within that makes it useful. Cut doors and windows into the walls of a room, it is these holes that make the room useful. Therefore it is profitable to have something but it is the void that makes the thing useful. (Chapter 11)
[27] Is it not that the space between heaven and earth is like a bellows? It is void and yet it is inexhaustible. The more movements that take place there the more comes out of it. (Chapter 5)
[28] A tree that fills the arms grew from a tiny sapling; a nine-storey terrace rose from a small lump of earth; a thousand-mile journey begins with a single step. (Chapter 64)
[29] The great *Way* pervades. It can be on the left and on the right, everywhere. The myriad things depend on it for their being, and it never rejects them. When it accomplishes something, it does not claim any credit. It clothes and nourishes the myriad things but never dominates them. (Chapter 34)

(D) Advance in reverse

[30] Seemingly moving in the opposite direction is how the *Way* progresses. Seemingly being weak is how the *Way* makes its achievements. (Chapter 40)
[31] If something is to be shrunk it must be let stretch first; if something is to be weakened it must be let strengthen first; if something is to be destroyed it must be let establish first; if something is to be taken away from a person he must be given it first. This is called "subtle wisdom". (Chapter 36)

(B) The use of the *Way*

[32] When spoken, the *Way* sounds plain and not exciting; when looked at, it is not much to see; when listened to, it is not much to hear; but when put to use, it is inexhaustible. (Chapter 35)

[33] In the past there were those who had got the *One*: Heaven got it and thereby became clear; the earth got it and thereby became settled; the gods got it and thereby became mythically efficacious; the valley got it and thereby became full; the myriad things got it and thereby became existent; the princes and kings got it and thereby became rulers of the world. (Chapter 39)
[34] The *Way* is the shelter for myriad things. It is what a good man treasures, and is an unfortunate man's refuge . . . Why did the ancients value this *Way*? Did they not say that by its guide they could gain what they prayed for and avoid crimes? (Chapter 62)

(C) The fall of the *Way*

[35] When the great *Way* was disregarded, there were benevolence and righteousness. When intelligence and cleverness emerged, there was great hypocrisy; when the six relations were not harmonious, there were filial piety and parental kindness; when the state was in disorder, there were loyal ministers. (Chapter 18)
[36] Thus after the *Way* was lost there was virtue; after virtue was lost there was benevolence; after benevolence was lost there was rectitude; after rectitude was lost there were the rites. Hence the rites were attenuated forms of loyalty and good faith, and the fountainhead of disorder. (Chapter 38)

(D) The Sage

(1) His character and qualifications

[37] Without stepping out of his door the Sage knows the world; without looking through his window the Sage sees the *Way* of Heaven. (Chapter 47)
[38] Be absolutely empty minded, keep steadily quiet. The myriad things would engage in all kinds of activities and I shall observe how they move back and forth because, though they are in flurry, each of them would return to its root. To return to the root is to be tranquil and is called to return to one's nature. To return to one's nature is to become Constant. One who knows the Constant is all-seeing. One who does not know the Constant and acts recklessly will court disaster. One who knows the Constant will be tolerant. Being tolerant one will be impartial; being impartial one becomes kingly; being kingly one becomes like the sky; being like the sky one is with the *Way*; being with the *Way* one will be long lasting and will not be in peril throughout one's life. (Chapter 16)
[39] A person who cultivates himself his virtue will become genuine, who cultivates his family the virtue of the family will be abundant, who cultivates his village the virtue of the village will grow, who cultivates his state the virtue of the state will be rich, who cultivates the world the virtue of the world will be prevailing. Thus a person can observe another person using his own person as a standard, observe another family using his own family as a standard, observe another village using his own village as a standard, observe another state using his own state as a standard, and observe the world using his own world as a standard. How do I know the world? It is by this method. (Chapter 54)

[40] In the past a person who practised the *Way* well was subtle, wonderful, profound, comprehending, and unfathomable. Because he was unfathomable we can barely describe him by his appearance: he was hesitant as a person wading a stream in the winter; timid as a person fearful of all around him; grave and courteous as a guest; evanescent as ice that is about to melt; simple as the primordial substance; vacant as a valley; cloudy as muddy water. (Chapter 15)
[41] One who has great virtues is like a newborn baby. Poisonous insects would not sting it, venomous snakes would not bite it, fierce beasts would not seize it, and birds of prey would not maul it. (Chapter 55)

(2) His objective

[42] When the primordial substance was dispersed its parts became useful objects, the Sage used them and became leader of the people. (Chapter 28)
[43] When one holds the Great Sign the world will follow him because wherever he goes there will be no harm but safety and peace. (Chapter 35)
[44] Man takes the earth as the model, the earth takes Heaven as the model, Heaven takes the *Way* as the model, and the *Way* takes nature as the model. (Chapter 25)

(E) The re-establishment of the *Way*

(1) The Sage's special tasks

(A) TO RID SOCIETY OF CONCRETE PROBLEMS

[45] The more taboos there are in a country, the people will be poorer; . . . the more laws and orders proliferate, there will be more thefts, robberies and mayhem. (Chapter 57)
[46] The people are starving because those above them consume too much in taxes; the people are difficult to govern because those above them are too fond of action. (Chapter 75)
[47] The Sage rejects excessiveness, rejects extravagance and rejects indulgence. (Chapter 29)
[48] Not to exalt the worthy will keep the people from contention; not to prize goods which are hard to procure will keep them from becoming thieves and robbers; not to reveal what you desire will keep their minds from being unsettled. (Chapter 3)

(B) TO MINIMISE THE ROOT OF SOCIAL PROBLEMS

[49] The five colours make man's eyes blind; the five tunes make his ears deaf; the five flavours injure his palate; galloping and hunting make his mind go wild with excitement. Therefore the Sage takes care of the belly, not the eye. He gets rid of those [allurements] and takes seriously this [what is basic]. (Chapter 12)
[50] In governing the people, the Sage empties their hearts but fills their bellies, weakens their wills but strengthens their bones. He always keeps them devoid

of knowledge and free from desire, and ensures that those who have knowledge never dare to act. (Chapter 3)
[51] In ancient times those who were good at pursuing the *Way* did not enlighten the people but made them ignorant. The reason why the people are difficult to govern is that they had too much knowledge. (Chapter 65)
[52] When the Sage governs the world he muddles the minds of the people. They will all have something to occupy their eyes and ears, and he treats them all like children. (Chapter 49)
[53] Stop learning, and there will be nothing to worry about. How much difference is there between an approval and a reproach? How much difference is there between good and bad? "What others fear I must also fear" – how barren and pointless this idea is! (Chapter 20)
[54] Eliminate sagaciousness, discard knowledge and the people will benefit a hundredfold; disregard benevolence, spurn righteousness and the people will again be filial and caring; dismiss ingenuity, abandon profit and there will be no more thieves and bandits. (Chapter 19)

(2) The Sage's attitude towards his work and his basic strategy

[55] Heaven and earth are not benevolent; they treat the myriad things as straw dogs. The Sage is not benevolent; he treats the people as straw dogs. (Chapter 5)
[56] Hold fast on to the *Way* of antiquity in order to keep in control what is here today. One who comprehends the beginning of antiquity knows the essence of the *Way*. (Chapter 14)

(3) His tactics

(A) To mix with the people

[57] A thing of great perfection seems chipped, and yet use will not wear it out; a vessel that is really full seems empty, and yet use will not drain it; a thing truly straight seems bent; a man with great skill seems clumsy; one of great eloquence seems tongue-tied. Strenuous activities repel cold; calm overcomes heat. One who is calm and quiet can rectify the world. (Chapter 45)
[58] He who knows does not speak. He who speaks does not know. (Chapter 56)
[59] The Sage knows but does not exhibit himself; he loves himself but does not engage in self-exaltation. (Chapter 72)
[60] The Sage has no fixed mind; he takes the mind of the people as his mind, [saying]: "What they regard as good I will regard as good; what they regard as bad I will regard as bad – my virtue is being sympathetic. What they trust I trust; what they distrust I will distrust – my virtue is being trusting." In the world the Sage withholds his own opinion and makes the minds of the people muddled. The people look at and listen to him. He treats all of them as children. (Chapter 49)
[61] The multitudes are merrily hustling as if enjoying a great banquet, or making a sightseeing trip up a terrace in spring; I alone am still, showing no signs, like an infant that has not yet learned to smile, appearing lost and knowing nowhere

to go. The multitudes already have more than they need; I alone seem to have nothing. My mind is like that of a fool, muddy and witless. All ordinary people are bright and alert; I alone seem befuddled. All the ordinary people are discerning; I alone am dull. I am as without desire as the sea, and as without purpose as the winds. (Chapter 20)

[62] Those who know do not speak; those who speak do not know. He who shuts his mouth, closes his door, dulls his sharpness, resolves disputes among the people, harmonises with them in their light, joins them in their dusty life. This is called the "mysterious unity". He who has achieved this unity cannot be treated familiarly or distantly; he cannot be benefited or harmed, honoured or disgraced. He is thus valued by all in the world. (Chapter 56)

(B) To appear selfless, humble, yielding and claim no credit

[63] The reason I have great trouble is that I have my body. When I no longer have my body, what trouble do I have? Therefore he who honours himself by working for the world, the world can be placed in his trust; he who loves himself by working for the world, the world can be placed under his care. (Chapter 13)

[64] A good soldier is not belligerent, a good fighter is not angry, a good conqueror does not engage in actual combat, a good employer is humble before his employee. This is called the virtue of not contending. (Chapter 68)

[65] The Sage's way is to do but not to contend. (Chapter 81)

[66] [The Sage] helps bring things into being and takes care of them. But while bringing them into being he was not possessive of them; while he does a lot for them he claims no credit; while he facilitates their growth he does not determine the outcome. This is called the "profound virtue". (Chapter 10)

[67] The Sage manages without action and teaches without words, and yet the myriad things develop. He helps them come into existence but does not possess them; he works for them but does not take credit; he accomplishes but does not dwell upon his success. It is because he does not dwell upon it he is never alienated from it. (Chapter 2)

[68] The reason why the river and the sea are able to be king of the hundred valleys is that they are good at taking the lower position. Therefore, desiring to rule over the people, one must in one's words humble oneself before them; desiring to lead the people, one must, in one's person, follow behind them. Thus the Sage places himself over the people yet they do not regard him as a burden; he places himself ahead of the people yet they do not consider him an obstruction. That is why the world joyously supports him and does not feel tired. Because he does not contend, no one in the world is able to contend with him. (Chapter 66)

(C) To appear inactive but engage in small efforts

[69] In a case where someone wishes to get hold of the world and do something to it, I see he cannot succeed. The world is a sacred object to which no one can

"do" anything. Anyone who does anything to it will damage it; anyone who tries to hold it will lose it. (Chapter 29)

[70] The softest thing in the world commands and drives the hardest thing in the world. What has no substance can enter where there is no space. Hence I know the advantages of no action. Few things are as effective as lessons without words and as beneficial as no action. (Chapter 43)

[71] He who studies increases his knowledge daily; he who practises the *Way* diminishes his action daily. He diminishes it and diminishes it again and arrives at doing nothing. When he is doing nothing there is nothing he cannot do. He who wins the world is usually by no action. When he begins to act he is never up to the job of winning the world. (Chapter 48)

[72] By no action one wins the world. How do I know? It is by this: the more taboos there are in the world the poorer the people; the more smart instruments the people have the greater disorder will be in the state; the more crafty skills the people possess the more strange contrivances will proliferate; the clearer the laws and orders are the more robberies and mayhem there will be. Therefore the Sage says, "When I am doing nothing, the people will transform themselves; when I am fond of quietude, the people will rectify themselves; when I do not take up any task, the people will grow rich by themselves; when I am without desire, the people will become simple themselves. (Chapter 57)

[73] Do the non-act. Tackle the non-task. Taste the tasteless. Enlarge the small. Multiply the few. Requite injury with kindness. Plan to face difficulty when it is still easy. (Chapter 63)

[74] Something that is at rest is easy to hold; something that has not taken shape is easy to take measures against; something that is brittle is easy to break; something that is tiny is easy to disperse. Act on a thing before it acquires a stature; manage a thing before it becomes disorderly. (Chapter 64)

[75] Plan to tackle a difficult task while it is still easy; begin to handle a huge job while it is still small. All difficult tasks in the world are sure to start in a form that is easy; all huge jobs are sure to begin in a shape that is small. For this reason the Sage never ventures into huge undertakings, and therefore he is able to accomplish great works. (Chapter 63)

[76] In governing the people and serving Heaven nothing is as good as frugality. It is because frugality is a sign of following the *Way* early. He who follows the *Way* early can accumulate strength fast. He who has accumulated strength will have nothing that he cannot overcome. Where he can overcome everything, others will not know his ultimate limit. Where others know not his ultimate limit, he can have the state. (Chapter 59)

[77] Governing a large state is like cooking a small fish. (Chapter 60)

(D) To advance in reverse

[78] The Sage puts his person last and it comes first; he treats it as alien to himself and it is preserved. Is it not because he is without personal interests that he can achieve his interests? (Chapter 7)

[79] The fish must not leave the deep water; the instruments of state government must not be revealed to the people. (Chapter 36, p. 28)
[80] What bends will be preserved, what curls will be straightened, what is depressed will be filled, what is worn will be renewed, what is deprived will gain, and what is excessive will be confused. That is why the Sage holds fast this single principle and serves as the model of the world. He does not display himself, so he shines; he is not self-assured, so he can be publicly acknowledged; he does not boast his ability, so he can have achievements; he does not brag, so he can have enduring success. It is because he does not compete that no one in the world can compete with him. (Chapter 22)
[81] The Sage says, "He who accepts the blame from his countrymen is to be the lord of the state; he who bears the calamities of the world is to be its king." Words of truth often sound paradoxical. (Chapter 78)
[82] In ancient times those who were good at pursuing the *Way* did not enlighten the people but made them ignorant . . . He who governs a state with cleverness is a scourge to the state; he who does not govern a state with cleverness is a good fortune to the state. (Chapter 65)

(4) *His possible achievement*

(A) A "SMALL STATE"

[83] Let there be a little state with a small population. Let the people continue to have tools that can save the labour of tens or hundreds of persons but not use them. Let the people value life and not migrate afar. Though they have boats and carts they have no use of them. Though there will be armour and weapons there is no place to display them. Let the people revert to the use of the knotted rope as reminders of something of importance. Let them find relish in their food, and beauty in their clothes, contentment in their abode, and happiness in their customs. Though neighbouring states are within sight of one another, and the sound of dogs barking and cocks crowing in one state can be heard in another, the people of one state will grow old and die without having had any interaction with those of another. (Chapter 80)

(B) SOLUTION TO DISPUTES AND CRIMES

[84] Where great grievances are settled there will be some remaining grievances. How can that be a good solution? Therefore the Sage holds the left half of the tally but does not make strict demands on others. (Chapter 79)
[85] Requite injury with kindness. (Chapter 63)
[86] Indeed the people have been long misguided. Therefore, the Sage corrects but does not cut down, rectifies but does not injure, straightens but does not overpower. (Chapter 58)
[87] If the people were always afraid of death, and if I were always able to arrest and put to death those who engage in prohibited activities, then who would dare to violate the prohibitions? (Chapter 74)

[88] When the people are not afraid of death, wherefore frighten them with death? (Chapter 74)
[89] There is a regular executioner in charge of execution. To execute on behalf of the executioner is like to hew wood on behalf of the master carpenter. In hewing wood on behalf of the master carpenter, there are few who escape hurting their own hands instead. (Chapter 74)
[90] The greater enforcer does not execute. (Chapter 28)
[91] The net of Heaven is spread wide. Its meshes are with large openings but it never lets anything escape. (Chapter 73)

(c) Solution to general disorder

[92] The *Way* never acts yet nothing is left undone. Should lords and princes be able to hold fast on to it, the myriad creatures will be transformed by themselves. After they are transformed, should they start to act up again, I shall press down with the nameless primordial substance. (Chapter 37)
[93] When the primal substance was scattered the remnants became useful implements, the Sage who has gained its use became the leader in government. (Chapter 19)
[94] Though the primal substance is small, the world cannot subdue it. If the ruler can hold on to it, the myriad things will transform themselves. (Chapter 32)

(F) Social relationships in Laozi's "small state"

[95] Heaven and earth are not benevolent, and they treat the myriad creatures as straw dogs; the Sage is not benevolent, and he treats the people as straw dogs. (Chapter 5)
[96] The highest type of ruler is one of whose existence the people are barely aware. The next is one whom they love and praise. The next is one whom they fear. The next is one whom they despise and defy. When a ruler is not enough to trust, there will be those who do not trust him. Appear casual and spare with words. When the task is accomplished the people will say, "It is what we have accomplished. It is only natural." (Chapter 17)

(G) Difficulties Laozi and his Sage encountered

[97] My words are very easy to understand and very easy to put into practice, but no one in the world can understand and practise them. My words have a theme and there is an objective for the matters I address. Because people do not know the theme and the objective they do not know me. Those who know me are few and those who follow me are preciously fewer. This is why the Sage wears coarse clothes and holds the jade in his bosom. (Chapter 70)
[98] The great *Way* is very level and yet people love the side paths – they keep their courts quite tidy, but leave their fields quite weedy and their granaries quite empty; they wear beautiful, ornamented dresses, carry sharp swords, feast on rich food and hoard superabundance of wealth and goods. This is the act of robbers and boasters, this is not the *Way*! (Chapter 53)

[99] When the top scholars heard the *Way*, they practised it diligently; when the mediocre ones heard it, they seemed to have got it at one moment but soon lost it; when the lowest ones heard it, they laughed out loud. If they did not laugh, it would be unworthy of being the *Way*. (Chapter 41)

Lao-zi 老子

PART 2
INTERPRETATION

Confucius had confidence in humankind and cherished civilisation. He realised that the situation of his time was depressing but believed that humans could change it for the better. This view was not shared by many of his contemporaries, however. Distressed and disgusted by the chaos and misery around them, they lost faith in humanity's ability to create a society and a lifestyle distinctively human and humane. They thought that the cause of all human problems was precisely humankind's attempt to have a way of life different from that of other creatures that simply follow the rules of nature. As they saw it, the right way to live is to be as much a part of nature as possible: that is, to have few desires other than those arising from the most basic biological and physical needs, and to satisfy those desires with the fruits of one's own labour so that one can be independent from all external control except, of course, that of nature. This kind of life may be harsh but it is better than a life of futile attempts to improve it that, in fact, make it far worse. The reason, in their opinion, is that the minuscule human ability is not up to the task. The more one meddles, the greater the mess one creates. In contrast, in following the rules of nature, one at least can have peace of mind, knowing that, if something goes wrong, one is not responsible. Of course, this is only a superficial benefit. More importantly, if everyone takes this road, few things will go wrong because there will be little competition and, hence, little contention and conflict. Everyone lives hand to mouth. There will probably be scarcity but certainly no strife. And, to those who had suffered enough violence and chaos, peace and order were of far greater value than the dubious rewards of human attempts to make life more prosperous and sophisticated.

There are many stories of such cynics, nihilists and primitivists. The most famous is probably that of Boyi 伯夷 and Shuqi 叔齊 It is told repeatedly in many classics.

Boyi and Shuqi were two brothers who tried to dissuade Ji Fa 姬發 (ruler of the state of Zhou 周) from taking up arms against the Yin Dynasty. Failing to do so, they fled to Shouyang mountains 首陽山 where they died of starvation rather than become subjects of the new Zhou Dynasty. Their motive was not simply political for they did not have a strong allegiance to the Yin. Rather, they were fearful that the uprising would bring great disaster upon the people, and the result would only be to replace one corrupt power with another.

Several encounters between Confucius and his critics are, as we have seen, recorded in *The Analects*. Regarding the political situation of their time hopeless, and becoming still worse in the future, they believed that men, even those as intelligent as Confucius, were incapable of making any meaningful change. So they withdrew from public life to live a private, primitive one. They even invited him to join them. When their invitation was declined they laughed at him for the futility in doing what he knew was impossible. To them such aspiration was preposterous.

What do these stories tell us? They described rather casual incidents, trifling anecdotes in Confucius's eventful seventy-three years of life. Why did his disciples record them in *The Analects*? A reasonable explanation is that they found the view of those critics disagreeable but could not be easily refuted. It was difficult because humans indeed have limited abilities to cope with the vicissitudes of life. Therefore, the idea that people should simply adapt to their environment and survive as other animals did was probably accepted long before the idea that encouraged human assertion. As we have seen, a theory supporting the latter was constructed by Confucius. One justifying the latter was expounded by Laozi probably sometime earlier.

Who was Laozi? Sima Qian 司馬遷, the great early Han Dynasty historian, was unsure. According to him, a person named Li Er 李耳, from the state of Chu who once served as the custodian of the archives of the central government of the Zhou Dynasty, was called upon by Confucius to ask about the rites. He left his post later to retire to the wilderness in the west and, before leaving the civilised world, he wrote a book of five thousand characters, later known as *Laozi*. Apart from these, Sima Qian had little to say about Laozi's life. He reported some legends saying that the man lived for 160 years or even two hundred years. Further, he reported that someone said there was a person named Lao Laizi 老莱子, also from the state of Chu, who wrote a book of fifteen chapters discussing the principles of the *dao* 道 and was a contemporary of Confucius. Then he said that, 129 years after Confucius's death, there was a person named Dan 儋, an official historian of the state of Zhou, who predicted the rise of the hegemony of the state of Qin and was recognised by some as Laozi, but denied by some others, and the world was unsure who was right. In any event, he said "Laozi" (老子 old man) was a recluse.[1]

So, quite probably, *Laozi* was not authored by a single person but was a compilation of short statements of wise elders of ancient times. Some of them, such as the recluses mentioned earlier, wished to escape from the world. The collective "Laozi" shared their view but, as we shall see, also wanted to change it. This dual intention caused some obvious contradictions in *Laozi*. They will be discussed in due course but, first, I shall present the major part of the book which has a consistent theme.

Most ancient Chinese thinkers were asked to explain the unsatisfactory situation of their time. Was it normal? If not, what existed before? If there had been order and happiness, what had made them possible and what had caused their disappearance? Would there be a better future? If so, how could it be brought about? Such questions inevitably led to conjectures about a utopian "primitive" society and theories of its evolution. Confucius thought society had been in a much better condition when people were less solipsistic but he did not draw a clear picture. A vivid image of a golden age in the past first appeared in *Laozi*. It existed when the *Way* prevailed. Though later lost, it could be restored.

(A) The *Way*

(1) Its nature and description

Like all ancient Chinese thinkers, Laozi talked much about the *Way*. His *Way*, however, was different from the *Way* widely accepted by others. He, like Confucius, did not believe it was based on the will of Heaven and on the wishes of gods and spirits but, unlike Confucius, he did not think it could be derived from similar human natures and common human experience. In his view, it was not created by anyone: it came into being prior to all else, including heaven and earth, and existed by itself. It was imperceptible, inaudible, intangible, impalpable, and yet universally present. It was elusive, perpetually moving, and yet eternally constant. It was above everything, all things came into being in accordance with it, and therefore, figuratively speaking, it gave birth to all things and regulated them all. But it did not have a purpose of its own; it did not have a will. Thus, though it was the cause of everything, it claimed no credit; though it governed everything, it exercised no authority. It did not dominate; everything obeyed it automatically.

Thus, the *Way* of Laozi was like the laws of natural science (indeed, he said the *Way* took its law from nature). At a time when a belief in some form of wilful superbeing was still popular, this will-less *Way* was something unimaginable to most people, a mystery. It was difficult even for Laozi to define. The best he could do was to give it a label – *dao* (道 *Way*). But, since that label had been used by others for other *ways*, he insisted that his *Way* was unique. It could be described but not in the more familiar terms describing other "*ways*". He emphasised that his *Way* was universal and constant but the others were not. His was "*the Way*".

(2) Its attributes and lessons

(A) MODERATION AND MODESTY

How did he know? Could it be just a mirage, a phantom, a product of his imagination? He said it actually existed because it had an essence which was very real and verifiable, which could be observed and tested by people in their everyday life. And it was his own observation that enabled him to know that the *Way* existed and had those characteristics.

He began his observation with some familiar phenomena: a gusty wind could not last all morning; a sudden downpour could not continue all day; things with sharp edges would become dull; one who was on tiptoe could not stand for long; excessive desires would be costly – multiple colours, tunes and flavours numbed people's senses; galloping and hunting made their hearts wild. Based on such observation, he concluded that there was a rule: things could not remain at extremes; they had to pull back and go to the middle, to the more stable mean. As further evidence, he pointed out that what was bent would become straight, what was hollow full, what was high lower, what was low raised, what was deprived compensated, and what was excessive curtailed. He likened these moves to the drawing of a bow – making the upper tip bend downwards and the lower tip bend upwards, reducing the excess and making up the inadequate – and said that was how the *Way* of Heaven worked.

Something that attracted his particular attention was water. He was impressed by the fact that it was soft and obviously never strove against anything, and yet, in attacking rigid obstacles, it was irresistible, it always won. He also noticed that big water (the sea) lay in a low place and attracted small waters (rivers, creeks) to it, and became their "king". In the same way, he noticed that things were pliable while alive, rigid when dead and that, in animals, in their interactions, the passive and submissive female always overcame the active and assertive male. From these facts he arrived at several conclusions: lying low, being soft and appearing submissive, and not striving were ways in which to survive and to prevail. He said this was the *Way* of Heaven.

(b) Selfless and devoid of emotion

More generally, he saw that life in various forms came into being spontaneously. Nature seemed accommodating to all things, showing no favour or disfavour to anything. This led him to extrapolate that the *Way* was devoid of emotion and without values. It was neither benevolent nor malevolent, had no preferences and was non-judgemental. To it everything was alike – nothing was good or bad, right or wrong – and, therefore, it preferred nothing and rejected nothing, rewarded nothing and punished nothing. It treated all things like a straw dog which, in ancient times, was used instead of a butchered animal as a sacrifice in the worship of gods and ancestors, and unsentimentally discarded after the ceremony.

(B) The use of the *Way*

(1) Inaction and covert action

The phenomenon, that nature seemed to have done nothing and yet myriad things came into existence and developed according to certain rules, fascinated

Laozi. Thus he thought that, in the same manner, nature, or the *Way*, did everything. This led him to see the *Way* as a net. It remained inactive but let nothing escape. It led him further to the idea that nature should be left to do what it had been doing; human efforts to make any change would be futile, so they should not be made at all. Thus, he compared the world to a *shen-qi* (神器 sacred object) – nothing should be done to it, and anyone who attempted to do anything would ruin it.

This idea that the *Way wu-wei er wu-bu-wei* (無為而無不為 did not do anything and yet nothing was left by it undone) was crucial to Laozi's theory. It sounded paradoxical but it had a philosophical basis and also a practical explanation. The former was his idea about *wu* (無 without) and *you* (有 with). He seemed to have deliberated about the origin of all things and concluded that, in the past, there was nothing, and it was from this void that something came, and therefore the void was crucial to everything. Practically, there had to be a void before some use could be made. For instance, it was the empty space in a bellows that produced wind. Hence, being empty was useful.

Then he observed that a tree which filled the arms grew from a tiny sprout; a nine-storey terrace rose from a small lump of earth; a thousand-mile journey began with a single step. These facts taught him that the *Way* to make something happen was to start and continue with small, easy endeavours. In the process, no effort was perceptible but, in the end, a tremendous result was achieved. Thus the *Way* seemed to be doing nothing but, in the end, accomplished everything.

From these observations Laozi arrived at another idea: the *Way* never claimed credit for what it had accomplished; it seemed to "retire" to the background. It was like water which was good at nourishing things but never conspicuously – it submerged into the soil.

(2) Advance in reverse

Laozi's other important discovery about the *Way* was that, when it acted, it appeared to be going in the direction opposite to that in which it would eventually arrive. He found this in the fact that, if something was to be shrunk, weakened or destroyed, it had to be already stretched, strengthened, or established; and, if something were to be taken away from a person, he must be given it first. Laozi called this awareness *wei-ming* (微明 subtle wisdom), and concluded that *fan-zhe dao-zhi-dong* (反者道之動 to advance in reverse was how the *Way* moved).

(C) The fall of the *Way*

One may wonder why Laozi used so much of his little book to write about the *Way*, which he confessed was not quite capable of explanation, and, indeed, while some of his explanations are commonsensical, some of his extrapolations defy logic. But the defects apparently did not bother him, and there was a reason. It was because he did not like the world of his time and wanted to change it for the better. For this purpose, he had to say that a better world existed before when his *Way* prevailed. Since his *Way* was not based on something people could easily comprehend, he had to describe it using esoteric language, metaphors and fables to make it sound profound and therefore command people's attention and belief.

Suppose people were convinced by him, they would ask him why, by his time, his *Way* evidently no longer prevailed and when it had ceased to be operative. Unlike the Ruists, who thought that their *Great Way* went into hiding when the first hereditary dynasty was established and everyone became solipsistic, Laozi seemed to think the unfortunate event took place much earlier because he did not talk about any of the ancient rulers, including Yao and Shun, much admired by other thinkers, apparently not believing that the world under them was much better. So, when had his *Way* disappeared? He does not enlighten us. But he did explain the process of its fall and vaguely hinted at the cause of the process. Here are his two famous statements:

> When the great *Way* was disregarded, there were benevolence and righteousness. When cleverness emerged, there were great artefacts; when the six relations were disharmonious, there were filial children and caring parents; when the state was in disorder, there were loyal ministers.

> When the *Way* was lost, there was virtue; when virtue was lost, there was benevolence; when benevolence, was lost there was rectitude; when rectitude was lost, there were the rites. Hence the rites were the attenuated form of loyalty and good faith, and the fountainhead of disorder.

How are we to understand these statements? They were both descriptive. The first described a fact – while in the state of nature, everyone was natural and indistinguishable; when that state was lost, some persons were recognised as being particularly benevolent, righteous, filial, loving or loyal. The second described a hierarchy of norms and suggested a process in which the higher ones were giving way to the lower ones. Both seemed to have hinted at a sequence but did not actually establish a cause and effect relationship. They conveyed only an impression that, when the *Way* prevailed, there was no need for artificial norms to define evil and virtue, right and wrong, and to make prescriptions and proscriptions; they came into being because it had fallen. Laozi did not answer the question as to why the *Way* had fallen.

The only clause in his statements that hinted a cause for the fall was "when *zhihui* (智慧 or 知慧 in some editions of *Laozi*) emerged *da-wei* (大偽 great *wei*) came into existence". Here we have enter into sinology – the word *Wei* is composed of two characters, *ren* (人 human being) and *wei* (為 act), and thus refers to artefacts, including artificial norms. Once humans began to make things for various purposes, they manipulated and, what originally existed, could no longer remain in its natural state; they could no longer follow the *Way* and it fell into disuse. Thus, it is fair to say that *zhihui* enabled the creation of artefacts and was thus the culprit for the fall of the *Way*.

What was *zhihui*? Nowadays, the term is generally used to mean intelligence and wisdom or cleverness but, if *zhi* was 知, it meant and means *zhishi* (知識

knowledge), and *zhihui* (知慧) would mean knowledge and wisdom or cleverness. In any case, there is a further question: where did knowledge and wisdom or cleverness come from? Laozi did not give an explicit answer. But he could not have argued that they came from human intelligence which is, by definition, innate to human beings. To use *zhi* in the sense of knowledge would, as we shall see, be more in congruence with other related points in *Laozi*.

(D) The Sage

Laozi evidently regretted the fall of his *Way* but, unlike the above-mentioned critics of Confucius, he was not a cynic or an escapist: he wanted the *Way* re-established. Unable to do it alone, he tried to show people how it could be done and, knowing that it was not easy, he gave instructions mainly to a special audience consisting of an extraordinary person and his followers. To them he needed only to point out what was hidden behind a facade that befuddled we ordinary people.

(1) His character and qualifications

Who was this special person? What were his qualifications? To begin with, because he was to restore the *Way*, he had to have the ability to know what it was. According to Laozi, this person "did not have to step out of his door, and yet knew everything under the sky; did not have to look out of his window, and yet saw the *Way* of Heaven". Laozi called this person *sheng-ren* (聖人 the Wise Man or the Sage).

Needless to say, the Sage had to be extraordinarily intelligent but how did he acquire an infinite amount of knowledge? Laozi never told us. Presumably he did what Laozi did, using objective investigation. According to Laozi, he would wipe himself absolutely clean of all preconceptions and prejudices and become absolutely empty minded, and he would remain completely tranquil and then carefully observe how the myriad things engaged in all kinds of activities and eventually came to rest in a stable condition – their "roots", their "destinies". Laozi called this condition *chang* (常 constancy) by which he actually meant the *Way* which was constant. When a person had grasped this "constancy" he became all-knowing, he was with the *Way*. According to Laozi, one who knows "'the Constant' will be tolerant, impartial and all-embracing like the sky and identified with the *Way*".

After thus learning the *Way*, a person could make himself, his family, his village, his state and the world virtuous, and, using his virtuous self, family, village, state and world as standards, he could know others and their villages, and so on.

What happened to a person with all the knowledge? He would be subtle and profound and yet appear hesitant as a person wading a stream in the winter, timid as a person fearful of all around him, grave and courteous as a guest, simple as the primordial substance. He was as innocent as a newborn baby and yet, because of his virtues, no one could bear harming him.

(2) His objectives

What this person was up to? Laozi said, "When *pu* 樸 was shattered, the remnants became useful implements and the Sage gained its use and became the leader of men." So the Sage was to lead the people, using the remnants of *pu*. What is *pu*? Ordinarily, the character is used as an adjective to mean pure and simple. It was used in this sense in *Laozi* twice. But Laozi also used it as a noun to mean *something* pure and simple, something never affected by human action – a primordial substance – on five occasions and here is one of them. In this use, the term is one of the most mystifying in *Laozi* which provided no explicit interpretation. But Laozi did say that, in the imperceptible, inaudible, intangible, elusive, impalpable *Way*, there was a matter, an essence, which was constant behind all things in flux and capable of influencing them in the most crucial sense. Therefore, it is possible that, here, Laozi meant this: when the Sage had grasped the essence of the *Way*, the constancy behind the flurries of superficial changes, he was in a position to use the various parts of it and regulate and lead the people; and they would follow him because he held *da-xiang* (大象 the Great Sign, another term Laozi used for the *Way*) and, wherever he went, there would be no harm but peace and order.

To where would the Sage lead the people? Ultimately, back to nature. So Laozi said, mankind should take the earth as a model as the earth takes Heaven, Heaven takes the *Way* and the *Way* takes nature.

So man should go back to a state of nature. Is that Laozi's ideal state? He did not make this point clear. He said that when the *xuan-de* (玄德 profound virtue) of the *Way* was operating, it would bring everything into being but not posses them; it would help them but not claim credit; and it would facilitate their growth but not determine the outcome. In other words, in an ideal state, everything was left alone although "produced", "enabled", and therefore dependent on the *Way*.

(E) The re-establishment of the *Way*

(1) His specific tasks

(A) To rid society of concrete problems

In any event, the Sage's road back to a state of nature was littered with problems. The problems were created by humans. When the Great *Way* was not followed, people got into trouble. A small number of clever and strong men grabbed more than they could produce by their own labour. They exploited the stupid and the weak who were the majority. And, to enforce this practice, moral principles, taboos and laws were made and government established to suppress disobedience. But the more prohibitions that were made, the more thefts and robberies were committed because the oppressed became poorer and hungrier. As time passed, those above the common people became more extravagant and coveted things that were hard to come by. So the government exacted heavy taxes and encouraged people to develop skills and employ ingenious devices. These measures made the producers of necessities fewer and poorer, and pushed more people into inventing and manufacturing wondrous objects. Consequently, while more people suffered, more desires arose and more competition, strife and violent crimes took place. Then the authorities were compelled to be more active, clever people were honoured and put in office, more levies were imposed, more laws made, more punishments inflicted, and more executions carried out. As this vicious circle continued, the state became less and less governable.

What was to be done to stop this downward spiral and reverse the course? Laozi suggested that rulers should drastically change their lifestyles. They should not have extravagant desires, treasure things hard to come by, honour the clever, and create unnatural norms, so that people would not have skewed values and be led to compete, contend and strive. They should then reduce taxes, abolish the taboos, rescind the laws and other artificial norms so that people could be spared from hunger and would not steal, rob, maim and commit other crimes. Generally, they should avoid being overactive and allow people to be calm and undisturbed.

(B) TO MINIMISE THE ROOT OF THE PROBLEMS

Though harshly critical of the rulers of his time, Laozi realised that they were not necessarily evil by nature. All humans had certain desires which had certain physiological and biological bases and, therefore, were irreducible. But desires could be fanned by external forces and, if a person indulged in gratifying many strong desires, harm would result. For instance, indulgence in the gratification of sensory needs would make a person ill – the five colours would make a person's eyes blind; the five tunes would make his ears deaf; the five flavours would injure his palate; galloping and hunting would cause his mind to go wild with excitement. It was therefore necessary to get to the root of the problems. Laozi suggested that the Sage should free people from these temptations and help them meet only their basic needs. He should empty their minds but fill their bellies, weaken their wills but strengthen their bones. He should transform them into infant-like simpletons who would want little apart from food, who would be like a fool, muddled and witless, befuddled and without purpose.

How could the Sage return people to a child-like state? Laozi said he would let them have something to occupy their eyes and ears, and, of course, food to eat but little else. He would not only refuse to enlighten them but actively muddle their minds and cause them to be ignorant. This was because when they became clever they would be difficult to govern.

How was the Sage to make people ignorant? Laozi suggested that he should make them *qi* (棄 discard) *zhi* (智, 知). As stated above, *zhi* can mean intelligence or knowledge. If *zhi* meant intelligence, its emergence must have been spontaneous and it could not be discarded. So it must mean knowledge. How could the Sage make people discard knowledge? He could deny them education. But, apparently since time immemorial, intelligent people had invented ways and means to make their lives easier and have passed on their knowledge to others: how could this practice be stopped? Laozi had another suggestion: *jue-sheng* (絕聖 eliminate sages or sagaciousness). The connotations of *sheng* are many. It can mean a sage or a learned person. Laozi could not have intended to eliminate the Sage. But, at his time, there were many learned persons who were called sages. In his view, they were different from the Sage, the true one. They were false sages and should be eliminated. It is unlikely that he meant to eliminate them physically; he must have meant that their claim of sagaciousness should be refuted and their practice of dissemination of limited knowledge, which misled the world into chaos, should be eliminated.

It might be possible for a government under the Sage to prohibit false sages from teaching publicly but how could he prevent the people learning from them in private? Laozi went a step further, arguing that there was actually little worth learning because, what the false sages taught, were norms and other artefacts but there was not much difference between good and bad, right and wrong, and the other artefacts – sharp tools, ingenious devices and clever methods – actually brought more trouble to society. Therefore he declared: "Stop learning, and there will be nothing to worry about." Everyone would expect very little from life and live happily.

Some people could be persuaded to refrain from acquiring knowledge and using its products – in short, abandoning civilisation. Many ascetics did so although it would be very difficult for them to deny the use of certain aspects of civilisation that had proven to be effective in helping to prevent starvation or cure illness, especially where their loved ones were involved. That was perhaps one of the reasons why true ascetics remained single. But it was unlikely that was what Laozi had in mind for most people to do. Another problem was how to keep the innate intelligence from emerging. This will be discussed later.

(2) His attitude towards his work and his basic strategy

So the Sage knew what he had to do to bring people back to nature. In a state of nature there are no feelings, Laozi said; Heaven and earth treat the myriad things as straw dogs. So, on the road of going back to nature, the Sage should be resolute and ruthless; he should have no feelings; he should treat the people as straw dogs. His strategy was to stick to the *Way*, hold fast to the *Great Sign* so that he could control the people and make them follow him to wherever he wanted them to go.

(3) His tactics

(A) TO MIX WITH THE PEOPLE

But people usually do not like to be told what to do. A person appearing to be different, clever and domineering would be repellent. It is better to mingle with the ordinary people unnoticed and to instigate inconspicuously from within their ranks, making them think that what they were doing was what they themselves wanted to do. That was how Laozi said the Sage should act. Though more intelligent and knowledgeable than the masses, he would not show off those qualities but seem to be quite stupid; he would not even speak much; he would seem purposeless, holding no strange ideas; he would thus fit in well with ordinary people and achieve *xuan-tong* (玄同 mysterious unity) with them but, in reality, he would muddle their minds, making them think that he was just one of them. So, when he acted and spoke, they looked at him and listened to him without suspicion, believing that he was acting and speaking for them. He became their alter ego and, as such, he would be cherished, valued and trusted.

(b) To appear selfless, humble, yielding and claim no credit

To be more specific, the Sage would appear selfless, sincere. It was because he was acting according to the *Way*, the law of nature. He regretted that he had his body which had its basic needs. But he would make his physical existence worthy by devoting it to save the world. He would not seek any benefit for himself let alone contend with others for it. He would practise *xuan-de* (玄德 profound virtue) – to help the people with their livelihoods but would not be possessive of them; to do a lot for them but would not claim credit; to help them grow but would not determine the outcome. He would take a low position and accept people as they were. By being so helpful and yet so selfless, so humble, he would attract people to him as the sea attracts the rivers. Because he would accept people as they were, no one would contend with him. He could then rule over them and meet no resistance.

(c) To appear inactive but engage in small efforts

When the Sage had the people behind him or when he was successfully integrated with them, what was he going to do? He was to help people meet their very basic needs for subsistence but Laozi did not say how. Apart from that, the measures he suggested for the Sage were mostly negative – to discard the artefacts, particularly the norms, and suppress education, but again he did not spell out how this was to be done. He used a lot of words to emphasise the futility of human efforts and the miraculous effect of inaction. He said that the more actions were taken, making contrivances, laws and orders, the more problems there would be. There is some truth in this observation that hyperactivity and overreach would produce undesirable results. But the examples he used to support his argument for inaction – that water, being soft, was able to attack something strong and rigid and that the female, being quiet and submissive, always prevailed over the boisterous and aggressive male – were specious. The serious point he made was that, when the people were left alone, they could do well with their lives. But this belief in laissez-faire was disingenuous because the world, according to him, was already trapped in chaos and going down a dangerous road towards greater misery; the ordinary people were lost, not knowing what was good for them, and the Sage should keep them or make them stupid and ignorant. So this exaltation of government inaction was a smokescreen, and a poorly made one, because, soon after setting it up, Laozi revealed what he really meant: The non-action was to cover up all actions. That was what the *Way* did and that was what the Sage was to do.

What the Sage should really do was to respond speedily before a situation had been developed and difficult to handle. If it was undesirable, he could nip it in the bud; if it was preferred, he could assist its growth. In both cases he would be *se* (嗇 frugal) in action – he would not take big ventures and engage in flurries of activities; he would make only small, necessary moves which would be almost imperceptible and yet produce great results. Thus, he would seem to be doing nothing but actually doing a lot – by making people do it. They would think that they were doing it on their own initiative and feel good and produce what he wanted. That was why Laozi said, "Governing a large state is like cooking a small fish" – under proper conditions the chef should not stir it much but let it cook itself.

(D) TO ADVANCE IN REVERSE SECRETLY

Laozi said that the *Way* of Heaven appeared to be in the direction opposite to where it was actually going: therefore, the Sage should do the same. Though he had an objective, an agenda – to lead the people back to the *Way* – he would act as if he were doing the opposite. Personally, he would not be assertive and display his talents but, rather, appear selfless, purposeless and clueless; in his relationship with the people, he would not contend or compete with them but would be humble and yielding, embracing them and accepting their ideas and, if anything went wrong, their complaints and blames. In this way, Laozi said, the Sage would become the lord of people. Does this sound paradoxical? Yes, it does, but what actually happened was that, when the Sage had gained people's trust, he would be able to control them. That was why Laozi said: "Words of truth often sound paradoxical."

While in actual control, the Sage would continue to wear a beneficent mask – when he was to take something away from the people, he would let them have it first; when he was to close something down. he would let it open first; when he was to crush something, he would let it stand first. Why did he do so? It was because he did not want to disclose his true intention. Why did he want to keep his intention secret? It was because he wanted people to do something extremely difficult, namely, to abandon what they had achieved with great effort to make their lives easier, more gratifying and more secure: in other words, civilisation. If his agenda was revealed, the people would suspect an ulterior motive in him and would certainly resist his scheme and even rise violently against him. He did not want to see this outcome so he had to be secretive. Laozi said, "The fish must not leave the deep water; the sharp tools for government must not be revealed to anyone." The Sage wielding the instrument of government would hide it. He would seem not to be pushing, nor even leading, them with any force but make them believe that his way was the right way and follow him under the illusion that they were doing it of their own volition.

(4) His possible achievement

Laozi wanted the Sage to re-establish the *Way*, to recreate a utopia where people would live in accordance with the law of nature. But even the Sage could not do it in a single step. Laozi seemed to suggest that he could first bring the people to a half-way stage. It would be a little state with a small population. There the people would have various labour-saving devices as well as boats, vehicles, and even armour and weapons, but would be persuaded by the Sage not to use them. He would also persuade people to abandon written language and revert to making rope knots as a way of reminding them of important things; to be content with what food and clothing they had; to be at peace with themselves and to enjoy their tradition. The neighbouring states would be within sight and the sound of their chickens and dogs would be audible but the peoples there would grow old and die without having any interaction.

That would certainly make for a peaceful state but there were problems. It was predicated on several preconditions, and here are two of the most obvious: the state must be able always to produce enough materials to sustain its people, and it could have no population growth. If these conditions were not met, the state would have to end its splendid isolation and seek help from its neighbours, or steal from them, and, in the case where its population outgrew the capacity of its territory, it would have to expand physically and enter into conflict with its neighbours. How was the Sage to solve these problems? Probably Laozi would say that he would continue to lead the people from the small state to give up more civilisation and enter the brave new world where the law of nature, or the *Way*, prevailed. In this state of nature, there would be no "states", no boundaries and no distinction between one person and another. Everyone would share everything and there would be no scarcity for anyone in particular; there would be no conflicts of any sort. But this is conjecture. Laozi never actually said that.

(5) His measures with which to deal with social problems

(A) DISPUTES AND CRIMES

What did Laozi say about the problems of the real world? Among such problems, the most common were disputes between people and crimes. Laozi's position on dispute settlement was negative. He did not believe humans were capable of solving serious discords. According to him, where great grievances were settled, there would always be some remaining grievances. So he would, instead of trying to redress injury, requite it with kindness. We remember that Confucius disagreed, asking with what would one respond to kindness and suggesting requiting injury with justice. Laozi seemed oblivious to this. As to crimes, he was opposed to punishments because, after all, the severest punishment was death but, if people, under overwhelming circumstances, were no longer afraid of death, how could the death penalty be a threat and a deterrent to them? If the authorities insisted on condemning certain people as criminals and executing them, the result would be harmful not only to the people but also to the authorities themselves. A better way was to correct the people but not execute them, to rectify them but not cause injury. This sounded wonderful but who could do so? It was the Sage, of course. How could he do so? Laozi did not give an answer. But he intimated that the law of nature would somehow in the end make all things straight. In his words: "The net of Heaven is spread wide. Its meshes may have large holes but it never lets anything escape." This is vintage Laozi, romantic and mystical.

(B) Social disorder

A more serious problem to Laozi was how to deal with the possibility that people already in his "little state" became dissatisfied with it, and some clever fellows wanted to make life easier by reverting or recreating civilisation again? Laozi said that the Sage had to be prepared. He should know the way of the forceful male while observing the way of the delicate female; he should, like a party of a contract holding the left half of a tally, be ready to demand specific performance by the other party holding the right half. When the clever ones were about to act he was to suppress them with *wu-ming-zhi-pu* (無名之樸 the nameless primordial substance).

Now we meet this "primordial substance" again. Laozi said it was something simple and pure. Why did he call it "nameless"? He said he did not know the name of the nebulous law of nature and only managed to give it a label – the *Way*. Here he was doing the same, making the mysterious "substance" even more inscrutable. He did describe the *Way*, and he also had a description of this nameless substance: It was small but nothing in the world could subdue it and, if the ruler could hold on to it, the myriad things would be subjugated by him. And now he said that the Sage could use it to suppress attempts to revive civilisation. So it must be more concrete than the *Way*. But what was it? Perhaps we could imagine it to be a tranquilising atmosphere created by the authorities? It could weigh heavily on a person and keep him still. His desires would be suppressed and his energy dissipated. He would be led into a state of transcendental peace and, in that state, he would see himself as having strayed from the *Way* and would be happy to return to it. This notion is not too far-fetched, for Laozi did say that this primordial substance "will make people devoid of desire, and when people are calm and devoid of desire the world will be settled by itself". And, alas, something like it did take place in history.

(F) Social relationships in Laozi's "small state"

What would the relationship between the ruler and the common people be like? According to Laozi, it varied. In an ordinary state, if the ruler was greedy, misguided and overactive – indulging in excessive desires, treasuring rare things, encouraging frivolous skills, promoting the clever, imposing heavy levies, propagating misleading moral rules, creating many taboos, and making numerous laws – and thus interfered and disrupted the lives of the common people, they would fear, resent, despise, and even defy him. If he was modest and refrained from those bad practices, they might respect and even love him.

What was the relationship between the people and the Sage? It was more complicated and nuanced. In several instances, Laozi said that the Sage should treat the people as children. One of the implications was that he cared for them. Judging by the enormous tasks Laozi said the Sage was to do for the people secretively, it could only be concluded that he must have the intention to help them meet their physical needs. But he did not want them to grow mentally. Instead, he wanted to muddle their minds, to make them stupid and devoid of desire and free will and behave like infants who would be easy for him to handle.

If we look more closely, we shall find that the relationship differed at different stages. While leading the people, the Sage had to be very nice to them and thereby hoodwink them, and make them follow blindly. If anyone accidentally deviated from the path, he would have to be more tactful to get that person back. But, when someone questioned the destination of the journey, showed suspicion of his motive and, worse still, made any attempt to revive civilisation, he would promptly use the nameless primordial substance to suppress the disbeliever and quash ruthlessly any potential challenge to his commands. He wanted to lead them eventually to a state of nature and he would not allow anyone to go astray and bring others with him.

In a state of nature the relationship would be different. Everyone would be free and on his own. Logically, since there was no further journey to make, the people would no longer need a leader. The Sage would retire but probably not disappear because, as we remember, a state of nature had once existed and had been lost evidently because of the development of human intelligence and the spread of knowledge. It happened once and might happen again. Therefore, the Sage had to be there, ready to prevent this possibility if it raised its head again. But, before that, he would truly mix with the people as if he was one of them. They might be aware of his existence but would pay him no attention.

How would the people think about the Sage and how would they treat him? In the beginning they would have had doubts and resisted him because, by the time he had appeared and tried to lead them to the *Way*, they had already travelled a great distance to escape from misery by creating things that could make their lives easier, and they cherished their achievements. The Sage wanted them to reverse that course, and they could not understand why inventions which could save labour and increase the production of necessities were bad and why a life of toil and scarcity was preferable. There could be some ascetics who shared his views and became his true believers but, when circumstances accommodating the idyllic, primitive life became tenuous, particularly when food became scarce, even they would begin to have doubts, and the ordinary people would become rebellious. They would revert to the old ways or invent new ones to ease their lives and thereby start the downward spiral once again, provoking the Sage to use the unnamed primordial substance to suppress them. Their attitude towards him would turn from reverence and love to hatred, and they would despise and reject him. The result would be total disaster for him.

Thus, in Laozi's theory, the relationship between the people and the authorities is complicated. It is mainly because he did not recognise that, despite their different social positions, people can be equal in the sense that they are all human beings. His ideal political leader, the Sage, is not a person cultivated through education and self-discipline but is one born with supernatural abilities and thus entirely different from the ordinary mortals who, according to this theory, are stupid and incapable of managing their own affairs. Supposedly, the Sage is to lead the people to a utopia but it is not necessarily what most of them want. When he pushes his own agenda, he has no feelings for them, he keeps them ignorant and treats them as infants or, more frankly, straw dogs. If they disobey, he will suppress them with the Orwellian "unnamed primordial substance". The relationship is terrifying and precarious.

(G) Difficulties Laozi and his Sage encountered

In spite of its many inherent difficulties, Laozi insisted that his theory was sound and easy to put into practice. It was the people's ignorance about his plan, or the primary objective and the reason behind it, that made them incapable of following him. Because those who did understand him were few, he was unable to see his theory implemented. Deeply disappointed, the Sage would hold the great *Way* to his bosom like a precious piece of jade and keep a humble, unremarkable appearance in coarse clothes. He harboured bitterness and criticised those who ignored him, branding them as petty and stupid for not choosing the *Way* but instead following a twisted path of thieves and boasters living a vulgar life – wearing beautiful, ornamented dresses, carrying sharp swords, feasting on rich food and hoarding wealth, keeping their homes tidy but letting their fields become weedy and their granaries empty – and thus creating their own misery. Even the intellectuals did not escape his censure. When they heard his *Way*, only the best ones practised it assiduously; the mediocre ones seemed to understand it at one moment but soon became perplexed. The lower ones laughed. Why? Because, incapable of understanding the Way, they though it ludicrous and laughable.

Laozi was indeed a difficult work. Its words often have uncommon meaning, making them susceptible to different interpretations; its style is concise, leaving the logic unclear; its narrative uses many analogies, making it mystical; and, above all, its themes are inconsistent, causing readers looking at the work from different points of view to entertain very different opinions. This last problem was especially acute in the cases of those who have not read the whole work carefully. They would, as the proverb says, *yi guan kui bao* (以管窺豹 to peek at a leopard through a thin tube), and have tunnel vision, seeing only the spots of its coat but not the animal as a whole. Trying to avoid this mistake, I have made a great effort to study the work and piece together most of its parts into a clear and consistent theory. Some parts which are in conflict with the theory are noted, and the inconsistencies analysed and explained when possible.

To put it simply, the theme of *Laozi* is as follows. The world was in chaos. It was the doing of those with little wisdom but great ambition. They made artefacts that caused people to abandon the simple life in accord with the laws of nature. The only way to save people from further strife was to lead them back to that idyllic, primitive life. It would take a wise man to do it. But making people to give up civilisation was difficult so he had to be tactful, hiding his agenda. He was like the

Pied Piper leading the children of Hamelin or like a shepherd herding his sheep. But there are important differences: the Sage was not to lead his "children" to their destruction, and he did not have his own interests at heart. He sincerely believed that there was a utopia and that the people should follow him there for their own well-being. He was thus not dishonest or dishonourable. He was only to make them observe the law of nature. Thus, perhaps a better metaphor would be that he was carrying out a scientific experiment. A scientist's task is primarily to find truth not to seek personal rewards. He is normally unemotional about his experiment and is ready to terminate it if his subject did not react as he has expected. This perhaps can better explain why the Sage is aloof to the people and treats them as straw dogs – or guinea pigs.

But, as a theory, Laozi's is problematic. First of all, he blamed the loss of the ideal state of nature not on some external elements but on human intelligence and knowledge. But intelligence is innate and knowledge useful. His suggestion of discarding them is unrealistic and impractical. In any case, he did not indicate how to do it; rather, he repeatedly asserted that the Sage did not have to do much. This is disingenuous because, to begin with, he had do a lot to disguise himself and plant in the minds of the people an irrational belief in him and then follow every step in the journey to the destination chosen by him, abandoning the hard-earned civilisation along the way. And he had to be constantly on the alert and prepared to use the "nameless primordial substance" to put down those who went astray.

Then there were Laozi's complaints that his theory was not understood by people. Those complaints are ironic and puzzling. Why call the people stupid? Didn't he say that they should be kept in ignorance? Why condemn them for being petty and stupid? Didn't the Sage find them so and wasn't that the very reason he wanted to save them? Why was Laozi so bitter? Was he supposed to have no feelings for the straw dogs?

The explanation is that Laozi was a mere social critic. He was much troubled by the situation of his time but did not have a practical way in which to bring about change. His advice: that one should be helpful in bringing things into being and facilitate their development but not possess them and determine their destiny; that one should be modest, tolerant and yielding; and that the authorities should not be hyperactive and meddle too much in people's lives are all excellent admonitions. People are attracted by them, and mesmerised and mystified by his metaphors and allegories. But he did not really engaged in the education of the people. Even in the case of Confucius who, with respect and sincerity, went to learn from him, he, instead of giving him a good lesson, turned the earnest young scholar away dismissively. This was what Sima Qian reported:

> Confucius came to the state of Zhou and was about to learn more about the rites from Laozi. Laozi said: "The persons [who made the rules] you want to talk about were long dead, only their words are left. A gentleman doing well at a fortunate time would [following the rites] ride a carriage, but when the time is not favour-

> able, he would just walk with a stick. A good merchant hides his merchandise as if he had nothing; a gentleman with high virtues appears to be stupid. Get rid of your air of haughtiness and many desires, pretentious appearance and excessive ambition. None of them will do you any good. This is all I can tell you."[2]

Being so summarily dismissed the poor confounded Confucius told his disciples:

> I know birds can fly, fish can swim and beasts can run. What runs can be caught by nets, what swims by fishing gears, and what flies by arrows. As to a dragon, I do not know how it can ride on winds and clouds and ascend to the sky. Today I met Laozi. He is like a dragon![3]

Perhaps Laozi was a dragon, a haughty and cynical one.

A comparison between him and Confucius is inevitable. It can help us understand both better. To be succinct, they held two divergent views about the world and the role humans should and could play. Though both were disappointed with their times and their own lives, Confucius was positive, constructed a reasoned theory for improvement, made great efforts to realise his ideas and accepted the outcome with equanimity. Laozi, was more complicated. Like Janus he had two faces: one, looking at the ordinary people, appeared passive and resigned, because, they were stupid and hopeless; the other, looking at the rulers, appeared positive and pushing, because they were to shepherd the masses. Therefore, on the one hand, he advised the ordinary people to be like infants, content with what they had; on the other hand, he urged the rulers to govern effectively, using various tactics. But his admonitions fell on deaf ears, and, according to legend, he fled the civilised world, riding a blue ox, into the wilderness in the west (a utopia in Chinese mythology), leaving a short work for people to puzzle over.

Notes

1. See "Biography of Laozi" in *Shi-ji*, vol. 63, p. 2140.
2. Ibid.
3. Ibid. and "Biography of Confucius" in *Shi-ji* vol. 47, p. 1909.

Mo-zi 墨子

PART 1
TRANSLATION

(A) The primitive world

[1] Mozi said, "Now we may imagine that in ancient times when humans first came into existence and there were not yet rulers, there was a saying, 'People had different ideas – each person had an idea, ten persons had ten ideas, a hundred persons had a hundred ideas. The more people there were, the more ideas there were.' As everybody regarded his own idea as correct and the ideas of others incorrect, they disputed. Even within the family, the father, the sons and the brothers harboured grudges against one another and were estranged, unable to live together in harmony. As a result, surplus energy would be wasted but not used to help others; useful knowledge would be concealed and not disseminated; and surplus goods would be left to rot but not shared. The world was a chaos just like that of the animals." (*Mozi Jian-gu* Chapter 12, "Shang-tong [II]" p. 47)

(B) Social authorities

(1) The need

[2] When it became clear that the chaos was the result of the absence of a ruler who could unify the ideas of what was right, a person of great virtue and wisdom was chosen and established as the Son of Heaven to achieve that unification. After being established, the Son of Heaven realised that, because of the limitations of his eyes and ears, he could not achieve this alone, so he chose from among the wise and virtuous three men and made them high ministers to help him. Realising that the world was vast and that it was difficult to unify the ideas of people in faraway places, they divided it into feudal states and appointed a ruler for each state to help achieve unification. Realising that it was difficult to unify the ideas of his people by himself, a ruler of a state chose from among them

some worthy and wise men and made them officials and officers and heads of districts and villages and ordered them to help him unify. (Ibid., pp. 47–8)

(2) The establishment

(A) BY HEAVEN AND ITS AGENTS – GODS AND SPIRITS

[3] Whence does rightness originate? Mozi said, "Rightness does not originate from those who are stupid and inferior in social status. It must originate from those who are wise and superior in social status. How do I know that? I know because rightness induces good government. How do I know that? I say rightness is good policy. How do I know? I say because when rightness prevails the world is in order; when it is disregarded, there is chaos. Moreover, the stupid and inferior do not govern the wise and superior but the wise and superior govern the stupid and inferior. By this fact I know rightness does not originate from the stupid and inferior but from the wise and superior. If so, who is the most superior and the wisest? I say, Heaven is, and therefore, rightness must originate from Heaven."

Now people of the world say, "It is clear that the Son of Heaven is superior to the rulers of the feudal states, and they in turn are superior to the officials. But we do not see how Heaven is superior to and wiser than the Son of Heaven." Mozi said, "There are many reasons why I know Heaven is superior to and wiser than the emperor. When the emperor does good, Heaven rewards him. When he does evil, Heaven punishes him. When he is suffering diseases and other misfortune he goes through ritual fast and bath and offers clean wine and rice as sacrifice to Heaven, and the spirits and Heaven will remove his problems. But I do not know that Heaven ever asks for blessings from the emperor. It is from these facts that I know Heaven is superior to and wiser than the emperor. Moreover, the Books of ancient sage kings which instruct us in the great and ineffable way of Heaven say, 'It is the brilliant and perspicacious Heaven that rules, like an overlord, the earth below'. Thus Heaven is more superior and wise than the emperor. Is there yet anyone who is superior to and wiser than Heaven? The answer is no, Heaven is the supreme and the wisest, that is all. Therefore rightness must originate from Heaven." (Ibid., Chapter 27, "Tian-zhi [II]" pp. 122–3)

[4] Mozi said, "In the past the sage kings of the Three Dynasties – Yu, Tang, Wen, and Wu – were obedient to the will of Heaven and obtained rewards – being made emperors in possession of the world and succeeded by descendants of many generations. The tyrants of the three dynasties – Jie, Shou, You and Li – opposed the will of Heaven and received punishments – being denied longevity and succession by a single generation." (Ibid., Chapter 26, "Tian-zhi [I]" p. 120)

[5] Mozi said, "After the death of the sage kings of the Three Dynasties of ancient times, the world lost rightness and the rulers of feudal states devoted their energy to war . . . and the world was left in disorder. Why did it happen? Because people doubted the existence of gods and spirits and were unaware that gods and spirits could reward the worthy and punish the violent. (Ibid. Chapter 31, "Ming-gui" [III] p. 138)

[6] Once Wang Liguo and Zhongli Jiao, two officials of Lord Zhuang of Qi, were involved in criminal litigation. For three years no judgment was reached. Lord Qi considered punishing them both but was afraid that one might be innocent. He also considered acquitting them both but was afraid that one might be guilty. He then ordered them to take a lamb to testify under oath of its blood in the altar of Qi. Both agreed. A small pit was dug, the throat of the lamb slit and its blood poured in. Wang Liguo presented his case first, and finished reading it. While Zhongli Jiao was less than half way through his testimony, the lamb jumped up and butted him, breaking his leg. Then a wizard priest emerged, hit Zhongli Jiao and killed him. All those present at the time witnessed the event; those not present heard of it, and it was recorded in the spring and autumn annals of Qi. The rulers of other states circulated the news around and said, "So speedy and severe is the punishment from gods and spirits to him who takes an oath in insincerity!" With such records in mind, how can we doubt that gods and spirits exist? (Ibid., Chapter 31, "Ming-gui" [III] pp. 144–5)

[7] Mozi said, "If the seeing and hearing of the ordinary people are thought to be not trustworthy, we may ask whether persons like the sage kings of the Three Dynasties, Yao, Shun, Yu, Tang, Wen and Wu, were. Everyone above mediocrity will say that they were. If so, let us review some of their deeds. After King Wu overthrew the Yin Dynasty and executed its last emperor Shou, he let the rulers of the feudal states share in the ceremony of worshiping the ancestors of Yin, saying, 'Those closely related to the Yin are to partake in the temple ceremony offering sacrifice to the Yin ancestors, those remotely related are to join in the outdoor ceremony offering sacrifice to the Yin state.' Thus it is safe to assume that King Wu believed in gods and spirits or he would not have initiated the ceremonies." (Ibid., Chapter 31, "Ming-gui" [III] pp. 145–6)

Moreover, in the past when the sage kings of the Three Dynasties – the Xia, the Shang, and the Zhou – first established their capitals, they selected the correct terrace for their ancestral temples, the best wooded place for the shrine of the dynasty patrons, the most virtuous of their elders as priests, the fattest animals, the most beautiful jades, the best grains and the finest wine for sacrifice in worshiping the gods and spirits. Thus, in governing the world, the sage kings place the gods and ghosts before the people. (Ibid., Chapter 31, "Ming-gui" [III] pp. 146–7)

[Then Mozi went to great lengths to say that, fearing their successors might not know the significance of their belief in the gods and spirits, the sage kings had premonitions for them written on bamboo slips and fabrics, carved in stones and inscribed on bronzes. And such premonitions were recorded in ancient books. Among them, the *Book of the Zhou*, the *Book of the Shang* and the *Book of the Xia* all mentioned how gods and spirits helped the founders of the dynasties achieve their great accomplishments. And, because of these books, Mozi argued, people should not have doubts about the existence and importance of gods and spirits.] (Ibid., Chapter 31, "Ming-gui" [III] pp. 147–50)

[Mozi argued that when the government was corrupt and cruel, as those headed by Jie of the Xia and Shou of the Yin were, calamities happened and, when a person committed serious crimes, punishment was inflicted on him because gods and spirits were watching and they brought the calamities and punishments even though Jie and Shou were powerful and the criminals might have acted in secrecy. This Mozi said was another proof that, in practice, gods and spirits existed and were active.] (Ibid., Chapter 31, "Ming-gui" [III] pp. 150–3)

[Mozi further said that, in the past as in the present, there were gods in Heaven, spirits of mountains and waters and ghosts of the dead . . . The dead were parents and elder brothers and sisters. If they existed as ghosts, the wine and rice offered as sacrifice in worship were for them to drink and eat. Was this not a great beneficence? If they did not exist as ghosts, what is offered was not lost because it was not to be thrown into the gutter but eventually consumed by family members and people of the same village. Thus, even if there were no gods and spirits, the ceremonies of worship could be a pleasant way in which to gather together the family and the neighbours of the village.] (Ibid., Chapter 31, "Ming-gui" [III] pp. 153–4)

(B) BY FATE (?)

[8] The fatalists say, "Where fate decrees that a man shall be wealthy, he will be wealthy; that he shall be poor, he will be poor; that there shall be abundance, there will be abundance; that there shall be scarcity, there will be scarcity; that there shall be order, there will be order; that there shall be chaos, there will be chaos; that a man shall live long, he will live long; that he shall die prematurely, he will die prematurely. Even if a person is determined and forceful [in pursuing his own goals, defying fate], what is the use?"

[Mozi then said that this doctrine had to be examined, and he pointed out that there were three ways in which to test a doctrine: first, to probe its foundation by checking it against the deeds of ancient sage kings; second, to investigate its validity by checking it against people's experience; and third, to evaluate it by applying it to government affairs and observing its logical effects on the people.]

Now some men believe that there is fate but have they studied the deeds of the sage kings? In ancient times, the disorder caused by Jie was inherited by Tang but turned into order; the disorder caused by Shou was inherited by King Wu but turned into order. The world did not change, nor did the people, yet, under Jie and Shou, there was disorder, and under Tang and Wu there was order. Can it be said that there is fate?

Now some men believe that there is fate but have they studied the books of the ancient kings? Those books meant for governing the country and benefiting the people were great constitutions. Did any of those constitutions ever say, "Blessing cannot be sought and disaster cannot be avoided; earnestness will do no good and violence no harm?" The rules for hearing litigations and deciding punishments were the penal laws. Did any of the penal laws of the ancient kings say, "Blessing cannot be sought and disaster cannot be avoided; earnestness will do no good and violence no harm"? (Ibid., Chapter 35, "Fei-ming" [I] pp. 163–5)

[9] The way I am to know whether there is fate or not is by checking with the people's testimony based on what they have heard and seen. If some people have heard it and some people have seen it, one can say that there is fate. If none has heard it and none has seen it, one can say there is no fate. So why not then check with people's experience? From antiquity to the present, ever since there were human beings, has anyone seen such a thing as fate, or has anyone heard the sound of fate? There is none.

If the common people are considered stupid and their hearing and sight unreliable, why not look into the recorded words of the state rulers? From antiquity to the present, ever since there were human beings, had any of the rulers said that he had heard the sound of fate or had seen such a thing as fate? None of them had. (Ibid., Chapter 36, "Fei-ming" [II] p. 169)

[10] If the doctrine of the fatalist were put into practice, those in superior status would not attend to government; those in inferior status would not attend to work. If the superiors do not attend to government, judicial and administrative tasks would be left in chaos. If the inferiors do not attend to their work, the supply of goods would become insufficient. (Ibid. Chapter 35, "Fei-ming" [I] p. 168)

[11] Therefore, the ancient sage kings promulgated laws and issued orders in order to establish standards for rewards and punishments and to encourage the worthy. Consequently, people were filial to their parents in the family and respectful to the elders in the village. They observed propriety at home, moderation abroad and decency between men and women. When made to manage a government warehouse, they would not steal; when ordered to defend a city, they would not surrender or rebel. When the ruler was in danger, they fought to the death for him; when he was banished, they escorted him in exile. Such was the conduct that the rulers would reward and the common people would applaud. Now the fatalist says, "Whoever is rewarded by the superior is predestined to be rewarded not because he is worthy; whoever is punished by the superior is predestined to be punished not because he is evil." In accordance with this doctrine, people would not be filial to their parents in the family and respectful to the elders in the village. They would not observe propriety at home, moderation abroad, and decency between men and women. When made to manage a government warehouse, they would steal; when ordered to defend a city, they would surrender or rebel; when the ruler is in danger, they would not fight to the death for him; when he is banished, they would not escort him in exile. Such is the conduct that the ruler would punish and the people would deplore.

Now the fatalist says, "Whoever is punished by the superior is predestined to be punished not because he is evil, whoever is rewarded by the superior is predestined to be rewarded not because he is worthy." In accordance with this doctrine, the ruler would not be righteous; the official would not be loyal; the father would not be caring; the son would not be filial; the elder brother would not be kind; and the younger brother would not be respectful. The unthinking adherence to this doctrine is the origin of pernicious ideas and is the way of the evil. (Ibid. Chapter 35, "Fei-ming" [I] pp. 166–7)

[12] Now the rulers go to court early and retire late, hearing lawsuits and attending to government business for the whole day, and dare not be negligent. Why? It is because they think that diligence will bring about order, and negligence, disorder; that diligence will induce safety, and negligence, danger. Now the officials exhaust their limbs and stretch their minds caring for the government coffers and collecting taxes to fill it, and dare not be negligent. Why? It is because they think diligence will procure honour and negligence procure dishonour; diligence will induce glory and negligence induce disgrace. Now peasants go to the field at dawn and return home at dusk, diligently sowing and planting various crops, and dare not be negligent. Why? It is because they think diligence will generate wealth, negligence poverty; diligence will create bounty, negligence famine. Now women get up early at dawn and retire late in the night, diligently weaving and spinning to make various fabrics, and dare not be negligent. Why? It is because they think diligence will generate wealth, negligence poverty; diligence will produce warmth, negligence cold.

Now, if they should believe in fate and behave accordingly, rulers would be negligent in hearing lawsuits and attending to government; officials would be negligent in caring for government business; peasants would be negligent in sowing and planting; and women would be negligent in weaving and spinning. When rulers are negligent in hearing lawsuits and attending to government, and officials are negligent in caring for government business, I should think the world would be in disorder. When peasants are negligent in sowing and planting and women are negligent in weaving and spinning, I should think clothing and food would be in short supply. If the doctrine of fatalism were applied in the government of the empire, in worshipping Heaven and the gods and spirits, they would not be pleased; and in nurturing the people, they would not be benefited. Instead they would be demoralised and would disperse and become unfit to be employed. As a result, there would be no strong defence at home and no victory abroad. And this was why the evil kings of the ancient Three Dynasties – Jie, Zhou, You and Li – ruined their countries and terminated their dynasties. Therefore, Mozi said, "If the men of the world really desire to promote what is beneficial and to eliminate what is harmful to the world, they cannot but rigorously refute the doctrine of fatalism. This doctrine is an invention of the evil kings and the practice of miserable men. It is not a doctrine of the humane. Those who are humane and righteous must examine it and refute it." (Ibid., Chapter 37, "Fei-ming" [III] pp. 175–7)

(3) The prerequisites for those to have social authority

[13] Mozi said, "In the past the sage kings of the Three Dynasties – Yu, Tang, Wen and Wu – acted in line with the will of Heaven and received Heaven's rewards. In the past the evil kings of the Three Dynasties – Jie, Shou, You and Li – acted against the will of Heaven and received Heaven's punishments." How did Yu, Tang, Wen and Wu received Heaven's rewards? Mozi said, "They worshipped Heaven with reverence, respected the gods and spirits, and loved the people. So

Heaven announced, 'They broadly love all I love and broadly benefit all I want to benefit. Their love is all-embracing and the benefit they bestow on people is so substantial!' Therefore Heaven had them honoured as Sons of Heaven, gave them the riches of the empire, and made their descendants of many generations to succeed them. History recorded their good deeds that spread all over the world, and to this day they are praised as sage kings."

Then how did Jie, Shou, You and Li received their punishments? Mozi said, "They blasphemed against Heaven, slandered the gods and spirits, and harmed the people. So Heaven announced. 'They discriminated against what I love and harmed what I want to benefit. Their hatred is all-embracing and their harm to the people so serious!' Therefore Heaven refused to permit them to live out their natural lives and to have any of their descendants survive them as kings. And to this day they are condemned as evil kings." (Ibid., Chapter 26, "Tian-zhi" [I] 120–1)

[14] Mozi said, "People of the past who did not know how to build houses, lived in hills and caves where it was damp and harmful to health. Therefore the sage kings built houses . . . People of the past who did not know how make clothing, wore coats of animal skin and belts of straw which were not light and warm in the winter or light and cool in the summer. The sage kings thought these unfit for people's need and taught women to produce silk and flax and to weave cloth and linen, therewith to make clothing for the people . . . People of the past who did not know how to make food, ate wild vegetables. The sage kings taught men to till the land and plant crops to provide for food . . . People of the past who did not know how to make boats and carts, could not move heavy loads and travel vary far. Thereupon the sage kings made boats and carts to facilitate the people . . ." (Ibid., Chapter 6, "Ci-guo" pp. 17–21)

(C) Social norms

(1) Origin and basic principles

[15] [Mozi alleged that, ultimately, rightness comes from Heaven, and Heaven has a will; it has its likes and dislikes. He then said] "What does Heaven desire and what does it abhor? It desires rightness and abhors wrongness. How can we know? It is because anything that is right lives, anything that is wrong dies; a person who is right is rich, a person who is wrong is poor; a state that is right is in order, a state that is wrong is in chaos. This is how I know Heaven desires rightness and abhors wrongness." (Ibid., Chapter 26, "Tian-zhi" [I] pp. 119–24)

[16] Now that we know we must not be careless about the will of Heaven, what does the will of Heaven desire and what does it abhor? Mozi said, "The will of Heaven does not want to see large states attacking small states, large households interfering with the affairs of small households, the strong oppressing the weak, the cunning deceiving the stupid, and the lofty disdaining the humble. Conversely, the will of Heaven desires people with strength to help others, those with knowledge to teach others and those with wealth to share with others.

Further, it desires that those of superior status diligently attend to government and those of inferior status diligently attend to their work." (Ibid., Chapter 27, "Tian-zhi" [II] pp. 123–4)

(2) Objectives and measures

(A) Promote universal love

[17] Mozi said, "I know with reason that Heaven loves the people dearly. It polishes the sun, the moon and the stars to give people light and guidance. It arranges the four seasons to regulate the people's activities. It sends down snow, frost, rain and dew to grow grain, and flax and silk so that the people can use and enjoy them . . . It appoints the various rulers to reward the virtuous and to punish the violent, and to make use of the metals, the wood, the birds and the beasts in order to help the people raise crops and meet their needs for food and clothing. It has never stopped doing all these since antiquity to the present.

Yet these are not the only reasons why I know that Heaven loves the people dearly. When one murders an innocent person, Heaven will inflict misfortune on the murderer. Who is the innocent? He is any ordinary man. From whom will the visitation come? It will come from Heaven. If Heaven did not love the people dearly, why should it inflict a misfortune on the murderer?

Yet this is not all by which I know Heaven loves the people dearly. There are those who love the people and benefit them and obey the will of Heaven and are rewarded by Heaven. And there are those who hate the people and harm them and oppose the will of Heaven and are punished by Heaven. Who are those who love the people and benefit them and are rewarded by Heaven? They were the ancient sage kings of the Three Dynasties, Yao, Shun, Yu, Tang, Wen and Wu . . . Who are those who hate the people and harm them and oppose the will of Heaven and are punished by Heaven? They were the ancient evil kings of the Three Dynasties, Jie, Shou, You and Li." (Ibid. Chapter 27, "Tian-zhi" [II] pp. 125–7)

[18] Mozi said, "A humane person's task is to help with his utmost ability promote what benefits the world and eliminate what harms it." At the present what are the greatest harms to the world? Mozi said, "It is the big states attacking the small ones, the big households interfering with the affairs of smaller ones, the strong oppressing the weak, the majority exploiting the minority, the cunning deceiving the stupid, and the lofty disdaining the humble. These are the harms to the world. In addition, the lack of kindness in the ruler, loyalty in the subjects, affection in the father, and filial piety in the son also harm the world. And so also do the mean people who injure one another with weapons, poisons, water and fire.

Now let us trace the origin of these harms. Do they originate from loving others and benefiting others? We have to say no and say they originate from hating others and injuring others. If we are to give different descriptions to the people of the world, should those who hate and injure others be called inclusive or discriminatory? We have to say that they are discriminatory. So it is mutual discrimination that produces great harm to the world and therefore discrimination is wrong."

Mozi said, "Replace discrimination with inclusiveness. Why? Where everyone regards the states of others as he regards his own state, who would attack other states? Where everyone regards the cities of others as he regards his own city, who would vanquish other cities? Where everyone regards the households of others as he regards his own household, who would interfere with the affairs of other households? When states and cities do not attack one another and households do not interfere with one another – is this result harmful or beneficial? It must be said that it is beneficial.

Now let us trace the origin of the benefits. Do they originate from hating others and injuring others? We have to say no and say that they originate from loving others and benefiting others. What makes people of the world love and benefit others? Is it because they are discriminatory or inclusive? We have to say that it is their being inclusive. It is mutual inclusiveness that produces great benefits to the world and therefore inclusiveness is right." (Ibid., Chapter 16, "Jian-ai" [III] pp. 71–2)

[19] The sage king who takes on himself the task of governing the empire must know the cause of disorder before he can put the empire in order. It is like a physician attending a patient. He must know the cause of the ailment before he can cure it.

What is the cause of disorder? It is the lack of mutual love. What is called disorder is just the lack of filial piety on the part of the official and the son towards the ruler and the father. Where a son loves himself but not his father, he will take advantage of his father to benefit himself. Where a younger brother loves himself but not his older brother, he will take advantage of his older brother to benefit himself. Where an official loves himself but not the ruler, he will take advantage of the ruler to benefit himself. These are called disorder.

Where the father shows no affection for his son, where the older brother shows no affection for his younger brother, and where the ruler shows no affection for his subjects, the situation is also called disorder. As the father loves only himself but not his son, he will take advantage of his son to benefit himself. As the older brother loves only himself but not his younger brother, he will take advantage of his younger brother to benefit himself. As the ruler loves only himself but not his subjects, he will take advantage of his subjects to benefit himself. Why is this so? It is due to lack of mutual love.

This is true even among thieves and muggers. As a thief loves his own family but not other families, he steals from other families to profit his own family. As a mugger loves his own person but not others, he injures others to benefit himself. Why is this so? It is due to lack of mutual love.

This again is true of the mutual interference among households and the mutual attacks among the feudal states. As an aristocrat loves only his own household but not others', he will interfere in the affairs of others' households to profit his own. The ruler of a feudal state who loves only his own state but not other states, will attack other states to profit his own. All the troubles in the world begin from this fact: that is, that there is lack of mutual love.

If everybody in the world loves universally, that is, loves others as one's self, will there still be any unfilial individual? When everyone regards his father, older brother, and ruler as himself, whereto can he direct any unfilial feeling? Will there still be any unloving individual? When everyone regards his younger brother, son, and subject as himself, whereto can he direct any disaffection? Therefore, there will not be any unfilial feeling or disaffection. Will there then be any thieves or any muggers? When everyone regards other families as his own family, who will steal? When everyone regards other persons as his own person, who will injure another? Therefore, there will not be any thieves or any muggers. Will there be mutual interference among the households and invasions among the feudal states? When everyone regards the households of others as his own, who will interfere? When everyone regards the state of others as his own, who will invade? Therefore there will be no interference among the households and no invasion among the feudal states.

If everyone in the world loves universally, states would not attack one another; households would not interfere with one another; theft and mugging would be extinct; rulers and subjects, fathers and sons, would all be affectionate and filial. Consequently, the world will be orderly. Therefore, how can the sage king who takes on himself the task of governing the empire not proscribe evil and encourage love? (Ibid., Chapter 14, "Jian-ai" [I] pp. 62–3)

(B) CONDEMN AGGRESSIVE WAR

[20] Now someone enters the orchard of another and steals some peaches and plums. Hearing of it, the public will condemn the act; getting hold of him, the authorities will punish him. Why? It is because he harms others to profit himself. As to grabbing dogs, pigs, and chickens from another person, it is considered a greater wrong than stealing peaches and plums. Why? It is because it harms the other person more, and the offender is thus considered more depraved and guilty of a more serious crime. When one enters into another's stable and seizes the other's horses and oxen, the offender is more depraved and his act more wrong than that of taking dogs, pigs, and chickens. Why? It is because it harms the other person more. When he harms others more, he is considered more depraved and guilty of a more serious crime. As to murdering an innocent person, stripping him of his clothing, robbing him of his spear and sword, it is an even greater wrong than entering another's stable and seizing his horses and oxen. Why? It is because it harms the other person more. When he harms others more, he is considered more depraved and his offence more serious.

The men of the world all know that they should condemn such behaviour and call it wrong. But when it comes to the greatest wrong of attacking a state, they do not know that they should condemn it. On the contrary, they applaud it, calling it right. Can they be said to know the distinction between right and wrong? (Ibid., Chapter 17, "Fei-gong" [I] p. 81)

[21] The murder of one person is called wrong and incurs the death penalty. Following this argument, the murder of ten persons would be ten times as wrong and would incur ten death penalties; and the murder of a hundred persons would be a hundred times as wrong and would incur a hundred death penalties. All the men of the world know murder to be wrong and condemn it. But when it comes to the greatest wrong of attacking a state, they fail to condemn it but rather applaud it, calling it right . . . (Ibid., Chapter 17, "Fei-gong" [I] pp. 81–2)
[22] [Mozi pointed out that the cost of war was horrendous – when a country goes to war in the spring many men will be taken away from tilling the land; when it goes to war in the autumn many men will be prevented from reaping the harvest. As a result, countless people will die from starvation. Moreover, countless weapons, armour and other military supplies will be sent to the front and will be lost; countless fat and strong horses and oxen will be sent and return thin and weak or not return at all; and, above all, countless soldiers will die or be maimed on the battlefield. Why then does the government harm the people to such a great extent?] A ruler might say, "I do it because I covet the fame of the victor and the spoils of the conquest." In reply Mozi said, "But count what is won, it is nothing of any use; and count what is gained, it is less than what is lost. Now, for the siege of a city with an inner wall of three *li* in perimeter and an outer wall of seven *li* in perimeter, it is impossible to avoid using troops and killing people. In fact, the number of persons killed will be thousands or tens of thousands before such a city can be seized. Now, the states of ten thousand chariots all have thousands of sparsely populated towns which can be developed without war; and they all have extensive territories which can be cultivated without war. So, land is abundant but people are few. To force people to their deaths and to increase the tension between the ruler and his subjects for the purpose of obtaining a devastated city is to discard what is scarce and to treasure what is already abundant. Whoever in government takes such an action is not serving his country well." (Ibid. Chapter 18, "Fei-gong" [II] pp. 83–4)
[23] Those who endeavour to gloss over offensive wars would say, "Look at the kings of Jing and Wu in the south, and the lords of Qi and Jin in the north. When their states were first established, none had a territory larger than a few hundred *li* square, and a population more than a few tens of thousands. By means of offensive wars, each has increased its territory to several thousand *li* square and its population to several million. So, offensive wars are not all that condemnable."

Mozi said, "The four or five states may have had their gains. But it is still not the right way. Take as an example the case of a physician treating patients. Where a physician prescribes the same medicine for all who are ill, if, among the ten thousand people who took it, only four or five were cured, it cannot be said that the medicine is right for all. A filial son will not give it to his parents, and a loyal subject will not give it to his ruler. Since ancient times, when feudal states were created, countless were extinguished by aggression – the earlier cases we've heard, the recent ones we've seen." (Ibid., Chapter 18, "Fei-gong" [II] p. 84)
[24] Now a state ruler fond of aggressive wars again glosses over their conduct to

refute Mozi, saying, "You condemn aggression as unjust and unprofitable? But, in ancient times, Yu made war on the chief of Miao, Tang on Jie, and King Wu on Shou. Yet they are regarded as sage kings. Why?" Mozi said, "You have not examined the terminology of my statements, and you do not understand the background of their conduct. Their actions were not to be called "aggression" but "punishment".

In antiquity, the three Miao tribes were in great chaos, and Heaven ordered their destruction. The sun rose at night and it rained blood for three days. Dragons emerged in the temple, and dogs cried in the marketplace. Ice came in summer, and the earth split and the cracks reached down to gushing groundwater. The five grains appeared in mutation, and the people were greatly shocked by all these. God Gaoyang in the celestial palace gave Emperor Yu the order of Heaven to conquer the Miao. Amid thunder and lightning, a god with the face of a man and the body of a bird and a jade tablet in hand was revealed waiting upon Yu. The commander of the Miao was struck down by an arrow and the Miao army was sent into great confusion. Since then, the Miao have been in decline. Having conquered the Miao, Yu separated the hills and rivers and established the great order for things high and low, near and far. Neither gods nor humans disobeyed, and the world was brought peace. This was why Yu made war on the Miao." [Mozi continued to point out that wars made by Tang on Jie and by King Wen on Shou were justifiable because Jie and Shou lost the Heavenly mandate and the wars were ordered by Heaven as punishments. And then he concluded that: judging by the deeds of these three sage kings, it is obvious that the wars which they made were not aggression but punishments.] (Ibid. Chapter 19, "Fei-gong" [III] pp. 91–5)

(c) Disparage music

[25] Humans are different from birds and beasts. Birds and beasts have their feathers and furs for coats, have their hoofs and paws for shoes, and have water and grass for drink and food. Therefore, the males do not sow or plant; the females do not spin and weave; and yet food and clothing are available. Humans are different. Those who work hard will survive; those who do not work will not survive. When men do not diligently attend to government, the government will be in chaos. When commoners do not diligently attend to their work, supply of materials will become insufficient . . .

Now if the rulers should love music and listen to it, they would not be able to go to court early and retire late to hear lawsuits and attend to government; then the state would be in chaos and danger. If the officials should love music and listen to it, they would not be able to use their full strength and employ their best intelligence in attending to the bureaucracy and collecting taxes to fill the government treasury and granaries; as a result, the treasury and granaries will be left empty. If the peasants should love music and listen to it, they would not be able to set out early and come home late to sow and plant and produce a large quantity of crops; as a result, there will be a shortage of food. If women should love music and listen to it, they will not be able to get up early at dawn and go to bed late in the night to spin and weave and produce various fabrics; as a result there will be a shortage of clothing . . . Therefore, Mozi said, "To make music is wrong." (Ibid., Chapter 32, "Fei-yue" [I] pp. 158–60)

[26] Mozi said, "The work of a humane ruler is to promote what benefits the world and to eliminate what harms the world. He will make himself a model for the world. What is beneficial to the people, he will do; what is not beneficial to the people, he will not do. Moreover, in planning for the world, the humane ruler does not do what delights his eye, please his ear, gratifies his taste, or comforts his body; if these are to deprive the people of their clothing and food, he will not do them." So the reason why Mozi condemns music is not that the sounds of big bells and drums, of lutes and flutes, are not pleasant; that the carvings and ornaments are not delightful; that the roasted, fried, baked, boiled foods not gratifying; or that the high terraces, grand palaces and quiet country villas are not comfortable. Though his body knows they are comfortable, his mouth knows they are gratifying, his eyes know they are delightful, and his ears know they are pleasing, yet he finds that having these enjoyments is not in accordance with the deeds of the sage kings of antiquity and do not contribute to the welfare of the people at present. Therefore, Mozi says: to make music is wrong. (Ibid., Chapter 32, "Fei-yue" [I] p. 159)

[27] The people have three worries: the hungry do not have food; the cold do not have clothing; and the tired do not have rest. These three are the greatest worries of the people. Now, suppose we strike the big bell, beat the sonorous drums, play the lute and the flute, and perform glorious dances, can the material for feeding and clothing the people be thus procured? I do not think that it is possible. Moreover, when large states invade small ones, large households interfere with the affairs of small ones, the strong oppress the weak, the many oppress the few, the lofty disdain the humble, bandits and thieves rampage everywhere and all these are unstoppable, can the chaos in the world be put into order by striking the big bells and beating the sonorous drums, playing the lute and the flute, and performing glorious dances? I do not think it possible. Therefore Mozi said, "To tax the people heavily and use the revenue to make the music of big bells and sonorous drums, lutes and flutes, is not to help promote what is beneficial to the world and to eliminate what is harmful to the world." Therefore Mozi said, "To make music is wrong." (Ibid., Chapter 32, "Fei-yue" [I] pp. 165–6)

[28] The ancient sage kings did collect taxes from the people to build boats and carts. When they were built, the people asked: "What are we to use them for?" The answer was: "The boats are to be employed on water and the carts on land, so that the gentlemen can rest their feet and the common people can rest their shoulders and backs. The people paid their taxes and did not complain. Why? It was because the boats and carts in turn benefited them. Thus, if musical instruments also contributed to the benefits of the people, I, too, would not dare to condemn them." (Ibid., Chapter 32, "Fei-yue" p. 156)

(D) CUT WASTE

[29] When a sage rules a state, its benefits can be doubled. When he extends his rule over the empire, its benefits can be doubled. The increase is not achieved by seizing land from without but by cutting out the wasteful expenditures within the state. (Ibid., Chapter 20, "Jie-yong" [I] p. 99)

[30] The ancient sage kings made the laws of economy, saying, "All you artisans and craftsmen – wheelwrights, cart-makers, tanners, potters, smiths, and carpenters – do what you can do. Stop when the needs of the people are satisfied." What causes extra expense but adds no benefit to the people is what the sage kings would not do.

The ancient sage kings made the laws regarding food and drink, saying, "Stop when hunger is satiated, breathing becomes strong, limbs are strengthened and ears and eyes become sharp. There is no need of combining the five tastes extremely well or harmonising the different sweet flavours. And efforts should not be made to procure rare delicacies from faraway countries."

The ancient sage kings made the laws regarding clothing, saying, "Make clothing of blue or grey silk in winter that is light and warm, and clothing of flax linen in summer that is light and cool, and stop. Anything in addition, which will increase the cost but not be of any benefit to the people, will not be done by the sage kings.

Because the wide rivers and broad valleys were once not crossable, the sage kings ordered boats and oars to be made. And these were made just so that they could cross the rivers. Even the three high ministers and the feudal lords would use the same type of boats, and the oarsmen wore no special outfits.

The ancient sage kings made the laws limiting funeral expenditure, saying: "Of shrouds there shall be three pieces in order to be enough to hold the rotting flesh. The coffin shall be 3 inches thick to be sufficient to hold the rotting bones. The pit shall be dug not deep enough to reach water but just so deep that the odours will not escape."

The sage kings made laws regarding houses. How are houses to be built? Mozi said, "Its sides can keep off the wind and the cold, its top can keep off the snow, frost, rain, and dew, its inside is clean for sacrificial ceremonies, its partitions in there are enough to separate the men from the women. What causes extra expenditure but does not add any benefit to the people, the sage kings will not do." (Ibid. Chapter 21, "Jie-yong" [II] pp. 101–4)

[31] After the death of the sage kings of the ancient Three Dynasties, the world has lost the right principles. Some gentlemen of later days considered lavish funerals and extended periods of mourning as humane and right, and as something a filial son should do, but some others disagree. (Ibid. Chapter 25, "Jie-zang" [III] p. 105)

[32] According to those who advocate lavish funerals and extended mourning, there must be several inner and outer coffins, and they must be buried deep; there must be many shrouds, elaborately embroidered, and there must be a massive

grave mound. If so, the death of a common man would exhaust the wealth of a family, and the death of a feudal lord would empty the state treasury . . . Moreover, there will be people to follow the deceased to the underworld. For the deceased emperor there will be between several scores to several hundreds; for a deceased high official there will be between several to several scores. (Ibid. Chapter 25, "Jie-zang" [III] pp. 106–7)

[33] What are the rules to be observed by the mourner? Those who advocate extended mourning said that he is to cry without restraint and sound as though he is choking. He is to wear a ragged dress of linen and a hat of flax. His tears and nose keep running, and he is to live in a mourning hut, sleep on a coarse mat of straw, and lay his head on a clod of earth. He is to abstain from food so as to be hungry, and to wear little so as to be cold. His cheeks and eyes are to be sunken and his complexion is to appear dark. His ears and eyes are to become dull, and hands and feet are to become weak and unusable. Moreover, they say that, in mourning, a gentleman of high status has to be supported in rising and has to lean on a cane to walk. And for him, all this is to last three years.

Taking such words as norms and putting them into practice, kings and lords would not be able to come to court early and retire late to hear lawsuits and attend administrative details; officials would not be able to run the bureaucracy, encourage the people to do farming and forestry and fill the government granaries and warehouses; peasants would not be able to set out early and come home late to do sowing and planting; craftsmen would not be able to make boats, carts and various wares; and women would not be able to get up early in the morning and retire late in the night to spin and weave. Thus, a careful calculation shows that a lavish funeral is to bury a lot of wealth, and extended mourning is to impose long abstention from work. Wealth already created is carried away into the grave, and what might be created is stopped by long abstention. To seek wealth in this way is like seeking a harvest by prohibiting sowing. Wealth is thus unattainable.

[Mozi then pointed out that the practice of prolonged mourning would reduce the population.] When a ruler died, the mourning period for everyone was three years; when a parent died, the mourning period for the children was three years; when the wife died, the mourning period for the husband was three years; when the firstborn son of a man's formal wife died, the mourning period for the father was three years; when an uncle, a brother or a son, other than the one mentioned above, died, the mourning period for a relative was one year; when a clansman died, the mourning period for other clansmen was five months; when an aunt, an elder sister, a maternal uncle or a nephew died, the mourning period was several months . . . During these periods, people had to suffer hunger, cold in the winter and heat in the summer. As a result, those who fell sick and died were countless. Moreover, during these periods, men and women were prohibited from intercourse. To want the population to grow under these circumstances was like seeking longevity by thrusting oneself upon a sword. (Ibid., Chapter 25, "Jie-zang" [III] pp. 107–9)

[34] Those who advocate lavish funerals and extended mourning said, "If lavish funerals and extended mourning were not the way of the sage kings, why then do the gentlemen of the Middle Kingdom practise them continually and follow them without any hesitation?"

Mozi said, "That's what is called finding convenience in habit and approval in custom. In the past, east of the state of Yue there was the state of Kaimu. Its people would, after giving birth to a first son, dismember and eat him, alleging that this would be propitious for his younger brothers. When the grandfather died, the people would carry the grandmother away and abandon her, saying that one should not live with the wife of a ghost. Such practices were enforced by officials as public policy and accepted by the people as established custom. The whole state followed continuously and no one had any hesitation. But were they humane and right? No. It is only because habit affords convenience, and custom carries approval. To the south of the state of Chu there was the state of Yanren. There, when the parents died, the son would cut out and throw away their flesh before burying their bones. By doing so, he was considered filial. To the west of Qin, there was the state of Yiqu. There, when the parents died, the son would burn their bodies on a pyre, and their souls were said to ascend to heaven with the smoke. By doing so, he was considered filial. Such practices were also enforced by officials as public policy and accepted by the people as established custom. The whole state followed continuously and no one had any hesitation. But were they humane and right? No. It is only because habit affords convenience and custom carries approval.

Obviously the practice of these three states is too heartless and that of the gentlemen of the Middle Kingdom is too extravagant. There should be a moderate middle ground between the extremes. Even in the case of food and clothing, which are necessary for the living, there should be moderation. How can funeral and burial, which are necessary for the dead, not follow certain rules of moderation?"

Drafting the rules for funeral and burials, Mozi said, "The coffin shall be three inches thick, just sufficient to hold the rotting bones. There shall be three pieces of shroud, just enough to hold the rotting flesh. The pit shall be dug not so deep as to strike water, and not so shallow as to allow the odour to ascend. The mound shall be just high enough to be identifiable. The surviving relatives may weep on the way to and from the burial. But, upon returning, they shall engage in production for food and clothing and also for the sacrifices as an expression of filial piety toward the deceased." Thus, according to his rules, the necessities of neither the dead nor the living are neglected. (Ibid., Chapter 25, "Jie-zang" [III] pp. 115–17)

[35] Now if those who advocate lavish burial and prolonged mourning are made to govern, the state will become poor, the population small and the judicial and administrative work disorderly. When the state is poor, the sacrificial offerings will not be rich and clean; when the population is small, there will be few people to worship Heaven and the gods and spirits; when the judicial and administrative work is disorderly, sacrifices will not be timely and regular . . . Heaven and

the gods and spirits will wonder whether it is better to have or not to have these people and decide that it makes no difference whether to have or not to have these people. Therefore, Heaven and the gods and spirits send judgements upon them and inflict on them calamities and punishments, and abandon them. (Ibid., Chapter 25, "Jie-zang" [III] p. 111)

(E) Increase production

[36] When a sage rules a state, it can be doubled . . . [Mozi pointed out that it was not difficult to double the amount of clothing, shelters, weapons, vehicles, animals and precious goods.] What is difficult to double? It is the population. But there is a way to double the population. In ancient times, the sage kings made a law prescribing, "No man of twenty should dare to be without a family; no girl of fifteen should dare to be without a husband." Such was the law of the sage kings. Now that the sage kings have passed away, the people have become loose. Some who like to have a family early marry at twenty. Some who like to have a family late marry at forty. When the late marriages are offset by the early ones, the average is still later by ten years than the legal requirements of the sage kings. If, on average, a child is born every three years, then two or three children should have been born by the time men now marry. Is it not clear that to require early marriage is a way to double the population?

But today those who govern the world diminish the population in more ways than one. They overwork and overtax the people and, as the people have not enough for subsistence, countless die of hunger and cold. Moreover, the rulers love to raise armies and make wars on neighbouring states. The campaigns might last a whole year or several months. Thus, men and their wives cannot see each other for a long time. This is another way to diminish population. Living in discomfort and eating and drinking irregularly, many people become ill and die. Participating in aggressive wars and engaging in sieges and battles, countless people die. Are these not the results of the policies of today's rulers that diminish the population? (Ibid., Chapter 20, "Jie-yong" [I] pp. 100–1)

(D) Enforcement of social norms

(1) Give correct directions

[37] In the past, King Ling of the state of Jing (Chu) loved slender waists. In his time, officials of that state ate no more than one meal a day. They had to lean firmly on a stick to stand up and touch a wall to walk. Now to diet like that was difficult and yet people did because that was what King Ling liked. Thus, within less than a generation, the people could be transformed in order to please those above them. King Goujian of the state of Yue admired military prowess and exhorted it to his officers and soldiers for three years. Unsure whether they had it, he set some ships ablaze and beat the drum to summon his men to fight the fire. They rushed forward, trampling those ahead, and died in flame and water in countless numbers . . . Now to be burnt alive was a great sacrifice, and yet it was

done because that was what King Goujian liked. Thus, within less than a generation, the people could be transformed in order to please those above them. Lord Wen of the state of Jin liked cheap clothing. In his time, the officials of that state wore garments of plain cloth, coats of sheepskin, hats of coarse silk and rough shoes. Thus dressed, they would go in and see the Lord and come out and attend government business in the court. It was uncomfortable in such ragged clothing, yet people wore it because that was what Lord Wen liked. Thus, within less than a generation, the people could be transformed to please those above them. Now to eat little, to be burnt, and to wear uncomfortable clothing were very hard for people to do, and yet, if that was what those above liked, in less than a generation the people of the world could be transformed. Why? Because they wanted to please those above them. (Ibid., Chapter 16 "Jian-ai" [III] p. 79)

(2) Exalt the worthy and employ the capable

[38] Mozi said: "All the rulers desire their states to be wealthy, their people to be numerous, and their government to be orderly. But what they get is not wealth but poverty, not a growing population but a diminishing one, not order but chaos. They are losing what they desire and getting what they dislike." Why? Mozi said: "It is because the rulers have failed to exalt the worthy and to employ the capable in the government. When the worthy are numerous in the state, order will prevail; when the worthy are scarce, order will break down. Therefore the task of the rulers is nothing but to have more of the worthy in the government." (Ibid. Chapter 8, "Shang-xian" [I] p. 25)

[39] When a prince or a great lord has a cow or sheep which he is unable to slaughter, he is sure to seek a good butcher. When he has a piece of cloth which he is unable to make into a dress, he is sure to seek a good tailor. For these tasks, he would not employ anyone whom he knows to be incapable even though the person is closely related to him, or rich and lofty but without merit, or simply good-looking. Why? It is because he is afraid that the person will spoil the matter. When the prince or lord has a sick horse which he is unable to cure, he is sure to seek a good veterinarian. When he has a defective bow which he is unable to use, he is sure to seek a good craftsman. For these tasks, he would not employ anyone whom he knows to be incapable even though the person is closely related to him, or rich and lofty but without merit, or simply good-looking. Why? It is because he is afraid that the person will spoil the matter. But, when it comes to governing the state, he is different. He would promote those closely related to him, those who are rich and lofty but without merit, and those who are good-looking. Then does it not seem that he loves his state less than he loves a defective bow, a sick horse, a piece of cloth, a cow or a sheep? Thus, I know that the gentlemen of the world understand only what is trivial but not what is significant. (Ibid., Chapter 10 "Shang-xian" [III] pp. 39–40)

[40] Therefore, in government, the ancient sage kings exalted the virtuous and advanced the worthy. If a person has the competence, even a farmer or an artisan, he would be promoted, given high rank, remunerated with generous emoluments,

trusted with important work, and empowered to issue definitive orders. For, if his rank were not high, people would not respect him; if his emoluments were not generous, people would not have confidence in him; if his orders were not final, people would not stand in awe before him. To bestow these three awards on the worthy is not so much to favour them as to bring about the success of their tasks. Therefore. in ancient times ranks were designated according to virtue, rewards given according to exertion, and emoluments according to achievements. Thus, officials were not constantly honoured, nor are the common people permanently humbled. Whoever was competent would be promoted, whoever was without competence would be demoted. This is what is meant by "elevate those who are right for the public, disregarding the fact that with whom the ruler has some private grudge". (Ibid., Chapter 8, "Shang-xian" [I] pp. 26–7)

[41] The ancient sage kings emphasised exaltation of the worthy and employment of the capable, and were not partial towards their relatives, the rich and lofty, and those with good looks. They exalted and promoted the worthy, enriched and honoured them, and made them officials and leaders; and they kept back and dismissed, dispossessed and degraded the unworthy, and made them labourers and servants. Thereupon, people were all encouraged by rewards and threatened by punishments and strove with one another after virtue. Thus, the worthy multiplied and the unworthy diminished in number. This was called "the exaltation of the worthy". Then the sage kings examined their words and acts to find out their capabilities and carefully assigned them to offices. This was called "the employment of the competent". Accordingly, those who were capable of governing the state were made to govern the state; those who were capable of running the bureaucracy were made to run the bureaucracy; and those who were capable of administering the districts were made to administer the districts. (Ibid., Chapter 9, "Shang-xian" [II] p. 29)

[42] When the worthy rule the country, they start the day early and retire late, hearing lawsuits and attending to administrative details. As a result, the country is well governed and laws are justly enforced. When the worthy run the bureaucracy, they retire late and get up early, collecting taxes to fill the treasury. As a result, the treasury is always full. When the worthy govern districts, they go out early in the morning and return late in the evening, engaging the people in sowing, planting, gathering and harvesting. As result, grain is bountiful, and the people are sufficiently supplied with food. As the country is well governed and laws are justly enforced, and the treasury is full and the people are well fed, there will be food and wine to offer to Heaven and the spirits; there will be money to use in diplomacy; and there will be enough wealth to care for all the people. Consequently, Heaven and spirits will bless the country, the neighbouring states will be friendly, and the people will be loyal. (Ibid., Chapter 9, "Shang-xian" [II] p. 29)

(3) Establish common values

[43] [Mozi pointed out that if, after the establishment of social authority, the people still did not have a common sense of rightness, rewards would not be enough to induce people to do good; punishments would not be enough to prohibit people from doing evil.] How do we know this is so? Mozi said, "When a ruler sets out to govern a country he proclaims, 'Whoever deserves reward, I will reward'. But if the people and the ruler do not share the same sense of rightness, whoever is rewarded by the ruler will be criticised by the people. When a person lives among the people who disapprove of something, even though he is to be rewarded by the authorities, the reward will not be enough inducement for him to do it. When a ruler sets out to govern a country, he proclaims, 'Whoever deserves punishment I will punish'. But, if the people and the ruler do not share the same sense of rightness, whoever is punished by the ruler will be applauded by the people. Thus, if something is approved by the community in which a person lives, even the punishment of the ruler will not be enough to deter him from doing it. If after the establishment of a ruler for the purpose of governing the people, his rewards are not enough to induce people to do good, and his punishments are not enough to deter people from doing evil, is the result not the same as in the beginning of human life when there were no rulers? If it is the same with or without the ruler, it is not the right way to govern the people." (Ibid., Chapter 12, "Shang-tong" [II] pp. 52–3)

[44] After the appointment of the feudal lords and leaders of the people, the emperor issued mandates, instructing the people, "Discovering good, you must report to your superior; discovering evil, you must report to your superior. What the superior regards as right all shall regard as right; what the superior regards as wrong, all shall regard as wrong . . ." Thus, in accordance with the emperor's mandate, the village head proceeded to standardise the sense of rightness in his village. Having accomplished this, he led the villagers to identify themselves with the head of the district, saying, "All you villagers are to identify yourselves with the head of the district and are not to have your own opinions. What the head of the district regards as right, all shall regard as right; what he regards as wrong, all shall regard as wrong. Discard your evil speech and learn his good speech; discard your evil conduct and learn his good conduct." As the head of the district is the most worthy of the district, if all the people in the district follow his example, how can the district not be well governed? Now, how is it that the head of the district could be so successful in governing the district? The answer is because he was able to establish a common sense of rightness among the people of the whole district. Having accomplished this, he led his people to identify themselves with the ruler of the state, saying, "All you people of the district are to identify yourselves with the ruler of the state and shall not have opinions of your own. What he regards as right, all shall regard as right; what he regards as wrong, all shall regard as wrong. Discard your evil speech and learn his good speech; discard your evil conduct and learn his good conduct." As the ruler of

the state is the most worthy of the state, if all the people in the state follow his example, how can the state not be well governed? Now, why did the ruler of the state succeed in governing the state? The answer is because he was able to establish a common sense of rightness among the people of the whole state. Having accomplished this, he led his people to identify themselves with the emperor, saying, "All you people of the state shall identify yourselves with the emperor and shall not have opinions of your own. What he regards as right, all shall regard as right; what he regards as wrong, all shall regard as wrong. Discard your evil speech and learn his good speech; discard your evil conduct and learn his good conduct." As the emperor is the most worthy in the empire, if all the people in the empire follow his example, how can the empire not be well governed? Now why was the emperor successful in governing the empire? The answer is because he was able to establish a common sense of rightness among the people of the whole empire. (Ibid., Chapter 12, "Shang-tong" [II] pp. 52–3)

(4) Be informed and keep control

[45] What is it that creates order among the people of a state? Mozi said, "When in government the ruler is well informed of the people's intentions and activities, there will be order; when he is ignorant of the people's intentions and activities, there will be disorder. When the ruler is well informed, he knows clearly who is good and who is evil. With this knowledge, he will be able to reward the good and punish the evil. When the good are rewarded and the evil are punished, the state is in order. When the ruler is ignorant of the people's intentions and activities, he does not know who is good and who is evil. Without such knowledge, he will not be able to reward the good and punish the evil. When the good are not rewarded and the evil are not punished, the state will be in disorder." (Ibid., Chapter 13, "Shang-tong" [III] p. 55)

[45] How can a ruler get to know the intentions and activities of his people? Mozi said, "Only by adopting a policy of making them identify their idea of rightness with that of their superiors." (Ibid., Chapter 13, "Shang-tong" [III] p. 55).

[46] The ancient sage kings were particularly careful about making the people identify their idea of rightness with that of their superiors . . . Communication between the people and their superiors flew freely . . . When someone, thousands of *li* away, did some good, the emperor was able to reward him even before the deed was known to all his family members and heard by all the people in his village. When someone, thousands of *li* away, did some evil, the emperor was able to punish him even before the deed was known to all his family members and heard by all the people in his village. As a result, everyone in the empire was fearful and trembling, and dared not be licentious and violent, saying, "The emperor is like a god in his seeing and hearing". (Ibid., Chapter 7, "Shang-tong" [II] p. 53)

[47] How can the people be made to identify their ideas of rightness with that of their superiors? Mozi said, "Why not start with the family? Let the patriarch proclaim to all the family members an order demanding that whoever sees someone who loves and benefits the family must report the fact; whoever sees someone

who hates and harms the family must report the fact. Whoever reports someone who loves and benefits the family loves and benefits it himself, and is therefore to be rewarded by the patriarch and applauded by the family members; whoever fails to report someone who hates and harms the family hates and harms it himself, and is therefore to be punished by the patriarch and condemned by family members. Wishing to receive reward and applause and to avoid punishment and condemnation, all members of the family would report who loves and benefits the family and who hates and harms it. The patriarch is thus able to reward the benefactors and punish the malefactors. As benefactors are rewarded and malefactors punished, it is certain that the family will be in good order. So why is a family put in order? The reason is that its members are made to identify their ideas of rightness with that of their superiors.

So a family is thus put in order; is that all for governing a state? No. The state is composed of many families, and each regards itself as right and the others as wrong. If the dispute is serious, there will be strife, and, if it is slight, there will be contention. Therefore, the family patriarchs are told to make the family members identify their ideas of rightness with that of the ruler of the state. The ruler should proclaim to the people of the state a law demanding, 'Whoever sees someone who loves and benefits the state must report that fact; whoever sees someone who hates and harms the state must also report. Whoever reports someone who loves and benefits the state loves and benefits it himself, and is therefore to be rewarded by the ruler and applauded by the people; whoever fails to report someone who hates and harms the state hates and harms it himself, and is therefore to be punished by the ruler and condemned by the people. Wishing to receive rewards and applause and to avoid punishment and condemnation, all people in the state would report who loves and benefits the state and who hates and harms it.' The ruler of the state is thus able to reward the benefactors and punish the malefactors. When benefactors are rewarded and malefactors punished, the state is in good order. So why is it that a state becomes orderly? The reason is that its subjects are made to identify their ideas of rightness with that of their superiors.

Now that the state is in order, is that all for governing the empire? No. The empire is composed of many states; each regards itself as right and the others as wrong. If the dispute is serious there will be wars, and if it is slight there will be struggles. Therefore, the state rulers are told to make their people to identify their ideas of rightness with that of the emperor. The emperor should proclaim to the people of the empire a law demanding, "Whoever sees someone who loves and benefits the empire should report the fact; whoever sees someone who hates and harms the empire must also report. Whoever reports someone who loves and benefits the empire loves and benefits it himself, and is therefore to be rewarded by the emperor and applauded by the people; whoever fails to report someone who hates and harms the empire hates and harms it himself, and is therefore to be punished by the emperor and condemned by the people. Wishing to receive rewards and applause and avoid condemnation and punishments, all the people in the empire will report who loves and benefits the empire and who hates and harms it. And the emperor will have those benefactors rewarded and the malefactors punished. As the benefactors are rewarded and the malefactors punished, the empire is in order. So, why is the empire orderly? The reason is that the people are made to identify their ideas of rightness with that of the emperor." (Ibid. Chapter 13, "Shang-tong" [III] pp. 57–9)

(5) Obey the will of Heaven and guard against human abuse

[48] If people identify their ideas of rightness only with that of the emperor but not Heaven, natural calamities will not stop. Heaven will cause unseasonable heat and cold, untimely rain and snow, failing crops, depleting flocks, and epidemics and plague; gale-force winds and incessant downpours come on the heels of one another. These are punishments that Heaven inflicts on the people to penalise their failure to identify their ideas of rightness with that of Heaven. (Ibid., Chapter 12, "Shang-tong" [II] p. 49)

[49] Mozi said, "The will of Heaven is to me like the compasses to the wheelwright and the square to the carpenter. The wheelwright and the carpenter measure the circular and square objects with their compasses and squares and say, 'What fits is correct, what does not fit is incorrect.'" (Ibid., Chapter 26, "Tianzhi" [I] p. 122)

[50] With the will of Heaven Mozi measures the administrative and judicial work of the rulers and the ideas and practices of the people. If a practice is in accordance with the will of Heaven, it is judged to be a good practice; otherwise, it is a bad practice. If an idea is in accordance with the will of Heaven, it is judged to be a good idea; otherwise, it is a bad idea. If the administrative and judicial work is in accordance with the will of Heaven, it is judged to be good work; otherwise, it is bad work. Thus, with the will of Heaven as the standard, to test the humanness and inhumanness of the rulers is as easy as distinguishing black from white. (Ibid., Chapter 27, "Tian-zhi" [II] p. 129)

[51] So Mozi establishes the will of Heaven as the standard. It is not just Mozi who takes the will of Heaven as the standard. A verse in the chapter "Daya" of the book of the sage kings [*Shi-jing*] reads, "God said to King Wen, 'I cherish those with virtue. They do not loudly and arrogantly pronounce laws and orders of their own. They do not inflict punishments on their own. They do not resort to knowledge and intellect of their own. They just obey the rules of God.'" That was to admonish King Wen to take the will of Heaven as the standard and comply with it. Now, if the gentlemen of the world really want to be humane and righteous and become the best officials, to follow the way of the sage kings, and to benefit the people, they must carefully observe the will of Heaven, for the will of Heaven is the most fundamental standard for rightness. (Ibid., Chapter 28, "Tian-zhi" [III] p. 137)

(E) Social relationships

[52] The will of Heaven desires people with strength to help others; those with knowledge to teach others; and those with wealth to share with others. And it desires that those in superior status diligently attend to government, and those

of inferior status diligently to attend to their work. When the superior attend to government diligently, the country will be in order. When the inferior attend to their work diligently, wealth will be sufficient. When the country is orderly and wealth is sufficient, there will be plenty of rice and wine to offer to the gods and spirits at home, and enough precious stones and pearls to give to the neighbouring states. When the neighbouring states have no complaints, there will be no wars on the borders. When there is enough for the care of the people, to keep the hungry fed and let the weary rest, the ruler will be benevolent and the people loyal; fathers will be loving, children filial, and siblings compassionate. Thus, when the will of Heaven is understood and widely obeyed in the world there will be justice and good government; all nations will coexist in harmony, and every state will be wealthy; the common people will be warmly clothed and well fed, and they will live in peace without worry. (Ibid., Chapter 27, "Tian-zhi" [II] pp.123–4)

Mo-zi 墨子

PART 2
INTERPRETATION

When people in ancient times looked at the mixed results of human efforts, some became enthusiastic, others dispirited. The enthusiasts, with a general belief in human ability, wanted to see it further developed to be a brave new world, where there would be peace, order, opportunities for individuals, and general prosperity and harmony in society. The dispirited, on the other hand, having little faith in humankind, wanted it to discard its achievements, ignore its potentials and return to a primitive form of life, which they believed to be more natural and hence preferable.

These were the two lines of thought articulated by Confucius and Laozi respectively. Confucian teaching, which was directed mainly at the ruling class and those closely associated with it, was quite widely studied. But, like most disciples living in the shadow of a great master, the Ruists were overwhelmed by his thought and felt that they could contribute little to his grand theory except by exploring some of its nuances and spelling out some of its details. They thus lost sight of the wide horizon and became rather trivial. And, because of their reduced vision and their obsession with trivia, they were unable to comprehend the larger problems of their time.

Such problems were already numerous in Confucius's time and continued to multiply. The upper class was unspeakably corrupt and constantly engaged in intrigues and wars; the lower class was ruthlessly exploited and lived in abject poverty. Many new measures and laws were introduced, some of them especially designed to improve the situation. But few worked well because society lacked common values and a shared sense of right and wrong. People had difficulty finding acceptable reasons for the existing norms, particularly many of the artificial laws.

Confucius's work was mainly to meet this need. But his theory, which reduced the emphasis on Heaven and gods, was difficult for ordinary people because, most importantly, it precluded a superbeing as the ultimate maker and enforcer of norms. Without such a superbeing, the theory could not easily convince people that the good would be rewarded and the evil punished, and, without this belief, ordinary people would have difficulty in seeing why they had to obey the norms which, after all, were mainly to distinguish good from evil. The theory's reference to fate, though quite rational, was incomprehensible to most people. Its emphasis on *li* was also problematic because, to many people, *li* was a meaningless formality. These problems called for a review and new solutions. The challenge was met by Mozi.

Sima Qian did not write a biography of Mozi but only a sentence attached to the biography of Mencius and Xunzi, saying, "Mo Di (墨翟 Mozi's formal name) was an official of the state of Chu who was versed in the military strategy of defence and advocated the principle of frugality. Some said he was a contemporary of Confucius; some said he was junior."[1] Neither Confucius nor any of his immediate disciples mentioned Mozi but, by Mencius's time, he was very famous. This fact suggests that he was younger than Confucius and older than Mencius. Several works of the Qin and the Han Dynasties support a view that he was born around 480 and died around 390 BCE. According to those works and to *Mozi*, he was probably from a lower class of artisans good at making ingenious objects, including a wooden bird that flew three days non-stop and many devices and equipment for defensive war. Probably because of his humble background, he was sympathetic towards the common people and resentful of the corruption of the ruling class. He once studied under some Ruists but became disenchanted, seeing the rites they taught and practised as frivolous and extravagant. Moreover, he found their theory irrational and elitist, aiding and abetting the wanton desires of the rich and powerful and ignoring the problems and sufferings of the poor and weak. To oppose them, he constructed a theory of his own and became a teacher and activist. He had hundreds of disciples and led them to stop the aggressive wars of their time. In one instance, he walked for ten days and nights to reach the state of Chu which was planning an attack on the state of Song. In an audience with the king of Chu, he demonstrated that he had effective means to repel any attack the Chu army could launch with the weapons and machines invented by Lu Ban 魯般, another great inventor of the time. The king called off the attack and the state of Song was saved. For such efforts and for his theory of universal love, he was much respected by those in power as well as by those who studied under him. Rulers of several states offered him government positions and lavish presents but he declined them when his advice was not accepted. As a result, he never served as an official in the Song, as Sima Qian had said, or in any other state, but lived frugally all his life. Because his moral principles were so high and because he actually practised them himself, his disciples were so moved that all of them were willing to die for his causes. Even Zhuangzi, who, of course, thought his efforts meaningless, called him "truly one of the best men in the world who never abandoned his principles while living in extreme poverty".[2]

The work known as *Mozi* is huge by the standards of Mozi's time. It might consist of some parts written by him but most of its chapters were apparently his disciples' notes of his speeches and discourses with them and with others. Several chapters were on defence technology, logic and science, of which some were probably added by later Mohists. Thus, the book has many unusual features. First, it has a unique style – it is repetitive. Not only is a point made many times and illustrated by many examples but also many sections in the book appear in three versions which, in most cases, are only slightly different from one another, though one may appear more succinct and cogent and the others more verbose and loosely organised. They were probably recorded by different students of Mozi.

Second, this work is disputatious – a feature common to works after *Lun-yu* and *Laozi*. The later thinkers had to repudiate others before establishing themselves. In Mozi's case, the positions he disputed most often were those of the Ruists.[3] Mozi was not openly critical of Laozi, probably because Laozi was not a popular teacher and his book was not yet widely read.

Third, this work is sometimes rather crude in its arguments. It routinely appeals to authority rather than to reason and repeatedly takes folklore as fact.

Finally, to support some of their unpopular positions, the authors sometimes twisted logic to produce arguments that conflict with common sense and challenge widely accepted beliefs. For this reason, some sections of *Mozi* were considered to be sophistry but, from a logical point of view, they are often very profound.

Nevertheless, Mozi's philosophy was powerful because he spoke for the poor and oppressed masses. For a while, it was very popular and considered to be as much a *xian-xue* (顯學 a prominent school of thought) as that of Confucius.

His theory begins with a view of the primitive world, and moves on to various questions concerning how people should live and what roles social authorities and norms should have in helping people to live prosperous and meaningful lives.

(A) The primitive world

The most striking passage in *Mozi* is about the primitive society. Neither Confucius nor Laozi discussed in detail what it was like but their theories presumed a past that was more orderly. Mozi's view was dramatically different and therefore he was compelled to describe it before presenting his solutions to the problems of his time. According to him, human beings are not, by nature, orderly creatures. Innately, they know only self-preservation; thus, in a primitive society, people were preoccupied by their immediate needs and were unable to discern common elements in varied matters, events, senses and situations. As an indication, they did not have a common language and, more importantly, a shared view of right and wrong. When people spoke a word, each had a different *yi* (義 meaning) for it and each would insist that his was the right *yi* and dismiss the *yi* used by others as incorrect. As a result, people were unable to communicate and form common ideas and take common action, and there was general dissension and strife, even among relatives and close associates.

(B) Social authorities

(1) The need

To escape from a state of dissension and strife, it is necessary, according to Mozi, to "unify people's *yi*", that is, to create common definitions for matters, events, senses, and situations with common elements – in other words, to establish a common standard, a common value system, a common view of rightness. In his mind, there could be peace and order in society only when these tasks were accomplished. This idea was not new or controversial – Confucius had insisted on "rectification of names". Laozi wanted people to take the order of the Sage as their sole guidance.

(2) The establishment

(A) By Heaven and its agents – gods and spirits

How are people's views to be unified, or standards to be established? Mozi said that there had to be a person of great virtue and wisdom whose uncommon qualities would enable him to rise above his immediate concerns and see the common interests of society as a whole. Only such a person could give a definition to each word, unify ideas and establish standards. And he should be chosen and made the emperor, or Son of Heaven, so that he would have the authority to ensure the acceptance by everyone of his definitions, views and standards. For this task, he needed assistants so he would choose wise and virtuous persons to be high ministers and feudal lords, and they in turn would choose wise and virtuous persons to be officials and heads of districts and villages. When this system was in place, the head of a district or village would unify the ideas of his people and make them conform to the ideas of the ruler of a state who would unify the ideas of his people and make them conform to the ideas of the emperor. Mozi called this process *shang-tong* (尚同 upward conformity)

Who would choose the emperor? It could not be the general public because, in Mozi's estimation, the people were too stupid and selfish to make the correct choice. It had to be Heaven. To prove this he constructed a tortuously long argument, starting with an affirmation that rightness would induce good government that would establish order. Then he asserted that only those who were wise and of superior social status were able to know rightness and act accordingly in governing those who were stupid and of inferior social status. Finally, he pointed out that Heaven was wiser than, and superior to, anyone on earth, and therefore he concluded that Heaven was to choose the emperor and supervise him.

How did he prove Heaven to be the wisest and the supreme? He pointed out as a fact that the emperor worshiped Heaven but not vice versa; Heaven rewarded and punished the emperor but not vice versa. This argument was crude and inadequate, "proving" only that Heaven was superior to the emperor but not wiser. Nevertheless, it was significant because, according to legend, there had been a time in the past when men with merit, such as Yao, Shun, Yu and Yu's son Qi, were chosen as rulers by a group of men in power and then approved by Heaven. But Qi let his son be his successor and thus, some eighteen hundred years before Mozi's time, began the tradition of political inheritance. Mozi's assertion that the emperor should be chosen from among the people was revolutionary because it implicitly challenged the, by then, well-established system of hereditary political succession.

Confucius and Laozi both talked about Heaven. Laozi's Heaven manifested itself in the form of laws of nature and was without a will; Confucius's seemed to have a will but it was inscrutable. Mozi's was different from both of theirs. It was a superbeing with intelligence and volition which were revealed through the being's agents, the gods and spirits, who were in everything – the sun, the moon, stars, mountains, rivers, animals and plants. To prove or disprove this and all propositions, Mozi suggested *sanbiao* (三表 three tests): namely to check against firstly, historical records, especially those of the ancient sage kings; secondly, well-known experience of the common people; and thirdly, the results after the proposition had been put into practice. According to him, there had been numerous cases since ancient times where people had seen gods and spirits, and had heard about them. For instance, when Wang Liguo 王里國 and Zhongli Jiao 中里徼, two officials of the state of Qi during the reign of Lord Zhuang 齊莊君, were tried by oath, the dying sacrificial lamb jumped up and butted Zhongli Jiao, breaking his leg and Zhongli Jiao was then killed by a wizard who emerged and hit Zhongli Jiao and killed him. This scene was witnessed by many people of the state of Qi, recorded in its annals, and was well known to people of other states.

If anyone would not trust what ordinary people had seen and heard, Mozi said let him look at the deeds of the sage kings of the past, which were numerous and recorded in the annals of ancient dynasties. Many examples were given by Mozi: for instance, before King Wu of Zhou was to attack King Shou of Yin, he offered sacrifices to his ancestors. He was seeking Heaven's mandate but prayed to the spirits of Zhou because he believed that they were Heaven's agents. If King Wu believed, could anyone doubt?

By giving such examples, Mozi was supposed to have proved that his proposition had passed the first two of his three tests but, since the events he mentioned were recorded in the annals, they had at best only passed the historical test. He did not provide evidence that people of his time had common experience of seeing gods and spirits and hearing about their deeds.

Then Mozi put his proposition through the third test and alleged that, in history, when people obeyed gods and spirits, there was order but, when they disobeyed, there was chaos. This is, of course, merely conjecture. Then he advanced a strange argument that, even if gods and spirits did not exist, the sacrifice people offered was not wasted; it would be consumed by people in a joyous feast which would help bring them together and improve their relationships. Here he offered a concession. It is utilitarian but unhelpful to his original proposition that gods and spirits do exist.

Why did Mozi insist that Heaven, gods and spirits existed? It was because his theory needed them. He realised that, by his time, many people had doubts. He was aware that Confucius's ambiguous attitude towards Heaven, gods and spirits further eroded people's trust in it. Moreover, he knew that people were seriously dissatisfied with the government and therefore disobedient, causing the established order to fall apart and the masses to live in chaos and misery. He wanted to create a new order for the world and, for this purpose, he needed someone with absolute authority. He thought it would be relatively easy to do it if he could revive the belief in Heaven because it could still be found in the back of many people's minds.

(B) By fate (?)

But he found that the task was not easy. Despite his appeal to authority and "history", he could not readily convince people that Heaven was in command of human affairs. Even if they conceded that its power existed, they had doubts about its fairness and consistency. Many of them turned to a belief in fate. They thought that every aspect of a person's life was predetermined by fate – whether he was to live long or die young, to be rich or poor, to occupy high or low social status. In moments of deep frustration, even Confucius used the word fate though he was hardly a fatalist. Nevertheless, Mozi accused him of promoting fatalism and considered it to be the most fallacious and damaging part of Confucian teaching. Using the first two of his "three tests", he asked: how could you prove the existence of fate? Had anyone ever seen or heard fate? No. Did the records of the past sage kings indicate they believed in fate? No. So, he concluded, there could be no fate.

Then he applied the third test, asking what would be the result if people really believed in fate? The result, he said, would be a complete end to all human endeavour – rulers would not rule, officials not administer, farmers not plant, and women not weave, because they were sure that what would happen would happen, and it would make no difference whether or not they did anything at all. But, actually, Mozi pointed out that there would be a difference – the cessation of the various types of work would lead to chaos and misery. For this reason, Mozi said, fate "is an invention of evil kings and the practice of miserable men, not something a person with a love of humanity should talk about".

Such arguments were not totally convincing. Why did Mozi make them? Was it an overreaction to a supposedly Confucian belief in fate? The real reason was that he wanted people to exert themselves to the utmost and not to use any excuse for relapse. Actually, Confucius held the same position and that was why he was called "the person who did what he knew was impossible". But Confucius was actually more realistic and philosophical. When he met failure after making great efforts, he retained his peace of mind, knowing that it was not his fault. Mozi did not allow himself or his followers this consolation. His position was more exaggerated.

(3) Prerequisites for those to have social authority

Under the hereditary political system that had been long established in Mozi's time, a ruler inherited his position regardless of his personal qualifications. Mozi objected to that. He said that, originally, the emperor had been chosen by Heaven. He was "the most virtuous and the wisest" of men. To be "virtuous", according to Mozi, was above all to have a true belief in Heaven and to worship it properly. The founders of the three ancient dynasties, Xia, Shang and Zhou, all had these virtues and were given the supreme reward of becoming "Sons of Heaven". The last rulers of the three dynasties were without these virtues, and Heaven punished them by having them dethroned and executed and their dynastic line terminated.

The ruler's "wisdom" was mainly to help people improve their lives. When people were living in caves, a wise ruler taught them to build houses; when they did not have proper clothing, he taught them to produce fabrics and make clothes; when they lacked transport, he taught them to make carts and boats.

It is noticeable that neither being humane, a paramount virtue of a Ruist noble man, nor being knowledgeable of natural law, a mysterious ability of a Laozi's sage, were to be prerequisites of Mozi's ruler who was only a religious person with practical know-how and skills – a model craftsman like Mozi himself.

(C) Social norms

(1) Origin and basic principle

But people needed not only the tools and skills to help meet their basic needs, they also needed to know how to interact with one another and avoid the perils of the primitive world; they needed rules governing their own behaviour; they needed norms. Who could help them? Mozi said it was the Son of Heaven because, as stated earlier, he alone knew *yi* (義 rightness) and was therefore capable of making norms that reflected rightness.

What is rightness? Mozi did not define it. He said only that it should originate from those who were wise and had superior positions. Since the Son of Heaven was the wisest and most superior among men, rightness must originate from him. He was to make norms prescribing what was right and what was wrong, and all people had to abide by those norms. But the Son of Heaven was not as wise and lofty as Heaven which had the power to reward or punish him. So rightness ultimately originated from Heaven. The Son of Heaven had to abide by Heaven's prescriptions of right and wrong and use them as the basis of the norms.

Mozi further said that Heaven had a desire to see the right to be upheld and the wrong rejected. This was what Mozi called *tian-zhi* (天志 the will of Heaven). He "proved" this by saying that a thing that is right lives, a thing that is wrong dies; a person who is right is rich, a person who is wrong is poor; a state that is right is in order, a state that is wrong is in chaos.

(2) Objectives and measures

(a) Promote universal love

Generally, according to Mozi, Heaven was interested in the well-being of the people. It loved them dearly. How did he know? He told people to look at what it had done for them – it made everything, including the sun, the moon, the plants and the animals, useful to them; it appointed rulers and officials to keep order for them. Because Heaven loved the people so much, it cherished those who benefited them, such as the sage kings of the Three Dynasties and abhorred those who harmed them, such as the evil kings of the same. In the case of ordinary people, one who murders an innocent person will suffer misfortune sent from Heaven.

Mozi talked about the desires of Heaven often. He said Heaven wanted those with strength to help others, those with knowledge to teach others, and those with wealth to share with others. He said Heaven desired that everyone should diligently attend to their own work (those of superior status the governing, those of inferior status the farming, manufacturing and weaving) and act properly towards other people (the ruler be humane, the subjects loyal; the father affectionate, the sons filial; the older brother caring, the younger brother respectful).

But apparently people did not take Heaven's wishes seriously. Mozi pointed out that the greatest harms of his time were the big states attacking the small ones, the big aristocratic houses interfering with the affairs of smaller ones, the strong oppressing the weak, the majority exploiting the minority, the cunning deceiving the stupid, and the lofty disdaining the humble. He also lamented that, at his time, the rulers were not kind, the subjects not loyal, fathers not caring and sons not filial. These he said also harmed the world no less than violent persons injuring people with weapons, poisons, water and fire.

What caused all these problems? Mozi said it was people's inclination not to *jian* (兼 inclusiveness) but to *bie* (別 discrimination) that made them not love but hate one another. This was not an innovation. Mozi was again reacting to the Confucian idea of grading human relations – the closer the relation, especially in the sense of kinship affinity, the more love there should be. This started with an emphasis on oneself and it set persons apart. In difficult times, this distinction could lead to discrimination. A person's behaviour would be dominated by self-love, not by sympathy and compassion, and would exclude others from sharing with him what was available or even take advantage of them in order to satisfy his own needs. Thus, Mozi said, "Where a son loves himself, but not his father, he will take advantage of his father to benefit himself . . ." And, according to him, this was true of families and states; hence the big states attacked the smaller ones. This was why Mozi advocated *jian-xiang-ai* (兼相愛 mutual love) and *jiao-xiang-li* (交相利 mutual benefit), and he almost considered *jian-ai* (兼愛 universal love) a panacea. In his words, "If everybody in the world loves universally, that is, loves others as one's self . . . states would not attack one another; households would not interfere with one another; theft and mugging would be extinct; rulers and subjects, fathers and sons, would all be affectionate and filial. Consequently, the world will be orderly."

This idea was considered by many of his contemporaries, as well as later critics, to be extreme and naive. But many in other cultures, particularly polytheists, also preach universal love. Monotheists are different. For instance, Jesus Christ made "Love thy neighbour" as one of the highest commands, but Christians do not love non-believers and positively hate heretics and infidels. Mozi had a similar problem. The Mohist Heaven is not indiscriminately all-loving. He said it had its dislikes and would punish what it disliked. If Heaven did not uphold universal love, how could humans?

Another problem was that here Mozi named a new cause for the troubles of the world. We recall that he said in the beginning, where there were no social authorities, people used different languages and had different senses of right and wrong, and, as a result, they were in disagreement and engaged in violent struggles against one another. Then Heaven established the emperor and a system of government which unified the language and created a universal standard for all things and produced peace and order. Here he introduced another cause for social troubles – the self-love of an individual, a family and a state. Apparently, it had not been eliminated by the Son of Heaven in the process of *shang-tong* and, somehow, at a certain point in history, it raised its ugly head again, and the ideal state created by the most wise and virtuous was lost.

This is a serious problem. We remember Laozi had to explain how the idyllic state of nature was lost. He blamed it on human intelligence. Is the self-love Mozi talked about also inherent in human nature? If so, the people's inclination to *bie* would be inevitable when the population grows and resources become scarce. People would not be able to *jian-ai* but would hate and harm one another, and society would be in chaos as it was when it had no social authorities. If so, would it be necessary to have another emperor to be chosen by Heaven as its "Son" to start the Sisyphean task once again?

(B) CONDEMN AGGRESSIVE WAR

The most flagrant act against universal love was aggressive war. This, Mozi said, was what Heaven abhorred most, and he characterised it as the most heinous of all crimes. Therefore, he advocated *fei-gong* (非攻 condemnation of aggression) and spelled out his reasons in detail. First, he pointed out that, in the cases of lesser crimes – theft, robbery and mayhem – people all knew that the offenders were wrong because they harmed the interests of the victims and should be condemned and punished, and that the more serious the harm, the heavier should be the punishment: murdering one person, the murderer was to receive one death penalty, murdering ten, ten death penalties . . . But, unfortunately, most people were unable to see this simple truth. In the case of aggressive wars, thousands of people were murdered and yet "the gentlemen of the world" hailed the victorious aggressors as heroes. Why? According to Mozi, they were dazzled by the glory of victory and blinded by the glitter of the spoils. But even if victory were assured, what would it bring to the victor, and at what cost? Mozi pointed out that countless goods would be destroyed and lives lost only to get wasted land in return, while every state of his time had empty lands but sparse populations. Therefore, aggressive wars were generally bad Pyrrhic deals. But someone accused him of oversimplifying the case for, after all, many states did gain from aggression. He answered this charge with an allegory: "Where a physician prescribed the same medicine for all who were ill, if, among the ten thousand people who took it, only four or five were cured, it could not be said that the medicine was right for all." He was correct. Since the creation of the feudal states though some had gained from aggressive wars, countless others had perished thereby.

Mozi also anticipated another question: were the wars launched by those ancient sage kings whom he so admired legitimate? Well, he said, those were not aggressive attacks but punitive actions ordered by Heaven. He then went on to prove his point using mythical tales. For instance, he said, once in ancient times the Miao tribes rioted against the Han Chinese authorities, causing great suffering among all people. Many warnings were sent from Heaven – the sun rose at night, blood rained from the sky, ice came in summer, the earth cracked open and water gushed forth from under the ground. As the riot continued, Heaven ordered the sage king Yu to put it down. When Yu arrived at the battlefield, a god with the face of a man and the body of a bird appeared in the sky above him amid thunder and lightning. With the god's blessing, Yu struck down the commander of the Miao army with a single arrow and vanquished his followers.

Thus Mozi was forced to concede that some offensive wars were justified but only in extreme cases where they were supported by gods. Creating justification for a war is a well-established practice common to both sides but, in the end, what is left is only that of the victor. Mozi was arguing for the victors of ancient times. Apparently, he thought it inadequate merely to list the wrongs of the vanquished, so he appealed to myths. Such appeals are not unusual. Essentially, it is not surprising that Mozi made them because, after all, his theory was built on the premise that gods and spirits existed and functioned as the agents of Heaven in carrying out justice. It is unclear how thinking people of his time reacted to his tales, but most of his followers probably accepted them because they had accepted his premise.

A more serious problem is the contradiction between Mozi's advocacy of universal love and his defence of justifiable war. In theory, if there is universal love, there should be no war but, in practice, "justifiable wars" were numerous in history. The need to campaign against aggression suggests the impracticability of universal love. It can be argued that the two ideas are two sides of the same coin which cannot be seen simultaneously. But, as parts of a theory, they made it inconsistent. A better explanation is that Mozi was a practical man whose real objective was to prevent war and was compelled to construct a theory based on universal love. The inconsistency between his practical objective and his theoretical basis did not bother him much.

Mozi was positive about defensive war but would prefer to prevent it than actually fight. It was reported that, after learning that the state of Chu was about to attack the state of Song with high-rising "cloud ladders" constructed by Gongshu Ban 公輸般, an especially ingenious craftsman, Mozi walked ten days and nights from the state of Qi in the north, with his swollen and bleeding feet wrapped in cloth ripped from his clothing, to reach the capital of Chu. He first talked with Gongshu Ban and convinced him it that was not right to invade Song, and then he explained to the king of Chu that the attack would be unprofitable. The king agreed but said that, since Gongshu Ban had already constructed the cloud ladders, the invasion should nevertheless go ahead. Mozi asked that he and Gongshu Ban be allowed to demonstrate in the presence of the king how the events could develop. Nine times Gongshu Ban showed how machines and methods were to be used in the attack; nine times Mozi demonstrated how he could defeat the attack. After failing to succeed, Gongshu Ban said he still had a way to win but would not divulge it. Mozi said he knew what that was: it was just to have him killed so that he would not be able to defend Song. But he said, he had over three hundred of his disciples in Song with his defensive mechanisms and techniques ready against the attack. Realising the futility of his plan, the king decided to scrap it.[4]

What were Mozi's defensive mechanisms and techniques? They were not spelled out in the story. But *Mozi* has twelve of his sixty-one chapters on these subjects, describing how to construct and defend a walled city; how to repel aggressors who used cloud ladders, tunnels, flood or fire, who climbed the city walls like ants, and who applied witchcraft; how to organise and train defensive forces and to reward the brave and punish the cowardly among them; and how to prepare for long sieges.[5] The details are incredible, extraordinary.

(c) Disparage music

Mozi also wanted to *fei-yue* (非樂 disparage music). His reasons were less obvious. In ancient times, people were apparently rather fond of music. As evidence, the poems collected in *Shi-jing* were songs, many sung by ordinary people expressing their spontaneous feelings. Later, some music became very elaborate and sophisticated, requiring ensembles of intensively trained musicians with expensive instruments. Some of this kind of music was played in public ceremonies and, in private, for the enjoyment of aristocrats and the rich while feasting, dancing or hunting. It was a crucial part of an extravagant lifestyle beyond the reach of the common people – though supported by their labour and the taxes they paid. It was a glaring symbol of social inequity and injustice. That was why Mozi condemned it and urged those in power to give it up together with their other habits of conspicuous consumption and waste. But, in his words, Mozi made it clear that he did not find sophisticated music and other forms of high living unpleasant. Rather, he objected to them because they were not only unhelpful in alleviating the hardship of ordinary people's lives but actually made it worse. He pointed out that, unlike birds and beasts, which had feathers and furs to fend off cold and widely available food to eat, humans had to work hard to keep warm and fed. Thus, the common people had three worries: namely, being hungry without food, cold without clothing, and tired without rest. So he asked rhetorically: "Can such worries be eliminated by striking the big bells, beating the sonorous drums, playing the lute and the flute, and performing glorious dances?" The answer was, of course, in the negative. And there were other social problems, such as big states invading small ones, the strong oppressing the weak, the many exploiting the few, and the lofty disdaining the humble. Could they be solved by music? Again the answer is no. On the contrary, people indulging in the enjoyment of music and entertainment would be less devoted to their work – the rulers to governing, farmers to tilling and planting, women to weaving and sewing – and, as a result, comes disorder, scarcity and hardship. Therefore, Mozi declared, *wei-yue fei-ye* (為樂非也 to make music is wrong).

It was another of Mozi's emotional reactions to the social injustice of his time and, in particular, another refutation of the Confucian position which held the rites as an important tool for social order and therefore emphasised the significance of music which usually accompanied the rituals. It is true that sophisticated music could be costly, and time spent on learning, playing and enjoying music could be used in the production of goods necessary for subsistence, but Mozi's extreme utilitarian view, which regarded music as wasteful, and all recreational, non-productive (in the narrowest sense) activities unworthy, ignoring their beneficial effects on people's mental and physical health, was crude and unreasonable.

(D) Cut waste

If music-making was to be stopped, so should all other unproductive and wasteful practices. Therefore, Mozi advocated *jie-yong* (節用 frugality in expenditure). According to him, the ancient sage kings made laws of economy about everything. Food was only to satiate hunger, increase vitality, strengthen the limbs and sharpen the eyes and ears. Clothing was only to keep a person warm in the winter and cool in the summer. Carts and boats were only to facilitate transport. Houses were only for keeping off the wind, the cold, the snow and the rain, and to provide a place for worshipping gods and spirits. All other goods were made only to meet the basic needs of the people. "What causes extra expense but adds no benefit to the people is what the sage kings would not do", he famously said.

But, apparently at his time, some people disregarded the sage kings' practices and indulged in many extravagant, unprofitable activities: among them, the two most distasteful to Mozi were *hou-zang* (厚葬 lavish burial) and *jiu-sang* (久喪 prolonged mourning), both quite popular then and supported by the Ruists. He observed that, according to those who advocated lavish burial, there must be several inner and outer coffins, and they must be buried deep; there must be many shrouds, elaborately embroidered, and there must be a massive grave mound. As a result, Mozi said, the death of a common man would exhaust the wealth of a family, and the demise of a feudal lord would empty the treasury of a state.

Moreover, as a part of the funeral rites, human sacrifice was offered. For a dead Son of Heaven, scores or even hundreds of people were killed and entombed; and for a lesser aristocrat, as many as several dozen would meet the same fate. This, as Mozi saw it, was a senseless way to decimate the population of a state or a family.

According to those who advocated prolonged mourning, Mozi noticed, the mourner must weep without restraint and sound as if he was going to choke. His tears were not to be wiped away, and he was to eat little food, wear few clothes and tremble in hunger and cold. His ears and eyes were to become dull, and his hands and feet feeble. He had to be supported in rising and lean on a cane to walk. And all this was to last for three years, during which he would not be able to do any work – as a ruler he would not rule, as an official he would not administer, as a commoner he would not toil.

Thus, lavish funerals sent much existing wealth into the grave; and prolonged mourning postponed the creation of wealth that was urgently needed. As a result, the survivors were left in poverty and, to Mozi, this was absurd and not to be tolerated.

But someone asked: if such practices were so counterproductive and harmful to people's welfare, why had they been followed by so many for so long? Because, Mozi answered, they had become customs but customs did not necessarily carry an inherent moral imperative. Moreover, different societies could have different customs and different ethical standards. For instance, Mozi pointed out that, in ancient times, there was a state in the far south where people would cut off and throw away the flesh of their deceased parents before burying their bones; and in the far west there was another state where people would burn the bodies of their dead parents. In both these states the children following such practices were considered filial. Who was there to tell them that their customs were wrong?

Thus, there was no moral imperative behind lavish burial and prolonged mourning. But then there was another question: was not lavish burial supposed to please and provide for the dead, and did not Mozi believe in spirits, that is, dead ancestors? Again he gave a pragmatic answer: the lavish burial would impoverish the living and cause disorder among them. When they were poor and in disorder they would be less capable of offering timely sacrifices to the spirits, leaving them in hardship. This was not what filial descendants should do, and the spirits in distress would think that there was no difference between having and not having such descendants and would inflict punishments on them and abandon them. Thus, in Mozi's theory, spirits were as pragmatic as he was, preferring regular maintenance, even though frugal, to lavish one-off provisions.

Therefore, Mozi wanted burial and mourning to be simplified. He suggested that the coffin should be 3 inches thick, just sufficient to hold the rotting bones; the body shroud be covered with three shrouds, just enough to hold the rotting flesh; the pit should be neither so deep as to strike water nor so shallow as to allow the odour to ascend; the mound should be just high enough to be identifiable; the surviving relatives should weep on the way to and from the burial but, upon returning, should promptly resume production of food and clothing.

(E) Increase production

Simply cutting waste and being frugal are, of course, not enough. To improve the welfare of the people, there should be an increase in production. Only when the pie grows, will the people have more to share.

At Mozi's time, the common people generally lived in scarcity. But he maintained that to increase the production of materials to meet people's needs was not difficult because there was a lot of unexplored land. What hindered production was a shortage of manpower. This simple truth did not dawn on the rulers. Instead, they diminished the population in more ways than one: they overworked and overtaxed the people, causing many to die of cold, hunger and exhaustion; they launched wars which, in addition to killing thousands, kept soldiers away from their wives for long periods, making the growth of population more difficult. This problem was aggravated by those who practised prolonged mourning which would cause many to become weakened and ill and then die, and prevented men and women from getting married and husbands and wives from having intercourse for months and years.

How could the population be increased? Mozi advocated early marriage. He said that the ancient sage kings had laws requiring men to get married at the age of twenty and women at the age of fifteen, and he wanted such laws to be strictly enforced.

Mozi was largely correct about the need to increase the population at his time. Confucius saw this need, too, and was pleased by the large population in the state of Wei and said that they should be enriched and educated. Mozi obviously thought a large population could produce more goods and, barring wasteful practices by the elites, make the common people's life easier. But he seemed to have stopped there without saying much else. Certainly, he wanted the people to have the same ideas as the authorities. But, as is to be analysed below, that was different from what Confucius had in mind.

(D) Enforcement of social norms

(1) Give correct directions

What is set out above resembles a political platform or a legislative, administrative and judicial agenda advocated by Mozi. How is it to be realised? First of all, how can the general principles be instilled in people's hearts – the moral precepts requiring everyone to love and not to hurt others? Confucius suggested education as a means. He particularly emphasised education by the personal example of the ruler, saying that the character of a noble man could influence that of the common people as the wind could bend the grass. Mozi shared the view that a ruler could give society clear directions by showing the people his preferences. To illustrate this point, Mozi told a number of stories. According to him, King Ling of Jing 荊靈王, King Goujian of Yue 越王勾踐 and Duke Wen of Jin 晉文公 who, simply by showing their personal preferences, induced their people: in one case, to go on a starvation diet; in another, to plunge into fighting fire; and, in the third, to wear ragged clothing.

There is obviously a significant difference between the positions of Confucius and Mozi. While Confucius's noble man would use nothing other than his admirable personal character gently to influence the common people, Mozi's rulers would resort to rewards and punishments to force their subjects to comply with their wishes. Thus, Mozi's method was not education but an appeal to ordinary people's basic self-interest. He thought that this method was enough to make people do practically anything the ruler wanted them to do – to starve, to freeze, even to die. In comparison, to ask them to work hard, to be frugal, to avoid doing harm to others, even to practise universal love would be easy. People would follow his orders like fire burning upwards and water flowing downwards. This belief in the effects of reward and punishment was revealed pervasively throughout Mozi's teachings. It had been, as discussed earlier, discredited by both Confucius and Laozi but Mozi was not bothered by their concerns.

(2) Exalt the worthy and employ the capable

To implement Mozi's agenda, there was a need for worthy and capable people to serve as officials. And they had to be extremely conscientious and diligent – starting their day early and retiring late to administer and adjudicate, to collect taxes, and to engage the people in sowing and planting, gathering and harvesting – so that the state would be in peace and order, the treasury full, the people well fed and sheltered. But such worthy and capable people were rare and often not fully appreciated by those in power. Mozi pointed out that, as a common practice of his time, when a person had a sheep to slaughter, he was sure to seek a good butcher; when he had a piece of cloth to be made into a dress, he was sure to seek a good tailor; when he had a sick horse, he was sure to seek a good veterinarian to treat it; when he had a defective bow, he was sure to seek a good craftsman to repair it. He would not give the work to an incompetent person, even if that person was closely related to him or rich and having high status or being very good-looking. Why? Because he would be afraid that such a man would fail at considerable cost. But when it came to governing the state, the ruler would do the opposite, promoting exactly such incompetent men.

A sage king, according to Mozi, was different. He would not be partial to his relatives, the rich and lofty, and those with good looks. Rather, he would choose the virtuous and capable regardless of their social origin and his personal relationship with them – even if they were farmers and craftsmen, and even if he had some grudge against them. When so identified, they would receive from him high honours, generous emoluments, important responsibilities, and the power to make final decisions, because he knew that: without high honours, they would not have the respect of the people; without generous emoluments, they would not have the confidence of the people; and without the power to make final decisions, they would not keep the people in awe. Having so endowed them, he would then check on their work and reward and promote those who did well and dismiss and punish those who failed.

(3) Establish common values

The importance of having shared values is obvious. Where they are absent or, worse still, where the values sanctioned by the ruler are in conflict with the values cherished by the people, the ruler's rewards would not induce people to do what he promotes and his punishments would not deter them from doing what he prohibits. But how can this result be avoided? Mozi went back to the notion of unification of ideas. According to him, first, a village head was to lead everyone in his village to comply with the ideas of the district magistrate, who was in turn to lead his people to comply with the ideas of the ruler of a state, who in turn was to lead his countrymen to comply with the ideas of the Son of Heaven. The reason behind this compliance with the superiors in the political hierarchy, according to Mozi, is that the government agents – village heads and others – were the wisest and most virtuous persons at each level, and the Son of Heaven was the wisest and most virtuous at the very top, and therefore his ideas were the absolute standards. What he regarded as right, all people must regard as right; what he regarded as wrong, all people must regard as wrong. No question was to be asked, no different opinion tolerated.

(4) Be informed and keep control

Exactly how were the village heads, and others, to lead people to comply with the ideas of the Son of Heaven? Practically, the procedure must be the reverse of that which Mozi suggested – the Son of Heaven must make his ideas known to the people and demand the government agents to impose them on the people. Conceivably, it could be done through propaganda but the result could never be certain. To ensure absolute conformity, Mozi had another suggestion: let people carefully and constantly look over one another's shoulders and inform the authorities whatever they discovered. When channels for this transmission were well established and maintained, Mozi said, communication between the people and their superiors would flow freely and, as a result,

> Someone, thousands of *li* (1 *li* is about 500 metres) away, does some good, the ruler is able to reward him even before the deed is known to all his clansmen and heard by all the people in his district; someone, thousands of *li* away, does some evil, the ruler is able to punish him even before the deed is known to all his clansmen and heard by all the people in his district. Consequently everyone is fearful and trembling, and dares not to be licentious and violent, saying: "The ruler is like a god in his seeing and hearing!"

A widespread network of informants could work. It is described by George Orwell in *Nineteen Eighty-four* and practised in Nazi Germany and other totalitarian states. But would people be morally and emotionally troubled by spying on others and reporting them to the authorities? Mozi assured them that they need not be because they would be doing a service to society as a whole. And the whole, in his opinion, was more important than any part. Indeed, as he saw it, saving the whole also saves the parts, including the deviant. To make this point easier to see, he told us to begin by looking at the family.

> What is needed is the head of a family to give orders to all its members that whoever sees something beneficial to the family must report it to its head. Whoever reports what is beneficial to the family benefits the family himself, and is therefore to be rewarded by the head of the family and applauded by its members. Whoever fails to report what is harmful to the family harms the family himself, and is therefore to be punished by the head of the family and condemned by its members. Wishing to receive reward and applause and to avoid punishment and condemnation, all members of the family would report what is beneficial and what is harmful to the family. The head of the family is thus able to reward the good members and punish the evil ones. As good members are rewarded and evil ones punished, the family is in good order.

What is true for a family, in Mozi's view, is true for the whole world.

(5) Obey the will of Heaven and safeguard against human abuse

But there is this nagging question: what if the authorities are wrong, their directions misleading and their values skewed? Mozi was realistic enough to know that, in reality, not all rulers were virtuous and wise. They could and, indeed, often did make mistakes, and sometimes intentionally did evil. So he said that there was an ultimate standard – the standard of Heaven. The Son of Heaven should not set up arbitrary standards; he must go a step further and comply with the will of Heaven. "If a practice is in accordance with the will of Heaven," Mozi said, "it is a good practice; otherwise, it is a bad one." And so is an idea or a government measure. And that is why Mozi said, "The will of Heaven to me is like the compass to the wheelwright and the square to the carpenter. The wheelwright and the carpenter measure all circular and square objects with their compasses and squares and accept those that fit as correct and reject those that do not fit as incorrect."

The will of Heaven, as discussed earlier, was to love the people. It was understood by the sage kings of the past, and they obeyed it strictly, never deviating from it, never innovating anything by themselves.

What if the behaviour of the Son of Heaven was not up to this high standard? Mozi said that there would be natural calamities. "Excessive heat and cold, untimely rain and snow, the failure of crops and depletion of flocks, epidemics and plague, gale winds and incessant downpours will be inflicted by Heaven on the people who fail to follow its will."

This sounds odd. When the ruler commits a wrong, the people are to suffer with him or, indeed, more than he does even though they have no control over him whatsoever. If Heaven is so vigilant and responsive, it is reassuring. But, by Mozi's time, it was widely noticed that the virtuous were not always rewarded and the wicked punished. It seemed to many that Heaven was negligent or unprincipled. Mozi would not even acknowledge these problems. He could not. His theory needs the ultimate leader to be good.

And then, being under pressure to inform the government, people might feel compelled to invent stories that they believed the authorities would like, producing unfounded information. Moreover, being under constant surveillance, people would inevitably be suspicious and distrustful towards one another. Social ties would be harmed and everyone isolated and living in fear. This would be contrary to Mozi's idea of universal love.

(E) Social relationships

What would the world be like after the will of Heaven was fully implemented? One of Mozi's statements seemed close to a depiction of his utopia: it intimates that, in this world, those with strength will help others, those with knowledge will teach others and those with wealth will share with others. The superiors will attend to government diligently and so will the inferiors attend to their work. The country will be in order and wealth will be sufficient. There will be plenty of rice and wine to offer to the gods and spirits at home, and enough precious stones and pearls to give to the neighbouring states. There will be no wars on the borders and there is enough to care for the people – keeping the hungry fed and letting those who toiled have rest. The ruler will be benevolent and the people loyal; fathers will be loving, children filial, and siblings compassionate. There will be rightness and good government, all nations will coexist in harmony, and every state will be wealthy; the common people will be warmly clothed and well fed, and they will live in peace without worry.

This vision is a rather modest one. The "ideal" world is to be dreary, perhaps like the world of ants, where everyone works and works for nothing apart from securing the very basic material needs for survival. There is no music, no joy, no relaxation and certainly nothing to look forward to in the future. It reflects Mozi's first and foremost concern: peace in the world and enough food and clothing for the common people. But, besides this concern, he emphasised another cause of social problems – people's divergent views on what was right and what was wrong. Other thinkers thought it necessary to address this by changing the people's moral and spiritual characters. And they thought that, to effect this change, arbitrary imposition from above about what was right and forcing people to adhere by coercion or crude inducements of rewards would not work but education would. Mozi was a teacher with many disciples but he did not think it necessary to help people find in their own hearts and minds how they should live and what life was for. It is regrettable.

(G) Relationship between the individual and the authorities

An important part of human life is interaction among individuals, particularly between those of different status. What would it be like in Mozi's ideal society? That society would be strictly hierarchical and highly regimented because, according to him, in the beginning each individual had a different set of views, values and objectives. In that way they were equal but the equality was their curse. They quarrelled and fought, and their lives were miserable, until a Son of Heaven appeared to impose upon them his will and drive them to co-operate and strive for a common goal. Then individual equality would be lost but social order established. People would be made not only to realise that government agents were superior to them in the political system but also to believe that such agents were wiser than they and therefore were justified commanding them and telling them not only what to do but also what to think. And then they would be forced, by a bleak choice between rewards and punishments, to obey or not to obey. Moreover, they would be indoctrinated to believe that everyone obeying the orders and helping the government maintain its control over one's fellows was for the good of oneself as well as for society as a whole. The head of the government was supposedly chosen by Heaven and was to obey its will which was to love the common people. But there was no way effectively to make him to obey or prevent him from deviation and punish him for violation. Thus, at best, he was a benevolent dictator but more likely a wilful tyrant. Against him, no one had freedom. Everyone, including those in his government, were like domesticated animals, at best loved but, because of their vulnerability, more probably abused. None of these effects had been even hinted at by Mozi but the implications were there embedded in his theory.

It is thus ironic and regrettable that Mozi, an apparently passionate advocate for the exploited and oppressed common people, could, in effect, become an apologist for absolute power. Why? A plausible explanation is that he had two conflicting views about the common people – on the one hand, they deserved sympathy and help; on the other, they could not be trusted to find ways to their own salvation. And he himself had two conflicting characters – at once a populist and an elitist who had sympathy for the people but no respect; he was someone who was disgusted by the ruling class but incapable of finding a realistic way to reform it, let alone replace it. Thus, in a rather emotional rush to induce change, he constructed a defective theory merely to condemn the behaviour of the rulers and then, in a cooler mood, he thought the common people could not be left to themselves but must be led by those intellectually and morally superior to them.

But persons of superior morality and intellect are hard to find, and are certainly not readily available among the hereditary rulers of Mozi's time. Therefore, he advocated a meritocracy. But he did not say how it could be initiated. The idea was subversive but Mozi could not envisage a real revolution. Instead, he said the new rulers were to be chosen by Heaven as its "Son" the ideal emperor. This escapist position became the Achilles heel of his theory – where the government was led by the Son of Heaven or a sage king, everything will be perfectly managed and people need no freedom of either thought or action. They should simply obey him.

Mozi thought his theory would help establish a new political and social order. But this was self-deceit. Society would still be under the control of privileged men traditionally in power with no one to control them. The theory was built on a myth and could not stand the test of actual human experience. Its emphasis on conformism and regimentation could easily lead to dictatorship and totalitarianism. The universal surveillance under the pretence of universal love would leave the individual destroyed; everyone, except the Son of Heaven, would no longer be a human being but, in effect, a cog in the machine of state.

After reading *Mozi*, one cannot but be deeply moved by his obvious compassion for the suffering masses and his selfless effort to help them, and hence see in him, as many in later times did, "a truly good man devoting his great talent, remarkable ability and the sincerest and kindest heart to the salvation of the world at immeasurable cost to himself".[6] To justify his actions he constructed a theory. It has some striking points but is imperfect. It is apparently not well reasoned – many of his ideas are not sufficiently supported by rational arguments. It is short-sighted – nothing more than order and subsistence living are forecast. It is surreal – an absolutely wise and virtuous superhuman is needed as the head of the political system. It is impractical – the system relies on people reporting on one another. It is self-contradictory – the idea of universal love is incompatible with the belief in a vindictive Heaven. Another unusual point is that not much is found in *Mozi* that discusses law and other norms. To maintain a system of collectivism, headed by an absolute ruler, law is of course necessary. Mozi did not talk much about it because, apparently in his mind, law was but the ruler's orders, or his *yi* which was to be accepted by all his subjects.

Perhaps he could be excused for being not quite comprehensive and consistent theoretically because he was not just a thinker but more a man of action. He was in a hurry to address what he perceived as extremely urgent problems of his time. He was like Zichan and all those who wanted to have immediate solutions. He did not achieve much but he practised what he preached, often at the risk of his own life, for the benefit others. This was truly extraordinary. Few others did the same. Were there more people like him, China, for better or for worse, would have been a different country.

Notes

1. See Sima Qian 史馬遷, *Shi-ji* 史記 Chapter 74 "Mengzi Xun Qing lie-zhuan" 孟子荀卿列傳 p. 2350.
2. For this account of Mozi's life see Fang Shouchu 方授楚, *Mo-xue yuan-liu* 墨學源流 pp. 3–37. According to it, Mozi was never an official of any state although he travelled to many states, presenting to those in power his ideas and ideals. For Zhuangzi's praise of Mozi see Guo Qingfan 郭慶藩, *Zhuangzi ji-shi* 莊子集釋 Chapter 33 "Tian-xia" 天下 pp. 464–8.
3. There are two chapters in *Mozi* devoted to criticising the Ruists – Chapter 38 "Fei-ru shang" 非儒上 and Chapter 39 "Fei-ru xia" 非儒下. The first was lost. For the second see Sun Yirang 孫詒讓, *Mozi jian-gu* 墨子閒詁 pp. 177–89. Some of the criticisms are polemic; the more serious ones in this chapter and elsewhere in *Mozi* are discussed in this study.

4. See Sun Yirang, *Mozi Jian-gu*, Chapter 50 "Gongshu" (公輸) pp. 292–6; *Lü-shi Chun-qiu*, Chapter 21 "Ai-lei" (愛類) p. 282.
5. See ibid., Chapters 52, 53, 56, 58, 61, 62, 63, 68, 69, 70, 71; pp. 297–374.
6. See Guo Qingfan, *Zhuangzi ji-shi*, *Zhuangzi*, "Tian-xia" (天下篇) pp. 461–81.

Zhuang-zi 莊子

PART 1
TRANSLATION

(A) Universal relativism and individual uniqueness

(1) Likes and dislikes

[1] If a person sleeps in damp places, he will have lower back sickness and will become half paralysed, but would this be true for an eel? If he lives in a tree, he will be fearful and tremble but will this be true of a monkey? Of these three which one knows the proper place to live? Humans eat vegetables and animal meat, deer eat grass, centipedes find tiny snakes tasty, and hawks and falcons relish mice. Of these four, which one knows what is the right taste? Apes associate with monkeys, deer mingle with elks, and fish swim with eels. Mao Qiang and Li Ji were admired by all people as beauties; but when a fish saw them it would dive deep, when a bird saw them it would fly high, and when a deer saw them it would abruptly run away. Of these four, which one knows the standard of beauty for the world? (Chapter 2, "Qi-wu-lun" pp. 44–5)

[2] Once a seabird alighted in the outskirts of the state of Lu. An aristocrat of Lu escorted it to his ancestral worship shrine where he entertained it with the *Jiu-shao* music and the *Tailao* feast. But the bird looked dazed and sad, not daring to eat a single slice of meat or drink a cup of wine, and died in three days. That was applying the way to provide for the aristocrat himself to provide for a bird, not applying the right way to provide for a bird. If one is to provide for a bird with what nourishes a bird, one should let it rest in deep forest, play in swamp, float on rivers and lakes, eat eels and small fish, fly and roost with its flock, and live freely as it likes. A bird hates to hear even the sound of human voices; why make all the noise for it? Hearing the music of *Xian-chi* and *Jiu-shao* performed in the fields around Lake Dongting, birds will fly off, animals run away, and fish dive deep, but people will gather around to enjoy the performance. Fish live in water and thrive; men staying long in water will die. It is because they are by

nature different and therefore have different likes and dislikes. (Chapter 18, "Zhi-le" pp. 274–5)

[3] When Huizi was prime minister of Liang, Zhuangzi went to visit him. Someone said to Huizi, "Zhuangzi is coming with the intention to replace you as prime minister!" So Huizi was frightened and searched all over the state for three days and three nights trying to find Zhuangzi. Zhuangzi then came to see him and said, "In the south there is a type of bird called the *yuan-chu*. Do you know about it? A *yuan-chu* will start from the South Sea and fly to the North Sea, and it will rest on nothing but phoenix trees, eat nothing but the seeds of bamboo, and drink nothing but the sweet spring water. Once there was an owl who had got hold of a rotten rat and, as the *yuan-chu* flew by, it raised its head, looked up at the *yuan-chu* and cried, 'Shoo!' Now that you have your state of Liang, are you trying to shoo me?" (Chapter 17, "Qiu-shui" p. 267)

(2) Nobility and meanness

[4] Ruo of the North Sea said, "From the point of view of the Way, nothing is noble or mean. From the point of view of things themselves, each regards itself as noble and the others as mean. From the point of view of convention, nobility and meanness are not determined by a thing itself." (Chapter 17, "Qiu-shui" p. 254)

(3) Big and small

[5] From the point of view of differences, looking at some aspect of a thing that is great, one will find that everything is great; looking at some aspect of a thing that is small, one will find that everything is small. If one can perceive the sky and the earth as a tiny grain and the tip of a hair a range of mountains, then one has grasped the essence of difference. (Chapter 17, "Qiu-shui" p. 254)

[6] There is nothing in the world bigger than the tip of a piece of autumn down, and Mount Tai is tiny. (Chapter 2, "Qi-wu-lun" p. 39)

(4) Life and death

[7] When Zhuangzi went to Chu, he saw a skull, dry and parched but intact. He poked it with his horsewhip and asked, "Sir, were your greedy for life and forgetful of reason and so came to this? Was your state vanquished and were you killed by a weapon, and so came to this? Did you do some evil deed and were you ashamed to bring disgrace upon your parents and family, and so came to this? Was it through the pangs of cold and hunger that you came to this? Or was it your old age that brought you to this?" When he had finished speaking, he dragged the skull over and, using it for a pillow, lay down to sleep. In the middle of the night, the skull appeared in his dream and said, "You talk like a rhetorician and all your words show the problems of a living man. The dead have no such problems! Would you like to hear the talk of the dead?" "Yes", said Zhuangzi. The skull said, "Among us the dead there are no rulers above, no subjects below, and no chores of the four seasons. Our springs and autumns are as endless as heaven and earth. A king facing south on his throne could have no more happiness than this!" Zhuangzi

couldn't believe this and said, "If I got the Administrator of Life to make you live again, add flesh to your bones, return you to your parents and family and your old home and friends, would you want that?" The skull frowned severely, wrinkling up its brow and said, "Why would I throw away more happiness than that of a king facing south on a throne and take on the troubles of a human being again?" (Chapter 18, "Zhi-le" pp. 272–3)

[8] Zhuangzi's wife died. When Huizi went to convey his condolences, he found Zhuangzi sitting with his legs sprawled out, tapping a pottery platter and singing. Huizi said, "You lived with her, and she brought up your children, grew old and died. It is already enough that you do not weep, but tapping a platter and singing, are you not going too far?" Zhuangzi said, "No. When she first died, how could I not grieve like a normal person would? But I looked at the very beginning and found that, before she was born, she did not have life. Not only that she did not have life, she did not have a body. Not only that she did not have a body, she did not have a spirit. She was like a mirage. Then imperceptibly a change took place and she had a spirit. The spirit changed and she had a body. Then she was born and had life. And now she changed again and became dead. It's just like the progression of the four seasons, spring, summer, autumn, winter. Now she's going to lie down peacefully in a vast room. If I were to follow after her bawling and sobbing, it would show that I don't understand anything about life. So I stopped." (Chapter 18, "Zhi-le" p. 271)

[9] Life is the companion of death; death is the beginning of life. Who understands their rules? Man's life is a coming together of air. When it is concentrated, there is life; when it disperses, there is death. If life and death are companions to each other, then what is there for us to be anxious about? (Chapter 22, "Zhi-bei-you" p. 320)

(5) Real and unreal

[10] He who dreams of drinking wine may weep in the morning; he who dreams of weeping may in the morning go off to hunt. While he is dreaming, he does not know it is a dream, and in his dream he may even try to interpret the dream. Only after he wakes does he know it was a dream. And someday there will be a great awakening when we know that this is all a great dream. Yet the stupid believe they are awake and clearly knowing about everything, calling this man ruler, that one herdsman – how obstinate! (Chapter 2, "Qi-wu-lun" pp. 49–50)

[11] Once Zhuang Zhou dreamt he was a butterfly, a butterfly flitting and fluttering around, happy with itself and doing as it pleased. It didn't know it was Zhuang Zhou. Then he woke up and surprisingly found he was Zhuang Zhou. But he didn't know if he was Zhuang Zhou who had dreamt he was a butterfly, or a butterfly dreaming he was Zhuang Zhou. (Chapter 2, "Qi-wu-lun" pp. 53–4)

(6) Right and wrong

[12] Suppose you and I have had an argument. If you have defeated me instead of me defeating you, then are you necessarily right and am I necessarily wrong? If I have defeated you instead of you defeating me, then am I necessarily right and are you necessarily wrong? Is one of us right and the other wrong? Are both of us right or are both of us wrong? If you and I don't know the answer, then other people are bound to be even more in the dark. Whom shall we get to decide what is right? Shall we get someone who agrees with you to decide? But if he already agrees with you, how can he decide fairly? Shall we get someone who agrees with me? But if he already agrees with me, how can he decide? Shall we get someone who disagrees with both of us? But if he already disagrees with both of us, how can he decide? Shall we get someone who agrees with both of us? But if he already agrees with both of us, how can he decide? Obviously, then, neither you nor I nor anyone else can know the answer. Who then should we wait for to make a decision? (Chapter 2, "Qi-wu-lun" pp. 50–2)

[13] From the point of view of preference, if we only look at an aspect of a thing that we consider as right, then among the myriad things, there are none that can be considered not right. If we only look at an aspect of a thing that we consider wrong, then among the myriad things, there are none that can be considered not wrong. If we know that Yao and Jie each thought himself right and condemned the other as wrong, then we may understand why there are preferences. (Chapter 17, "Qiu-shui" p. 255)

(B) The inborn nature, its importance and protection

[14] Innate nature is unchangeable. (Chapter 14, "Tian-yun" p. 235)

[15] The Lord of the South Sea was called Shu, the Lord of the North Sea was called Hu, and the Lord of the central region was called Hundun. Shu and Hu from time to time came together for a meeting in the territory of Hundun, and Hundun treated them very generously. Shu and Hu discussed how they could repay his kindness. "All people", they said, "have seven orifices so they can see, hear, eat, and breathe. But Hundun alone doesn't have any. Let's try to drill him some." Every day they drilled a hole and, on the seventh day, Hundun died. (Chapter 7, "Ying-di-wang" p. 139)

[16] Therefore, although the duck's legs are short, it would be worried if they were to be extended; although the crane's legs are long, it would be saddened if they were to be shortened. What is long by nature is not to be shortened; what is short by nature is not to be extended. (Chapter 8, "Pian-mu" p. 143)

[17] Horses have hoofs to tread frost and snow and fur coats to keep out wind and cold. They eat grass, drink from the stream, lift up their feet and gallop – this is the true nature of horses. (Chapter 9, "Ma-ti" p. 149)

[18] In the bald and barren north, there is a dark sea, the Pond of Heaven. In it is a fish which is several thousand *li* in width, and no one knows how long. His name is Kun. There is also a bird there, named Peng, with a back like Mount

Tai and wings like clouds filling the sky. It beats the whirlwind, leaps into the air, and rises up 90,000 *li*, cutting through the clouds and mist, shouldering the blue sky, and then turns south, intending to journey to the southern darkness. A small swamp quail laughs at it, saying, "Where does it think it is going? I leap up, not more than 10 or 12 yards before I come down fluttering among the weeds. And that is the best kind of flying. Where does it think it is going?" (Chapter 1, "Xiao-yao-you" p. 8)

[19] Yao wanted to cede the empire to Xu You. Xu You said, "When a small bird builds its nest in the deep forest, it uses no more than one branch. When a beaver drinks at the river, it takes no more than a bellyful. Go home and forget the matter, my lord. I have no use for the empire." (Chapter 1, "Xiao-yao-you" pp. 12–13)

[20] The states of Han and Wei were fighting over a piece of land. Zihuazi went to see Lord Zhaoxi of Han. The lord had a worried look on his face. Zihuazi said, "Suppose all men of the world were to draw up a written agreement in your presence, reading: 'Seize it with your left hand and you will lose your right hand; seize it with your right hand and you will lose your left; yet he who seizes it will certainly gain possession of the world.' Would your lordship like to seize it?" "I would not!" said Lord Zhaoxi. "Very good!" exclaimed Zihuazi. "From this I can see that your two arms are more important to you than the world, your body as a whole is more important than your two arms, and the state of Han is far less important than the world. Now this piece of land that you are fighting over is far less important than the state of Han but your lordship worries about not getting this piece of land and thereby harms your health?!' (Chapter 28, "Rang-wang" pp. 416–17)

[21] Shinan Yiliao called upon the Lord of Lu. The lord had a worried look. Shinanzi asked, "Your lordship has a worried look. Why?" The lord said, "I study the way of the former King Wen, I carry on the work of my ancestors, I respect the spirits, honour the worthy, and I personally followed their principles and never for an instant relax, and yet I can't seem to avoid disaster. That is why I am so worried." Shinanzi said, "Your tactics to avoid disaster are superficial. The richly furred fox and prettily spotted leopard dwell in the mountain forests and crouch in the cliff-side caves, very quietly. They go abroad by night but rest at home by day, very cautiously. Though hunger, thirst, and hardship press them, they go separately to the wilderness to seek food, very thoughtfully. And yet they can't escape the disaster of nets and traps. What guilt do they have? They have none. It is their fur which is the cause of their disaster. Now is not the state of Lu your coat of fur? I hope you would strip away your form, rid yourself of this fur, wash clean your mind, abandon your desires and wander in the uninhabited wilderness . . . I hope you would leave your state, discard its tradition and go with the Way. (Chapter 20, "Shan-mu" pp. 294–5)

[22] When people of ancient times spoke of fulfilment of ambitions, they did not mean to have high status with fine carriages and ornamental hats as its symbols. They meant simply that their joy with what they had was so complete that it

could not be made greater. Nowadays, when people speak of fulfilment of ambitions, they mean to have fine carriages and ornamental hats. But carriages and hats are only for a person's body, not for what is essential to his nature and life. Such things from time to time may happen to come a person's way. They are like temporary deposits. As such, when they arrive, a person cannot resist them; when they depart, he cannot stop them. Therefore, he who is not elated and licentious for having carriages and hats or depressed and vulgar for being poor and humble, but is just as happy in either condition, will have no worry. Now, when some temporary deposits are gone, a person is unhappy. From this result, it is obvious that, while being happy, such a person is never without worry. Therefore, it is said, those who sacrifice themselves for outside things and lose their inborn nature in pursuit of what is vulgar are called the "upside-down people". (Chapter 16, "Shan-xing" pp. 246–7)

[23] Hence it is said, "The essence of the Way is for caring for one's person; its residue is for managing the state; its waste is for governing the empire." With this view, the accomplishments of emperors and kings are superfluous affairs to the sage because they are not what to keep the body whole and to care for life. Now many gentlemen of the present vulgar world endanger themselves and throw away their lives in the pursuit of trifling matters. Aren't they pitiable! When the sage makes a move, he will certainly investigate where he is going and what he is to do. Now suppose there is a man here who takes the priceless pearl of the Lord of Sui and uses it as a pellet to shoot at a sparrow 1,000 yards up in the air – the world will certainly laugh at him. Why? Because what he is using is of great value, and what he is trying to acquire is trifling. And life is surely of greater value than the pearl of the Lord of Sui! (Chapter 28, "Rang-wang" pp. 417–18)

[24] Once, when Zhuangzi was fishing in the Pu River, the king of Chu sent two officials to see him and announce to him: "I would like to trouble you with the administration of my realm". Zhuangzi held on to the fishing pole and, without turning his head, said, "I have heard that there is a sacred tortoise in Chu that has been dead for 3,000 years. The king keeps it wrapped in cloth and boxed, and stores it in the ancestral temple. Now would this tortoise rather be dead and have its bones left behind and honoured? Or would it rather be alive dragging its tail in the mud?" The two officials said, "It would rather be alive and drag its tail in the mud." Zhuangzi said, "Then go away. I'll drag my tail in the mud!" (Chapter 17, "Qiu-shui" pp. 266–7)

[25] Someone invited Zhuangzi to office. Zhuangzi replied to the messenger saying, "Have you ever seen a sacrificial ox? They dress it in embroidery, feed it with grass and beans. But when at last they lead it into the great ancestral temple, then, though it might wish it could become a lonely calf once more, can it get its wish?" (Chapter 32, "Lie Yu-kou" p. 460)

[26] Yao wanted to cede the empire to Xu You, but Xu You did not accept. Then he tried to give it to Zizhou Zhifu. Zizhou Zhifu said, '"Making me the emperor? That should be all right. But I happen to have a deep-seated and worrisome illness which I am just now trying to cure, so I have no time to manage the empire."

Now the empire is a thing of supreme importance, yet he would not allow it to harm his life. How much less, then, any other thing! (Chapter 28, "Rang-wang" p. 414)

(C) The inborn nature and the *Way*

[27] The Way has its reality and its signs but is without action or form. One can transmit it conceptually but cannot receive it concretely; one can get it perceptively but cannot see it physically. It is its own source, its own root. Before there were heaven and earth, it existed already. It gave spirituality to the spirits and gods; it gave birth to heaven and earth. It poses beyond the extreme height, and yet it is not lofty; it delves beneath the extreme depth and yet it is not deep. It was born before heaven and earth, and yet it has not been there long; it is earlier than the earliest time, and yet it is not old. (Chapter 6, "Da-zong-shi" p. 111-12)

[28] Wushi said, "The Way cannot be heard; heard, it is not the Way. The Way cannot be seen; seen, it is not the Way. The Way cannot be described; described, it is not the Way. Do you know that which gives form to the formed is itself formless? There is no name that fits the Way." (Chapter 22, "Zhi-bei-you" p. 330)

[29] The Way is the route which the myriad things travel. All things that miss it would die; all that get it would live. (Chapter 31, "Yu-fu" p. 448)

[30] Dongguozi asked Zhuangzi, "The so called "Way" – where does it exist?" Zhuangzi said, "There is no place it does not exist." Dongguozi said, "Please be more specific." Zhuangzi said, "It is in the ant." "Why is it so low?" "It is in the panic grass." "But that's lower still." "It is in the tiles and shards." "But that's lower still." "It is in the piss and shit." Dongguozi did not respond. Zhuangzi said, "Sir, your questions simply don't get at the substance of the matter. When market superintendent Huo asked the butcher how to test the fitness of a pig, he was told that the lower down on the pig's legs you press, the nearer you come to the truth. But you must not expect to find the Way in any particular place – there is not a thing that escapes its presence. Such is the Perfect Way, and so too are the truly great words. 'Complete', 'universal', 'all-inclusive' – these three are different words with the same meaning. All point to a single reality [that the Way is omnipresent]." (Chapter 22, "Zhi-bei-you" pp. 326–27)

[31] The Way is the reason [behind all things]. (Chapter 16, "Shan-xing" p. 242)

[32] One who knows the Way can grasp the reasons. One who grasps the reasons can clearly see the circumstances. He who can clearly see the circumstances will not sacrifice himself for trifling things. (Chapter 17, "Qiu-shui" p. 259)

[33] Confucius said to Lao Dan [Laozi], "Today you seem to have some leisure, may I ask about the Ultimate Way?" Lao Dan replied, " . . . Heaven cannot but be high, the earth cannot but be broad, the sun and the moon cannot but revolve, the myriad things cannot but multiply. This is the Way." (Chapter 21, "Zhi-bei-you" pp. 323–4)

[34] Does heaven turn? Does the earth stay still? Do sun and moon compete for a place? Who determines all this? Who keeps the order? Who, resting inactive

himself, effects the push that makes things go this way? Perhaps there is some mechanism that would not let them do what they want? Perhaps they just move and turn and cannot stop? Do clouds exist to make rain, or does the rain make the clouds? Who puffs the clouds up, who showers the rain down? Who, resting inactive himself, stirs up all this for licentious joy? The winds rise in the north, blowing now west, now east, whirling up to wander on high. Whose breaths and exhalations are they? Who, resting inactive himself, huffs and puffs them about like this? Wu Xiantiao said, "Come. I will tell you. Heaven has the six directions and the five constants. When emperors and kings go along with these, there is good order; when they move contrary to these, there is disaster." (Chapter 14, "Tian-yun" pp. 218–20)

[35] The *kui* [a mythical, one-legged animal] pities the millipede, the millipede envies the snake . . . The *kui* said to the millipede, "I use this one leg that I hop along, no one can walk as simply as I do. Now how in the world do you manage to work all those ten thousand legs of yours?" The millipede said, "It is not as difficult as you think. Haven't you ever watched a man spit? He just gives a hawk and out it comes, some drops as big as pearls, some as fine as mist, falling down in countless numbers. Now all I do is put in motion the heavenly mechanism in me, but I'm not aware of how the thing works." The millipede said to the snake, "I use many legs to move, but can't keep up with you who have no legs. How is that?" The snake said, "It's just the heavenly mechanism moving me along, how can I change the way I am? Why do I have to use legs?" (Chapter 17, "Qiu-shui" pp. 261–2)

[36] To act through inaction is called Heaven. (Chapter 12, "Tian-di" p. 183)

(D) The world of "Perfect Virtue"

[37] People of antiquity lived in a state of primordial haziness throughout their lives indifferent to the interests of others and therefore attained tranquillity. At that time the *yin* and *yang* were harmonious and still, ghosts and spirits worked no mischief, the four seasons kept to their proper order, the myriad things knew no injury, and living creatures were free from premature death. Though people had knowledge, they did not use it. This was called the Perfect Unity. At that time, no one acted with a special motive, and everything existed according to its nature. (Chapter 16, "Shan-xing" p. 243)

[38] I have heard that, in ancient times, birds and beasts were many and people few. Therefore, people all nested in the trees in order to escape danger, during the day gathering acorns and chestnuts, at sunset climbing back up to sleep in their trees. Hence, they were called the "nest-building people". In ancient times, people knew nothing about wearing clothes. In summer, they heaped up piles of firewood, in winter they burned them to keep warm. Hence, they were called "the people who know how to stay alive". In the age of Shennong, people lay down in peace, woke up in contentment. They knew their mothers but not their fathers, and lived side by side with the elk and the deer. They ploughed for their food, wove for their clothing, and had no thought in their hearts of

harming one another. This was Perfect Virtue at its height! (Chapter 29, "Dao Zhi" p. 429)

[39] You do not know of the age of Perfect Virtue? In the past, during the time of Rongcheng, Dating, Bohuang, Zhongyang . . . [names of fictitious ancient leaders], people knotted ropes and used them [as a means of reminding themselves of something]. They relished their food, cherished their clothing, enjoyed their customs, and were content with their abode. Though neighbouring states were within sight of each other, and people in one state could hear the cries of dogs and chickens in another state, they grew old and died without ever interacting with one another. In a time like this, the world was in Perfect Order. (Chapter 10, "Qu-qie" p. 162)

[40] In a time of Perfect Virtue the gait of men was slow and idle, their gaze steady but aimless. In that time, mountains had no paths or tunnels, lakes and rivers no boats or bridges. The myriad things lived closely together. Birds and beasts formed their flocks and herds, grass and trees grew tall. Thus, one could tie a string to a bird or a beast and walk with them, or climb a tree and peer into the nest of the birds. (Chapter 9, "Ma-ti" p. 151)

[41] In an age of Perfect Virtue the worthy were not honoured and the talented not employed. Rulers were like the high branches of a tree and the people were like wild deer in the wilderness. They acted properly but did not know that was rightness; they loved one another but did not know that was benevolence; they were devoted but did not know that was loyalty; they were faithful but did not know that was trustworthiness; they engaged in plain activities helping one another but did not think they were doing any favour. Thus, they moved without leaving any trail behind, acted without leaving any records. (Chapter 12, "Tian-di" p. 199)

[42] In Nanyue there is a town named "The State of Established Virtues". Its people are naive and simple, few in thoughts of self, scant in desires. They know how to make things, but not how to store them away; they give, but look for nothing in return. They do not know what accords with rightness, and what conforms to rites. Without plans and aims, they move as their instincts lead them and, in this manner, they tread the path of the Great Way. Their life is enjoyable; in death they are buried in peace. (Chapter 20, "Shan-mu" p. 295)

(E) The fall of the *Way*

[43] In an age of Perfect Virtue people lived together with birds and beasts and mingled among the myriad things. Who then knew anything about "gentleman" or "petty man"? As people were uniformly without knowledge, their virtue did not depart from them. Being uniformly without desire, they were all plain and simple. Being plain and simple, they preserved their nature. Then along came the sage, strenuously trying to do benevolence, standing on tiptoe to reach rightness, and the world for the first time had doubts; indulging in music and fussing about the rites, and the world for the first time was divided. Thus, if the virgin wood had not been destroyed, who could make wine vessels? If the white jade had not been

shattered, who could make the ceremonial tablets? If the Way and the Virtue had not been discarded, why was there the need for benevolence and rightness? If the inborn nature had not departed, why would there be any use for rites and music? If the five colours had not been mixed, who was there to make decorations? If the five notes had not been confused, who was there to create the six tones? Destroying the virgin wood in order to fashion implements was the crime of the artisan. Destroying the Way and the Virtue in order to create benevolence and rightness was the fault of the sage. (Chapter 9, "Ma-ti" pp. 152–3)

[44] A horse's hoofs can tread frost and snow, its fur can keep out wind and cold. It eats grass, drinks from the stream, lifts up its feet and gallops – this is the true nature of a horse. If it had great terraces and fine halls, it would have no use for them. Then along comes Bole, saying, "I am good at handling horses" and proceeds to singe them, shave them, pare their hoofs, brand them, bind them with martingale and crupper, tie them up in stable and stall. By this time, two or three out of ten horses have died. He goes on to starve them, make them go thirsty, race them, prance them, pull them into line, force them to run side by side, give them the pain of bit and rein in the front, and the terror of whip and crop in the behind. By this time, over half the horses have died. (Chapter 9, "Ma-ti" pp. 149–50)

[45] When horses live on the plain, they eat grass and drink from the streams. While happy, they twine their necks together and rub; while angry, they turn back to back and kick. This is all horses know how to do. But if you put on their neck yokes and crossbars connected to pulling poles, and on their head and body armour, they will learn to snap the crossbars, break the yoke, rip the carriage top, champ the bit, and chew the reins. Thus, horses learn how to commit the worst kinds of mischief. This is the crime of Bole. In the days of Hexu [a fictitious leader of ancient times], people stayed home unconscious of what they wanted to do, walked about without knowing where they wanted to go. With food in their mouths, they played around; with bulging bellies, they frolicked. They were able to be so at ease. Then the sage came along using rites and music to alter people's behaviour, exalting benevolence and rightness to reform people's minds. Then, for the first time, people learned to stand on tiptoe and covet knowledge, to fight to the death over profit, and there was no stopping them. This was the fault of the sage. (Chapter 9, "Ma-ti" pp. 153–4)

[46] So it is said, "When the Way was lost, then there was virtue; when virtue was lost, then there was benevolence; when benevolence was lost, then there was rightness; when rightness was lost, then there were rites. Rites are the frills of the Way and the forerunners of disorder." (Chapter 22, "Zhi-bei-you" p. 319)

[47] When Virtue began to dwindle and decline, Suiren and Fuxi [two legendary ancient leaders] began to manage the world and thus there was compliance but no longer any unity. When Virtue further dwindled and declined, Shennong and the Yellow Emperor began to manage the world, and thus there was security but no longer compliance. When Virtue further dwindled and declined, Yao and Shun began to manage the world – they set up various measures to regulate and

transform and, in doing so, defiled purity and shattered simplicity. Their path deviated from the Way and their acts were devoid of Virtue. After this, people abandoned their common nature and each one followed his mind's directions. The minds would gain knowledge but it was not enough to give the world stability. After this, "culture" was added on, and "broad learning" was increased. "Culture" destroyed people's basic nature, "broad learning" drowned their minds and, after this, people began to be confused and disorderly. They had no way to revert to the true form of their inborn nature or to return once more to the original conditions. (Chapter 16, "Shan-xing" pp. 243–5)

[48] Zigong [a disciple of Confucius] said [to Lao Dan], "The Three Sovereigns and the Five Emperors ruled the world in different ways, but similarly gained praise and acclaim. Yet Sir, you alone do not regard them as sages, why?" Lao Dan said, "Young man, come a little closer. Why do you say that they ruled in ways that were not the same?" Zigong replied, "Yao ceded the throne to Shun. Shun ceded the throne to Yu. Yu wore himself out for it. Tang had to resort to war [to seize the throne from Jie, the last emperor of the Xia Dynasty]. King Wen obeyed Shou [the last emperor of the Shang Dynasty] and dared not rebel. King Wu rebelled and refused to obey. Therefore, I said that their ways were not the same." Lao Dan said, "Young man, come closer and I will tell you how the Three Sovereigns and the Five Emperors ruled the world. In ancient times the Yellow Emperor ruled the world by making the hearts of the people one. Therefore, where some person did not wail at the death of their parents, others did not censure them. Yao ruled the world by making the hearts of the people affectionate. Therefore, where some person mourned for longer or shorter periods according to the degree of kinship of the deceased, others did not censure him. Shun ruled the world by making the hearts of the people rivalrous,. Therefore, pregnant women gave birth in ten months, babies were able to talk five months after birth, and before being one year old, they began to distinguish others. It was then that premature deaths first occurred. Yu ruled the world and caused people's hearts to be varied. It was recognised that each person had a heart of his own, that recourse to arms could be justified and that killing a robber was not a case of murder. Every person made himself the standard and wanted all others to cup their ears and listen to him. As result, the world was greatly shocked and the Ruists, the Mohist and all the other schools rose to the occasion. At first, they created ethics but now they do not observe their own rules. What can you say? So let me tell you this: in name, the Three Sovereigns and the Five Emperors had ruled the world; in reality they brought it the utmost disorder. Their little knowledge blotted out the brightness of sun and moon above, sapped the spirit of hills and streams below, and overturned the round of the four seasons between. Their knowledge was thus more fearsome than the tail of the scorpion; down to the smallest animals, not a living thing was allowed to keep its life and rest in the true form of its nature. And yet they considered themselves sages! Was it not shameful – their lack of shame!" (Chapter 14, "Tian-yun" pp. 232–4)

[49] As long as those in high places covet knowledge and are without the Way, the world will be in great disorder. How do I know this is so? When people have much knowledge about making bows, crossbows, nets, stringed arrows, and like contraptions, birds fly in confusion to the sky. When people have much knowledge about making fishhooks, lures, seines, dragnets, trawls and weirs, fish dive in confusion to deep water. When people have much knowledge about making pitfalls, snares, cages, traps, and gins, animals flee in confusion to the swamps. When people have much knowledge to cheat and deceive their fellow men, to make sophisticated arguments separating the hardness from the whiteness of a thing and distinguishing the similarities and differences of things, common customs are confused by sophistry. Thus, the world is frequently plunged into great confusion. The blame lies in this coveting of knowledge. (Chapter 10, "Qu-qie" pp. 163–5)

[50] Zhi [Knowledge] wandered north to the banks of the Black Water, climbed the Mound Yinfen and there by chance came upon Wu-wei-wei. Zhi said to Wu-wei-wei, "There are some things I'd like to ask you. How to ponder and deliberate can one get to know the Way? How to position and conduct oneself can one rest in the Way? What direction to go and path to follow can one get to the Way?" Three times the questions were repeated but Wu-wei-wei did not answer. It wasn't that he just did not answer, he didn't know how to answer. Zhi, failing to get any answer, returned to the south of the White Water, climbed the Hill Huque, and there caught sight of Kuang-qu and asked the same questions. "Ah – I know!" said Kuang-qu. "And I'm going to tell you." But just when he was about to say something, he forgot what it was he was about to say. Zhi, failing to get any answer, returned to the imperial palace and saw the Yellow Emperor and posed his questions. The Yellow Emperor said, "Only when you do not ponder and deliberate can you get to know the Way. Only when you do not take any position and do any act can you rest in the Way. Only when you take no direction and follow no path can you get to the Way." Zhi said to the Yellow Emperor, "You and I know but those other two that I asked didn't know. Which of us is right, I wonder?" The Yellow Emperor said, "Wu-wei-wei is the one who is truly right. Kuang-qu appears to be so. You and I in the end are nowhere near it." (Chapter 22, "Zhi-bei-you" pp. 318–19)

[51] Heaven and earth have their great beauties but do not speak of them; the four seasons have their clear rules but do not discuss them; the myriad things have their principles of being but do not expound them. The sage goes to the origin of the beauties of Heaven and earth and arrives at the principles of the myriad things. Thus the Perfect Man does not act, the Great Sage does not invent. They just observe everything between heaven and earth. (Chapter 22, "Zhi-bei-you" p. 321)

(F) The rule makers

[52] There is no one more highly esteemed by the world than the Yellow Emperor, and yet even he could not keep his virtue whole and fought [against Chiyou, a

legendary leader of the Miao tribe] on the field of Zhuolu until the blood flew a hundred *li*. Yao was an unkind father [who killed his eldest son Dan-zhu]. Shun was an unfilial son [who banished his father Gu-sou]. Yu was partially paralysed [because he worked hard to gain power]. Tang exiled his sovereign Jie and King Wu attacked his sovereign Shou. All these six men are held in high esteem by the world, and yet a close look shows that all of them in order to pursue worldly gains confused what was of true value to them and forcibly turned against their own nature. Their behaviour was indeed shameful. (Chapter 29, "Dao Zhi" p. 430)

[53] Man Goude [a fictitious person] said, "The petty thief is imprisoned but the big thief becomes a feudal lord. Inside the doors of feudal lords 'benevolence' and 'rightness' are kept. In the past Xiaobai, Duke Huan of Qi, murdered his elder brother and took his sister-in-law for a wife, and yet Guan Zhong served him as a minister. Tian Chengzi Chang [a minister of the state of Qi] murdered his sovereign and stole his state, and yet Confucius accepted gifts from him. In words they condemned them but, in practice, they bowed before them. Thus, this contradiction of words and deeds must have fought in their hearts, and isn't this a trouble? So the Book says, 'Who is bad? Who is good? The successful becomes the head, the unsuccessful becomes the tail.'" (Chapter 29, "Dao Zhi" p. 434)

[54] Man Goude said, "Yao killed his eldest son and Shun banished his brother; had they the proper kindred relationship? Tang exiled his sovereign Jie and King Wu killed his sovereign Shou; had they the rightness between the superior and the inferior? King Ji [instead of his elder brothers] inherited the throne and Lord Zhou killed his older brothers [who rebelled against his rule]; had they the order of the senior and the junior?" (Chapter 29, "Dao Zhi" p. 434)

(G) Man-made rules

(1) Some are outdated and irrelevant

[55] While Confucius was visiting the state of Wei in the west, his disciple Yan Yuan asked Maestro Jin of Wei, "What do you think of my master's course?" Maestro Jin said, "A pity! Your master is heading towards a dead end." Yan Yuan said, "How so?" Maestro Jin said, "Before a straw dog is offered in sacrifice it is stored in a bamboo trunk and covered with embroidered material. The priest will fast and bathe and then take it to the sacrificial site. Having been so used, passers-by will trample on its head and spine, and firewood gatherers will burn it. If a person picks it up and puts it back in a bamboo trunk and covers it with embroidered material, and lingers or lies down beside it, even if he does have a nightmare, he will have troubles. Now your master takes the straw dogs that had been used by the previous kings and gathers his disciples to linger and lie down beside them. That was why when he was in Song, people cut down the tree under which he stayed; when he left Wei, people erased all signs of his visit. Those were his troubles in lands formerly of the Shang and the Zhou dynasties. Were these not nightmares to him? Then he was besieged by fighting soldiers between the states of Chen and Cai for seven days without cooked food and

barely existed between life and death. Were these nightmares to him? Now nothing is as good as a boat for going on water; nothing is as good as a cart for going on land. But, if someone who having seen a boat going on water wants to push it over land, he will for his entire life not be able to move much distance at all. Are the past and the present not like the water and the land, and the Zhou and the Lu not like a boat and a cart? To practise the ways of the Zhou times in the state of the present day Lu is like pushing a boat over land – a great deal of hard work, no accomplishment, and certain harm to the person who tries to do so. It is because he does not know the principle that turning without fixation is the way to respond to the infinite changes of things. Moreover, have you not seen the well-sweep? Pull it, and down it comes; let it go, and up it swings. It is pulled by men and it does not pull them. So it goes up and down and never gets blamed by anybody. Thus the rites, rightness, laws and measures of the Three Sovereigns and the Five Emperors are valued not for their uniformity but for their ability to bring about order. Therefore they are like the haw, the pear, the orange, and the citron. Their flavours are very different but all pleasing to the mouth. Therefore the rites, rightness, laws and measures are things that change in response to the times. If you take a monkey and dress him in the robes of the Duke of Zhou, he will chew and tear them until he gets rid of them completely. The difference between the past and the present is like that between the monkey and the Duke of Zhou. Xishi frowned while walking in her village because of a pain in her heart. Seeing her and admiring her beauty in such a gesture an ugly girl of the same village put her hands over her heart and frowned too. When the rich people of the village saw her they tightly closed their doors and stayed inside. When the poor people saw her they took their wives and children and fled. The ugly girl thought frowning beautiful but did not know why it was beautiful. What a pity! Your master is going to have trouble likewise!" (Chapter 14, "Tian-yun" pp. 225–8)

(2) Some are meaningless

[56] When Lao Dan died, Qin Shi went to mourn for him but, after giving three cries, he left the room. "Weren't you a friend of the Master?", asked Laozi's disciples. "Yes." "And you think it's all right to mourn him this way?" "Yes," said Qin Shi. At first he thought they were all Lao Dan's true believers but after finding that some of the older mourners wept as if they were weeping for a son and some of the younger ones wailed as if they wailed for a mother, he realised that they were not . . . He then said: "Your master happened to come because it was his time, and he happened to leave following a natural course. If you find the timing agreeable and the course acceptable, grief and joy have no way to enter into your heart. In the old days, this was called being freed from painful bondages." (Chapter 3, "Yang-sheng-zhu" pp. 59–60)

[57] Master Sanghu died. He had not yet been buried when Confucius, hearing of his death, sent Zigong to assist at the funeral. On arrival, Zigong found one of the dead man's friends arranging the funeral songs, another one strumming a

lute and together they sang this song: "Ah, Sanghu! Ah, Sanghu! You have gone back to your true form while we remain as men, O!" Zigong hastened forward and said, "May I be so bold as to ask is this the rite to sing over the corpse?" The two men looked at each other and laughed. "What does this man know of the meaning of rites?" they said. Zigong returned and reported to Confucius what had happened and asked, "What sort of men are they? They pay no attention to proper behaviour, disregard their personal appearance and, without so much as changing the expression on their faces, sing in the very presence of the corpse! I can think of no name for them! What sort of men are they?" "They", said Confucius, "are wanderers outside the confines of the ordinary; men like me wander within them. Those outside and those inside can never meet. It was stupid of me to send you to offer them condolences. They join with the Creator to wander in the single breath of heaven and earth. They look upon life as a swelling tumour, a protruding cyst, and upon death as the draining of a sore or the bursting of a boil. To men such as these, how could there be any concern about life and death, before and behind? They take elements of different things and house them in the same body. They forget liver and gall, cast aside ears and eyes, turning and revolving, ending and beginning again, unaware of where they start or finish. Idly they roam beyond the dust and dirt, and wander free and easy in the business of inaction. How could they fret and fuss about the rites of the vulgar world and make a display for the ears and eyes of the common people?" (Chapter 6, "Da-zong-shi" pp. 120–3)

[58] [Confucius said to an old fisherman], "Please, may I ask what you mean by being 'True'?" The fisherman said, "By being 'True' I mean being absolutely pure and sincere. He who is not pure and sincere cannot move others. Therefore, he who forces himself to lament, though he may sound sad, will awaken no grief; he who forces himself to be angry, though he may appear fierce, will arouse no awe; he who forces himself to be affectionate, though he may smile, will create no air of harmony. True sadness need make no sound to awaken grief; true anger need not burst out to arouse awe; true affection need not smile to create harmony. When a man has the Truth within himself, his spirit may move external things. That is why the Truth is to be valued. When applied to human affairs it will enable one to serve one's parents with love and filial piety; to serve the ruler with loyalty and integrity; to be merry and joyful while drinking; to be sad and grievous while mourning . . . In providing comfort to parents, one does not question the means to be employed. In seeking merriment in drinking, one does not fuss over what wares are to be used. In expressing grief in mourning, one does not quibble over the exact ritual to be followed. Rites are something created by the vulgar men; Truth is what one receives from Heaven. It is natural and cannot be changed. Therefore the sage takes Heaven as his model and values the Truth, and does not allow himself to be constrained by vulgar rules. The stupid man does the opposite of this. He is unable to follow the way of Heaven and instead frets over human concerns. He does not know enough to prize the Truth but, instead, plodding along with the crowd, he allows himself to be changed by vulgar ways,

and so is never content. Alas, that you fell into the slough of human hypocrisy at such an early age, and have been so late in hearing of the Great Way!" (Chapter 31, "Yu-fu" pp. 446–7)

(3) Some contradict nature and are thus harmful to people

[59] The potter says, "I am good at handling clay, making pots perfectly round with the compass or perfectly square with the T-square." The carpenter says, "I am good at handling wood, making it perfectly arched with a curve or straight with a stretched string." But how is it possible that the clay and the wood by their inborn nature wished to be subjected to the compass, the T-square, the curve or the stretched string? (Chapter 9, "Ma-ti" p. 150)

[60] If we have to use curve, stretched string, compass, or square to make something right, it means we are to cut its inborn nature; if we have to use cords and knots, glue and lacquer to make something firm, it means we are to violate its natural character. So the crouching and bending for the performance of rites and music, the smiles and beaming looks for showing benevolence and rightness with the intention to comfort the hearts of the world, in fact, destroy their normal conditions. The world has its normal conditions. The normal conditions is this: things are arched not by the use of the curve, straight not by the use of the stretched string, rounded not by compasses, squared not by T-squares, joined not by glue and lacquer, bound not by ropes and strings. Thus, all things in the world naturally live but do not know how they happen to live; all things similarly get what they need and do not know how they happen to get it. This principle has been the same in the past as well as at the present. Nothing can do injury to it. So what is the use of having benevolence and rightness to intrude between the Way and the Virtue like glue and lacquer, ropes and strings? They only make the world confused! (Chapter 8, "Pian-mu" pp. 144–5)

(3) Some can be easily abused and become harmful to society

[61] A follower of Robber Zhi asked him, "Does the thief too have a Way?" Zhi replied, "How could he get anywhere if he didn't have a Way? Making shrewd guesses as to how much booty is stashed away in the room is intelligence; being the first one to break in is bravery; being the last one to get out is rightness; knowing whether the job can be pulled off or not is wisdom; dividing up the loot fairly is benevolence. No one in the world ever succeeded in becoming a great thief if he didn't have all five!" From this we can see that, without the Way of the sage, a good person cannot establish himself; without the Way of the sage, Robber Zhi could not have succeeded in his profession. (Chapter 10, "Qu-qie" pp. 156–7)

[62] To guard against a thief who is to break open and ransack trunks, bags, and boxes, one must bind them with cords and ropes and make them fast with locks and hasps. This is what the ordinary world calls wisdom. But, if a great robber comes along, he will shoulder the boxes, hoist up the trunks, sling the bags over his back, and dash off, only worrying that the cords and ropes, the locks and

hasps are not fastened tightly enough. In that case, the man who earlier was called wise was, in fact, only hoarding goods for the benefit of a great robber. Thus, is it not true that what the ordinary world calls a wise man is, in fact, someone who hoard things for the benefit of a great robber? And to pursue this argument further, are there any of those the world calls wise persons who do not hoard for great robbers? Are there any of those the world calls sages who do not stand guard for the benefit of great robbers? How do I know this is so? Formerly in the state of Qi, there were neighbouring towns within sight of each other where the cries of the dogs and chickens of one could be heard in another. The area where the people spread their nets and seines, and ploughed and cultivated the earth, measured over 2,000 *li* square. Did not those who presided over this land within its four borders, established ancestral temples and altars, and governed its towns and villages abide by the laws of the sages? Yes, but one day, Tian Chengzi murdered the ruler of Qi and stole his state. And it was not only the state he stole. Along with it, he also stole the laws which the wisdom of the sages had devised. Thus, though Tian Chengzi had the name of thief and bandit, he was able to rest as peacefully as a Yao or a Shun. The smaller states did not dare condemn him, the larger states did not dare to attack, and thus he gained control of the state of Qi. . . . Is this not a case where he stole the state of Qi together with its sagacious and wise laws for the safeguarding of a thief and a bandit? (Chapter 10, "Qu-qie" pp. 154–6)

(H) Enforcement of man-made rules

(1) Giving orders

[63] Jianwu went to see the madman, Jieyu. Jieyu said, "What was Zhongshi telling you the other day?" Jianwu said, "He told me that the ruler of men should, according to his own judgement, promulgate principles, standards, ceremonies, and regulations. Who would dare not to obey and be transformed?" The madman Jieyu said, "This is fraudulent! To try to govern the world like this is like trying to walk on the ocean, to drill a hole in a river, or to make a mosquito shoulder a mountain! When the sage governs, does he govern what is on the outside? He makes himself right first, and then he acts. He makes certain that things can do what they are supposed to do, that is all. The bird flies high in the sky to escape the danger of stringed arrows. The field mouse burrows deep down under the sacred hall to avoid the worry of being dug up or smoked out. Have people got less sense than these two creatures?" (Chapter 7, "Ying-di-wang" pp. 131–2)

(2) Using benevolence and love

[64] In ancient times the Yellow Emperor first used benevolence and rightness to meddle with people's minds. Yao and Shun followed him and worked till there was no more muscle on their thighs, no more hair on their shins, trying to nourish the people of the world. They grieved their five vital organs in the practice of benevolence and rightness, exhausted their blood and breath in the

establishment of laws and standards. But there were still some people they could not win over, and so they had to exile Huandou to Mount Chong, cast the Sanmiao tribes to the region of Sanwei, and banish Gonggong to Youdu. This shows that they did not win over the world. By the time the kings of the Three Dynasties appeared, the world was in great consternation. On the lowest level there were men like the tyrant Jie and Robber Zhi, on the highest, men like Zeng and Shi, and the Ruists and Mohists rose up all around. Then those in joy and those in anger suspected one another; the stupid and the clever cheated one another; those who approve and those who object refuted one another; those sceptical and those credulous ridiculed one another; and the world sank into a decline. There was no more unity to the Great Virtue, and the inborn nature shattered and fell apart. The world coveted knowledge and the common people were thrown into turmoil. Then there were axes and saws [penal instruments] to control them, ink and stretched string [rites and laws] to trim them, mallets and gouges [corporal punishments] to maim them, and the world fell into great disorder. The guilt lay in this meddling with people's minds. As a result, worthy men crouched in hiding below the great mountains and yawning cliffs, and the lords of ten thousand chariots fretted and trembled above in their courts and halls. In the world today, the victims of the death penalty lie heaped together; the bearers of cangues tread on each other's heels; and the sufferers of punishment are never out of each other's sight. And now come the Ruists and Mohists, waving their arms, striding into the very midst of the fettered and manacled people. Alas! that they should go this far, that they should be so brazen, so lacking in any sense of shame! I am unsure that "sagely wisdom" is not in fact the wedge that fastens the cangue, that "benevolence and righteousness" are not in fact the loop and lock of these fetters and manacles! How do I know that Zeng and Shi are not the whistling arrows that signal the approach of Jie and Zhi? Therefore, I say, cut off sagacity, cast away wisdom, and the world will be in perfect order." (Chapter 11, "Zai-you" pp. 169–72)

[65] Lao Dan asked Confucius, "Please, what do you mean by benevolence and righteousness?" Confucius said, "To have peace and be joyous in heart, to embrace universal love and to be without partisanship. This is the essence of benevolence and rightness." Lao Dan said, "Hmm, but the last part is questionable. 'Universal love' is a rather nebulous ideal, isn't it? And to be without partisanship is already a kind of partisanship. Do you want to keep the world from losing its direction? Then you should know heaven and earth always have their constant ways, the sun and moon their brightness, the stars their ranks, the birds and beasts their flocks, the trees and shrubs their stands. You have only to go along with Virtue in your actions, to follow the Way in your journey, and already you will be there. Why exert yourself upholding benevolence and righteousness, as though you were beating a drum and searching for a lost child? Alas, you are bringing confusion to people's nature!" (Chapter 13, "Tian-dao" pp. 213–14)

[66] Confucius went to see Lao Dan to talk about benevolence and rightness. Lao Dan said, "When one winnows rice, its chaff blurs one's eyesight and, in

his eyes, the heaven and earth and the four directions seem to have shifted their place. When mosquitoes or horseflies sting one's skin one cannot sleep for the whole night. Benevolence and righteousness are like poisons that damage people's minds, causing the greatest confusion. If you can prevent the world from losing its simplicity, you can also move with the prevailing wind and hold your virtue and stand firm. Why do you have to strenuously holding up benevolence and rightness as if carrying and beating a big drum in search of a lost child? The crane does not take a daily bath to stay white, the crow does not daily dye itself to stay black. Black and white in their simplicity offer no grounds for argument, fame and praise in their appearance provide no basis for pride. When the springs dry up and fish are left stranded on the ground, they spew each other with moisture and wet each other down with saliva. But it would not be as good as in the case where they could forget each other in the rivers and lakes." (Chapter 14, "Tian-yun" pp. 230–1)

(3) Resorting to rewards and punishments

[67] In the past when Yao governed the world, he made it elated, and people let their nature indulge in merriments, and they had no calmness. When Jie governed the world, he made it weary, and people's nature suffered in hardship, and they had no joy. To have no calmness and no joy is to go against Virtue, and there has never been anyone in the world who could go against Virtue and survive for long. When people are exceedingly merry they will do damage to the *yang* element. When people are exceedingly angry they will do damage to the *yin*. When both *yin* and *yang* are damaged, the four seasons will not come duly, heat and cold will fail to achieve their proper harmony, and this in turn will do harm to a person's body. It will make people lose a proper sense of joy and anger, to move abnormally, to think wildly, and to behave irrationally. Thus, the world begins to become disputatious and confrontational, and then appear the ways of Robber Zhi, Zeng, and Shi. As a result, the means of the entire world is inadequate to reward the virtuous ones, and the means of the entire world is insufficient to punish the evil ones. Huge as the world is, it cannot supply enough rewards and punishments. Since the Three Dynasties, the rulers of the world hustled and bustled in doing nothing but making rewards and punishments. How could they have the time to give peace to people's nature and life? (Chapter 11, "Zai-you" pp. 165–7)

(3) The need for a higher principle

[68] In the past Shun asked Yao, "As the Heavenly king, how do you use your mind?" Yao said, "I am not arrogant to those who have no one to appeal to, nor do I reject those in poverty. I grieve for the dead, love children and am sympathetic to women. It is on these people I use my mind." Shun said, "That is, indeed, admirable but not yet great." Yao said. "Then what should I do?" Shun asked. "When heaven is settled, the earth rests in peace, the sun and the moon shine and the four seasons move about, the day and the night take turns regularly

and the clouds move and the rain falls." Yao said, "How fussy and restless am I. Your way is to join Heaven. Mine is only to join with the people." The way of heaven and earth has been held as great since antiquity. It was commonly praised by the Yellow Emperor, Yao and Shun. So what did those who ruled the world in ancient times do? To follow the way of heaven and earth, that was all. (Ch. 13, "Tian-dao" p. 212)

(I) The way to clear up chaos and return to order

(1) To get rid of the rules and dismiss their makers

[69] Zigong travelled south to Chu and, on his way back through Jin, passing along the south bank of the Han River, he saw an old man preparing his vegetable garden for planting. The old man hollowed out a way by which he entered the well and from which he emerged, lugging a pitcher of water to irrigate the fields. Grunting and puffing, he used up a great deal of energy and produced very little result. Zigong said to him, "There is a machine which can water a hundred fields in a day, using very little strength but producing great results. Wouldn't you like one?" The gardener raised his head and looked at Zigong and asked, "How does it work?" "It is a contraption made of wood. The back end [of a pole] is heavy and the font end light, and it brings up the water as though it is pulling it out, and it is so fast that the water seems to be gushing and springing up by itself. It is called a well sweep." The gardener appeared vexed and said with a scornful laughter, "I have heard from my teacher: 'One who uses machines must be doing some clever tricks. One who does clever tricks must have a scheming heart. With a scheming heart in one's breast, one's simplicity and purity are lost. Not being pure and simple, one's mind knows no rest. One with a restless mind cannot follow the Way.' It's not that I don't know about your machine. I would be ashamed to use it!" Zigong blushed with embarrassment, looked down, and made no reply. After a while, the gardener said, "What do you do?" "I am a disciple of Kong Qiu." The gardener said, "So are you not one of those who learn broadly in order to ape the sages, who brag about their knowledge to get above the common people, who pluck the strings and sing sad songs all by themselves in hopes of buying fame in the world? If you can forget your arrogant air, let down your lofty posture, then you might be all right. Now you don't even know how to look after your own body, how do you have any time to think about looking after the world! On your way now! Don't interfere with my work!" (Chapter 12, "Tian-di" pp. 193–5)

[70] [The old fisherman said to Confucius], "Once there was a man who was afraid of his own shadow and hated his own footprints, and so he tried to get away from them by running. But the more he lifted his feet and put them down again, the more footprints he made, and no matter how fast he ran, his shadow never left him. So, thinking that he was still going too slowly, he ran faster and faster without a stop until he exhausted his strength and fell dead. He didn't understand that, by staying in the shade, he could have got rid of his shadow and, by resting in quietude, he could have put an end to his footprints. His stupidity was

extreme! Now you have scrutinised the realm of benevolence and righteousness, examined the borders of sameness and difference, observed the changes between stillness and movement, followed the rules of giving and receiving, regulated the emotions of like and dislike, harmonized the degrees of joy and anger, and yet you barely manage to escape harm. If you were diligent in cultivating yourself, careful to hold fast to the Truth, and would let others have what were theirs, you could avoid these entanglements. But now, without cultivating yourself, you make demands on others, are not you stepping outside of the Way?" (Chapter 31, "Yu-fu" p. 446)

[71] In the world good persons are few and bad people are many so, in fact, the sage brings little benefit to the world, but much harm . . . When the sage is born, the great thief appears. Criticise the sages and forgive the thieves and bandits; then the world will begin to be ordered! When the rivers become dry, the valley is empty; when the hills are flattened, the deep pool becomes filled with earth. When the sage is dead, no more great thieves will arise. The world will then be peaceful and free from problems. (Chapter 10, "Qu-qie" p. 157)

[72] Until the sage is dead, great thieves will never cease to appear. To give weight to the sage, in the hope of bringing the world to order, is actually to give more profit to Robber Zhi. Make pecks and bushels to measure things, and he will steal the pecks and bushels as well. Make scales and balances to weigh things, and he will steal the scale and balance as well. Make tallies and seals to insure trustworthiness, and he will steal the tallies and seals as well. Make benevolence and righteousness to reform people, and he will steal benevolence and righteousness as well. How do I know this is so? He who steals a belt buckle pays with his life; he who steals a state gets to be a feudal lord, and inside the doors of the feudal lords are "benevolence" and "rightness" kept. Is this not a case of stealing benevolence and rightness and the wisdom of the sages? So for those who follow the steps of the great thief, establish themselves as feudal lords, steal benevolence and rightness, and take the profits by peck and bushel, scale and balance, tally and seal, even the rewards of carriages and caps cannot induce them, even the threat of the executioner's axe cannot be deter them. Thus giving heavy profits to Robber Zhi and making him impossible to deter is all the fault of the sage! (Chapter 10, "Qu-qie" pp. 158–60)

[73] Therefore it is said, "The fish should not leave the deep water; the sharp tools of the state should not be shown to the people." The sage is the sharp tool of the world. He is not for enlightening the world. Therefore, dismiss sagacity and discard knowledge, and the great robbers will cease. Discard the jades, crush the pearls, and the petty thieves will not rise. Burn the tallies, shatter the seals, and the people will be simple and guileless. Chop up the bushels and break the scales and the people will not wrangle. Destroy the laws of the sages made for the world, and the people will then be able to participate in discussions. Confuse the six tunes, ruin the pipes and cut the strings of the lute, plug the ears of Maestro Kuang, then people of the world can retain their natural keen hearing. Eliminate designs and decorations, disperse the five colours and glue up the eyes of Li Zhu,

then the people of the world can retain their natural clear eyesight. Eliminate the curve and the stretched string and abandon the compass and the square, and fracture the fingers of Craftsman Chui, then the people of the world can retain their natural dexterity. Refute the ways of Zeng and Shi, gag the mouth of Yang and Mo, refute and reject benevolence and righteousness, and for the first time the Virtue of the world will reach the state of Transcendent Uniformity. (Chapter 10, "Qu-qie" pp. 160–1)

[74] Where people can retain their natural eyesight, the world will not be dazzled; where people can retain their natural hearing, the world will not be confused; where people can retain their natural wit, the world will not be bewildered; where people can retain their inborn virtue, the world will not be corrupted. Persons such as Zeng, Shi, Yang, Mo, Maestro Kuang, Craftsman Chui, and Li Zhu all displayed their special virtues on the outside and confounded the world. Such virtues are of no use to the right Way. (Chapter 10, "Qu-qie" pp. 161–2)

(2) To govern by inaction

[75] Tiangen was wandering on the sunny side of Yin Mountain. When he reached the banks of Liao River, he bumped into Wu-ming-ren [nameless man] and asked, saying, "Please may I ask how to rule the world?" Wu-ming-ren said, "Get lost, you stupid and lowly man! How inept is the question! I am just about to be with the Creator. And if I get bored with his company, I shall ride on the ethereal bird out beyond the six directions, wandering in the country of nothingness and staying in the vast empty field. Why do you come to disturb my mind with this talk of governing the world?" But Tiangen repeated his question. Wu-ming-ren said, "Let your mind wander in simplicity, blend your spirit with the empty, follow along with things the way they are, and make no room for personal views, then the world will be governed." (Chapter 7 "Ying-di-wang" pp. 132–3)

[76] I have heard of letting the world be, of leaving it alone; but never heard of governing the world. You let it be for fear of corrupting the inborn nature of the world; you leave it alone for fear of distracting the Virtue of the world. If the nature of the world is not corrupted and the Virtue of the world is not distracted, why should there be any governing of the world? (Chapter 11, "Zai-you" p. 165)

[77] Cui Qu asked Lao Dan, "If you do not govern the world, how can you have people's hearts settled?" Lao Dan said, "You should be careful not to meddle with a person's heart! If you disparage, it sinks low; if you praise, it flies high. Such ups and downs make a person a prisoner or a fighter, easily turning from submission to overbearing. At once he may be crude and then refined. He can be as hot as fire and cold as ice. Such change can be so fast as if, in a moment, he could move beyond the four seas. He may stay tranquilly like a pool of deep water and he may jump suddenly and reach the sky. So wild and uncontrollable is this thing – the human heart!" (Chapter 11, "Zai-you" pp. 168–9)

[78] When a great sage rules the world, he lets the minds of his people roam freely to form their own guidelines and customs, avoid harmful influences and pursue their own objectives. Since people do all these in accordance with their

inborn nature, they are not conscious of why they are doing so. In this way, what need has the sage to revere the way in which Yao and Shun taught their people and reverentially following it? He wants the people only to be in agreement with their native virtues and to repose their minds in peace. (Chapter 12, "Tian-di" p. 193)

[79] Therefore, if a Noble Man had no choice but to preside over the world, there is no better course for him than to be inactive. With inaction he can then let his nature and life be in peace. Therefore it is said, "He who values the world as he values his own body can be entrusted with the world. He who loves the world as he loves his own body can be handed the world. If a gentleman can keep from displaying his five vital organs [his intentions] and from showing off his hearing and eyesight [his knowledge] but can stay in corpse-like stillness and yet appears like a dragon [with great potential], keep the silence of deep pools and yet sounds like thunder [with great effects], then, when his spirit moves, the world follows; when he remains at leisure and inaction, the myriad things evolve like smoke in the wind. Then he will say, 'Why do I have to find time for governing the world?'" (Ch. 11, "Zai-you" p. 168)

[80] King Wen was sightseeing at Zang when he noticed an old man fishing. Yet he was not using any bait. He was not holding the fishing pole to fish for something. He just held the pole steadily. King Wen wanted to elevate him and hand over the government to him but was afraid that the high officials and the seniors in his family would be uneasy. He thought perhaps he had better forget the matter and let it rest, and yet he couldn't bear to let the people not be properly cared for [by such an extraordinary person]. At dawn the next day he reported to his ministers, saying, "Last night I dreamt I saw a fine man with dark complexion and beard, mounted on a dappled horse that had a red hoof. He commanded me, saying, 'Hand over your rule to the old man of Zang, then perhaps the ills of the people may be cured!'" The ministers, awestruck, said, "It was the late king, your father!" King Wen said, "Then perhaps we should divine to see what ought to be done." The ministers said, "It is the command of your late father. Your Majesty must not have second thoughts. What need is there for divination?" So the old man of Zang was escorted to the capital and handed the government. The existing laws and precedents remained unchanged, and no skewed orders were issued. After the end of three years, King Wen made an inspection tour of the state and found that the local notables had dismissed their leaders and disbanded their cliques, that the heads of government bureaux did not display any special achievements of their own, and that persons entering the four borders from other states no longer dared to bring their own measuring cups and bushels with them. The local notables had dismissed their leaders and disbanded their cliques because they had learned to identify with their superiors. The heads of government bureaux displayed no special achievements of their own because they worked together with all concerned. Persons entering the four borders from other states no longer dared to bring their own measuring cups and bushels with them because other feudal lords had ceased to distrust the local measures.

Thereupon, King Wen exalted the old man as Grand Master and, facing north, asked him, "Can your governance be extended to the world?" The old man from Zang looked blandly, made no response, and unceremoniously departed. In the morning he was conducting government business, in the night he escaped, and for the rest of his life nothing was ever heard about him. (Chapter 21, "Tian Zifang" pp. 314–15)

[81] Those who know do not speak; those who speak do not know. Therefore, the sage practises the teaching that has no words. The Way cannot be reached; the Virtue cannot be forced to come . . . So it is said, "He who practises the Way does less every day. Doing less and less he arrives at the point where he does nothing. Doing nothing he has nothing that he does not do." Now we have been doing all kinds of things and want to return to the roots [the Way]. Wouldn't it be difficult? Perhaps only a truly great man can find it easy. (Ch. 22, "Zhi-bei-you" pp. 319–20)

(J) Social relationships

(1) Relationships between individuals

[82] When Confucius was besieged between the states Chen and Cai by mobs [mistaking him to be Yang Huo, a man who looked like him, and did them harm before]. For seven days he did not have cooked food. Taigong Ren went to express his sympathy, saying, "You almost perished?" Confucius said, "That is right." "You hate to die?" "Yes." Then Ren said, "Let me tell you the way not to perish. In the East Sea there is bird whose name is Yidai. It flutters about slowly, seemingly listless. It flies in a group and rests in a flock. In advancing, it dares not be in the lead, when withdrawing it dares not be at the rear. In eating, it dares not take the first bite; it picks only the leftovers. So, when it flies with other birds in a file, they do not push it aside, and outsiders never get to harm it. This is how it avoided disasters. The tree with straight trunks is the first to be cut down; the well with sweet water is the first to be drawn dry. You intend to demonstrate your knowledge to astound the ignorant and improve yourself to throw light on the defective, going around as if carrying the sun and the moon on your shoulder. That is why you were unable to avoid the calamity. I have heard from a man of great accomplishment saying, 'He who brags will have no success, if he had succeeded he will fall, if he were famous his name will be decimated.' Who can abandon success and fame and return to join the masses? If a person can make his way prevail and not claim success, make his virtue popular and not claim fame, remain simple and ordinary just like the ignorant, wipe away the traces of his deeds and discard his position and not work for achievements and reputation, he will make no demands on others, and others will make no demands on him. An ultimate man is unknown to others. Why do you love to be recognised?" Confucius said, "Good!" and then excused himself from his acquaintances and left his disciples and fled into a great swamp. There he wore animal fur and coarse cloth, ate nuts, walked among the beasts without scaring the herd, mixed with

the birds without alarming the flock. If even birds and beasts did not dislike him, how could humans do? (Chapter 20, "Shan-mu" pp. 297–9)

[83] Confucius asked Zi Sanghu, "I was twice driven out of Lu. People of Song cut down the tree under which I stayed. My traces in Wei were wiped out. My ventures in Shang and Zhou were fruitless, and I was besieged between Chen and Cai. I suffered these disasters and my relatives and associates have drifted further and further away from me, and more and more of my disciples have left me. Why?" Zi Sanghu said, ". . . [They were close to you because of profit.] People joined by profits break apart when pressed by loss and poverty, misfortune and disaster . . . Thus, the friendship of noble persons is plain like water; the friendship of petty men is as sweet as wine. Noble persons can stay close because their relationship is plain and incorruptible; petty men break apart because their relationship is sweet and easily becomes sour." Confucius said, "Respectfully I have heard your instruction." Then he slowly and calmly walked home, stopped his studies and discarded his books. His disciples no longer bow before him and yet loved him even more than before. (Chapter 20, "Shan-mu" pp. 299–300)

(2) Relationship between the ruler and the people

(A) HOW THE RULER IS TO TREAT THE PEOPLE: HAVE SELF RESTRAINT, BE CAREFUL AND CONSIDERATE

[84] A true sovereign's work is based on Virtue and completed in accordance with the Way of Heaven. Therefore it is said that sovereigns of great antiquity ruled the world through inaction, merely observing the virtue of Heaven and nothing more . . . Therefore, it is said that, in ancient times, those who cared for the world were without desire, and the world was satisfied; without action and the myriad things were transformed; being calm and silent and the people were at rest. The Record says: "Be with the One and the myriad tasks will be accomplished; get rid of desires and gods and spirits will bow in respect." (Chapter 12, "Tian-di" pp. 181–2)

[85] The border guard of Changwu said to Zilao, "When running the government you must not be haphazard; in ordering the people you must not be careless. In the past I used to grow grain. I ploughed in a haphazard way and got a haphazard crop in return. I weeded in a careless way and got a poor crop in return. The following year I changed my methods, ploughing deeper than before and raking with great care – the grain grew thick and luxuriant, and I had all I wanted to eat for the whole year!" (Chapter 25, "Ze-yang" p. 387)

[86] In ancient times, the rulers attributed what success they had to the people and what failure they had to themselves, attributed what was right to the people and what was wrong to themselves. Therefore, if there was something wrong with a single person, they would retire and take the blame upon themselves. Now it is different. They make things obscure and then blame people for not understanding; they enlarge the difficulties and then punish people for not have the courage to tackle them; they pile on responsibilities and then penalise people

for not being able to fulfil them; they make the journey longer and then chastise people for not reaching the end of it. When their knowledge and strength are exhausted, the people will go on with pretence. When the ruler puts out false pretence day by day, how could the people not resort to pretence? When strength is insufficient people will pretend; when knowledge is insufficient people cheat; when goods are insufficient people steal; when theft and robbery are widespread, who should be blamed? (Chapter 25, "Ze-yang" pp. 389–90)

(B) How the people are to treat the ruler

(i) Do not covet rewards and lose freedom and integrity

[87] Long ago, when the Zhou Dynasty first came to power, there were two gentlemen who lived in Guzhu named Boyi and Shuqi. They said to each other, "We hear that in the western region there is a man who seems to possess the Way. Let us try going to take a look at him." When they reached the sunny side of Mount Qi, King Wu, hearing of them, sent his younger brother Dan to meet them. He offered to draw up a pact with them, saying, "You will be granted emoluments of the second order and offices of the first rank, and the pact will be sealed in animal blood and buried." The two men looked at each other and laughed, saying, "Hah – how peculiar! This is certainly not what we would call the Way! In ancient times, when Shennong held possession of the empire, he performed the seasonal sacrifices with the utmost reverence but he did not pray for blessings. In his dealings with men, he was loyal and trustworthy and observed perfect order but he did not seek anything from them. He delighted in ruling for the sake of ruling, he delighted in bringing order for the sake of order. He did not use other men's failures to bring about his own success; he did not use other men's degradation to lift himself up. Just because he happened along at a lucky time, he did not try to turn it to his own profit. Now the Zhou, observing that the Yin has fallen into disorder, suddenly wants to govern the world, emphasising schemes, handing out bribes, relying on weapons to maintain its might, offering sacrifices and drawing up pacts to impress men with its good faith, lauding its achievements in order to please the masses, killing and conquering in order to seize profits. This is simply to push aside disorder and replace it with violence! We have heard that the gentlemen of old, if they happened upon a well-ordered age, did not run away from public office but, if they encountered an age of disorder, they did not try to hold on to life at any cost. Now the world is in darkness and the virtue of the Zhou in decline. Rather than remain together with the Zhou and defile ourselves, it would be better to run away and thus protect the purity of our conduct!" The two gentlemen thereupon went north as far as Mount Shouyang, where they eventually died of starvation. (Chapter 28, "Rang-wang" pp. 425–6)

[88] A man of the state of Song, named Cao Shang, was sent by his king as envoy to the state of Qin. On his departure, he was assigned a few carriages. The king of Qin liked him and bestowed on him an additional hundred carriages. When he returned to Song, he went to see Zhuangzi and said, "Living in a poor

neighbourhood of cramped alleyways, oppressed by poverty, weaving one's own sandals, with withered neck and sallow face, is what I'm no good at. But winning instant recognition from the ruler of a state of ten thousand chariots and returning with a hundred carriages in one's retinue is what I excel at!" Zhuangzi said, "When the king of Qin falls ill, he calls for his doctors. The doctor who lances a boil or drains an abscess receives one carriage in payment but the one who licks his piles for him gets five carriages. The lower down the area is to be treated, the larger the number of carriages. Is it possible that you treated his piles? Otherwise why did you receive so many carriages? Get out!" (Chapter 32, "Lie Yu-kou" p. 454)

[89] When King Zhao of Chu lost control of his state, the sheep butcher Yue fled and followed King Zhao into exile. When King Zhao regained control of the state, he set about rewarding his followers but, when it came the turn of the sheep butcher Yue, Yue said, "When His Majesty lost control of the state, I lost my job as sheep butcher. Now His Majesty has regained the state, and I have also got back my job butchering sheep. So my 'title and emolument' have already been restored to me. Why should there be any talk of a reward?" "Force him to take it!" ordered the king. But the sheep butcher Yue said, "The fact that His Majesty lost the kingdom was no fault of mine, therefore I would not venture to accept any punishment for it. And the fact that His Majesty has regained the kingdom is no accomplishment of mine, therefore I would not venture to accept any reward for it." "Bring him to see me!" ordered the king. But the sheep butcher Yue said, "According to the laws of the state of Chu, a man may be granted an audience with the ruler only when he was to receive weighty awards for great accomplishments. Now I was not wise enough to save the state, nor brave enough to die in combat against the invaders. When the armies of Wu entered the city of Ying, fearful of the dangers ahead, I escaped from the invaders. I did not purposely follow after His Majesty. Now His Majesty wishes to disregard the laws and break the precedents by granting me an audience. But this is not how I am to win a reputation in the world!" The king said to Ziqi, his minister of war, "The sheep butcher Yue is a man of mean and humble position, and yet his pronouncements on rightness are lofty indeed! I want you to promote him to one of the 'three-banner' offices." When told of this, the sheep butcher Yue said, "I am fully aware that the 'three-banner' rank is a far more exalted place than a sheep butcher's stall, and that the emolument of 10,000 *Zhong* of grain is more wealth than I will ever acquire slaughtering sheep. But how could I, merely out of greed for title and emolument, allow my ruler to gain a reputation for irresponsibly handing out such favours? I dare not accept. Please let me go back to my sheep butcher's stall." And, in the end, he refused to accept the position. (Chapter 28, "Rang-wang" p. 419)

(ii) Do not succumb to pressure and live in disgrace

[90] Shun wanted to cede the empire to his friend, a man from the north named Wuze. Wuze said, "What a peculiar man this ruler is! Initially he lived in the fields and ditches, and then he wandered inside the gates of Yao's palace. Not

content to let it rest at that, he now wants to use what he got by his disgraceful doings to defile me. I would be ashamed even to see him!" Thereupon he threw himself into the Clear-and-Cold Abyss. Having overthrown Jie, Tang offered to cede the throne to Bian Sui. Bian Sui refused, saying, "When he was plotting to attack Jie, he came to me for advice, so he must have thought I was capable of treason. Now he has defeated Jie and wants to cede the throne to me, so he must think I am avaricious. I was born into this world of disorder, and this unprincipled man repeatedly came and tried to defile me with his disgraceful doings! I can't bear to go on listening to such proposals again and again!" Thereupon he threw himself in the Chou River and drowned. Tang then tried to cede the throne to Wu Guang, saying, "The wise man plans, the military man completes the task, and the benevolent man presides over the government. That has been the way since antiquity. Now why will you not accept the position?" Wu Guang declined, saying, "To depose your sovereign is no act of rightness; to slaughter the people is no act of benevolence. To enjoy the benefits after others have overcome the difficulties is no act of integrity. I have heard it said, 'If the man is without rightness, do not accept his awards; if the world is without the Way, do not tread its soil.' And you expect me to accept such a position of honour? I can't bear the sight of you any longer!" Thereupon he loaded a stone on to his back and drowned himself in the Lu River. (Chapter 28, "Rang-wang" p. 424)

(iii) Appear useless and preserve life

[91] Carpenter Shi went to Qi and, when he got to Quyuan, he saw an oak tree worshipped by the local people as the earth god. It was broad enough to shelter several thousand oxen and measured 100 spans around, towering above the hills. After soaring up to 70 feet, its branches began to spread out, among them more than ten could be made into boats. There were so many sightseers that the place looked like a fair, but the carpenter didn't even glance around and went on his way without stopping. His apprentice stood staring for a long time and then ran after Carpenter Shih and said, "Since I first took up my axe and followed you, Master, I have never seen timber as beautiful as this. But you don't even bother to look, and go right on without stopping. Why is that?" "Forget it, say no more!" said the carpenter. "It's a worthless tree! Make boats out of it and they'd sink; make coffins and they'd rot in no time; make vessels and they'd break at once. Use it for doors and it would sweat sap; use it for posts and the worms would eat them up. It's not a timber tree, there's nothing it can be used for. That's how it got to be that old!" (Chapter 4, "Ren-jian-shi" pp. 77–8)

[92] Zhi-li-shu was a cripple with chin stuck down to his navel, shoulders pushed up above his head, his pigtail pointed at the sky, his five organs placed at the top inside his torso, his two thighs pressed against his ribs. By sewing and laundering, he got enough to fill his mouth; by handling a winnow and sifting out the good grain, he made enough to feed ten people. When the authorities called out the troops, he loitered wobbling among them; when they ordered a great work, he was spared the corvée because of his permanent disability. But when they doled

out grain to the ailing, he got three big measures and ten bundles of firewood. With a crippled body, he was nevertheless able to look after himself and finish out the years Heaven gave him. How much better, then, than if someone had crippled virtue! (Chapter 4, "Ren-jian-shi" pp. 82–3)

[93] The mountain trees are liable to be felled, the fat is liable to be burned. The cinnamon is edible and so it gets cut down; the lacquer tree can be used and so it gets sliced apart. All men know the use of the useful; nobody knows the use of the useless! (Chapter 4, "Ren-jian-shi" p. 85)

(K) Human life and objective

[94] Humans living between the heaven and the earth are like passing by a white colt seen through a crack in the wall. The event lasts only an instant. In this moment all things emerge, sprouting and growing, and then in silence they slide and slip into oblivion. They transformed into life and then into death. All living things grieve over this change and humans mourn it. But death is actually a relief from confinements, like untying the Heaven-made bow bag and cracking open the Heaven-made sword case. After the spirit is freed like smoke, the body follows. This is the great returning. (Chapter 22, "Zhi-bei-you" pp. 325–6)

[95] To be deliberate in thought, lofty in action, aloof from the world, different from convention, indulgent in high-sounding talks and be critical, all for the purpose of appearing superior, is what is liked by the gentlemen of the mountains and valleys and those who disapprove of the world and prefer to be starved and drown in deep pools. To discourse in benevolence, rightness, loyalty, and trust, and to be deferential, frugal, modest, and yielding, all for the purpose of cultivating one's virtue, is what is liked by the gentlemen of the world in order to educate people and engage them in studies. To talk about great accomplishments, establish great fame, make the ruler and the officials behave according to the rites, and to rectify the action of the superior and the inferior, all for the purpose of good governance, is what is liked by gentlemen of the court who honour the ruler and strengthen the state, strive for achievements and acquisition of territory. To repair the thickets and ponds, live in idleness and remain unoccupied, all for the purpose of being inactive, is what is liked by gentlemen of the rivers and seas who withdraw from the world and pursue leisure. To pant, puff, breath, exhale the old, inhale the new, stretch the neck like a bear, extend the legs like a bird, all for the purpose of attaining longevity, is what is liked by gentlemen who practise the art of health to nourish the body, like Pengzu and others who enjoyed extraordinary old age. Then there are those who do not deliberately appear to be high minded, who cultivate their virtue without practising benevolence and righteousness, who help govern without accomplishments and fame, who are at ease without living on rivers and seas, who are long living without practising healthy living. It is because they have nothing that they cannot forget and, as a result, there is nothing they do not have. They are calm and with few desires and yet all that is beautiful comes to them. This is the great Way of Heaven and earth. This is the perfect virtue of the sage. (Chapter 15, "Ke-yi" pp. 237–8)

[96] Is there or is there not perfect happiness in the world? Is there or is there not some way to make living worthwhile? What is one to do, what is one to rely on, what to avoid, what to stick to, what to approach, what to keep away, what to enjoy, what to hate? What the world honours are wealth, eminence, longevity and fame. What the world likes are comfortable living, rich food, pretty clothes, beautiful sights and charming music; what it dislikes are poverty, low status, premature death and a bad name; what the world is bitter about are no rest for the body, no rich food for the mouth, no pretty clothes for the figure, no beautiful sights for the eye, no charming sound for the ear. Those who do not have what they want become greatly worried and fearful. To treat oneself like this is, indeed, stupid. (Chapter 18, "Zhi-le" pp. 268–9)

[97] He who comprehends the essence of life does not work on what is unnecessary. He who comprehends the essence of fate does not work on what is inevitable. To nourish the body it is necessary to resort to goods. But there are those who have more than enough goods and yet are unable to nourish their bodies. To have life it is necessary not to leave the body unattended. But there are those who do not leave their bodies unattended and yet lose their lives. When life comes it cannot be declined, when it leaves it cannot be stopped. Sadly, people of the world believe that to have their bodies nourished they can keep their lives. If nourishing the body is not enough to preserve life what is the world to do? Though a person knows that something is not worth doing and yet feels obliged to do it, his work is useless. If he wants to avoid doing useless work for his body, he can do no better than abandoning the world. When he abandons the world he will have no burdens. When he has no burdens he can be straight and balanced. When he is straight and balanced his life will be renewed along with everything. (Chapter 19, "Da-sheng" pp. 277–8)

[98] Tian Zifang waited on Lord Wen of Wei and, on numerous occasions, praised Dong-guo shunzi . . . saying that, as a person, he was true and, though he looked like others, he was free from prejudices and kept being true. (Chapter 21, "Tian Zifang " p. 306)

[99] What is meant by "the True Man"? The True Man of ancient times did not know to love life and did not know to hate death. He came into this world without delight and left it without resistance. He came and left naturally, that was all. He did not forget how he began and he did not try to find out how he was to end. He accepted what came to him gladly but forgot about it and gave it back readily. This means that he did not use his mind to harm the Way and did not make man help out Heaven [nature]. Such a man is called the True Man. (Chapter 6, "Da-zong-shi" pp. 103–4)

[100] One who does not take anything very close and does not keep anything very distant, who holds his own virtue and yet goes along with the world, is called a True Man . . . The True Man of ancient times treated people according to the natural ways of Heaven but did not let people interfere with the Heaven's ways. Such a man was the True Man of ancient times. (Chapter 24, "Xu Wu-gui" pp. 374–5)

[101] External punishments are administered by implements of metal and wood; internal punishments are caused by overaction and by regretting mistakes. When a man incurs external punishments he suffers under the implements of metal and wood; when a man incurs internal punishments he is consumed by the fight between *yin* and *yang* [right and wrong]. Only the True Man is capable of avoiding both the external and the internal punishments. (Chapter 32, "Lie Yu-kou" p. 456)
[102] The True Man of ancient times . . . could climb up to high places without being frightened, merge in water without getting wet, and enter into fire without getting burned. (Chapter 6, "Da-zong-shi" pp. 102–3)
[103] A man of perfect virtue will not be burned by fire, drowned by water, harmed by cold and heat, injured by birds and beasts. I am not saying that such results will not happen when he is actually in close contact with those things. I am saying that he is clear about what is safe or dangerous, calm about fortune and misfortune, and careful about approaching or keeping away. Consequently, none of those things can hurt him. (Chapter 17, "Qiu-shui" pp. 259–60)

Zhuang-zi 莊子

PART 2
INTERPRETATION

What interests we humans most are, naturally, human problems – physical, psychological, social, environmental and so on. Most ancient Chinese thinkers were engrossed in social problems concerning a person's relationship with his fellows. Little of their attention was paid to other things. They were anthropocentric. They thought everything, including a superbeing, existed for humans, and they thought that for all human problems there was a human solution or, more specifically, a societal solution – a solution that could be devised and carried out by an organised society.

The biggest problems for humans are how to meet their physical and psychological needs, develop their talents, realise their aspirations, live in peace with others, and help society reach its goals. Confucius recognised all these problems and recommended self-cultivation and a hierarchical social structure where people would have mutual obligations and behave according to a set of time-honoured rules of propriety. Mozi did not think much about the individual. He wanted a more tightly organised society where people were like automatons sharing the values of a supreme ruler, obeying his orders and striving for his objectives, all in the hope that chaos and misery could thus be avoided, and individual well-being achieved as part of the general well-being of society as a whole. Laozi seemed to oppose this view but, in fact, wanted a sage to lead people back to a small, self-sufficient society where they would live a simple life, under the watchful eye of that sage.

These societal solutions to human problems share two crucial presumptions and leave one important question unanswered. The first presumption is that all humans have something in common. It can be called human nature or by some other name. In any case, it is supposed to be very basic to being human. The second presumption is that this basic human quality is capable of being changed.

The three thinkers whom we've discussed so far did not have the same degree of belief in these presumptions. Confucius believed that humans do have a common nature, or at least a similar one, when they are young, though it may become different in each person when he grows up, as a result of his education and experience. This is why Confucius saw great promise in education for solving human problems. But he also thought that there is a limit. Human beings are unique because of a special characteristic which may be called humanness. You can change a person only to a certain degree. Beyond that, his humanness will be destroyed.

Laozi did not say much about human nature but, in the description of his utopia, we can clearly see that he implicitly recognised that a human has an innate good nature which makes communal life possible. Unfortunately, this precious nature was corrupted by false sages but, if the corrupting influence is removed, the good nature can be restored.

Mozi did not believe that a human has a good nature but he seemed to think that humans are infinitely malleable. Thus, he advocated standardisation of people's behaviour and thought.

To realize their solutions to human problems, all three thinkers stated that they would need sages as rulers. Now, even if we do not ask where sages would come from, how they would carry out their missions, and what would happen to the people if a sage-ruler overstepped his authority, we cannot avoid this question: is this the way individuals should live in a society – more or less like sheep in a herd being led by a shepherd? None of the three thinkers answered this question. They did not even ask it. It was raised and answered by Zhuang Zhou.

Zhuang Zhou 莊周 (365–290 BCE), respectfully called Zhuangzi, was once a minor official of the state of Song who lived in poverty but refused high offices offered by the state of Chu.[1] Not known for having many disciples, he probably wrote down his own thoughts in a volume, *Zhuangzi*, though some parts of it were obviously written by others.[2]

By Zhuangzi's time, more than a century-and-a-half after that of Confucius, and a century after Mozi, the world had fallen into greater disorder. More people franticly tried to change the situation, and Zhuangzi was one of them. His work was a reaction to the prevailing theories and practices of the Ruists and the Mohists and, to a lesser degree, an endorsement of the ideals of Laozi. Its main theme was to emphasise the importance of nature, both human and cosmic, and therefore to refute the efforts of humans to change nature. More specifically, Zhuangzi condemned the efforts of organised society against individual freedom. As he saw it, society, with its authorities and norms, was itself a problem. Only when individuals were emancipated from the authorities and norms, and left completely alone, could human problems be solved and true peace and happiness realised. Probably because his views were too unconventional to be presented in conventional language, he resorts to a special narrative method, using fantastic dialogue or soliloquy or the behaviour of fictitious persons and imaginary things to argue or illustrate his points. This method freed him from common sense and strict logic, and invited his reader to forget the ordinary and think the unthinkable.

(A) Universal relativism and individual uniqueness

To begin with, Zhuangzi asks us to start looking at things from an unusual angle – a cosmic, rather than anthropocentric, one. From this angle, we see that everything appears to be unique, has a value of its own and is an end in itself. Therefore, everything is entitled to have its point of view and opinion, and all different views and opinions are relative – none is absolute, none has an inherent value greater than the other, and none is completely right or completely wrong. Thus, he pointed out, the likes and dislikes of different species are different – humans and monkeys prefer different places to live; beautiful women charm men but scare the fish and deer; the legendary bird *yuanchu* 鵷鶵 ate only the seeds of bamboo; the owl eats rotten rats; a seabird being treated like a human (fed with meat and wine and entertained with orchestral music) died in three days. So, Zhuangzi asked rhetorically, who could claim to have the right tastes? Here, of course, he was not emphasising the differences among different species; rather, he wanted to illustrate the differences among different persons, though the allegories were not strictly appropriate – a common problem for those who speak in allegories and metaphors rather than in straightforward language.

Besides tastes, all other judgements are, according to Zhuangzi, equally relative. Whether a thing is big or small, noble or mean, real or unreal depends entirely on who is looking at it and in what context or framework it is viewed. Zhuangzi told a story that, in a dream, he found himself to be a butterfly but, when awake, he found himself to be Zhuangzi, and he was unsure which had had the dream – the butterfly or Zhuangzi – and which was real. Are dream and day life, fantasy and reality relative? Are life and death also relative? If a person believes in existence after death, then, to him, life and death are not really very different but only two stages in a continuous process, like dreaming and awakening. There is no reason for such a person particularly to cherish life because, from his point of view, the existence after death might be more enjoyable. This lesson was what Zhuangzi learned from an old skull (while in a dream) which refused to regain life, and that was why he was found tapping a pottery jar and singing after his wife's death – he was happy that she was relieved from the misery of life.

The most important point that Zhuangzi wanted to make is that there can be no commonly accepted right and wrong. Everyone is partial; no one is above personal bias to make objective judgements. Moreover, in everything, there is always certain rightness, and also certain wrongness. As different people have different focuses of attention, the rightness and wrongness exist only in the eyes of the beholder. Therefore, Zhuangzi said, "The world cannot decide what is right and what is wrong."

(B) The inborn nature, its importance and protection

If right and wrong are purely subjective, is there anything that is objective for everyone? What about the "human nature" discussed by other thinkers – the characteristics that supposedly make human different from other animals? Zhuangzi did talk about this subject. According to him, human beings have a "constant inborn nature". But it is only to seek food when hungry and warmth when cold. It is, therefore, not uniquely human but, rather, common to all animals. Thus, he did not really believe in a common "human" nature. When he talked about people's "inborn nature", he was actually talking about the unique character of each individual.

This denial of a common human nature is crucial to Zhuangzi's philosophy. It explains why he thought that it was acceptable that everyone takes what agrees with his "nature" as right and rejects what disagrees with it as wrong. It also explains why he thought no one is in a position to make decisions for anyone else. In another allegory, he pointed out that the duck's legs are short and the crane's are long but, in each case, they serve their function well. Therefore, he warned, do not try to stretch or shrink them because you will maim the bird and it will not be happy. Similarly, while an eagle wants to reach the skies and travel to the end of the world, a little sparrow enjoys hopping over tall grass; while Yao wanted to rule the world, his friend Xu You 許由wished only to live a simple life like a sparrow or a mole. Can and should anyone force anyone else to do what one thinks to be the right thing?

Therefore, Zhuangzi maintained, the most important thing to a person is his unique character, or "inborn nature". All other things – wealth, honour, prestige, glory, and so on – are secondary and not worth pursuing, certainly not at great cost, such using a priceless pearl as a pellet to shoot at a sparrow 1,000 yards up in the air, and worse still, if the pursuit would damage one's own vital interests. To illustrate this point Zhuangzi told a story of the states of Han and Wei fighting over a piece of land. A man named Zihuazi 子華子 went to see Lord Zhaoxi 昭僖侯 of Han and asked him whether he would seize the empire if he were to lose a hand, and got from him a negative answer.

In another story Zhuangzi made up, the Lord of Lu was worried by problems of his state. Shinanzi 市南子, another wise man, told the lord that the state was like the beautiful fur of a fox or leopard that attracts hunters, and advised the lord to abandon the state and get lost in the wilderness and become happy with the Way.

The lesson of the first story – to seize something of relatively small value at great cost – can be readily accepted. But Zhuangzi obviously went too far with the metaphor in the second story. The fur is an inherent part of an animal's body, not something external to it which can be abandoned. And it is also not a feasible solution to the troubles of a state if its ruler simply quits. This is a problem common to thinkers who push a point to its extreme. But, to a certain extent, Zhuangzi had a good point: one should not risk one's physical well-being, moral integrity, inner peace and true happiness in pursuit of something superficial, such as social position, power and wealth, manifested in carriages and high hats and other goods, because, in the final analysis, they are peripheral and transient, attached to a person only temporarily. Unfortunately, such misguided persons who, in pursuit of things external to themselves, lose their inborn nature are legion. Zhuangzi had a name for them: *daozhi zhi min* (倒置之民 the upside-down people or people of wrongly inverted priorities).

Zhuangzi himself, needless to say, would not sacrifice so much for so little. Thus, when offered a post in the government of the state of Chu, he told the king's messenger to get out of his sight and let him be as free as an old turtle dragging its tail in the mud or a lonely calf grazing in the pasture. He was, of course, following the steps of such legendary wise men as Xu You and Zizhou Zhifu 子州支父 who both declined Yao's offer of the empire.

(C) The inborn nature and the *Way*

Besides escaping from a problem, an often unrealistic option, how is one to live happily with one's inborn nature intact? Zhuangzi suggested strict observation of the Way. All Chinese thinkers of old times talked about "the Way". Zhuangzi said it is something real, with its own body and roots. Yet it is formless and thus it can be perceived but not seen. It can be understood intuitively but not talked about in ordinary language. It has been in existence before heaven and earth, given birth to everything, and regulated the movements of everything. With it everything lives; without it everything dies. Does not this sounded like what Laozi said? Indeed, because both these thinkers used similar language of myth in describing *dao* (道 the Way), they were called the Daoists though, as we shall see, their Ways are quite different.

We may recall that the Way of Laozi is universal and external to all things. Only a true sage can "see" it. Zhuang thought the Way is intrinsic, existing in the nature of everything. Thus, he said, the Way could be found in an ant, in weeds, in tiles and shards, and in piss and shit.

Because everything has its own Way, everything follows its own Way – the skies turn round and round, and the earth stays immobile, not because something external is causing them to do so, they simply cannot but do so. And when things follow their own Ways, they act naturally with no obvious effort. Thus, to the mythical animal *kui* 夔 which had only one foot to hop around, it was a pity that a millipede had to manoeuvre a thousand feet to make a move. But, as Zhuangzi pointed out, the millipede did not have to make an effort to manoeuvre its feet; it merely puts in motion the *tianji* (天機 heavenly mechanism) built in its body, and that was easy.

(D) The world of "Perfect Virtue"

Therefore, in an ideal state which, according to Zhuangzi, existed in the past, everything was left alone, with its inborn nature unadulterated, and it behaved using its *tianji* and obedient to the rules of its inborn nature. Human beings lived in peace with the birds and beasts, and the myriad things coexisted in harmony. If there was social organisation, people would not have been aware of it. The authorities, if any, would be like high boughs, and the people would be like wild deer. They would have little to do with each other.

How did a human being in this golden past meet his basic needs? If we believe Zhuangzi, this primitive person was probably a vegetarian. He certainly did not hunt. He played with animals and evaded some of them by living in a tree house; he would climb high to watch birds in their nests but would not harm them. He ate only the grains he grew and wore only the textiles he wove. So we might say he was good-natured. But Zhuangzi would not characterise human nature as good. He thought that to label it one way or another was meaningless.

Another distinctive character of this person in Zhuangzi's utopia was innocence. We see that he was intelligent enough to plant and weave but he had no intention of developing his intelligence and acquiring more knowledge. He had few desires and no goals to strive for. He was not conscious of his activities but merely followed his nature – though he was actually upright, loving, faithful and trustworthy, he knew nothing about righteousness, benevolence, loyalty and honesty. He was aware of the activities of others but he passed no judgements. Indeed, he did not see things as good or bad, right or wrong. He had no arbitrary standards and knew no social norms.

A person like this, according to Zhuangzi, was happy. Life was simple but carefree; death was not feared but considered as another phase in an endless cycle.

(E) The fall of the *Way*

Unfortunately, this paradise did not last for long. The situation, according to Zhuangzi, began to deteriorate when people accumulated knowledge. According to him, people in great antiquity had no knowledge and lived carelessly and happily together with everything in the world. In his utopia people had some rudimentary skills to grow food and make clothing. But then someone with more know-how came and taught people to make gadgets and contrivances which were to save labour and make life easier. He did not explain why someone saw the necessity of making life easier or how that person acquired the know-how to make the gadgets and contrivances. He just said that it happened, and to illustrate this occurrence, he told a story of an imaginary encounter between an old man who, through a trench, carried water from a deep well to irrigate his fields, and Zigong 子貢, a disciple of Confucius, who tried to convince the old man about the utility of a device called *gao* (槔 well-sweep), which was designed to save time and energy in bringing water from a well and thus to help increase productivity. Apparently, Zigong did not invent the device; he simply spread the knowledge of it. The old man did not dispute the utility of the device and thus implicitly admitted that his own work was hard. But he pointed out something that had escaped Zigong's attention: those who have *jixie* (機械 gadgets) will do *jishi* (機事 clever things); those who do clever things must have *jixin* (機心 scheming hearts); those who have scheming hearts are no longer innocent and have no peace of mind. Therefore the old man said that he had heard about the well-sweep before but decided to avoid it and stick to his simple, albeit hard, way of life rather than be sucked into a spiral of wanting to have ever more gadgets, and engaging in endless pursuit of schemes.

In addition, Zhuangzi gave many more examples of why the Way fell – the myriad things lost their inborn nature: the horse trainer Bole 伯樂 tortured horses to turn them into draught animals; the ancient sage rulers made people into competitors, rivals, rebels, sophists, thieves and robbers. In all cases, it was because the culprits used their knowledge, specifically the petty knowledge of making gadgets and rules.

On this point Zhuangzi agreed with Laozi and both believed that there was a different kind of knowledge – in Laozi's case the knowledge of the Way; in Zhuangzi's case the knowledge of the Ways. They also differed on how one can gain that knowledge. Laozi said a true sage could know the Way of Heaven without leaving his room. Zhuangzi did not think one can easily know the Ways. More definitely, he thought no one could learn them from another person because they could not be expressed in any language. Thus, in the chapter entitled *Zhi-bei-you* (知北遊 Knowledge wandered north) in *Zhuangzi*, he said that Huangdi (黃帝 The Yellow Emperor) who answered the question raised by the fictitious figure Zhi about how to know the Way, did not know the Ways; another fictitious figure, Kuang-qu (狂屈 the wild but witless one), who thought he knew but forgot what he could say, probably knew something about the Ways; only the third one, Wu-wei-wei (無為謂 the one with nothing to do and nothing to say), who did not give any answer, really knew the Ways. According to Zhuangzi, heaven, earth, and the myriad things between all have their Ways but will not reveal them. Only a great sage, who carefully observes everything between heaven and earth, is able to perceive the Ways of things – their different inborn natures.

(F) The rule makers

It is not easy to perceive the various Ways of the myriad things. Even the ancient rulers – *San Huang* (三皇 Three Sovereigns) and *Wu Di* (五帝 the Five Emperors) – were incapable of doing so. To begin with, Zhuangzi pointed out that, though much hailed by the world as sage kings, they were actually of questionable character and deeds – When the Yellow Emperor fought Chiyou 蚩由, the leader of the Miao tribes, countless people died, their blood flowed 100 *li*. Yao was a cruel father who killed his oldest son. Shun was an unfilial son and an unkind brother who exiled his father and younger sibling. Yu over worked and became partially paralysed [and thus hurt his inborn nature]. Tang banished his sovereign Jie, and King Wu murdered his ruler Shou. As to the norm makers of later times, Zhuangzi observed, Duke Huan of Qi 齊桓公 killed his elder brother and married his widowed sister-in-law; Tian Chengzi 田成子 murdered his king and usurped the throne of Qi. Why then did they become rulers and make rules for others to follow? It was the victor's Way. That is why, Zhuangzi pointed out, the petty thief is punished but the big thief is made a feudal lord. Those ancient kings were able to impose their rules on others because they were successful big thieves.

Secondly, Zhuangzi thought that those ancient rulers who tried to make rules for the world did not have the ability to do so. Their governments actually made the world worse off: first, they made the people lose unity, and then general compliance, and finally simplicity and purity. People became mutually alienated, distrustful, and contentious, and everyone became confused and deprived of his inner peace. Why so? Because those rulers made norms that violated people's inborn nature. And, after the problems they created, the Ruists and the Mohists and various other schools sprang up, trying to fix the situation by spelling out more and more norms of lesser and lesser inherent virtue. Why so? Because, said Laozi, these self-proclaimed wise men, like the rulers, had inadequate knowledge and little wisdom. Zhuangzi agreed and added that, even the so called sage kings of the past, did not know enough to understand why the sun and the moon shone, why mountains stayed and rivers flowed, and why the four seasons rotate endlessly – in short, they did not know the rules of nature, or the Ways. They misunderstood and misinterpreted, causing confusion and conflicts, and inducing the creation of numerous contradictory theories and strife. Their knowledge was thus more poisonous that the tail of a scorpion.

A little knowledge is a dangerous thing. A person who is capable of knowing only partial truth is more dangerous than a completely ignorant one because he, like the legendary blind man who learns about an elephant by touching only a part of it, would insist that what he knows was the truth and would dismiss all other views as false. And, more unfortunately, he would hold high his knowledge as good and condemn that of others as evil.

(G) Man-made rules

(1) Some are outdated and irrelevant

Now let us take a look at the norms made by the so-called sages and later holders of power. From Zhuangzi's point of view, most of them were not worthwhile. While many of his contemporaries, particularly the Ruists, hailed the norms made by rulers of the ancient times, he pointed out that, as time passed and society changed, those rules were outdated. Thus, he compared applying rules of the early Zhou Dynasty in the state of Lu in his time to pushing a boat over land.

(2) Some are meaningless

Some other rules were meaningless, ludicrous or absurd. Among them, Zhuang particularly (and repeatedly) named those that required mourners to wail in a certain manner. First of all, he saw life and death only as phases of a natural cycle, like successive dreams, or the forming and bursting of a boil, and therefore mourning was meaningless. He conceded that certain expression of spontaneous feelings towards the deceased is acceptable but to turn it into a ritual is ridiculous. He was reacting to the practices and theories of the Ruists who had made funerals elaborate ceremonies that provided jobs for them as directors and for others as professional wailers.

(3) Some contradict nature and are thus harmful to people

Some other norms actually harmed people. To illustrate his point, Zhuangzi told us to look at the horses. As wild animals, they were perfectly happy with what they had – hoofs to tread frost and snow, a fur coat to keep out wind and cold, grass to eat, and stream water to drink – and they wandered and galloped as they pleased. Then, along came Bole, the horse trainer. "I am good at handling horses", he announced and proceeded to singe them, shave them, pare them, brand them, bind them with martingale and crupper, and tie them up in stable and stall. After all this, two or three out of ten horses would be dead. Then he went on to starve them, make them go thirsty, race them, make them prance, pull them into line, force them to run side by side, control them with bit and rein, and terrorise them with whip and crop. After all this, over half the horses would be dead, and the remaining half were turned into draught animals. Though subdued, they occasionally would act with anger and snap the crossbars, break the yoke, or even hurt people.

Now let us look at the people. In a time of Perfect Virtue, Zhuangzi said, the gait of men was slow and ambling; their gaze was steady and mild . . . In other words, they were innocent and happy. Then along came the sage, huffing and puffing about benevolence, reaching on tiptoe for righteousness, and the world for the first time had doubts; mooning and mouthing over his music, snipping and stitching away at his rites, and the world for the first time was divided. Some people would be called gentlemen and given privileges because they were supposedly benevolent and righteous, and they played music and observed rites. Others would be branded petty persons, and were oppressed and exploited because they had doubts about benevolence and righteousness and did not have the means and leisure to toy with music and rites.

This division, of course, caused friction and conflict. But, more unfortunately, the new norms made no one happy because everyone was constrained by them like horses by the bit and rein. Or, as Zhuangzi said in another passage, everyone was forced to conform to the norms like materials being shaped into circles and squares or bound tight by glue and rope. In any case, they would lose their inborn nature and be miserable. As Zhuangzi saw it, they sacrificed themselves at the altar of benevolence and righteousness.

(4) Some can be easily abused and become harmful to society

Worse still, many norms could be easily abused and become harmful to society as a whole. To begin with, Zhuangzi pointed out that rules are like tools which can be used to do good or evil depending on the person who uses them. For instance, pecks and bushels, scales and balances, are fashioned to establish standards and ensure fairness but people use them to cheat. In one of his most sarcastic passages, he said that the same rules for a good ruler are followed by a successful robber: "Making shrewd guesses as to how much booty is stashed away in the room is sagacity; being the first one to break in is bravery; being the last one to escape is righteousness; knowing whether the job can be pulled off or not is wisdom; dividing up the loot fairly is benevolence." Thus, the way of the robber was the same as the way of the sage. Similarly, benevolence, righteousness and other norms are created to reform people but people can use them to camouflage their wrongdoing. Thus, a petty criminal, who simply breaks standards and norms, gets caught and pays with his life but a great one, who uses the standards and norms artfully, becomes a ruler. Thus, Zhuangzi observed, "inside the doors of the feudal lords 'benevolence' and 'righteousness' are kept".

Indeed, the more effective a set of norms is the easier the norms can be abused. To illustrate this, Zhuangzi first pointed to a simple fact: to guard against thieves, the owner of a treasure box would have it secured with strong ropes and locks to prevent it from being easily broken open but a great robber would simply carry it on his back and run away, worrying only that the ropes and the locks were not strong enough. Then, Zhuangzi referred to a historical event: the ruler of the state of Qi made numerous strict laws to preserve order and his own position but Tian Chengzi, a treasonous minister, simply murdered him and took over his state and its laws. The people of Qi offered no resistance because, having become strictly law-abiding, they were incapable of making independent decisions about right and wrong, and simply subjected themselves to whoever in the government held the same laws.

(H) Enforcement of man-made rules

(1) Giving orders and using rewards and punishments

Thus, Zhuangzi showed us that artificial norms were defective. He further pointed out that such norms were difficult to enforce. First, he refuted the allegation of some simple-minded persons who thought that to govern the world a ruler needed only to issue orders for the people to obey. He called this fraudulent, saying that to try to govern the world in this way was like walking on the surface of the ocean, drilling a hole in a river, or making a mosquito carry a mountain. Even Yao and Shun, the most praised rulers in ancient times, who established laws and standards and worked hard for the people, were unable to get everyone to obey and therefore had to exile the Sanmiao (三苗) tribes to the region of Sanwei, and banish Gonggong to the Youdu.

So, to enforce the rules it was necessary to punish the violators. But Zhuangzi noted that, in his time, the victims of the death penalty lay heaped together, the bearers of cangues trod on each other's heels, and the sufferers of punishments were never out of people's sight. These facts demonstrated the futility of punishment as a means to enforce norms. Then there was the suggestion that rewarding those who obey the rules would help. But, he said, if many people were law-abiding, there would not be enough resources for the rewards.

(2) Using benevolence and love and resorting to higher norms

Many ancient thinkers believed that the solution was in resorting to higher norms. Confucius and Mozi suggested that, if people would abide by the principles of benevolence, righteousness, and universal love, they would not only avoid violating the lower norms, such as laws and orders, but actually find them superfluous. Zhuangzi also thought a high norm essential but it is not benevolence and righteousness, and so on, because they, like all other artificial norms, constrain people and force them to do what they do not naturally do. They are like bit and rein, whip and crop that control and compel horses to become draught animals. The idea of making people love benevolence, and so on, is as preposterous as making a horse love bits, and so on. Therefore, these norms are not good enough. What he had in mind was the norm of letting everything follow its inborn nature, its own Way. If everyone was left free to act according to his Way he would be naturally right and could very well fend for himself without receiving any form of help from anyone else. The snowbird is white by itself, needing no one to help bathe it, the crow is black by itself, needing no one to dye it. And, in any event, when one is prevented from following one's own Way, benevolence from others is never adequate. When fish are stranded on land splashing each other with moisture and wetting each other with saliva, this does not save them. Why not simply let them go back to rivers and lakes and forget one another? That is the Way for them to do well.

(I) The way to clear up chaos and return to order

(1) To get rid of the rules and dismiss their makers

Thus, originally, when people had their inborn nature intact, the world had peace and order. This state was damaged by people who invented gadgets and norms. These artefacts were defective and difficult to use but easy to abuse because their makers had only small talents and petty knowledge but grotesque pretensions, outrageous ambition and questionable intentions. Therefore, they and their norms were the cause of human problems not the solution to them. We have seen that Zhuangzi used the conversation between Zigong, a disciple of Confucius, and an old farmer about the well-sweep to make the point. Unfortunately, the norm-makers did not realise this. When problems became more serious and numerous, more norms were made. Zhuangzi used an allegory to illustrate the futility and disastrous result of this effort. "Once there was a man", he said, "who was afraid of his own shadow and hated his own footprints. So he tried to get away from them by running. But the more he lifted his feet and put them down again, the more footprints he made. And no matter how fast he ran, his shadow never left him. Thinking that he was still going too slowly, he ran faster and faster without a stop until his strength gave out and he fell down dead." This man was really stupid, Zhuangzi commented, "He did not understand that by lolling in the shade he could have got rid of his shadow and by resting in quietude he could have put an end to his footprints."

The lesson is obvious. People should stop making more norms and thereby causing more problems. But what about the norm-makers and the norms they had already made? Zhuangzi, like Laozi, suggested *juesheng qizhi* (絕聖棄知 discredit the sage and discard knowledge). When we discussed *Laozi*, we tried to work out what he meant by *zhi* – 智 intelligence or 知 knowledge. In his work, Zhuangzi clearly used *zhi* to mean knowledge. We recall that, in the chapter "Zhi-bei-you", Zhuangzi maintained that the Ways of the myriad things are unknowable to ordinary people. What they can have is only petty knowledge which is, by nature, inadequate. A true sage who has studied everything may know their Ways but he is unable to transmit his knowledge to others. Moreover, since true sages and evil people used the same sort of knowledge and there are always more evil people than true sages, knowledge is more likely to be misused. Zhuangzi wanted people to see that everything has its own Way and therefore all values are relative. It is meaningless to assign to a thing an artificial value and cause people to vie for it. Thus, he said, "Break the jades, crush the pearls, and petty thieves will no longer rise up." He then wanted people to abandon the arbitrary devices of measurements, such as bushels and balance, tallies and seals, that were to determine and affirm the values of things, so that the people will no longer dispute and wrangle. Finally he wanted to "dismiss and wipe out the laws that the sage has made for the world". Only then, he argued, will people be free from outside constraints that distort their nature and, at last, they can be engaged in a discourse about their behaviour which is meaningful to them.

Laozi also wanted people to dismiss "sages" and discard knowledge, and suggested that ordinary people should stop acquiring petty knowledge; false sages who disseminate such knowledge should be discredited; and a true sage should make sure that the ordinary people stay innocent, or ignorant. Zhuangzi did talk about a *da sheng* (大聖 great sage) and a *jun-zi* (君子 noble man) "who has no choice but to direct and look after the world". But, unlike Laozi, Zhuangzi did not specify what unusual qualities this person had to have. He said only that a person who loves the world like he loves his body can be trusted with the world. What he meant was that only a person who cares for his own inborn nature knows the value of the inborn nature of all things and takes care of it. In other words, the great sage must have great wisdom and great knowledge. He must know the rules of nature, or the nature's Ways.

(2) To govern by inaction

Now what was the great sage to do? In one passage, Zhuangzi warned those who are in government against meddling with the people's hearts because they are wild and uncontrollable. In another passage, he said, when a great sage rules the world, he lets the minds of the people roam freely to form their own guidelines and customs, to wipe out harmful thoughts and to pursue their own objectives.

Anyone who says he can do any of these for others was, in Zhuangzi's eyes, a fool or a fraud whose task is impossible, like walking on the surface of the ocean, drilling a hole in a river, or making a mosquito shoulder a mountain. Therefore, he said, when a noble man has no choice but to direct and look after the world, the best course for him is inaction. He should keep the stillness of a corpse and the silence of a deep pool. He should not exert himself to do much for the world because he understands that he cannot do much and that, when left alone, a person can do much more for himself than others can ever do for him. To illustrate this point, Zhuangzi told us that even animals do well for themselves – the bird flies high in the sky where it can escape the danger of arrows; the field mouse burrows deep down under the sacred hall where it will not have to worry about men digging and smoking it out. In addition, he made up a story in which King Wen trusted his state to an old fisherman who, for three years, did nothing – he never changed the existing laws and issued no new ones – and yet, at the end of that period, the state was transformed and there was trust, peace and unity.

Thus Zhuangzi's true sage is less active than Laozi's. It is because Laozi believed in a Way that is external to man and the myriad things and guides them from the outside. When people are misled by false sages and stray from this Way, the true sage has to remove the misleading factors and bring them back to it. It is a lot of work for him. But Zhuangzi's Way is within everything itself so, when people were misled and stray from their own Ways, the true sage needs only to remove the misleading factors and leave people alone. They will return their own Ways by themselves. He has only a part of the work of Laozi's sage.

Nevertheless, how is Zhuangzi's sage actually to remove the misleading factors? In the story of the old fisherman, he did not abolish the existing laws. Presumably, he simply left them unenforced. But what about the problems they had already caused – the disputes and conflicts, and so on? Is Zhuangzi's sage going to let the people fight it out among themselves? What will be the outcome? Zhuangzi did not answer these questions. Here we see a difference between him and Laozi. Though it is a small book, *Laozi* devotes many passages to the tactics of implementing his plans. Reading them, we get a sense that he was serious about his plan. In *Zhuangzi*, a much larger work, there are only brief statements about a general strategy – to discredit sageness and abandon knowledge – and a few somewhat specific measures – to destroy goods that are difficult to get (pearls, jades, and so on), implements that are to ensure trust (seals, tallies, and so on), tools that are to establish standards (balances, pecks, and so on), and, above all, the norms created by sages. As discussed in the chapter on *Laozi*, it is not easy to carry out such a strategy and measures because people had spent long time and great effort to gain knowledge and invent the gadgets for a purpose, and they are unwilling to give them up. The great sage of Zhuangzi, like the sage of Laozi, had to have schemes and a secret agenda, which is to enable people to find their own Ways. Thus, though being an "efficient tool", it is not to "enlighten", let alone compel them. It is to be kept hidden, like fish in deep water. So, here again, while using similar language, Zhuangzi is different from Laozi.

(J) Social relationships

(1) Relationships between individuals

While Zhuangzi dreamed about his utopia, he realised that people lived in a less ideal society where few of them were left alone by themselves. They had to interact with one another according to certain rules which were not necessarily in agreement with everyone's own Way. How should each one behave? First, because each individual has his own Way, everyone is equal and should recognise and respect this fact. A person should not try to distinguish himself from others by reaching for special achievements because what he considers as valuable may not be appreciated by others and, besides, Zhuangzi pointed out, a thing of distinction becomes extinguished more quickly than the ordinary: a person who boasts about his achievements is sure to be criticised and fall into disgrace – a particularly straight tree gets cut down first; a well of sweet water is emptied first.

Thus, according to Zhuangzi, a person should be modest and yielding and then he will not be attacked and harmed. He will be able to mix in with the masses anonymously, becoming just one of them. And, as a result, he will to a degree be left alone unnoticed and he will be able largely to keep to his own Way and be safe and happy.

Another piece of advice from Zhuangzi is that a person should not have a very close relationship with anyone, especially a mutually profitable relationship because, when the profit becomes less tangible, the relationship will become untenable. Thus, when Confucius was experiencing difficulties, his disciples began to desert him. "Therefore," Zhuangzi said, "the friendship of noble persons is plain like water; the friendship of petty men is sweet as wine. Noble persons can stay close because their relationship is plain and incorruptible; petty men break apart because their relationship is sweet and easily becomes sour."

In short, what is suggested by Zhuangzi is simply to keep as much room as possible for one's own Way. To seek recognition of one's achievements by others is to subject oneself to their scrutiny and criticism. To become closely tied up with others is to be tied down physically and emotionally with them. In either case, one will lose a certain amount of freedom and will live for others. This is not how to keep one's own Way and be happy.

(2) Relationships between the people and their ruler

Since great antiquity people had lived in social systems under the control of a ruler. What should their relationship be? How should they interact? Practically all ancient Chinese thinkers, including Laozi despite his protestations, maintained that a ruler should lead and the people should follow. Zhuangzi had some very unusual ideas. In his utopia, there is no distinction between the ruler and the ruled. Even in a less ideal situation, where there is such distinction, he said, the ruler should be like the top branches of a tall tree and the people like wild deer – the two do not have much interaction at all. But, in a still less ideal situation, where interaction was inevitable, he had some practical suggestions.

(A) How the ruler is to treat the people: have self-restraint, be careful and considerate

According to Zhuangzi, those who ruled the world in ancient times had remarkable self-restraint. They were almost without desire and were not overactive. They were silent and unfathomable, and yet the world was satisfied, the myriad things settled, and the people rested in peace. Zhuangzi's emphasis on the ruler ridding himself of desire and refraining from action is based on his belief that the ruler cannot do much for the people without depriving them of their freedom and dignity and, more importantly, damaging their inborn nature and thereby making them less capable of fending for themselves.

Thus, in case a noble man has no choice but to rule, he should try to do little and, when he does something – such as getting rid of sagacity and knowledge or, more specifically, abandoning those things that establish standards for measurements and social behaviour – he should not act haphazardly and ruinously. In other words, he should treat the people with care and compassion.

In another passage Zhuangzi, said the rulers of old attributed what success they had to the people and what failure they had to themselves. What he meant is probably this: an ideal ruler realises that the people, following their innate nature, can do no wrong; whatever problems they have must be the result of his doing and, therefore, he takes the blame whenever something goes awry. In the same passage, Zhuangzi noted that the rulers of his time did exactly the opposite – they made things obscure and then blamed people for not understanding; they increased the difficulties and then punished people for not being able to cope with them; they piled responsibilities on people and penalised them for not being able to fulfil them; they made the journey long and then chastised people for not reaching the end of it.

But when people were pushed to the limit, Zhuangzi pointed out, they would first cheat and then revolt, just as a horse yoked and lined up in harness and shafts and overworked would learn to snap the harness, break the yoke, rip the carriage top, champ the bit and chew the reins. That was why Zhuangzi said, "Things are lowly and yet must be used in accordance with their nature; the people are humble and yet must be governed in accordance with their wishes."

(B) How the people are to treat the ruler

But that statement was only a gentle reminder to those in the government. Zhuangzi said nothing about what the people could do when those in the government ignored the reminder and abused their power. Instead, he turned to the people and offered three pieces of advice on how to keep their personal freedom and dignity in their relationship with the authorities.

(i) Do not covet rewards and lose freedom and dignity

First, Zhuangzi advised the people not to covet the ruler's rewards. He used a story of Cao Shang 曹商 to illustrate that to earn a favour from a ruler one has to pay a steep price. In this case, Zhuangzi suggested Cao was probably rewarded with one hundred carriages by King of Qin for licking the sovereign's piles. It was a nasty remark. The point is that, in human relations, a person's dignity and freedom can be preserved only if he is not excessively dependent on another person for the satisfaction of his desires. If he is, then the other person can use what he can give to force this person to be enslaved.

One way to avoid this dependency and subjugation is to lower one's desires so that it will be easy to resist temptation. That was why Zhuangzi preferred a simple life and was able to refuse office. The story of the sheep butcher Yue 屠羊說 provides another example of such a self-denying but dignified, independent, and freedom-loving person. He fled the state of Chu simply because he lost his job after the state was overrun by enemy forces. But the king insisted on interpreting Yue's behaviour as loyalty and wanted to press some rewards on him. It was an act of a typical power-holder who saw a political reason behind everything and believed that everyone depended on him, wanted favour from him, and therefore was subjected to him. But this humble sheep butcher declined his rewards and preserved his freedom and dignity. It is a great story.

(ii) Do not succumb to pressure and live in disgrace

Zhuangzi's second piece of advice for the people was not to compromise their principles under political pressure. He gave five legendary persons, Beiren Wuze 北人無擇 (The Choiceless Northerner), Bian Sui 卞隨 Wu Guang 務光, Boyi 伯夷 and Shuqi 叔齊, as examples of those who stood up to coercive power. In the first three cases, each person was offered the empire and each declined because, in every case, the offerer had acquired the empire by treason. In none of the cases was the offer bona fide; it was made to win over the receiver or silence him. The refusal was a form of criticism. It was not to be tolerated, and all three knew that. So they committed suicide instead of succumbing to the traitors.

In the cases of Boyi and Shuqi, because they removed King Wu's mask and revealed the ugly face of a rebel, they were not to be allowed to live in peace, disseminate the truth and disrupt his designs. They knew that, and that was why they fled into the mountains and starved to death. To them, death was less painful than becoming accomplices of the devil. And, because they were willing to give up life, they were free to speak their minds and to die as dignified and free men.

(iii) Appear useless and preserve life

Should people think death too high a price to pay for freedom and dignity, Zhuangzi offered them an alternative: to make themselves useless to the ruler. If they appear useless they will not be used. They will receive no rewards but will not be exploited either. The parables of the ancient oak with gnarled features and Zhi-li-shu 支離疏 were used to illustrate this point. Both were useless and therefore left alone while more useful trees were cut down, and more capable persons were made to toil for the powerful and to die in battle. No wonder Zhuangzi lamented that "all men know the use of the useful, but nobody knows the use of the useless".

(K) Human life and objective

So what is human life for? It is so short. Zhuangzi compared it to the passing of a galloping colt glimpsed through a crack in a wall. During this blink of an eye, most people set their minds on pursuing fame and wealth. Some try to discover the problems of the world, others to enlighten it, others to govern it and a few would try to escape from it. Many go to extraordinary lengths to gain personal health and longevity. Zhuangzi thought all of them stupid and called them the upside-down people because they had their priorities wrongly inverted.

Zhuangzi noted that there are those who would chase none of those objectives. Such people, according to him, were sagacious. He called them *zhenren* (真人 True Men).

What did Zhuangzi mean? He said the True Man is someone true to himself. By *zhen* he meant the way that is natural to a person, inborn and unalterable. A True Man comes to life naturally and dies naturally. He is not known to love life and to hate death because he sees life and death as just two phases of a phenomenon. He does not desire anything but accepts what comes to him gladly and lets it go without resisting. Because he does not strive to gain or reject anything, he is at peace with himself and, not interfering, let alone competing with others, and therefore he can escape harm from both inside and outside himself.

In other words, a True Man is a person without a purpose. If the world is populated by such people, there is no need for human relationships, no need for society, no need for norms and no need for authorities. They come into being naturally, stay alive naturally, and pass away naturally.

For lesser mortals purpose is necessary. It is, Zhuangzi said, to be as natural as possible, to live according to one's inborn nature, not for any outside values.

Like Laozi, Zhuangzi was a social critic. They were both appalled by the social conditions of their time and wished to bring about change. A quick reading of their works shows that they had similar viewpoints on the causes of the problems, and came up with similar solutions, but a more careful study reveals that any similarities were superficial and their differences fundamental. A comparison should be helpful to make both theories clearer.

First, they both believed that there is a right way for people to follow which is more natural than that which they actually follow. But Laozi thinks it is a Way with an independent existence that can only be understood by an extraordinary person, a true sage. To Zhuangzi there is no such Way but that there are innumerable ways, each natural to a person.

Second, while Laozi believes in an absolutely correct Way, Zhuangzi denies such a thing and thinks nothing is absolute, everything is relative.

Third, they both believe that there was a time when a Way or myriads of ways governed and the world was a utopia, and they both alleged that it was lost because people driven by excessive desires strove to gain more and more petty knowledge and created needless gadgets and wrong norms.

Fourth, Laozi maintains that artificial gadgets and norms violate the Way, Zhuangzi thinks they violate the natural ways of individuals.

Fifth, to reverse the situation of the dystopia of their time, Zhuangzi simply wants the gadgets and norms abandoned so that each individual follows his natural way. He says that this can be realised by the leaders refraining from doing anything that positively interferes with people's lives. Laozi stresses the same strategy but actually designs an elaborate scheme tactically to lead people to the Way. Zhuangzi's idea is unrealistic, Laozi's dishonest.

Sixth, both implicitly acknowledge that gaining knowledge is possible because people have intelligence and therefore suggest knowledge should not only be discarded but also that those who have extraordinary intelligence should be discredited. Laozi recommends a programme of making people ignorant. Zhuangzi probably believes that, in a utopia, intelligence is useless and therefore will not emerge but this assumption, of course, contradicts another, namely that utopia was lost because people with intelligence gained knowledge. He can be excused for this logical lapse because he simply cannot accept any coercive measure to suppress what is natural.

Seventh, both allege that, in a utopia, the natural Way (or ways) rules. But, before reaching that utopia, government is necessary to eliminate artificial obstructions. At a later stage of this journey, according to Zhuangzi, the authorities resemble a high branch of a tall tree, and people live like wild deer beneath it, having little to do with each other. In Laozi's vision, a temporary roadside stop is a little state with a small population living in peace and splendid isolation. Both allegations are disingenuous – Zhuangzi's is illogical because, if the authorities already have little to do, they do not need to exist; Laozi's is a lie because, on the way to his utopia from this roadside stop, the true sage has to be continuously vigilant about human intelligence raising its ugly head and to be ever ready to suppress it with "the nameless primordial substance". He has a lot to do and there is no end in sight to a point when human intelligence is completely extinguished.

Eighth, in neither case is it clear what the utopia is for. Why should Laozi's true sage or Zhuangzi's reluctant noble man bother to bring people to it? Why should people abandon what they have achieved and return to a more primitive way of life? Zhuangzi says that, in his utopia, individuals are left alone to follow their own natural ways and therefore are free and happy. Whether that can be the case practically is another question; logically, at least, he has a valid argument. Laozi is inconsistent. He also lauds the way of nature but it is a unique Way not intrinsic to, and readily knowable by, ordinary individuals. People cannot by themselves live according to the Way and be happy; they have to be led to it by a true sage and, if they disagree with him, he will use various tactics to induce or coerce them. This is not natural. If people cannot live according to their natural ways, what is the objective of their lives? Laozi does not enlighten us.

In addition to the comparisons above, another, between Zhuangzi, on the one hand, and Confucius and Mozi, on the other, can also help make Zhuangzi's theory clearer. In short, while they affirm human uniqueness, value human achievements and want to continue and advance civilisation, he dismisses all these, regarding human efforts as superficial, if not harmful, and the products of such efforts become fetters so that he wants to set people free. While they have difficulty in reaching their goals, his is rather unrealistic. Basically, his philosophy is incompatible with organised society; it is nihilist and anarchic. When misused, it can lead to revolution and, indeed, some revolutionaries of later times were inspired by it. Many others took his advice to avoid social responsibilities and become escapists and solipsists.

Finally what is Zhuangzi's contribution to Chinese jurisprudence? Again, a comparison will help us to understand. Practically all other thinkers, including Confucius, Laozi, Mozi and those we are to discuss later in this book, exalt society above the individual. They argue that, at their time, an individual cannot survive outside society. And, because he exists only as a member of society, he should live for the good of society. Indeed, values are created and decided by society, and a value of an individual which is different from, and independent of, societal values is a fantasy. Zhuangzi refutes this view, pointing out that people have different preferences. From this fact, he concludes that people have different kinds of inborn nature, and then he argues that protecting this inborn nature is more important for an individual because, if he loses it, he is no longer an individual human being, he becomes an automaton. The life of an automaton is not worth living.

So Zhuangzi points out that there is a different value system which, in his view, is higher than the value system adopted by other thinkers. The difference comes from his belief that human life has an end in itself. An individual does not live because and for society; society is created by individuals to help them live their lives. Therefore, when society poses a threat to the ways of life individuals prefer, society, not the individual, should be changed.

Apart from wanting to abandon all artificial devices, norms and institutions, and to discredit creative minds, Zhuangzi has not suggested any practical measure to help implement the value system of the individual. He only advises that an individual who does not want to be forced to fit into the value system of society should not be enticed or coerced to do so by the authorities. Such advice sounds rather negative but, in practice, has been followed by many Chinese and has given comfort to those oppressed by the authorities like a small light in the darkness of their lives.

More importantly, Zhuangzi's emphasis on the worth of the individual and equality among individuals is, indeed, of great significance. We realise that it is this respect for the individual that has been largely responsible for pushing the West into developing a legal system that balances the interests of the individual and with those of society. The balance is not perfect but the effort is remarkable. Traditional China neglected this task and, as a result, not only in practice but also in theory, the protection of the individual was minimal. Zhuangzi at least provides some philosophical justification for correcting this gross imbalance in favour of society. Therefore, it is easier for Chinese people today to look at the Western legal system and accept some of its features, which echo Zhuangzi's emphasis on individual values, and devise a more balanced system that enables individuals to live more at ease with themselves and with society as a whole. Thus, Zhuangzi may not have contributed much to the jurisprudence of traditional China but he has had an important influence on Chinese legal thinking and practice at the present and will continue to do so in the future.

Notes

1. Sima Qian wrote only two short paragraphs about Zhuang Zhou. He noted that Zhuang Zhou was learned and wrote a work of over 100,000 words, mostly metaphors and fables, critical of Confucius and expounding Laozi. See *Shi-ji*, Chapter 63 "Laozi Han Fei Lie-zhuan" p. 544.The second part of Sima Qian's observation, as I shall explain, is erroneous.
2. Most obviously the last chapter includes a section commenting on Zhuangzi's theory. See *Zhuangzi*, Chapter 33 "Tian-xia" pp. 461–81.

Meng-zi 孟子

PART 1
TRANSLATION

(A) Criticism of Yang Zhu and Mozi

[1] Gongduzi 公都子 said, "Outsiders all say that you, Master, are fond of disputation. May I ask why?" Mencius said, "I am not fond of disputation, I cannot help doing so. The world has been around for a long time, sometimes in peace, sometimes in disorder. During the time of Yao water reversed its natural course and inundated the Central Kingdom . . . Yao ordered Yu to tame the flood . . . and then people were able to live on the plains. After the death of Yao and Shun the Way of the Sages declined and tyrants arose successively . . . During the reign of Shou 紂 [last ruler of the Yin Dynasty] the country was in chaos. Duke Zhou assisted King Wu in toppling Shou . . . and the world greatly rejoiced . . . Then the world again fell into disorder, the Way became unclear, and heresies and violence spread again. There were subjects killing their rulers and sons killing their fathers. Confucius was frightened and composed *Chun-qiu* [commenting on those events] . . . No sage king appeared since then. The feudal lords have been indulging in wanton behaviour and scholars strenuously expressing their unorthodox views. The words of Yang Zhu 楊朱 and Mo Di 墨翟 have filled the world. The opinions held by the people are either those of Yang or those of Mo. Yang advocates everyone for oneself, and therefore denies the importance of the ruler. Mo advocates universal love, and therefore denies the importance of the father. One who dismisses his ruler and his father is a bird or beast . . . When the ways of Yang and Mo are not extinguished and the way of Confucius is not made prominent, specious theories will beguile people and take over the place of the principles of benevolence and righteousness. When the principles of benevolence and righteousness are crowded out beasts will be led to feast on people, and people will feast on one another. Frightened by this I studied the ways of former sages in order to refute Yang and Mo and expel the excessive views. Specious ideas should not be allowed to arise. When they arise in one's

mind one's undertakings will be adversely affected. When people's undertakings are so affected government work will be harmed. If a sage again emerges, he will not dispute these words of mine . . . In the past . . . when Confucius completed the *Chun-qiu*, the disorderly officials and injurious sons became fearful . . . I too want to rectify people's minds, extinguish the specious talks, repel the egregious behaviour, banish the excessive views and thus continue the work of the three Sages [Yu, Lord Zhou and Confucius]. I am not fond of disputation. I cannot help it. Anyone who can with words repel Yang and Mo is a disciple of the Sages." (Chapter 6 "Teng Wen-gong xia" 滕文公下 Section 9, pp. 263–72)

(B) Need of social organisation, norms and authority

[2] Chen Xiang 陳相 saw Mencius and said, quoting the words of Xu Xing 許行, "The ruler of Teng is indeed a worthy one. However, he has not yet learned the Way. A worthy ruler tills the land together with his subjects, eats what he produces, and rules while cooking his own meals. Now the state of Teng has granaries and treasuries. This indicates that its ruler exploits the people to provide for himself. How can he be considered truly worthy?" Mencius asked, "Does Xuzi eat only the grain he has grown himself?" "Yes." "He wears only cloth he has woven himself?" "No. He wears coarse hemp." "Does he wear a cap?" "Yes." "What kind of cap does he wear?" "It is plain raw silk." "Does he weave it himself?" "No. He trades grain for it." "Why does he not weave it himself?" "Because weaving will interfere with his work in the fields." "Does he use a metal pot and a pottery utensil for cooking, and iron implements for ploughing?" "Yes." "Does he make them himself?" "No. He trades grain for them." "Trading grain for implements is not exploiting the potter and the blacksmith. The potter and the blacksmith also trade their wares for grain. In doing so, surely they are not exploiting the farmer either. Why does Xuzi not work as a potter and a blacksmith as well so that he can get everything he needs from his own house? Why does he indulge in such multifarious trading with men who practise the hundred crafts? Why does he put up with so much bother?" "It is naturally impossible to combine the work of tilling the land with that of a hundred different crafts." "Then, is ruling the country such an exception that it can be combined with the work of tilling the land? There are tasks of great men, and there are chores of small men. A person's life is made possible by the use of products of hundreds of others. If everyone must make everything he uses, the country will be led along the path of incessant toil. Thus it is said, 'Some people labour with their mind, some labour with their muscle.' The former rule; the latter are ruled. Those who are ruled support those who rule; those who rule are supported by those who are ruled. This is a common principle in the world. In the time of Yao, the world was not yet settled. The flood raged unchecked, inundating the country; vegetation overgrew; birds and beasts multiplied; the five grains were not planted and harvested; wild animals encroached upon men, and their trail criss-crossed the Middle Kingdom. Yao was particularly worried. He elevated Shun to deal with it. Shun put Yi 益 in charge of fire. Yi burned the mountains and swamps, and the birds and beasts went into hiding. Yu

禹 dredged the Nine Rivers . . . He spent eight years in the country and passed by the door of his home three times but did not enter. Even if he wished to plough the fields could he have done so? . . . The way of the common people is this: once they have sufficient food, warm clothes and comfortable lodging but no education their behaviour will be close to that of birds and beasts. The Sage Yao was worried and appointed Xie 契 as minister of education to teach the people human relationships: love between father and son, duty between ruler and subject, distinction between husband and wife, precedence of the old over the young, and faith between friends. Fangxun 放勳 [Yao's name] said [to his ministers]: 'Toil for the people and gather them, guide them and make them straight, assist them and protect them, enable them to stand up on their own and then educate them and help them become virtuous.' The sage cared about the people so much, could he still have the leisure to plough the fields?"(Chapter 5 "Teng Wen-gong shang" 滕文公上 Section 4, pp. 215–28)

(C) Good and bad governments

[3] [King Xuan of Qi asked Mencius,] "May I hear about the rule of a True King?" Mencius replied, "In the past when King Wen ruled the area Qi 岐, tillers of land paid one ninth of their produce as taxes; officials held hereditary fief estates; at border stations and marketplaces there was inspection but no levy; there was no prohibition against fishing in the ponds created by weirs; punishment did not extend to the wife and children of an offender. Old men without wives, old women without husbands, old persons without children, and young children without fathers are the four types of the most destitute people who have no one to turn to for help. When King Wen enforced benevolent policies, he always started with these four types. (Chapter 1 "Liang Hui-wang shang" 梁惠王上 Section 5, pp. 79–81)

[4] Mencius said: "Boyi fled Shou 紂 and settled on the shore of the northern sea. Learning the rise of King Wen, he said, 'Let me go to him. I hear that the Count of the West is good at taking care of old people' . . . When there is someone who is good at taking care of old people, men of virtue will go to his place as their home. If a family with a house and five *mu* 畝 [a *mu* is roughly 667 square metres] of land around it plants mulberry trees by the walls and has a woman to raise silkworms, its old people will have dresses of silk. If the family has five hens and two sows kept breeding at the right time, its old people will not be deprived of meat. If a man has a field of 100 *mu* to plant crops his family of eight persons will not go hungry. The saying 'the Count of the West was good at taking care of old people' meant that he regulated the distribution of land, taught people what trees to plant and what livestock to breed, guided the womenfolk and children in the way of taking care of the aged. For after the age of fifty, one is not warm without silk clothing and, after seventy, one is not satisfied without meat. To have neither warm dress nor a full belly one will be freezing and starving. Among the subjects of King Wen, there were no old people freezing and starving. This is what the saying meant." (Chapter 13 "Jin-xin shang" 盡心上 Section 22, p. 537)

[5] [Mencius said to King Xuan of Qi] "Nowadays, the regulations for the distribution of property to the people make it difficult for a man to care for his parents and provide for his wife and children. In a year of good harvest they endure no hardship; in a year of disasters they cannot avoid death." (Chapter 1 "Liang Hui-wang shang" Section 7, p. 57)

[6] King Xuan of Qi 齊宣王 asked, "The royal park of King Wen was seventy *li* [a *li* was about 500 metres] square. Is it true?" Mencius replied, "It is so recorded." "Was it really as large as that?" "Even so, the people found it small." "My park is only forty *li* square, and yet the people consider it too big. Why?" "King Wen's park was seventy *li* square, but people could go in there to log, cut hay and catch pheasants and hares. As he shared it with the people, is it any wonder that they found it small?" . . . "When I first reached at the border I inquired about the major prohibitions of your state before I dared to enter. I was told that in the outskirts of the capital there is a park forty *li* square, in which killing a deer is as serious an offence as killing a man. If this is true the forty *li* square is a trap in the midst of the state and isn't it fitting that your people consider it too big?" (Chapter 2 "Liang Hui-wang xia" 梁惠王下 Section 2, pp. 63–5)

[7] [Mencius told King Hui of Liang] "There is fine meat in your kitchen and fat horses in your stable, but your subjects look hungry and in the countryside there are corpses of starved people. This is like leading animals to eat people." (Chapter 1 "Liang Hui-wang shang" Section 4, p. 37)

[8] [Mencius said to King Hui of Liang] "If when dogs and pigs are eating what is fit for human consumption the ruler does not know to save and store food, and when corpses of starved people are strewn in the road the ruler does not know to open the stores and distribute alms; instead, after people die he says 'It is not my fault, it is that of the weather and harvest.' How is his act different from stabbing people and killing them and then saying, 'It is not me but the weapon that kills'?" (Chapter 1 "Liang Hui-wang shang" Section 4, pp. 36–7)

[9] King Hui of Liang said: "The way I am to my country is to give my whole heart to it. When there is famine in the He-nei area I move its people to the He-dong area, and ship grain from the Hedong to the Henei, and when the Hedong suffers famine, I reverse the action. I see no ruler of any neighbouring state governing as wholeheartedly. And yet the population of the neighbouring states has not decreased, and the population in my state has not increased. Why?" Mencius replied: "Your Majesty likes warfare, so let me use a military analogy. When drums roll and weapons cross, a group of soldiers fled, discarding their armour and dragging their weapons. Some stopped after 100 steps, some after 50 steps. What would you say if those who stopped after 50 steps laughed at those who stopped after 100 steps?" "It is not right. Those who laugh only fled less than 100 steps, but they fled just the same." "Knowing this, your Majesty should not expect your subjects to be more numerous than those of your neighbouring states." (Chapter 1 "Liang Hui-wang shang" Section 3, pp. 31–2)

[10] [King Xuan of Qi said to Mencius] "I would like to pursue my great ambition" . . . [Mencius said] "Your 'great ambition' is conceivable. It is to enlarge

your territory, make the rulers of Qin and Chu pay homage to you in your court, rule over the Central Kingdom and pacify the barbarians on its borders. But to pursue your ambition by doing what you now do is like seeking fish by climbing a tree." (Chapter 1 "Liang Hui-wang shang" Section 7, pp. 53–4)

[11] Mencius said, "The Five Hegemons [the five strong feudal lords of the Chun-qiu Period: Duke Huan of Qi 齊桓公, Duke Wen of Jin 晉文公, King Zhuang of Chu 楚莊王, Duke Xiang of Song 宋襄公, and Duke Mu of Qin 秦穆公] were offenders against the Three Kings [the founders of the Xia, the Shang and the Zhou Dynasties]; the present-day feudal lords are offenders of the Five Hegemons; the present-day great officials are offenders of the present-day feudal lords. When a True King visits the fiefdom of a feudal lord and sees that the land is opened up and the field cultivated; the aged are taken care of, the worthy honoured, and the talented in government posts, he rewards the feudal lord with additional land. When he enters a feudal state and finds the land lies in waste, the aged are neglected, the worthy ignored, and cruel persons in government positions, he reprimands the feudal lord . . . Thus, a True King punishes but does not attack. The Five Hegemons coerced some feudal lords to follow them in their attacks against some other feudal lords; thus they were the offenders of the way of a True King. Among the Five Hegemons, Duke Huan of Qi was the most prominent. At a meeting in Kui-qiu, convened by him, the feudal lords swore to the following orders: first, punish the impious sons, do not change the lawful heir, and do not make a concubine the wife. Second, honour the worthy and cultivate the talented. Third, respect the aged, be kind to the young, and do not neglect the guests and travellers. Fourth, the rank of *shi* [the lowest government officer] is not to be made hereditary; different posts are not to be held concurrently by one person; the selection of officials must be appropriate; and no official should be executed by the order of a feudal lord alone. Fifth, do not curve dykes, do not suppress the sale of grain, and do not give fief to a subordinate without reporting to the king . . . The present-day feudal lords violate all these five prohibitions, and therefore I say that they are offenders of the Five Hegemons. The crime of passively letting the evil deeds of a ruler grow unabated is small; the crime of actively greeting the evil deeds of a ruler is bigger. The present-day high officials all greet the evil deeds of their rulers; therefore, I say, the present-day high officials are offenders of the present-day rulers." (Chapter 12, "Gaozi xia" 告子下 Section 7, pp. 495–550)

[12] King Xuan of Qi said "I have a weakness – I am fond of material goods." Mencius replied: "In the past Gong Liu 公劉 [an ancestor of King Wen] was fond of material goods. *The Book of Odes* says, 'He stocked and stored; he bound up provisions in bags and sacks; and he thus gathered his people and led his people to safty . . . ' If you are fond of material goods and can share this fondness with the people, it will not prevent you from becoming a True King." The king said: "I have another weakness – I am fond of beautiful women." Mencius replied: "In the past, Tai-wang 太王 [King Wen's grandfather] was fond of women, and loved his wife . . . At his time, there were no lonely spinsters in homes and no unmarried

men abroad. If you are fond of women and can *yu-min tong-zhi* (與民同之 share this fondness with the people), it will not prevent you from becoming a True King." (Chapter 2 "Liang Hui-wang xia" Section 5, pp. 81–3)

[13] [King Xuan of Qi told Zhuang Bao 莊暴 that he was fond of music. Mencius said to the king] "If your Majesty is really fond of music, the state of Qi will be faring very well. But now when your Majesty has music played here, the people, upon hearing the sound of the bells and drums and the note of flutes and pipes, raise their aching heads with knitted eyebrows and say to one another 'Why is our king's love of music causing such extreme pain to us – making fathers and sons not see each other and the brothers and wives and children dispersed?' The reason is nothing but this: You did not *yu-min tong-le* (與民同樂 share with the people in enjoying the same pleasure)." (Chapter 1 "Liang Hui-wang shang" Section 1, p. 60)

(D) Critical problems and Mencius's solutions

[14] [King Xiang of Liang 梁襄王 asked,] "How could the world be settled?" Mencius replied, "It will be settled when unified." "Who can unify the world?" "The one who is not addicted to having people killed." "Who would follow him?" "None in the world would refuse to follow him. Does Your Majesty know that, in the seventh and eighth moons of the year when there is a drought, the rice shoots will wilt. When clouds gather and rain pours down, they spring up again and no one can suppress them. Now few of the rulers of the world are not addicted in having people killed. If there is one who is not so addicted, the people of the world will stretch their necks looking for him. In such a case, the people will come to him like water rushing towards a low place. It will be so forceful. Who can prevent it?" (Chapter 1 "Liang Hui-wang shang" Section 6, pp. 42–4)

[15] At the present, the territories of the various states are roughly the same size, and their governments are roughly of the same quality, and, as a result, none is able to dominate the others. There is no other reason than that every ruler is given to employing those he can instruct, not those who can instruct him." (Chapter 4, "Gongsun Chou xia" 公孫丑下 Section 2, p. 154)

[16] Mencius went to see King Hui of Liang. The king said, "Sir, you came from 1,000 *li* away. Do you have some way to profit my state?" Mencius replied, "Your Majesty, why do you have to talk about profit? What is needed is benevolence and righteousness. If your Majesty asks 'How can I profit my state?' Every great official will ask 'How can I profit my house?' and every officer and commoner will ask 'How can I profit my person?' Then those in high positions and those in low ones will try to gain profit at the expense of the others, and the state will be in danger. In a state of 10,000 chariots the person who commits regicide must be from a house of 1,000 chariots; in a state of 1,000 chariots the person who commits regicide must be from a house of 100 chariots. A thousand out of ten thousand or a hundred out of a thousand is not insignificant but, if profit is put before righteousness, one will not be satisfied until one grabs the whole. No benevolent person neglects his parents; no person of righteousness neglects his

ruler. All your Majesty needs to talk about is benevolence and righteousness. Why is it necessary for you to talk about profit?" (Chapter 1 "Liang Hui-wang shang" Section 1, pp. 21–6)

[17] Gongsun Chou 公孫丑 said, "The Way [of benevolence and righteousness] is indeed lofty and beautiful but, to approach it, is like climbing up to the sky which is beyond one's reach. Why not make it less remote so that people can have hope to get to it and therefore diligently make the effort?" Mencius said, "A master craftsman does not put aside the stretched string for the benefit of a clumsy worker; Yi 羿 [a master of archery] did not lower his standard of drawing the bow for the benefit of a clumsy archer. The gentleman shows people the best stance like Yi would draw the bow to the full extent but did not release the arrow, which would appear ready to fly. The gentleman would stand right in the centre of the Way and those of capability will follow his example." (Chapter 13 "Jin-xin shang" Section 41, pp. 555–6)

(E) Re-establishment of good government: possibility and timing

[18] Mencius said, "One who virtuously practices benevolence will become a True King. A True King does not need a big state to start with. Tang 湯 [the first ruler of the Shang Dynasty] started with a state of 70 *li* square; King Wen started with one of 100 *li* square. (Chapter 3, "Gongsun Chou shang" 公孫丑上 Section 3, p. 130)

[19] Mencius said, "If the ruler of a big state today takes King Wen as model he will need five years to have his policies prevail in the world; if his state is small he will need seven years . . . If a ruler inclines to be benevolent none in the world can be his enemy." (Chapter 7, "Li Lou shang" 離婁上 Section 7, p. 292)

[20] Mencius said to King Hui of Liang, "A land of 100 *li* square is sufficient for its ruler to become a True King . . . It is said that the benevolent man has no match. I beg you not to doubt this." (Chapter 1, "Liang Hui-wang shang" 梁惠王上 Section 5, p. 40)

[21] Duke Wen of Teng 滕文公, while still crown prince, on his way to Chu passed through Song and went to see Mencius. Mencius talked about human nature being inherently good and said nothing but praise for the way of Yao and Shun. On his way back from Chu, the prince again saw Mencius. Mencius said, "Does Your Highness doubt my words? There is only one Way. Cheng Jian 成閒 [a man known for his courage] once said to Duke Jing of Qi 齊景公, 'He is a man, and I am a man. Why should I be in awe of him?' Yan Yuan 顏淵 [Confucius's best disciple] said, 'What kind of a man was Shun, and what kind of a man am I. One who aspires to great achievements should be like him.' Gongming Yi 公明儀 [a wise and worthy man] said, 'King Wen is my teacher and [in Duke of Zhou I trust, he] would not mislead me.' Now the territory of Teng, being roughly calculated, is about 50 *li* square. It is big enough to be made a good state. A passage in the *Book of Historical Documents* says, 'If the medicine does not make a patient dizzy, it will not cure his illness.'" (Chapter 5 "Teng Wen-gong shang" Section 1, pp. 188–9)

[22] Mencius said, "Jie 桀 and Shou 紂 [last rulers of the Xia and the Yin Dynasties

respectively] lost the world as a result of losing its people. They lost the people as a result of losing their hearts. There is a way to win the world: win the people and you will win the world. There is a way to win the people: win their hearts and you will win the people. There is a way to win people's hearts: share with them what you want, and do not impose upon them what you dislike. The people turn to the benevolent as water flows downwards or as animals run to the wilderness. Thus it is the otter that drives the fish to the deep waters; it is the hawk that drives the sparrows to the bushes; and it was Jie and Shou that drove the people to Tang 湯 and Wu 武 [founders of the Shang and the Zhou Dynasties respectively]. Today, if a ruler is fond of practising benevolence, all the feudal lords will be driving their people towards him. Even though he would not like to be a King, he cannot help but be one. (Chapter 7, "Li Lou shang" Section 9, pp. 295–7)

[23] Mencius said, "Every five hundred years a True King should arise and, in the interval, there should be someone who would rectify the names of the world. From the beginning of the Zhou Dynasty to the present it is more than 700 years. The 500-year mark has been passed and the time is ripe. It must be that the Heaven does not yet wish to have the world settled in peace and order. If it wishes to have the world so settled, who is there at the present time to help the rectification other than I myself?" (Chapter 4, "Gongsun Chou xia" Section 13, pp. 183–4)

[24] Mencius said, "The appearance of a True King has never been longer overdue than today; and the people have never suffered cruel government more than today. The hungry are easy to feed, and the thirsty easy to have their thirst quenched . . . At the present time, if a state of 10,000 chariots were to carry out benevolent policies the people would be so happy it would be like being released from hanging by the heels. As a result, people today can, with half the effort, achieve twice as much as those in ancient times." (Chapter 3, "Gongsun Chou shang" Section 1, pp. 109–10)

(F) Conceptual bases of good government and norms

[25] Mencius said, "Everyone has a heart that cannot bear to see others suffer . . . Now when a man sees that a child is about to fall into a well, he will feel fear and compassion, not because he wants to get in good grace with the child's parents, nor because he wants to gain praise from his neighbours and friends, nor because he dislikes the child's cry." (Chapter 3, "Gongsun Chou shang" Section 6, p. 138)

[26] [King Xuan of Qi asked Mencius,] "How virtuous must a man be before he can become a True King?" [Mencius replied,] "He becomes a True King by protecting the people, and no one can stop him." "Can someone like me protect the people?" "Yes." "How do you know that I can?" "I heard from Hu He 胡齕. He said that while Your Majesty was sitting in the hall someone walked by with an ox. Your Majesty noticed and asked 'Where is the ox going?' The man replied, 'Its blood is to be used for consecrating a new bell.' 'Spare it.' Your Majesty said, 'I cannot bear to see it trembling like an innocent man going to the place of execution.' 'In that case, should the ceremony be abandoned?' 'How

can it be abandoned? Use a lamb instead.' I wonder if this was true" "It was." "The heart behind your action is sufficient to enable you to become a True King. The people all thought that you were stingy, but I am sure that you were moved by pity for the animal." The king said, "Indeed, there are those who thought so. But though Qi is a small state I am not quite so stingy about an ox. It was simply because I could not bear to see it trembling in fear, like an innocent man going to the place of execution, that I used a lamb instead." "You must not be surprised that the people thought you stingy. You just used a small animal in place of a big one, how could they see the difference? If you were pained by an innocent animal going to its death, what was there to choose between an ox and a lamb?" The King laughed and said, "Indeed, what was really in my mind, I wonder? It is not true that I was stingy about the expense, but I did use a lamb instead of the ox. I suppose it was only natural that the people should have thought me stingy." "There is no harm in this. It is the way of a humane man. You saw the ox but not the lamb. The attitude of a noble man towards animals is this: once having seen them alive, he cannot bear to eat their flesh. That is why the gentleman keeps his distance from the kitchen." (Chapter 1, "Liang Hui-wang shang" Section 7, pp. 47–50)

[27] Mencius said, "Men all have something they cannot bear. When this becomes a guide to their behaviour it is called benevolence. Men all have something they will not do. When this becomes a guide to their behaviour, it is called righteousness." (Chapter 14 "Jin-xin xia" 盡心下 Section 31, p. 591)

[28] Mencius said, "What a person can do without having to learn it is his innate capability; what a person can know without having to deliberate it is his innate knowledge. There are no children who do not know about loving their parents. When they grow up none of them does not know about respecting their older brothers. Loving one's parents is benevolence; respecting one's older brother is righteousness. Why? These virtues are but extensions of those feelings towards others." (Chapter 13 "Jin-xin shang" Section 15, p. 529)

[29] One without a compassionate heart is not human; one without a heart of shame and aversion is not human; one without a courteous and modest heart is not human; one without a heart of right and wrong is not human. The compassionate heart is the seed of benevolence; the heart of shame and aversion, the seed of righteousness; the courteous and modest heart, the seed of observance of the rites; the heart of right and wrong, the seed of wisdom. Man has these four seeds just as he has four limbs. (Chapter 3, "Gongsun Chou shang" Section 6, pp. 138–9)

[30] Gongduzi said [to Mencius], "Gaozi 告子 said, 'human nature is neither good nor bad.' Others said, 'Human nature can be either good or bad. Thus with the rise of King Wen and King Wu the people were given to virtue; with the rise of King You 幽王 and King Li 厲王 [two cruel kings of the Western Zhou Dynasty] the people were given to violence.' Still others said, 'There are those who are by nature good, and there are those who are by nature bad. Therefore while Yao was the king he had Xiang 象 [Shun's younger brother, an inferior person] as

a subject, while the Blind Old Man was the father he had Shun as a son. And because Shou 紂 was the son of their older brother, Princes Qi 啟 and Bigan 比干 [two uncles of Shou, known for their virtues] made him the king.' Now you say human nature is good. Were those people all wrong?" Mencius said, "Let a man follow his own inclination and he can be virtuous. This is why I say human nature is good. As for a man becoming bad, it is not the fault of his nature. The compassionate heart is possessed by all men, the heart of shame is possessed by all men, the courteous heart is possessed by all men, and the heart of right and wrong is possessed by all men. The compassionate heart leads to benevolence, the heart of shame to righteousness, the courteous heart to observance of rites, and the heart of right and wrong to wisdom. Thus, benevolence, righteousness, rites, and wisdom are not gilded on me from outside, they are intrinsic to me." (Chapter 11, "Gaozi shang" 告子上 Section 6, pp. 441–6)

[31] Gaozi said, "Human nature is like whirling water. Give it an outlet in the east and it flows east; give it an outlet in the west and it flows west. Human nature has no preference for good or bad. It is like water, which has no preference for east or west." Mencius said, "Indeed water has no preference for east or west, but does it not have a preference for high or low? Human nature is good like water seeks to low ground. No man is by nature bad, no water does not flow downwards. Now if splashed, water can spring upwards, shooting higher than a person's forehead; if forced, it can go up a hill. But how can these actions be expressions of the nature of water? It is the circumstances that make it to act so. Man can be made to be bad. His nature is like that of water." (Chapter 11, "Gaozi shang" Section 2, pp. 433–4)

[32] Mencius said, "There was a time when the trees were luxuriant on Ox Mountain. But, being on the outskirts of a big city, the trees are constantly cut by axes. Is it any wonder that they are no longer fine? When they had some respite for days and nights, and moistened by rain and dew, there was no lack of new shoots coming out, but then the cattle and sheep came to graze. As a result the mountain is now bare. People, seeing only its bareness, tend to think that it never had any trees. But can this possibly be the nature of a mountain? Can what is deep in a man be completely lacking the heart of benevolence and righteousness?" (Chapter 11, "Gaozi shang" Section 8, p. 456)

[33] Mencius said, "All things of the same kind have similarities. Why should there be any doubt about humans? . . . Hence it is said, 'all palates have the same preference in taste, all ears in sound, and all eyes in beauty.' Then why do hearts alone have nothing in common? What is common to all hearts? It is reason and rightness." (Chapter 11, "Gaozi shang" Section 7, pp. 449–50)

[34] Cao Jiao 曹交 asked, "Everyone can be a Yao or a Shun, is that right?" Mencius said, "That is right . . . The way of Yao and Shun is just to be filial to one's parents and loving to one's brother. If you do the acts Yao did, you will be like Yao." (Chapter 12 "Gaozi xia" Section 2, pp. 477–80)

[35] Mencius said, "Treating with proper care the old of my own family and extending the same treatment to the old of other people's families, and treating

with proper love the young of my own family and extending the same treatment to the young of other people, I can roll the world in my palm. The *Book of Odes* says, 'First set myself as an example for my wife and my brothers, I can then rule my family and my state.' In other words, it is to use one's own heart as a standard and apply it to others. Thus if a ruler can extend his benevolence he can keep in order what is within the four seas. If he does not, he cannot even protect his wife and children." (Chapter 1, "Liang Hui-wang shang" Section 7, pp. 51–2)

[36] [After pointing out to King Xuan of Qi that a ruler who could protect the people would become a True King, and no one would be able to resist him,] Mencius said, "Should someone say to you, 'I am strong enough to lift 100 *jin* [about 50 kilograms] but not a feather; I have eyes that can see the tip of fine autumn down but not a cartload of firewood,' would Your Majesty believe him?" "No." "Now your kindness is enough to reach the animals but not to the people, why? Where a feather is not lifted it is because the person's strength is not used, where a cartload of firewood is not seen it is because the person's eyesight is not focused, and where the people are not protected it is because their ruler's kindness is not extended. Thus, in your case of not becoming a True King, it is because you did not make an effort, not because you are incapable." "How do you describe the difference between not making an effort and not being capable?" "If, referring to a feat of striding over the North Sea with Mount Tai carried under the arm, a person says he is incapable, he is indeed incapable. if, referring to taking a deep bow to an elder, a person says he is incapable, he is not making an effort but not really incapable. Your failure to be a True King is not in the category of striding over North Sea with Mount Tai carried under your arm, but in the category of taking a deep bow to an elder." (Chapter 1, "Liang Hui-wang shang" Section 7, pp. 50–1)

[37] Mencius said, "Every man has a compassionate heart. The ancient kings had compassionate hearts and therefore had compassionate policies. With a heart of compassion in carrying out compassionate policies to govern the country it can be as easy as rolling it in the palm." (Chapter 3 "Gongsun Chou shang" Section 6, p. 138)

(G) Members of society

(1) The common people

[38] Mencius said, "The people are of the highest value, the temple of the gods of earth and grain are of the next, and the ruler is of the least." (Chapter 14 "Jin-xin xia" Section 14, p. 573)

[39] Mencius said, "Yao's worry was about not finding Shun; Shun's worry was about not finding Yu and Gaoyao 皋陶 [a Minister of Justice during the reign of Shun]. One who worried about not cultivating well 100 *mu* of crop land is a farmer." (Chapter 5 "Teng Wen-gong shang" Section 4, p. 229)

[40] Mencius said, "The common people who are without constant means will have no constant hearts. Lacking constant hearts they will become unprincipled

and excessive, stopping at nothing. When they fall into crimes and the authorities punish them. It is entrapment." (Chapter 1 "Liang Hui-wang shang" Section 7, p. 56)

[41] Mencius said, "The way of the common people is this: once they have sufficient food, warm clothes and comfortable lodging but no education, their behaviour will be close to that of birds and beasts." (Chapter 5 "Teng Wen-gong shang" Section 4, p. 226)

(2) The "superior men"

[42] Mencius said, "He who nurtures what is small in him is a small man; he who nurtures what is great in him is a superior man." (Chapter 11, "Gaozi shang" Section 14, p. 14)

[43] Gongduzi asked, "Although all men are human, some are superior men, some are small men, why?" Mencius said, "Those who follow what is of great importance in them are superior men; those who follow what is of small importance in them are small men." "All men are human, but some follow what is great in them; some follow what is small in them. Why?" "The ears and eyes are organs that do not do thinking and can be affected by what have impacts on them. The heart is the organ that does thinking. Thinking helps a person know what is right. This is what nature gives men. If a man is firm on what is of great importance to him, what is of small importance will not be able to mislead him. This is how he becomes a superior man." (Chapter 11, "Gaozi shang" Section 15, p. 467)

[44] Mencius said, "What makes a gentleman different from others is the way he keeps his heart. A gentleman keeps his heart right by following the principles of benevolence and the rites. (Chapter 8 "Li Lou xia" 離婁下 Section 28, p. 350)

[45] Mencius said, "A superior man is one who never loses his innocent heart like that of a newborn baby." (Chapter 8 "Li Lou xia" Section 12, p. 327)

[46] Mencius said, "A man who stays in the world's broad place, occupies the world's proper position, walks the world's great road, shares his bounty with the people when his aspiration is fulfilled, follows the right course by himself when his aspiration is not fulfilled, incorruptible by wealth and high position, uncompromised by poverty, and unbowed by force and authority, is called a 'great man'." (Chapter 6 "Teng Wen-gong xia" Section 2, p. 246)

[47] Mencius said, "In ancient times a man who had achieved what he aspired to, he spread his benefits among the people. When he was unable to achieve what he aspired to, he cultivated his personal virtue and showed it to the world. In obscurity he made himself alone good; in prominence he made the world good as well." (Chapter 13 "Jin-xin shang" Section 9, p. 525)

[48] Mencius said, "A great man is one who rectifies himself and then helps rectify the myriad things." (Chapter 13 "Jin-xin shang" Section 19, p. 533)

[49] Mencius said, "Sages are teachers to hundreds of generations. Such were Boyi and Liuxia Hui 柳下惠. Among those who have heard the way of Bo Yi, the corrupt become clean and the cowardly begin to have high ambitions. Among those who have heard the way of Liuxia Hui, the mean-spirited become generous

and the narrow-minded become tolerant. These two rose a hundred generations before and, a hundred generations thereafter, those who have heard their ways also rise to their standards. Can anyone less than a sage produce such effects? And how much more effect would a sage have on those who have learned from him in person?" (Chapter 14 "Jin-xin xia" Section 15, p. 574)

[50] Mencius said, "Yan Yuan remarked, 'What kind of a person was Shun, and what am I? One who wishes to achieve something significant should be just like him.'" (Chapter 5, "Teng Wen-gong shang" Section 1, pp. 188–9).

[51] Prince Dian 墊 [a prince of the state of Qi] asked, "What does a gentleman do?" Mencius said, "Keep and realise high aspirations." "What do you mean?" "Just to be humane and right, that is all. To kill an innocent man is inhumane; to take something to which one is not entitled is not right. Where is the place for one to settle? It is in humanity. Which is the way for one to walk? It is in rightness. Stay in humanity and follow rightness. That is what a great man does." (Chapter 13 "Jin-xin shang" Section 33, p. 546)

[52] Gongsun Chou asked, "May I ask what you, Master, are good at?" Mencius said, "I can know what is behind one's remarks, and I am good at nurturing my great broad spiritual energy." "May I ask what this broad spiritual energy is?" "It is difficult to explain. This energy is most vast and most strong. When properly nourished and not harmed, it fills the space between heaven and earth. It closely associates with rightness and the Way. Deprived of them, it collapses . . . It also collapses when a person's conduct is disagreeable to his own heart." (Chapter 3 "Gongsun Chou shang" Section 2, pp. 117–19)

[53] Mencius said, "Fish is what I desire; the bear's paw is also what I desire. When I cannot have both, I will give up fish and choose the bear's paw. Life is what I desire; rightness is also what I desire. When I cannot have both, I will give up life and choose rightness." (Chapter 11 "Gaozi shang" Section 10, p. 461)

[54] Mencius said, "Specious ideas should not be allowed to arise . . . I, too, want to rectify people's minds, extinguish the specious talk, repel the egregious behaviour, banish the excessive views and thus continue the work of the three Sages [Yu, Lord Zhou and Confucius]. (Chapter 6 "Teng Wen-gong xia" Section 9, p. 272)

[55] Wan Zhang 萬章 asked, "The *Book of Odes* says, 'How does a man take a wife? He must first report to his parents.' If one is sincerely to believe in that teaching, it should not be more so than Shun. But he married without reporting to his parents first, why?" Mencius said, "If he reported he would not have been allowed to marry. A man and a woman living together as husband and wife is the most important human relationship. If he had reported, he would have had to abandon this most important relationship and he would become resentful of his parents. That is why he did not report." (Chapter 9 "Wan Zhang shang" 萬章上 Section 2, p. 364)

[56] Wan Zhang asked, "Xiang devoted himself every day to plotting against Shun's life. When Shun was established as the Son of Heaven, he banished Xiang, why?" Mencius said, "He assigned Xiang a fief, although some called the

act banishment." Wan Zhang said, "Shun banished Gong Gong 共工 to Youzhou, exiled Huan Dou 驩兜 to Chongshan, killed Sanmiao 三苗 at Sanwei, executed Gun 鯀 at Yushan. His acts on these four culprits made the world bow to him in obedience because he punished the wicked. Xiang was extremely wicked and yet Shun assigned him a fief in Youbi. What wrong did the people of Youbi do? Should a benevolent man act like this: in the case of other culprits punish them; in the case of his brother assign him a fief instead?" "Against a brother a benevolent man will not harbour anger or nurse a grudge. He simply loves him. Because of this love he wants him to have rank and wealth. Letting him have Youbi as a fief was to give him rank and wealth. If, as the Son of Heaven, Shun left his brother Xiang to be a mere commoner, could he be considered to love his brother?" "May I ask why some people called Shun's act 'banishment'?" "Xiang was not allowed to take any action in his fief except receive tributes and taxes from it. That was why some called the arrangement 'banishment'. How could Xiang mistreat the people of Youbi?" (Chapter 9 "Wan Zhang shang" Section 3, pp. 370–2)

[57] Tao Ying 桃應 asked, "If, when Shun was the king and Gaoyao the judge, the Blind Old Man [Shun's father] killed someone, how was the case to be handled?" Mencius said, "Arrest the killer. That is all." "Shun would not try to stop the arrest?" "How could Shun stop it? Gaoyao's action had good grounds." "Then what would Shun have done?" "Shun regarded abandoning the kingdom as no more than discarding a worn shoe. He would have secretly carried the old man on his back and fled to the edge of the sea and lived there happily, never giving a thought to the kingdom." (Chapter 13 "Jin-xin shang" Section 35, pp. 548–9)

[58] Kuang Zhang 匡章 said, "Is Chen Zhongzi 陳仲子 not truly a man of clean character? When he was in Wuling, he was without food for three days and, as a result, could neither hear with his ears nor see with his eyes. By the well was a plum, more than half of it already worm-eaten. He crept up and ate it. Only after three bites was he able to hear and see." Mencius said, "Among the gentlemen of the state of Qi, I have to regard Zhongzi as prominent. Nevertheless, how can he be considered completely clean? Pushed to its utmost limits, his way of life would only be possible for an earthworm which eats the dry earth above and drinks the yellow spring below. Was the house in which Zhongzi lived built by Boyi? Or was it built by the Bandit Zhi 跖? Was the millet he ate grown by Boyi? Or was it grown by the Bandit Zhi? The answer cannot be known." "What does it matter? He himself made sandals and his wife made hemp and silk thread to barter for these things." "Zhongzi came from an old established family. His older brother Dai 戴 had a government salary of 10,000 bushels of grain a year but he considered it unjustified and refused to benefit from it, and he considered his brother's house ill-gotten and refused to live in it. He lived in Wu-ling, apart from his brother and mother. One day, when he came for a visit and found someone had given his brother a live goose as a present, he knitted his brow and said, 'What does one want this honking creature for?' Another day, his mother killed the goose and gave it to him to eat. His brother came home and said, 'This is the meat of that honking creature.' He went out and vomited it all up. He ate what

his wife provided but not what his mother did. He lived in Wu-ling but not in his brother's house. Can such a person push his principles to the utmost limits? Pushed to the utmost limits, his way of life would only be possible if he were an earthworm." (Chapter 6 "Teng Wen-gong xia" Section 10, pp. 273–7)

[59] Mencius said, "Chen Zhongzi would refuse the state of Qi were it offered to him against the principles of rightness, and everyone believed him. But what he calls rightness is merely the rightness of refusing a basketful of rice and a bowlful of soup. Nothing is more wrong than repudiating the fundamental relationship between parents and children, between the ruler and the subjects and between a superior and an inferior. How can we, on the grounds of his small virtue, trust him with important matters?" (Chapter 13 "Jin-xin shang" Section 34, pp. 546–7)

[60] Gongduzi said, "Kuang Zhang is called an impious son by the entire state. Why do you, Master, not only associate with him but treat him with courtesy?" Mencius said, "Customarily a person is called impious as a son for any of five reasons: first, he neglects caring for his parents because of laziness; second, he neglects caring for his parents because of indulgence in gambling and drinking wine; third, he neglects caring for his parents because of stinginess with money and excessive love of his wife and children; fourth, he shames his parents because of his abandonment to sensual pleasures; and fifth, he endangers his parents because of his aggressive behaviour. Has Zhangzi a single one of these problems? In his case, father and son are at odds from taxing each other over a moral issue. It is for friends to demand goodness from each other; for father and son to do so seriously undermines the affection between them. Do you think that Zhangzi does not want to be with his wife and sons? Because of his offence, he is not allowed near his father. Therefore, he sent his wife and sons away and refused to allow them to look after him. To his way of thinking, unless he acted in this way, his offence would be greater. That is all Zhangzi is guilty of." (Chapter 8, "Li Lou xia" Section 30, pp. 352–4)

[61] Mencius was about to go to see the king [King Xuan of Qi] when a messenger from the king came with an instruction: "I was to come to see you, but I have a cold and cannot be exposed to the wind. Tomorrow morning I shall, however, hold court, and I wonder if I shall have the opportunity of seeing you then." To this Mencius replied, "Unfortunately, I too am ill and shall be unable to come to court." The next day, Mencius went on a visit of condolence to the Dongguo 東郭 family. Gongsun Chou said, "Yesterday you excused yourself on the grounds of illness, yet today you go on a visit of condolence. This is, perhaps, not quite right?" "I was ill yesterday, but I am recovered today. Why should I not go on a visit of condolence?" The king sent someone to enquire after Mencius's illness. When a doctor came, Meng Zhongzi 孟仲子 [a cousin of Mencius] said, "Yesterday when the king's summons came, Mencius was ill and was unable to go to court. Today he is a little better and has hastened to court. But I am not sure that he can make it." Then Meng Zhongzi sent several men to intercept Mencius with the message, "Please do not return home but go straight to court." Mencius was compelled to go and spend the night with the Jingchou 景丑 family. Jingzi 景子 said, "Within

a family the most important principle is that governing the relation between the father and the son; without, it is between the ruler and the subjects. Between the father and the son, the chief emphasis is on mutual love; between the ruler and the subjects, it is on mutual respect. I have seen the king showing you his respect but I have yet to see you showing your respect to the king." "Oh! What kind of talk is this! No one in the state of Qi talks to the king about humanity and righteousness. Do you think it is because they do not think these nice? In their minds, they say, 'How can we talk about humanity and righteousness to a person like him?' There is nothing more disrespectful than this. I have never dared to put before the king anything short of the Way of Yao and Shun. Thus, no man of Qi respects the king as much as I do." Jingzi said, "No, that is not what I had in mind. According to the rites, 'When summoned by one's father, one should not simply say, yes. When summoned by one's ruler, one should not wait for the carriage horse to be harnessed.' You were actually about to go to see the king but, on hearing his instruction, you stopped. It seems that your act is in contradiction to the rites." "Is that what you meant? . . . A ruler who is to achieve great things must have subjects he does not summon. If he wants to consult them, he goes to them. If he does not honour virtue and delight in the Way in such a manner, he is not worthy of being helped towards the achievement of great things . . . Tang 湯 first received instructions from Yi Yin 伊尹 and then appointed him a minister. As a result, Tang became a True King without much personal effort. Duke Huan 桓公 first received instructions from Guan Zhong 管仲 and then appointed him a minister. As a result the duke became a hegemon without much personal effort . . . The duke did not dare to summon Guan Zhong. If Guan Zhong could not be summoned, how much would be the case for someone who has no wish to be merely like him?" (Chapter 4 "Gongsun Chou xia" Section 2, pp. 150–5)

[62] Peng Geng asked, "With tens of carriages and hundreds of followers in tow, you, sir, went from state to state and received hospitality from the feudal lords. Is this not rather excessive?" Mencius said, "If one's conduct is not in accordance with the Way, one should not accept even a basket of food from another. If it is, Shun accepted the world from Yao and did not think it was excessive. But you think it was?" "No. But it is not right for a gentleman not to earn his keep." "If there is no exchange between people of different trades to meet inadequacy with surplus, farmers would have surplus grain and weavers surplus cloths. If there is exchange then carpenters and carriage-makers all deserve to be fed. Here is a man who is filial at home and brotherly abroad, acts as a guardian of the ways of the sage kings for the benefit of students of later times. But in your view he does not deserve to be fed? Why do you honour the carpenter and carriage-maker more than the man who practises benevolence and righteousness?" "The intention of a carpenter or carriage-maker is to make a living. Is the intention of a gentleman following the Way also to make a living?" "Why do you mention intention? Whoever has accomplished something worthwhile to you, you will feed him. Do you do so on account of his intention or his accomplishment?" "On account of his intention." "If here is a builder who obviously intended to make a living but

broke your tiles and soiled your wall, would you feed him?" "No." "Then you feed a person on account of his accomplishment not his intention." (Chapter 6 "Teng Wen-gong xia" Section 4, pp. 251–3)

[63] Mencius said, "A superior man will not observe a 'rite' that is contrary to the spirit of the rites, nor will he do a 'right act' that is contrary to the spirit of righteousness." (Chapter 8 "Li Lou xia" Section 6, p. 325)

[64] Mencius said, "A superior man need not always keep his word, nor does he have to see his action through to the end. He only aims at what is right." (Chapter 8 "Li Lou xia" Section 11, p. 327)

[65] Mencius said, "The conduct of a gentleman is indeed not easy for ordinary people to understand." (Chapter 12 "Gaozi xia" Section 6, p. 492)

[66] Mencius said, "Teaching can be done in many ways. My reluctance to teach a person is also a way to teach him." (Chapter 12 "Gaozi xia" Section 16, p. 516)

(3) The officials

[67] Zhou Xiao 周霄 asked, "In the past did gentlemen seek government posts?" Mencius replied, "Yes, they did. It was reported that when Confucius was out of government employment for three months he felt unsettled." . . . "If to be employed by the government is so important why does a gentleman find it so difficult to get employed?" "When a boy is born, his parents wish that he may one day find a wife; when a girl is born, her parents wish that she may one day find a husband . . . But, if without waiting for neither the command of the parent nor the arrangement of a matchmaker, a man and a woman bore a hole in the wall to peep at each other or climb over the wall to get together, they will be despised by their parents and countrymen. In ancient times, though gentlemen wanted to serve in the government, they disliked taking office not according to the proper way. When a man takes an office not according to the proper way, his act is in the same category as boring a peephole in the wall." (Chapter 6 "Teng Wen-gong xia" Section 3 pp. 247–51)

[68] Wan Zhang said, "Some said that Yi Yin 伊尹 tried to attract the attention of Tang by his cooking skills; was that the case?" Mencius replied, "No, that was not. Yi Yin tilled fields in Youshen and delighted in the Way of Yao and Shun. He would not accept the position of governing the world if the offer was not right and in accordance with the Way . . . Three times Tang sent envoys to make the offer. Yi Yin changed his mind, saying, 'To work in the fields and enjoy the Way of Yao and Shun is not as good as to make the ruler one like Yao or Shun, and not as good as to make the people like those of Yao and Shun . . . ' He thought about every man and woman who had not enjoyed the benefits of Yao and Shun and felt as though he had left them in ditches. Because he wanted to take on himself the heavy responsibility of bringing peace to the world, he went to Tang and persuaded him to fight the Xia Dynasty and save the people." (Chapter 9 "Wan Zhang shang" Section 7, 385–7)

[69] Mencius said, "Shun rose from the fields. Fu Yue 傅說 was raised to office from among the building sites, Jiao Ge 膠鬲 from the fish and salt market, Guan Yiwu

管夷吾 from prison . . . Thus, when Heaven is to place great responsibilities on a man, it is first of all to trouble his mind and test his will with difficult problems, and then to make his muscles and bones toil, to let him suffer hunger and other forms of depravation, and to thwart his efforts, all for the purpose of motivating his heart and toughening his character and improving his abilities. A man can make corrections only after learning many of his own mistakes and can innovate only after frustration and careful thinking." (Chapter 12 "Gaozi xia" Section 15, p. 510)

[70] Mencius said, "When all his close attendants say a certain person is worthy, the ruler will not take it as enough; when all the high officials say so, he will not take it as enough; when all the people in the country say so, he will then carefully investigate, and employ that person only after finding him indeed worthy. When all of his close attendants say a certain person is not suitable, the ruler will not listen; when all the high officials say so, he will not listen; when all the people in the country say so, he will then investigate, and dismiss that person only after finding him indeed not suitable. When all of his close attendants say a certain person should be executed, the ruler will not listen; when all the high officials say so, he will not listen; when all the people in the country say so, the ruler will carefully investigate and order the execution only after finding him indeed guilty." (Chapter 2 "Liang Hui-wang xia" Section 7, pp. 85–6)

[71] Chenzi 陳子 asked, "Under what conditions would a gentleman of the ancient times take office?" Mencius said, "There are three conditions under which he would take office, and there are also three conditions under which he would relinquish it: first, when he was greeted with respect in accordance with the rites, and told that his advice was to be put into practice, he would take the offer. When the respectful treatment of him was not reduced but his advice was not put into practice he would leave. Second, though his advice was not to be put into practice, but he was greeted with respect in accordance with the rites, he would take an office, and when the respect is reduced he would leave. In the worst case, he lacked food and was unable to leave his house because of hunger. A ruler heard about this and said, 'I am unable to follow either in a significant sense the Way he advocates, nor more practically his specific advice. Now he is starving in my land. I am ashamed!' Consequently, provisions were delivered to him. It was all right for him to accept the handouts to save him from death." (Chapter 12 "Gaozi xia" Section 15, pp. 509–10)

[72] Mencius said, "To serve in the government is not to save one from poverty, though sometimes it does save one from poverty . . . Confucius once served as a clerk of government storage and said, 'My job is only to keep the accounts correct'. He once served as a keeper of a government animal farm and said, 'My job is only to ensure the cattle and sheep grow well'. When an official in a low post talks about lofty measures, it is offensive; when an official in the court of the state is unable to implement the Way, it is shameful." (Chapter 10 "Wan Zhang xia" 萬章下 Section 5, pp. 417–18)

[73] Mencius said, "Boyi . . . would not serve the wrong kind of ruler and govern the wrong kind of people. When the country was in order he served, when it was

in chaos he retired . . . Yi Yin said, 'What kind of ruler would I not serve? What kind of people would I not govern?' He served when the country was in order and served also when the country was in chaos, saying 'Heaven gives birth to all people and makes those who have attained understanding of the Way early enlighten those who are slow in attaining such understanding. I, being one who understood early, am going to enlighten the common people' . . . Liuxia Hui was not ashamed to serve a ruler of tarnished reputation and did not decline an offer of small office . . . saying 'You are you; I am I. Even though you are naked beside me, how can you tarnish me?'" (Chapter 9 "Wan Zhang xia" Section 1, pp. 395–6)

[74] Mencius said, " . . . Confucius would serve in the government of a state where the ruler was capable of implementing the Way, where the ruler treated him according to the correct rites, and where the ruler was sincere in providing for the worthy." (Chapter 10 "Wan Zhang xia" Section 4, p. 416)

[75] Mencius said, "There are those who simply serve the ruler, they merely please him. There are those who intend to bring peace to the state, they achieve satisfaction through realisation of their aspiration." (Chapter 13 "Jin-xin shang" Section 19, p. 533)

[76] Mencius said: "Today, one in the service of a ruler will say to him, 'I can extend your territory and fill your treasury'. This so-called good official of today would be known in the past as a thief stealing from the people because, where a ruler has no intention of following the right way and no will to practise benevolence, to enrich him is like enriching Jie. Similarly, today one will say to a ruler, 'I can form an alliance between your state and others, and I can make you victorious in military campaigns.' This so-called good official of today would be known in the past as a thief harming the people because, where a ruler has no intention of following the right way and no will to practise benevolence, to help him fight forcefully is to assist a Jie. (Chapter 12 "Gaozi xia" Section 9, p. 504)

[77] Mencius said, "While serving as the manager of the House of Ji 季氏 [the chief minister of the state of Lu] Ran Qiu 冉求 was unable to change the moral character of his master but doubled his income of previous times. Confucius said, 'Qiu is not a follower of my principles. You, my disciples, can beat a drum and attack him!' From this it is obvious that one who enriches a ruler who does not practise benevolent policies is dismissed by Confucius. How much more would Confucius disapprove of one who fought forcefully for a ruler? In a war to gain land, the slain will fill the field; in a war to capture a walled city, the slain will fill the city. This is called making the land feast on people's flesh and, for this crime, the death penalty should not be spared. Hence, those who are skilful in warfare should receive the most severe punishment; those who arrange military alliances should receive the next most severe punishment; those who opened up waste land and make people toil over it to increase revenue for the government should receive the next most severe punishment. (Chapter 7 "Li Lou shang" Section 14, pp. 302–4)

[78] When governing the state of Zheng, Zichan 子產 let his own carriage take people across the fords of the Rivers Zhen and Wei. Mencius said, "He was kind

and generous but did not know how to govern. In the eleventh month, footbridges should be built and bridges for carriages by the twelfth month. The people would have no difficulty in crossing the fords. When a good official governs properly, it is enough to open a way for the people. How could he take everyone across the fords? Thus, if a person in government wanted to please everyone, he would find his day is not long enough." (Chapter 8 "Li Lou xia" Section 2, pp. 320–1)

[79] Gongsun Chou asked Mencius, "Sir, if you can have your way in the state of Qi, could the achievements of Guan Zhong and Yanzi 晏子 [another able chief minister] be repeated?" Mencius said, "You are indeed a man from Qi, knowing only Guan Zhong and Yanzi. Someone asked Zeng Xi 曾西 [a grandson of Confucius's disciple Zengzi 曾子], 'You, sir, and Zilu 子路 [another disciple of Confucius], who are better and wiser?' Zeng Xi appeared uneasy and said, 'He was the one my late grandfather held in awe.' 'Then who is better and wiser, you, sir, or Guan Zhong?' Zeng Xi looked offended and said, 'How can you compare me with Guan Zhong? He was so trusted by the ruler and governed the state for so long, and yet his achievements were so low. How can you compare me with such a man?' Guan Zhong was what Zeng Xi would not like to be, and you think I would like to be?" "Guan Zhong made his ruler a hegemon, Yanzi glorified his ruler. They were not worth your emulation?" "To make the ruler of Qi a True King is as easy as turning over one's hand." "If so, I, as a student of yours, am even more confused. Virtuous as King Wen was, he did not succeed in extending his governance over the world when he died at the age of one hundred. It took King Wu and Duke Zhou to continue his effort to make it prevail. Now you say to be a True King is easy. Is King Wen an unworthy model?" "How can one stand comparison with King Wen! From Tang to Wu Ding 武丁 [an able ruler of the Yin Dynasty], there were six or seven worthy and wise monarchs. The world was long content with the rule of the Yin Dynasty. Where there was this long rule, it was difficult to change. Wu Ding commanded the homage of the feudal lords and governed the country like turning it in his palm. Shou was not far removed from Wu Ding, the tradition of the old regime, the custom and good government policies were still in existence. Moreover, there were many great officials . . . all of them wise and virtuous, who helped and supported Shou. That was why he lasted quite a long time before losing his throne . . . Nevertheless King Wen rose up from a state of only 100 *li* square. That was why it was difficult . . . Now it is easy . . . Qi has land [more than 10,000 *li* square] and [a large] population . . . If the ruler practises benevolent government, he will become a True King, and no one can resist him." (Chapter 3 "Gongsun Chou shang" Section 1, pp. 102–9)

[80] Mencius said, "When Confucius was the chief judge of the state of Lu, his advice was not followed. He participated in a sacrifice but was not given a piece of meat from the sacrificial animal afterwards. He promptly left Lu without taking off his ceremonial cap. Those who did not understand him thought that he left for not being given the meat; those who claimed to understand him thought that it was because, in treating him, the ruler of Lu failed to abide by the proper rites. But what Confucius wanted was to give an impression of leaving because of a

misdeed rather than to leave without a reason." (Chapter 12 "Gaozi xia" Section 6, p. 492)

[81] Gongsun Chou asked Mencius, "Is it an ancient practice to serve in government without accepting remuneration?" Mencius replied, "No. After I had my first audience with the king [King Xuan of Qi] I already had the intention of leaving. [Although I stayed as a guest official] I declined remuneration because I did not want to appear to have changed my principles." (Chapter 4 "Gongsun Chou xia" Section 14, p. 184)

[82] After Mencius left Qi, Yin Shi 尹士 said to someone, "If he did not know that the king is incapable of acting like Tang and King Wu, he is not bright. If he knew and yet came, he is to seek government pay. He came from 1,000 *li* away to see the king and left after failing to gain the king's trust but stayed in the town of Zhou for three nights. Why was he so slow in departing? I am not pleased." Gaozi 高子 told this to Mencius. Mencius said, "What does Yin Shi know about me? Coming from 1,000 *li* away to see the king was what I wanted. Failing to gain his trust and therefore leaving is not what I wanted. I could not help it. In my heart I felt that leaving after staying three nights in Zhou was too hasty. I wished that the king would change his mind. If he did, he would ask me to return. After leaving Zhou and not being chased by anyone sent by the king to recall me, I had a strong desire to return home. However, did I give up on the king? If he is still capable of doing good and employs me I will not only bring peace to the people of Qi but also to all the people in the country. If only the king would change his mind – that is what I hope every day. I am in no way like those petty men who, after their advice to the king is rejected, take offence and show resentment on their faces, and when they leave, they exhaust themselves by a day-long journey before putting up for the night." Yin Shi heard this and said, "I am indeed a petty man!" (Chapter 4 "Gongsun Chou xia" Section 12, pp. 181–2)

(4) The ruler

[83] Wan Zhang said, "Is it true that Yao gave the kingdom to Shun?" "No", Mencius replied, "The king cannot give the kingdom to another person." "If so, who gave the kingdom to Shun?" "Heaven gave it him." "By 'Heaven gave it him', do you mean that Heaven earnestly told him so?" "No. Heaven does not speak but reveals itself through its acts and deeds." "How does Heaven do so?" "The king can recommend a man to Heaven but he cannot make Heaven give this man the kingdom . . . In the past Yao recommended Shun to Heaven and Heaven accepted him; he presented him to the people and the people accepted him. Hence I said, 'Heaven does not speak but reveals itself by its acts and deeds.'" "May I ask how he was accepted by Heaven when recommended to it and how he was accepted by the people when presented to them?" "When he was put in charge of sacrifices, the hundred gods enjoyed them. This showed that Heaven accepted him. When he was put in charge of government affairs, they were kept in order and the people were content. This showed that the people accepted him. Heaven gave it to him, and the people gave it to him. Hence I said, 'The king

cannot give the kingdom to another person.' Shun assisted Yao for twenty-eight years. This is something which could not be brought about by man, but only by Heaven. Yao died and, after the mourning period of three years, Shun shunned Yao's son and withdrew to the south of the Southern River, yet the feudal lords of the kingdom came to pay homage to him, not to Yao's son; those who were engaged in litigation went to him, not to Yao's son; and ballad singers sang the praises of him, not of Yao's son. Hence I said, 'It was brought about by Heaven.' Only then did Shun return to the Central Kingdom and ascend the imperial throne. If he had just moved into Yao's palace and ousted his son, it would have been usurpation of the kingdom, not receiving it from Heaven. The 'Tai shi' [a chapter of the *Book of History*] says, 'Heaven sees with the eyes of its people; Heaven hears with the ears of its people.' This describes well what I meant." (Chapter 9 "Wan Zhang shang" Section 5, pp. 379–81)

[84] Wan Zhang asked, "It is said by some that virtue declined with Yu who chose his own son to succeed him, instead of a good and wise man. Is this true?" "No, it is not", replied Mencius. "If Heaven wished to give the kingdom to a good and wise man, it would be given to a good and wise man; if Heaven wished to give it to the son, it would be given to the son. In the past, Shun recommended Yu to Heaven, and died seventeen years later. When the mourning period of three years was over, Yu shunned Shun's son and withdrew to Yang Cheng, yet the people of the kingdom followed him just as those followed Shun instead of Yao's son after Yao's death. Yu recommended Yi 益 [a minister] to Heaven, and died seven years later. When the mourning period of three years was over, Yi shunned Yu's son and withdrew to the northern slopes of Mount Ji. Those who came to pay homage and those who were engaged in litigation went to Qi 啟 [Yu's son] instead of Yi, saying, 'This is the son of our lord'. Ballad singers sang the praises of Qi instead of Yi, saying, 'This is the son of our lord'. . . . Confucius said, 'Yao and Shun abdicated, Xia, Shang and Zhou practised hereditary succession, but the principle they followed was the same.'" (Chapter 9 "Wan Zhang shang" Section 6, pp. 381–5)

[85] Mencius said, ". . . Danzhu 丹朱 [Yao's son] was depraved, as was the son of Shun. Over a period of many years Shun assisted Yao, and Yu assisted Shun. Thus the people enjoyed their benefits for a long time. Qi was worthy and able to follow Yu's way. Yi assisted Yu for only a few years, and benefited the people not long. Shun and Yu differed from Yi greatly in the length of time they assisted the king, and their sons were worthy and unworthy. All this was due to Heaven and could not have been brought about by man. When a thing is done, though no one has actually taken any action, then it is the work of Heaven; when a thing comes about, though no one brings it about, then it is determined by fate." (Chapter 9 "Wan Zhang shang" Section 5, pp. 382–3)

[86] Mencius said, ". . . A common man who comes to possess the kingdom must not only have the virtue of a Shun or a Yu but also the recommendation of a king. That is why Confucius never possessed the kingdom. On the other hand, he who inherits the kingdom is only put aside by Heaven if he is as evil as Jie or Zhou.

That is why Yi, Yi Yin and the Duke of Zhou never came to possess the kingdom." (Chapter 9 "Wan Zhang shang" Section 5, p. 383)

[87] Mencius said, "[If a ruler wishes to have glory and avoid humility it is best] to value virtue and respect the learned, have the good and wise in high office and the talented and capable on the jobs; then, while the state is at peace and the people have leisure, make clear his policies and laws; then even the great states will stand in awe of him." (Chapter 3, "Gongsun Chou shang" Section 4, p. 132)

[88] Mencius said, "Li Lou 離婁 had keen eyesight, Gongshuzi 公輸子 had deft hands, but not using instruments for circumference and right angle, they could not make perfect circles and squares . . . One who knows the Way of Yao and Shun but does not implement benevolent policies, cannot bring peace to the world . . . Thus it is said, 'Good intention alone is not sufficient for government. A rule cannot be effective by itself.'" (Chapter 7 "Li Lou shang" Section 1, pp. 279–84)

[89] Mencius said, "The carpenter's compasses and square are the ultimate instruments for making perfect circles and right angles. The Sage is the ultimate model for human beings . . . A ruler who does not govern the subjects as Yao governed his subjects, is harming one's subjects." (Chapter 7 "Li Lou shang" Section 2, pp. 288–9)

[90] Mencius said, "The Three Dynasties won the country through practising benevolence; they lost it for being no longer benevolent. This is true for the rise and fall, survival and collapse, of a state. An inhumane king cannot keep his kingdom; an inhumane feudal lord cannot keep his state; an inhumane official cannot keep his family line and its ancestral temple of worship; an inhumane officer or commoner cannot keep his four limbs." (Chapter 7 "Li Lou shang" Section 3, pp. 289–90)

[91] Mencius said, "The common people who do not have constant material means will not have constant hearts. Without constant hearts they will become unprincipled and excessive, stopping at nothing. To punish them when they have fallen into crimes is to trap them. Can a benevolent man in authority trap people? Therefore when an enlightened ruler makes regulations regarding the material means of support a man needs, he ensures that it is sufficient for the man to care for his parents, wife and children . . . If Your Majesty wishes to put this into practice you should go back to the basics: let the family with 5 *mu* of land around its house plant mulberry trees, then those over fifty years old will have silk to wear. Let chickens and pigs not miss their breeding periods, then those above seventy years will have meat to eat. Let a peasant have a plot of 100 *mu* and ensure he does not miss the farming season, then a family of eight will not go hungry . . . When the aged have silk to wear and meat to eat and the common people are neither hungry nor cold, it is impossible that you will not be a True King." (Chapter 1, "Liang Hui-wang shang" Section 7, pp. 56–8)

[92] Mencius said, "Benevolent government must begin with land demarcation. When boundaries are not properly drawn, the distribution of land to the tillers will be unfair and the income of officials derived from the land will be inequitable

. . . I suggest that . . . in the countryside a piece of land of 1 *li* square be divided into nine plots, each to pay a tax of one tenth of the produce; inside the walled city, people be required to pay one twentieth of their income voluntarily . . . A plot of land in the countryside of 1 *li* square will be divided in the form of the character *jing* 井, each consisting of 100 *mu*. The plot of 100 *mu* in the middle of the *jing* 井 will be public land. The eight plots surrounding it will be distributed to eight families. The eight families will work jointly in the public field first and then in their own plots separately . . . This is a broad outline; the details are up to your ruler and you people." (Chapter 5, "Teng Wen-gong shang" Section 3, pp. 205–14)

[93] Mencius said, "A worthy ruler is modest and frugal, and treats those below him according to the rites and takes from the people with restraint . . . In collecting land taxes, the rulers of the Xia adopted the *gong* system, those of the Yin the *zhu*, and those of the Zhou the *che*. In fact, in all three cases the rate was the same: one in ten." (Chapter 1, "Teng Wen-gong shang" Section 3, pp. 196–7)

[94] Mencius said [to King Hui of Liang], "If your majesty practises benevolent government towards your people – using fewer punishments, collecting less taxes, and letting the farmers have enough time and energy to plough deeply and weed frequently – and teaches the able-bodied men in their spare time the principles of filial piety, brotherly love, loyalty to the state and trustworthiness in their relations with others so that they know how they are to serve their fathers and older brothers in the family, and the elders and superiors outside of it, you can have them taking up simple wooden clubs against the strong armour and sharp weapons of the states of Qin and Chu." (Chapter 1, "Teng Wen-gong shang" Section 5, p. 40)

(H) Social relationships

(1) Between individuals

[95] Mencius said, "A man who debases himself is not worth talking to; a man who abandons himself cannot be trusted with an endeavour. He who refuses to talk about the principles of the rites and righteousness debases himself. He who says 'I am incapable of abiding by humanity or of following righteousness', abandons himself. Benevolence is a man's peaceful abode and righteousness his proper path. It is lamentable for anyone not to live in his peaceful abode and not to follow his proper path." (Chapter 7 "Li Lou shang" Section 10, p. 298)

[96] Mencius said, "If a man in a subordinate position cannot win the confidence of his superiors, he will be unable to regulate the people. There is a way for him to win the confidence of his superiors – if he is not trusted by his friends, he cannot win the confidence of his superiors. There is a way for him to win the trust of his friends – if, in serving his parents, he fails to please them, he cannot win the trust of his friends. There is a way for him to please his parents – if, upon reflecting on himself, he finds that he has not been true to himself, he cannot please his parents. There is a way for him to become true to himself – if he does

not understand goodness, he cannot be true to himself. Hence being true is the Way of Heaven; to be true is the Way for man. There has never been a man totally true to himself who fails to move others. On the other hand, one who is not true to himself can never hope to move others." (Chapter 7 "Li Lou shang" Section 12, p. 299)
[96] Mencius said, "All things [about human relations] are there in oneself. If on reflection, one finds oneself being sincere, one will have no greater happiness. Doing one's best to treat others as one treats oneself is the shortest way to be benevolent. (Chapter 13 "Jin-xin shang" Section 4, pp. 520–1)
[97] Mencius said, "He who is benevolent loves people; he who observes the rites is respectful to people. He who loves people is loved by them; he who is respectful to people is respected by them. In case there is a person who treats others outrageously, a gentleman facing this will reflect on himself thinking 'I must not have been benevolent and courteous towards him, otherwise how can this mistreatment come to me?' If, upon this reflection, he found that he had been benevolent and courteous, and yet the outrageous treatment continues, he will reflect again thinking, 'I must have failed to do my best in dealing with him'. If, upon this reflection, he found that he had done his best and yet the mistreatment continues, he will say, 'This is a person not knowing what he is doing. As such he is no different from a bird or beast. Why should I be troubled by a bird or beast?'" (Chapter 8 "Li Lou xia" Section 28, pp. 350–1)
[98] Mencius said, "In the world there are three most highly honoured things: rank, age and virtue. In government, rank is supreme; in the local community, age; for assisting the government and educating the people it is virtue." (Chapter 4 "Gongsun Chou xia" Section 2, p. 154)

(2) Between the ruler and the common people

[99] Mencius said to King Xuan of Qi, "If a ruler treats his subjects as his hands and feet, they will treat him as their belly and heart. If he treats them as dogs and horses, they will treat him as a stranger. If he treats them as mud and weeds, they will treat him as an enemy." (Chapter 8 "Li Lou xia" Section 3, p. 322)
[100] Mencius said, "There is a common expression – the kingdom, the feudal state, the family. The basis of the kingdom is in the state; that of the state is in the family, and that of the family is in the individual person." (Chapter 7 "Li Lou shang" Section 5, p. 290)
[101] Mencius said, "The people are most valuable, the temple of the gods of earth and grain are the next, and the ruler is least. Thus, he who has the trust of the people can be the king; he who has the trust of the king can be a feudal lord; he who has the trust of a feudal lord can be an official. When a feudal lord endangers the temple of the gods of earth and grain [symbols of the kingdom] he is to be replaced. When the sacrificial animals are properly prepared, grains and other offerings and vessels are clean, and ceremonies are performed in time, and yet there is drought and flood, the temple should be replaced." (Chapter 14 "Jin-xin xia" Section 14, p. 573)

[102] Mencius said to King Xuan of Qi, "Suppose a subject of yours entrusted his wife and children to the care of a friend and went on a trip to the state of Chu. Upon returning, he found the friend had let his wife and children suffer cold and hunger. What should he do?" The king said, "Discard the friend." "If a superior judge were unable to give guidance to lower judges, what should be done?" "Dismiss him." "If things within the four borders of a state were not in order, what should be done?" The king turned to his attendants and changed the subject. (Chapter 2 "Liang Hui-wang xia" Section 6, pp. 83–4)
[103] King Xuan of Qi asked, "Is it true that Tang banished Jie and King Wu launched punitive campaigns against Shou?" Mencius replied, "It is so recorded." "Is regicide permissible?" "A man who cripples humanity is a crippler, and one who mangles righteousness is a mangler. He who is both a mutilator and a crippler is a 'lone despot'. I have heard of the punishment of the 'lone despot Zhou', but not of regicides." (Chapter 2 "Liang Hui-wang xia" Section 8, p. 86)

(3) Relationship between the "superior men" and those in power

[104] Wan Zhang said, "May I ask why you do not go to see the feudal lords?" Mencius said, ". . . According to the rites, before being appointed to a government office a commoner would not dare to see a feudal lord." "When a commoner is summoned to corvée labour he goes to serve. Why then should he refuse to go when he is summoned to an audience with the state ruler?" Mencius said, "It is right for him to go and serve but it is not right for him to see the ruler. Moreover, for what reason does the ruler wish to see him?" "For the reason that he is learned or that he is virtuous and wise." "If it is because he is learned, even the king does not summon his teacher, let alone a feudal lord. If it is because he is virtuous and wise, then I have never heard of summoning such a man when a ruler wishes to see him." . . . Wan Zhang said, "When summoned by the ruler, Confucius went right away without waiting until his carriage was ready. So Confucius was wrong?" Mencius replied, "Confucius at that time was already holding an office. He was summoned as an official in government service." (Chapter 10 "Wan Zhang xia" Section 7, pp. 424–7)
[105] Chen Dai 陳代 said, "In declining to see the feudal lords you appear to be abiding by a rather petty principle. Once you see one of them, you may, in the best case, make him a True King, or, at least, make him a hegemon. Moreover, it is said, 'Bend the foot, straighten the yard'. To me this rule seems worth applying." Mencius said, "To bend a little in small matters in order to get the big ones straight is a practice in seeking profit. If there is profit, would bending the yard to straighten the foot also be worth doing? . . . You are wrong. One who bends himself can never straighten others." (Chapter 6 "Teng Wen-gong xia" Section 1, pp. 240–4)
[106] Mencius said, "When speaking to a person of lofty position do not be impressed by his trappings but look at him with disdain. He may have halls several yards high with eaves extending out several feet but if, I could have my aspirations fulfilled, I would not have those. When he dines, there may be in

front of him a table tens of feet square, full of dishes, and there may be hundreds of female attendants waiting on him but, if I could have my aspirations fulfilled, I would not have those. He may have great bands playing music while he gives parties and thousands of chariots following him while he engages in galloping and hunting but, if I could have my aspirations fulfilled, I would not not do so. All those things valued by him are what I do not care about. What I will do is all in accordance with norms established since antiquity. Why should I cower before him?" (Chapter 14 "Jin-xin xia" Section 34, pp. 596–8)

[107] Wan Zhang said, "Gentlemen do not rely on the generosity of a feudal lord for living. Why?" Mencius said, "He would not dare to think it is correct. When a feudal lord has lost his state, he would depend on other feudal lords for protection, and it is in accordance with the rites. A gentleman relying on a feudal lord for living is not in accordance with the rites." Wan Zhang said, "If a ruler gives grain to him, would he accept?" "He would." "On what principle does he accept?" "The ruler always gives charity to people in need." "Why would the gentleman accept charity but not regular gifts?" "Because he would not dare to think it is correct." "May I ask what do you mean by 'would not dare to think it is right'?" "Gatekeepers and watchmen receive wages from the authorities because they have regular jobs. Those who do have regular jobs and accept regular pay from the authorities are not presumptuous." "If one can accept charity or gifts from a ruler can this practice be continuous?" "To Zisi 子思 [Confucius's grandson], Duke Mu of the state of Lu 魯繆公 frequently sent his greetings and pots of meat. Zisi was not pleased. Finally, he directed the messenger out of his front door, faced north, bowed twice and declined the gift, saying, 'Now I know the ruler treats me as his dogs and horses'. Since then no more gifts came. In spite of his claim of liking the worthy, if a ruler can neither elevate them to high office nor properly take care of them, can his claim be called true?" "May I ask how, if a ruler wishes to take care of a worthy man, can this be done properly?" "For the first time a messenger should be sent under the order of the ruler to present the gifts. The worthy man would bow twice and accept them. Afterwards, the granary keeper would continue to present grain and the chef to present meat but no longer do so as a being carried out as a special order from the ruler. Zisi considered that requiring him to bow repeatedly for each delivery of a pot of meat was not the way to provide for a gentleman. To take care of Shun, Yao ordered his nine sons to work with Shun, married his two daughters to Shun, made the hundred officials and cattle and sheep and the granary ready to serve Shun while he was still labouring in the fields, and finally raised him to high office. This is how a king honours a worthy man." (Chapter 10 "Wan Zhang xia" Section 6, pp. 419–24)

[108] Duke Mu frequently went to see Zisi and asked, "In ancient times, how did a ruler of a state with a thousand chariots make friends with gentlemen?" Zisi was displeased and said, "What the ancients would say was *to serve*, not *to befriend* them." The reason for Zisi's displeasure was: "In terms of position, you are the ruler and I am your subject. How dare I befriend you? In terms of virtue, it is you

who ought to serve me. How can you befriend me?" (Chapter 10 "Wan Zhang xia" Section 7, p. 425)

[109] Mencius resigned from office in the government of the state of Qi and was about to go home. The king of Qi came to see him saying, "Previously I wished to meet you but did not have the honour of a meeting. Then I had the pleasure of attending the same court and was delighted. Now you are abandoning me and going home. I wonder whether from now on there will be further opportunities to see you again." Mencius said, "That is just what I wish though I did not dare make the suggestion." On another day, the king said to Shizi 時子 [an official], "I would like to give Mencius a house in the central part of my capital, and a pension of 10,000 *zhong* [a *zhong* was about 6,400 handfuls] of grain for the support of his disciples, so that my officials and my people will have a model to look up to. Go and say this to him for me." Shizi delivered the message through Chenzi 陳子 [a disciple of Mencius]. Mencius said, "I see, but how could Shizi not realise that it will not work. If I wish to get rich would declining 100,000 *zhong* [the yearly emolument for Mencius when he was an official of Qi] and accepting 10,000 *zhong* be the way to do it?" (Chapter 4 "Gongsun Chou xia" Section 10, pp. 175–7)

(4) Between the ruler and the officials

[110] King Xuan of Qi said, "The rites prescribe that a subject should observe the rule of mourning for a ruler he has once served. Under what circumstances is this rule to be observed?" Mencius said, "Where a subject whose advice has been adopted by the ruler for the benefit of the people has a reason to relinquish his post and leave the country, the ruler sends someone to conduct him beyond the border, and a messenger is sent in advance to the place he was heading for to prepare his way. Only if, after three years, he decides not to return, will the ruler take over his land. This is known as the three courtesies. If the ruler behaves in this way then it is the subject's duty to observe the rules of mourning for him. Today when a subject whose advice has been rejected by the ruler to the detriment of the people has a reason to leave, the ruler forces him to go under guard, makes things difficult for him in the state he is going to and takes his land the day he departs. This ruler can be called an enemy. What mourning rules are there for an enemy?" (Chapter 8 "Li Lou xia" Section 3, pp. 322–3)

[111] King Xuan of Qi asked about ministers. Mencius said, "What kind of ministers is Your Majesty asking about?" "Are there different kinds of ministers?" "Yes. There are ministers from the ruler's same lineage and those from families of a different surname." "What about ministers from the same lineage?" "If the ruler made serious mistakes, they would remonstrate with him; when repeated remonstration fell on deaf ears, they would depose him." The king promptly displayed an astounded and angry expression. Mencius said, "Your Majesty, please do not find my answer strange and unpleasant. You asked me and I dare not to give an incorrect answer." After regaining his composure, the king asked about ministers from families of different surnames. Mencius replied, "When the ruler makes a

mistake they will advise against it. If repeated advice fell on deaf ears, they would leave their posts. (Chapter 10 "Wan Zhang xia" Section 9, pp. 429–30)

[112] Gongsun Chou said, "Yi Yin said, 'I cannot tolerate those who do not follow the Way' and he banished Tai Jia 太甲 [successor to King Tang, founder of the Shang Dynasty] to Tong. The people were greatly pleased. When Tai Jia became worthy, Yi Yin welcomed him back to the throne and the people were greatly pleased. So where a wise and virtuous man is an official and the ruler is not worthy, it is all right for the official to banish the ruler?" Mencius said, "It is all right if the official had Yi Yin's noble objective. If not, the act is usurpation." (Chapter 13 "Jin-xin shang" Section 31, p. 545)

Meng-zi 孟子

PART 2
INTERPRETATION

At Zhuangzi's time China was in chaos, much worse than before and progressively becoming more so. The central government of the Zhou was further enfeebled; the feudal states were constantly at war, fighting for land, people and survival. Many small ones were vanquished by bigger ones and several big ones split into smaller ones as a result of internal power struggles. The people lived in poverty and despair, but the ruling class indulged in obscene luxury and became confounded and incapable of proper government. The need for talents to deal with the problems was pressing, and the traditional political system was not able to meet the need. More *shi* (士 intellectuals) rose to the occasion, circulating around the various states and proffering their solutions. Mencius (Meng Ke 孟軻, c.390–305 BCE) was one among them. He was nearly a 150 years after Confucius but a great admirer of the Master. Like Confucius, he was a commoner. In youth, he studied under a student of Zisi 子思, a grandson of Confucius. At the age of thirty he started teaching. In his forties, known as an erudite Ruist, he visited the states of Qi, Song, Teng, Liang, and Lu for nearly twenty years seeking office. For a few years he was appointed a *ke-qing* (客卿 guest minister) in Qi. He retired at the age of sixty-one and devoted his time to teaching and writing. He died at eighty two.[1]

Sima Qian wrote a brief biography of Mencius, pointing out that, at his time, because of the fierce struggle among the warring states, men specialising in political control, diplomatic manoeuvre and military campaign, such as the Legalist Lord Shang 商君 and the war strategist Sunzi 孫子, were in great demand but Mencius preached the virtues of Yao, Shun and the Three Dynasties as the means to achieve good government, and was therefore disagreeable to the contemporary rulers.[2]

Indeed, what Mencius wanted was not simply to help the rulers be victorious; he wished to help one who would listen to him become kingly like Yao and Shun.

The greatest obstacle to this achievement, in his view, was not lack of economic strength and military might, but the proliferation of erroneous conceptions and ideas. In his time, he said the most popular ones were those of Mozi and Yang Zhu (楊朱, *c.*395–335) which "filled the entire world". We have discussed Mozi's theory. Yang Zhu was characterised by Mencius as somewhat of an egoist whose position was almost the opposite of that of Mozi. But, more importantly, both were opposed to the teachings of Confucius.

As we have seen, Mozi advocated universal love and criticised Confucius's hierarchical social system and some of the Ruist practices of the rites; Yang Zhu posed a more fundamental challenge to Confucian principles, which was similar in nature to that made by Zhuangzi in denying human ability to create civilisation and live a life different from that guided blissfully by the law of nature. Mencius thought those ideas pernicious and took it upon himself to scrutinise and refute them. Since Zhuangzi was about twenty-five years his junior, Mencius did not name him in his discussion but criticised Yang Zhu, his contemporary. Though Yang Zhu's words must have been well known to him, in writing they were mostly lost, except for a few passages quoted in the books of other authors which are quite in agreement with Zhuangzi's ideas. We can, therefore, only infer from *Zhuangzi* in what way Mencius was critical of Yang Zhu though there are possibly some differences between the two.

Mencius's own work, *Mengzi* 孟子, was apparently written by him, and its authenticity has not been seriously questioned through history. It expresses his ideas mostly in the form of dialogues between him and rulers, officials, friends and disciples. (It is therefore convenient to arrange the narrative in this format below.) His language was straightforward and fluent though some of his arguments were rather argumentative. As we shall see, he was, indeed, criticised for this by his contemporaries.

Mencius did not engage in examining the contemporary problems in detail and suggest practical solutions. Instead, he took on the difficult task of clearing up the wrong ideas of many thinkers that were at the root of the problems, and establishing a set of what he considered to be the correct ideas. He began with a criticism of Mozi and Yang Zhu, and affirmed the need for a stratified society, various norms, and government authorities, and then proceeded to create a theory about human nature and to formulate rules for good government and proper human relationships. He argued strongly for the feasibility of his theory and expressed confidently that, after its realisation (with the help of someone like him), the chaos of his time could be resolved and a world of peace, prosperity and bright civilisation, similar to that during the reign of sage kings Yao and Shun, could emerge again.

(A) Criticism of Yang Zhu and Mozi

First, Mencius disagreed with Yang Zhu and Mozi. It was interesting that, though he said their words "filled the world", his comments on them were rather brief, mainly in a short statement: "Yang advocates everyone for oneself and therefore denies the importance of the ruler; Mo advocates universal love, and therefore denies the importance of the father. One who dismisses his ruler and his father is a bird or a beast." The criticism was harsh but crude. What Mencius could have said more fully is as follows. The theories of Yang and Mo would damage the functions of the family and society and make human life difficult, unless every person can live like a bird or beast that can survive with complete independence.

It is easy to see that denying the special position of the father and, by extension, the special positions of other members of the family, will make family life, as people knew it, difficult. It is less clear that people also have to live like birds and beasts if they do not have a ruler. Mencius obviously thought that Mozi's idea of universal love would make people regard a ruler as just another ordinary person. In fact, as we have seen, Mozi did not deny the importance of a ruler. On the contrary, he advocated an extremely regimented society with a ruler at its top wielding almost absolute dictatorial power. Why did Mencius make such criticisms? Actually, he was disagreeing with another misconception of his time and trying to explain why government authorities and norms were necessary. That misconception was the product of those known later as *nong-jia* (農家 Agriculturists).

(B) Need of social organisation, norms and authority

Many people of Mencius's time were disgusted by the wasteful lifestyles of those in power and their incompetence in governing. Among them there was a group who admired Shen-nong (神農 the ancient legendary inventor of agriculture) and argued that a ruler should toil in the fields together with his subjects and receive recompense proportionate to his work. Mencius disapproved of this egalitarian stance though he, too, condemned extravagance.

To begin with Mencius did not think Shen-nong was a good model for the rulers of his time. Unlike Mozi, Laozi and Zhuangzi, who had fantasies of a primitive world and a common wish to return to it, Mencius, like Confucius, did not indulge in such ideas and harbour such a wish. He never speculated about what a world of great antiquity was like. The earliest period he spoke about was that of Yao 堯, the legendary sage ruler of the twenty-fourth century BCE and the first hero of Chinese civilisation exalted by the Ruists. According to him, the world of that time was dangerous – there were widespread floods, little easily available food, and many dangerous animals that posed a threat to humans. Life was harsh and far from peaceful. People had to be organised and led by competent leaders, such as Yao and his colleagues, to modify the hostile environment and establish liveable conditions and civilisation.

To accomplish that much, everyone had to work hard. Hard work was hailed as a high virtue by Mozi, an admirer of Yu 禹 who, under Yao's order to tame the flood, laboured so much that no hair was left on his legs and he later became partly paralysed. But not everyone had to do the same work. Mencius pointed out that, to survive, a person needs the help of hundreds of others. Even Xu Xing 徐

行, the leading Agriculturist of the time, was unable to meet his personal needs with the fruits of his own work but had to engage in bartering his products for those of potters, blacksmiths, and so on. This proved that division of labour was necessary and that trade was inevitable. And to produce the goods for everyday life is not the only work people have to do. There are other tasks to ensure their survival, including, for instance, taming floods and overcoming other natural disasters. For such tasks, it is necessary to have norms and government authorities. To make good norms and exercise authority properly, it is necessary to have extraordinary persons. Thus, Mencius observed that there are tasks for superior men and chores for lesser men. The superior men use their minds and worry about the general welfare of all people; the lesser men use their muscles and worry about how well their land is cultivated and their wares are made. The superior men have no time for agriculture and crafts even if they had the skill; they have to give their undivided attention to making and enforcing the norms and maintaining good governance. They are the rulers and the lesser men are the ruled. In their daily lives, the rulers depend on the ruled for sustenance, and the ruled provide the rulers with their basic needs. In short, people have different jobs and roles. Governing is an important job, and it is necessary to have people do it professionally. Extreme egalitarian ideas are therefore erroneous.

(C) Good and bad governments

Government, in Mencius's view, is to co-ordinate people's efforts to make a peaceful, prosperous and civilised way of life. He pointed out that there were, in history, many examples of this objective being reached under good rulers. Yao and Shun 舜 commanded the high officials to work hard for the common people, give them peace and order, help them become self-reliant, educate them and make them virtuous. And these officials obeyed this command conscientiously. For instance, in nine years, while taming the great flood, Yu passed by his house three times, heard his son crying, but never entered the door. The other officials did their jobs with similar diligence, and Yao and Shun were constantly searching for the right people to serve in the government and carefully supervising their work.

What was a good government, one of a True King, like? According to Mencius, it distributed adequate amounts of land to people so that they could have a house, grow crops and raise pigs, chickens and silkworms to produce food and clothing material; it opened government land, including the royal garden, to the public so that they could enjoy it, collect wood and hunt small animals there; it taxed people lightly and gave special care to the destitute; it educated people and punished only those who were personally guilty, never extending punishments to their wives and children.

In the time of the five Hegemons [strong feudal lords of the Chunqiu Period: Duke Huan of Qi 齊桓公, Duke Wen of Jin 晉文公, King Zhuang of Chu 楚莊王, Duke Xiang of Song 宋襄公, and Duke Mu of Qin 秦穆公] governments were less well run but they still observed some general rules, insuring that social mores and political establishments were upheld, the worthy respected, the talented employed, the old and the young cared for, domestic and international order kept, and commonly recognised crimes punished.

At Mencius's time the situation had deteriorated drastically. The rulers were wilful and incompetent; most officials, lacking personal integrity, flattered and facilitated the evil deeds of their superiors; the government treasury and granary were full, and the kitchens of the rich and powerful filled with meat and grain – much of which was for their dogs and horses; the common people did not have enough land to produce food, and the corpses of the starved were strewn along the roads. The worst rulers did not know what to do and blamed the weather for poor harvest, an excuse Mencius compared to blaming a murder on a knife. A more conscientious ruler tried to move the people from one area to another to escape famine. His action was only slightly less wrong and left the root problem unsolved. For him to disparage the more inept rulers was, in Mencius's words, like a soldier who ran 50 steps away from an enemy laughing at a fellow soldier who ran 100 steps away – the pot calling the kettle black.

Thus Mencius accused the rulers of his time of violating the rules of better governance established by the Five Hegemons who, in turn, had violated the rules of the even better governance established by the three True Kings, and, therefore, the present rulers offended against the Five Hegemons and the Five Hegemons offended against the three True Kings.

But the feudal lords of Mencius's time had a particular problem that the good rulers of the past did not have, namely, preventing their states from being conquered by their neighbours. To survive it was necessary to make the state strong. The way generally taken by an ordinary ruler to achieve this was to squeeze his own people and launch predatory expeditions against his weaker neighbours. A ruler of a big state would want that state not only to survive but become dominant. This was what King Xuan of Qi 齊宣王 slyly called his *da yu* (大欲 great desire) of becoming the hegemon of the feudal lords. Because of this desire, his state was constantly involved in military conflicts and his people lived in fear and poverty, and many perished in the endless skirmishes and battles.

In addition to that serious and common problem, ordinary rulers might have personal shortcomings. For instance, could one like King Xuan of Qi, who frankly admitted that he had several weaknesses, including love of material goods and beautiful women, achieve good governance? Mencius was well aware of the vices of the power-holders of his time and did not expect them to be saints. He had, as we shall see, several practical suggestions for achieving good governance but, to the king, he gave a short answer: Yes, in principle he could. He said that it was all right for the king to have such desires as long as he cared not only for his own satisfaction but also realised that other people had similar desires and would take measures that would enabling them to be similarly satisfied. To prove his point, Mencius said ancestors of King Wen of Zhou 周文王 were fond of material goods and women, and they made sure that the people had enough provisions and that all men and women could have spouses. He further said that King Wen enjoyed his royal garden and opened it to the people. Therefore he concluded, if a ruler could *yu-min tong-le* (與民同樂 share with the people in the enjoyment of the same kind of pleasures) his "weakness" would not prevent him from becoming a True King.

(D) Critical problems and Mencius's solution

This principle was not recognised by the rulers of Mencius's time, however. Most of them tried to make their states strong and engaged in wars to snatch more territories and people. As a result, the common people were exploited to death at home and slaughtered abroad on battlefields. The world was in chaos, and even a mediocre ruler, such as King Xiang of Liang 梁襄王, wondered how it could be settled.[3] Mencius replied that it will be settled when it is unified. "Who can unify it?", asked the king. "The person who is not addicted to having people killed", Mencius replied. The answer was terse and blunt. Needless to say it would take more than such a person to unify the country but Mencius was expressing a deep frustration about the situation of his time and a particular contempt for the king who, evidently, was not such a person. And, to add more weight to his assertion, he stressed that when, such a person appears, the entire world would respond exuberantly like parched plants reacting to copious rainfall. No one could prevent him from becoming a True King.

Why could none of the current rulers be such a person? Mencius had another simple answer: they were all ignorant, stupid and egotistical. There were people who had spent their lives studying social problems and knew the right way to govern but were despised by the rulers. Instead of learning from such people, a typical ruler would arrogantly force them to obey his commands. It is as inappropriate as a man wishing to have a house built telling the master carpenters to forget their knowledge and skills and take instructions from him on how to cut timber.

Who were those people from whom rulers should learn? At Mencius's time there were many who preached Ruism, Daoism, universal law, and solipsistic or anarchistic principles. Mencius hailed Confucius and readily dismissed the others, who were little heeded by the current rulers, anyway. But there was another group he had difficulty in dealing with. They were those, such as Zichan 子產, who devoted themselves to solving the urgent, practical problems of the time: how to enable a state to survive in the great struggle against domestic turmoil and foreign conquest. Mencius could not ignore this problem but he objected to the answer those pragmatists gave which was simply to empower the government to be more decisive and effective in making and enforcing ad hoc decisions thereby seeking immediate gain at the expense of long-term benefit.

An opportunity was presented to Mencius to make his point when he had an audience with King Hui of Liang 梁惠王 [King Xiang's more capable father]. The king greeted the elderly gentleman [Mencius was in his fifties] graciously and asked how he was to *li* his state. [The word *li* 利 could mean "benefit" or simply "facilitate". But the Ruists often used it in the sense of "profit" as opposed to *ren*

仁 "enevolence" and *yi* 義 "righteousness".] Choosing to read *li* in this narrow and utilitarian sense, Mencius gave an extraordinary lecture on the evil of seeking profit. He branded the attempt as an abominable act of greed and pointed out that, when everyone did it at the expense of everyone else, the state would be soon be in a disastrous situation – a powerful minister would commit regicide and usurp the throne. The reason was simple: although the minister was already rich and powerful, if he sought profit before thinking about righteousness, he would not be content until he had seized the ultimate prize. After presenting this scenario, Mencius tried to persuade the king to adopt a different approach – to strive only for benevolence and righteousness and never talk about profit. According to him, such an approach would make the ruler safer because those who were benevolent and righteous would not harm others but would help one another in a common pursuit of the long-term objectives of peace and prosperity for the whole country.

But, if one understands *li* in a broader sense, one would find Mencius's sermon to King Hui of Liang rather uncalled for. He burst into a tirade against profit because of his belief that profit gained by exploiting people and winning wars would be short-lived. The states would engage in an arms race and be trapped in incessant wars. He said the country would be settled when it was unified but did not foresee the possibility of one state becoming strong enough to vanquish all its rivals and unify the country. Instead, he pessimistically thought the status quo would persist indefinitely and that the warring states would bring endless suffering to their people. So, he condemned this short-sighted objective of seeking profit and the pernicious methods used in its pursuit. He was quite emotional about this and it was because of this emotion he rebuked the king.

While Mencius's aversion to short-term profit was strong, his belief in benevolence and righteousness as the means to achieve peace, prosperity and even unification of the world was sincere. Because of this belief, he travelled for more than ten years to various states proselytising on it and, when he retired to write his book, he made it the first topic of the first chapter.

But, to many people, his efforts seemed impractical if not quixotic. Even Gongsun Chou 公孫丑, a disciple, was ambivalent about it and said, "The Way [of benevolence and righteousness] is indeed lofty and beautiful but to approach it is like trying to climb to the sky." And then he pleaded with Mencius to make his theory less remote so that people can hope to reach it and will try diligently to do so. It was a reasonable request. We may recall that Confucius suggested a simple and easy way to make a person benevolent by restraining his desires and following the rites. Mencius, as we shall see, also had some advice for individuals to improve themselves and for states to achieve order but he did not give it to Gongsun Chou as a direct reply. Instead, he insisted that high standards should be kept by those who really wanted to be good.

(E) Re-establishment of good government: possibility and timing

Mencius stressed that it was not difficult to follow the way of benevolence and righteousness and that it was possible to re-establish good norms and governance. He pointed out that a ruler who governs in accordance with the principles of benevolence and righteousness can be a True King even though he does not have a large state. Tang of the Shang began with an area of 70 *li* square; King Wen of Zhou started with one of 100 *li* square. And it will not take long. Taking King Wen as a model, the ruler of a big state needs only five years, and one of a small state seven years. He said this to King Hui of Liang (a big state of over 1,000 *li* square) and also the heir apparent of Teng (a small state of 50 *li* square) because, according to Mencius, the same principles apply to all states whatever their size: where a ruler is benevolent and righteous, no one in the world can resist him. On the other hand, if a ruler acts against that principle and treats his people with cruelty and neglect, he will lose their hearts as well as his state, and he will drive his people towards his opponents in the way that a hawk drives sparrows to the bushes. A ruler who has not tried to follow the principles may, like the Crown Prince of Teng, have doubts. But Mencius, citing as examples a few well-known persons with ambition and self-respect, assured him that he, just like any one of them, could do it, and that the principle was like a good medicine which was difficult to take but was the only thing that could cure the illness of a state of that time.

Moreover, Mencius said, the world was at just the right time for the re-establishment of good government. He looked at history and found that every five hundred years or so a True King would emerge and that, in the interval, there would be those who could assist his rise. From the beginning of the Zhou Dynasty to his time, more than seven centuries had passed. The appearance of a True King was long overdue; and the people had never before suffered more cruel government. Like the hungry and thirsty, they were easy to feed and their thirsts easy to quench, so that people would flock to a state with benevolent government, and its ruler could win the world with half the effort of the former True Kings.

And then Mencius revealed his ambition: to be the one who assists in the rise of a True King. Considering his own situation, however, which was rather unfortunate, he lamented, saying, "It must be that Heaven does not yet wish to have the world settled in peace and order. If it wishes to have the world so settled, who is there at the present time to provide help other than I myself?" This shows how very self-assured and yet disappointed he was. But, like Confucius, he was not a fatalist. By "Heaven", he meant certain conditions not yet under his control. And he was not going to give up. This point was proven by his tireless efforts to search for opportunities for realisation of his ambition.

(F) Conceptual bases of good government and norms

To realise his ambition, Mencius had to take several concrete steps. After refuting wrong ideas and spurious theories and hailing benevolence and righteousness as the best medicine, he proceeded to construct a theory for a positive course of action.

Firstly, what are benevolence and righteousness? We have seen that Confucius hailed benevolence as the paramount virtue and the fundamental principle to guide a person's behaviour towards others – a man should treat other men as he wants them to treat himself. Mencius took the same line but wanted to make the point clearer. Why should the self be the standard? This prompted him to initiate a theory that human nature is "good". If human nature is good, a man need only follow his nature and he will behave correctly.

Confucius did not say much about righteousness as an abstract concept. He associated it with *zhi*, or correctness, and thought it could be a relative idea. Mencius said righteousness comes from human nature and has a definite connotation.

How did Mencius prove that human nature is good? We saw that Confucius merely said that humans have a similar nature and ceased speculating on whether it is good or bad. Mencius was more specific. First, he alleged that all things have a unique *xing* (性 nature), and humans have a uniquely human nature. As proof, he pointed out that any man who sees a child about to fall into a well will be frightened and feel concern. This feeling is what he called *bu ren ren zhi xin* (不忍人之心 the heart of not being able to bear seeing others suffer) or *chu ti ce yin zhi xin* (怵惕惻隱之心 the sympathetic and compassionate heart). He noticed that King Xuan of Qi could not even bear to see an ox slaughtered. Thus, this "heart" is innate to every human being. Then, without providing further evidence, he extrapolated that everyone also has a heart that can feel shame and aversion, a heart that knows courtesy and modesty, and a heart that can distinguish right from wrong. And he further asserted that these "hearts" are the seed of virtues – the compassionate heart that of benevolence, the heart of shame and aversion that of righteousness, the courteous and modest heart that of proper and refined behaviour, and the heart of knowing right and wrong that of wisdom. In another paragraph, Mencius said, "Men all have something they cannot bear. When this becomes a guide to their behaviour, it is called benevolence. Men all have something they will not do. When this becomes a guide to their behaviour, it is called righteousness."

Based on these premises, Mencius declared that human nature is *shan* (善 good). This idea was controversial. Other thinkers had different views. As we shall see, Xunzi believed the very opposite – human nature is bad. At Mencius's time, his most prominent detractor was Gaozi 告子 who held that human nature is neutral and malleable, and argued that a person can become good or bad depending on what outside forces he is subjected to. Mencius acknowledged the influence of outside forces. Thus, he observed that, when forced, water can go uphill but he emphasised that, left alone, it flows naturally downwards. A man's good "hearts" can be corrupted by external influence just as a mountain can be denuded of its originally luxuriant vegetation by continuous assault by loggers and sheep. So, basically, Mencius agreed with Gaozi that a man is a product of his environment but, nevertheless, he strenuously disputed Gaozi's position as yet another misconception and insisted that all virtues – benevolence, righteousness, and so on – are intrinsic to humans. Anyone without the four "hearts" is not human, and everyone whose "hearts" are not damaged will naturally behave according to those virtues. In his words, "This is recognised by all the people of the world", as simple as that.

These statements are arbitrary but Mencius was not bothered. He went on to say that, because everyone can find in his heart the "seeds" of benevolence and righteousness, just let the seeds grow naturally and a person can become as good as Yao and Shun. More specifically, if a person can use his own "hearts" as a standard, he will respect his parents and extend that respect to other people's parents, care for his children and extend that care to other people's children, and become benevolent and righteous. In other words, to be benevolent and righteous is to treat others as a person wants others to treat him – the same principle Confucius advocated – but all for good without recognising any possibility of masochism or cruelty towards others.

Moreover, Mencius said that, if a ruler can extend his "hearts", particularly the compassionate and sympathetic heart, in treating his people, he will be able to *bao-min er wang* (保民而王 protect the people and become a True King). This, according to Mencius, is not difficult. It is not a feat of "striding the Northern Sea carrying Mount Tai under the arm"; it is like "taking a deep bow to an elderly man". By treating others as one's own family, one can make the world "roll in one's palm".

All these assertions are based on the presumption that human nature is good. But, in all fairness to Mencius, this presumption is shaky, and his conclusions are rather simplistic. At the root of his problem is that he did not address the obviously important question: from where does the bad influence come? If a thing exists in the natural environment, it may harm a man's health but it is not bad in a moral sense. If people do not just die under adverse circumstances (like plants which die during a drought) but become bad (committing evil acts such as theft or robbery), there must be some "seed of badness" in human nature. Mencius did not recognise this possibility.

Why did Mencius make such crude, unsubstantiated assertions? Here is a plausible answer: he characterised human nature as good in order to say that the virtues he exalted are intrinsic to human beings, not prescribed by outside authorities, and cannot be dismissed or belittled by those authorities. A person can be forced to be bad but, once the influence is removed, his good nature and his inherent virtues will return to guide his behaviour. Outside authorities can make rules which are in conflict with those virtues and impose them upon a person but those rules will ultimately be judged by people's inherent virtues, and the degree of a person's observance of those rules should and will be dependent on this judgement. This interpretation of Mencius's view is supported by another of his assertions: what is common to all hearts is reason. Reason, unlike virtues, is not subjective. It is not relative but absolute, not individualistic but universal. If all men have the heart, or ability, to reason, and come to the conclusion that benevolence and righteousness are preferable, then benevolence and righteousness, being supported by reason, are absolute as well.

There is another possible explanation: Mencius wanted to boost people's self-respect and faith in their own potential. If every person has the "four hearts" and is capable of being benevolent and righteous, every person should hold himself high and do his best to develop his capability. He who claims inability to be benevolent and righteous abandons himself and is thus unworthy. In supporting this argument, Mencius reported Confucius's favourite student Yan Yuan 顏淵 saying, "What kind of a person was Shun, and what am I? One who wishes to achieve something significant should be just like him." Further, he quoted the *Book of Historical Documents*: "When Heaven sends down calamities, there is still the possibility of avoiding them; when a person brings disaster on himself, there is no hope of surviving it", and the *Book of Odes*: "Always act in accordance with natural reason and seek good fortune by yourself".[4]

Thus Mencius's assertion about human nature is not meant to be a statement about fact but a conceptual notion. The "good" human nature was used by him as a basis on which good government could be built and a justification for persuading people to better themselves. In short, it was the foundation of his theory for the re-establishment of good society and good government.

In reality, to establish good government is not easy. Mencius said in a different context: "When people have sufficient food, warm clothes and comfortable lodging but no education, their behaviour will be close to that of birds and beasts." We have seen that he likened those who followed the teachings of Yang Zhu and Mozi to birds and beasts and we have tried to interpret what he might have meant. What did he mean in this statement? It should be assumed that he was not contradicting himself regarding human nature nor did he mean birds and beasts are bad in nature. He could have meant that birds and beasts are different from humans because they can live individual lives without much co-operation. On the basis of this assumption, it is possible to argue that what he really meant is this: because men cannot live without the help of others, they have to have division of labour and co-operation. This led him to an examination of various types of people in a society, what roles they each played and how they should interact with one another.

(G) Members of society

(1) The common people

Sociopolitical structure, according to Mencius, had three levels: the country, the feudal states, and the families. The common people formed the base of this structure. They engaged in various undertakings to produce the materials for life. Those at higher levels existed to help the common people and relied on their support for sustenance. From this fact Mencius said, "The people are of the highest value, the temples of the gods of earth and grain (symbols of state) are of the next, and the ruler is of the least."

But the common people had many weaknesses. First of all, they lacked vision. Each individual saw his immediate interest and did his own small job. He could not see long-term, large-scale problems. Thus, Mencius said a farmer would worry about not cultivating well his little plot of land, but not much else. When larger problems, such as a great flood, arise, the people need leaders and rules in order to become organised and make concerted efforts to find solutions.

Second, a common person had to be anchored to something definite. According to Mencius, if an ordinary man does not possess land, he becomes rootless and will behave in a disorderly way. In his words, "The common people who are without constant means will have no constant hearts. Lacking constant hearts they will become unprincipled and excessive, stopping at nothing." For this reason it is necessary to enable them to acquire a certain amount of land.

Third, when ordinary people were assured of the necessities of life, they would not live in the way that humans should: their behaviour will be similar to that of birds and beasts. On this point, Mencius obviously showed an anthropocentric bias against other species but, as discussed above, he harboured no malice towards them. He just emphasised the human need for society.

These weaknesses made the common people generally "small" – caring only for their personal physical needs. Mencius was sympathetic. That was why he repeatedly emphasised their value. His evaluation was counter-intuitive to that of most people of his time who generally placed the power-holders above the commoners, and a typical ruler often acted as if he was the state. It was thus remarkable that Mencius championed the cause of these common people whom he characterised as *xiao ren* (小人 small men) but without any sense of belittlement or disdain.

(2) The "superior man"

In contrast to the "small men", there was a class of people Mencius called *da ren* (大人 superior men) or *jun-zi* (君子 gentlemen). They were some of the commoners and aristocrats who shared a few distinctive characteristics. Generally, a "superior man" is a thinking person who knows what is right and thinks and cares about something big – something greater than that which the sensory organs could discern. He cares about his heart – he keeps it as innocent as that of a newborn baby – and he is benevolent and righteous and has great aspirations. When his aspirations are not yet realised, he cultivates his personal virtues and becomes a *da-zhang-fu* (大丈夫 great man) who cannot be corrupted by wealth or high position, is uncompromised by poverty, and not bowed by force and authority. When his aspirations are fulfilled, he shares the benefit of his achievements with the people. Thus, he serves as a role model and helps make people right. Mencius mentioned several persons of the past and of his own times as such "superior men" and praised them as "teachers to hundreds of generations", whose examples cleansed the corrupt, made the coward ambitious, the mean-spirited generous, and the narrow-minded tolerant.

Mencius made an important point that a person is not born superior or small. It depends on how he is nurtured. According to him, Yan Yuan said that one who wishes to achieve something significant can strive to be as great as Shun. If one has the lesser ambition of becoming just a "gentleman", it is not at all difficult. One need only be humane and righteous.

Mencius himself strove to be a superior man of a high order and believed that he had succeeded. With little modesty, he made the esoteric remark that he was good at nurturing his *hao-ran zhi qi* (浩然之氣 broad vitality or spiritual energy) which he described as a kind of willpower to propel a person to the Way. It germinates from the heart (the "four hearts") and, being properly nurtured and unharmed, it reaches everywhere between heaven and earth and affects everything. Then he explained, in less abstruse terms, that this *qi* is, in essence, benevolence and righteousness and manifests itself in benevolent and righteous actions. Thus, when faced with a choice between life and righteousness, he, with this *qi*, would give up his life and choose righteousness.

In more concrete terms, Mencius said that he would like to be as good a learner and teacher as Confucius was, and he wanted to carry on the mission of Confucius and the sages, which included teaching people of hundreds of generations to come and helping a ruler to become a True King. We have seen that, on this last point, he even boasted that, at his time, no one was better prepared than he was to do the work.

A "superior man" is thus very different from ordinary people. Yet he is not easily recognised as such. Sometimes he acts contrary to convention and is therefore considered bizarre rather than "great". This posed a problem which Mencius found necessary to address, using actual people as examples.

The first example was Shun. Many in Mencius's time found Shun's behaviour inscrutable. To begin with, why did he get married without seeking permission from his father, as required by the rites? Mencius replied that, if he had, he would not have received permission and would have remained single, violating the principle that a man and a woman should live together as husband and wife to form the most important human relationship, and that he would then become resentful of his father for obstructing the formation of this relationship.

Second, why after becoming king, did Shun give a fief to his brother, Xiang 象, who was depraved, cruel and attempted several times to kill Shun? What wrong did the people of that fiefdom commit that made them deserve an evil lord? Mencius replied that a loving man, being the king, would not leave his brother in poverty. Shun let Xiang enjoy the income from the fiefdom but did not allow him actually to rule the people.

Third, suppose Gu Sou (瞽叟 the "Blind Old Man", the nickname of Shun's father) murdered somebody, what would Shun do? Mencius replied that Shun would let the minister of justice arrest Gu Sou and then he would break into the jail, carry his father on his back, escape to the remote seashore and live there happily together in exile, never giving a thought to the kingdom because, to him, abandoning it was no more than discarding a pair of worn-out shoes.

Mencius's answers to those questions are themselves strange and raise further questions: in the first case, if the relationship between a man and a woman as husband and wife was "the most important", then the relationship between father and son must be secondary, and filial piety a lesser virtue than matrimonial love. But what would happen if the father dislikes the daughter-in-law and the two cannot get along? Is it not a traditional rule for the son in such a case to divorce his wife? In the second case, is nepotism, no matter how it is practised, not a violation of the principle of good government? Finally, are not jailbreaking and helping a murderer to flee serious crimes, abandoning office a dereliction of duty, and living outside the reach of law as fugitives bad examples? It might be argued that relinquishing the position of the ruler and living in the wilderness were enough punishments for Shun but what about a person without his status who followed his examples?

Besides these remarks about Shun, Mencius had some comments on the behaviour of a few of his contemporaries that were strange as well. Chen Zhongzi 陳仲子, a member of an established clan in the state of Qi, was known for being extraordinarily scrupulous. He subsisted in poverty away from his family estate where his widowed mother and rich older brother, a high official, lived so that he could avoid being contaminated by the wealth of his brother of which some, in his view, was ill-gotten. While being admired by many in Qi, he was dismissed by Mencius as not clean enough. To be absolutely clean, Mencius said, a person has to become an earthworm that would eat only soil and drink underground water. Chen Zhongzi was far from that because he survived on things that might have been produced and processed by corrupt people. In any case, living away from his mother and not taking care of her was immoral.

On the other hand, Kuang Zhang 匡章 was known in Qi as an impious son for living away from his father but Mencius befriended him and treated him with courtesy. Why? Mencius's answer: Kuang Zhang did not neglect caring for his father, nor shamed him, nor endangered him. He and his father disagreed on some moral issues. When he declined to bend his principles, his father expelled him. As a way to express his regret he lived alone without the company of his wife and sons. He was wrong but for an understandable reason.

Mencius's own behaviour was often in question. Once, he was about to see King Xuan of Qi as a visitor to see a host but, when the king's messenger came to summon him to the royal court the next day, Mencius lied that he would not be able to go because of illness. The next day he went to pay his condolences to the family of a deceased friend. When the king sent a physician to inquire about his illness, he hid in the house of another friend. Being questioned about his action by this friend he gave a long lecture on the mistake of a ruler summoning an older subject of superior moral standing and the correctness of such a subject refusing to obey the summons, alleging that a ruler who is to aspire to some great achievements must have subjects whom he should not summon.

Then, why did Mencius go to many states and accept lavish gifts from the rulers? This was his reply: If one's conduct is not in accordance with the Way, and one has not accomplished some worthy task for the good of society, one should not accept even a basket of food from another. If the opposite is the case, then one deserves to be compensated adequately. Shun did not consider it excessive to accept the kingdom Yao offered. He, Mencius, as a teacher of moral principles and as a role model for the people, certainly deserved the stipends and honorariums, just as a carpenter should be paid for the work he accomplished.

In conclusion, Mencius said, "The conduct of a gentleman is indeed not easy for the ordinary people to understand." For such a man, the supreme norm is the fundamental principles of benevolence and righteousness. These principles are more profound than ordinary people think they are. Thus, a superior man will not blindly observe a "rite" if it is contrary to the spirit of the rites; he will not do a "correct act" if it is contrary to the spirit of righteousness. He will not rigidly keep his word nor will he see his action through to the end. Such behaviour is, indeed, hard to comprehend, but what is mentioned here is the easy part – the superior man's inaction. More perplexing is that a superior man sometimes actively violates a norm, for instance, telling a lie. Mencius did that and gave an implicit justification that rejecting a summons was a way to teach King Xuan of Qi a lesson in the hope of making him a better ruler. More generally, Mencius said, "Teaching can be done in many ways. My reluctance to teach a person is also a way to teach him." It explains why, in several instances, Mencius refused to answer questions from people of high positions. It probably was also the reason why Confucius refused to receive Rubei 孺悲, pleading falsely that he was ill. Looking at these instances, an ordinary person could be excused for being dumbfounded.

Thus, like Confucius, Mencius also saw a hierarchy of norms with benevolence and righteousness at the top and the various other norms beneath. To observe a higher norm, a lower one can be ignored. The guideline for a person to make the choice, according to Mencius, is that he should always aim at what is right. But what is rightness in a particular case? Mencius had a simple answer: just search your own heart. The seeds of righteousness and other virtues are all there and, when developed, they give rise to all norms. But actually, this search is not easy. Only the "superior men" can do it. Seeing this ability in them, but not in ordinary people, Mencius was showing a bias often found among intellectuals.

(3) The officials

A ruler intending to govern well needs good officials. Mencius said that Yao worried most that he could not find Shun and other able assistants. The need became more urgent for less sagacious rulers. Among whom is a ruler to find good candidates? What qualifies them? What are they to do while in office? From his high praise of the "superior men", it should be clear that Mencius thought candidates should come from their ranks.

How could a good candidate be found? We have seen that, in *Zhuangzi*, there was a story that King Wen of Zhou found an old fisherman and made him a minister. But that was unusual, to say the least. More probably, it was the superior man who went to the ruler to offer his services. It was reported that Confucius, after three months not being in the service of a ruler, felt unsettled and sad and, while abroad, he always carried some symbolic gifts to give to a ruler when he had a chance to see one. There was even a story that he, with the help of Mi Zixia 彌子瑕, a favourite attendant of Duke Ling of Wei 衛靈公, went to see Nanzi 南子, the duke's wife, in order to gain an appointment in the government of Wei.[5] Why was it so difficult for a superior man to be employed, someone asked. Mencius replied that, in seeking office, a superior man had to observe certain principles and, to explain his point, he gave this analogy: a man wishing to get married should first receive permission from his parents and then go through certain procedures arranged by a matchmaker. If without the permission and the procedures a man drilled a hole in the wall of a woman's house to peep at her and climbed over the wall to get together with her, he might get a wife but would be despised and the union viewed as illicit Therefore, Mencius rejected the rumour that Yi Yin 伊尹 tried to attract the attention of Tang by his cooking skills. A superior man would never resort to unseemly tactics to gain office; he wanted office only because of a noble objective to help improve government.

However a superior man is found, it is up to the ruler to offer him an office. How is the ruler to make the decision? A superior man may hail from a low social position but has undergone many tests and proven his worthiness. According to Mencius, before being lifted to high government positions, Shun and many superior men had lived in humble circumstances and gone through numerous trials. After hearing from all his attendants, officials and the common people, saying a certain person is worthy, the ruler should investigate personally and make the final decision.

When an offer is made, a superior man should decide whether or not to accept it. Mencius said there are three conditions under which a superior man would take office: first, when he was greeted with respect in accordance with the rites, and told that his advice was to be put into practice. Second, though his advice was not to be put into practice, he was greeted with respect in accordance with the rites. In the third and worst case, when he was in abject poverty and starving, he would take the offer without insisting on any conditions. Unfortunately, many a superior man was in that situation because he neither tilled the land nor engaged in ordinary trades that brought him any income. Mencius noted that, when he was young and poor, Confucius took several low government posts. So Mencius observed, "To enter into government service is not to save a person from poverty, but sometimes it is." And he even recognised that, in some extreme circumstances, a superior man might have to accept alms from the government.

In addition to those three conditions, a superior man may have other considerations. According to Mencius, Boyi would not serve the wrong kind of ruler and govern the wrong kind of people but Yi Yin and Liuxia Hui 柳下惠 did not make such choices, and Confucius would serve under three circumstances: where the ruler was capable of implementing the Way; where the ruler treated him according to the correct rites; and where the ruler was sincere in providing for the worthy. Why did they react differently? Mencius replied: Boyi wanted to preserve his personal integrity; Yi Yin wanted to modify and save the world; and Liuxia Hui, confident in his own incorruptibility, wanted to do what little he could to help the people. In Confucius's case, Mencius offered no explanation but probably thought that it was more reasonable because, while obviously the Master wanted to help restore the Way, he was poor and had to have a job if it was offered to him in an appropriate manner.

While in office, an official should observe certain norms. Mencius said that some officials work for high objectives of bringing peace and order to the country; others simply serve the ruler, flatter him and do his bidding slavishly for the sole purpose of remaining in his favour. Needless to say, Mencius strongly condemned the latter type. Then there were other types of officials who alleged that they were capable of either extending the ruler's territory and filling his treasury or forming alliances between his state and others and leading his armies in victorious military campaigns. Mencius called the first type "thieves stealing from the people" and the second type "thieves harming the people". To illustrate his point, Mencius recalled an event where Ran Qiu 冉求, a disciple of Confucius, who, as the manager of the House of Jisun 季孫, the chief minister of the state of Lu, doubled its income of previous times. Confucius condemned the act and disowned Ran Qiu. Then Mencius went on to maintain that Confucius would have even more harshly censured those who fought forcefully for aggressive rulers because wars would inevitably lead to countless people being slain: thus, conducting a war to gain land, would be like making the land feast on people's flesh. Therefore Mencius declared, "Those who are skilful in warfare should receive the most severe punishment; those who arrange military alliances should receive the next most severe punishment; those who opened up waste land and make people toil over it to increase revenue for the government should receive the next most severe punishment."

What should an official try to accomplish? Zichan, a chief minister of Zheng, and Guan Zhong 管仲, a chief minister of Qi, were much admired for their achievements. Zichan kept his small state in peace and order and fended off aggressive designs on it by bigger neighbouring states. Confucius praised him as a benevolent man. But Mencius was more critical. Commenting on the story that Zichan let his carriage be used to ferry people across a ford, Mencius said that he was kind and generous but did not know how to govern. Instead of doing ad hoc, small personal favours for a few people, a good official should implement policies that will promote the general welfare of the people as a whole.

Guan Zhong was different. He made Duke Huan of Qi 齊桓公 a hegemon of the feudal lords and successfully defended the Middle Kingdom against the barbarians on its borders. For these feats, he was hailed by Confucius: "So benevolent, so benevolent!"[6] But Mencius was not satisfied, insisting that, since Guan Zhong had the complete trust of the duke, he should, and could, have made him a True King, and brought peace and prosperity not only to Qi but to the entire country. Again why did Mencius take this extreme position? Probably he himself had such aspiration but did not have the good fortune of being offered an opportunity.

What should a good official do when he realised that there is no possibility of achieving his high objectives? Mencius said that, if such an official was still treated with respect in accordance with the rites, he could remain in office but, when respect was reduced, he should resign. Confucius stayed on in his job as a chief judge of the state of Lu and remained respectful to Duke Ding 定公 though his advice was often ignored. Only when the duke failed to send him the meat used in state sacrifice did he decided to resign and leave Lu. Mencius was stricter. When he was a *ke-qing* (客卿 guest official) in Qi and found that his advice was not well received by King Xuan, he decided to stay only temporarily in office but refused to accept a salary. Nevertheless, when he left Qi, he departed slowly because he eagerly wished to carry out his plans for making the world better and he still hoped that the king might regret what had happened and send someone to recall him. He was disappointed and never offered a responsible office by any feudal lord. He paid a price for upholding his principles but established a standard for good officials in the future.

(4) The ruler

The ruler is at the top of a political system. The first questions about him are how does he become a ruler and on what grounds is he justified in keeping the position? In the *Book of Historical Documents* and the *Book of Odes* Yao, Shun and the founders the Xia, the Shang and the Zhou Dynasties were described as persons of great virtue and accomplishments who saved the people from natural and human-made disasters. It is not clear how Yao became king. Reportedly, he abdicated in favour of Shun who did the same for Yu but Yu passed his throne to his son Qi 啟 and began the tradition of hereditary royal succession. Mencius was asked why a king was allowed to "give the kingdom" to someone of his choice. He thought the idea was yet another misconception and his reply was creative. The king cannot. He can only recommend a candidate to Heaven and assign him to government jobs and see whether the gods accept his offer of sacrifice and the people are satisfied with his work. Yao did so to Shun for twenty-eight years and, after Yao's death, the whole kingdom went to pay homage to Shun and made him king. It was in the same way that Yu succeeded Shun after being tested for seventeen years.

The case of Qi succeeding his father Yu was different. Yu recommended and tested Yi 益 but, only seven years thereafter, Yu died and the people saluted Qi, saying, "He is the son of our lord Yu!" and enthroned him. But the difference was only in appearance; in reality, the choice was also made by the people and approved by Heaven since "Heaven sees as the people see and hears as they hear". And that was why, according to Mencius, Confucius said, "Yao and Shun abdicated, Xia, Shang and Zhou practised hereditary succession, but the principle they followed was the same."

Then Mencius addressed an implicit but thornier question: Why were some men of great virtue and accomplishments not made kings and why did some of the unworthy men inherit the throne and remain unchallenged. His answer was clever: a common man who comes to possess the kingdom must not only have the virtue of a Shun or a Yu but also the recommendation of a king. Confucius never possessed the kingdom because no king recommended him. On the other hand, he who inherits the kingdom is only put aside by Heaven if he is as evil as Jie 桀, the last king of Xia, or Shou 紂, the last king of Shang. Yi 益 and Yi Yin 伊尹, the prime minister of King Tang of Shang, and Duke of Zhou 周公, a younger brother of King Wu of Zhou, respectively, never possessed the kingdom because the kings of their times were not so bad.

The principles governing the kings should be applicable to the feudal lords as well. But, in reality, more court coups and regicides happened for which only flimsy reasons were offered or no justification was made at all, and many hereditary feudal lords remained in power in spite of their incompetence or cruelty or both. Mencius's explanation was probably that they were still not as bad as Jie and Shou.

But Mencius did list certain norms for a ruler to observe. First of all, a ruler, like everyone else, should be virtuous, especially benevolent. But, as stated earlier, being familiar with the rather low quality of the rulers of his time, Mencius did not expect them quite to meet the requirement. He did not regard it as sinful for them to have some "weaknesses" as long as the people could enjoy similar pleasures. But he strongly condemned extravagance and waste, censuring rulers for letting their horses and dogs eat better than the people, dismissing their action of providing ad hoc relief as inadequate, and ridiculing them for blaming a poor harvest on bad weather and by saying it is weapons and not men that kill.

It is important to note here a difference between Mencius and Confucius. While Confucius emphasised that the ruler should serve as a model for the people, Mencius did not; he was more realistic and tried only to reach for the second best result: making the ruler's vice less salient and harmful to the people; while Mencius strongly censured the rulers' extravagance and waste, Confucius did not; he only charged rulers with living according to the rites. A possible reason is that, at Confucius's time, the rulers' exploitation of the people was not yet extreme.

A more obvious norm for the ruler is to concentrate on governing. As mentioned above, a ruler need not do the same type of work of the common people; his responsibility is to make conditions conducive to good life for all his subjects. Nor should a ruler pay attention to trifling matters, as King Xuan of Qi did in ordering the slaughter of a sheep instead of an ox. Instead, a ruler should think big and aim high – to become a True King and to give peace and prosperity to his subjects.

Apart from following those norms for his personal behaviour, a ruler needs to do more. First of all, he should find wise and virtuous persons, appoint them to high office, and evaluate their performance. In doing this, he should listen to the opinions of many, conduct his own investigation and finally make the decision himself.

But a ruler cannot personally make all decisions; he has to promulgate some rules and guidelines for his officials, as well as the common people, to follow. Mencius said, *tu shan bu-zu-yi wei-zheng* (徒善不足以為政 good intentions alone are not sufficient for government). Just as a carpenter cannot always make a perfect circle without a compass, a ruler cannot reach the objectives of good government without good laws and policies. What objectives should a government have? At Mencius's time, most states wanted to increase their strength in order to survive the incessant wars. We have seen that, when Mencius met King Hui of Liang, the first question the king asked was how was his state to be "profited" by the elderly gentleman, and that this question provoked Mencius to make a spirited refutation of seeking profit as an objective of a state. In his view, the ultimate objective of a state should be benevolence and righteousness. The founding fathers of the Three Dynasties initiated benevolent policies and won the world; the last rulers of the Xia and the Shang discarded benevolent policies and they lost their thrones.

Generally what Mencius meant by benevolent policies or *ren zheng* 仁政 are humane measures that take care of the people. The ordinary people, according to him, who had no *heng chan* (恆產, "constant property", or property that one is to possess indefinitely) could not have *heng xin* (恆心, "constant heart", or settled behaviour). They would feel rootless and behave in unpredictable and probably harmful ways. If, after they had so strayed, the government punishes them it is entrapment. How could a humane ruler do such a thing? That is why, Mencius said, the sage kings of the past made fair distribution of land a priority.

In ancient times all land was owned by the Son of Heaven. He divided it up and allowed aristocrats and the common people own some of it. In so doing, he should be careful that the distribution was equitable so that everyone could have enough for a living. That was why Mencius said the very first benevolent policy should be proper "demarcation" of land. According to him, the Three Dynasties all had a system of dividing a piece of land into nine parts in the shape of # or the Chinese character *jing* 井, assigning to eight able-bodied commoners one part each of about 100 *mu* (畝, 1 *mu* being approximately 666.7 square metres), for production of food for his family, and an additional 5 *mu* of land around his family home for growing mulberry trees for silkworms to produce silk for warm clothing for the elderly. The remaining one part was to be cultivated jointly by the eight men to provide revenue for the government. In addition, the Three Dynasties had a system of taxation and corvée service which Mencius said was basically the same: a tithe on the harvest, and the people were called to do public works only after the farming seasons. He recommended these systems to Teng Wen-gong but did not spell out the details for their actual implementation which, he said, was to be worked out by those with government responsibilities.

The last, but not the least important, policy is to educate the people. According to Mencius, Yao, being worried by the fact that people without education would act like birds and beasts, appointed Xie 契 as the minister of education to teach the people human relationships: love between father and son, duty between ruler and subject, distinction between husband and wife, precedence of the old over the young, and loyalty between friends. This may sound strange to us, because we have learned from him that everyone as a child innately loves his parents and, when grown up, knows that he should respect his older brother. Why do people still need to be so educated? This is yet another inconsistency in Mencius's theory. A possible explanation is that, actually, love of parents, and so on, has to be done in a proper way (the rites) that has to be learned. It is discussed in *The Analects* but not mentioned in *Mengzi*.

Mencius fully endorsed those policies. He observed that, if a man has a field of 100 *mu* of land to plant crops, a family of eight persons will not go hungry. If a family has a 5 *mu* plot on which to grow mulberry trees for silk worms, five hens and two sows, its old people will have silk to wear and meat to eat. If taxes are light and corvée labour limited and timely, those with grey hair will not be carrying loads on the roads. If people are taught during their leisure time, the principles of filial piety, brotherly love, loyalty to the state and trustworthiness in their relations with others, so that they know how they are to serve their fathers and older brothers in the family, and the elders and their superiors abroad, they will be willing and able to defend what they have by taking up wooden clubs to fight against the strong armour and sharp weapons of big, aggressive powers.

Needless to say, good laws and policies are also essential but they are not enough. After pointing out that good intentions are not enough for government, in the same breath, Mencius added, *tu fa bu-neng zi-xing* (徒法不能自行 norms cannot be effective by themselves). Laws and policies have to be properly enforced by good men. By this simple statement, he presciently pointed out the fallacy in the arguments that were to rage in later times for and against the rule of humans and the rule of law.

Here we also find a difference between Mencius and Confucius and most other ancient thinkers. While they predicted a day when a great ruler, who implemented the specific principles and policies they suggested, could *wu wei er zhi* (無為而治 govern without much doing). We have seen that Laozi and Zhuangzi promoted this view. Confucius, in praising Shun's sagacious rule, said he had little to do but *gong-ji zheng-nan-mian* (恭己正南面 to hold himself upright to face the world). Mencius never considered such an extraordinary result. Instead, he saw that, to make a society function, there is always a need for government authorities diligently to make decisions and enforce them.

When a good ruler does his job well, his state will have peace and prosperity. But, at Mencius's time, a typical ruler was extravagant, greedy, and cruel, and levied heavy taxes on the people, demanded frequent corvée service from them and sent them to war frequently. As a result, he lost the hearts of his people and drove them away like a hawk drives sparrows to hide in the bushes. But, if a ruler followed Mencius's advice and implemented *ren zheng*, he would win the hearts of people of other states who would come to seek asylum in his, and the rulers of other states would stand in awe of him. He would become a True King in quite short period of time even though his state might be relatively small.

Was Mencius unduly optimistic? Most feudal lords of his time apparently thought so and thus none offered him important government positions, prompting him to assume that Heaven was not yet ready to let him help bring order and prosperity to the world.

(H) Social relationships

A common problem in all societies is how people should relate to, and interact with, one another. Mencius suggested some general rules for the relationships between individuals, and some more specific ones for those between the ruler and the common people, the ruler and the "superior men", and the ruler and the officials.

(1) Between individuals

Mencius emphasised that, in dealing with others, a person must be first of all have self-respect and confidence, believing that he can be virtuous and able to engage in worthy endeavours just like anyone else. That was why he quoted Yan Hui, 顏回, the favourite student of Confucius, saying, "What kind of a person was Shun and what am I? One who intends to achieve something worthy should do just like Shun did." By this Mencius implied that people are equal and capable of reaching high objectives, and he spelled out how to realise one's potential. He must be true to himself and understand the principles of benevolence and righteousness. Then he can sincerely treat others as he treats himself. When he does so there will be good relations. In Mencius's words, "He who is benevolent will be honoured; he who loves others will be loved; he who is courteous to others will be respected." If a person encounters some unexpectedly disagreeable action of another person, he should reflect on his own conduct and make necessary changes to be benevolent and righteous. If he finds that he is not at fault, he could simply dismiss the other person as a beast.

In addition to the general principles, people should observe certain special rules in special circumstances: in the government, a rule that emphasises rank – a superior should be respected by an inferior; in a community a rule that emphasises age – a senior should be respected by a junior; in the country, a rule that emphasises virtue – a person with virtue that enables him to help and govern the people should be respected by everyone.

(2) Between the ruler and the common people

Mencius recognised that the ruler is to govern and the common people are to be governed, and he stressed that the ruler is to see the big picture of society and care for all its members, and the commoners are to provide for the needs of the ruler. Thus, to Mencius, the relationship is interdependent and reciprocal. This view prompted him to put the relationship in a light not seen before, and to make this statement: "If a ruler treats his subjects as his hands and feet, they will treat him as their belly and heart. If he treats them as his horses and dogs, they will treat him as a stranger. If he treats them as mud and weeds, they will treat him as an enemy." At his time such a statement was quite shocking. He justified it by quoting the adage: "The kingdom, the feudal state, and the family." According to him it should mean that the basis of the kingdom is in the state; that of the state is in the family, and that of the family is in the individual person. In other words, the individual common person is the building block of the political and social structures, the most basic, essential element of all human institutions. Based on this interpretation, Mencius alleged that the people are more valuable than the ruler and, for this reason, the individual common person should be respected by those in power in the kingdom, the state, and the family, and they are accountable for the tasks he entrusts to them.

For the ruler the primary task is to keep good governance. If he fails in that he should be dismissed, just as a person should who has failed to take care of the wife and children of a friend who is away and has placed them in his trust. Here is Mencius's reasoning: he who has the trust of the people can become the king; he who has the trust of the king can become a feudal lord; he who has the trust of a feudal lord can become an official. When a feudal lord endangers the temple of the gods of earth and grain (symbol of a particular regime of the country) he is to be replaced; when the government fails and the country falls into chaos, the regime is to be replaced.

In the absence of a peaceful way to replace a regime, the long-suffering people would revolt. This had happened in the past: people led by Tang banished Jie of Xia and by King Wu of Zhou killed Shou of Shang. King Xuan of Qi was troubled by these stories and asked Mencius whether they were true. Mencius replied that it was recorded in history. But, the king demanded, is it permissible for a subject to commit regicide? Mencius said, "One who harms humanity is a mutilator; one who harms rightness is a crippler. He who is both a mutilator and a crippler is called 'a lone despot'. I have heard of killing the lone despot Shou but not of regicide." By this Mencius provided a justification for revolution.

(3) Between the "superior men" and those in power

This was a rather new relationship and very problematic. The "superior men" offered help but also posed challenges to the rulers. In the past, such helpers and challengers were officials, never persons outside the government. Confucius was one of the first of those who, after having acquired knowledge by self-education, sought government appointments and discussed the right way of governance.

By Mencius's time, such people, known as *shi* (士 cultivated men or gentlemen), were many and their interactions with rulers of feudal states were numerous and frequent. Occasionally, a ruler would approach a well-known *shi*, seeking his advice and requesting his service. More frequently a *shi* went to rulers to seek office. We have seen what Mencius said about how a *shi* was to approach a ruler for that purpose. If a *shi* is not actively seeking an office, his relation with the ruler is different. He does not take the initiative to present himself. That was how Mencius acted. When he was travelling through several states, obviously seeking office, he never displayed an intention of that. He was already famous and his reputation preceded him. When he was in a state, often with a large retinue of disciples, a prominent man in the government would inform the ruler of his presence but Mencius would not go to see the ruler. His disciple, Wan Zhang, was puzzled and asked why. Mencius said that, according to the rites, a commoner should not present himself to a feudal lord before being appointed to a government office. Wan Zhang said that, when a commoner was summoned to do corvée labour, he would go but why, when a ruler wanted to see a commoner, should the commoner refuse the summons. Mencius said that to do corvée labour was an obligation but to see a ruler was not. And then he asked why a ruler would want to summon a commoner. If the commoner was known for being learned, he should be treated as a teacher, and the Son of Heaven would not dare to summon his teacher. If the commoner was known as wise and virtuous, it was unheard of that such a person could be summoned. Wan Zhang was more puzzled because it was reported that Confucius responded to a summons from the ruler of Lu promptly walking before his carriage was ready. Why? "It was because, at that time, Confucius was already an official", Mencius replied.

The same question was put by another disciple, Chen Dai 陳代, who thought Mencius's refusal to answer the summons of the feudal lords to be an act of abiding by a rather petty principle because, if he ignored it, he might turn a ruler into a True King or a hegemon. To support his opinion, Chen Dai quoted an old saying *qu chi zhi xun* (屈尺直尋 bend the foot, straighten the yard). We may recall that Zixia 子夏, a distinguished disciple of Confucius, said "If one does not overstep the bounds of major norms, one can be allowed some discretion in observing minor norms." Indeed, Confucius was flexible about some of his personal principles in showing a willingness to accept calls from two power-holders who rebelled against legitimate rulers, hoping that he could transform them and achieve what he aspired for – a government similar to that of Lord Zhou. But Mencius was more rigid. He rejected the adage and gave Chen Dai a lecture: "To bend a little in small matters in order to get the big ones straight is a practice in seeking profit. If there is profit, would bending the yard to straighten the foot also be worth doing? . . . You are wrong. One who bends oneself can never straighten others." Why was Mencius so adamant? A reasonable guess is that he had realised, as Confucius probably did after being criticised by his disciple Zilu 子路, that such a hope was illusory, and that he had seen too many officials lose their personal integrity without achieving anything worthwhile. A worthy commoner should not fall into this trap.

If a proper arrangement was made for a ruler to come to see a worthy commoner, how should the interview go? Mencius said the commoner should act with dignity and not be cowed by the ruler's trappings of power and authority. In an outburst of self-righteousness, Mencius said, "When speaking to a person of consequence, I would not be impressed by his lofty position but look at him with disdain. He may have halls several yards high with eaves extending out several feet but, if I could have my aspirations realised, I will not have those. When he dines there may be in front of him a table tens of feet square full of dishes and there may be hundreds of female attendants waiting on him but, if I could have my aspirations realised, I will not have those. He may have great bands playing music while he gives parties and thousands of chariots following him while he engages in galloping and hunting but, if I could have my aspirations realised, I will not do so. All those things valued by him are what I do not care about. What I will do is all in accordance with norms established since antiquity. Why should I be cowed before him?"

Therefore, in an interview with a ruler, a worthy commoner should present his ideas straightforwardly and try to convince the ruler of their righteousness, not just the profits they could produce. Above all, he should never bend his principles to suit the ruler's desires.

While in a state, it is all right for a worthy commoner to be provided for by the ruler. In some unfortunate cases, the commoner in distress can accept charity from a ruler like any other people in a similar situation. Under ordinary circumstances, the provisions can be considered as gifts but not presumed to come indefinitely, and should not be accepted if they are not properly presented with respect. When Zisi 子思, grandson of Confucius, was in Lu, its ruler Duke Mu 繆公 frequently sent messengers to ask after him and bestow upon him cooked meat. After a few times, Zisi ejected the messenger and declined the food, saying, "Now I realise the duke treats me as he treats his dogs and horses." Mencius hailed Zisi's action and blamed the duke for not placing Zisi in a high government position and not treating him as a worthy man. How should a ruler treat such a person? According to Mencius, when the duke sent gifts to Zisi for the first time, they should have been presented by a messenger with his greetings. In response, Zisi would have expressed his gratitude in deep bows. Thereafter, meat and grain should be delivered regularly by cooks and granary-keepers, and Zisi would not have to perform the ritual of thanks repeatedly. Mencius further pointed out that, in the case of Yao and Shun, Yao sent his nine sons to serve Shun, gave his two daughters to Shun as wives, and ordered his hundred officials to provide cattle, sheep and a granary for Shun's use while Shun was still working in the fields as a farmer, and then raised Shun to high office. That, Mencius said, was how a True King treated the worthy.

While being provided for by a ruler, a worthy commoner will keep his relationship with the ruler formal; he will not let it become familiar or even friendly. It was reported that, on one occasion, Duke Mu of Lu tried to make friends with Zisi, and Zisi was displeased. Mencius imagined that Zisi would have said in response to Duke Mu's initiatives, "In terms of position, you are the ruler and I am your subject, how dare I befriend you? In terms of virtue, it is you who ought to serve me, how can you befriend me?" In other words, the relationship can only be one between a superior and inferior, never one between equals. Mencius's rule was that a ruler should treat a superior man of virtue as a teacher and learn from him before appointing him to an office, and then the superior man would serve under the ruler as an official of his government.

It has been mentioned above that Mencius himself as a commoner accepted lavish gifts from many feudal lords and justified his behaviour by the saying that he had served society well as a teacher to rulers and a model for the people. But he also declined gifts from some rulers he thought unworthy. In a particular case, having realised that his policy suggestions were not to be accepted by the king of Qi, Mencius decided to resign from the post of guest minister and leave the state. The king sent a messenger to make him an offer: "I would build a house for Mencius in the centre of the capital, and provide him with a pension of 10,000 *zhong* [鍾 1 *zhong* is roughly 768 catties in weight; 1 catty is about 500 to 600 grams] of grain a year to support him and his disciples, so that the officials and the people can have a model to look up to." Mencius was not impressed, saying that if he was after wealth why would he decline the guest minister's salary of 100,000 *zhong* a year and accept a pension of 10,000 *zhong*? What irked him was the king's crass thinking – paying a little for a decoration to the state of Qi. His aspiration was to realise his ideals of giving order and prosperity to the country, not simply be honoured as a symbol, especially in such a cheap way.

(4) Between the ruler and the officials

Norms regulating this relationship were established early. The officials were to suggest solutions to government problems; the ruler was to make final decisions. In doing so, the ruler should first of all learn about the questions to be decided; he should learn from the good officials. He should respect them. According to Mencius, a *da-you-wei zhi jun* (大有為之君 a ruler with great achievements) is always meticulously careful in dealing with his officials. He will have some *bu-zhao zhi chen* (不召之臣 officials not to be summoned). When he wants to consult them, he goes to see them. He should never tell his officials to give up what they were prepared to do and listen to his instructions. He listens to their advice and implements the good advice earnestly. When he disagrees with them, he is never dismissive. Even in a case where an official decides to resign and leave the country, the ruler should send someone to conduct the official beyond the border, dispatch a messenger in advance to the place the official intends to go to prepare for his entrance, and take over the official's fief three years after he had left and decided not to return.

What is to happen if the ruler is seriously wrong and rejects the good advice of the officials? Their reaction, according to Mencius, should depend on their status. When they are from outside the ruler's family, they should leave his service; when they are his close relatives, they can depose him. In an extraordinary statement, Mencius said an official could temporarily remove a ruler from the throne, and gave Yi Yin as an example. As the prime minister appointed by Tang, Yi Yin banished Tang's successor Tai Jia 太甲 for being unruly, and reinstated him when he repented and changed his behaviour. Such dramatic actions were permissible because Yi Yin had no intention of usurpation but the good intent of preserving order in the state. To describe this historical event in this light was novel. It was Mencius's way of challenging the conventional norms governing the relationship between the ruler and the officials.

When his ideas are not accepted or he is not treated properly in accordance with the rites, an official should withdraw and leave, but slowly, hoping that the ruler may discover his own mistake and send a messenger to recall him. Only when no such messenger came, would he leave with a peaceful mind and no regrets. That was what Mencius did when he left the state of Qi, a sad scenario for a great "superior man" with ambition to save the world and continue the tradition of Yao, Shun, Yu, Tang, King Wen, Duke Zhou and Confucius.

Reading *Mengzi* one gets the impression that he was, indeed, disputatious and often argumentative, disapproving of many widely held commonsensical propositions but, in some instances failing to prove his own arguments, or pushing them beyond their logical limits, or contradicting himself, or sounding esoteric and mysterious. He said he was compelled by his circumstances and could not help it. Indeed, the situation of his time was far from ideal and many intellectuals suggested solutions; his were not particularly persuasive though they were presented rather stridently.

Seeing government authorities and norms as necessary for getting people organised to tackle difficult tasks and keep peace and order, Mencius found it necessary to reject solipsism, nihilism and absolute egalitarianism. Not being a revolutionary, he grudgingly accepted the political status quo. But his misgivings about it were fundamental. The traditional affairs of the states had been changing and the hereditary rulers were ill-prepared for the new situation. He was dissatisfied with the way government was run (by incompetent rulers and officials) and policies made (in disregard of the vital interests of the common people). He worried about the authorities becoming more arbitrary and the government more incompetent. There was little that could be done to bring about necessary changes. He invoked the power hidden in everyone's heart. He wanted the people, especially the superior men among them, and the officials, as well as the rulers, to use this power to change the world.

He pointed out that human beings are capable of being sympathetic and compassionate, and then extrapolated that everyone is also capable of feeling shame, knowing modesty and distinguishing right from wrong, and therefore everyone has the potential of being benevolent, righteous, and virtuous in many ways. His arguments were crude but his purpose, though implied, was not hard to detect. We may find that this is his logic: if virtues are embedded in human nature, they can be used as a force to make society and life better. More specifically, the heart with all the good innate to it can be used as the standard to test all artificial norms and the actions taken by the government authorities. In other words, everyone has the ability and the right to check on the norms and on the authorities.

On this premise, Mencius developed a theory in which the bases of norms and authorities were discussed, though it failed to address the question of whence came evil and how it could be controlled. He also suggested some norms for personal behaviour and some economic and political measures for government action. But they were not well received. The behavioural norms could not be disputed in principle but their interpretation and application were far too idealistic and situational, and therefore only the "superior men" could know and observe; ordinary people were often puzzled. The economic and political measures were not practical because land was no longer freely available and thus the most crucial measure of distributing a plot of considerable size to every man could not be implemented.

In human relations, he created a set of rules for interaction between people of different social strata, particularly rules between the "superior men" and those in power. Basically, he preached that people should treat one another with respect and compassion. But his advice for the "superior men" to hold those with lofty positions in contempt is rather emotional. It was a reflection of the self-righteousness of the rising intellectual class but it did not work out well for those who adhered to it. His statements that the people are the most valuable and the ruler is the least, and that killing a "lone despot" is justifiable, provided a rationale for revolution, but he did not trumpet it. Aside from his high-sounding words, he made little pragmatic effort to change the status quo. Indeed, his behaviour actually caused some scepticism among his friends and contributed to the decline of the influence of the more rational and commonsensical Ruist teachings. His theory was accepted only by his true believers but largely rejected by the rulers who did not believe in the utility of benevolence and righteousness and were hell-bent on pursuing more tangible "profits" to make their states rich and strong.

Nevertheless, Mencius's legacy was remarkable. By insisting that human nature is good, he lifted the dignity of individual humans. He pointed out that both government authority and norms have to have basis in human nature and thus created a standard to test them. He emphasised the need of both good men and good norms for good government is an idea more balanced than those of Xunzi and the Legalists which are to be discussed later. Personally, he did not achieve much in terms of his own ambition of helping establish a government like that of Yao and Shun but he instilled in people, especially the intellectuals, the aspiration of becoming superior men or *da-zhang-fu* who cannot be subjugated or corrupted by power and wealth. Indeed, he helped mould the Chinese character of self-respect and spiritual insubordination to oppressive authority. This character, above all, enabled the Chinese people to survive domestic despots and foreign aggressors, and made Chinese civilisation resilient under adverse circumstances through the past millenniums. He was honoured as *ya sheng* (亞聖 the Second Sage) after Confucius as *zhi sheng* (至聖 the Foremost Sage) for a good reason.

Notes

1 See Lü Tao, *Mengzi Ping-zhuan*.
2 See Sima Qian, *Shi-ji*, Chapter 74 "Mengzi Xunqing Lie-zhuan" pp. 594.

3 The king was an average ruler but was particularly despised by Mencius. After having an audience with the king, Mencius said, "Being looked at from a distance, he does not appear like a ruler; being approached he does not inspire awe." See *Mengzi*, Chapter 1 "Liang Hui-wang shang" Section 6, pp. 41–2.
4 *Mengzi* Chapter 3 "Gongsun Chou shang" p. 133.
5 See Liu Baonan, Lun-yu zhen-yi, Chapter 7 "Yong-ye" p. 131. Sima Qian. *Shi-ji* Chapter 47 "Kong-zi shi-jia" p. 487. Zhang Bingnan, *Kong-zi zhuan*, p. 140
6 *Lun-yu Zheng-yi*, Chapter 14 "Xian-wen" Section 16, p. 311.

Shang-jun-shu 商君書

PART 1
TRANSLATION

(A) Social evolution and need of government authority

[1] After heaven and earth were settled, humans came into existence. In the beginning people knew their mothers but not their fathers. Their way was to love their relatives and to cherish what they privately had. Because of their love of their relatives, they were discriminating, and, because of their partiality to what they privately had, they fell into disorder. At that time, people bent to surpass one another and acted aggressively. Such behaviour led to competition and contention. If these could not be settled justly, no one could live in peace. Therefore, men of wisdom and virtue defined equity and justice and extolled impartiality, and people become appreciative of benevolence. Then, the practice of loving only one's relatives was abandoned and that of exalting the wise and virtuous established.

Now the virtuous practised universal love and the wise proffered various ways to solve problems. As population multiplied and their behaviour unrestrained; the virtuous and the wise, continuing such activities of loving others indiscriminatingly and suggesting different solutions, eventually caused disorder again. Then some sages rose to the situation. They divided land and property into proper shares, and assigned men and women to different positions. But such moves could not be carried out without enforcement measures, so the sages prescribed coercions. Since coercions could not be effective without those who administer them, so the sages appointed officials. Since officials could not act without someone to unify their actions, so the sages established the ruler. Once a ruler had been established, the practice of exalting the wise and virtuous was abandoned and that of respecting the government stations created . . . These three historical stages did not represent contradictory ways. It was because when people's custom degenerated and what was emphasised by them changed. When the affairs of the world varied the way to manage them became different. (Chapter 7, "Kai-sai" 開塞 pp. 15–16)

[2] In antiquity, before the time when there were rulers and subjects, superiors and inferiors, the people were disorderly and were not governable. So the sages created a system of noble and humble status with ranks, titles and designations, all for the purpose of defining the different roles of the ruler and the subjects, the superiors and the inferiors. As the territory was extensive, the people were numerous, and things were many, the sages set up five kinds of officials to administer them. As the people were numerous, and wickedness and depravity multiplied, the sages enacted laws and regulations and created weights and measures in order to prohibit them. (Chapter 23, "Jun-chen" 君臣 p. 38)
[3] In the past when people lived densely together in disorder, they desired a ruler. Thus the reason why the world was glad to have a ruler was that he would create order . . . Indeed, there is no greater benefit for the people than order, and there is no firmer order to be obtained than by establishing a ruler. (Chapter 7, "Kai-sai" p. 17)

(B) Prerequisites of government authority

(1) Extraordinary intelligence

[4] The wise see an event upcoming before it has sprouted. (Ch. 1, "Geng-fa" p. 1)
[5] A sage knows the right course which must be followed and the right time and circumstances for action. Therefore he can carry out the necessary government measures . . . A sage sees the fundamentals of government and knows the principles that must be followed. Therefore his administration of the people is like making water flow from a high position to a lower one, or like making fire approach what is dry and avoid what is wet. (Chapter 18, "Hua-ce" 畫策 p. 33)
[6] A sage or bright ruler is not a person who is able to get to the bottom of all things but is one who understands what is essential in all things. Therefore, his administration of the state is only to examine what is essential. (Chapter 3, "Nong-zhan" 農戰 p. 6)
[7] What is meant by "bright" in the case of a ruler is for nothing to escape his sight, so that the multitude of officials dare not commit treachery and the people dare not do wrong. Thus, the ruler will repose on a couch and listen to the sound of string and wind instruments, and yet the state will be well governed. (Chapter 18, "Hua-ce" p. 33)

(2) Unusual attitudes towards the people

[8] A ruler who governs the people as if they are generally good will inevitably make the state fall into disorder and be decimated. A ruler who governs the people as if they are essentially wicked will certainly lead the state to order and strength. (Chapter 5, "Shuo-min" p. 10)
[9] A sage cannot, with what the world thinks easy, overcome what it thinks difficult; he must, by means of what it thinks difficult, overcome what it thinks

easy. So, if the people are stupid, he can overcome them by means of knowledge; if the world has knowledge, he can overcome it by means of force . . . So when Shen-nong 神農 taught ploughing and attained supreme leadership, it was by means of his knowledge. When Tang 湯 and Wu 武 made themselves strong and attacked other feudal lords, the subjugation was induced by means of force. (Chapter 6, "Suan-di" p. 14)

[10] Therefore, it is said: "When the people are stupid, by knowledge one may become king; when the world has knowledge, by force one may become king." (Chapter 7, "Kai-sai" p. 16)

[11] A sage, in administering a country, is able to consolidate its strength and also to dissipate it. When standards and measures are clear, the people's strength is consolidated; if it is consolidated but not used, nothing can be accomplished. (Chapter 8, "Yi-yan" 壹言 p. 18)

(C) Responsibilities of government authority

(1) Determining the course of development of the state

[12] Duke Xiao of Qin 秦孝公 was planning the affairs of the state with three ministers, Gongsun Yang 公孫鞅, Gan Long 甘龍, and Du Zhi 杜摯 in attendance. They considered the changes in the world, searched the bases on which to correct the laws and sought for a way of guiding the people. The duke said, "Do not forget, at his succession, the spirits of the soil and of grain, is the way of a ruler; to shape the laws and to take the responsibility of governing the people are the tasks of the ministers. I intend now to alter the laws so as to achieve good government, and to reform the rites so as to educate the people, but I am afraid the world will criticise me."

Gongsun Yang said, "I have heard it said, 'He who hesitates in action will have no accomplishment; he who hesitates in an undertaking will have no achievement.' Your Lordship should decide quickly about changing the laws and heed not the criticism of the world. Moreover, he who conducts himself as an outstanding man is surely viewed negatively by the world; he who can consider affairs with uncommon wisdom is inevitably criticised by the common people. The saying runs, 'The stupid do not understand a task even after it has been completed but the wise see it even before it has sprouted. The ordinary people are unable to participate in deliberating on an initiative but they can share in the rejoicing over its completion.' According to the principle of Guo Yan 郭偃 [a minister of the state of Jin 晉 who helped reform laws of the state], 'He who is concerned about the highest virtue is not in harmony with popular ideas; he who realises great accomplishments does not counsel with the multitude.' The law is to care for the people; the rites are to facilitate undertakings. Therefore, when a sage finds some new measure that can help strengthen the state, he will not observe the laws of the past; and he would not adhere to the established rites, if by not adhering he could benefit his people."

Duke Xiao said, "Good."

Gan Long said, "Not so. I have heard it said, 'A sage guides the people without changing their characters, and a wise man achieves good government without altering the laws.' Where one guides the people in accordance with their characters, success can be achieved effortlessly; where one governs according to the established law, officials will be accustomed and the people settled. Now, if Your Lordship changes the laws, refuses to adhere to the old customs of the Qin state, and teaches the people reformed rites, I am afraid that the people of the world will criticise Your Lordship, and I wish that you would reflect on this matter with great care."

Gongsun Yang said, "What you said is conventional. Ordinary people are accustomed to old practices, and academics are immersed in what they have learned from books. These two kinds of men, while fit for holding office and maintaining the law, are unworthy to talk to in a discussion that goes beyond the law. The founders of the Three Dynasties became kings following different rites, and the five Hegemonic Lords have attained their dominance by different laws. Thus, a wise man creates laws but a foolish man is controlled by them; a man of talent reforms rites but a stupid man is constrained by them. A man who is constrained by rites not worthy to speak to about important affairs; a man who is controlled by laws is not worthy to discuss with about reform. Your Lordship should not hesitate any more."

Du Zhi said, "I heard that unless the profits can be hundredfold, one should not alter the law; unless the utility can be tenfold, one should not change a ware. I heard that, in observing precedents, one makes no mistakes, and, in following established rites, one commits no wrong. Your Lordship should consider these ideas with care."

Gongsun Yang said, "Former generations did not follow the same doctrines, so which past precedents should one obey? Emperors and kings of the past did not copy one another, so what rites should one follow? Fuxi 伏羲 and Shen-nong 神農 educated and did not punish. Huangdi 黄帝, Yao, and Shun punished but were not angry. Wen and Wu both established laws fit for their times and prescribed rites appropriate for the activities. Thus, rites and laws should be in accordance with what was opportune; regulations and orders should be expedient; weapons, armour, wares and equipment practical. Therefore, I say, there is more than one way to govern the world and there is no necessity to imitate antiquity in order to benefit the state. Tang and Wu rose to be kings without following antiquity; Yin and Xia lost their dynasties without their rites bing changed. Hence those who acted counter to antiquity did not necessarily deserve blame; nor did those who followed established rites merit much praise. Your Lordship should have no more doubts."

Duke Xiao said, "Excellent! I have heard it said that in poor neighbourhoods, many people are easily surprised by anything new; and people with little learning are often argumentative. What makes the foolish laugh makes the wise sad; the joy of the uninitiated is the worry of the talented. The world might criticise me, but I have no doubts anymore." Then, he issued the order to bring waste lands under cultivation. (Chapter 1, "Geng-fa" 更法 pp. 1–2)

(2) Choose social values and policy orientations

(A) CORRECT VALUES AND ORIENTATIONS

[13] Those who govern a state would want the people to engage in agriculture. If the state is not so engaged in its struggle against its rivals, it will not be able to hold its position because the strength of its people will not be sufficient. The other states will take advantage of its weakness and encroach upon its territory and render it feeble and, when these happened, it would be too late for remedy. A sage knows what is essential in administering a state, and so he induces the people to devote their attention to agriculture. If their attention is devoted to agriculture, they will be simple and easy to correct, diligent and easy to command. (Chapter 3, "Nong-zhan" p. 7)
[14] A sage king, realising that kingship is obtained through military might, will charge the entire country with military service. He who enters a state and studies its administration will find it strong if its army is ready to fight for the state. How does he know the people are ready to fight? If they, on perceiving war, behave like hungry wolves on seeing meat, they are ready. Generally, war is what people hate; he who succeeds in making people delight in war attains supremacy. In a strong state, when the father, in making a parting bequest to his son, the older brother to his younger brother, the wife to her husband, all say, "Do not return unless you win". And further they say, "If you incur death by disobeying the law or by deviating from orders, we too shall die." . . . Thus the soldiers of the armies will obey the orders like running water ad, in danger of death, they will not turn on their heels. (Chapter 18, "Hua-ce" p. 31)
[15] If the intelligent as well as the stupid, the noble as well as the humble, the brave as well as the timorous, the talented as well as the uninitiated will all apply to the full whatever knowledge they may have in their minds, exert to the utmost whatever strength they may have in their limbs, and will be at the service of their ruler even to death, then the ambitious and talented of the whole world would follow him, like flowing water, then, his army will have no equal, and his orders will be carried out throughout the whole world. A state of ten thousand chariots will not dare challenge his soldiers in the battlefield; nor will a state of a thousand chariots dare defend a walled city against his march. Should a state of ten thousand chariots challenge his soldiers in the battlefield, he will in one single battle rout its army; and should a state of a thousand chariots defend a walled city against his march, he will by one attack raze that town. (Chapter 17, "Shang-xing" 賞刑 p. 28)
[16] Therefore, in administering a state, a sage makes its people stick to agriculture at home and plan for war abroad . . . If at home, the people are directed to use their strength to the fullest, the fields will not lie fallow; and, if abroad, they are directed to fight to the death, they will conquer their enemies. If enemies are

conquered and fields do not lie fallow, wealth and power can be achieved without difficulty. (Chapter 6, "Suan-di" p. 13)

(B) Incorrect values and orientations

(i) Academic studies and sophisticated arguments

[17] Honour academicians who talk about nothing but *The Book of Odes* and *The Book of History* are held in esteem, people will become restless and think lightly of their ruler. (Chapter 6, "Suan-di" p. 14)

[18] Even though there is a bundle of *The Book of Odes* and *The Book of History* in every village, and a student of them in every family, they have no beneficial effect on the establishment of good government. (Chapter 3, "Nong-zhan" p. 7)

[19] Sophisticated words are difficult to understand even for the highly intelligent. (Chapter 26, "Ding-fen" 定分 p. 43)

[20] Sophistry and cleverness are aids to disorder. (Chapter 5, "Shuo-min" p. 10)

[21] The rhetoricians form columns and talk profusely in embellished language but their words are of no practical use. (Chapter 3, "Nong-zhan" pp. 7–8)

[22] When study [of rhetoric] becomes popular, people will abandon agriculture and engage in talks of highly abstract topics and discussions with false arguments, and they will thus leave the farm and travel around seeking food, and mutually exalt one another with their words. Therefore, the ordinary people would become estranged from the ruler and there will be crowds of disloyal subjects. This is a way which leads to the impoverishment of the state and to the weakening of the army. (Chapter 3, "Nong-zhan" p. 8)

[23] When scholars study with those rhetoricians, the common people will lose touch with reality and just recite empty words. Thus, their strength will decrease and transgression will increase, and, if the ruler does not realise this and deploys them in battle, they will make him lose his generals, and, in defence of a city, they will sell it to his enemy. (Chapter 25, "Shen-fa" 慎法 p. 40)

(ii) Moral precepts

[24] A benevolent man may benefit others but cannot make others benevolent; a righteous man may love others but cannot make others loving. From this we know benevolence and righteousness are not sufficient for keeping the world in order. (Chapter 18, "Hua-ce" p. 33)

[25] Kindness and benevolence are the mothers of transgression. (Chapter 5, "Shuo-min" p. 10)

[26] Where recluses are held in esteem, people will become estranged and criticise their superiors; where the brave are held in esteem, people will become contentious and think lightly of prohibitions. (Chapter 6, "Suan-di" p. 14)

(iii) Rites and music

[27] Rites and music are invitations to excessiveness and licentiousness. (Chapter 5, "Shuo-min" p. 10)

(iv) Popular reputation

[28] Popular reputation is the rat that carries evil designs. (Chapter 5, "Shuo-min" p. 10)
[29] A person whom the world calls worthy is supposed to be one whose words are correct. The reason why his words are correct is because their partisans say so. Hearing his words one may takes him to be capable and, on asking his partisans, one thinks that he is indeed so. Therefore, one would honour him without waiting for him to have achieved anything . . . This practice gives corrupt officials precisely the opportunity to realise their wicked and dangerous designs, and small-minded men the opportunity to apply their crafty tricks. (Chapter 25, "Shen-fa" p. 40)

(v) Commerce and crafts

[30] If craftsmen are valued, the people will become volatile and easily move their places of abode; if merchants are allowed to live in luxury and make profits with ease, people will blame and criticise their superiors. (Chapter 6, "Suan-di" p. 14)

(vi) The "parasites"

[31] The "six fleas" are: rites and music, *The Book of Odes* and *The Book of History*, moral culture and virtue, filial piety and brotherly love, sincerity and faith, chastity and integrity, benevolence and righteousness, repudiation of arms, and being ashamed of fighting. If there are these twelve things, the ruler is unable to make people farm and fight, and then the state will be poor and eventually dismembered. (Chapter 13, "Jin-ling" 靳令 p. 23)
[32] In a state where the "eight things" – sophistry and cleverness, rites and music, kindness and benevolence, popular trust and reputation – are numerous, the people overwhelm the government . . . In a state where these "eight things" are absent, the government controls the people. (Ch. 5, "Shuo-min" p. 10)
[33] A ruler who, in governing his state, ignores his authority and listens to sophisticated talk he will toil much but achieve little. Therefore, where five types of persons [rhetoricians, recluses, the brave, the craftsmen, and merchants] are held in esteem by the state, the land will lay in waste and the military will be weak. The capital of the rhetoricians engaging in exotic speeches lies in their mouths; that of the recluses in their will; that of the brave in their strength; that of craftsmen in their hands; that of merchants in what they personally possess. For them the world is one single house and their capital is in their bodies. They can carry their capital around with them and make any place their home . . . It was difficult even for Yao and Shun to deal with them, and it was why King Tang

of Shang and King Wu of Zhou banned them and achieved great accomplishments. (Chapter 6, "Suan-di" p. 14)

[34] If in a state there are ten evils – *The Book of Odes* and *The Book of History*, rites and music, virtue and the cultivation thereof, benevolence and integrity, sophistry and intelligence – the ruler will have no one whom he can employ for defence and warfare. If a state is governed by means of these ten things, parts of its territory will be lost, as soon as an enemy invades, and, even if no enemy invades, it will be poor. (Chapter 3, "Nong-zhan" p. 6)

[35] If in a country there are ten evils – rites, music, *The Book of Odes*, *The Book of History*, virtue, moral cultivation, filial piety, brotherly love, integrity, and sophistry – the ruler cannot make the people fight, loss of territory is inevitable, and extinction will follow. (Chapter 4, "Qu-qiang" 去彊 pp. 8–9)

[36] The reason why the people are unhelpful to the government is that they see those who are itinerant scholars can be honoured, those in commerce can enrich their families, and those who practise crafts can make a living. When the people see that these undertakings are easy and profitable, they will certainly avoid agriculture. Avoiding agriculture, the people will regard their residence with little care and, as a result, will not defend their homes and fight for the ruler. (Chapter 3, "Nong-zhan" p. 7)

[37] If the people in the country all say that agriculture and war can be avoid and yet office and rank can be acquired, the talented and ambitious men will all change their occupations to apply themselves to the study of *The Book of Odes* and *The Book of History* and cultivate influence from abroad. If the best of them can actually achieve prominence, the mediocre can acquire offices and ranks, and the least talented can occupy themselves with trade, arts and crafts and thus avoid agriculture and war, the state will be in a dangerous situation. Where the people are given to such professions, it is certain that such a state will be decimated. (Chapter 3, "Nong-zhan" p.5)

[38] Therefore is it said, "If there are a thousand people engaged in agriculture and war, and only one in the study of *The Book of Odes* and *The Book of History* and clever rhetoric, then those thousand will all be remiss in agriculture and war; if there are a hundred people engaged in agriculture and war and only one in the arts and crafts, then those hundred will all be remiss in agriculture and war. (Chapter 3, "Nong-zhan" p. 6)

[39] As a result, the people in the country change and become fond of sophistry, take pleasure in study, pursue trade, practise arts and crafts, and shun agriculture and war and so [the ruin of the state] will not be far off. When the state is in trouble, the learned people will hate law, merchants will become profiteers, and artisans will refuse to be useful. That is why the state will be easily destroyed. Indeed, if farmers are few, and those who live idly on others are many, the state will be poor and in danger. Take the various kinds of crop-eating insects as an example. They are born in spring and die in autumn yet, once they appear, the people will be short of food for many years. Now, if one man tills and a hundred live on him, the harm is far greater than those insects. (Chapter 3, "Nong-zhan" pp. 6–7)

(3) Pursuit correct values and objectives

(A) Human dispositions and inclinations

[40] People seek food when hungry, rest when tired, amusement when suffering hardship, honour when humiliated. Such are the natural inclinations of the people. When seeking profits, they neglect the rules of proper behaviour; when seeking fame, they lose the norm of their nature. How can we conclude it is so? Now those who rob or mug violate the prohibitions of the ruler and conduct themselves improperly as subjects and, consequently, their reputations are ruined and their lives in danger, and yet they do not desist. It is because of the profit they want to gain. The gentlemen of antiquity wore clothes that did not warm their skins, ate food that did not fill their bellies, and yet they exhausted their minds, fatigued their four limbs and impaired their five internal organs, in order to increase their reputation. This is not in accordance with the norm of human nature but they did it for the sake of fame. Therefore is it said, "Where fame and profit go, the people will follow." (Chapter 6, "Suan-di" 算地 p. 13)
[41] Shame and disgrace, labour and hardship are what the people dislike; fame and glory, ease and joy are what the people work to get. (Chapter 6, "Suan-di" 算地 p. 15)
[42] Generally, the desire of people for riches and honour does not cease before their coffins are closed. (Chapter 17, "Shang-xing" p. 30)

(B) Ways to effect change

(i) Establishing a single goal

[43] I heard that the way to guide the people is for the ruler to go ahead of them. Thus, the people can be made to engage in farming and fighting, or to travel around seeking official appointments, or to pursue knowledge, all depending on what the ruler values. Where the ruler values agricultural productivity and military valour, the people will engage in farming and fighting; where the ruler values *The Book of Odes* and *The Book of History*, the people will pursue academic knowledge. The people run after profits like water runs to low places, they have no other choice. (Chapter 23, "Jun-chen" p. 38)
[44] What the people desire is tens of thousands in number but, if profit comes only from one single source, the people who do not concentrate on that source will not attain their desires. (Chapter 5, "Shuo-min" p. 11)
[45] A state that allows profits to come from one single source is invincible. One that allows two sources is half as strong. One that allows ten sources is undefendable. (Chapter 13, "Jin-ling" p. 24)
[46] Block the private ways to end the people's ambitions and open a single door to let them attain their desires. (Chapter 5, "Shuo-min" p. 11)
[47] In ruling a state, a sage knows what is fundamental and orders the people to concentrate their minds on agriculture. When they concentrate, they are

simple and easy to keep right; when they are all engaged in agriculture, they are easy to deploy, they can be trusted to defend their homes and engage in wars because, when they concentrate on a single undertaking, they will be less treacherous but value settlement; when they are engaged in a single undertaking, they can be moved by rewards and punishments; when they are engaged in a single undertaking, they can be employed for ventures abroad. (Chapter 3, "Nong-zhan" p. 7)

[48] When the people see that the ruler honours those who engage in agriculture and war, depreciate craftsmen and artisans, and despise itinerant scholars, they concentrate on a single task [agriculture and war]. As a result their families will become rich and they will be personally honoured by the state . . . In governing a state, one who can make the people concentrate on a single goal will make the state strong. (Chapter 8, "Yi-yan" p. 18)

[49] The ruler, in order to increase the strength of the people, opens to them the way to public profits and blocks the door to private interest. Work made for private interest will not be glorified in the country and favours of the ruler cannot be gained through the gate of private intrigue. As a result, merit and public fame will be effective in encouraging the people, orders from above will be enforced, waste land reclaimed, licentious people stopped, and evil deeds prevented from breaking out. In governing a state, he who can increase the people's strength by making them concentrate on a single task will make the state strong; he who can work on the fundamentals and prohibit the frivolous will make the state rich. (Chapter 8, "Yi-yan" p. 18)

[50] Presently most of those who govern have no grasp of the fundamental principle. While talking about governance in the court, they have numerous divergent ideas striving to replace one another. As a result, the ruler is puzzled and the officials confused. The people become guideless and idle and unwilling to engage in agriculture. They will learn sophisticated knowledge and participate in endless debates, or engage in commerce, or practise various crafts – all for the purpose of avoiding farming and fighting. In this way, the state will soon be ruined because, when it is in trouble, the academics will hate the law, the merchants will change their allegiance, and the craftsmen will avoid government service (Chapter 3, "Nong-zhan" p.6)

(ii) Rewards and punishments

[51] People are born with likes and dislikes, and therefore they can be governed. The ruler must be careful about what the people like and dislike. What the people like and dislike are the bases for rewards and punishments. By nature, humans love titles and rewards and hate punishments and penalties. A ruler uses the two to guide people's intentions and meet their desires. Titles should be bestowed on people who have made their utmost efforts, and rewards should follow after people have achieved merit. If a ruler can, by making such consequences as clear as the sun and moon and thus win the people's trust, his army will have no equal. (Chapter 9, "Cuo-fa" p. 20)

[52] What a ruler uses to prohibit and encourage are punishments and rewards. Rewards should follow merit; punishments should follow crime. (Chapter 24, "Jin-shi" 禁使 p. 39)
[53] What a ruler uses as a means to encourage people is official posts and titles; what enables a state to rise is success in agriculture and war . . . The way all good rulers follow in educating the people is that, to reach official posts and titles, there is a single opening [to engage in agricultural work and war] . . . The people who see that profit from above comes through one single opening will be simple. Where they are simple, they will not be lazy and licentious. Where the people are not lazy and licentious, they will have strength. Where the people have strength, the state will be strong. (Chapter 3, "Nong-zhan" p. 5)
[54] Of the external affairs of the people, there is nothing more dangerous than warfare . . . Of the internal affairs of the people, there is nothing harder than agriculture. (Chapter 22, "Wai-nei" 外内 p. 37)
[54] Agriculture makes the people suffer hardship, war makes them face danger. To make them endure hardship and ignore danger is a tactic based on their own calculations. They will calculate about the profit they can get in their lifetime, and they do care about the reputation they leave behind them after death. It is therefore important for the ruler to determine from where the people can obtain fame and profit. If the profit comes from the land, people will use their full strength to farming; if fame results from war, they will fight to the death. (Chapter 6, "Suan-di" p. 13)
[56] The people will love farming and enjoy warfare because they see that the ruler honours such undertakings. (Chapter 8, "Yi-yan" p. 18)
[57] In ruling the state, the sage unifies rewards, unifies punishments and unifies education. When rewards are unified, the army will have no equal; when punishments are unified; orders will be carried out; when education is unified, inferiors will obey their superiors. (Chapter 17, "Shang-xing" p. 28)
[58] What is meant by "unification of rewards" is that profits and emoluments, office and titles should come only from military merit and no other source. Thus, the intelligent and the stupid, the noble and the humble, the brave and the timorous, the virtuous and the unworthy, will all exhaust what knowledge they may have in their minds and what strength they may have in their limbs to serve their ruler until death. The heroic and the virtuous of the world will follow this path like flowing water. As a result, the ruler's army will have no equal and his orders will be implemented throughout the world. (Chapter 17, "Shang-xing" p. 28)
[59] What is meant by "unification of punishments" is that punishments are not to have degrees and grades but that, from the ministers and generals down to officers and ordinary people, whosoever does not obey the king's orders, violates the prohibitions of the state, or rebels against the laws adopted by the ruler, should be punished with death and not pardoned. Achievements of the past should not cause a decrease in the punishment for later failures, nor should good deeds of the past cause any mitigation of the law for later wrongdoings. (Chapter 17, "Shang-xing" p. 29)

[60] What is meant by "uniform education" is that those who are known for their wide learning, argumentative talk, cleverness, integrity, scrupulousness, expertise in rites and music, cultivation in conduct, participation in partisan groups, and engagement in commendations and criticisms, are not allowed to become rich and honoured, to comment on punishments, and independently to present their private views to the superiors. The strong should be broken and the sharp blunted. Though one may be called wise or learned or clever or eloquent or generous, or honest, yet one cannot gain the ruler's favours without having achieved merit. The gate to riches and honour lies in war only. He who is capable in war will walk through the gate to riches and honour; he who is wilful and disobedient will suffer established punishments with no pardon. (Chapter 17, "Shang-xing" p. 30)

[61] The former kings were able to order the people to walk on sharp swords and face arrows and stones. The people were willing, not because they had learned to like it, but because they wanted to avoid harm. Therefore, my teaching is to command those who desire profit to get it by no means other than farming, and those who want to avoid harm to escape it by no means other than engaging in war. All the people in the state will first devote themselves to agriculture and war and then get what they are happy with. As a result, even though the land may be scarce, the produce is plentiful, even though the population is small, the army is strong. For he who can achieve these two results in his state, the road to becoming a hegemon or king of the world is fully prepared. (Chapter 25, "Shen-fa" p. 41)

(iii) Control and use of the people

[62] In the past, he who could control the world would first control his own people; he who could overcome strong enemies would first overcome his own people. The basic task of overcoming the people is to gain control over them, like a smelter will do to the metal and a potter to the clay. (Chapter 18, "Hua-ce" p. 31)

[63] When the people are weak, the state is strong; when the state is strong, the people are weak. Therefore the state that has the right way for governance will do its best to make its people weak. (Chapter 20, "Ruo-min" 弱民 p. 35)

[64] When the people are made humble, they value the titles and ranks awarded by the government; when they are made weak, they hold the officials in awe; when they are poor, they cherish the rewards given by the authorities. Controlled by punishments, the people will be happy to be employed by the government . . . To rule the people, they must be humbled by punishments. (Chapter 20, "Ruo-min" pp. 35–6)

[65] When the people are stupid they are easy to govern. (Chapter 26, "Ding-fen" p. 43)

[66] When the people are stupid, one with wisdom can be the king; when they are sophisticated, one with power can be the king . . . It is the nature of people that, when stupid, they want to know, and, after devoting to learning, they have no strength left and become obedient to force. (Chapter 7, "Kai-sai" p. 16)

[67] When standards and measures are clear, the people's strength is consolidated. If it is consolidated but not dissipated, it is not useful; if it is used but not for a specific purpose, there will be disorder. Therefore, for one who administers a country, the purpose for consolidating its strength is to make the state rich and its army strong. The way to dissipate its accumulated strength is to make the people engage in agriculture and attack the enemy. If many other ways are open, and are not barred, there will be those who choose the easier ways, and, if they are not punished, there will be treachery. If the easy ways are barred, the people will be simple and devote themselves to a single goal and become strong. If their strength is not dissipated, there will be those who live like parasites. Therefore, consolidating the people's strength is brought about by making them take up a single occupation; dissipating their strength is brought about by making them attack the enemy. (Chapter 8, "Yi-yan" p. 18)

[68] He who governs a state values making the people simple-minded. When simple-minded, they engage in agriculture. When engaging in agriculture, they are diligent. When diligent, they become rich. When they are rich, their wealth should be reduced by exchanging it for government titles so that they will not become extravagant. Those who become extravagant will be subdued by punishments and by making them engage in agriculture. Therefore, if a ruler is able only to consolidate strength but not to use it, disorder ensues; and a ruler who is able only to reduce strength but not consolidate it, will perish. A bright ruler, who knows how to combine these two measures, will have a strong state; a ruler who does not know how to combine these two, will have his state decimated. (Chapter 8, "Yi-yan" p. 18)

[69] People would not be able attain their desires without concentrating on a single undertaking, so they concentrate. When they concentrate, their strength is consolidated. When their strength is consolidated, they become strong. When the consolidated strength is properly used, the state will become stronger. Thus, a state that can consolidate its people's strength and use it properly is called an "enemy-attacking state". It will inevitably become powerful . . . A state that can consolidate its people's strength but cannot use it is called a "self-attacking state". It will inevitably become decimated. (Chapter 5, "Shuo-min" p. 11)

[70] A poor state that launches wars will send its poison to the enemy and rid itself of its six fleas. As a result it will inevitably become strong. A rich state that does not launch wars will have idle elements breeding inside, and there will be the six fleas, so that it will inevitably become weak. (Chapter 13, "Jin-ling" p. 23)

[71] Therefore a state that knows how to produce strength but not how to reduce it, is called one that "attacks itself", and will certainly be decimated. So it is said that, where there is a true king, the state does not store its strength and the family does not hoard grain. The state does not store its strength because the people are readily employed; the family does not hoard grain because it is kept in government granaries. (Chapter 5, "Shuo-min" p. 11)

(c) Concrete measures

[72] Among the external affairs of the people none is more difficult than warfare. Therefore, weak law cannot make people do it. What is a "weak law" ? It is one that gives few rewards and has little punishing force and therefore cannot bar depraved ways. What is a "depraved way"? It is to honour sophisticated rhetoricians, to employ itinerant office-seekers, give prominence to those known for academic works and private reputation. When these three are not barred, the people will not engage in warfare and the state affairs will fail. For, when rewards are few, those who obey the law will receive no profit; when the punishing force is weak, those who violate the law will find no harm. Therefore, opening the depraved way to entice the people and then using weak law to combat their transgression is like using a wild cat as the bait to catch a mouse. Would it not certainly fail? So he who wants to make his people engage in warfare must make the law strong. The rewards must be generous, the punishing force must be harsh, the depraved ways must be barred. Those who engage in sophisticated talk and clever arguments will not be honoured; those who travel to seek government appointments will not be employed and those who are learned and have private reputation will not be made prominent. Seeing that rewards for fighting are generous, the people will forget the danger of death, and seeing punishments for not fighting they will find life miserable. When the people forget the danger of death because of the generous rewards, and find life miserable because of the heavy punishment, and all deviant routes for escape are blocked, they will meet the enemies like shooting a falling leaf with a crossbow of 100 catties' capacity. What can they not vanquish? (Chapter 22, "Wai-nei" p. 37)

[73] Among the internal affairs of the people, none is harder than farming. Thus, weak measures cannot make them engage in it. What are "weak measures"? They are those that make the farmers poor and the merchants rich, the foodstuff cheap and money dear. When foodstuff is cheap, the farmers are poor; when money is dear, the merchants are rich; when frivolous undertakings are not forbidden, the craftsmen will have profits and those who rely on others for a living will multiply. Farmers endure extreme hard labour and earn little profit – not as much as that gained by merchants and craftsmen. If the number of merchants and craftsmen can be restricted, it is impossible to prevent a state from becoming rich. Therefore, it is said that, if a state is to be enriched through agriculture, foodstuff must be expensive, taxes on non-agricultural population numerous, and levies on markets heavy. As a result, people have to farm. Those who do not farm will have to buy food; food will be expensive and farmers will have profits. Where farming is profitable, many people will farm. When food is expensive and dealing in it is not unprofitable but heavily taxed, people cannot but abandon commerce and crafts and engage in agriculture. (Chapter 22, "Wai-nei" pp. 37–8)

(i) Rules to win people's trust in the government

[74] Tax people according to the amount of grain their lands yield. In this way the government will be applying a uniform measure, and the people wild think it equitable. When the government is consistent, the people will have trust in it. When the government is consistent, the officials will not dare to do evil. When the people feel there is justice, they will be prudent. When the people are prudent, they will not easily change . . . The adults will diligently engage in agriculture and the young will tirelessly learn to do the same. As a result waste land will be reclaimed. (Chapter 2, "Ken-ling" 墾令 p. 2)
[75] Government action should not be delayed overnight so that crooked officials would have no time to make any private gains from the people. When the government work in the hands of various officials is not delayed, the people would have more time to farm, and the waste land will certainly be reclaimed. (Chapter 2, "Ken-ling" p. 2)
[76] Do not give government posts and titles to those who cultivate and receive support from foreign powers; then people will not value learning and belittle agriculture. When people do not value knowledge they will be ignorant. When they are ignorant, they will not engage in establishing foreign connections. When they have no foreign connections, they will diligently engage in agriculture and will not try to find easy ways of life. When people do not belittle agriculture, the state will be secure and in no danger. When the state is secure and in no danger, and the people diligently engage in agriculture and do not try to find easy ways of life, the waste land will certainly be reclaimed. (Chapter 2, "Ken-ling" p. 3)
[77] The different districts in the country should each have the same administrative system and follow the same operating rules so that departing officials could not cover up their wrong deeds and succeeding officials could not make unwarranted changes . . . As a result, the number of officials will be small and the people will not be overworked. When officials are not crooked, the people will not escape from them. When the people do not have to escape from crooked officials, their undertakings will not be ruined. When the number of officials is small and the demands on the people for public service are not numerous, the people will not be overworked but will have more days for farming. When there are more days for farming, the demand for public service is less; and if farming is not obstructed, the waste land will certainly be reclaimed. (Chapter 2, "Ken-ling" p. 4)

(ii) Rules against misconduct by officials

[78] Great ministers and high officials should be prohibited from engaging in broad learning and sophisticated disputation, and in moving their residences about. When they are not allowed to travel to the districts and live there, the farmers will not hear and see ways that might change their behaviour . . . but know only farming and will not leave what they are accustomed to do. When ignorant farmers do not know anything new and have not become fond of knowledge . . . they will diligently engage in farming. When they only know farming

and do not depart from their custom, the waste land will certainly be reclaimed. (Chapter 2, "Ken-ling" p. 4)

[79] Sophisticated music and fine dress should not be allowed to be heard and seen in the districts. While doing their work, the people will not have such dress to look at, and, while resting, will have no such music to listen to. When there is no such music to listen to, the people's mood will not become volatile; when there is no such dress to look at, the people's minds will be focused. When their minds are focused and their mood not volatile, the waste land will certainly be reclaimed. (Chapter 2, "Ken-ling" p. 3)

[80] The price of wine and meat should be high and the taxes on them should be ten times the price. As a result, there will be fewer wine merchants, farmers will not develop a love for alcohol, and officials cannot indulge in drinking and feasts. When wine merchants are few, grain will not be wasted; when people do not drink excessively, farming will not be neglected; when the great officials are not self-indulgent; the affairs of state will not be delayed . . . Then the waste land is sure to be reclaimed. (Ch. 2, "Ken-ling" p. 3)

(iii) Rules against vagabonds and idle dependants

[81] Prevent people from migrating, and then those who are crafty and interfere with farming will have no place to get food and will have to farm. When those who are stupid but have many desires become focused, the farmers will be calm. When such people want to farm, the waste land will certainly be reclaimed. (Chapter 2, "Ken-ling" pp. 3–4)

[82] Ban the hostels along travel routes, then those crafty and deceitful people, and those who are unsettled and engaging in clandestine dealings and who create doubts in the minds of farmers, cannot travel. When travellers cannot find places to eat, they will have to turn to agriculture and, as a result, waste land will certainly be reclaimed. (Chapter 2, "Ken-ling" p. 3)

[83] Those who, with generous government remunerations and numerous fief tax incomes, keep large households with many mouths to feed, will ruin agriculture. They should be taxed heavily according to the number of their dependants, and their dependants should be made liable to corvée service. As a result, excessive lifestyles will be curbed, and the idle and unsettled will not have places to get food. When they have no place to get food, they have to engage in agriculture, and the waste land will certainly be reclaimed. (Chapter 2, "Ken-ling" p. 3)

[84] Prohibit the employment of large numbers of helpers and labourers; then high ministers and heads of great families cannot start major construction works, their pampered sons cannot live idly, the indolent will not be able to shy from hard work, and those seeking employment with the ministers and great families will find no place to get food and will have to engage in agriculture, and the waste land will certainly be reclaimed. (Chapter 2, "Ken-ling" p. 3)

[85] Sons of an aristocrat, other than the firstborn and customarily the heir apparent, must be enlisted for government employment according to established rules. They will not be allowed to go in and out of government office buildings

freely. The compensation for their work is distributed under the strict supervision of government functionaries. They will not be allowed to escape corvée service. Not being certain to get high office and not being allowed to go to serve other aristocrats, they will have to engage in agriculture, and then the waste land will certainly be reclaimed. (Chapter 2, "Ken-ling" p. 4)
[86] Place the mountains and large lakes under government control so that those who are lazy will have nowhere to get food easily and will have to engage in agriculture, and, as a result, the waste land will certainly be reclaimed. (Chapter 2, "Ken-ling" p. 3).

(iv) Rules against merchants

[87] Prohibit merchants from buying grain and farmers from selling it as merchandise. Where the farmers are prohibited from selling grain, even the indolent will work hard [in order to earn government rewards]. Where the merchants are prohibited from buying grain, they will not be happy in a year of good harvest [and hoard up surplus] and will not gain large profits in a year of poor harvest. When there is no large profit to be gained, the merchants will be reluctant and will want to engage in agriculture. When even lazy farmers work hard and the merchants want to engage in agriculture, the waste land will certainly be reclaimed. (Chapter 2, "Ken-ling" p. 3)
[88] Prohibit people from privately delivering foodstuff into the military market so that evil schemes will not develop clandestinely. Those who deliver foodstuff to the military will not be allowed to linger in the military market, and the shifty and idle will not be allowed to loiter there. When the privately delivered foodstuff cannot be sold in the market, no one will privately deliver foodstuff to the military market and, when the shifty and idle are not allowed to loiter in the military market, the farmer will not be enticed by them, and the waste land will certainly be reclaimed. (Chapter 2, "Ken-ling" p. 4)
[89] Those who transport grain [to government granaries] are to be prohibited from charging fees and from carrying goods on their return trip. The cart and the ox should be registered and inspected. When extra goods are carried, the carrier will be charged to do extra corvée service. As a result, the round trips will be rapid, farm work will not be obstructed, and the waste land will certainly be reclaimed. (Chapter 2, "Ken-ling" p. 4)
[90] Impose heavy taxes on merchandise at the check points and in the market, then the farmers will hate to engage in commerce, and the merchants will have doubts and be restrained. As a result, the waste land will certainly be reclaimed. (Chapter 2, "Ken-ling" p. 4)
[91] Let only those registered as merchants engage in commerce and pay the prescribed tax and do the prescribed corvée service. The servants and labourers employed by a merchant must be registered and made liable for corvée service. As a result, farmers will have more leisure; merchants will be more burdened with corvée service. When farmers have more leisure, land will not lie uncultivated; when merchants are more burdened with corvée service, they will have less time

to travel around . . . Then the waste land will certainly be reclaimed. (Chapter 2, "Ken-ling" p. 4).

(v) Rules against potential and actual criminals

[92] Inflict heavy punishments on the guilty and collective penalties on their relatives, then those who are devious will not quarrel; those who are obdurate will not litigate; those who are lazy will not move around seeking handouts; those who are extravagant will not be excessive; and those who are wicked, obsequious and evil minded will not corrupt people's hearts. When these five types of persons are not living within the borders, the waste land will certainly be reclaimed. (Chapter 2, "Ken-ling" p. 3)
[93] No one should be allowed to petition the officials, asking for permission to provide food for a convict. Then the wicked will have no master. When the wicked have no master, they will not enthusiastically engage in evil deeds. When they are not so engaged, they will have little to gain. When they have little to gain, farmers will not be harmed. When farmers are not harmed, the waste land will certainly be reclaimed. (Chapter 2, "Ken-ling" p. 4)

(D) Law

(1) Basis

[94] In governing a state, a sage does not simply follow the past as a model or go along with the trend of the present. He governs after taking into consideration the situation of the time and creates laws after evaluating the prevailing customs. A law adopted without first examining the people's feelings will not succeed. Government actions in agreement with the conditions of the time will be carried out without interruption. (Chapter 8, "Yi-yan" p. 19)

(2) Objectives and functions

[95] The way to have a ruler established is no more crucial than to have effective laws. (Chapter 7, "Kai-sai" p. 17)
[96] A sage's way of government is to make prohibitions numerous in order to limit the people's opportunity of using their talents, and to reward the people only for their labour so that fraud and trickeries can be eliminated. (Chapter 6, "Suan-di" p. 14)
[97] The basic principle that guides the people is the law. Therefore, he who is good at governing will restrain the people with law. (Chapter 18, "Hua-ce" p. 31)
[98] A ruler is not more virtuous in conduct than the ordinary people, not more knowledgeable than they, and not braver and stronger than they. Nevertheless, even with greater virtue and knowledge, they dare not plot against him; even with greater valour and strength, they dare not kill him; even in greater number they dare not overrule him. When he posts heavy rewards none among the millions of them dares to dispute; when he inflicts punishments none of them dares to complain. Why? It is because there is the law. (Chapter 18, "Hua-ce" p. 32)

[99] When a rabbit runs in the field, a hundred people chase after it. It is not that they all want the particular rabbit; the market is full of rabbits on sale but even a thief dare not take one because the legal title to it has been settled. Therefore, where the legal title of a rabbit was not settled Yao, Shun, Yu and Tang would all swiftly chase after it; when the legal title is settled, greedy thieves will not take one. (Chapter 26, "Ding-fen" p. 43)

[100] The early kings hung the scales for weight and fixed the measuring ruler for length. These instruments are still in use today because they make the measurements clear. If one discards the scales in deciding the weight of something or abolishes the rule in measuring the length of something, even if his appraisals are accurate, the merchants will not use his kind of skill because it does not always yield definitive results. Those who discard law as a measuring tool and rely on private judgement do not know how to make correct decisions. The only person who could decide the talents and worthiness of another was Yao but not everyone in the world is a Yao. Therefore, the early kings, knowing that personal judgements and private evaluations were unreliable, established laws to determine the correct measure, rewarded those who met the standards and punished those who violated them. Because the laws prescribing rewards and punishments were not misapplied, the people did not contend. When offices and titles are not awarded for merit, loyal officials will not be promoted; when rewards and remunerations are not given for achievement, brave warriors will not be employed. (Chapter 14, "Xiu-quan" 修權 pp. 24–5)

[101] Law is what the people depend upon for their life . . . Trying to govern the people while eliminating law is like wanting to be not hungry while eliminating food, or wanting not to be cold while eliminating clothes, or wanting to be in the east while going west. It is clear that the wishes cannot be realised. (Chapter 26, "Ding-fen" p. 43)

[102] Therefore, the sages made laws and appointed officials. The officials were appointed to be teachers to the people of the world. The measures were to define everyone's position. When positions were defined, even the very cunning would become scrupulous and trustworthy, and the ordinary people would all become honest and guileless, each one restraining himself. Thus, having everybody's position defined is the road that leads to orderly government; not having everybody's position defined is the road that leads to disorder. (Chapter 26, "Ding-fen" p. 43)

(3) Making and enforcing law

(A) Make law the supreme norm

[103] A benevolent man can be benevolent to others but cannot make others benevolent; a virtuous man can love others but cannot make others loveing. Therefore we know that benevolence and righteousness are not enough to keep the world in order . . . A sage does not value virtue, he values law. (Chapter 18, "Hua-ce" p. 33)

[104] When the population is large, evils and transgressions breed. To prohibit them the legal system is established and standards created . . . If, after the establishment of the legal system, privately preferred practices are allowed, the people will not be fearful of the proscriptions. (Chapter 23, "Jun-chen" p. 38)
[105] If laws and standards are dismissed and private judgements preferred, wicked ministers will peddle their influence and seek bribes; government personnel will deceive the people and extort them. Thus, it is said, "Where woodworms are multitudinous the wood breaks, where there is a large fissure the wall collapses." So, if ministers of state vie with one another in selfishness and do not care for the people, then inferiors are estranged from superiors. When this happens, there is a fissure in the state. If government personnel deceive and extort from the people, they are like woodworms to the people. Therefore, it is rare in the world that a state with fissures and woodworms does not become extinct. This is why an intelligent king relies on the law and avoids private judgements, and his state is free from fissures and woodworms. (Chapter 14, "Xiu-quan" p. 25)
[106] A bright ruler cherishes his power of making the final decisions, and values the people's trust, and does not harm the law because of his private interests. (Chapter 14, "Xiu-quan" p. 24)
[107] If the ruler abandons the law and allows people do what they like, wickedness will proliferate. (Chapter 20, "Ruo-min" p. 35)
[108] After the law has been established, no one should damage it with words of virtue . . . If after the law is fixed, a ruler is fond of employing the "six fleas", his state will be ruined. (Chapter 13, "Jin-ling" p. 23)
[109] Therefore, a bright ruler is careful about the law. Words that are not in accordance with the law, he will not listen to; actions that are not in accordance with the law, he will not exalt; deeds that are not in accordance with the law, he will not do. He harkens to words that are in accordance with the law, exalts actions that are in accordance with the law, and performs deeds that are in accordance with the law. As a result, his state will be in order and its territory will be widened, his army will be strong and he will be honoured. This is the climax of good government and an imperative for a ruler of men to examine. (Chapter 23, "Jun-chen" p. 39)
[110] The officials and the common people of the world, even those who are virtuous and wise, cannot say a word that twists the law; those who are rich with 1,000 taels of gold cannot use one single coin to bend the law. Consequently, the clever and deceitful, as well as the worthy and talented, will all obey the law and behave properly, keeping their own affairs in order, and observe public policies. (Chapter 26, "Ding-fen" p. 42)
[111] In ordering the people a bright ruler will make them do their best and evaluate their achievements. Where there are achievements, rewards of wealth and honour will follow. He does not do private favours. (Chapter 9, "Cuo-fa" p. 20)

(B) Make law clear and definitive

(i) General principle

[112] If laws and orders are not clear and their prescriptions are not definitive, everyone in the world can criticise them, and the criticisms differ from person to person and there will be no agreement. If the ruler at the top makes the laws, but the people at the bottom criticise them, this is to make the laws uncertain and to let the inferiors supersede their superiors . . . This is the way that will cause wickedness and wrongdoings to rise greatly, the ruler to be despoiled of his power and authority, the state ruined and the temple of its patron gods destroyed. (Chapter 26, "Ding-fen" p. 43)

[113] I heard that the bright rulers of old established law and the people are devoid of evils . . . It was because the law was clear and people were benefited by it. (Chapter 9, "Cuo-fa" p. 19)

[114] Where the law is not clear, it is impossible to demand the people to follow orders. Where orders are not followed it is impossible to keep the ruler honoured. Even if he had the wisdom of Yao and Shun, he cannot govern. (Chapter 23, "Jun-chen" p. 38)

[115] Words whose meaning is subtle and mysterious are difficult even for those highly intelligent to comprehend. Those who are always correct without the guidance of laws and standards are but one among tens of thousands. The sage governs the world according to rules applicable to people in tens of thousands. Thus, a rule that only a highly intelligent person understands cannot be made law because the people are not all so intelligent. A rule only a virtuous person understands cannot be made law because the people are not all virtuous. Therefore, in making a law, the sage will make it clear and easy to understand. He will use the correct terms that the stupid as well as the intelligent can all understand. He will appoint law officials and clerks as teachers for the people of the world to enable the multitude of people not to fall into peril. Thus, where the sage is established as the ruler, no one in the world will die of punishments. It is not that he does not punish and execute, it is because the law is clear and easy to understand, and law officials and clerks are appointed as teachers to guide the people to a proper understanding of the law. Then the thousands of people all know what to avoid and what to approach – to avoid disasters and approach prosperity and thus regulate themselves. Thus, a bright ruler governs when there is already order and achieves great order in the world. (Chapter 26, "Ding-fen" p. 43)

(ii) Specific measures

[116] Records of laws and orders should be made in duplicate. One set is to be kept in the imperial palace. For the second set a Forbidden Room should be built . . . After the second set is placed in it, the room is locked and secured with a seal. Anyone who, without authorisation, breaks the seal, enters the room to see the

laws and orders, or alters a word thereof, shall be sentenced to death and there will be no pardon. (Chapter 26, "Ding-fen" p. 42)

[117] The duke asked Gongsun Yang, saying, "After having adopted appropriate laws in time, I want them to be clearly known and applied correctly without bias by all government officers and the people throughout the world the very next day. How can this be brought about?" Gongsun Yang replied, "Officials and clerks should be specifically appointed for the sake of law. Those who are capable of understanding the meaning of law and serve as a model for the people should be reported to the emperor. The emperor will appoint them as law officials. They will receive orders to go to their posts to administer law. Any one of them who applies the law incorrectly will be given the punishment prescribed by that law." (Chapter 26, "Ding-fen" pp. 41–2)

[118] The emperor shall set up three law officers, one in the palace, one, together with clerks, in the office of the Censor, and one in the office of the prime minister. In the various vassal states and districts, each shall be appointed one law officer together with clerks . . . They will all receive laws from the Forbidden Room and learn their meaning. Other officials, and the people who want to know the laws and orders, should all ask these law officers. (Chapter 26, "Ding-fen" p. 42)

[119] The law officers are required to learn the meaning of the laws and orders. A schedule will be set up, and they are required to learn the meaning of the laws and orders accordingly. For those who fail to meet the schedule, a law to punish the lax shall be enacted. Those who dare to alter the laws and orders, adding or erasing even one single word, shall be sentenced to death without pardon. (Chapter 26, "Ding-fen" p. 42)

[120] Whenever government officials or the people have questions about the meaning of the laws and orders and ask a law officer, he should in each case address the reason why the question is raised and answer clearly regarding the law asked about. And, in each case, he should make a tally of the length of 1 feet and 6 inches, with clear inscription of the year, month, day and hour, as well as the name of the law about which questions were asked and the answer given. If a law officer refuses to give the content and explain the meaning of a law asked by someone, he is to be punished with the same penalty prescribed by the particular law. The left half of the tally will be given to the questioner. The law officer will keep the right half in a wooden box and store it in a special room which will be secured with a seal especially made for the law records. If, eventually, an affair concerning this law should arise after the death of one of the parties to this encounter, it should be handled according to the question and answer recorded on the tally. (Chapter 26, "Ding-fen" p. 42)

[121] As government officials, as well as the people of the world who want to know a law, can ask the law officials about it, none of the officials and the people of the world will be ignorant about the law. As an official knows that the people know the law, he would not dare to treat them unlawfully; as the people know the law, they would not dare to violate the law and offend the law officer. (Chapter 26, "Ding-fen" p. 42)

(c) Encourage reporting

[122] If a state is in disorder, it is not because the law is disorderly, nor because its law is not used. All states have laws but not a law that guarantees that the laws are always enforced. All states have laws that prohibit crime and wickedness, and punish those who steal, rob and maim, but not a law that guarantees that such evil and wicked people, those who steal, rob and maim, will always be caught. If those who commit evil, wickedness, steal, rob and maim are punished with death, and yet evil and wickedness, theft, robbery and maiming do not cease, it is because they are not always caught. (Chapter 18, "Hua-ce" pp. 31–2)
[123] If punishments are applied to accomplished crimes, wrongdoing will not be stopped; if rewards are bestowed for actions which the people consider to be righteous, it will not help deter misconduct. If punishments cannot stop wrongdoing, nor can rewards help deter misconduct, there certainly will be disorder. Therefore, a true king inflicts punishment on those who are about to commit wrong, so that major offences will not occur; he rewards those who inform the authorities about vice, so that small transgressions will not go unnoticed. (Chapter 7, "Kai-sai" p. 17)
[124] Where an official knows and reports someone in the same department who has violated the king's law, the informer will be exempted from punishment and, regardless of his position, high or low, will be made to succeed to the official rank and government emolument, including land and salary, of the head of the department. (Chapter 17, "Shang-xing" p. 29.)
[125] Where the government is at its best, husband and wife, friends and acquaintances, regardless of their closeness, cannot mutually cover up each other's evil deeds and mistakes. Ordinary people cannot mutually conceal one another's crimes. (Chapter 24, "Jin-shi" p. 40)

(d) Emphasis on rewards and punishments

(i) A general principle

[126] Since it is the nature of the people to love titles and government emoluments and hate punishments and penalties, the ruler establishes the two measures to guide the people's intentions and reach what he wants. When the people exhaust their strength in what they are told to do, titles will follow; when they have achieved military merit, rewards will follow. (Chapter 9, "Cuo-fa" p. 20)
[127] A true king uses rewards to prohibit and punishments to encourage. He wants to find what is evil not what is good. He uses punishments to eliminate punishment. (Chapter 7, "Kai-sai" pp. 17–18)
[128] When virtue is publicised, wrongdoings will be hidden. When wickedness is exposed, criminals will be punished. (Chapter 5, "Shuo-min" p. 10)
[129] He who is good at governing punishes the evil but does not reward the virtuous . . . Rewarding the virtuous is not right, it is like rewarding those who do not commit theft and robbery. (Chapter 18, "Hua-ce" p. 32)

[130] Where punishment is used as the means of government, the people will be kept in fear. When in fear, they will not do evil deeds. Where they do no evil deeds, they are at peace and happy with what they can enjoy. Where virtue is used as the means to teach people, they will be free to do what they like. When they indulge in what they like, there will be disorder. Where there is disorder, they will be hurt by what they dislike. (Chapter 7, "Kai-sai" p. 17)
[131] What the world now calls just is to establish what people like and abolish what they dislike, and what the world calls unjust is to establish what people dislike and abolish what they like. In fact, the two words –just and unjust – are mistakenly used and what they denote are the very opposite. If you establish what people delight in, then they will suffer from what they dislike but, if you establish what the people dislike, they will be happy in what they like. How do I know that this is so? Because, while in anguish, people think and, in thinking, they become resourceful; while happy, they are dissolute and, in dissoluteness, they become excessive. The punishment I talk about is the foundation of justice. What the world calls justice is the fountainhead of violence. It is because, in making people correct, if what they dislike is used as a means, they will in the end attain what they like. On the contrary, if what they like is used as a means, they will be in the end be ruined by what they dislike. (Chapter 7, "Kai-sai" pp. 16–17)

(ii) Make rewards few and inexpensive

[132] Making punishments severe and rewards slight is the way in which the ruler loves his people and why they die for him. Making rewards great and punishments light is the way in which the ruler does not love his people and why they do not die for him. (Chapter 4, "Qu-qiang" p. 9)
[133] The state of a true king applies punishments in nine out of ten cases of the people's affairs and gives rewards in just one; a state of strength applies punishments in seven cases and gives rewards in three; a state in decline applies punishments in five cases and gives rewards in five. (Chapter 4, "Qu-qiang" p. 9)
[134] The way to use the soldiers is to make government rewards uniform. (Chapter 6, "Suan-di" p. 14)
[135] What is meant by the "uniform reward" is that profits, emolument, offices and titles are awarded only to soldiers of merit and no one else. (Chapter 17, "Shang-xing" p. 28)
[136] The gate to riches and titles opens only to those who fought in wars. (Chapter 17, "Shang-xing" p. 30)
[137] In the past, Tang was endowed the feudal estate Zanmao, King Wen was endowed the feudal estate Qizhou. Each had a land of 100 *li* square. Tang fought Jie in the field of Mingtiao; King Wu fought Shou in the middle of Muye. In both cases, Tang and King Wu smashed the nine armies of their enemies. They then divided up the land of the vanquished, made their officers feudal lords, and gave each soldier who participated in the battles the tax revenue from scores of households of the conquered people . . . If they were to use their own grain to reward

their followers each person will not get even a single cup. If they were to use their own money to reward their followers, each person will not get even a single coin . . . What they did was to use the goods of the whole world to reward the people of the world. Thus great, clever rewards are not costly to the ruler. (Chapter 17, "Shang-xing" pp. 28–9)

(iii) Make punishments numerous and harsh

[138] In the state of a true king, punishments are applied in nine out of ten cases and rewards are given in one. If, in nine cases, punishments are applied, the six kinds of indulgence will be stopped . . . If the six kinds of indulgence are stopped, the state will be without evil schemes. (Chapter 5, "Shuo-min" p. 11)

[139] If criminals were always caught and yet there are still evil and wicked persons and those committing theft, robbery and maiming, it is because the punishments are light. Where punishments are light the criminals cannot be eliminated. (Chapter 18, "Hua-ce" p. 32)

[140] In the application of punishment, minor offences should be given heavy penalties so that minor offences will not occur. If minor offences do not occur, major ones have no chance of emerging . . . If, in the application of punishment, major offences are given heavy penalties and minor offences are given light penalties, then minor offences will not be stopped, and consequently there will be no means of stopping the serious ones. (Chapter 5, "Shuo-min" p. 11)

[141] Since a wrong can be serious or trivial, the punishment should be correspondingly heavy or light; since a good act can be of great or small significance, the reward should be correspondingly of more or less value. These are the two principles the world commonly applies. But, if punishments are applied to crimes that have been carried out, wrongdoing will not be stopped; if rewards are bestowed for actions which the people consider to be righteous, it will not help deter misconduct . . . Therefore, a true king inflicts punishment on those who are about to commit wrong, so that major offences will not occur; he gives reward to those who inform the authority about vice, so that small transgressions will not go unnoticed. (Chapter 7, "Kai-sai" p. 17)

[142] The former kings, in order to prohibit people from homicide or murder, prescribed punishments of amputation of a foot or of a tattoo on the face. It is not that they sought to harm the people; they wanted to suppress wickedness and prevent crime. There is no better means of suppressing wickedness and preventing crime than by making punishments heavy. If punishments are heavy and the culprits are always apprehended, people will not dare to test how far they can go against the law and, as a result, no one in the state will be punished. This result proves the saying, "When punishments are made absolutely clear, they will not actually harm the people." (Chapter 17, "Shang-xing" p. 29)

[143] Thus, it is said, "Giving heavy punishments and imposing collective responsibility on those related to a criminal will make the people dare not test the law." Because people dare not to test the law, there will be no punishment. (Chapter 17, "Shang-xing" p. 29.)

[144] Where punishment is used to remove the need for punishment, the state is in order; where punishment causes the need for more punishment, the state is in disorder. Thus it is said, "In using punishment, make it heavy for minor offences, and the need for punishments will be removed and the state will be strong; make it heavy for serious offences and light for minor offences, and it will produce more offences, and the state will be decimated. (Chapter 4, "Qu-qiang" p. 9)
[145] Duke Wen of Jin 晉文公 wanted to make clear the punishments in order to establish a close rapport with the people. He assembled together all the feudal lords and great officers in the Shi-qian Palace. Dianxie 顛頡 arrived late, and the law officer asked for punishment. The duke said, "Let the law be carried out." Thereupon the law officer broke Dianxie's spine, causing his death. The people of the state of Jin all became frightened, saying, "Dianxie was a favourite of the ruler and yet his spine was broken and he died, how it would fare with us!" Then the duke raised an army and attacked Cao and Wu-lu, razed the parapets on the ramparts of the state of Zheng, made the dividing paths between the farmlands of the state of Wei run east–west [to let his troops pass easily], and defeated the army of the state of Chu at Cheng-pu. The soldiers of his three armies were so disciplined that, when ordered to halt, they would immediately stop as if their feet were cut off, and, when ordered to march, they would go like flowing water. None of the soldiers of his three armies dared to transgress his prohibitions. So, by breaking Dianxie's spine to demonstrate that severe punishments would be applied even in cases of minor offences, the duke put the state of Jin in order. (Chapter 17, "Shang-xing" p. 29)
[146] Formerly Dan 旦, Duke of Zhou, killed his older brother Guan 管, and banished his younger brother Huo 霍, saying, "They transgressed the prohibitions." The multitudes in the empire all said, "If, when the ruler's own brothers commit a fault, he does not deviate from the law, how it would fare with those who are distant and far off!" As the empire knew that sword and saw were used in the court of Zhou, order prevailed within the seas. This is the reason for the saying, "When punishments are made utterly clear, the result will be no need for punishments." (Chapter 17, "Shang-xing" p. 30)
[147] If the purpose of war is to eliminate future wars, it is all right to engage in war; if the purpose of execution is to eliminate homicide, it is all right to execute; if the purpose of punishment is to eliminate the need for punishment, it is all right to use severe punishments. (Chapter 18, "Hua-ce" p. 31)

(E) Effects of law being properly made and enforced

(1) The rule of law

[148] What are known as virtues are merely that subjects be loyal to the ruler, children be filial to the parents, the junior be courteous to the senior, and man and woman keep their distinctive rules of behaviour. But the established law makes a hungry person not eat if it is not lawful and a person about to die not struggle for life if it is not lawful. Thus, a sage king does not value virtue but

values law. He makes law clear and orders carried out. That is all. (Chapter 18, "Hua-ce" p. 33)

[149] A good ruler makes a man like Zhi 跖 [a robber] trustworthy, how much more, then, a man like Boyi 伯夷; an incapable ruler makes a man like Boyi mistrustful, how much more a man like Zhi! If conditions are such that one cannot commit crimes, then even a man like Zhi will be trustworthy; but, if conditions are such that it is possible to commit crimes, then even a man like Boyi will be mistrustful. (Chapter 18, "Hua-ce" p. 32)

(2) Self-government by the people

[150] When the people all know what to pursue and what to avoid – to avoid disasters that follow violation of law, and to pursue fortune that results from obeying the law – they can govern themselves. When a bright ruler takes advantage of this situation to govern, the state will be in great order. (Chapter 26, "Ding-fen" p. 43)

[151] Where punishments are removed because heavy punishments are prescribed for minor offences, where affairs are conducted by regular officials according to established rules, where punishments are eliminated because people are strictly organised in local security units, rewards are not unduly given, and evil deeds are always reported to the authorities, then individuals can make judgements in their own minds. (Chapter 5, "Shuo-min" pp. 11–12)

[152] Where the people know how to properly respond to orders from above, and decisions made in the family are acceptable to the authorities, then judgements can be made in the family . . . In a state that is orderly, judgements are made in the family; in a state that is disorderly judgements are made by the ruler. (Chapter 5, "Shuo-min" p. 12)

[153] In a state where judgements are made in the family, the state is kingly; where judgements are made by officials, the state is strong; where judgements are made by the ruler, the state is weak. (Chapter 5, "Shuo-min" p. 12)

[154] In a well-governed state it is valued that judgements are made below. Thus, where judgements are made within the local community of 10 square *li*, the state is weak; where judgements are made within the local community of 5 square *li*, the state is strong; where judgements are made within the family, the state will have strength to spare. It is therefore said that, where judgements are made immediately during the day when a problem occurred, the state is kingly; where judgements have to be made by officials who do not have enough time during the day and have to work into the night, the state is strong; where judgements are made by the ruler and their delay is inevitable, the state will be chaotic and decimated. Therefore, in a state that has good order, its government does not listen to the ruler and its people do not follow the officials. (Chapter 5, "Shuo-min" p. 12.)

(F) Social relationships

[155] A ruler who governs well has no loyal ministers, and a loving father has no filial sons. He does not want pleasant talk but wants their relationships to be governed by the law. (Chapter 18, "Hua-ce" p. 32)

(G) Ideal government

[156] Thus a bright ruler reclines on his couch, listens to the music of strings and wind instruments, and the world is well governed. (Chapter 18, "Hua-ce" p. 33)
[157] A sage is not one who knows all things. Therefore, in governing a state, he holds up the basic principles that are applicable to all things. It is true that this maxim is easy to understand but difficult, even for a sage, to implement. But, actually, in governing a state, a sage does not have to make extra efforts and an average ruler need not regard the task as impossible. As long as the law of the state is clear, to execute a person is not an act of cruelty, and to reward a person is not an act of benevolence. When a ruler appoints a person to office or bestows titles on him because of his achievements, the worthy will not worry about being ignored. When he forgives no wrong deeds and spares no punishments, the wicked will not arise. (Chapter 17, "Shang-xing" p. 30)
[158] In governing the state, an intelligent ruler recognises people's efforts, not their virtue. As a result, he will have no worry and need make no exertion and yet achievements will be made. (Chapter 9, "Cuo-fa" p. 20)

Shang-jun-shu 商君書

PART 2
INTERPRETATION

Law was not discussed much by the thinkers studied above. Nevertheless, it was on the minds of people in ancient times; they had some ideas about its peculiar characteristics and functions, and some of the ideas were recorded in *Shu-jing* (*The Book of Historical Documents*). Those ideas were further developed and written down in works by thinkers of later times; *Shang-jun-shu* (商君書 *Book of Lord Shang*) is an example. It is attributed to Lord Shang (商君 390–338 BCE) but contains many references to events that occurred long after his death. Thus, the book is actually a collection of ideas shared by thinkers before and after him who were later known as the Legalists. It is included here because it introduced some very distinctive ideas.

Lord Shang, originally named Gongsun Yang (公孫鞅), also known as Wei Yang (衛鞅 because he was formerly a minor aristocrat of the state of Wei) and Shang Yang (商鞅 because he was made Lord Shang while serving as a chief minister of the state of Qin), was a contemporary of Mencius. The times were turbulent; there were constant interstate wars and unrest in every state. The state of Qin was first established in 770 BCE, became strong during the reign of Duke Mu 穆公 (659–620) but fell into disorder because of internal political struggle and foreign invasions. Duke Xiao 孝公 (361–338) inherited a small and weak country, and was frustrated at home by the hereditary aristocrats and despised abroad by rulers of six major powers in the east. Trying to get out of this situation, he introduced some changes in domestic politics but was unable to achieve more. He then publicised a plan to recruit talent from abroad.

According to Sima Qian 司馬遷, Gongsun Yang, then a junior official in the state of Wei but enjoying no trust of its ruler, went to Qin and had four interviews with the duke. When he talked about *di-dao* (帝道 the way of the sage emperors) and *wang-dao* (王道 the way of the sage kings) the duke grew bored and fell asleep. The duke showed some interest when the subject was *ba-dao* (霸道 the way of the hegemons) but said that he did not have time for those achievements; he was in haste. Then Gongsun Yang presented *qiang-guo zhi shu* (強國之術 tactics to strengthen the state) and the duke unconsciously moved closer to him and listened attentively for several days. Finally Gongsun Yang succeeded winning the duke's trust.[1]

The ideas of *di-dao*, *wang-dao*, and *ba-dao* were often discussed by the Ruists. Basically, the first two refer to the ways of the more idealised ancient rulers who were benevolent and righteous. *Ba-dao* was the way of hegemon rulers of the Chunqiu Period (722–468) who made their states strong and rallied the lesser feudal lords in defence against non-Han invaders but were unsuccessful in promoting the general well-being of everyone. "The tactics that strengthen a state" presented by Gongsun Yang will be discussed in some detail later. It is interesting to point out here that, according to Sima Qian, Gongsun Yang actually regarded such tactics less worthy than the way of the hegemons. So perhaps he was more in agreement with the ideals of the Ruists but pursued the lesser goals only as a compromise.

Sima Qian's biography gave no hint, however, that Gongsun Yang ever regretted what he had achieved. During his tenure in the Qin government (eight years as a high minister, ten years as the premier), he made laws and enforced them ruthlessly, punishing those who hindered his moves, including two tutors of the crown prince (for an offence he committed) and several close relatives of the duke,[2] and, according to another historian of the Han period, Liu Xiang 劉向, once tried and executed seven hundred criminals by the Wei River, making the water flow red with blood.[3] In the end he did, indeed, make Qin strong and laid the foundation for the final conquest of all its rivals and the unification of China.

The urgency Duke Xiao expressed was felt by other statesmen of the Chunqiu and Warring State periods. Zichan, a prime minister of Zheng, also said that he was in a hurry to strengthen his state, fend off foreign threats, and solve social, political problems at home. One of his more salient actions was to promulgate new laws. His act was soon followed by governments of all other states, including Qin under Duke Xiao and Gongsun Yang.

To support the new laws, Gongsun Yang must have had his ideas and justifications presented in an orderly way. But the book *Shang-jun-shu* is not in this form. The major points are scattered through, and repeated in, many chapters, sometimes inconsistently. They are sorted and organised to appear as a self-consistent theory below.

(A) Social evolution and need of government authority

Gongsun Yang, like most thinkers discussed above, was worried about the chaos of his time and believed that order was possible. But, unlike those who saw order and disorder alternate as a result of cyclic changes of dynasties, he said the changes were lineal due to social evolution. According to him, at first people lived only in families, loved only their relatives and not outsiders, and were partial to what they had. As a result, they were discriminatory and biased. When population grew and interaction among people of different families increased, the discrimination and biases caused friction and disorder, followed by competition and contention. Some persons of wisdom and virtue rose to define justice and extolled impartiality, and people began to enjoy indiscriminating humanity, weaning them from the practice of loving only one's relatives, and to establish a new practice of respecting and following the wise and virtuous.

But when population grew and people were all altruistic, benevolent and loving to everyone without restraint, there was disorder again. Another set of wise and virtuous persons responded by creating a social hierarchy to place each person in a specific category (the noble and the humble, the superior and the inferior, and so on), an economic system to distribute land and other resources, laws and prohibitions against acts that went against these systems, and a bureaucracy headed by a ruler to enforce the laws. After these measures were established, the people switched to a new practice of submitting to the government authorities instead of following the wise and virtuous.

Gongsun Yang called these three practices *qin-qin*(親親 loving one's relatives), *zun-xian* (尊賢 respecting the wise and virtuous) and *gui-gui* (貴貴 honouring the authorities), and alleged that they were established in response to three stages of social evolution. To him the third was to last indefinitely because a ruler with ultimate authority was absolutely necessary in keeping order, and order was the supreme good. This is the justification for his doctrine of the supremacy of the ruler.

(B) Prerequisites of government authority

(1) Extraordinary intelligence

To be the ruler of a state and to be an effective one are two different things. According to Gongsun Yang, to be effective a ruler has to have certain uncommon qualities. First of all, he has to be extraordinarily intelligent; in particular, he must have the ability to know *bi-ran zhi li* (必然之理 the inviolable logic or course that must be followed) in order to carry out *ben-ran zhi zheng* (本然之政 the necessary measures of government) at the right time, in the right circumstances. But he does not have to get to the bottom of everything; others should do the investigation for him; as a result, nothing will escape his notice and he will be able to judge everything according to their essence and the fundamental principles.

Extraordinary intelligence as a prerequisite for leadership was, of course, commonly recognised by most thinkers but, by *bi-ran zhi li* and *ben-ran zhi zheng*, Gongsun Yang meant, as we shall see, something quite different from what the thinkers discussed above did.

(2) Unusual attitudes towards the people

Another prerequisite of an effective ruler is an unusual set of attitudes towards the people. First, Gongsun Yang said that, in governing a state, the ruler must think of the people as basically wicked; if he treats them as basically good, his state will fall into disorder and be destroyed. This perception puts the ruler and his people in opposite camps and leads to the conclusion that, if the state is to be governed well, the ruler must overcome the people as a whole by various means which, as we shall see, Gongsun Yang was to discuss at great length later.

Second, Gongsun Yang talked a lot about how to *tuan-li* (摶力 consolidate the strength) of the people and thus make the state strong. Having consolidated the strength of the people, he must know how to *sha-li* (殺力 dissipate that strength) or it will cause problems. This suggests that, in Gongsun Yang's view, the ruler should regard the people as domestic animals. We can imagine that Gongsun Yang was comparing the people to a horse: in raising a horse, you do not want it to be idle and cause trouble or get fat and become useless; you feed it to build its strength and you use it to get your work done, and keep it lean and fit. Other thinkers also talked about how to treat and employ the people but none was so cynical, and their objectives in doing so were different.

(C) Responsibilities of government authority

(1) Determining the course of development of the state

After an exceptional person was made the ruler, his primary responsibility, according to Gongsun Yang, is to guide the development of his state, especially when it is facing existential crises such as the weak state Qin was in during the early Warring States Period. How to survive and become strong were the subjects of a debate among Gongsun Yang and two high ministers in the presence of Duke Xiao.

Facing strong enemies on the borders, powerful aristocrats at home and rigid tradition in the government, the duke was frustrated and wanted to break out of this situation but was worried about popular resistance to change. Gongsun Yang advised him not to heed the opinions of the people, asserting that all great men of outstanding achievements met resistance from petty persons. In his words, "an outstanding man is, as a matter of course, disapproved of by the world". Why? Because "the stupid would not understand something that is complex even after it has happened, but the wise see it even before it has begun". Therefore, "he, who is concerned about the highest good, is not in harmony with popular ideas; he, who accomplishes great works, does not take counsel with the multitude". A great man "cannot let the people share in the plan to start a project, but they can be allowed to share in the rejoicing over its completion". Gongsun Yang was an elitist.

But Gan Long 甘龍, one of the ministers in the debate, had doubts. Even if a great man did not have to heed the common people, could he also ignore tradition? Yes, Shang Yang replied. Only ordinary people would abide by old practices. Great men would not. The sage kings who founded the three ancient dynasties initiated different laws and institutions, and so did the five hegemonic lords of the Spring and Autumn period. Why? Because, after all, "laws were to care for the people, and rites were to make things run smoothly". "Therefore," Gongsun Yang argued, "a sage would not obey the laws of antiquity if, by not obeying, he could strengthen his state; and he would not adhere to the established rites if, by not adhering, he could benefit his people." In short, he concluded, "A wise man creates laws, but a foolish man is controlled by them; a man of talent reforms rites, but a stupid person is enslaved by them."

Du Zhi 杜摯, the other minister, questioned the wisdom of drastic changes. Quoting an old saying he emphasised, "Unless the benefit is to be increased a hundred times, one should not reform the law; unless the efficiency is to be improved tenfold, one should not alter a tool." In other words, if a thing isn't broken, don't fix it. He was not sure that any reform could bring good results. Gongsun Yang rejected this cynicism by pointing out that "former generations did not follow the same doctrines, so which past precedents should one obey?" After all, he argued, "Rites and laws were fixed in accordance with what was opportune; regulations and orders were all expedient." Therefore, he said, "There is more than one way to govern the world," and the past ways had proved ineffective. If so, he asked in effect, why not try something new?

Gongsun Yang was preaching to the converted and wiping out some slight remaining doubts that troubled the duke who, now assured by Gongsun Yang's arguments, promptly ordered the preparation and promulgation of a completely new set of laws known as *Ken-cao-ling* (墾草令 Wasteland Reclamation Edicts).

What we see here is something truly remarkable. It was a conceptual victory of the progressive over the conservative, and of positive law over customary rules. We have observed that practically all other schools of thought believed in a golden past and maintained, in one sense or another, that improvement of the current conditions meant a return to that past. Gongsun Yang's view represents an abrupt departure. It demonstrates an absolute faith in human beings' ability to chart new courses. It says, in effect, that human beings are capable of controlling their own future; they need not be tied down by the past. Moreover, it shows an unusual faith in artificial law. None of the other thinkers believed that positive law alone, being a low norm compared with humanity, righteousness, and so on, could achieve social change.

(2) Choose social values and policy orientations

(A) CORRECT VALUES AND ORIENTATIONS – AGRICULTURE AND WAR

Apart from some basic physiological and psychological needs, people have different values. In Gongsun Yang's view, some values are good for society because they lead it to prosperity and order; some others have the opposite effects. He thought that, for the state of Qin, people should value agricultural production and military service. It is easy to see the importance of agriculture, which was the main source of wealth and the basis of a state's strength, without which the state would become easy prey of stronger rivals. Moreover, engaging people in agricultural activities had many latent benefits for the state and its ruler. Gongsun Yang pointed out that farmers were "simple and easy to correct; diligent and easy to command". It may be added that, if many people were encouraged to bring waste land under cultivation, the state would be strengthened in more ways than one because waste land did not belong to any of the aristocrats but to the state. When such land was cultivated, the tax would go directly to the state treasury, and the people who worked on such land would come directly under the control of the ruler. As these people could come only from the farms of the aristocrats or neighbouring states, the result was that, while building his own strength by gaining more people and revenue, Duke Xiao would also weaken his rivals at home and enemies abroad. This purpose was not voiced but was undoubtedly on the minds of Gongsun Yang and the duke.

To honour military service was important because Gongsun Yang wanted not only to ensure survival of the state but also its expansion. (Therefore when he talked about war he meant both defensive and offensive ones.) These purposes were also served well by the laws that encouraged cultivation of waste land. When the duke got the additional revenue from the reclaimed land and direct control over the farmers, he would be able to raise a greater army. But that was not enough for Gongsun Yang: he wanted the entire nation, on anticipating war, "to behave like hungry wolves on seeing meat". He wanted the father, the older brother, and the wife of a soldier, on sending him off to a battle, to say to him: "If you incur death by disobeying the law or orders, we too shall die". Only when the whole nation becomes a fierce fighting machine can it survive and conquer. Aggression is the best defence.

(B) Incorrect values and orientations

(i) Academic studies and sophisticated arguments

On the other hand, Gongsun Yang thought that some values which were popular at his time were harmful to society and therefore incorrect. First, he condemned the study of *The Odes*, *The History* and what he called "rhetoric", "clever talk", "high-sounding, ingenious, empty words" – the kind of vain babblings and artful speeches made by itinerant, office-seeking intellectuals of his time – because they would confuse the people, make them neglect their work, lose touch with reality, and become cynics and disloyal subjects.

(ii) Moral precepts

The second target of Gongsun Yang's attack was moral tenets. According to him, they, too, were useless. "A benevolent man may benefit others but cannot make others benevolent; a righteous man may love others but cannot make others loving." Moreover, moral tenets actually induced evil. In his words, "Kindness and benevolence are the foster mother of transgressions." What he meant was that such virtues would lead to unjustified leniency which, in turn, would encourage wrongdoing.

Even the virtue of being scrupulous and keeping oneself clean and away from worldly affairs and government service was disparaged. For, if such a person, known as *chu-shi* (處士 recluse), is esteemed by the people, they will, according to Gongsun Yang, become estranged from the state and criticise the authorities.

(iii) Rites and music

Rites and music were believed by the Ruists to be capable of regulating people's behaviour and were therefore given great value. But, to Gongsun Yang, they were "symptoms of excess and licence". His logic was simple. Rites and music were playthings of the aristocrats and the idle rich. To emphasise and spread them is to invite extravagance and licentiourness.

(iv) Popular reputation

Many people seek public recognition as a value and it often brings about certain desired results, including some government rewards. But Gongsun Yang saw popular reputation as a "rat that carries evil designs" because it is usually created by partisan people. When a person is "publicly" regarded as worthy, he is actually praised only by members of his close circle who want him to be promoted. If a ruler asks about his character and ability, they will sing in unison of his worthiness. Thus, in Gongsun Yang's words, "This practice gives evil people precisely the opportunity to realise their wicked and dangerous designs and crafty tricks."

(v) Commerce and crafts

In traditional China, there was a view that belittled commerce and craft. In comparison to agriculture, these trades were considered easy. Those engaged in them did not produce anything essential to life; they lived on the farmers who were the real creators of true wealth. And yet the income of merchants and craftsmen was much greater than the farmers'. Gongsun Yang shared this view and was concerned by the fact that merchants and craftsmen were mobile, not bound to the land – they took their skills and capital with them and travelled a great deal, seeking the best employers and customers. They thus lacked firm allegiance to any state or community and were difficult to control. It was a serious problem for Gongsun Yang who wanted the people to devote themselves to agriculture and be supervised by local security units.

(vi) The parasites

Together the six types of values and the people pursuing them earned an epithet *liu-shi* (六蝨 six fleas) invented by Gongsun Yang. In his book, many others, whose lives were considered by him as parasitic, were lumped together under this and some other derogatory or dismissive labels such as *shi-bai* (十敗 the ten rotten ones), *shi-zhe* (十者 those ten types), *ba-zhe* (八者 those eight types), *wu-zhe*

(五者 those five types), *shi-er-zhe* (十二者 those twelve types) or, more vividly, *ming, te, ke, zhu* (螟螣蚵蠋 various kinds of crop-eating insects). The fact that they are discussed in so many passages is an indication of the vehement distaste Gongsun Yang had for them. Elsewhere he simply referred to them as *jian-min* (姦民 wicked people) and wanted them eliminated. His simple justification is that, if allowed to exist or, worse still, if just a few of them were given government posts and honours, they would lure others away from agriculture and military service and leave the state in weak and perilous conditions.

(3) Pursuit correct values and objectives

(A) Human dispositions and inclination

Gongsun Yang wanted to change the situation and thought the first thing to do was to make clear to the people the correct values and objectives. To do so was not easy, because people usually have their own views on this subject, but he thought change was possible because people have some general dispositions and inclinations – "when hungry they seek food; when tired they seek rest; when suffering hardship they seek amusement; when humiliated they seek honour". These are the obvious *li* (利 profits) that a person needs for personal survival and comfort. After having met these needs, he sometimes acts altruistically to gain *ming* (名 fame) both current and posthumous. For profits and fame, people will go to the extremes, including taking risks and violating prohibitions, until the very end of their lives. But, while the desires are inherent, the actual behaviour with which to satisfy them is not fixed because, in the final analysis, people are calculating. If a ruler knows this, he has a way to change people's behaviour. This is why, as we shall see, Gongsun Yang often talked about the need for a ruler to "investigate the people's wishes", and "to study the people's likes and dislikes". He was not talking about finding out the people's opinion on any particular subject; he meant only that it was necessary to recognise this calculating human disposition and to manipulate it.

(B) Ways to effect change

(i) Establishment of a single goal

The first steps, according to Gongsun Yang, are for a ruler to demonstrate clearly his own view of the correct social values, and then to establish a single goal for the people to pursue those values. The values are agricultural productivity and military valour. To make the pursuit of these values the single goal for the people, the ruler should, on the one hand, *qi yi-men* (啟一門 open a single door) for people to go through to reach for profit and fame, and, on the other hand, *sai yin-dao* (塞淫道 block the various deviant routes) for them to satisfy their desires. The single door opens to farming and warfare; the deviant routes are those of academic knowledge, crafts, commerce, and so on. This is of utmost importance because, Gongsun Yang pointed out, "A state that has profits and fame coming from a single source is strong; one that allows two sources is half as much; one that allows ten sources is undefendable." The reason is that, when the people see that the ruler honours those who engage in agriculture and war and despises itinerant scholars and others in non-productive professions, they will concentrate on a single undertaking – agriculture and war. When they are so concentrated, they are simple and easy to control. In Gongsun Yang's words "When they are at one, they will be less volatile but value settlement; when they are at one, they can be moved by rewards and punishments; when they are at one, they can be used for ventures abroad." This plain truth was, however, not clear to many state rulers at his time, and he therefore lamented: "Presently most of those who govern have no grasp of the fundamental principles. While talking about governance in the court they have numerous divergent ideas striving to replace one another. As a result the ruler is puzzled, the officials confused and the people become guideless and idle and unwilling to engage in hard work. They will learn sophisticated knowledge and participate in endless debates, or engage in commerce, or practise various crafts – all for the purpose of avoiding farming and fighting. In this way, the state will soon be ruined because, when the state is in trouble, those pursuing learning will hate the law, the merchants will leave and the craftsmen will not obey orders . . . Therefore, the sage who knows the fundamental principles of government makes the people devote their minds to farming."

(ii) Rewards and punishments

Exactly how can a single goal be established? A dictator can prohibit his people from doing certain things but how can he make them carry out a particular act? Gongsun Yang pointed out that the ruler has two ways to accomplish it. Because people love profits and fame and are calculating, the ruler can, on the one hand, entice them with rewards (government employment, emoluments, honour, titles) to do one act and, on the other hand, chastise with punishments (disfigurement, enslavement, death, collective punishments) those who refuse this act but choose to do something else. While he insisted on making agriculture and war the only goals for the people, Gongsun Yang recognised that agriculture is hard work and war is dangerous. But, if the ruler can offer sufficient rewards and inflict overwhelming punishments, people will do as he wants, both because they are calculating and because they have no choice. They will be like a horse led with food in the front and driven by cracking whips in the rear while and all escape routes are blocked. It has no choice but to go the way its master sets for it.

To make rewards and punishments effective they must be made, in Gongsun Yang's word, *yi* (壹 one, uniform). He insisted on *yi-shang* (壹賞 uniform reward) and *yi-xing* (壹刑 uniform punishment) meaning that rewards in various forms of profits – government appointments, honour, titles, and emoluments – will be given only to people who have military merits, and that the same punishments will be inflicted on everyone who violates the same law or order, regardless of his position, achievements and previous good deeds. As a result, he said, the people will become accustomed to pursuing the goals set for them by the ruler. They will even love them because to reject them will bring, with absolute certainty, unbearable disasters.

(iii) Control and use of the people

Thus, with the right mix of rewards and punishments, the ruler can make the people do anything – walk on sharp swords and face arrows and stones, let alone toil in the fields. Those measures presented attractive and compulsive forces that are irresistible but may be resented. To suppress any resentment, Gongsun Yang advocated *yi-jiao* (壹教 uniform education) that would not only make clear to the people what they should and should not do but also create in the people's minds an idea that they are *yu* (愚 stupid), *ruo* (弱 weak), *ru* (辱 humble) vis-à-vis the ruler and, therefore, a willingness to submit to the authorities. These measures would, Gongsun Yang said, enable the ruler to *sheng-min* (勝民 overcome the people), *zhi-min* (制民 control the people) and *zhi-min* (治民 rule the people).

When the people are well controlled and governed, the state will be rich and strong. Then the ruler should proceed to use the people, reducing their strength, lest they fall into idleness and be parasitic, engage in academic learning, crafts and commerce, indulge in sophisticated talk and criticism of the government, avoid farming and fighting and, as a result, the state will become "self-attacking" and eventually ruined. Instead, the ruler should make the state "enemy attacking". This idea seems to have obsessed Gongsun Yang. Thus, he said, even a poor state should engage in wars to send its *du* (毒 poison) – the "six fleas" – to its enemy. For a rich state, wars were more profitable. When the strength of its people is fully used, its army will have no equal and its ruler's orders will be carried out throughout the whole world. Indeed, after the state of Qin became rich and strong, thanks to Gongsun Yang's policies, it launched incessantly aggressive wars and finally conquered all its rivals and united China.

(c) Concrete measures

Unlike other thinkers, Gongsun Yang had not only a theory but also the opportunity to realise many aspects of it. Some of the concrete measures he suggested were adopted as laws: among them, the most specific was the "Order for Reclamation of Waste Land".

The Order was issued mainly to address the economic and financial problems of the state of Qin. The state was divided into many small fiefdoms where agricultural productivity was low and the revenue went to the feudal lords. But, on the state's undefined border, particularly that of the west, there was large area of vacant land occasionally used by nomads. The main purpose of the Order was to drive Qin people to cultivate this waste land. The work would be hard and the profit meagre, and, for the more resourceful, there were other ways in which to make an easier and more comfortable living, including trade and crafts, and peddling knowledge. Therefore, the Order was not positively to encourage the reclamation but, rather, negatively to punish avoiding agricultural work in general. The rationale for this is spelled out succinctly in various chapters other than the one entitled *Ken-cao* (墾草 to weed).

The Order does not appear in the form of a law. Instead of articles it had twenty passages reading like policy suggestions. They can be grouped into five categories.

(i) Rules to win people's trust in the government

The first one concerns government operation, obviously designed to win people's trust in the government. It suggest that all taxes are to be paid in grain; that government actions affecting the interests of the people should be prompt; that government posts and honours should not be awarded to people who do not engage in agriculture; and that the various parts of the state should have the same government system and follow the same operating rules.

(ii) Rules against misconducts of officials

The second category consists of rules against misconduct by officials, suggesting that they should be prohibited from academic studies and sophisticated disputations as well as travelling to, and living in, the countryside to display their luxurious lifestyle; and that the price of wine and meat should be high and taxes on them be heavy to prevent officials and the common people from indulging in drinking and feasts that would impede agricultural work and waste food.

(iii) Rules against vagabonds and idle dependants

In the third category are prohibitions against vagabonds and idle dependants. People should be banned from migration. Hotels along travel routes are to be closed. Aristocrats who keep large households with many dependants are to be taxed heavily and the dependants will be liable to corvée service. They will be prohibited from employing many servants and craftsmen on large construction projects, and their sons will not be allowed to stay idle but are to work for the government. Mountains and lakes are to be placed under government control so that those unwilling to engage in farming cannot go there freely to make a living as loggers, hunters and fishermen.

(iv) Rules against merchants

The fourth group of rules is against the merchants. They and their employees and servants will be registered and made liable for corvée service. They are prohibited from buying and selling grain for profit, doing business in military camps, and charging fees for transporting grain while doing it as a corvée service.

(v) Rules against potential and actual criminals

Finally, there is a set of rules against potential and actual criminals. Those who are quarrelsome, litigious, lazy, extravagant and wicked, and those who actually disrupt social order are to be punished severely and their relatives and associates held collectively responsible. No one is allowed to petition officials, asking permission to provide food for the convicts.

Obviously these measures were designed mainly to make life difficult for those who tried to avoid agricultural work. But, in order to facilitate their implementation, Gongsun Yang sensibly included a number of rules to win the people's trust in the government, Including, for instance, a uniform tax rate. It is interesting to note that, at the end of every passage spelling out a measure, he concluded: "As a result the waste land will certainly be cultivated".

(D) Law

Besides the Order for cultivation of waste land, the state of Qin had, of course, other laws, many enacted when Gongsun Yang was in power. It is reported that he made laws regulating many mundane and trifling aspects of people's lives: such as punishing them from throwing dirt in the street and using incorrect measuring instruments; prohibiting parents and adult children from living in the same room; fining gown-up brothers who remain in a single household; and condemning men marrying into their wives' family.[4]

(1) Bases

Shang-jun-shu has also numerous passages on jurisprudence concerning the bases, objectives, functions, and enforcement of law. Other thinkers have perceived rules of nature or human dispositions or social relationships as the bases of law; Gongsun Yang said that, in making law, the ruler has to take into consideration the people's feelings and the social conditions, otherwise law cannot be carried out smoothly. But he made a twist here. He did not mean that law should provide what the people obviously want and adapt to the existing social conditions. As analysed above, the ruler needs only to know that people want to have profit and fame and avoid deprivation and hardship, danger and disgrace. On the basis of this knowledge, law is to be made to encourage people to work hard and risk danger or suffer greater hardship. Gongsun Yang would argue that, eventually the people will achieve profit and fame but the beneficiary may very well not be the individual but the state and the ruler.

(2) Objectives and functions

Indeed, Gongsun Yang said that laws are to "restrain the people", to "limit their opportunities of using their talents", and to "establish an effective ruler" whom even the people with greater virtue and knowledge, valour and strength, and in overwhelming numbers, dare not challenge.

Thus law is a means for the ruler to control the people, to keep everyone in his place and play an appointed role. This function of the law is of crucial importance to prevent disorder. To illustrate this point, Gongsun Yang told us that, when a wild rabbit runs in the field, hundreds of people will consider it as fair game and try to catch it but no one in a market full of rabbits on sale will glance at them without intending to buy any. It is because when the ownership, or *ming-fen* (名分 legal title), of the rabbits is settled, people cannot raise contending claims.

We have seen the word *ming* (名 name) was given great significance by Confucius who emphasised rectification of names as the first step correctly to identify a thing and justify an action. Here, Gongsun Yang added the word *fen* (分 share) to *ming* to make clear that an appropriate share of resources will go to a person of a certain position. There is a chapter in *Shang-jun-shu*, under the title of "Ding-fen" (定分 fix the shares), in which this subject is discussed. In Gongsun Yang's view, positions and shares should be assigned by law. When a person's position and share are unclear, they can be determined by the law just as weight can be determined by scales and length by a ruler. It is not that no one can determine weight and length without these instruments, it is that no one can always determine accurately without them. So, when an objective standard is used, the result will always be accurate and there will be no disputes. People can thus live in peace, "even the very crafty would become scrupulous and trustworthy and the ordinary people would all become honest and guileless, each one restraining himself", Gongsun Yang asserted.

(3) Making and enforcing law

(A) Make law the supreme norm

In any society, there are many norms competing for people's attention. Law is but one of them made by political authorities. It is often arbitrary. People do not readily observe law; often they prefer other norms which may be perceived as more rational or more in agreement with human feelings. But, in Gongsun Yang's view, as mentioned above, this preference has three problems: first, moral principles are ineffective in making people good and keep the world in order. Second, since those norms do not provide universal standards, they let the wicked cheat and cause chaos. Third, rules that guide people to pursue values other than those sanctioned by the authorities create "six fleas" and *du* (蠹 woodworms) and bring about disorder and destruction. Therefore, if a ruler allows his people to follow those principles and rules in defiance of the law he adopted, his state will be ruined.

The authority of law can also be undermined in two other ways. If, after law is established, a ruler, in making decisions, disregards it and relies on his personal judgement, and, if he listens to opinions that may conflict with and contradict the spirit of the law, in both cases, the law will be uncertain and not respected.

Therefore, Gongsun Yang said, a bright ruler is careful about the law. "He will not listen to words that are not in accordance with the law, exalt actions that are not in accordance with the law, and perform deeds that are not in accordance with the law." He will do the opposite. And "his officials, clerks and the common people, even those who are virtuous and wise, would not dare say a word that distorts the law, and even those who are rich with 1,000 taels of gold would not dare use a single coin to bend the law". This, according to Gongsun Yang, is "the height of good government and an imperative for a ruler to examine". In other words, a good ruler shall make law the supreme norm to which no challenge is allowed. This is a drastic departure from the teachings of all other thinkers discussed above.

(B) Make law clear and definitive

(i) General principle

If law is to be observed, the people must know its prescriptions and proscriptions. To enable the people to know, law must be expressed in plain, straightforward language, otherwise there will be problems for, as Gongsun Yang said, arcane words and abstruse statements are difficult even for the highly intelligent. That is why sages formulate law in such a way that its meaning can be clearly and definitively understood by everyone, clever or stupid.

When law lacks clarity and definitive meaning, people can legitimately criticise it in many ways. When there are many criticisms, the law cannot be readily enforced and there will be disorder: the people will challenge the authorities and the wicked will do evil.

Of course, when people clearly and definitively understand a law, they may still dislike it and be unwilling to obey it. But that was not Gongsun Yang's concern because, in his view, the law is imposed upon the people and, when it is made clear and definitive, criticisms will not be tolerated. The people will have no choice but to obey. Knowing what the law promotes and what it prohibits, they will learn what to approach and what to avoid. Thus, there will be order before the law is actually applied. This is how a clever ruler achieves order in his state. There is a simplistic optimism underlying Gongsun Yang's theory which will be discussed further in due course.

(ii) Specific measures

To avoid misunderstanding and misinterpretation of law, a number of suggestions for the safekeeping of law records and dissemination of correct knowledge of law were spelled out in the chapter "Ding-fen". Because some government positions and institutions mentioned were created long after Gongsun Yang's time, the chapter was clearly not written by him. The points made in it seem to be consistent with his ideas, however, and, for this reason, they are briefly summarised below.

Copies of laws and orders are to be kept in the royal palace and in Forbidden Rooms in government offices. Law officials will be appointed and assigned to the central and local governments. They will study the laws and orders. Other officials, as well as the common people, who want to know about the prescriptions and proscriptions of a law can ask a law official. He has to give them the correct answer and write the question, the answer and the date down on a pair of wood tallies, give the questioner the left part and keep the right part in the Forbidden Room. If a dispute arises, the two parts are to be brought together to show the correct answer. In this way, the people will know the law. As the official who administers law knows that the people also know it, he will not dare to misuse it.

(c) Encourage reporting

To make law effective, it is not enough that its prescriptions and proscriptions are clearly set forth and easily understandable. There must be ways in which to identify those who violate it. Gongsun Yang knew this well as he said, "All states have laws that prohibit crime and wickedness, and punish those who steal, rob and maim, but no law guarantees that such evil and wicked people always get caught." Actually, he thought that always catching the culprit after a law has been violated is not good enough; it is better to catch him when he is about to commit a crime. In his words, "If punishments are applied to accomplished crimes, wrongdoing will not be stopped; if rewards are bestowed for actions which the people consider to be righteous, it will not help deter misconduct. If punishments cannot stop wrongdoing, nor rewards help deter misconduct, there certainly will be disorder. Therefore a true king inflicts punishment on those who are about to commit wrong, so that major offences will not occur; he gives reward to those who inform the authority about vice, so that small transgressions will not go unnoticed." Therefore, Gongsun Yang established the reporting system: anyone who knows someone's criminal design must report it to the authorities; the informant will be exempted from penalty for conspiracy and given material rewards, and, in case the suspect has a title or official post, it will be taken away and bestowed upon the informant. When this system operates in the best way, Gongsun Yang said, not only can ordinary people not conceal one another's crimes, "husband and wife, friends and acquaintances, regardless of their closeness cannot mutually cover up each other's evil deeds and mistakes". As a result, no offences, big or small, will escape the ruler's notice and punishments.

We have seen that such reporting was strongly censured by Confucius who analysed its terrible consequences. But, apparently, they never occurred to Gongsun Yang to be a problem.

(d) Emphasis on rewards and punishments

(i) A general principle

It has been mentioned that Gongsun Yang considered it a basic principle that, in governing the people, they should be presumed "essentially wicked". He further advocated that a good ruler should find out what is evil in the people but not publicise their good deeds. He should punish the wicked but not reward the virtuous. In his words, "Rewarding the virtuous is like rewarding those who do not steal and rob."

Moreover, he had a rather unusual view about justice. To understand it, a complete passage from *Shang-jun-shu* is quoted here:

> What the world now calls just is to establish what people like and abolish what they dislike, and what the world calls unjust is to establish what people dislike and to abolish what they like. In fact, the two words – just and unjust – are

> mistakenly used and what they denote are the very opposite. If you establish what people delight in, they will suffer from what they dislike but, if you establish what the people dislike, they will be happy in what they like. How do I know that this is so? Because, while in anguish, people think and, by thinking, they become resourceful; while happy they are dissolute and, in dissoluteness, they become unprincipled . . . Thus, in making people correct, if what they dislike is used as a means, they will in the end attain what they like. On the contrary, if what they like is used as a means, they will be in the end ruined by what they dislike.

This sounds paradoxical. But the idea is the same as that which Gongsun Yang presented in the policy discussion with Duke Xiao and two other ministers summarised earlier, namely the common people are short-sighted, capable of seeing only the immediate results of an action, not its long-term consequences. But the two views are usually in conflict, and pursuit of instant gratification often brings lamentable results in the future. Knowing this, a good ruler would use punishments to prohibit people from seeking what they instinctively like and force them to seek eventual, long-lasting benefits. This is *yi* (義 just). A bad ruler will do the opposite and that is *bu-yi* (不義 unjust). Thus, Gongsun Yang said the *xing* (刑 punishments) he talked about is *yi zhi ben* (義之本 the foundation of justice) and what the world calls *yi* is actually *bao zhi shou* (暴之首 the fountainhead of violence).

(ii) Make rewards few and inexpensive

Because of the ideas that, in governing the people, all of them should be presumed basically bad, and that rewarding the virtuous is like rewarding those who do not steal and rob, it follows that a ruler should seek out the people's faults but not their good deeds and that rewards should be few. Gongsun Yang observed that, in a well-governed state, the ruler uses punishments nine times more often than rewards, and that the more rewards are given the weaker the state will be because its resources are limited. A better way to use reward is to give it only to those who are meritorious in military campaigns against foreign enemies. When a state is victorious in an aggressive war, it can divide up the land and the people of the defeated and give them to its officials and soldiers. The rewards will cost the victorious state nothing but make the recipients greatly satisfied, encourage them to fight for more spoils, and thus make the state stronger and more aggressive.

(iii) Make punishments numerous and harsh

Nevertheless, Gongsun Yang believed that punishment is a far more effective means of government. It is not only to chastise criminals but to deter people from committing crime and, ultimately, make punishment unnecessary. To achieve these objectives, he suggested two measures: to make punishments numerous and to make them harsh. The first measure will criminalise many activities that seem to be innocent to many ordinary observers. They include pursuits of many values disapproved by the government and attempts to avoid agriculture and war. Because those engaged in such activities are numerous, a "true king", in managing the people's affairs, applies punishments in nine cases out of ten.

It is one thing to make numerous prohibitions; it is another to catch all those who breach them. And then there is yet another puzzling fact that, even when culprits are always caught and punished, crimes continue to rise. Why? Gongsun Yang had a simple answer: because the punishments were too light. Therefore, he proposed the second measure. He recognised that it was commonly held that, because there are trifling as well as serious wrongs, there should be correspondingly severe and lenient punishments. This position was especially stressed by the Ruists but, to Gongsun Yang. it was a misconception. People are calculating and, when punishment is made to fit the crime, a reckless person can be tempted to take a chance to get what he wants. If he is caught, he may already have enjoyed the fruits of his crime and face only proportionate punishments. Since criminals are not always caught, those who have escaped will become more audacious and commit more serious crimes. This is not the way to prevent offences but to allow them to proliferate. In his words, "If in application of penalty, major offences are given heavy penalties and minor offences light penalties, the minor offences will not be stopped and, consequently, there will be no means of stopping the major ones."

In support of his suggestion of harsh punishments, Gongsun Yang observed that the sage kings of the past prescribed such corporal punishments as amputation of a foot or a tattoo on the face for persons who committed minor offences. In his view "it is not that they sought to harm the people; they wanted to suppress evil and stop crime", and "there is no better means of suppressing evil and stopping crime than by making punishments heavy". A punishment whose harshness far outweighs the seriousness of a crime is the most effective deterrent to potential wrongdoers. To follow the "sage kings", Gongsun Yang expanded the numbers of crimes punishable by corporal punishment and the death penalty, and, according to *Han-shu* (漢書 *The History of the Han Dynasty*), he added drilling the skull, extracting the sinews, and boiling alive in a pot. Furthermore, he initiated laws of collective criminal responsibility, making all members of a serious criminal's father's, mother's and wife's clans liable to the same punishment given the criminal.[5] To him, and according to him, "the sage kings" too, the ultimate purpose of such punishments is to make the calculatingly minded people stop violating prohibitions and, consequently, to make all punishments unnecessary.

To demonstrate that this result is possible, Gongsun Yang gave two historical examples. In the past, when Duke Zhou 周公 served as the regent of the young King Cheng 成王, two of his own brothers were disobedient. Duke Zhou executed one of them and banished the other. The people were frightened and sufficiently warned, and order was established. Recently, when Duke Wen of the state of Jin 晉文公 held court, one of his favourite officials arrived late. The duke ordered law officers to execute him by breaking his spine. The people were frightened and sufficiently warned. Thereafter, when the duke sent his army into battles, the soldiers were so well disciplined that they marched like flowing water and stopped as if they had had their feet cut off, and vanquished his enemies.

Having his belief that disproportionately heavy punishments can prevent crimes thus proven, Gongsun Yang went further, hailing the righteousness of *yi-xing qu-xing* (以刑去刑 using punishments for elimination of the need of punishment) and compared it to *yi-zhan qu-zhan* (以戰去戰 launching war for the purpose of eliminating future wars). When, as a result, punishment is no longer necessary, the people will live in peace and become virtuous. Obviously, it never occurred to him that excessive punishments could brutalise the people and that they, being widely subjected to such punishments, might find life not worth living and, as Laozi said, would no longer fear death, and then the most severe punishment – death – could no longer deter them from committing ever more serious crimes.

(E) Effects of law being properly made and enforced

(1) The rule of law

Gongsun Yang had faith in the mysterious character of the law. First of all, as discussed above, he believed it is automatically applicable in solving social problems in the way that scales could determine weight and a ruler could measure length. In this sense, he believed in the rule of law. Law must be used mechanically. Anyone who misinterprets a law, let alone alters a word of it, will be punished.

Second, he asserted that law is more effective in regulating human behaviour than other norms. According to him, virtues, at best, merely make a subject loyal, a child filial and a junior courteous to the seniors, but law makes a hungry person not eat if it is not lawful and not live and avoid death if it is not lawful. The law will make all people scrupulous, even a robber, such as the notorious Zhi 跖, trustworthy. How so? He told us that human nature can be manipulated with the use of rewards and punishments.

(2) Self-government by the people

Gongsun Yang asserted that, when his policies are properly implemented – where affairs are conducted by officials according to law; where punishments are eliminated because people are strictly organised in local security units; rewards are not unduly given; and evil deeds are always reported to the authorities – the state would be well governed by the people themselves. It is because they were taught law and told to ignore other norms that they knew what to pursue and what to avoid and were not confused by other considerations. Whenever something unusual happens, proper judgements about its correctness are made by each individual, family, village, and district. He called such process *xia-duan* (下斷 judgements being made below). The result will be remarkable. In his words, "Where the people know how properly to respond to orders from above, and decisions made in the family are acceptable to the authorities, then judgements can be made in the family . . . In a state where judgements are made in the family, the state is kingly; where judgements are made by officials, the state is strong; where judgements are made by the ruler, the state is weak." When correct judgements are made at the bottom, the decision-making process is simplified and speeded up. Gongsun Yang observed that where decisions are made quickly, the state is strong; where they are delayed the state is disorderly.

But self-government was not voluntary. People were only observing the law which prescribed what was right and wrong. Any deviation would bring extremely severe punishments.

(F) Social relationships

Thus, in Gongsun Yang's "self-governing" state there, is a very strange human relationship – in his words, "A bright ruler had no loyal ministers and a loving father had no filial sons". Why? It is because he believed that mutual affection and care made people partial to their relatives and discriminate against those outside their clans and tribes and caused strife among them. To keep a large state cohesive, all its members should be loyal to a single ruler who could keep them in order and catch those who broke it. Laws should be made to require everyone to report wrongs committed by others and to punish those who failed to do so. In such a state everyone would be under the surveillance of everyone else and treat one another as a potential danger to one's own interests and safety. As a result, mutual trust would be lost; loyalty, filial piety, friendship, sympathy and compassion become luxuries few could afford. People had no emotional connections; each person was alienated from the next one and tried to have as little to do with each other as possible.

(G) Ideal government

The ruler was, of course, different. Being the operator of the state machine, he had to have control over everything. In order to do so, according to Gongsun Yang, he had to be incredibly intelligent and knowledgeable of human needs and weaknesses, skilful in exploiting them, using various tactics to "weaken", "overcome" and "control" the people, to manipulate them and make them into what he wanted them to be like a potter would do to clay and a smith to metal. In particular, he would use rewards and punishments to force them to achieve what he wanted – making the state rich and strong, and his own position unassailable. It would be a wonderful feat that only a Sage could accomplish, and it is, indeed, a lesson which a careful reader of Gongsun Yang's book would certainly get. Yet, at the end of the book, there is this strange passage insisting that the task was easy. When the law was made supreme and clear, and strictly applied, the people would regulate themselves and the ruler could govern without much to do. This reflected a blind faith in law. As we shall see, it is one of the serious problems in Gongsun Yang's theory.

Among the thinkers we study here, Gongsun Yang was the only one who exercised government power and accomplished much. The book *Shang-jun-shu* is supposed to provide the theory behind his actions but the result is unsatisfactory. It is because many of his ideas are flawed and therefore the arguments to justify them are controversial.

The most serious problem with his theory is the absence of a vision for society and its individual members. Unlike the Ruists, Mohists and Zhuangzi, who visualised a state where individuals are allowed to develop their best potentials and society to have happiness and harmony, Gongsun Yang merely wanted the state to be rich and strong; beyond this, no higher and broader prospects are manifest in his book. It is possible that, when a state is rich, its wealth can trickle down and improve the well-being of the common people. But Gongsun Yang did not want to have this result because, he said, when people are well off they become lazy and indulge in idle activities, such as academic studies. So he suggested that, when the people have surplus strength, the ruler should dissipate it by sending them to aggressive wars. What is a state to do after conquering all its rivals? Gongsun Yang did not enlighten us.

Gongsun Yang's focus on agriculture as the only means for wealth creation is naive, and his condemnation of other values and undertakings misguided. We have seen that this view was advocated by the Agriculturalist School and definitively refuted by Mencius who pointed out that, for a person to survive, he needs many others to provide for his necessities. It is only too obvious that craftsmen making various tools – including weapons – and educators teaching behavioural rules – including law – are necessary. Even the much criticised merchants are indispensable in moving goods around to meet needs in different locations.

Gongsun Yang realised that agricultural work is hard and war dangerous but he believed that people can be made to engage in them by rewards and punishments because people are calculating. But this idea is itself a miscalculation – there is a limit to what rewards and punishments can accomplish. We have already mentioned Laozi's argument against excessive punishments. Zhuangzi also pointed out that, when a horse suffers too much abuse, it will rebel. So it is false for Gongsun Yang to assume that human behaviour can be completely changed. More importantly, his idea reflects a simplistic view of human nature. People are not all self-centred; to many, there are things more precious than worldly gain and more dreadful than death. Mencius gave a good example to illustrate the point that, in certain circumstances, people will act without considering profit and fame. And there are many stories in *Zhuangzi* about famous historical personages committing suicide in defence of moral principles.

Gongsun Yang insisted that law must be made the paramount, if not the only, norm. This is the source of the problems of his legal theory. It is generally recognised that, for a norm system to be effective, it should have certain characteristics. First of all, it should be justifiable. A command from a mere mortal is usually not enough to be accepted as a norm. That is why advocates of a legal system often claim as its bases something more profound, such as the will of god, or rules of nature or common human dispositions. Gongsun Yang did not try to deify the ruler who made law. He said that the ruler should be more far-sighted than others but did not say that artificial law should be in agreement with natural law or human nature. He did say that the ruler should know that people have their likes and dislikes but, instead of helping them achieve what they like, he said the ruler should manipulate their desires, guiding them to pursue the objectives of the state. He did not recognise an immutable natural law known to many thinkers as "the Way". He thought law must change along with changes in society. When it is made by a ruler who claims to know the circumstances and decides to change it, his law should be supreme.

The trouble is that artificial law cannot be comprehensive. A law can be made very broad and general but, to apply it to real cases involving circumstances not precisely foreseen by the law-maker, it needs innovative interpretations which may be inconsistent or even conflicting. Or, each time a new case arises, a new law is adopted and applied retroactively, but this will result in uncertainty and impair judicial authority. On balance, a law must be specific enough for a particular category of cases, and flexible enough to accommodate the different circumstances of each case. But this was not recognised by Gongsun Yang. For strict application of the law, he saw it as a measuring instrument, such as scales and rulers, that can correctly and uniformly determining right and wrong in human affairs. But humans affairs involve more complicated elements. Therefore, in its application, a law inevitably needs to be interpreted and, because it is not self-justifiable, interpretations have to be based on something beyond and above it. Hence, making law a set of grossly imperfect and hardly well-received rules the supreme norm will induce disagreement, contention and litigation, a result quite opposite to that which Gongsun Yang predicted.

Another problem is that artificial law cannot be free from bias and arbitrariness. This problem has no solution because everyone is a product of his circumstances; even sages of the past, as Gongsun Yang himself pointed out, were limited in their views. Laws perceived as unjust or ineffective can be changed but new ones will harbour new bias and arbitrariness. This is why other thinkers raised higher norms as standards for law to pursue. Gongsun Yang's dismissal of the higher norms makes law forever a victim of the whims of political power.

Being so defective, law cannot easily win wide and enthusiastic support of the people. It has to be imposed upon them and implemented by force. Gongsun Yang was quite aware of this and, to support his policy of making law supreme, he gave two novel theorems: first, he narrated a three-stage social development that ends at a time when order was finally and definitively established under the rule of a single political authority who is completely free to makes laws for everyone to obey and exercises absolute power to enforce his laws; second, he argued for an uncommon connotation of justice that mandates harsh, disproportionate punishments that will force absolute obedience and eventually make punishments unnecessary. Obviously, by these arguments, he wished to justify authoritarian rule and a brutal legal system to facilitate it. But the first proposition is mere conjecture. There were long periods of peace and order in ancient Chinese history when the government and the people followed not laws made by a single authority but by customs and rites. The second proposition contradicts human experience. As pointed out by Laozi, when there is general disorder, the disenchanted and aggrieved will not be deterred by the death penalty. Even in ordinary times, a thinking person may even commit a more serious crime to get more of what he wants because, if he is caught, the result would be the same as if he committed a less serious crime. This is why oppressed people will rebel against the government – the ultimate "crime". The ideal of a society without crime is not new. Confucius wished to make litigation unnecessary and, by implication, crimes rare. The difference between him and Gongsun Yang is in the means to this end. To Confucius it was moral education; to Gongsun Yang it was punishments. Moral education may not be sufficient; harsh punishments may momentarily deter some offenders but, in the end, brutalise the whole population and make crimes multiply.

Finally there is a problem that underlies all of Gongsun Yang's other problems. He said that, when his laws and policies are fully carried out, the government will be left with little to do. The ruler can "recline on his couch, listen to music, and the world will be in perfect order".

This ideal of *wu wei er zhi* was popular among all ancient Chinese thinkers but none of them was naive enough to think it easy to realise, and Gongsun Yang was no exception. Though, according to his theory, when the absolute rule of law is realised, people can govern themselves, he recognised that there has to be a *ming-zhu* (明主 clever ruler) who, though supposedly reclining on a couch, nothing can go unnoticed by him. But, regrettably, Gongsun Yang did not tell us where to find such an extraordinary man. Indeed, he himself admitted as much – in another passage, he more realistically said, "In managing the affairs of a state, it is easy to know the principles but difficult, even for a sage, to carry them out".

Thus both in the views of the other thinkers we studied, and by Gongsun Yang's own admission, his theory is flawed. It was put into practice only because he had the support of Duke Xiao, a ruler who had no higher ideals than making his state rich and strong. Together, they forced draconian measures on the people who submitted but were resentful. Gongsun Yang knew this and his own precarious situation. It was reported that, at the zenith of his career, he would not venture outside his home without an extraordinary security arrangement – his vehicle would be surrounded by guards marching along with long spears and sharp swords, followed by several tens of chariots carrying armoured soldiers.He was accused of treason immediately after the duke's death. While on the run, he could find no shelter because he lacked travel permits; when captured and killed, his body was torn apart and put on public display, and his entire clan extinguished. Thus, in the end he became the victim of his own brutal laws.[6]

His tragic end was not viewed with much sympathy. Sima Qian called him *tian-zi ke-bo ren* (天姿刻簿人 a man of mean nature) obviously because he made harsh laws and enforced them cruelly. But some of his critics did point out that, as an official, he was completely devoted to his duties, doing everything for the state, nothing for his own interests; and, in implementing law, he was absolutely upright and incorruptible, neither yielding to the powerful nor cheating the weak.[7] Thus, he established standards for an administrator of justice. This must be recognised as an important contribution to the Chinese legal system but, because he enforced law mechanically, giving no consideration to reasonable mitigating circumstances, this commendable character of his was largely ignored. It is regrettable. More unfortunately, many judicial personnel of later times without his personal integrity followed his way of automatic application of law and caused great injustice. They corrupted his standards; he must be turning in his grave!

Notes

1. See Sima Qian 司馬遷, *Shi-ji* 史記, Chapter 5 "Qin ben ji di-wu" (秦本紀第五) pp. 202–3; Chapter 66 "Shang-jun lie-zhuan" 商君列傳 p. 2228.
2. Ibid., pp. 2231–2.
3. See Zhao Shanyi 趙善詒, *Xin-xu shu-zheng* 新序疏證 (by Liu Xiang 劉向) "Notes and postscript" 序跋 (by Liu Xin 劉歆) p. 317. The note is also attached to Sima Qian, *supra*, p. 2238.
4. See Sima Qian., "Shang-jun lie-zhuan" (商君列傳) p. 2232.
5. See Ban Gu, *Han Shu*, "Xingfa zhi" (漢書刑法志 Essay on Criminal Law in *The History of the Han Dynasty*) p. 1096.
6. See Sima Qian, *Shi-ji*, "Shang-jun lie-zhuan" (商君列傳) p. 2235
7. See Liu Xiang 劉向 ed. *Xin-xu* (《新序》) p. 317

Xun-zi 荀子

PART 1
TRANSLATION

(A) Man, Heaven and Fate

[1] When stars fall and the trees cry, the people are afraid, asking, "Why?" The answer: "There is nothing to it. They are just the natural changes in heaven and earth and the transformation of Yin and Yang. They are unusual, and we may wonder, but should not fear. Eclipses of the sun and the moon, unseasonable rain and wind and the occasional appearance of strange stars are not uncommon in all ages. When the ruler is wise and the government just, these events might come together at once but they could do no harm. When the ruler is stupid and the government unjust, even though none of these strange events occurs, their absence would have no beneficial effects." (Chapter 17, "Tian-lun" 天論 p. 209)
[2] It rains after a prayer for rain is performed. Why? The answer: "There is no reason. It also rains when no one prays for it. When there is an eclipse, people try to rescue the sun or the moon; when there is a drought, people pray for rain; when an important decision is to be made, people consult the divining devices first. It is not that such results can be achieved when people perform those acts. Such activities are merely stylised expressions of wishes. The gentleman realises this is so but the common people believe that they can thus get help from deities. He who thinks it is only a way to express wishes is fortunate; he who thinks deities are involved is unfortunate. (Chapter 17, "Tian-lun" p. 211)
[3] Heaven has its own constant way to move. This way does not exist for Yao or disappear because of Jie. Respond to it with good government and there will be good results; respond to it with bad government and there will be bad results. If people are diligent in their basic work and economical in their expenditures, Heaven cannot make them poor; if they have enough nourishment and exercise at the right time, Heaven cannot make them ill; if they cultivate their virtue and do not deviate from it, Heaven cannot send them misfortune. Thus, flood and drought cannot make such people starve and thirst; cold and hot weather cannot

make them ill; evil spirits cannot make them suffer. On the contrary, if people neglect their basic work and are wasteful in their expenditure, Heaven cannot make them rich; if they have inadequate nourishment and exercise little, Heaven cannot keep them healthy; if they reject the Way and act wantonly, Heaven cannot make them fortunate. Thus, even if flood and drought do not come, there will be hunger; even if extreme cold and hot weather do not occur, there will be illness; even if supernatural powers do not act, there will be calamity. The natural circumstances of these people are the same as those of the people living under a good government but their experiences are different. They cannot blame their miseries on Heaven. It is their own way that has brought about the results. (Chapter 17, "Tian-lun" p. 205)

[4] The gentleman carefully cultivates what is within himself and does not desire what is up to Heaven. The small man neglects cultivating what is within himself and desires what comes from Heaven. As he cultivates what is within himself and does not desire what is up to Heaven, the gentleman progresses everyday; as he neglects cultivating what is within himself and desires what comes from Heaven, the small man regresses everyday. (Chapter 17, "Tian-lun" pp. 208–9)

[5] How can exalting Heaven and wishing for its blessings be compared with raising things and gaining control over them? How can following Heaven and praising it be compared with getting hold of its rules and applying them to one's advantage? How can hoping for a good time and waiting for it be compared with adapting to the times and doing something appropriate? . . . Therefore a person who neglects what men can do and hopes for what Heaven may do misses the right course in doing everything. (Chapter 17, "Tian-lun" pp. 211–12)

[6] Confucius was on his way to the state of Chu in the south and was trapped between the states of Chen and Cai. For seven days, there was no cooked food, no rice, but shoots and roots of some wild plants. His disciples appeared hungry. Zilu 子路 approached Confucius and asked, "I heard that to those who do good Heaven rewards them with fortune and to those who do evil Heaven sends them misfortune. Now you, sir, have done so much good for so long and yet you are trapped under these miserable conditions. Why?" Confucius said, "You 由[Zilu's formal name], you do not understand; let me tell you. Do you think a wise person must be appreciated? Wasn't Prince Bigan 王子比干 [an uncle of King Shou of the Shang Dynasty] executed and his heart opened? Do you think a loyal person must be appreciated? Wasn't Guan Longfeng 關龍逢 [a worthy official of the Xia Dynasty] given corporal punishment? Do you think a person who gives candid advice must be appreciated? Wasn't Wu Zixu 吳子胥 [an able minister of the state of Wu 吳 during the Warring State Period] stoned to death outside the East Gate of Gusu city? Whether a person is appreciated depends on the external circumstances of his time; whether a man is worthy or unworthy depends on his own character. Many learned and thoughtful gentlemen did not live in the right time; I am not alone. But, just as an orchid growing in deep forest will not stop being fragrant because no one is there to appreciate it, the gentleman cultivates him-

self not to seek worldly rewards. The purpose is to enable him to live in poverty without depression and in grief without despair, and to know the changes of good and bad fortune and not to be perplexed. So, whether or not a person is worthy or unworthy is due to his own character; whether he does or does not do good is up to himself; whether he is appreciated is decided by the circumstances of his time; and whether he is to live or die under a particular condition is determined by fate. Now here is a man whose circumstances are not favourable, how can he, though worthy, have his way? But when the circumstances are favourable, what difficulty at all will such a person have? This is why the gentleman studies broadly, thinks deeply, cultivates his virtue, keeps his behaviour correct, and waits for his opportunity." (Chapter 28, "You-zuo" 宥坐 pp. 345–6)

(B) Human nature

(1) It is inborn and universal

[7] The nature of a thousand persons or ten thousand persons and that of a single person is the same. (Chapter 3, "Bu-gou" p. 30)
[8] What is known as the "nature" is something made by Heaven. It cannot be learned. It cannot be cultivated. (Chapter 23, "Xing-e" p. 290)
[9] Every person has something in common with others. When hungry, he desires to eat; when cold, he desires to be warm; when toiling, he desires to rest; he desires what is beneficial and hates what is harmful. Man is born with these desires; he does not have to wait to have them; in these respects Yu and Jie were alike. (Chapter 4, "Rong-ru" 榮辱 p. 39)
[10] These are man's dispositions: for food he wants to have meat, for clothing he wants to have embroidered fabric, for travel he wants to have carriages and horses. In addition, man desires surplus wealth and keeps accumulating it. He works hard year after year and generation after generation for all these desires and never becomes contented. These are human dispositions. (Chapter 4, "Rong-ru" p. 42)

(2) It is "bad"

[11] To be as lofty as the emperor and as rich as the owner of the world is what everyone wishes. But if this wish were granted to everyone, the circumstances would become unbearable, and the resources would become inadequate. (Chapter 4, "Rong-ru" p. 44)
[12] While people's likes and dislikes are the same, there are not sufficient goods to satisfy everybody, and hence there will inevitably be strife. (Chapter 9, "Wang-zhi" 王制 p. 96)
[13] By nature man is born with a desire for profit; if it is allowed to develop freely, strife and robbery will result and courtesy and yielding will disappear. Man is born with certain dislikes; if they are allowed to run wild injury and destruction will follow and loyalty and faithfulness will disappear. Man is born with sensory craving and sexual lust; if they are allowed to grow unchecked, excess and disorder will follow and modesty, righteousness and civilised behaviour will disappear.

Therefore, if left to their nature and disposition, men will contend and grab, violate the right guidelines and cause disorder. (Chapter 23, "Xing-e" p. 289)

[14] Yao asked Shun, "What is human nature like?" Shun answered, "Human disposition is rather ugly. What is the point of asking about it! When a man has a wife and children, his filial piety to his parents diminishes; when a man's desires are satisfied, his fidelity towards friends diminishes; when a person has obtained titles and position, his loyalty towards his ruler diminishes. Human disposition! Human disposition! it is rather ugly! What is the point of asking about it?!" (Chapter 23, "Xing-e" pp. 296–7)

[15] Mencius said, "Human nature is good." I say this is not the case. It is a result of not knowing the human nature and not distinguishing human nature from human artefact. Human nature is what is made by Heaven. It cannot be learned and cannot be cultivated . . . What can be learned and cultivated is called human artefact . . . The nature of man is that, when hungry, he desires repletion; when cold, he desires warmth; when toiling, he desires rest. This is human nature. But now, when hungry, a man dares not eat ahead of some elders but yields to them. When working, he dares not seek rest but toils for them. The son's yielding to his father and the younger brother's yielding to his older brother, the son's toiling for his father and the younger brother's toiling for his older brother, are two kinds of behaviour that are contrary to human nature and repugnant to human disposition. But they are the way of the filial son and fine expressions of propriety and rectitude. Thus, if one follows one's nature and disposition, one will not be courteous and yielding; if one is courteous and yielding, one will be acting against one's natural and disposition. From these, it is clear that human nature is evil, and man's goodness is artificial. (Chapter 23, "Xing-e" pp. 290–1)

[16] Mencius said, "The nature of man is good." I say this is not the case. In all times and places, "goodness" means righteousness, order, peace and justice, while "evil" means prejudice, malice, rebellion and disruption. This is the difference between good and evil. If human nature is, indeed, righteous, orderly, peaceful and just, why is there the need for sage kings? Why is there the need for rites and justice? What can the sage kings and the norms add to good order and just government? Now that is not the case. The nature of man is evil. Realising that human nature was evil and that it was partial, biased, rebellious and disorderly, the ancient sages established rulers to govern humankind, made clear principles of the rites and other norms to transform humans, created laws and policies to guide humans, imposed heavy punishments to prohibit humans from doing wrong, so that the world was made orderly and humankind in conformity with virtue. That was the result of the good government of the sage kings and the influence of rites and justice. Now suppose we remove the authority of the ruler, the influence of rites and justice, the law, the policies, and the punishments, and observe how the people interact with one another. The strong will harm the weak and rob them, the majority will oppress the minority and divide them, and the whole world will fall into chaos and mutual destruction in no time. From this it should be clear that human nature is bad. What is good is acquired

pretence. Thus, those who are good at talking about the past must verify the validity of what they say with what happens in the present; those who talk about Heaven must check their views with what is in the human affairs. Those who make arguments should value evidence showing a correlation between their words and the reality. In this way, those who sit down and discuss a matter will be able to get up and practise what they say. Now Mencius said man's nature is good but he had no evidence to support his words, and therefore he could sit and talk but was unable to get up and prove what he said. Isn't it rather wrong? Thus, if human nature were good, sage kings would have been dismissed, and rites and justice put aside. If human nature were bad, the sage kings had to be followed, and rites and justice valued. As the invention of wood-bending devices was for crooked timber and the creation of the carpenter's stretched string was for things that are not straight, the establishment of rulers and rites and justice was for the fact that human nature is bad. From this it should be clear that human nature is bad. What appears to be good is acquired pretence." (Chapter 23, "Xing-e" pp. 293–4)

(3) Its expression can be changed

[17] Nature is what I cannot do anything about, but it can be transformed. Personal disposition are not what I naturally possess but I can do something about it. By learning and practice, human nature can be transformed. (Chapter 8, "Ru-xiao" 儒效 p. 91)

[18] Though human desires are limitless, they can be limited. Though human desires cannot be eliminated, they can be restricted . . . The right Way is to limit desires and restrict them. (Chapter 22, "Zheng-ming" 正名 p. 285)

[19] A man who practises hoeing and ploughing becomes a farmer; a man who practises chopping and carving becomes a carpenter; a man who practises selling goods becomes a merchant; a man who practises rites and justice becomes a gentleman . . . None of these outcomes is determined by human nature. All of them are results of continuous cultivation. (Chapter 8, "Ru-xiao" pp. 91–2)

[20] "The man on the street can become a Yu 禹" – what does it mean? I say the reason Yu was Yu is because he acted in accordance with the principles of benevolence, justice, law, and uprightness. These principles can be rationally comprehended and actually practised. As any man on the street can have the capability of comprehending and the ability to practise these principles, it is clear that he can become a Yu. (Chapter 23, "Xing-e" p. 295)

[21] While it is right that anyone on the street can become a Yu, it is not true that everyone on the street will become a Yu. Though one may not become a Yu, it does not invalidate that one can become a Yu. (Chapter 8, "Ru-xiao" p. 296)

(C) Need of social organisation

[22] It takes hundreds of special skills to produce goods to meet the needs of a single person; yet no one is able to have numerous skills and manage multiple jobs. If men live separately and do not serve one another, there will be poverty. If they live together in a group without classification there will be strife. Poverty breeds hardship and strife produces calamity. To alleviate hardship and eliminate calamity, it is best to form social organisations and keep social classification clear. (Chapter 10, "Fu-guo" 富國 pp. 113–14)

[23] Man's strength is not equal to that of an ox; his running is not equal to that of a horse; yet oxen and horses are used by him. Why? It is because men can form social organisations but the animals cannot. How is it that men can form social organisations? It is because men are separated into different classes. What makes this separation work? It is justice. If the division is in accordance with justice there will be harmony. Where there is harmony there is unity. When men are united they have great strength. When they are strong they can dominate other things. (Chapter 9, "Wang-zhi" p. 104)

(D) Need of government authority

[24] Where two persons are both of high social status, they cannot serve each other; where two persons are both of low social status, they cannot employ each other. This is natural. Where people have equal status and power and the same likes and dislikes and there are not enough resources for satisfaction, they inevitably compete. Competition will inevitably lead to disorder and disorder will result in poverty. The ancient kings hated the disorder, so they established rites and justice to separate the people into different classes of the poor and the rich, the privileged and the humble, and thus enabling some to supervise the others. This is the most fundamental arrangement for the care of the world. (Chapter 9, "Wang-zhi" p. 96)

[25] When social classes were not established, people's positions were determined by their personal relations. But, if a descendant of a king, a feudal lord, an official or officer cannot follow rites and justice, he is to be relegated to the class of commoners. If a descendant of a commoner has acquired learning, developed a good character, and is able to observe rites and justice, he is to be elevated to the class of officials. (Chapter 9, "Wang-zhi" p. 94)

(E) Need of social norms

[26] Someone asked, "If human nature is evil, where do rites and justice come from?" The answer: "Rites and justice are products of sages. They do not come from human nature . . . The sage deliberates and learns about customs and creates rites and principles of justice and establishes the laws. Thus rites, justice and the laws are creations of the sages, not the outcome of human nature. (Chapter 23, "Xing-e" p. 291)

[27] Whence come the rites? Man born with desires. When desires are not

satisfied, he cannot but search for satisfaction. When this search is carried out without restraint, there cannot but be strife. When there is strife, there will be disorder; when there is disorder, there will be poverty. The ancient kings hated this disorder, so they created rites and justice to dispel it and to satisfy man's desires and end his search. They wanted man's desires not to exceed the resources and the resources readily available for man's desires. They want the two to be co-related and developed together. It is for this reason that rites were created. (Chapter 19 "Li-lun" 禮論 p. 231)

(F) To learn the norms

(1) Need of education

[28] Man is born petty. Without teachers and norms he can only see what is profitable . . . With only his mouth and stomach to care for, how could he know rites and justice, courtesy and modesty, shame and virtue? He would only eat and chew to keep his belly full. Without teachers and norms a man's mind sets only on his mouth and stomach. (Chapter 4, "Rong-ru" p. 40)
[29] Without teachers and norms those who are intelligent will commit theft; those who are brave will physically injure others; those who are talented will cause disorder; those who are discriminating will become eccentric; those who like to debate will become argumentative. (Chapter 8, "Ru-xiao" p. 90)

(2) Objectives

[30] The mind must not be ignorant of the Way. If it is, it might disapprove of the Way and approve the wrong way . . . If a person who disapproves of the Way is to choose company, he will side with those who do not follow the Way, and this will be the source of disorder . . . Therefore, the most important thing for establishing order is to know the Way. (Chapter 21, "Jie-bi" 解蔽 p. 263)
[31] True knowledge is to know what is right as right and what is wrong as wrong. Ignorance is to take what is right as wrong and what is wrong as right . . . Rectitude is to say what is right is right, what is wrong is wrong. (Chapter 2 "Xiu-shen" 修身 p. 14)
[32] Not hearing about something is not as good as hearing about it; hearing about a thing is not as good as seeing it; seeing it is not as good as knowing it; knowing it is not as good as practising it. The ultimate objective of learning is to put into practice the lessons one has learned. (Chapter 8, "Ru-xiao" p. 90)
[33] As for the objectives, the initial one is to be a gentleman; the final one is to be a sage. (Chapter 1, "Quan-xue" 勸學 p. 7)

(3) Methods

[34] He who lives in Chu becomes a man of Chu; he who lives in Yue becomes a man of Yue; he who lives in Xia becomes a man of Xia. (Chapter 8, "Ru-xiao" p. 92)

[35] At what point should one start one's formal education and what is its end? I say that, as far as book-reading is concerned, it is to start with reciting the Classics and to finish with reading books on rites. (Chapter 1, "Quan-xue" p. 7)
[36] The gentleman knows that his knowledge will not be good enough if it is not comprehensive and pure. Therefore, he repeatedly reads the Classics to find their central themes; he ponders on related problems to achieve a general understanding; and then tests it by placing himself in the situation of the persons encountering problems. (Chapter 1, "Quan-xue" p. 11)
[37] When enough earth is gathered to form a mountain, wind and rain will originate there. When enough water is accumulated to form a lake, dragons will breed there. When enough good deeds are done, a person becomes self-content and sage-like. Therefore, without taking single steps one would not travel 1,000 *li*; without accumulating water from small streams, rivers and seas cannot be formed. A fast horse in one leap cannot cover 10 paces but an old, worn-out nag walking for ten days can travel a long distance. What matters is perseverance. Without perseverance one cannot break a piece of decayed wood; with perseverance one can carve metal or stone. The earthworm has no sharp claws and teeth, no strong sinews and bones, and yet it can eat the hard clay and drink the deep groundwater, because it can concentrate; a crab has six legs and two pincers, yet it has no shelter other than the holes of snakes and eels, because it is impatient. Thus, he who has no unwavering determination will have no conspicuous achievements; he who does no patient preparation will have no shining success. (Chapter 1, "Quan-xue" pp. 4–5)
[38] With teachers and norms, those who are intelligent will quickly become knowledgeable; those who are brave will quickly become awesome; those who are talented will quickly become successful; those who are discriminating will quickly find the truth; those who like to debate will quickly arrive at correct conclusions. Thus, teachers and norms are the greatest treasure a man can have, and the lack of teachers and norms is the greatest misfortune a man can suffer. (Chapter 8, "Ru-xiao" p. 91)
[39] Hua-liu, Qi-ji . . . were good horses of antiquity. But they had to have reins to guide them, whips to drive them and Zao-fu 造父 [a great charioteer] to steer them before they could reach 1,000 *li* a day. In the case of man, even those who have good character and high intelligence must follow a wise teacher and associate with good friends. With a wise teacher, one could hear about the way of Yao, Shun, Yu and Tang; with good friends, one could learn the acts of loyalty, faithfulness, respect and modesty. As a result, one would become increasingly humane and righteous everyday without knowing it. That is because the change is gradual, subtle and accumulative. (Chapter 23, "Xing-e" pp. 299–300)
[40] Tall grass growing among shafts of hemp plants becomes straight without support. (Chapter 1 "Quan-xue" p. 3)

(4) Result

[41] [Having learned the Way], a man sitting in a room can see the world within the boundaries of the four seas; living in the present he can discuss what is far in the past and the future; glancing at the myriad things he can know their characteristics, reviewing the order and disorder in history and comprehend the rule . . . He is thus called a "Great Man". (Chapter 21 "Jie-bi" p. 265)
[42] A gentleman is called competent not because he can do everything others do; a gentleman is not called erudite because he knows everything others know . . . To plant crops a gentleman is not as good as a farmer; to conduct commerce a gentleman is not as good as a merchant . . . What a gentleman is good at is that, in speaking, his words are in accordance with reason and, in doing a job, his work fits the task. (Chapter 8, "Ru-xiao" pp. 78–9)
[43] A gentleman does not look at what is not right to see, listen to what is not right to hear, speak what is not right to say, ponder what is not right to think . . . As a result, his aims cannot be distracted by force and wealth, changed by the wishes of the masses, or overturned by the possibility of dominating the world. He lives and dies for these objectives and his acts are called "Practices of Pure Virtue" and with such practices a person can be settled. When settled he can respond properly in all circumstances. He who is settled and capable of responding properly in all circumstances is called an "Accomplished Man". (Chapter 1 "Quan-xue" pp. 11–12)
[44] Where a person's objective and intention are cultivated, he can be prouder than the rich and powerful; where his emphasis is on the right Way and justice, he can dismiss the princes. This is because, when a person pays attention to what is within himself, what is outside becomes of little importance. The Record says, "A gentleman makes things work, a petty man works for things." This is what the saying means. (Chapter 2, "Xiu-shen" p. 16)
[45] Where justice is at stake, he is never subdued by the powerful and never considers what profit he can gain. When he is given the authority to govern a whole country, he does not change his views. He values his life but will uphold justice and not bend his principle. This is the courage of a gentleman. (Chapter 4, "Rong-ru" p. 35)
[46] If a man's manner is respectful, his heart loyal and faithful, his behaviour according to rites and principles of justice, his attitudes toward others loving and benevolent, he can go anywhere in the world, even being trapped among barbarians, and be honoured. If a person would press ahead of others in doing something arduous but is willing to yield to others in doing something enjoyable, and if he is upright, faithful, sincere and trustworthy, he can go anywhere in the world, even being trapped among barbarians, and be trusted. (Chapter 2, "Xiu-shen" pp. 16–17)
[47] The gentleman may exalt the virtues and praise the good deeds of others but his act is different from flattery. He may, for the sake of justice, directly point out other people's faults but his act is different from petty criticism. He may talk about the results of his own cultivation, compare them with those of Shun and

wish them to be in harmony with heaven and earth but his act is different from self-aggrandisement. He may softly bend like a reed when the circumstances so require but his act is different from cowardice. He may be firm, forceful and determined to realise his word, but his act is different from insolence and foolhardiness. This is because he is responding to the changes outside himself according to the principles of propriety, and because he knows what is right and what is wrong. (Chapter 3, "Bu-gou" pp. 25–6)

[48] The gentleman is ashamed of not being virtuous but not ashamed of being insulted; he is ashamed of not being trustworthy but not ashamed of not being trusted; he is ashamed of not being capable but not ashamed of not being employed. Thus he is not enticed by flattery and not fearful of criticism. He strictly follows the Way, carefully rectifies himself, and does not falter because of external influences. This kind of person is called a "True Gentleman". (Chapter 6, "Fei-shi-er-zi" 非十二子 p. 64)

[49] The gentleman scarcely seeks profit, quickly stays away from harm, fearfully avoids disgrace, and courageously follows the Way. He keeps his high aspirations while in poverty, and maintains his modesty while with wealth and honour. He does not let down his spirit while resting, and appear worn out while tired. (Chapter 2 "Xiu-shen" pp. 21–2)

[50] It is easy to approach a gentleman but difficult to become familiar with him. He can be frightened but not threatened. He is fearful of harm but will not avoid death for the sake of justice. He desires benefits but will not do wrong to gain them. He can be close to people but will not become partisan. He can be eloquent but will not resort to sophistry. He is open and straight and thus distinctive in the world. (Chapter 3 "Bu-gou" p. 24)

[51] The gentleman is tolerant but not indulgent, scrupulous but not nitpicking, disputatious but not contentious, observing but not censorious, free-standing but not dominating, strong but not overpowering, soft but not drifting along with the current. He is respectful, careful and friendly towards others. (Chapter 3 "Bu-gou" p. 25)

[52] There are those who superficially follow the way of the early sage kings and thereby cause disorder in the world; who have learned disorganised lessons and do not know how to follow the later sage kings in unifying institutions and standards; who do not really observe rites and principles of justice and truly embrace the lessons of *The Book of Historical Documents* and *The Book of Odes*; . . . who merely talk about the way of the early sage kings to dazzle the stupid people and thereby make a living; . . . who obey their leaders . . . like slaves having no will of their own. They are "the vulgar Ruists". (Chapter 8 "Ru-xiao" p. 88)

[53] There are those who follow the teachings of the later sage kings, know how to unify their learning about institutions and standards; who earnestly observe rites and principles of justice and understand the lessons in *The Book of Odes* and *The Book of History*; whose remarks and actions are in accordance with great principles and yet there are things their intelligence cannot deal with – whenever they encounter something about which they have not learned from

their education or personal experience, they do not know how to categorise it; who will say they know when they really know and will say they do not know when they do not know, and thus would not deceive themselves or others; who revere the virtuous and wise, respect the law, and dare not be neglectful and arrogant. They are "the refined Ruist intellectuals". (Chapter 8, "Ru-xiao" p. 89)

[54] There are those who observe the teachings of the ancient sage kings; who are well versed in rites and principles of justice and know the unifying principles behind social institutions and standards; who are capable of dealing with the complicated by learning from the simple, of dealing with the present by learning from the past, of dealing with ten thousand by learning from one . . . When a strange thing, or a bizarre twist in circumstances never heard or seen before, suddenly appears, they are able to categorise it and respond by applying a general principle without any hesitation. The existing rules will be expanded to cover the case, and there will be a perfect match. They are "the great Ruists". (Chapter 8, "Ru-xiao" p. 89)

[55] In straightening himself, the gentleman uses the stretched string to make a straight line. In correcting others, he gives a helping hand. Because he is strict with himself, he is worthy of being a model for the world; because he is considerate to others, he can be tolerant in achieving the desired results and thus realise great success in the world. (Chapter 5, "Fei-xiang" 非相 p. 54)

(G) To make a better world

(1) Objectives and general operating principles

[56] Marquis Ying 應侯 [chief minister of the state of Qin] asked Xunzi, "What have you found since coming to the state of Qin?" Xunzi said, "Its borders are well fortified and secure; its geography is convenient for expansion; its mountains, forests, rivers and valleys are beautiful and its natural resources abundant. It is thus well-endowed. After entering into the state, I observed its customs and found that its people are simple, their music is not vulgar, their dress not garish, and they are very respectful and obedient to the officials. They are thus like people of an older, better age. When I arrived at a government office in a city, I found all the clerks are quiet, serious, diligent, and never invidious. They are thus like clerks of an older, better age. When I entered the capital, I observed the officials and found that, after leaving their homes, they head for their offices, and, after leaving their offices, they head for home, and none of them engage in any private dealings. They are impartial and not cliquey but open and fair in their actions. They are thus like officials of an older, better age. I observed the royal court and found that decisions are quickly made and nothing is left in neglect. As a result, it appears as if nothing is there to be done. It is like the court of an older, better age. It is for these reasons that, in the short period of four reigns, Qin has become victorious. It is not due to good fortune but to good management. These are what I have found. It is therefore said that the ideal government is at ease and yet

governs well; its measures are simple and yet leave no details uncovered; it is not overly active and yet accomplishes a lot. This is the ultimate form of governance, and the government of Qin is nearly like this. Nevertheless, Qin has its problems. It has all these favourable conditions and yet, compared with those of a great kingdom, its achievements fall far short. Why? The reason is that it does not have great Ruist scholars." (Chapter 16, "Qiang-guo" 強國 pp. 202–3)

[57] What the Ruists will do is different . . . They will make policies and orders fully implemented and custom elegant. (Chapter 11, "Wang-ba" pp. 149–50)

[58] A great king enriches the people; a hegemonic feudal lord enriches the gentry; one who merely preserves his state enriches his ministers; one who rules a vanquishing state fills his coffers and his treasury. (Chapter 9, "Wang-zhi" pp. 97–8)

[59] If a ruler does not care for his subjects and benefit them, he cannot expect them to be close to him and love him; if they are not close to him and do not love him, he cannot expect them to serve him and die for him; if they would not serve him and die for him, he cannot expect his army to be strong and his cities secure; if his army is not strong and his cities not secure, he cannot hope that his enemies will not attack; if his enemies attack, he cannot hope that his state will not be decimated and vanquished. (Chapter 12, "Jun-dao" p. 154)

[60] A ruler who neglects his primary responsibilities but takes care of the petty needs of the people – embrace them, chat with them, give them rice in the winter and millet and fruits in the summer – in order to win their temporary praises, is following the way of a thief. He may indeed win temporary praise from some cunning people but it is not a lasting way. His projects will not be completed and his achievement not established. It is a fraudulent way to govern. A ruler who hastily employs the people to do some work and pushes them for quick achievements, taking criticisms lightly and forgetting the hardship on the people, may have the work done but the people will be resentful. This is going to the other extreme. His project will soon collapse and what achievement he has had will be reversed. Thus it is not right for a ruler to neglect his primary responsibilities and to care for only petty needs of the people, not is it right for a ruler to pursue achievements and forgot the hardship they inflict on the people. Both are fraudulent ways to govern. The ancient rulers did differently. They made people not suffer scorching heat in the summer and freezing cold in the winter, not exhausted in carrying out urgent projects and not lag behind schedule in doing ordinary work. As a result, many tasks were completed, great achievements established, everyone up and down in the country became better off, and the people all loved their superiors and turned toward them as water flowing downward, happily regarded them as if they were their parents and were willing to die for them with no regret. The reason was simple. Towards their people the ancient rulers were extremely loyal and faithful, fair and just. Thus if such a ruler wanted people to have a task done in a hurry, his fairness and justice made them work faster than any harsh orders could push them, and his loyalty and caring made them more pleased than any rewards they might receive from him. (Chapter 10, "Fu-guo" pp. 122–3)

[61] There are three ways to win the people's allegiance: first, by the use of virtue; second, by the use of power; third, by the use of wealth . . . The state which wins the people's allegiance by the use of virtue becomes a true kingdom; the state which wins the people's allegiance by the use of power becomes weak; the state which wins the people's allegiance by the use of wealth becomes poor. This is true both in the past and in the present. (Chapter 15, "Yi-bing" 議兵 p. 191)

[62] In governing a state, he who succeeds in establishing justice becomes a great king; he who succeeds in establishing trust becomes a hegemonic lord; he who resorts to treachery will soon be vanquished. (Chapter 11, "Wang-ba" 王霸 p. 131)

[63] When the law is well maintained, the officials wise and capable, the people faithful, and the customs pleasing, the state is in a superb condition. (Chapter 11, "Wang-ba" p. 143)

[64] Someone asked how to govern a state. Xunzi said, "I have heard about how to cultivate oneself but not about how to govern a state. The ruler is like a pole in the sun and the subjects the shadow it produces. When the pole is upright the shadow is straight. The ruler is like a vessel and the subjects are like water. When the vessel is round the water in it will appear round. If the ruler likes archery, the subjects will practise with bow and arrow. When King Zhuang of Chu 楚莊王 loved slender waists, there were hungry men in his court. Therefore I say, 'I have heard about how to cultivate oneself but not about how to govern a state.'" (Chapter 12, "Jun-dao" 君道 p. 154)

(2) Concrete measures

(a) Staff government with good people

[65] What is a ruler? He is someone who can gather people together. How can someone gather people together? He is good at caring for them, at distinguishing them, at properly employing them and at protecting and educating them. (Chapter 12, "Jun-dao" p. 156)

[66] The king said, "What would a Ruist be like when he is a ruler?" Xunzi said, "When he is a ruler, he is great. He will have high objectives established in his mind and proper conduct cultivated in his court; laws and correct measures will be maintained by his officials; loyalty, faithfulness, love and mutual assistance will be common among his people. He would not do one unethical act nor kill one innocent man to get the empire. His rightness is trusted by men everywhere, and they respond to his actions like echoes . . . He is therefore called the teacher of man." (Chapter 8, "Ru-xiao" pp. 76–7)

[67] The state is an important institution, and to govern it is a heavy responsibility. A ruler must therefore carefully select a proper place to put it and a proper way to lead it . . . Putting the state at a proper place does not mean to give it a particular piece of land. It means to give it the right laws and to let it be governed by the right men. Thus, a ruler who follows the laws of great kings and gives the

government to men with the virtues of the great kings will himself become a great king; who follows the laws of the hegemonic lords and give the government to men with hegemonic skills he will become a hegemon; who follows the laws of a fallen state and gives the government to men with liability to cause the fall of the state he will become a ruler to lose his state. (Chapter 11, "Wang-ba" pp. 134–5)

[68] The assignment of government responsibilities: . . . The Minister of the Interior should know the details of the conditions and products of the cities, the countryside, and the various feudal fiefs. The Minister of War should know the details of the armour, chariots, soldiers, battalions and regiments . . . To erect embankments and bridges, to keep the ditches and canals clean, to drain off overflow water, to build reservoirs and to control the water flow so that, despite flood or drought, people will be able to farm are the responsibilities of the Minister of Public Works . . . To repress the unprincipled and restrain the overbearing, to guard against the wicked and remove the vicious, and to punish them with the five penalties so that the violent and overbearing will change their behaviour, and the wicked and the vicious will not arise are the responsibilities of the Minister of Justice. To establish policy, to correct laws, to oversee every government programme, to check on the officials regularly and give them appropriate reward so that they will be diligent and the people will not be lazy are the responsibilities of the Prime Ministers. Carefully to observe the rules of rites and music, to correct their own behaviour, to spread education, to rectify customs, to care for all their subjects and unify them are the responsibilities of the feudal lords. To perfect his personal virtue, to seek the highest ideals, to improve the institutions and the culture, to unify the empire, to enable even the most humble to do his best, and to make the people of the entire world loyal and obedient are the responsibilities of the king. Thus, when government is in disorder, the guilt is with the Prime Minister; when a state has lost its good customs, the fault is with the feudal lord; when the world is not unified, the king is not the proper person. (Chapter 9, "Wang-zhi" pp. 106–9)

[69] The ancients had a way of selecting people . . . Check a person's behaviour against the principles of rites and observe whether he carefully follows and is at ease with them. Place him under changing circumstances and observe whether he is capable of proper response. Let him have leisure and comfort and observe whether he lapses into frivolity. Confront him with sex, power, anger, and danger and observe whether he can hold his position. Whether he is worthy or not worthy will be as clear as black and white. (Chapter 12, "Jun-dao" p. 159)

[70] King Zhao of Qin 秦昭王 asked Xunzi, "Are Ruist scholars of no use to a state?" Xunzi said, "Ruist scholars follow the ways of the ancient kings and exalt principles of rites and justice. They are careful subjects and they honour their superiors. If the ruler would employ them, their presence in the court would help make it proper. If they are not employed, they would retire among the people and become honest and obedient subjects . . . If one of them is placed above the

people, he has the ability to be an excellent ruler. If he is placed below a ruler, he will be a capable servant to the state and a great asset to the ruler. Even if he lives the life of a recluse in a poor alley in a house with a leaking roof, all people honour him because he earnestly practises the Way. When Confucius was about to become the Minister of Justice, Shen You shi 沈猶氏 dared not make his sheep drink water in the morning . . . And the traders of cattle and horses in the state of Lu would no longer dare post unfairly high prices. All these people corrected themselves in expectation of his appointment. When Confucius was living in Que as a commoner, the people who engage in hunting and fishing separately would pool their catches and let those who had living parents take more than their share because they were transformed by him as a model of filial piety and respect for the elders. Thus, a Ruist scholar in the court helps make government good; one in the country helps make customs good. This is how a Ruist scholar would be in an inferior position." (Chapter 8, "Ru-xiao" pp. 75–6)

[71] The achievements of a great Ruist: When King Wu died, and King Cheng 成王 was a minor, Duke Zhou protected King Cheng and succeeded King Wu in order to preserve the empire because he did not want the empire to rebel against the house of Zhou. He took the throne of the emperor and made decisions for the country, acting as if the position was naturally his, yet the world did not call him greedy. He killed Guan-shu 管叔 and destroyed the state of Yin 殷, yet the world did not call him brutal. He controlled the empire, established seventy-one states assigning fifty-three of them to the members of his own Ji 姬 clan, yet the world did not call him biased. He educated and guided King Cheng, making him understand the Way and follow the path of King Wen and King Wu, and then returned the throne. The world did not stop obeying the Zhou Dynasty and he himself in the imperial court faced north and acted as a subject of King Cheng . . . This is something none other than a sage can accomplish. This is known as the achievement of a great Ruist scholar. (Ch. 8, "Ru-xiao" pp. 73–4)

(B) Choose and apply good norms

(i) Hierarchy of norms

[72] Confucius said, "A ruler whose behaviour meets both the high and the low norms is a superior one. A ruler whose behaviour is in conformity with the high norms but at variance with the lower ones is a medium one. As to a ruler whose behaviour contradicts the high norms, though in conformity with the lower ones, I do not care to see what else he does." (Chapter 9, "Wang-zhi" p. 97)

(ii) Application of norms

[73] There are hundreds of sage kings; which one shall I follow? Ancient laws and institutions, after the passage of a long period of time, are now lost; ancient music, after the passage of a long period of time, is no longer heard; hereditary officers who enforced the law, after the passage of a long period of time, are now in oblivion. Therefore, it is said, "If you want to see the legacy of the sage kings,

look at the clearest ones available, and they are those left by the later kings." (Chapter 5, "Fei-xiang" pp. 50–1)

[74] Duke Ai of Lu 魯哀公 asked Confucius, "If one obeys one's father, is he a filial son? If one obeys one's ruler, is he a loyal subject?" The questions were repeated three times but Confucius gave no answer. [After coming out of the court, Confucius told Zigong 子貢, a disciple, what happened and asked what he thought about the encounter.] Zigong said, "One who obeys one's father is a filial son, and one who obeys one's ruler is a loyal subject. What is there for you, sir, to answer?" "You are indeed too young to know," said Confucius, "In the past, if a state of ten thousand chariots had four officials who would argue with their ruler, its territories would not be encroached upon; if a state of a thousand chariots had three officials who would argue with their ruler, the temples of its patron gods would not be desecrated; if a feudal family of a hundred chariots had two officials who would argue with their master, its ancestral shrine would not be destroyed; if a father has a son who would argue with him, he would not fall into impropriety; if a person had a friend who would argue with him, he would not commit serious wrong. Hence, if one simply obeys one's father, how can he be considered filial? If a subject simply obeys his ruler, how can he be considered loyal? Only the person who carefully scrutinises what is to be obeyed can he be considered filial and loyal." (Chapter 29, "Zi-dao" pp. 347–8)

[75] To be filial to one's parents at home and respectful to the elders abroad are behaviours of small significance. To be obedient to one's superiors and magnanimous to one's inferiors are behaviours of medium significance. To follow the Way but not one's superior and to obey justice but not one's father are behaviours of great significance. (Chapter 29, "Zi-dao" 子道 p. 347)

[76] Under three circumstances, a filial son would not obey the orders of his parents. If obedience would leave them in danger but disobedience would keep them in safety, the filial son would disobey, and his act would be characterised as proper. If obedience would bring them disgrace but disobedience would bring them honour, the filial son would disobey, and his act would be characterised as just. If obedience would make him appear bestial but disobedience would make him appear cultured, the filial son would disobey, and his act would be characterised as reverential. Thus, in a case where a son could obey but he disobeys, he is not filial. In a case where a son could not obey but he obeys, his act is not proper. A son who knows the distinction between when he ought or ought not obey, and is capable of carefully keeping the distinction when he acts, can be called a son of great filial piety. This is what is meant by the saying, "follow the Way but not the ruler; obey rightness but not one's father". (Chapter 29, "Zi-dao" p. 347)

[77] Where there is a law, act accordingly; where there is no law, place the case in the category of similar ones, look at their common basis to know their ramifications, look at their left side to know their right side. Hundreds of things may appear different but obey the same rules. Rewards and punishments can be widely usable only when they can be applied by analogy in similar cases. (Chapter 27, "Da-lüe" 大略 p. 329)

[78] If law is applied without careful deliberation, anything which is not explicitly covered by a law will be left unregulated. (Chapter 11, "Wang-zhi" p. 96)
[79] Though learned, a person who knows only the letters of a law but not its spirit will inevitably be at loss when he encounters a problem. (Chapter 12, "Jun-dao" p. 151)
[80] The use of the tally and the written contract is to ensure honesty but, if the ruler loves treachery, his officials, clerks and the wicked and fraudulent will use them to cheat. The use of the lottery is to ensure openness but, if the ruler loves secrecy, his officials and clerks will use it to cover up their secrete designs. The use of scales is to ensure fairness but, if the ruler is partial, his officials and clerks will use them to defraud. The use of the peck and bushel is to ensure exactness but, if the ruler is covetous, his officials and clerks will use them to take more and give less and thus exploit the people. Thus, the various mechanical devices of measurement are mere tools to achieve order but not the source of order. The ruler is the source of order. The officials apply the tools; the ruler cares for the source. When the source is clean, the water downstream will be clean; when the source is dirty, the water downstream will be dirty. Thus, if the ruler upholds propriety and justice, employs the wise and capable, and is himself not covetous, the officials will be modest, loyal, faithful, and behave carefully. Then even the common people will be honest without the use of the tally and the written contract, open without a lottery, fair without scales, exact without a peck. (Chapter 12, "Jun-dao" pp. 151–2)
[81] There are rulers who cause disorder; there is no state that becomes disorderly by itself. There are people who can establish order; there is no law that can establish order by itself. The method of Yi 羿 [a legendary great archer] was not lost but his disciples could not always hit the bullseye. The laws of Yu were still existent but his descendants could not continue to be emperors. Thus, laws cannot stand by themselves and precedents cannot automatically govern. When there is the right person, they will be properly used; when the right person is gone, they will fall into disuse. The law is the starting point of good government. The ruler is the fountainhead of law. Thus, if there is a good ruler, the law may be simple yet it will be sufficient. If there is not a good ruler, the law may be comprehensive yet, when the circumstances change, there will be no proper action taken and the result will be chaos. (Chapter 12, "Jun-dao" p. 151)
[82] There has been disorder under good laws; but there has never been disorder under a good ruler – from antiquity to the present, this is unheard of. It is said, "good government springs from a good ruler; bad government springs from a petty man". This is what it means. (Chapter 9, "Wang-zhi" p. 96)

(iii) Rites as the norm of choice

[83] Whence do rites arise? Man by birth has desires. When satisfaction cannot be readily had, he cannot but search for it. When this search is carried out without restraint, there cannot but be strife. When there is strife, there will be disorder; when there is disorder, there will be poverty. The ancient kings hated

this disorder so they created rites to dispel it and to satisfy man's desires and end his search. They wanted man's desires not to exceed the means of satisfaction, and the means of satisfaction readily available for man's desires. They wanted the two to be co-related and develop together. It is for this that rites were created. (Chapter 19, "Li-lun" p. 231)

[84] Rites are to distinguish the honoured from the humble and the senior from the junior, and to put the rich and the poor, the important and the unimportant, all in their right places. (Chapter 10, "Fu-guo" p. 115)

[85] Without rites a state cannot be kept right. The principles of rites determine the right course of a state just as the scales determines the right weight, the stretched string determines the straightness, the square determines whether something square is truly square and the compass determines whether a round thing is truly round. When it is applied, nothing can deviate from it without being recognised as wrong. (Chapter 11, "Wang-ba" p. 136)

[86] When the string is properly stretched, there can be no doubt about what is crooked and what is straight; when the scales are properly hung, there can be no doubt about heavy and light; when the square and compass are properly used, there can be no doubt about whether a thing is square or round; and when the gentleman is well versed in the principles of rites, he cannot be fooled by deceit and artifice. The stretched string is the ultimate standard of straightness, the scale the ultimate standard of evenness, the square and compass the ultimate standards of squareness and roundness, and rites the ultimate standard of the Way of man. (Chapter 19, "Li-lun" p. 237)

[87] For those who wade through fords, signs to mark the depth of the water are set up to save them from sinking; for governing people, a standard marking what is disorder is established to save the people from falling into it. Rites are such signs. The ancient kings made the sign to mark what is disorder. Now rites are being discarded, it is like discarding the sign to save people from disorderly conduct, and this is why people are perplexed and fall into disasters, and why criminal punishments proliferate. (Chapter 27 "Da-lüe" p. 323)

[88] In using one's strength, will power and intellect, he who follows rites will be successful; he who does not will be confused, careless and fail. Regarding food, clothing, lodging and movement, he who follows rites will be comfortable and appropriate; he who does not will become sick and encounter difficulties. Regarding appearance and conduct, he who follows rites will be elegant; he who does not will be rude, unreasonable, contrary to accepted wisdom and wild. Thus, man cannot live without rites, a task cannot be accomplished without rites, the country cannot be peaceful without rites. (Chapter 2, "Xiu-shen" pp. 13–14)

[89] Rites are, indeed, the utmost standards . . . Observing them, a country will be well governed; not observing them, it will be in disorder. Observing them, a country will have peace; not observing them, it will be in danger. Observing them, a country will survive; not observing them, it will perish. (Chapter 19, "Li-lun" p. 236)

[90] Rites should be based on people's hearts. Therefore, a rule that is not recorded in the canons of rites but is based on people's hearts can be a rule of rites. (Chapter 27 "Da-lüe" p. 324)
[91] The superiors love the inferiors and restrain them with rites . . . This is a common principle held by the hundred kings and is the basis of rites and law. (Chapter 11, "Wang-ba" p. 144)
[92] Rites are the guiding principle of law and the governing rule for precedents. (Chapter 1, "Quan-xue" p. 7)
[93] Rites of worshiping ancestors are rich with ceremony. A person not being sagacious would not know why. Sages clearly know, educated gentlemen perform the rituals with a peace of mind; officials hold on to them as required; the common people simply observe them as a custom. The gentlemen take the worship as the proper way to be man; the common people think it is to serve the spirits. (Chapter 19 "Li-lun" p. 250)
[94] Rites. The common people observe but do not know the reason behind them. The sages observe them and know the reason. (Chapter 30 "Fa-xing" 法行 p. 350)

(c) Enforcement of norms

(i) Use of rewards and punishments

[95] To reward the meritorious and punish the guilty . . . are to demonstrate appreciation of the good and displeasure with the evil. (Chapter 16 "Qiang-guo" p. 196)
[96] These are principles of the true king: men without virtue shall not be honoured; men without ability shall not be employed; men without merit shall not be rewarded; men without guilt shall not be punished. In the government no one attains a position by luck; among the guilty no one escapes punishment by luck. The worthy shall be honoured and the able employed, and none of them shall be left unrewarded. The violent shall be repressed and the evil restrained, and punishments shall be meted out without error. The common people clearly understand that, if they do good at home, they will be rewarded in the court; if they do evil in secret, they will be punished in public. These are known as the established principles, the principles of the true king. (Chapter 9, "Wang-zhi" pp. 101–2)
[97] When the punishment fits the crime, it is a deterrent; when the punishment does not fit the crime, it is despised. When a title befits the worth of a man, it is valued; when it does not, it is debased. In ancient times, the severity of the punishment would not exceed the seriousness of the crime, and one's rank would not surpass his virtue. Therefore, the ruler would kill a [guilty] father and employ his [innocent] son; or kill an older brother and employ his younger brother. Punishment and reward would not be excessive but would fit the crime and merit encouraged the virtuous and discouraged the wicked. As a result, punishments were rarely used and yet they prevailed as a powerful deterrent against crime. (Chapter 24, "Jun-zi" 君子 p. 301)

[98] It is a principle accepted by all kings that a murderer should die and that whoever injures another should suffer punishment. The origin of this principle is unknown. But it is clear that when the punishment fits crime there is order; when one does not fit the other there is disorder. Therefore, under a good government, punishments should be heavy; under a bad government punishments rightly should be light, because disruption of order is a more serious offence than increase of disorder. (Chapter 18, "Zheng-lun" p. 219)

[99] Those who follow popular tradition say that, in ancient times when the world was orderly, there were no corporal punishments but only symbolic ones – instead of being tattooed, the criminal's face was painted black; instead of having his nose cut off, the criminal was made to wear a straw hat; instead of being castrated, the criminal was made to wear a dress without the knee cover; instead of having his feet amputated, the criminal was made to wear straw sandals; instead of the death penalty, the criminal was made to wear an ochre-coloured dress without collar. Such were the punishments of the past when there was good government." This is not true. If there was truly good government, there would be no criminals, hence no need even for symbolic punishments. If some people did commit crimes and were given such light punishments, the result would be that murderers would not die, and a man who injured another would not suffer. When the crime is extremely serious but the punishment extremely light, the common people will have no fear, and the consequences will be very grave indeed. The main objective of punishment is to suppress violence, to demonstrate strong disapproval of evil, and, above all, to deter their occurrence. To allow a murderer to live and a man who has injured another not suffer is not to demonstrate disapproval of evil but to show favour to the violent and leniency to thugs. For this reason, it is obvious that symbolic punishments did not originate from the past when there was good government. Instead, it originated in the present where there is bad government. In the past, when there was good government, the situation was not like what it is today. In the past, the giving of reward and the imposition of punishment responded to people's deeds. The cause and response corresponded in kind. When the response does not correspond to the cause, disorder begins – when one's virtue does not befit his position; when one's ability does not befit his office; when the reward does not befit the merit; when the punishment does not fit the crime, nothing can be more disastrous. (Chapter 18 "Zheng-lun" 正論 pp. 218–19)

[100] Reward should not be unwarranted, punishment should not be indiscriminate. Unwarranted reward benefits the petty man; indiscriminate punishment harms the gentleman. If, unfortunately, there is excess, let it be unwarranted reward rather than indiscriminate punishment. Rather than harm the good, it is less evil to benefit the undeserving. (Chapter 14, "Zhi-shi" 致仕 p. 175)

(ii) Use of compassion and education

[101] When men act only to win rewards and praises, then they will stop when they see danger and harm. Therefore, rewards, punishments, force, and deceptive

schemes are insufficient to make men exhaust their strength or risk their lives for the ruler. If the ruler treats the common people not in accordance with the principles of rites, loyalty, and good faith, but rely solely upon rewards, punishments, force, and deceptive schemes, he can oppress them and get some kind of service and achievement out of them but, when a great invader comes, those who are entrusted with the defence of a threatened city will surely rebel; those who are led into battle will invariably be defeated; those who are assigned difficult and demanding tasks will certainly run away; and the inferiors will turn upon, and seize control of, their superiors. Thus, the way of using rewards and punishments, force and deceptive schemes is the way to deal with hired labourers and traders but not the way in which to unify the population or bring glory to the nation. Therefore, a good ruler in the past was ashamed to follow such ways. Instead, he would lead the people by virtuous action, guide them by making clear rites and principles of justice, care for them with devotion and good faith, keep their social order by honouring the worthy and employing the talented, improve their morale by bestowing on them titles and rewards. Moreover, he would let people work in the proper seasons and would lighten their corvée duties so that they could have respite. He would nourish them and care for them as one does for infants. Thus, good governance would be established and people's customs unified. If there should be those who depart from the customs and disobey their superiors, all the common people would hate them and want to get rid of them as if to have an evil exorcised. Then punishments could be used. What greater disgrace could there be? If a person tries to profit by evil ways, he will find himself confronted by severe punishment. Who but a madman or a fool, perceiving such an outcome, would fail to reform? After all these, the common people will become enlightened and will learn to obey the laws, follow the ways of their ruler, and find rest and delight in the outcome . . . This process is known as "unification by grand transformation". (Chapter 15, "Yi-bing" 議兵 pp. 189–90)

[102] If people are punished before being educated, punishments will proliferate and yet evils cannot be repressed. If, after being educated, people are not punished for doing wrong, the wicked will not be restrained. If there are only punishments but no rewards, hard-working people will not be encouraged. If punishments and rewards do not fit crimes and merits, people will have doubts, their behaviour will be treacherous, and they cannot be unified. Therefore, the ancient kings unified the people by teaching them rites and principles of justice; loved them by being loyal and faithful to them; kept them in proper social positions by promoting the virtuous and employing the able; encouraged them by bestowing upon them titles and rewards; eased their lives by using their labour only in the right season and giving them light workloads. In short, they broadly protected them and nurtured them as if caring for infants. As a result, the wicked could not prosper and thieves could not rise but the virtuous were encouraged. (Chapter 10, "Fu-guo" pp. 123–4)

[103] While Confucius was the Minister of Justice of the state of Lu, there was a father and a son suing each other. Confucius kept them in custody but, for three

months, did not make a decision. The father asked to withdraw the suit; Confucius released both of them. Jisun 季孫 [the chief minister] heard about this and was displeased, saying, "That old man cheated me. He told me that to govern a state one must exalt the virtue of filial piety. Now here is an opportunity to kill one person to warn against impious behaviour, yet he let it go." Ranzi 冉子 reported this to Confucius. Confucius sighed, saying, "Alas, after the ruler has lost the Way, the officials kill the stray people. Is this permissible? To adjudicate cases before educating people is like killing the innocent. When the army is routed, the fleeing soldiers should not be executed; when the judicial system is not in order, the people should not be punished – because the real fault is not theirs. To be casual in issuing orders but strict in carrying out punishments is to main the people; to tax the people without restriction is to devastate them; to demand results without first educating the people is to treat them with cruelty. Stop these three practices and then punishments can be applied. *The Book of History* says, 'Even in cases of justified punishments and executions, do not carry them out immediately. I have to say that I did not do my work well.' What it meant is that education should be given before the punishments. Therefore, after having displayed the Way, the ancient kings themselves followed it first. When the people could not see its value, virtuous and wise persons were promoted to educate them. When the people still did not see its value, the unworthy among them were dismissed as a warning. After three years, at most, the people will be following the examples of the king. If some wicked persons still did not follow, they were then given punishments, and the people as a whole would know what crimes were . . . At the present it is different. Education is in disarray, and punishments in profusion. When people are perplexed and fall into wrongdoing, the authorities follow them with penalties. This is why, while punishments proliferate, they cannot deter the crimes." (Ch. 28, "You-zuo" pp. 342–3)

[104] Within seven days after acting as Chief Minister of the state of Lu, Confucius ordered Shaozheng Mao 少正卯 to be executed. His disciples came and asked, "Shaozheng Mao was a famous person of Lu. You, sir, executed him before anyone at the very beginning of your government. Was it not a wrong move?" Confucius said, "Sit. Let me tell you the reason. There are five kinds of evil people, and robbers and thieves are not among them. They are, first, those whose mind is sharp but treacherous; second, those whose behaviour is deviant but obdurate; third, those whose remarks are deceitful but eloquent; fourth, those whose knowledge is ghastly but profound; and fifth, those who follow the wrong way and glorify it. Anybody with the character of any of these five kinds will not escape execution by the gentleman ruler. Now Shaozheng Mao had all five. Thus, while at home, he was able to gather a large crowd of disciples; with his words, he was able to conceal the wrong and deceive the masses; with his strong will, he was able to resist any pressure and have his own way. He is thus the greatest among the petty men, and he had to be executed. This is why Tang executed Yin Xie 尹諧; King Wen executed Pan Zhi 潘止; Duke Zhou executed Guanshu 管叔; Taigong (first ruler of the state of Qi) executed Hua Shi 華仕; Guan Zhong

executed Fu Liyi 付里乙; Zichan executed Deng Xi 鄧析 and Shi Fu 史付. These seven persons were of different times but had the same character and all deserved execution." (Chapter 28, "You-zuo" pp. 341–2)

[105] Someone asked how to govern. I replied, "In the case of worthy and able men, promote them without waiting for their turn to come up. Dismiss the inferior and incompetent men, promptly without hesitation. In the case of evil men who initiate criminal offences and head the criminal gangs, punish them without advance warning." (Chapter 9, "Wang-zhi" p. 94)

(iii) Result

[106] When the supreme Way was manifested in its majestic form, rites were exalted, the laws strictly obeyed, so the state was under steady guidance; the worthy were honoured and the talented employed, so the people know what is right; various opinions are openly studied, so that the people will not be suspicious; the meritorious are rewarded and the deceitful are punished, so the people will not neglect their duties . . . As a result the common people will change their customs, the petty men will reform their hearts, the crooked and deviant will return to straightness and honesty. This is called the paramount achievement of governance and education. As a result, the emperor does not look and yet sees; does not listen and yet hears; does not study and yet knows; does not move and yet accomplishes. He sits alone like a block and yet the whole world follows him like the four limbs obey the mind. This is called the great manifestation. (Chapter 12, "Jun-dao" pp. 157–8)

(H) Social relationships

(1) Basic assumption

[107] See [20], [21]

(2) General rule

[108] In the presence of the ruler one should act according to the principles governing the behaviour of a subject; in the presence of village people one should act according to the principles governing the behaviour of the seniors and the juniors; in the presence of an elder one should act according to the principles governing the behaviour of a son or younger brother; in the presence of a friend one should act according to the principles of rites, justice, modesty and yielding; in the presence of an inferior or a junior one should act according to the principles of admonition and tolerance. One should be compassionate to all and courteous to all and not contentious to anybody. One should be all-embracing like the heaven and the earth that embrace myriads of things. Being so, one will be honoured by the worthy and loved by the less capable. (Chapter 6, "Fei-shi-er-zi" p. 63)

(3) Relationship between people of different social status

(A) Father and son

[109] See [74], [76]

(B) Ruler and officials

[110] See [75].
[111] Where the ruler has a wrong policy or some wrong conduct which is to endanger the state or the government, the high officials and seniors in his family should present their advice to correct the wrong, and leave their posts or the country if the advice is rejected. Such behaviour is known as arguing against a wrong. If they commit suicide when their advice is rejected, their behaviour is known as fighting against a wrong. If they can unite and lead all the officials in an effort to challenge the ruler, thus making him uncomfortable and yet unable to refuse their requests, and thereby eliminating the great danger and restoring the ruler and the state in peace, their behaviour is known as rectifying the ruler. If they resist the ruler's order, take away his power, act on his behalf and, as a result, save the state from disaster, and the ruler from humiliation, and achieve great success for the state, their behaviour is known as defying the ruler. These persons, who argue with the ruler, fight him, rectify him, and defy him, are great officials of the state, and valuable assets of the ruler. They are the ones whom a wise ruler honours and respects. (Chapter 13, "Chen-dao" 臣道 pp. 165–6)
[112] Serving a sage ruler, one should only obey but never argue or fight with him. Serving an average ruler, one should argue and fight with him but never flatter him. Serving a tyrant, one should try to correct his mistakes but never challenge or defy him. When people live during a time of disorder in a state under a brutal ruler with nowhere to escape to, they can only praise what little beauty there is in him and publicise what little good there is in him; avoid what he dislikes and refrain from exposing his failures; talk about his talents and keep silent about his shortcomings. (Chapter 9, "Chen-dao" p. 167)
[113] Be reverential and modest, prompt in following his orders, venture no decisions by themselves and make no private gains and favours; just obey him and make his will their own. These are the principles for officials to serve a sagacious ruler. Be loyal and faithful but never flattering; argue with him but never merely follow his orders; hold oneself upright and do not waver; say yes to what is right and no to what is wrong. These are the principles for officials to serve an average ruler. Be accommodating but not simply go along; be obedient but do not bend under pressure; be tolerant but do not join him in committing evil; enlighten him with the great Way and try to make his actions fit it; change his character and restrain his behaviour. These are the principles for officials to serve a tyrannical ruler. Their job is like riding an untrained horse, or nursing an infant, or feeding a hungry man. They can work on his fear to make him correct

his mistakes, work on his worry to make him learn the cause, work on his likes to lead him to the Way, work on his anger to eliminate the cause of his grievance. This is known as reaching the goal by indirect ways. (Chapter 13, "Chen-dao" pp. 167–8)

(c) The sovereign and the common people

[114] Heaven populated the world with people but not for the ruler. It instead installed the ruler for the people. (Chapter 27, "Da-lüe" p. 332)

[115] King Tang and King Wu followed the Way and acted in accordance with justice. They promoted what was beneficial for the empire and eliminated what was harmful. The people of the entire empire came to them as their subjects. They then set themselves up as examples of virtue for the people, made clear to the people rites and principles of justice as guidance of their conduct, demonstrated their love for the people with loyalty and faithfulness, rewarded the wise and capable among the people with ranks and honours, summoned the people for government service at the right time and made their work light, broadly protected and assisted the people as if nurturing infants. In raising the people, they were lenient; in employing the people they were reasonable. They conscientiously administered the law and government in order to care for the people of the empire. They would not impose an unreasonable government measure, even though of little consequence, upon even the least resisting people – orphans, widows, widowers, and the old and childless. For these reasons, the people honoured them as gods, loved them as parents, and were happy to die for them. (Chapter 11, "Wang-ba" p. 147)

[116] During a time of disorder the situation is quite different. The ruler leads the people in dirty tricks and stealthy deeds, demonstrates for them the art of treachery and subversion. He causes disorder in government by employing the disqualified, and making the stupid teach the wise and the wicked supervise the virtuous. In managing the economy he makes people poor; in using their labour he makes them exhausted. Therefore the people despise him like a snake or pig and hate him like a demon. Every day they seek the opportunity to banish him and trample on him. (Chapter 11, "Wang-ba" pp. 147–8)

[117] If horses are frightened of the carriage, the gentleman cannot ride in safety; if the common people are frightened of the government, the gentleman cannot occupy his post in safety. If horses are frightened of the carriage, the best thing to do is to calm them down; if the common people are frightened of the government, the best thing to do is to treat them with kindness. Select men who are worthy and good for government office, promote those who are kind and respectful, encourage filial piety and brotherly affection, look after orphans and widows and assist the poor, and then the common people will feel safe and at ease with their government. And once the common people feel safe, the gentleman may occupy his post in safety. This is what is meant by the saying, "The ruler is the boat and the common people are the water. The water bears the boat up, the water also capsizes it." Therefore, if the gentleman desires safety, the best thing

for him to do is to govern fairly and to love the people. If he desires glory, the best thing is to observe rites and treat person of quality and integrity with respect. If he desires to win fame and merit, the best thing is to promote the worthy and employ men of ability. (Chapter 11, "Wang-zhi" p. 97)

Xun-zi 荀子

PART 2
INTERPRETATION

The six thinkers studied above, being troubled by the problems of their times, suggested the existence of a better era in the past when there was peace and order, and lamented its disappearance. Each of them had different explanations for the loss but agreed on one main cause – the wrong ideas and actions of someone else. We notice that Confucius blamed those who violated good norms, particularly rites that assigned social positions and prescribed civilised behaviour. Laozi and Zhuangzi condemned those who deviated from the laws of nature. Mozi denounced the petty Ruists, for their obsession with frivolous rites, and castigated the aggressive warmongers. Mencius despised those who sought "profit" and harshly criticised those who advocated solipsism and universal love. Gongsun Yang censured those who refused to seek profit for the state. Now we shall see most of them being critiqued by Xunzi.

According to a brief biography by Sima Qian, Xun Kuang (荀況 *c*.313–238 BCE) hailed from the state of Zhao 趙. At the age of fifty he was in the state of Qi as the oldest among the scholars honoured by King Xiang 齊襄王 (r. 283–265) and was made the head of the royal academy. Later, he moved to the state of Chu and served as the magistrate of a district. He was a teacher. Two of his students were famous – Li Si 李斯, the chief minister of the state of Qin who helped it vanquish its rivals and unify China, and Han Fei 韓非, the consummate Legalist theoretician. By his time, many intellectuals held distinctive ideas about life and society and influenced great numbers of common people. Xunzi found twelve such intellectuals particularly popular, placed them in six categories, two in each, as representatives of views he considered misconceived, and used one chapter "Fei-shi-er-zi" (非十二子 criticisms of twelve scholars) of his book to refute them.[1] This is an established academic practice – before presenting your own views critique the rival ones first. We shall therefore briefly mention his criticisms here.

First, he mentioned Ta Xiao 它囂 and Wei Mou 魏牟 who, in pursuing their personal freedom, followed their own inclinations and dismissed all social norms and authorities, and were thus unfit for life in civilised, orderly society. He was apparently criticising those sharing the views of Zhuangzi who reportedly admired Wei Mou.

In the second category were those of the opposite type who strictly controlled their personal emotions and desires, and acted dramatically differently from ordinary people and, therefore, were unable to associate with others and play a role in community. He listed Chen Zhong 陳仲 and Shi Yu 史魚 in this group. We have seen in Chapter 5 Mencius's critique of Chen Zhongzi. Confucius said Shi Yu was "straight as an arrow when the state is in order and also straight as an arrow when the state is in disorder" but did not particularly appreciate his rigid "straightness".[2] Xunzi apparently thought it would make difficult for such a person to fit into society.

Thirdly there were people such as Mozi and Song Jian 宋銒 who were ignorant of how a state would work and yet wished to create a good one, overemphasised hard work, frugality and altruism, and ignored different degrees of human relationship and, as a result, were unable to establish a necessary and viable political system.

Then, he listed Shen Dao 慎到 and Tian Pian 田駢 in the fourth category, saying that they exalted law but did not know its essence; they initiated numerous statutes, obeyed the wishes of the ruler, followed the customs of the people and talked endlessly about the written provisions but, when questioned about the ultimate objective of law, were unsure what it was and, therefore, were incapable of governing the state and establishing the correct positions for the various people in society. Obviously, Xunzi was criticising the Legalists but he did not mention Gongsun Yang. It is perhaps because, though he found shortcomings in the Legalist theory he, as we shall see, admired Gongsun Yang's achievements.

In contrast, there was the fifth group – those who ignored the teachings of the early sage kings and disregarded rites and principles of righteousness, liked to discuss mysterious subjects and played with esoteric words. Their investigation into a topic was often extremely painstaking but brought no substantive benefits; their arguments were sophisticated but of no practical use. They talked much but achieved little and, therefore, could not be employed to guide the people. Among them, Xunzi included Hui Shi 惠施 and Deng Xi 鄧析. The former was known for debating Zhuangzi; the latter, a litigation master, who reportedly taught people how to argue both sides of an issue and thus caused trouble for Zican 子產, the chief minister of the state of Zheng.

Finally there were those who largely followed the early sage kings as models but did not know their unifying principles. They were talented and had great ambitions. They learned ancient ideas widely and created their own theories which were difficult to understand but supposedly intended to expound the teachings of Confucius. Among them Zisi 子思 [a grandson of Confucius] began the narrative, Mencius [a student of Zisi] elaborated it and the multitude of lesser

Ruists followed in a cacophony without knowing their mistakes. Therefore, Zisi and Mencius were guilty of misrepresenting Confucius and Zigong 子弓 [a disciple of Confucius and the mentor of Xunzi]. As we shall see, Xunzi famously disagreed with Mencius about human nature. He also found Mencius's high-sounding ideas about society and government impractical and objectionable.

After criticizing the six types of persons, Xunzi went on to praise those who were able to understand the broad, fundamental principles of things and events, who cultivated themselves and educated the masses accordingly, and who, when not in government, would, like Confucius and Zigong, serve as models for all men; and, when in government, would, like Shun and Yu, be sage kings for the world.

Obviously with the ambition of emulating Confucius, Xunzi tried to establish the true teachings of the Master. His thoughts were recorded in *Xunzi* though some parts of it were probably added by his disciples. The book is more verbose than *Lun-Yu*, less argumentative but more repetitive than *Mengzi*.

(A) Man, Heaven and Fate

Arguably the most fundamental questions about human existence are what a human being is; how he perceives himself among the myriad things around him, including other human beings; what relationships he has, and should have, with them; how much freedom he has; how much inside and outside himself he can control; how much he is controlled by others; and, finally, what he can look forward to in the course of his life. Before a person has clear answers to these questions, he would have difficulty in deciding what to do and his action might not produce the result he wanted. For those who do not care about the outcome, these questions may not mean much but most humans do care. At least, they evidently want to preserve the lives of themselves and their loved ones. For these very basic purposes they have to find out how much they can master the forces that facilitate or retard the realisation of their aspirations. In ancient times, people found many elements inside and outside themselves which were inimical to their health and life, and frustrated their efforts for self-protection and development. Having little confidence in themselves, they imagined that their lives were controlled by numinous forces – spirits, deities, ancestors, and, in a general and abstract sense, "Heaven" which had a will and overwhelming power to enforce it. They therefore worshipped it, tried to divine its intentions, and strove to follow its way, hoping that it would reward their submission and piety. As civilisation developed, more careful observation made people realise that Heaven did not always respond to their actions, let alone answer their prayers. They became puzzled. Some began to think that perhaps they should not pay so much attention to Heaven but concentrate more on what humans could do. Others, though equally unsure about the relation between man and Heaven, had profound doubts about people's ability to control their own destinies.

It can be argued that true believers in nature, such as Zhuangzi, were in the second camp because they believed that every event is predetermined by the law of nature and, by following that law and discarding all artificial rules, a person can be truly free. In this sense, Laozi was a fake – while preaching that law, he actually wanted to manipulate it as a tool for his "sage" to make a deceptive "small state" where *his* law controls everything. All the other thinkers were more or less openly in the first camp. Confucius did not dismiss gods and spirits but advised people to revere them from a distance, and urged people to do their utmost to achieve what was socially worthy and accept without complaint when success eludes them. He called the failure "fate", not in the sense of being predetermined but, rather, as a shorthand for the result of inadequate effort. Mozi emphasised the power of gods, spirits and Heaven yet had a strong faith in the common people's ability to improve their lot. Mencius tried to provide a theoretical basis for this faith by asserting that men are basically "good" and capable of great achievements, though his idea of developing the good human nature and nurturing the *hao-ran zhi-qi* (浩然之氣 broad vitality) as the manifestation of this nature is mystifying. Gongsun Yang and the Legalists were, of course, true believers in the capacity of man, particularly that of the powerful political authorities. But they did not address the problem of the abuse of this capacity and, as a result, their theory brought disasters upon countless people, including themselves.

Xunzi was scientific. He realised that there are rules which govern the natural world, and that many things out there affect humans. But he did not believe that the law of nature also governs human behaviour. Therefore, he wanted people to abandon anthropocentricism, cut the umbilical cord that supposedly connects them to Heaven, rely on themselves, and do their very best to solve their own problems. According to him, when strange natural phenomena appear, we may marvel at them but should not be frightened because they appear in all ages, good or bad, and there is little mutual influence between them and human affairs.

But why does it rain after a ritual praying for rain is performed? He said that there is no explanation, and pointed out that it also rains when no one prays for it. Why do people always consult their divining devices before making important decisions? Well, Xunzi said, those who are wise know that it is just a formality which makes the decision seem more careful. In short, he said, nature follows its own course, which will not change for people. And though nature has an effect on human affairs, the effect is not absolute; though people cannot make nature grant their wishes, they can try to limit its influence – if people are diligent in their work and economical in their expenditures, Heaven cannot make them poor; if they always have enough nourishment and exercise regularly, Heaven cannot make them ill. Therefore, people should try to do what they can and should not dream about something that might fall from Heaven. From this position, Xunzi went so far as to suggest *zhi-tian* (制天 controlling Heaven), namely, learning its rules and applying them to one's advantage, and he pointed out that an enlightened gentleman cultivates his own capability but does not look up to what is outside of him; an ignorant, petty man leaves his own strength undeveloped and expects what he might receive from Heaven and, as a result, the gentleman progresses every day, while the petty man regresses every day.

But there is a problem. Why is the outcome of human efforts so uncertain? Why did Confucius suffer hunger and humiliation, and some famous persons of great virtue and achievements meet violent deaths at the hands of depraved scoundrels? Xunzi could not answer these questions. Like Confucius, he took the way out of using "fate". In his words: "Whether or not a person is appreciated is decided by his circumstances; whether he is to live or die at a particular time is determined by Fate." This statement smells of fatalism. Here, we sense a difference between him and Confucius. But, because of his great emphasis on human efforts, the difference is nominal.

If, however, people are generally capable of controlling their own lives and environment to a large degree, why didn't individuals live by themselves happily as Zhuangzi said that they would? Why did they get involved in one another's affairs and make such a mess of the world? This led Xunzi to create a theory about innate human nature and artificial human behaviour.

(B) Human nature

(1) It is inborn and universal

Practically all ancient Chinese thinkers talked about *xing* (性 nature). Confucius said humans have similar natures; Mencius said they have a common nature which is good; both used the term to mean something innate to humans but malleable. Xunzi was more specific. His *xing* (or *qing* 情 or *qing xing* 情性) refers only to some inborn likes and dislikes which are universal and unchangeable. In his words, "the nature of a thousand persons or ten thousand persons and that of a single person is the same"." This "nature" is innate, not something a person can get through learning or self-cultivation. It is like the ability of the eye to see, the ear to hear, the mouth to taste. It is common to everybody, whether he is a Yu 禹 [founder of the Xia Dynasty] or a Jie 桀 [last ruler of the Xia]: he desires to eat when hungry, to be warm when cold, to rest when toiling.

The trouble with human desires is that they are insatiable. Xunzi pointed out that people all want meat, clothing, carriages, and countless other things in greater and greater quantity and better and better quality, and, above all, as much power as an emperor has.

(2) It is "bad"

Having an infinity of desires clashes with a fact of living: freely available resources for the satisfaction of such desires are finite, and human ability to create such resources is limited. (Xunzi told us to look at an ordinary individual – his strength is not equal to that of an ox and his speed is not equal to that of a horse.) When there are more people than the things they desire, there cannot but be competition and strife; and, when there is competition and strife, courtesy and principles of rightness may be in jeopardy.

But, if the undesirable consequences were produced by competition and strife, and competition and strife were unavoidable because of a mismatch between supply and demand, human nature is merely self-oriented or selfish. Selfishness is, of course, often equated with badness but Xunzi apparently thought human nature is worse than selfish. He pointed out that certain desires inevitably lead to egregious behaviour: for instance, in seeking material gain, greed and rapaciousness will result. For this reason, he said, "If human nature is left to itself, men will contend and grab, violate the right guidelines and cause disorder." Further, he said (attributing the words to Shun) "After a man has a wife and children, his filial piety towards his parents diminishes . . . when he has obtained titles and positions, his loyalty towards his ruler diminishes." So human nature is "ugly".

These two statements are problematic. The first is sweeping, making a possible connection between two events inevitable. The second, finding humans ungrateful and treacherous under fortunate circumstances, is rather counterintuitive and not supported by evidence. Attributing the observation to Shun, one of the sage kings, was only an arbitrary appeal to authority. Thus, Xunzi's allegation, "Human nature is evil", is conjectural and presumptive, and can be taken only as a postulate for his theory.

If human nature is evil, however "evil" is defined, why do we see around us behaviour, such as submission and other more serious forms of sacrifice of one's own interests for the benefit for others, which cannot be characterised as evil but is commonly regarded as "virtuous"? Xunzi, like Mencius, believed that any behaviour which is contrary to human nature is caused by external forces but, unlike Mencius, he thought that virtue, not evil, is forced upon people from without. He pointed out that, following human nature, a person will want to eat when he is hungry but, in the presence of his seniors, he dares not rush ahead of them to reach food; he yields to them. This person, in Xunzi's view, is acting against human nature which would drive him to grab the food in total disregard of the same need of everyone else. He acts virtuously because a norm requires him to do so, and he has either internalised the norm or is compelled by his fear of the punishment prescribed for its violation. To reinforce his theory, Xunzi made two long statements refuting Mencius's postulate.

In essence he argued, firstly, Mencius did not prove that human nature is good, and, secondly, the fact that society needs laws, punishments, rulers and government proves his view that human nature is evil. The first point is valid but the second one could be challenged by Laozi and Zhuangzi, arguing that laws, punishments, and so on are the very artefacts which caused human strife. Of course, their theory applies to a society where people are few and natural resources are abundant and readily available, circumstances that did not exist in Xunzi's time. Nevertheless, is it true that, in every case of scarcity, there will always be strife but are laws, punishments and so on the only answer to the problem? Xunzi's assertion is not totally convincing.

(3) Its expression can be changed

After refuting Mencius's theory, Xunzi asserted that people's virtuous behaviour was *wei* (僞 [a character composed of two parts: *ren* 人 – human, and *wei* 為 – do] man-made outward appearance). He said, "*Xing* is what I cannot do (*wei* 為) anything about but it can be transformed (*hua* 化); *qing* is not what I possess but I can do something to it." It sounds puzzling but there is a likely explanation. While Xunzi often used *xing* and *qing* interchangeably, meaning nature, here he was using *xing* to mean nature and *qing* to mean the outward expression of nature. Thus, while nothing can be done to nature, something can be done to affect its outward appearance: for instance, a hungry man cannot be made not to want food but he can try to reduce the amount of food he consumes or change the manner in which he gets it in the presence of others. If he continues the practice, it becomes a habit and his behaviour becomes different from that of one who does not so practise. When many practices are *ji* (積 accumulated), one's *qing* is formed. If the practices are virtuous, one becomes a virtuous person. Thus, virtue is something acquired; it is different from the innate human nature; it is something added on to it, like a coat of paint, and, if it is thick enough, the nature, though not altered, will be covered and appears in a different form – thus "transformed".

(2) It can be made good

People are born evil but Xunzi wanted them to become virtuous. What is "virtue"? He did not define it. He only hinted that virtuous behaviours are those in accordance with the principles of rites, rightness, law and other appropriate measures. People will be good if they observe those principles and measures. And he said that those principles and measures can be known by every ordinary person and that such a person has the ability to know them. Therefore, every person has the potential to follow these principles and become as good as a Yu, the sage king who tamed the great flood and made life liveable for all. The fact that not everyone is a Yu does not invalidate this argument. It is because not everyone has tried hard enough to realise his potential.

Thus, Xunzi and Mencius shared the view that human nature can be made to appear good or bad. Why did they differ on the original character of "human nature"? It is fair to say that Mencius wanted to give the individual freedom and dignity and a justification for standing up against the increasingly oppressive government authorities; Xunzi, on the other hand, wanted individuals to be more restrained and society better organised and make people, both in and out of government, better educated and know right from wrong, and prevent government from overreaching itself.

(C) Need of social organisation

Having resolved the conceptual problem about *xing* and *wei*, Xunzi went on to construct his theory about social organisation, government authorities, and norms. First, about the need of social organisation, he stated that an individual has limited physical and intellectual capacity but many needs and desires, and is incapable of solving his problems entirely by himself; he has to live in *qun* (群 group) where there is division of labour and co-operation. For this purpose, people have to be "classified", professionally, as farmers, merchants, craftsmen, scholars, and so on, each devoting to a special task which can mesh with others to produce the optimum amount of goods and services. When these steps are taken organised society is formed. Without social organisation, people will not be able to meet their needs and will inevitably fight one another to seize what is available. The strong will exploit the weak, the majority oppress the minority, and there will be robbery, mayhem, war, revolts and general disorder in which peaceful existence is impossible. This is easy to see and had been discussed by Mencius. Xunzi elaborated on it and offered his own explanation as to why people need social organisation and how it was created and maintained. According to him, unlike other animals, humans formed social organisation because of their ability to *qun* (群 join together) in a group for common interests and to *fen* (分 divide) into smaller ones for different tasks. But this is a fine point. More significantly, he differed from Mencius on how social organisation was actually formed. Mencius implied that it happened naturally; Xunzi maintained that it was accomplished under the direction of sages. This is obviously because Mencius had faith in the goodness of human nature but Xunzi believed it is bad and therefore the ordinary people can not do much without guidance from someone wiser and more just than they are. With such guidance, the result is remarkable. In his words, "If the division is in accordance with principles of rightness there will be harmony. Where there is harmony there is unity. When men are united they have great strength. With strength they are strong and they can dominate other things."

(D) Need of government authority

While it may not be absolutely necessary for people to be guided by a sage to form social organisation, it certainly cannot be maintained for long without some persons making division of labour and co-operation work smoothly. Plans have to be made to co-ordinate the separate undertakings; orders have to be issued and obeyed. But Xunzi pointed out that "two persons of equal status cannot serve or employ each other", therefore, he said, in addition to professional groups, people have to be stratified into two political levels – the rulers above and the ruled below. There is, of course, nothing new in this idea but he added something unusual, saying that, when this political order was not established, there was disorder and "hating disorder, the ancient sages established principles of rites and principles of rightness to separate the people, dividing them into different classes of the poor and the rich, the privileged and the humble, and thus enabling some to supervise the others" and he claimed that this is "the most fundamental arrangement for the care of the world". It may sound a bit odd that the poor are to serve the rich but, of course generally, the rich are more closely associated with political power than the poor are.

A more important point is that, after saying how the political levels are established, Xunzi immediately emphasised that this "stratification" is not to be cast in stone. Rather, in his words, "If a descendant of a king, a feudal lord, or an official cannot follow the rules of propriety and principles of rightness, he is to be relegated to the class of commoners; if a descendant of a commoner has acquired learning, developed a good character, and is able to observe the rules of propriety and principles of rightness, he is to be elevated to the class of officials." To put it simply, there should be social mobility and meritocracy. At a time when many government positions were hereditary, Xunzi's argument was revolutionary.

(E) Need of social norms

How are social authorities to do their work? First, they are to establish social norms. Norms, according to Xunzi, are rules used by the authorities for two purposes – *ding-fen* (定分 to determine positions) and *zhi-zheng* (止爭 to stop strife). The latter is easy to understand; the former needs some explanation. Most classical thinkers maintained that, in an organised society, every person should be assigned a specific position. In that position he is given certain responsibilities and, when they are successfully met, he is allowed certain benefits. The word *fen* (份, more accurately in this context) is thus used to connote the ideas of a "position", a responsibility, and a share of the benefits produced by society. The importance of establishing *fen* was generally recognised. It was implied in Confucius's idea of "rectification of names" and in his famous remark, "a ruler should be a ruler, a subject a subject, a father a father, and a son a son". Gongsun Yang illustrated it by pointing out that, when a rabbit is in the wilderness, everyone competes to catch it but one would not look at the hundreds of rabbits in a market if one does not intend to buy any. Xunzi emphasised that it was for the purpose of determining a person's *fen* and thereby restraining his unlimited desires that the sages created the norms – rites and principles of rightness.

A careful reading of *Xunzi* shows that, when he said that a person can receive a "share" of benefits – goods and services for his physical needs and perhaps some honours – from society, Xunzi did not mean that a person can receive something unconditionally. It depends on what is available and how much the person has contributed to society. Then what happens to a person who is incapable of making a contribution? Xunzi did not have a direct answer but, as we shall see, he emphasised that the ruler should care for all his people like infants. Therefore, in other words, no one has a "right" to claim any benefit from society but society has a "responsibility" to provide the necessary care for the needy.

(F) To learn the norms

(1) Need of education

If norms are created by sages, they cannot, as Mencius alleged, be found in human hearts; they have to be learned. Pessimistic about human nature but optimistic about the malleability of its appearance, Xunzi constructed an elaborate theory of education. First of all, he pointed out the necessity because humans are not only by nature evil, they are born petty, capable of seeing only the requirement for gratifying his basic physical needs but not much beyond that. Even in the case of a person with considerable potential, it can only be realised with the help of outside influence and, if the result is to be good, the influence has to be good – good teachers, good norms and good friends. If left alone, Xunzi said, the intelligent will become thieves; the brave will become thugs; the resourceful will cause disorder; those who are discriminatory will become eccentric; those who like to debate will become contentious.

(2) Objectives

Therefore, the general objective of education is to *hua xing* (化性 transform people's "nature") and *qi wei* (起偽 create artificial behaviour, or "pretence"); in other words, to change the appearance of human nature for good. Generally, it is to make people know the right Way; in Xunzi's words, it is to help them "know what is right as right and what is wrong as wrong". More specifically, he said, the initial purpose is to make a man a cultivated gentleman, and the final goal is to help him become a sage. Such is the faith he had in education!

(3) Methods

How is this great power of education to be exercised? Xunzi said a person's conduct is conditioned by his environment; thus he who lives in a place will become a man of that place, speaking its dialect and following its customs. But to become an enlightened gentleman there is a more specific way, which, according to Xunzi, is to start with reciting the Classics and to finish with practising rites. This shows his belief in the value of civilisation created by great men of the past and recorded in the such works as *The Book of Historical Documents* and *The Book of Odes*, and his emphasis on the rules of elegant behaviour formulated on the bases of custom, reason, ethics, practicality and propriety. In other words, Xunzi wanted a person aspiring to be a good man first to learn the principles of proper conduct and then act accordingly.

This process is not easy. It is not enough for a person to memorise the texts of the Classics; he has to "find their central themes and ponder on related problems to achieve a general understanding, and to test it by placing himself in the situation of the persons encountering certain problems". And, most important of all, he has to have determination and perseverance and make continuous efforts to complete his education. Xunzi warned against the wish of covering a big distance by a single jump. Instead, he advised taking one small step after another, as an old horse does, slowly but relentlessly, and eventually arriving at a far-away destination. Only by this method can a man gain great knowledge and achieve his high and distant objectives. Here is a good admonition from Xunzi: "He who has no unwavering determination will have no conspicuous achievements; he who does no patient preparation will have no shining success."

Needless to say, the study of the Classics can be more effective with the help of a teacher who can help explain the subtle points, make clear the important themes, provoke further questions and thinking, and finally guide students to the Way. In Xunzi's words, "With a wise teacher, one could hear about the way of Yao, Shun, Yu and Tang." Equally important, a good teacher can steer students out of harm's way, and, in Xunzi's words, "make the intelligent quickly knowledgeable, the brave awesome, the talented successful, the discriminating find truth, the debate-loving arrive at correct conclusions". More generally, a good teacher will help men to break out of the pettiness they are born with, so that they can see the high objectives human life should pursue. Besides good teachers, a man should have good friends. Xunzi pointed out that grass growing among shafts of hemp plants becomes straight without support; with friends of good character, a person can learn the acts of loyalty, faithfulness, respect and modesty. Consequently, a man with good teachers and friends will "become increasingly humane and righteous every day without knowing it because the change is gradual, subtle and accumulative".

(4) Result

The result of education is the production of better men. Because Xunzi believed that good society and government begin with good men, he spent a great deal of space in his book to spelling out what a good man is. According to him, having learned the norms and practised rites, a man will become a *jun-zi* (君子 gentleman). A gentleman is different from ordinary people in many ways. Most noticeably he is enlightened. Though he does not know the details of everything others know, he is able to grasp the essence of all things and he understands the rules of their development. He knows right from wrong and always strives to do what is right. He has high objectives for himself and for society and is determined to reach them. He is extremely demanding of himself and is content while following the Way. He shies from seeking personal gain and will not be distracted by wealth and power, nor will he be depressed by poverty and misfortune because, in comparison with the virtues he keeps within himself, everything else is of less value. He avoids harm but would willingly die for principles of rightness. In interacting with others, he is considerate, loyal, benevolent, just, modest, submissive, courteous, sincere and trustworthy, and therefore anywhere he goes, he is well received and respected, even by the barbarians. He praises the virtues and good deeds of others but never flatters. He may criticise others but never in a way that is unjust and petty. He takes the sages as his model and aspires for good achievements but never self-aggrandisement. He may softly bend as circumstances require but never submits. He can be firm and forceful but never insolent and overbearing. In short, he is a product of what the best education can help achieve. As such, he would receive from Xunzi the label *da-ren* (大人 great man) or *cheng-ren* (成人 accomplished man).

But, of course, not every educated person deserves these labels. Xunzi realised that there were some scholars who had learned the Classics only superficially and some others who had learned them well but were unable to apply their principles under varying circumstances. Because the Classics were used as teaching materials mostly by Ruists, with Confucius as their model, Xunzi called the first type *su-ru* (俗儒 vulgar Ruists) and the second type *ya-ru* (雅儒 refined Ruists). In contrast to what he called *da-ru* (大儒 great Ruists) who are *da ren*, these two types are on lower levels. What society and government need are, of course, the great Ruists.

(G) To make a better world

(1) Objectives and general operating principles

The objective of education is to produce many superior men who, with transformed expression of nature and knowledge of the Way, can help make the world better. What will a better world be like? In *Xunzi*, many passages allude to this question. A particularly interesting one reports Xunzi's impression of the state of Qin. He generously praised what he observed on a visit: the people and the officials devoted to their jobs and engaging in no activities beyond their callings; and the administration was efficient, making decisions on various government businesses quickly and calmly. All these were like what was expected of a state at a time in the past where everything was in good order. And yet he said, in comparison with great kingdoms of earlier times, the state of Qin fell short because it did not have great Ruists.

What was a great kingdom of the past like and what can a great Ruist do to bring about such a utopia? Xunzi's answer to the first question appears in many chapters of his work. To put it succinctly, he insisted that a great kingdom is not only orderly and efficient, rich and strong. In addition, it is harmonious, it has pleasing customs and fine culture, and its people are at ease and happy. To achieve these objectives, Xunzi had a long list of specific things for a great Ruist to do. They will be discussed later. But here are some general operating principles to guide a state to greatness. First its authorities should focus on the broad, long-term interests, as the Duke of Zhou 周公 did – after his brother King Wu 武王 died, he set aside his nephew the young King Cheng 成王, assumed the throne, suppressed rebellions and ruled for a long period of time before returning the government to King Cheng, and he thus succeeded in preserving the Zhou Dynasty and saving the people from chaos and suffering. This, Xunzi said, was *da-ru zhi xiao* (大儒之效 the achievements of a great Ruist).

In less challenging cases, the objective of the government should be to keep order and help create prosperity. Basically, the ruler needs to care for his subjects and be benevolent to them – to enable them to support themselves and not to impede their effort by numerous burdens, including badly timed conscription and heavy taxes. He is to make laws just and appoint honest and efficient officials to administer the laws. The ancient sage kings did all these and won the loyalty of their people.

Though rather simple, these basic principles were often ignored by rulers of later times. Many of them neglected their primary responsibilities and tried to solicit short-term praise from the people by providing them with some food and comfort in time of need. It was a misunderstanding of the meaning of benevolence. It was, in Xunzi's view, *tou-dao* (偷道 the way of a thief) to steal a temporary reprieve. This practice cannot be regular because it will make the state poor. At the other extreme, there were those rulers who employed the people at the wrong time and forced them to overwork, disregarding their sufferings. This way was characterised as *pian-dao* (偏道 deviant way). Both ways lead to serious problems.

Therefore, good governance begins with the ruler. When asked how to govern a state, Xunzi said it is up to the ruler. For, in his words, "The ruler is like a sundial and the subjects the shadow it produces . . . When King Zhuang of Chu 楚莊王 loved slender waists, there were hungry men in his court." In other words, the people will follow their ruler. If he wants them to behave in a certain way, he should give them a direction and, better still, make himself a model for them to follow.

(2) Concrete measures

(A) Staff government with good people

Who can be a good ruler? Xunzi listed a few essential qualities. First of all he should be one who can "gather people together". He can do this if he is good at caring for them, at establishing rules and institutions to govern them, at assigning various government positions to proper persons, and at making the system of social classes and political stratifications function well with appropriate rewards and punishments. He does not have to have skills in many trades but must be knowledgeable of the Way and capable of finding truth and solutions to social problems. With this knowledge, he can manage the various government affairs. In another passage, Xunzi said a great Ruist could be a good ruler because he will establish high objectives and maintain proper conduct; he will make sure that there will be correct laws and policies; he will make officials faithful and people mutually helpful; he will not do any unethical act nor kill any innocent man in order to get the empire; his rightness is trusted by men everywhere, and they respond to him like echoes. Thus, in the final analysis, to be a good ruler is first of all to be a good man. So, on another occasion when someone asked about how to govern a state, Xunzi replied that he had heard how the ruler is to cultivate himself but not about how to govern a state.

Even a good ruler cannot manage all government affairs alone. He needs helpers, and it is his responsibility to select them with the utmost care. Xunzi suggested that a candidate should first be given some general tests to see whether he can follow rites with ease, respond to changing circumstances properly, avoid frivolity in leisure and comfort, and hold his position without being distracted by sex, power, anger and danger. Having passed such tests and been appointed to a government post, he is to be assessed according to his performance. Each office-holder has a set of responsibilities. For instance, the Minister of Justice is to "suppress the unprincipled, restrain the overbearing, guard against the wicked and punish the evildoers by imposing upon them the five penalties"; the Chief Minister is "to establish policies, correct laws, oversee government programmes, check on the office-holders regularly, discipline them when they make mistakes and give them appropriate rewards so that they will be diligent and the people will not be lazy".

Who are the candidates? At Xunzi's time, educated men of various schools vied for government offices. Some rulers had doubts about the ability of the Ruists. Xunzi was upset by this view and devoted a lengthy chapter to argue against it. According to him, a good Ruist is a person who knows well the principles of government; therefore, he will do all the right things to make his state orderly and prosperous, and much better. He is a *ren shi* (人師 teacher of man), a model for all people. Confucius was such a person. According to Xunzi, when the great master lived in Que as a commoner, the people who engaged in hunting and finishing together would pool the catch and let those who had living parents take more than their shares. When he was about to take the office of the Minister of Justice of the state of Lu, Shen You 沈猶, a shepherd, dared not make his sheep drink water in the morning to add weight before he was to sell them; Gong Shen 公慎 divorced his adulterous wife; the debauched Shen Kui 慎潰 escaped beyond the borders; and the traders of cattle in the state would no longer dare to post false prices. That was how a great Ruist can change people for the good even before taking government office. Needless to say, his influence will much greater when he is in government, either as an official or as the ruler. More than Confucius accomplished, Duke Zhou achieved the greatest possible success of a Ruist. We have seen how Xunzi praised the duke's achievements. It is mainly because he did something that an ordinary person would not do – temporarily take over the throne and save the newly established Zhou Dynasty. That was, Xunzi said, the legacy of a *da ru*.

In short, Xunzi emphasised that government posts, including that of the ruler, ought to be given to men of virtue and ability. Many intellectuals advocated the same but he was more explicit in exalting a system dominated by the Ruists.

(B) Choose and apply good norms

(i) Hierarchy of norms

Mencius said that it is not enough for those in government to have good intention; they have to apply norms. Norms are many and, according to him and Confucius, they are of different importance, forming a hierarchy. At the top are the moral principles which can be found in one's heart and in human relations which are natural, comprehensive and comprehensible. Law is at the bottom. As the product of political authorities used to address specific problems, law is narrow in scope, often arbitrary and not readily understandable. Between are rites and customs, the former created by sages for proper and elegant behaviour; the latter formulated by people through practice. In each category, there are several levels; some are more significant than others. Xunzi attributed to Confucius a statement saying that there are higher and lower norms and that a ruler who observes both the high and the low norms is a superior one; one who observes the high but not the lower norms is a medium one; and one who observes only the lower norms is unworthy. Obviously, Xunzi shared this view and, as we shall see, he also endorsed the other points about norms made by Confucius and Mencius.

(ii) Application of norms

First, according to Xunzi, there was an abundance of norms, some established by *xian-wang* (先王 early sage kings), some by *hou-wang* (後王 later sage kings). By "early sage kings" he probably meant Yao, Shun, Yu and Tang; by "later sage kings" he evidently meant the founders of the Zhou Dynasty. The two sets of norms were basically in agreement but might vary in some minor points. Xunzi advised people to observe those of the later time because they were more recent and thus their contents were clearer.

Second, Xunzi addressed the problem of actual, proper observance of norms. He used filial piety and political loyalty as examples because, apparently, how to be filial and loyal often puzzled people. To illustrate this, Xunzi told a story: Duke Ai of Lu 魯哀公 asked Confucius, "If one obeys his father, is he a filial son? If one obeys his ruler is he a loyal subject?" Three times the question was raised but not answered. Then Confucius told Zigong 子貢, a disciple, about this encounter, and Zigong said the answers should obviously positive. That was apparently the common understanding of most people. But Confucius thought differently, saying a person had to scrutinise carefully what is to be obeyed.

What is to be obeyed? According to Xunzi, to obey the orders of one's father or one's superior is only *xiao-xing* (小行 behaviour of small significance); one should instead obey principles of rightness and the Way, that is *da-xing* (大行 behaviour of great significance). Therefore his commandment: "To follow the Way but not one's superior and to obey principles of rightness but not one's father."

Specifically, he warned that, under three circumstances, a filial son should not obey the orders of his father: if obedience would leave them in danger; if obedience would bring them disgrace; and if obedience would make him appear bestial. Thus, after receiving an order from his father, a person has to ponder its possible results. In a case where a son could obey but disobeys, he is not filial; in a case where a son should not obey but obeys, he is not filial. A son who knows the distinction between when he ought or ought not to obey, and is capable of carefully keeping the distinction when he decides on his action, can be called truly filial. Xunzi did not spell out the situations in which a subject should or should not obey the order of the ruler. But the same principle should apply.

Then Xunzi went a step further. When a person is in a situation where he ought not to obey his father or the ruler, he should not just disobey but should argue against the order. In the story mentioned above, Xunzi said Confucius told Zigong that, if a state had four officials who would argue with their ruler, its territories would not be encroached upon and the temples of its patron gods would not be desecrated; if a feudal family had two officers who would argue with their master, its ancestral shrine would not be destroyed; if a father has a son who would argue with him, he would not fall into impropriety. Hence, if one simply obeys one's father, he cannot be considered filial; if a subject simply obeys his ruler, he cannot be considered loyal.

Thus a person always has to "scrutinise" the circumstances and then determine how properly to implement a norm. This is no mean feat, especially when some higher principles are involved because they are usually general and abstract and not quite as simple as they seem. Therefore, when confronted with such choices, ordinary people are often lost, and, when told about difficult decisions made by "great men" such as Shun and Confucius, they were, as Mencius pointed out, befuddled, incapable of understanding the reasons. Confucius and all Ruists knew this and hence they emphasised rites. Xunzi took the same position, which will be discussed later.

(iii) Application of law

Law is different. It is more specific and so its application should be easy. Xunzi said, "Where there is a law, act accordingly." But, in fact, it is not that simple. To begin with, while some cases may fall squarely within the scope of a law, many may have some aspects which were not foreseen by the law-makers and therefore the law cannot be automatically applied. Second, in many other cases, no law has ever been enacted or there may be several conflicting laws and none strictly fits the circumstance. These problems are common but solutions may vary. In theory, the inadequacy of law could be addressed by making more laws but there are always situations that are not foreseen. If a post hoc law is made and applied retroactively, it would be a most egregious offence against principles of rightness. This is why, where no clearly applicable law is available, most legal systems require judges to resort to custom and jurisprudential principles in civil cases, and allow them to abstain from action in criminal cases. In traditional China, judicial authorities were obliged to act on all cases brought before them. What should they do? Xunzi said that they should *yi lei ju* (以類舉 to place a case in a category of similar one and then decide). Why? He said that some things, which were different in some details, may have the same roots, they can therefore be considered to be of the same type. Human conduct can also be so categorised. Thus, a law made for one case may be applicable to another. But this cannot be done mechanically. A judge must carefully study the legislative background to determine why a law was adopted, what its immediate objective is, and what effects it may have on society in the long run. He called this investigation *yi* (議 to deliberate) the *yi* (義 the true meaning, or the spirit, and the ramifications) of a law. After this investigation and a careful examination of the facts of the case at hand, the judge will be able to decide whether the law can be applied analogically. This process is not easy for a judge but it is necessary. In Xunzi's words, a judge who knows the spirit of law will be able to handle all cases; a judge who knows only the letter of the law will inevitably be at loss when he encounters a case not clearly covered by an existing law.

Xunzi was not the first person who recognised the problem and suggested a solution. Both have been mentioned in *The Book of Historical Documents*.[3] Xunzi's recommendation was generally accepted and became a rule known as *bi-fu yuan-yin* (比附援引 to compare and apply by analogy) incorporated into criminal codes of later periods.[4] But this practice leads to another problem – the "spirit of law" is nebulous and therefore can be interpreted in different ways, making the result of a trial uncertain – a judge may come to different conclusions in similar cases and different judges may decide the same case differently. The unpredictable outcomes will be highly injurious to the judicial system. Though not difficult to see, this problem was not addressed by Xunzi.

Besides honest differences, judges could misuse law because of prejudice or evil intention. Thus, after saying that the scale, the peck, the bushel and other instruments of measurement, which are supposedly to ensure fairness and exactness, can be abused, Xunzi pointed out that law is also a mere instrument and, by itself, not "the source of order", but can also be misused or abused. Whether it can be used to achieve principles of rightness depends on the person who uses it. Therefore humans are the source of order. When the person using law is just, law can bring justice; when he is dishonest, law can become a tool for injustice. In Xunzi's words, "when the source is clean the water downstream will be clean; when the source is dirty, the water downstream will be dirty".

This logic led Xunzi to support the rule of the good person and reject the rule of law in the sense that it be applied mechanically in all circumstances. He argued that the laws of the ancient sage kings continued to exist through the later periods but the descendants of those kings did not continue to be rulers. The simple reason is that the later rulers did not use law properly. "Thus," he famously said, "laws cannot stand by themselves and precedents cannot automatically govern. When there is the right man, they will be properly used; when the right man is gone, they will fall into disuse." But Xunzi was not simply dismissive of law; he just emphasised its limits; hence his axiom: "The law is the starting point of good government; the ruler is the fountainhead of law. If there is a good ruler, the law may be simple yet it will be sufficient; if there is not a good ruler, the law may be comprehensive yet, when the circumstances change, there will be no proper action taken and the result will be chaos." As a proof, he pointed out that there had been disorder under good laws but there had never been disorder under a good ruler – from antiquity to his time that was unheard of. Indeed, his observation has been verified by Chinese history after his time as well.

(iv) Rites as the norm of choice

Thus, neither high principles nor law is easy to apply. It was undoubtedly for the purpose of solving this problem that another set of norms was created. Known as *li* (禮 rites), they were rules for proper and refined behaviour initially designed for the upper classes from the rulers down to the *shi* (士 lowest officers). According to *Li-ji* (禮記 *Notes on Rites*), some of them were created by ancient sages but most others had their basis in custom, human feelings, common sense, and reason.

As mentioned earlier, Xunzi thought rites necessary because people have limitless desires but the means to satisfy them are finite. This fact leads to competition, strife and disorder. Hating disorder, the ancient sage kings established rites as guidelines for people to follow a safer course in their search for the satisfaction of their desires. Thus, rites are also likened to water-level markers for people to avoid danger. Xunzi hailed rites as "the ultimate standards" for human conduct and assigned extraordinary importance to them, saying that, in personal life, rites guide people to live correctly and behave elegantly; in society, rites prescribe how people of different classes are to live and behave, to stay in their right places and interact with one another amicably; and that, in a country, rites lead to good governance and ensure peace and prosperity. Discarding rites, people will bring misfortune and calamity upon themselves, on society, and on the country.

Why were rites given so much weight by Xunzi (and other Ruists)? We can see that rites are more concrete than moral principles and less limited and rigid than law, and that, while being specific rules for practically every conduct, rites allow reasonable flexibility under some circumstances, and therefore are easier to observe than moral principles as well as the law. Xunzi did not explicitly make this argument. Instead, he reiterated that there are high principles to govern people which are the *shu-yao* (樞要 essence) of rites and law but rites are the *da-fen* (大分 guideline) of law and the *gang-ji* (綱紀 governing rule) of the precedents. In other words, rites are the middle road between high principles and law and are thus preferable.

There are some problems with Xunzi's position. First, unlike the authors of *Li-ji*, who recognised multiple origins of rites, he insisted that rites were created by ancient sage kings. But, apparently, those wise men did not write down the details of their creation,[5] so that, when they were gone, its content could become unclear. At Confucius's time, many people were ignorant about what a rite for a particular occasion should be. Another problem is that the sage kings apparently did not explain why a rite should be in a particular form. That was why Mozi criticised the forms of certain rites, particularly those for funerals and burials, as meaningless. Xunzi had to admit that the rites of worshipping ancestors, for instance, were so rich with ceremony that only a sage could understand why.

As time passed, and the social conditions changed, the problems were compounded. Certain rites became clearly outdated and were actually ignored. As a type of norm, rites had to evolve, and Xunzi was aware of this necessity. But, on what bases should rites change? He said, "Rites should have their bases in people's hearts. Therefore, a rule that is not recorded in *li-jing* (禮經 classic works about rites),[6] but is based in people's hearts can be a rule of rites." We remember that Mencius stated that people's "five hearts" are the *source* of norms because human nature (their "hearts") is good. But Xunzi said human nature is bad. How can rites as norms be based on it? A closer look shows that he did not say rites should come from human "hearts" but only should be *ben* (本 based on) them. Since norms are to correct people's "natural" behaviour, they have to be "based" on, or take into consideration, people's bad "heart" (desires and feelings). Then there is another question: if rites were created only by sage kings, who in their absence is to enable them to evolve? If they are the government authorities, a new rite will be just a law in another name. If ordinary people can take into consideration bad human nature and make the change, rites could be varied from person to person. Because of these problems, Xunzi's argument for rites to be the norm of choice is not quite convincing.

(c) Enforcement of norms

(i) Use of rewards and punishments

Norms, especially artificial ones, cannot be effective automatically. They have to be enforced. A common way to enforce norms is by giving rewards and inflicting punishments. Xunzi explored the objectives of reward and punishment, and the problem of how to make them effective. In principle, he said, rewards and punishments are to demonstrate the appreciation of good and the disapproval of evil. In practice, rewards are to encourage meritorious conduct and punishments to chastise the guilty and deter crime. For these purposes, reward and punishment should only be given to those who deserve them, and it should be made certain that the result is inevitable. When the truly worthy and meritorious are certain to be rewarded and the truly evil and guilty certain to be punished, the people will clearly understand that "if they do good at home they will be rewarded in the court; if they do evil in secret they will be punished in public". This is what Xunzi called *wang-zhe zhi lun* (王者之論 principles of the true king).

Then he addressed the more difficult question about the relationship between crime and punishment. We remember that Gongsun Yang advocated severe punishment for minor offences. Xunzi objected strongly, arguing that punishments and offences should match, in his word *dang* (當 corresponding in kind and fitting in degree) – a murderer should die an whoever physically injures another, should suffer corporal punishment. The origin of this idea, he said, is not known but its result is clear: "when punishment fits the crime, it is a deterrent, when it does not, it is despised".

By Xunzi's time, punishments were generally severe. As a reaction, there was a popular saying that, in ancient times when there was good government, punishments were light – there were no real corporal punishments but only symbolic ones: for instance: the punishment of tattooing was actually carried out in the form of covering the face with black cloth or paint. This was recorded in *The Book of Historical Documents*.[7] But Xunzi said it was wrong. As he saw it, if there was truly good government, there would be no criminals, hence no need even for symbolic punishments. If some people did commit crimes and were given symbolic punishments, the result would be that murderers were not to die, and a man who injured another was not to suffer. When the crime is very serious, but the punishment rather light, the common people will have no fear, and the consequences will be very grave indeed.

While recognising the usefulness of punishment Xunzi, realised that it can be misused and, being a Ruist, he maintained that when, unfortunately, punishment is mistakenly used, it is better to err on the side of leniency. It is less egregious to release a guilty person than to harm an innocent one.

Xunzi said less about reward, except emphasising that it should not be unwarranted because unwarranted reward benefits the undeserving, petty person. Generally, it, like punishment, should be proportionate, though disproportionate reward is less harmful. In his words, "If unfortunately there is excess, let it be unwarranted reward rather than indiscriminate punishment. Rather than harm the good it is less evil to benefit the undeserving."

(ii) Use of compassion and education

Thus, Xunzi's faith in the effectiveness of rewards and punishments as a means of enforcing norms is limited. According to him, "It is the way with all men that, if they do something only for the sake of winning rewards and benefits, then, the moment they see that the undertaking may end unprofitably or in danger, they will abandon it. Therefore, rewards and punishments, force and fraudulent schemes, are not enough to make men put forth their full efforts or risk their lives for the state. They are *yong-tu yu-mai zhi dao* (傭徒粥賣之道 the way to deal with hired labourers and traders) but not the way to unify the people or bring glory to the nation."

Instead, Xunzi said, the ruler should lead the people by virtuous action and good faith, guide them by making clear rites and the principles of rightness, employ the talented and honour the worthy among them to improve their morale, let the common people work in proper seasons and lighten their corvée duties so that they can have respite. In short, he should treat them like infants, nourish them, educate them and care for them. They will be transformed and ultimately be alike in their behaviour. He called this process *da-hua zhi-yi* (大化至一 becoming unified as one by grand transformation). If, after all this labour of love on the part of the authorities, there is a person who departs from the law, a less demanding set of norms, the community as a whole will turn against him. Then, and only then, can punishments be effectively applied and the people will learn to be right.

Xunzi told a story to illustrate this point: While Confucius was the Minister of Justice of the state of Lu, a father and a son sued each other. Confucius kept them in custody for three months without making a decision. The father asked to withdraw the suit, and Confucius released them both. Jisun 季孫, the ruling aristocrat of Lu, heard about this and was displeased, saying, "That old man cheated me. He told me that to govern a state one must exalt the virtue of filial piety. Now here is an opportunity to kill one person to warn others against impious behaviour, and he let it go." Upon hearing this complaint, Confucius sighed, saying, "Alas, after the ruler has misled the people, the officials kill them. Is this permissible? To judge people before educating them will result in killing many of the innocent. When an army is routed, the fleeing soldiers should not be executed; when the judicial system is not in order, the people should not be punished." Jisun was probably unmoved by this comment. Confucius's behaviour in this case must have contributed to his eventual dismissal as Minister of Justice.

Then there is another story in *Xunzi* saying that Confucius, just seven days in office as acting Chief Minister, ordered the execution of Shaozheng Mao 少正卯, a public person of great notoriety in the state of Lu. Neither previous warning nor actual trial was recorded. Confucius justified his abrupt action, pointing out that, with his words, this person was able to conceal truth and deceive the masses; with his strong will, he was able to resist pressure and have his way. "He was", Confucius concluded, "the most dangerous among the mean people, and therefore should be executed." Xunzi apparently approved, saying, in another passage, that evil men who initiate criminal offences and head criminal gangs could be punished "without advance warning".

Neither story was recorded in *Lun-Yu*. The first one is believable because Confucius was reluctant in adjudicating lawsuits; he preferred to let the parties settle their dispute in more peaceful and amicable ways. The second story first appeared in *Xunzi* and was embellished by writers of later times. The fact that no other work reported this story before *Xunzi*, which was written more than two hundred years after Confucius's death, raises questions about its veracity. More significantly, its lesson, that a person who knowingly violates a norm can be punished without first being warned and then properly tried, is fundamentally in conflict with Confucius's teaching and also conspicuously contradicts Xunzi's own theory that education must precede punishment. Thus, it is probable that the story was invented by some of Xunzi's disciples who were disgusted by the many sophists making paradoxical speeches which caused dissention among the people and disorder in society. These disciples wanted to condemn such sophistry. Among them, Han Fei, the most prominent Legalist theoretician, said so honestly. It was the less candid ones who inserted the story in *Xunzi*. Xunzi might also be troubled by the sophists; indeed, in numerous instances, he refuted their ideas, and there is a chapter "Zheng-lun" (正論 the correct arguments) in his book devoted to this purpose but he always presented his views straightforwardly, and would not put dubious words into other people's mouths, certainly not Confucius's.

(iii) Result

What will be the result after good norms were enforced by good men in government? To Xunzi it would be a utopia. As we have seen, the other classical thinkers had their ideal states in which there are peace and prosperity and, somehow, little for the government to do. Xunzi shared this vision and described his utopia as a state where rites are exalted, laws strictly obeyed, and the state is under steady guidance; where the worthy are honoured, the talented employed, and the people know what is right; where various opinions are openly studied and the people are not suspicious; where the virtuous are rewarded, the deceitful punished, and people do not neglect their duties; where the common people will improve their customs, the petty men reform their hearts, and the dishonest and devious will return to straightness and honesty; where great achievements will be made while the ruler seems to do little.

Thus, the common ideal of *wu wei er zhi* (無為而治 govern by inaction) could be achieved. Xunzi did not use that term but named this condition *zhi-dao da-xing* (至道大形 the grand manifestation of the supreme Way). It was the result of *zheng-jiao zhi ji* (政教之極 the ultimate consequence of good policy and education) which was produced by the elaborate process he called *da-hua zhi-yi* mentioned above. From these terms, we can appreciate his keen awareness of how difficult it is to realise his utopia, and his firm conviction that, with proper education and policy, it is nevertheless realisable.

(H) Social relationships

(1) Basic assumption

Xunzi believed that humans are alike – they are by nature all bad but can be transformed by education. According to him, everyone in the street could become as good as a Yu 禹. This implies that people are in principle equal and therefore should treat one another according to rules that ensure equality.

(2) General rule

In a society where there are many norms enforced by various authorities, how is an individual to conduct himself and interact with others, particularly those in different social positions? Xunzi said that where there is a clearly applicable law, one should obey it. But an ordinary person may not know all the laws, and then there are situations where there are no applicable laws. Xunzi replied that the person need not know all the laws, not even the details of rites; as long as he acts according to the *yi* (義 principles), underpinning the relationships between him and the other side, his behaviour should be acceptable. He did not spell out these principles, presuming that they were widely known. But, if that was not the case, he suggested a more general rule. It is only essential for a person to be sympathetic and respectful in his social relations. A person who acts in this way will be treated likewise by others, and honoured by the worthy and loved by the less able. This suggestion is in agreement with Confucius's dictums: "Do not do to others what you do not want them to do to you" and "Help others establish themselves as you want to establish yourself."

(3) Relationship between people of different social status

(A) Father and son

Apart from the general rule, Xunzi discussed in some detail the relationships between people of different social status. The first one he addressed is that between father and son. Like other Chinese thinkers of the past, he had little to say about a father's responsibility towards a son but more about a son's filial piety towards the father. But, like Mencius, Xunzi pointed out that filial piety does not mean blind obedience. As discussed above, he insisted that a son should follow what is right, not just the father's order.

(B) RULER AND OFFICIALS

If a son should not simply follow his father's orders, Xunzi argued, a subject should be even more careful about following the orders of the ruler. This is especially so in the case of high officials. They should be loyal and faithful but never obsequious and subservient, let alone flattering and actually promoting the interests of a misguided ruler. They should always think of the interests of the state and the people first and defend such interests against any wrong actions of the ruler. They should argue with him and, if their advice is rejected, resign from office or even commit suicide. But it would be better if they could unite and challenge the ruler, making him uncomfortable yet unable to refuse their advice, and thereby avoiding the dangerous results of his actions and restoring authority to the throne and peace in the state. In an extreme case, it is even permissible for them to reject the ruler's wrong orders, to take away his power, and to act in his place in order to save the state from disaster and the throne from humiliation, and eventually to achieve great success for the country. Xunzi called these four types of action, *jian* (諫 to admonish), *zheng* (爭 to argue), *fu* (輔 to rectify) and *fu* (拂 to defy), and hailed the officials who acted in these manners as *guo-jun zhi bao* (國君之寶 the ruler's treasure) whom a wise ruler should honour and respect.

But the measures for these great officials to take are drastic. Was Xunzi serious in advising them to struggle against their ruler over noble causes? Well, his advice was conditional. It was only for officials who were serving an average ruler. Serving a sage king, the officials should be reverential, modest, and prompt in following his orders; they should not initiate anything but simply obey him and make his will their own. To serve a tyrant is an entirely different task. According to Xunzi, officials should try to correct his mistakes but never challenge or defy him. They should be accommodating without simply going along with his every desire; be obedient without bending under pressure; be tolerant without acquiescing in his commission of evil. They should try to influence his thinking and restrain his behaviour, enlighten him in the Way and make his actions in agreement with it. This is, of course, difficult. That was why Xunzi compared their job to riding an untrained horse, and observed that they have to play on the tyrant's fear to make him correct his mistakes, on his worry to make him learn the right course, on his likes to lead him to the Way. This is known as *qu de* (曲得 reaching the goal by indirect routes.)

Unfortunately, most rulers of Xunzi's times were tyrannical or incompetent, and the hereditary aristocracy, which once exercised some control over them, was in rapid decline. Many high officials were intellectuals from lower middle social strata without any power base of their own. There was, in fact, little chance that they could follow Xunzi's advice and succeed. Of course, he knew this; nevertheless he expressed his view of how an official *should* behave vis-à-vis the sovereign. It was a quixotic but genuine Ruist view. We have seen Confucius and Mencius taking similar position. They all emphasised that, even in circumstances of extreme adversity, an official should retain his integrity and follow the highest norms. Only the techniques could be adjusted, never the principles.

(c) The sovereign and the common people

The common people are more remote from the sovereign. They were subjugated, exploited and neglected, and had practically no power against the authorities. But Xunzi saw a different aspect of the relationship. According to him, "Heaven populated the world with people not for the ruler. It instead installed the ruler for the people." Therefore, the ruler should love the people and be loyal and faithful to them, promote what is beneficial and eliminate what is harmful to them, reward the virtuous, punish the wicked, and educate the ignorant among them, use their service only at the right time and tax them lightly. He should not impose an unreasonable measure, even one of little consequence, upon even the most defenceless among them –orphans, widows, widowers, and the old and childless. If there is a ruler like this, Xunzi said, the people will come to him, honour him as a god, love him as a parent, and will be happy to die for him. But. if a ruler leads the people in dirty tricks and stealthy deeds, demonstrates for them the art of treachery and subversion, disrupts government business with favouritism and nepotism, and makes the stupid teach the wise and the wicked supervise the virtuous; if in managing the economy, he impoverishes the people, and. in using their labour he exhausts them, then, Xunzi predicted, the people will look down on him as if he were a snake and hate him as if he were a demon. Every day they will seek the opportunity to banish him and trample on him. We may recall that Mencius emphasised the same relative relationship.

Thus, as Xunzi saw it, in their relationship an ordinary ruler depends on the people more than the people do on the ruler. This is why he used the metaphor: "The ruler is the boat and the common people are the water. It is the water that bears up the boat, and it is the water that capsizes it." In another passage he said more specifically, "It is the responsibility of the emperor to perfect personal virtue, to seek the highest ideals, to improve the institutions and the culture, to unify the empire, to enable even the most humble to do his best, and to make the people of the entire world loyal and obedient . . . Thus, when the empire is not unified, the emperor is not the proper person." The implication is clear: the emperor should be removed from the throne. But, less courageous than Mencius, Xunzi did not take that position openly. In any case, unfortunately, in Xunzi's time, most people did not see the relationship between the ruler and the people in this light, and he realised that. Thus. he feebly observed, "When people live under an oppressive tyrant, having no place to escape, they can only praise what little beauty there is in him and publicise what little good there is in him. They have to avoid what he dislikes and refrain from exposing his failures, talk about his talents and keep silent about his shortcomings." How miserable and sad!

At the beginning of this chapter, it was mentioned that Xunzi critiqued six types of intellectuals before and of his time. A closer look shows that they occupied a continuum between two extremes – on the one hand, those like Zhuangzi who had little regard for human ability and thought that man should simply live according to the law of nature; on the other hand, those like Gongsun Yang who were overconfident in human ability and believed that humans can create a world of their choice. Between the two extremes, Xunzi found those like Mozi and Mencius. He criticised Zhuangzi as unrealistic, Mozi as degrading, Mencius as naive.

In *Xunzi* Gongsun Yang was mentioned as Wei Yang and characterised as one of the Military Strategists,[8] but Xunzi actually considered the ideas behind his policies as Legalist and criticised them as simplistic. This may sound strange: after all, Xunzi, more than the other thinkers outside the Legalist School, recognised the importance of law. But he, more than the others, clearly pointed out the shortcomings of law and its easy misuse and abuse. He wanted to keep and improve its utility and avoid its pitfalls. His suggestions were to make law in agreement with the higher principles and the law enforcement personnel learn how to apply law in this way. More noticeably – and this shows his true colour as a Ruist – he suggested that rites should be made a norm of choice. But his arguments were not very convincing.

Nevertheless, Xunzi's emphasis on rites can be seen as a meaningful effort in building a bridge between law and the higher norms. His statement, that rites should be the "essence" of law, is significant. It is because rites, though not definitive, are more concrete than morality, and, therefore, it is easier to translate the spirit behind a rite into the letter of the law. And, in practice, it must be admitted that, if a person follows rites as rules of refined behaviour which conveys a sense of courtesy, respect, sympathy and compassion, it is less likely that he will get into trouble with the law. In this sense, rites can be a step that leads law to comply with higher norms.

Confucius believed in the malleability of human character and therefore emphasised education and advocated as its objective to make a person restrain his desire, follow rites and finally reach for *ren* (仁 the highest form of humanity). Xunzi echoed Confucius and criticised Mencius for his unfounded faith in the goodness of human nature and his claim that norms could be found in man's own heart. His real purpose was to stress the need for educating the ruling class which is, of course, generally recognised by thinkers in all civilisations. He placed particular weight on it because he believed that human nature is bad. A ruler without high principles instilled in his character by good education is sure to go astray and bring harm to his people. Whether good education can produce good rulers is uncertain but that is the only way that men, who lived under a political system not of their own choosing, could think of.

In such a system ordinary people's position was precarious. Mencius, representing a newly risen class of intellectuals outside the system, had the audacity to challenge it. For this reason more than any other, he was lauded by the intelligentsia of later times and honoured as second only to Confucius. Xunzi, who lived in a time when power was concentrated more in the hands of the rulers, was less courageous. He insisted that officials should uphold high principles and retain their personal integrity but advised them and the common people not to defy the political authorities, especially the tyrants, who were many at his time. Though more pragmatic, this was one of the reasons why he was less highly regarded.

There was another reason – his position towards law. He recognised its importance but wanted to distinguish it from rites. He was not quite successful because of some of the language he used. For instance, he compared rites to scales, the square and so on, just as the Legalists compared law to the same measuring instruments and tools. More importantly, if tools can be misused, can rites also? There is thus a defect in his theory. This defect, in particular, was emphasised by his two prominent disciples, Han Fei and Li Si. Because of these facts, he was considered not to be a *chun-ru* (純儒 pure Ruist) and was relegated to a place lower than Mencius in the Ruist pantheon. But this is because of a lack of complete understanding of his views, and, to blame him for what his disciples did, is unfair.

His reputation rose many centuries later during the Qing Dynasty when more scholars studied his book. But, in fact, since the Han Dynasty, intellectuals had begun to do what he intended – make law more in agreement with higher moral principles. We shall discuss this in the final chapter of this book. Here I just want to point out that he did accomplish a task of significance, namely, to help move an era of rule by uncertain norms – morality, rites – to one of rule by law. He never endorsed the idea of the "rule of law" in the sense that law is the supreme norm and should be applied invariably under all circumstances to all men, which he though unrealistic and undesirable. His ideal state is one under the rule of good men with law. Of course, truly good men are rare, and that was why Xunzi placed so much emphasis on education. It is questionable whether the kind of education he suggested can achieve the result he wanted but, besides education, there is no way a better world can be brought into existence.

Notes

1. See Wang Xianqian 王先謙, *Xunzi ji-jie*, Chapter 6, pp. 57–66.
2. See *Lun-yu zheng-yi* Ch. 15, p. 335.
3. A passage in the chapter "Lü-xing" briefly requires a judge *shang xia bi zui* (上下比罪 to compare a crime that is not specifically proscribed with one that is more or less serious and is clearly proscribed). Various annotators agree that it means that, where there is no clear law governing a particular case, a judge is to search for a law or precedent governing similar cases and *bi fu xing zhi* (比附行之 to apply by analogy). See Sun Xing-yan 孫星衍, *Shang shu jin gu wen zhu shu* 尚書今古文註疏 Chapter 27.
4. See *Tang-lü shu-yi* pp. 134, 522; *Da Qing Hui-dian shi-li* vol. 739, pp. 8b–9b, vol. 740, pp. 20b–21a.
5. The two classics, *Yi-li* (儀禮 *The Book of Rites*) and *Li-ji* (禮記 *Notes on Rites*), appeared as written books in much later times. And so was *Zhou-li* (周禮 *Zhou Li*), which is about government structure and supposedly existed in early Zhou, not about rites.

6. Since rites were not codified, here the term cannot refer to a particular work we know of but generally to some works about rites known to people of Xunzi's time.
7. *Shang-shu jin-gu-wen zhu-shu* Chapter 27, p. 522.
8. See *Xunzi Ji-jie* Chapter 15, pp. 182–3.

Han-fei-zi 韓非子

PART 1
TRANSLATION

(A) Symptoms of disorder

(1) Useless and harmful people

[1] A state with a land of 1,000 *li* of rock cannot be called rich; a state with a million soldier figurines cannot be called strong. It is not that the land is not large and the figurines not numerous; it is because rocky land cannot grow crops, and figurines cannot fight enemies. Now merchants and officials, artisans and craftsmen eat but do not till. A land not tilled is the same as a piece of rock; scholars and swordsmen holding fame and honour without military merit are as useless as figurines. (Chapter 50, "Xian-xue" 顯學 p. 354)

[2] In a disorderly state, the scholars hail the ways of the former kings to support their theory about benevolence and rightness, and resort to extravagant costumes and rites and speak sophisticated words to cast doubt on laws of the time and cause the ruler to be indecisive. The pleaders create false premises and fraudulent arguments and use external help to promote their private goals at the expense of the interests of their own state. The swordsmen gather bands of followers, create their own standards of behaviour to establish their fame, and violate the prohibitions of the government. Those close to a powerful official give him big bribes and, with his help, gain government rewards at the expense of those with merit. The craftsmen make inferior goods and the merchants, with considerable wealth, hoard them, to gain profit from the peasants in a time of need. These five types of persons are the woodworms of the state. (Chapter 49, "Wu-du" 五蠹 p. 350)

[3] Xu You 許由, Xu Ya續牙 . . . twelve famous persons of the past, were known for not being glad to see profits, and not being afraid when meeting dangers . . . Those who are not pleased by profits will not be encouraged by rewards the ruler offers; those who are not afraid of dangers will not be deterred by severe

punishments the ruler threatens. These are called "persons unresponsive to government orders". They die in caves, wither away in woods, starve in mountains or drown in rivers. Even the ancient sage kings could not make them loyal subjects, so how can a ruler of the present find any use for people like them? (Chapter 44, "Shuo-yi" 說疑 pp. 307–8)

(2) Specious intellectuals and outrageous swindlers

[4] After Confucius and Mozi died, the Ruists divided into eight groups and the Mohists into three. Each had different takes on their respective masters' teachings, and yet all claimed to be true Confucians and true Mohists. The two masters cannot come to life again: who is here to determine for now and for posterity the truth of their teachings?

Both Confucius and Mozi allegedly followed the way of Yao and Shun; although they differed in accepting and rejecting certain parts of it, each claimed what he followed was the true way of Yao and Shun. Now Yao and Shun cannot come to life again, who is to determine the truth of the claims of the Confucius and Mozi?

The present is more than 700 years from the time of the Yin and the Zhou Dynasties, and more than 2,000 years from the time of the dynasties of the Yu and the Xia. If one cannot determine the truth of Confucius and Mozi and yet wants to investigate the way of Yao and Shun of 3,000 years ago, I would think it is quite impossible. He who resolutely affirms something he cannot examine and verify its truth is stupid; he who acts according to a way he cannot affirm is fraudulent. (Chapter 50, "Xian-xue" p. 351)

[5] There was once a guest artist who painted for the king of Qi. The king asked him what was the most difficult to paint. "Dogs and horses are the most difficult," the artist replied. "What is the easiest?" "Ghosts and spirits," the guest said. Dogs and horses are difficult to portray because they are close to people, in their sight every day. Ghosts and spirits, being shapeless, invisible to people, are therefore easy to depict. (Chapter 32, "Wai-chu-shuo zuo-shang" 外儲說左上 p. 202)

[6] The King of Yan advertised for fine craftsmen. A man from Wei came and proposed to carve a monkey at the tip of a thorn. The king was pleased and kept him with a stipend equal to the salary of an official of five carriages.

One day the king said, "I would like to see the monkey you carved on the tip of a thorn." The guest said, "If a ruler wants to see it, he must, for half a year, refrain from going into his harem, drinking wine and eating meat. And then he has to wait for a moment when the rain just stopped and the sun is coming out. At such a moment if he stares at the thorn, held against the silver lining of the dark clouds, the monkey will be visible." Thereupon the king kept supporting the man from Wei but never could see the monkey.

A blacksmith from Tai-xia in the state of Zheng, came and talked to the king of Yan, saying, "I, your servant, am a maker of carving knives. When one carves a small object one must use a carving knife smaller than the object to be carved. Now as the tip of a thorn has no room even for the sharpest edge of a carving knife, it is impossible for anyone to carve it. If Your Majesty can have a look at the knife that guest of yours uses, you will know whether he can do what he proposed to do."

The king said, "Excellent!" and said to the man from Wei, "My guest, how do you carve the thorn?" "With a carving knife." "I would like to see the knife." "Let me go to my hostel to fetch it," said the guest, and he escaped. (Chapter 32, "Wai-chu-shuo zuo-shang" p. 200)

[7] When King Xuan of Qi 齊宣王 ordered people to play pipes he always wanted three hundred of them playing together. A man from the southern suburb of the capital asked to play pipes for the king. The king was pleased and provided him with the same stipend as he gave the other three hundred players. After the death of King Xuan, King Min 湣王 ascended the throne. As he loved to listen to the players one by one, the fellow from the southern suburb fled. (Chapter 30, "Nei-chu-shuo shang – qi-shu" 內儲說上七術 p. 173)

[8] Someone presented the elixir of life to the king of Jing. The court usher took it in hand and entered the palace. A palace guard asked, "It is edible?" "Yes," the usher said. The guard snatched and ate it. The king was enraged and ordered the guard executed. The guard sent someone to plead with the king on his behalf, saying, "What the visitor presented was supposed to be elixir of life, but if Your Majesty can put me to death after I ate it, then it must not be elixir but a mortal drug and the visitor must be cheating Your Majesty. Now to kill an innocent man to demonstrate someone cheating Your Majesty is not as good as to release me. (Chapter 22, "Shuo-lin shang" 說林上 p. 130)

(3) Treacherous officials

[9] There are six origins of disorder: the queen dowager, the queen and consorts, the ruler's children, his brothers, grand ministers, and those with great honours and talents. (Chapter 48, "Ba-jing—Qi-luan" 八經—起亂 p. 332)

[10] There are five types of wicked officials . . . There are those who lavishly use their wealth to buy good reputation; those who richly reward people to change their actions; those who form partisan groups, court the shrewd and honour the intellectuals to advance their schemes; those who grant leniency and pardon criminals to flaunt their authority; and those who cater to the opinion of the masses, display their personal talents, make sophisticated speeches and appear in splendid attire to dazzle and awe the people. (Chapter 44, "Shuo-yi" p. 313)

[11] Officials exhaust their strength to purchase favour from the ruler; the ruler uses offices and emoluments to purchase their service. Between the ruler and the officials there is not love like that between father and son; they act according to calculation. (Chapter 36, "Nan-yi" 難一 p. 267)

[12] Bo Yi said to Zhao Jian Zhu: "Your Majesty's state is well fed in the middle." Jian Zhu was pleased and asked, how so. Bo Yi replied, "Your treasury is empty, your people are hungry, but your wicked officials are becoming richer every day." (Chapter 35, "Wai-chu-shuo you-xia" 外儲說右下 p. 260)

[13] Officials have no bonds of flesh and blood which tie them to their ruler; they were forced by the circumstances to serve him. Hence, those who act as ministers never for a moment cease trying to spy into the ruler's mind. (Chapter 17, "Bei-nei" 備內 pp. 82–3)

[14] All wicked officials want to please the ruler and gain his trust and affection. Thus, when he likes something, they all praise it; when he dislikes something, they all decry it . . . After winning his trust and affection, they will promote or dismiss other officials . . . and will deceive him and accomplish their private schemes. As a result, he will be hoodwinked and they become powerful. These are known as "the officials that control their ruler". (Chapter 14, "Jian-jie-shi chen" 姦劫弒臣 p. 68–9)

[15] The officials have eight strategies to realise their evil schemes. The first is to make use of the ruler's "bedfellows". Who are they? They are the court ladies and young boys who are charming and pretty. The ruler is beguiled by them. If they ask for something they desire when he is at ease and satiated with food and wine, their requests are sure to be heeded. The wicked officials will treat them with gold and jewels and employ them to delude the ruler.

The second is to make use of the ruler's "attendants". Who are they? They are the jesters and entertainers, attendants and favourites who are close to the ruler, and always say "Yes, yes!" before he makes a command, and "Of course, of course!" after he gives an order. They guess his intention and predict his wishes, and they watch his face and observe his expression. This is how they are able to anticipate his moves. In unison they step forward and in unison they retire, and they answer and respond in identical tones and words. This is how they are able to move his mind. The wicked officials will treat them with gold, jewels, pets, and playthings, and do illegal favours for them, and thus employ them to influence the ruler.

The third is to make use of the ruler's "fathers and brothers". Who are they? They are princes from a side line of the ruler's clan whom he loves, and the grand officials and court officers with whom he deliberates and makes important decisions. When they insist on some point, the ruler always listens. The wicked officials provide these princes with musicians and entertainers, and win over the grand officials and officers with flattery and suggest that they propose to the ruler projects that are certain to be concluded successfully and they will be certain to receive rewards and promotions. In this way, they delight the hearts of these men and persuade them to act against their ruler.

The fourth is to indulge the ruler in "baleful pursuits". What are they? Rulers love to beautify their palaces, terraces, and pools, and to decorate their female attendants, dogs and horses for their amusement. As such pursuits are detrimental to the rulers' true interests, the officials will exhaust the energies of the people in constructing beautiful palaces, terraces, and pools, and make heavy demands on the people to provide trinkets, for decoration of the attendants and fine dogs and horses in order to delight the ruler and bring disorder to his mind, indulge his desires and exact some private gain in the process.

The fifth is to manipulate the "opinion of the people". How is that to be done? The wicked officials will distribute public funds to please the people, and hand out small private favours to win their hearts. By making everyone in both the court and the countryside praise them and causing the ruler to be insulated from other opinions, they can achieve what they want.

The sixth is to make use of "overwhelming arguments", How is that to be done? Because the ruler, being isolated from public discussions and insulated from opportunities of hearing different opinions, can be easily moved by cunning arguments, wicked officials recruit sophisticated debaters from abroad and patronise able speakers at home, and employ them to plead their special causes. With clever and elegant phrases, fluent and compelling words, such men show the ruler the prospects of gain, terrify him with predictions of hazards, and overwhelm him with their empty preaching.

The seventh is to usurp "authority and power". How is that to be done? A ruler's authority and power are dependent on the support of the officials and common people. Hence, whatever they approve of, he approves of; whatever they disapprove of, he disapproves of. The wicked officials will gather bands of armed men around them and support men who are willing to die in their cause, in order to show their might. They make it plain that whoever works in their interest will profit; whoever does not will perish. And, in this way, they manage to intimidate the lesser officials and common people and further their private interests.

The eighth is to make use of "foreign states". How is that to be done? A small state will do the bidding of larger states; a weak army will stand in fear of stronger armies. When a large state makes a demand, a small state has to heed; when a strong army approaches, a weak one cannot but succumb. Therefore, the wicked officials will impose heavy taxes on the people, empty the treasury, and exhaust the state in the service of the great powers, and then make use of their influence with those powers in their efforts to entrap the ruler of their own state. The worst of them may send troops to the border to increase tension there in order to enforce their will within the state; the less evil ones will, from time to time, call in envoys from abroad in order to shock the ruler and fill him with terror. (Chapter 9, "Ba-jian" 八姦 pp. 36–8)

[16] Duke Huan of Qi 齊桓公 asked Guan Zhong 管仲, "What is the greatest headache concerning governing a state?" Guan Zhong replied, "The greatest headache is those rats in the Temple of the Earth." "Why so?", the duke asked. "Has Your Majesty noticed how the Temple is constructed?" Guan Zhong replied, "First, one builds the wood wall and then one plasters it with clay. The rats will then make holes in the wall and stay inside there. If one wants to smoke them out, one is afraid that the wood might be burnt; if one wants to flood them, one is afraid that the plaster might disintegrate. This is why temple rats cannot be caught. Now those who are close to the ruler would, while outside of the court, use their power to extort the people; and, while inside the court, gang up on and cheat the ruler, spy on him and leak inside information to their friends outside.

As a result, they become important both inside and outside of the court, and all officials and clerks become their assistants. If the law officer does not punish them, he will be disregarding the law; if he does, the ruler will be uneasy. Thus, they come into possession of the state. They are thus the temple rats of the state." (Chapter 34, "Wai-chu-shuo you-shang" 外儲說右上 p. 242)

[17] Grand officials gang up for a single purpose – to hoodwink the ruler. Secretly, they are good to one another but, publicly, they appear as adversaries to show that they have no shared private interests. They will serve as each other's ears and eyes spying on the ruler. He will be duped and deprived of ways to know the truth and thus become a ruler only in name, his power and authority usurped by those ministers. (Chapter 17, "Bei-nei" p. 85)

[18] Where a ruler, with no standards of his own to evaluate his officials, determines according to the words of others . . . a treacherous official will spend all his family property to form a gang of partisans in the court and establish connections with persons outside for the purpose of raising his reputation. He will enter into secret agreements with other officials to secure his position and will promise bounties to the common people, saying, those who are with him he will benefit, those who are against him he will harm. When the people, craving for his largess and fearing his power, praise him, his fame spreads all over the country and reaches the ears of the ruler who, incapable of finding the truth, will believe that he is, indeed, talented and worthy. In addition, he will employ some deceitful persons to disguise themselves as favoured envoys from other states, furnishing them with carriages and horses, giving them forged credentials, coaching them in what to say, and providing them with valuables to be presented to his ruler so that they can have an audience and pretend to discuss some topics of mutual concern to the two states but actually speak for the benefit of him . . . The ruler, being pleased by them and their words, will think that he is indeed a worthy fellow of the world. (Chapter 44, "Shuo-yi" pp. 310–11)

[19] In the time of Duke Ling of the state of Wei 衛靈公, Mi Zixia 彌子瑕 was in favour and dominated the government of the state. One day a dwarf jester went to see the duke and said, "My dream is realised". "What dream?" asked the duke. "In my dream I saw a stove. Now I see Your Highness." This made the duke angry, retorting, "I heard that when a person is to see his ruler, he dreams of seeing the sun. Why do you say you dreamed of seeing a stove before seeing me?" "The sun shines on all things in the world," the dwarf replied, "its rays cannot be blocked by a single object; the ruler sees all things in a state, his view cannot be blocked by a single man. That is why before a man is to see his ruler he dreams of seeing the sun. In the case of a stove, when one person blocks its opening, its fire cannot shine on others behind that person. Perhaps there is someone blocking Your Highness's view? If so, is it not right that I dreamed of seeing a stove before seeing Your Highness?" (Chapter 30, "Nei-chu-shuo shang – Qi-shu" pp. 161–2)

[20] The "mighty men" are those who, in the absence of orders from the ruler, take matters into their own hands; those who twist the law for private gain;

those who enrich their family at the expense of the state; those who are powerful enough to control the ruler. (Chapter 11, "Gu-fen" 孤憤 p. 55)

[21] The Chief Minister Zihan 子罕 of Song said to his ruler, "Since the people all love rewards and favours, you should bestow them yourself; since they hate punishments and death sentences, I beg to be allowed to dispense these for you." The ruler of Song said, "Fine". Thereafter, whenever punishments were to be inflicted on ordinary people and death sentences considered for great officials, the ruler always said, "Consult Zihan". As a result, great officials became fearful of him and common people became obedient to him. After a year, Zihan killed the ruler of Song and took over the government. (Chapter 35, "Wai-chu-shuo you-xia" pp. 252)

[22] Zhou Huazhi 周滑之, Gongsun Shen 公孫申 . . . , twelve notorious officials of the past, were known for thinking about petty profits and forgetting law and justice. While in the court, they suppressed the talented and the worthy and thus hoodwinked the ruler; while out of government, they disrupted the work of other officials and caused disorder. Thus, when they were close to the ruler and gained his trust, it was not difficult for them to ruin the state and kill the people. With officials like those, even sage kings would be in fear of being usurped, so how can a stupid ruler not lose his throne? (Chapter 44, "Shuo-yi" p. 309)

[23] According to the annals several tens of states perished since the time of King Xuan of Zhou 周宣王, many being the result of ministers killing their rulers. Thus, altogether, the numbers of such disasters initiated from within a state and those from abroad were about equal. (Chapter 44, "Shuo-yi" p. 312)

[24] The so called "sage rulers" and "bright kings" of the past did not obtain their positions through inheritance according to certain order; they raised their partisans, gathered their clansmen and private gangs, forced the ruling monarchs to abdicate or murdered them to take over their states. Someone asked "How do you know that?" I say, "Shun coerced Yao, Yu coerced Shun, Tang banished Jie, and King Wu attacked Shou. These four kings were the ones who, as officials, killed their rulers and yet the world praised them. An investigation of the minds of these four kings shows that there was nothing but avarice. An examination of their behaviour shows that it was violent use of military force. Thus, owing to their self-aggrandisement, the world hailed them as great; owing to their self-promotion, the world lauded them as brilliant. Because their power was enough to overwhelm the world and their largess enough to win over the people, the entire world fell to their schemes. (Chapter 44, "Shuo-yi" p. 311)

(4) Unwise but wilful rulers

[25] Where the great officials are in control of the government and exercise dictatorial power, and the ruler does not know how to restrain them, it is because he is not intelligent. (Chapter 11, "Gu-fen" p. 58)

[26] These are the "Ten Faults" [of a ruler]: first, to practise the petty loyalty and thus violate the great loyalty; second, to care for small gains and thus jeopardise

big gains; third, to be eccentric, arrogant and impolite to fellow feudal lords and thus bring about personal ruin; fourth, to be addicted to music and heedless to government problems and thus cause endless troubles; fifth, to be greedy for profits and thus lead to destruction of the state and personal demise; sixth, to indulge in the pleasures of women and ignore the government affairs and thus ruin the state; seventh, to travel afar from the seat of government against the advice of others and thus endanger personal safety; eighth, to be obdurate after making mistakes and disregard remonstration from loyal subjects and thus lose his reputation and become a laughing stock; ninth, to have an unrealistic estimate of domestic strength but rely on the help from abroad and thus have the state dismembered; and tenth, as the ruler of a small state, to disregard the rites and dismiss the good advice of faithful officials and thus to arrive at a position of the downfall of his state. (Chapter 10, "Shi-guo" 十過 p. 40)

[27] These are the hazardous ways for the ruler: first, to cut short what is prescribed by law; second, to stretch beyond what is proscribed by law; third, to profit by what harms people; fourth, to rejoice in people's disasters; fifth, to endanger what people are at peace with; and sixth, failing to keep close to what one should love and keep away from what one should hate. (Chapter 25, "An-wei" 安危 p. 147)

[27] [In forty-seven circumstances a state is surely to perish; some of them are directly created by the ruler, including the most serious ones below.]

[No. 2] Where the ruler neglects laws and prohibitions, indulges in personal deliberation, and disregards self-defence and relies on foreign friendship and support.

[No. 4] Where the ruler is fond of palaces, chariots and curios and thereby tires his people and exhausts his treasury.

[No. 5] Where the ruler believes in astrology, worships spirits and gods, trusts divination and lavishes money on sacrifices.

[No. 6] Where the ruler listens only to the high officials but does not check their words against those of others to find truth and thereby lets only one door open for his information.

[No. 8] Where the ruler is slow-minded, incapable of making timely and firm decisions, and unable to form an opinion on what is right and take a position.

[No. 10] Where the ruler is prone to use harsh punishments but does not make laws complete, fond of ideas and arguments but does not put them into practice.

[No. 11] Where the ruler is naive, reveals what he has in mind and never conceals any thought but communicates openly with his officials.

[No. 12] Where the ruler is stubborn and uncompromising, resistant to remonstrance and fond of winning debates, careless about the conditions of the state and trusting only his own judgements.

[No. 13] Where the ruler relies on the help of big, far-off powers but ignores and insults the neighbouring states.

[No. 16] Where the ruler does not use the talented persons in his own country but seeks foreigners, does not test people's worth against their achievements but employs or dismisses them according to their reputations, exalts and honours expatriates above members of old staff at home.

[No. 23] Where the ruler humiliates great officials and yet depends on them in the government, punishes petty attendants and yet uses them in the court, and thus causes both of them harbour anger and feel shame and eventually carry out treasonous schemes.

[No. 27] Where the ruler is fond of using his wits to twist laws, mixing his personal interests with those of the state, changing laws often and issuing orders frequently.

[No. 32] Where the ruler is easily provoked and fond of resorting to arms but neglects agricultural work and military training and ventures into aggressive wars heedlessly

[No. 42] Where the ruler, upon seeing a great profit, does not quickly seize it; after learning of a threat, does not prepare against it; takes lightly what he should strive for but decorates himself with what is called benevolence and righteousness. (Chapter 15, "Wang-zheng" 亡徵 pp. 78–81)

[28] Su Dai 蘇代 went to the state of Yan as an envoy of the state of Qin, and found that, if he did not have something that would benefit Zizhi 子之 [the chief minister of Yan], he could accomplish nothing on that mission and no rewards would be bestowed upon him on his return to Qin. So, when he had an audience with the king of Yan he praised the king of Qi. The king of Yan asked, "Being so wise and virtuous, is the king of Qi eventually going to be the ruler of the world?" Su Dai said, "He has hardly the time to save his state from ruin. How can be the ruler of the world!" "Why?", the king of Yan wondered. "Because", said Su Dai, "he does not fully trust the minister he liked." The king of Yan asked, "Why would that lead a state to ruin?" In reply Su Dai said, "In the past Duke Huan of Qi liked Guan Zhong, honoured him as 'Uncle' and let him manage all home affairs and decide all foreign relations, entrusting the whole country to him. As a result, the entire world was rectified and, for nine times, all the feudal lords were rallied under the leadership of Qi. But now the king of Qi does not fully trust the minister he likes and, for this reason, I know Qi is to be ruined." The king of Yan responded, "I have put my full confidence in Zizhi but the world is not yet aware of this." On the following day he called an assembly of all officials in the court and entrusted Zizhi with all state affairs.

[Having heard about this interview, Zizhi had someone give Su Dai 100 *yi* (about 240 ounces) of gold.]

Then Pan Shou 潘壽 said to the king of Yan, "It would be better if Your Majesty abdicated and gave the state to Zizhi. The reason why people call Yao wise and virtuous is because he gave the world to Xu You 許由. As Xu You was never to accept the throne, Yao gained the fame of abdicating in favour of Xu You while, in fact, he was not to lose the world. Now, if Your Majesty offers the state to Zizhi, he is not to accept it, and Your Majesty would have the name of abdicating in favour of Zizhi and become as famous as Yao." Consequently, the king of Yan committed his whole state to Zizhi, and Zizhi became all the more powerful.

According to another report, Pan Shou was a recluse. The king of Yan sent someone to invite him to court [to discuss abdication]. He said to the king, "I am afraid that Zizhi is going to be like Yi 益 [Yu's chief minister]." "Why Yi?", the king asked. Pan Shou replied, "In the past when Yu was dying he was about to give the world to Yi. But followers of Qi 啟 [Yu's son] joined one another in attacking Yi and established Qi. Now Your Majesty loves Zizhi and wants to give the state of Yan to him. But, while the followers of the Crown Prince were in power holding seals of government offices, none of Zizhi's men were in the court. Should one day unfortunately Your Majesty pass away, Zizhi would suffer just as Yi did." Thereupon, the king recalled all the seals from the officials and ordered all those whose emolument was above 300 *shi* [about 30,000 litres] of rice to answer to Zizhi. Zizhi became immensely powerful.

The means the ruler uses as a mirror to look at himself are envoys from other feudal lords but now all those envoys are partisans of private individuals. The means the ruler uses to assist himself are those who are detached from worldly affairs and live in rocky caves but now all those recluses are actually guests of private individuals. Why is that so? It is because the power of bestowing and depriving is held in the hands of such individuals as Zizhi. (Chapter 35, "Wai-chu-shuo you-xia" pp. 256–7)

[29] Duke Xiang of Song 宋襄公 fought the army of the state of Chu at Zhuo-gu. When the Song troops had already formed a battle line on the bank of the Zhuo River, the Chu forces had not yet completely crossed the river. Gou Qiang 購強, the Vice Minister of War ran to Duke Xiang and urged, "As the Chu forces are numerous and the Song forces are few, please attack the Chu forces when only half of them have crossed the river and not yet formed a battle line. They are sure to be defeated." Duke Xiang replied, "I heard it said by noble people, 'Do not harm those who have already been injured, do not capture soldiers with grey hair, do not push the enemy into a dangerous position, do not force them while they are in distress, and do not attack those who have not yet formed a battle line. Now to attack the Chu forces while they have not fully crossed the river is violating the principle of righteousness. Let the Chu forces finish crossing the river and complete forming a battle line and then beat the drum of attack." The Vice Minister of War said, "Your Majesty does not love the people of Song and does not protect what is vital to you, just for the sake of righteousness?!" The Duke ordered, "If you do not return to your line, I am going to enforce the martial law." The Vice Minister returned to his line, and the Chu forces finished crossing the river and completed forming a battle line. The Duke ordered the attack and suffered a crushing defeat. He was wounded in the thigh and died in three days. This is the calamity of yearning after benevolence and righteousness. (Chapter 32, "Wai-chu-shuo zuo-shang" pp. 211–12)

[30] There is a proverb saying: "The leper feels pity for the king." . . . It refers to the kings that had been coerced and murdered. Where a ruler has no law and tactics to control his officials . . . the fear he harbours in his heart and the pain

his body suffers are much greater than those that a leper endures. (Chapter 14, "Jian-jie-shi chen" p. 76)

(B) Causes of disorder

(1) Self-interest

[31] Humans do not have thick body hair or feathers, thus they are cold without clothes. Unlike those in heaven or those grown from the earth, it is vital for humans to have food in their stomachs and intestines – if they do not eat they cannot live. This is why they cannot avoid desires for what can benefit them. (Chapter 20, "Jie-Lao" 解老 pp. 106–7)
[32] To pursue safety and benefit and to avoid danger and harm – this is human nature. (Chapter 14, "Jian-jie-shi chen" p. 69)
[33] Eels look like snakes; silkworms look like caterpillars. Seeing a snake, people become frightened; seeing a caterpillar they develop goose pimples. Nevertheless, women pick up silkworms, and fishermen hold eels. Whenever there is profit to be made, people forget their dislikes and all become as brave as Meng Fen 孟賁 and Zhuan Zhu 專諸 [two persons known for their bravery]. (Chapter 23, "Shuo-lin xia" 說林下 p. 173)
[34] A physician often sucks men's wounds clean and holds the bad blood in his mouth, not because he is bound to them by any tie of kinship but because he knows there is profit in it. (Chapter 17, "Bei-nei" p. 83)
[35] The carriage-maker making carriages hopes that men will grow rich and eminent; the carpenter making coffins hopes that men will die prematurely. It is not that the carriage-maker is kind-hearted and the carpenter cruel. It is only that, if men do not become rich and eminent, the carriages will never sell and, if men do not die, there will be no market for coffins. The carpenter does not hate people; he has a profit in their death. (Chapter 17, "Bei-nei" pp. 83–4)
[36] Where labourers are hired to plough and sow the field, the landlord will spend a lot to feed and pay them well, not because he loves them but because he thinks that, by doing so, he can induce them to plough deeply and weed thoroughly; the labourers, on the other hand, will exhaust their strength in ploughing and weeding, use their best skill in forming the crop rows, not because they love the landlord but because they think that, by doing so, they can induce him to provide good food and pay good money. (Chapter 32, "Wai-chu-shuo zuo-shang" pp. 204–5)
[37] This is how parents treat their children: After giving birth to a boy, they congratulate each other. After giving birth to a girl, they kill her. Now boys and girls both come from their parents' bosoms, and yet, if it is a boy, they are congratulated; if it is a girl, they kill her. Their consideration is for future convenience; their calculation is for long-term interests. Thus, even in treating their children, parents resort to a calculating heart. (Chapter 46, "Liu-fan" 六反 p. 319)
[38] The ordinary people's intellect is as useless as that of an infant. In the case of an infant . . . if he has an abscess and does not have it cut open, the disease is

going to worsen. To have his abscess cut open, it is necessary to have someone hold him down and his mother to do the cutting. Still, he will continually cry and scream. It is because the infant does not know how to endure a small suffering in order to have a big benefit. . .

Formerly, Yu rechannelled the Jiang [the Yangzi River] and dredged the He [the Yellow River] but the people piled up tiles and stones [to prevent his work]; Zichan removed the barriers between agricultural plots but the people of the state of Zheng slandered him; Yu benefited the world, Zichan saved the state of Zheng, and yet they both were vilified. In view of these facts, it should be clear that the intellect of the ordinary people is not sufficient for any use. Therefore, to make policies that are agreeable to the people is the beginning of chaos, not the method to achieve good government. (Chapter 50, "Xian-xue" pp. 356–7)

(2) Conflict of interests

[39] Once in the state of Wei, a husband and a wife prayed together. The wife said, "Please let us have no trouble, and let us have a hundred bundles of cloth." The husband asked her, "Why so few?" "If we get more," the wife answered, "you are going to buy a concubine." (Chapter 31, "Nei-chu-shuo xia – Liu-wei" 內儲說下一六微 p. 183)

[40] In some cases, the queen or consort of a ruler of a state of a thousand or ten thousand chariots would, after her son is made the crown prince, wish the ruler to die early. Why? Because husband and wife are not related by bones and flesh, when there is love, they are close, when love is lost, they are estranged. The adage says, "When the mother is pretty, the son is embraced." Then the opposite must be "When the mother becomes comely the son is alienated." Now a man in his fifties still lusts after beautiful women but the beauty of a woman in her thirties is fading. A woman with fading beauty serving a husband lusting after beautiful women will be distanced, even disgraced by him, and her son will not be allowed to succeed to the throne. This is why a queen or consort would like her husband to die early. (Chapter 17, "Bei-nei" p. 83)

[41] In the state of Chu there was a man of rectitude. When his father stole a sheep, he reported the theft to the authorities. But the prime minister said, "Execute him." It was because the prime minister thought that, though the man showed rectitude in the service of his sovereign, he harmed his own father. The case was so decided and the punishment carried out. Thus, we see that a man who shows rectitude as a subject of his sovereign may be a cruel son to his father.

There was a man of the state of Lu who accompanied his sovereign to war. Three times he went into battle, and three times he ran away. When Confucius asked him the reason, he replied, "I have a father in old age and, if I should die, there would be no one to take care of him." Confucius, considering the man filial, recommended him to the sovereign. Thus, we see that a man who is a filial son to his father may be a traitorous subject to his lord.

The prime minister of Chu executed a man and, as a result, crimes stopped being reported to the authorities; Confucius rewarded a man and, as a result, the people of Lu thought nothing of surrendering or running away in battle. The interests of those up in the government and those down among the masses are as disparate as this! (Chapter 49, "Wu-du" p. 344–5)

[42] The interests of the ruler and those of the officials are different . . . The interests of the ruler are in appointing to office those who are able; the interests of the officials are in getting appointments without proven competence. The interests of the ruler are in giving titles and emoluments to those with merit; the interests of officials are in obtaining wealth and honours without it. The interests of the ruler are in having heroic and talented people in his service; the interests of officials are in forming partisan groups to advance private schemes. (Chapter 11, "Gu-fen" p. 59)

[43] The mind of the ruler and that of an official are different. The ruler employs officials out of calculation and the official serves the ruler out of calculation. Thus, their engagement is mutually calculating. Suffering personal harm in order to benefit the state is what an official will not do; harming the state in order to benefit an official is what the ruler will not do. (Chapter 19, "Shi-xie" 飾邪 p. 93)

[44] Huangdi黄帝 said, "The superiors and inferiors fight a hundred battles a day." (Chapter 8, "Yang-quan" 揚權 p. 34)

(3) Conflict of values

[45] Those who fear death and avoid difficulties are men who would surrender or retreat in a battle but the world honours them as "life-loving gentlemen". Those who study the Way and create their own theories are men who would neglect the law but the world honours them as "cultured gentlemen". Those who travel around and accept generous hospitality are men who beg for a living but the world honours them as "talented gentlemen". Those who twist their language and pretend profundity are fraudulent and deceitful men but the world honours them as "eloquent and intelligent gentlemen". Those who brandish swords and attack and kill are violent, savage men but the world honours them as "hardy and courageous gentlemen". Those who save culprits and hide plotters are men who deserve the death penalty but the world honours them as "chivalrous and admirable gentlemen". These six types of people are those whom the world praises.

Those who run risks and die in honesty are men who steadfastly uphold principles but the world disparages them as "miscalculating persons". Those who are simple and obey orders are men who help make law effective but the world disparages them as "uncouth and naive persons". Those who work hard to make a living are men who create profits but the world disparages them as "small-talented persons". Those who are generous and ingenuous are men who are good and upright but the world disparages them as "silly and stupid persons". Those who follow orders and are careful in carrying out their assignments are men who revere their superiors but the world disparages them as "cowardly and faint-hearted persons". Those who suppress the criminals and prevent plotters are men who help the ruler uncover troubles but the world disparages them as "flattering and slanderous persons". These six types of people are those whom the world despises.

Thus the six types of wicked, fraudulent, useless persons are so praised by the world, and the six types of useful persons who engage in agriculture and war are so despised by the world. This is called "the six contradictions". (Chapter 46, "Liu-fan" p. 318)

[46] He who carries out private favours for old acquaintances is called a loyal person who "does not abandon what is antiquated". He who distributes alms using public money is called a "benevolent man". He who makes light of government emoluments and gives weight to his personal reputation is called a "noble man". He who bends the law to protect the interests of his relatives is called "virtuous". He who gives up government post in order to cultivate certain friendships is called "chivalrous". He who deserts the world and avoids all superiors is called "high-minded". He who quarrels with people and disobeys orders is called a man of "strong character". He who bestows largess on people to win their support is called "popular".

Now, in effect, to praise someone who does not abandon his old acquaintances will indulge officials in their corrupt practices; to praise someone as a benevolent man is to waste state wealth; to praise someone as a noble man is to make people difficult to command; to praise someone as a man of virtue is to lead to the destruction of laws and institutions; to praise someone as a chivalrous man is to encourage people to disregard government offices; to praise someone as high-minded is to cause people to neglect their duties; to praise someone as a man of strong character is to encourage people to disobey the law; and to praise someone as popular is to isolate the ruler. The characters and behaviours that win private praises for individuals are the causes of great disasters for the ruler. (Chapter 47, "Ba-shuo" 八說 pp. 324–5)

[47] Creating titles is to honour but now the world characterises as "lofty" those who belittle titles and their benefits. Instituting ranks is to establish hierarchy but now the world characterises as "worthy" those who slight the ruler and refuse to ask for an audience. Authority and profit are to enforce orders but now the world characterises as "dignified" those who desire no profit and disregard authority. Laws and commands are to achieve order but now the world characterises as "self-respecting" those who disobey laws and commands and pursue private good. Government offices and honours are to encourage people but now the world characterises as "heroes" those who like fame and belittle office. Punishments are to demonstrate authority but now the world characterises as "fearless" those who make light of law and avoid neither corporal punishment nor death. Because people are so much more eager in seeking fame than profit, how can wilful people, who are without much to lose, not go to live in caves in great hardship in order to compete for fame in the world? Therefore, the cause of disorder in the world is not the fault of the inferiors but the ruler's loss of the proper way of government – he values what causes disorder and depreciates what encourages disorder. As a

result what the people want is in conflict with what the ruler hopes to maintain order. (Chapter 45, "Gui-shi" 詭使 p. 314)

(C) Erroneous responses

(1) The basic, critical mistake

[48] What enables the ruler to establish order are punitive rules but now those who adhere to private standards are honoured; what keeps the state stable is calm but now those who are quarrelsome and litigious are made officials; what make the people follow their leader is his trustworthiness and his virtue but now those who are perfidious and manipulative are appointed his agents; what helps to enforce the law and establish authority are people who are respectful and obedient to their superiors but now those who retire to the mountains and caves and criticise the government are given prominence; what fills the granary is the product of the farmer but now those who make luxury goods and do ingenious crafts are made rich; what gives the ruler fame and expands his territories are the soldiers but now, while entertainers ride in carriages and wear silk, orphans of those who have died in battles line the street as beggars; what makes the people do their best and willingly risk their lives in war are rewards but now, while fortune tellers who speak pleasing words in the presence of the ruler receive gifts daily, soldiers who have suffered in battles share no rewards; what gives the ruler the authority to decide issues of life and death are laws and established measures but now, while those who lie with their sweet words and depraved practices get to see the ruler often, those who want to serve him loyally by upholding the law and observing the established measures can have no audience with him; what help the ruler govern well are those who act strictly in accordance with the law, make sure that the punishment fits the crime, apply established rules strictly and put to death the wicked but he keeps them away and stays close to those who endanger the state by flattering him, going along with his wishes and trying to satisfy all his desires; what helps fill the treasury is to collect taxes and make people concentrate on their undertakings but now many avoid work and hide from war by taking shelter with the mighty in order to evade taxes and military service, making tens of thousands of such people beyond the reach of the ruler; what encourages the soldiers are good land and nice houses as rewards but now, while men with pretty daughters or sisters, and great officials and close attendants with few merits, can choose the houses and land they want, the family of a soldier who has died on the battlefield has no house to live in and has to forfeit the land that was assigned to him earlier; what influences the people are the rewards from the ruler but now, while those who retire to the mountains are given prominence, fighting men get no promotion. If the ruler uses these practices as examples to teach the people, how can the titles he creates not to be despised and his own position not to be endangered? (Chapter 45, "Gui-shi" pp. 315–16)

(2) Misguided practices of benevolence and righteousness

(A) THEY ARE SELF-CONTRADICTORY

[49] [Shun went to work with the quarrelling farmers and fishermen, and with the potters who lacked the skill to make good pottery, and, in each case, spent a year in improving their conditions.] Confucius sighed deeply, saying, "Farming, fishing, and making pottery were not Shun's business, and yet he went in order to solve the problems, he personally endured the hardship, and made the people follow his principles. He is benevolent, indeed, and this is why it is said that the virtue of a sage transforms."

Then someone asked a Confucian, "At that time [when Shun did all those things] where was Yao?" The Confucian replied, "Yao was the emperor." "Then why did Confucius praise Yao as a sage? When a sage was the ruler supervising the affairs of the world, he was supposed to free the world from evil. As a result, the farmers and fishermen should not be quarrelling, and pottery should not be of poor quality. If so, who was Shun to transform with his virtue? If Shun was needed to solve the problems, then Yao must be at fault. If you praise Shun as a man of great talents, you have to deny that Yao exercised effective government; if you laud Yao as a sage, you have to deny that Shun transformed people with his virtue. You just cannot praise them both."

"There was a man from Chu who peddled spears and shields. First, he advertised his shields, saying, 'My shields are so tough that nothing can pierce them.' Then he advertised his spears, saying, 'My spears are so sharp that there is nothing they cannot pierce.' Someone asked, 'What would happen if your spear is used to pierce your shield?' The peddler was unable to respond. Now, just as a shield that cannot be pierced and a spear that pierces anything cannot coexist in the same world, Yao and Shun cannot both be praised. To do so is self-contradictory." (Chapter 36, "Nan-yi" pp. 264–5)

(B) THEY ARE INEFFECTIVE IF NOT USELESS

[50] Moreover, in saving the troubles, Shun solved one problem in a year and three problems in three years. His life was limited but the problems of the world are endless. If he attempted to solve the endless problems in his limited lifetime, what he could solve would be few. (Chapter 36, "Nan-yi" p. 265)

[51] A mother's love for her young son is so great that no other kind of love is comparable. Yet, when the son behaves improperly, she sends him to his teacher for discipline; when he is ill, she sends him to a physician for treatment. If not disciplined, he may eventually be punished under the law; if not treated, he may die. Though she loves him, her love is not enough to help him avoid punishment or death. Therefore, what helps preserve a son is not just love. Now the relationship between mother and son is based on natural love; the relationship between the ruler and his subjects is based on self-interests. If a mother cannot preserve her family with love, how can a ruler govern a state with it? (Chapter 47, "Ba-shuo" p. 328)

[52] Now here is a young man of bad character. His parents angrily scold him but he does not reform; the neighbours criticise him but he is unmoved; his teachers admonish him but he refuses to modify his ways. Thus, though three fine influences are brought to bear on him – the love of his parents, the advice of the neighbours, and the wisdom of his teachers – yet he remains indifferent and refuses to change so much as a hair on his shin. But let the local magistrate send out officers to enforce the law and search for miscreants, and then he is filled with terror, reforms his conduct, and changes his ways. Thus, the love of parents is not enough to make children learn what is right; the effort must be backed up by the strict penalties of the local officials; for people by nature grow insolent on love but they listen to authority. (Chapter 49, "Wu-du" p. 343)

[53] Now both the Ruists and the Mohists say that the ancient kings practised universal love and treated all people in the empire like their children. How do they know this? They say, "When the law officer was to administer the death penalty, the king would not have music performed in court and, upon hearing the report of an execution, he would shed tears." This is how they praised the ancient kings.

If it is true that there will invariably be order when the ruler and the subjects are like father and son, then it must be presumed that there can be no disorderly fathers and sons. Among people's natural feelings, none is more prominent than the love of parents towards their children but there is not always order in the family. The ancient kings could not love their people more than parents love their children and, as children are not always orderly, how can the people always be kept in order under the ancient kings? Thus, a ruler who sheds tears upon hearing an execution according to the law only shows his kind heart but not how to establish order. Shedding tears and wishing not to execute are, indeed, signs of benevolence, and yet, that the penalty must be inflicted is the command of the law. The fact that the ancient kings upheld the law, in spite of their own tears, indicates clearly that benevolence is not useful in keeping order.

Moreover, while most people will naturally defer to authority, few of them can be moved by righteousness. Confucius was one of the greatest sages of the world; he perfected his conduct, learned the Way, and travelled throughout the area within the four seas but, in all that area, those who rejoiced in his benevolence, admired his righteousness, and were willing to become his disciples numbered only seventy. It is because to practise benevolence and to adhere to righteousness is not easy; therefore, in the vast world, only seventy men became his disciples, and only one man – he himself – was truly benevolent and righteous . . . Nowadays, when intellectuals counsel a ruler, they do not urge him to wield authority, which is the certain way to success, but, instead, insist that he practise benevolence and righteousness to become a true king. This is, in effect, to demand that the ruler rises to the level of Confucius and that all the ordinary people are to be like his disciples. This is absolutely impossible. (Chapter 49, "Wu-du" pp. 342–3)

[54] When children are at play, they use dirt for rice, mud for soup, and wood for meat but, when it is late, they must go home for dinner because the dirt rice and

mud soup are good only for playing but not for eating. Now reports of the past achievements sound good but are not verifiable; the praises of the ancient kings' benevolence and righteousness do not contribute to the government of a present state. This is because such talk too is good only for playing but not for actual governing. (Chapter 32, "Wai-chu-shuo zuo-shang" p. 204)

(c) They are actually harmful

(i) They make rewards and punishments inappropriate

[55] Intellectuals of the world today who counsel a ruler do not advise him to use his august position of authority and power to subdue wicked subjects. Instead, they all say, "Practise nothing but benevolence, righteousness, magnanimity and love." The ruler, being attracted by the appealing names of benevolence and righteousness never investigates what they really mean. As a result, in a serious case, his state will be ruined and he will lose his life, and, in a lesser case, his territory will be diminished and he will be humiliated. How can this be explained? To give charity to the poor and destitute is what the world regards as acts of benevolence and righteousness, and to have pity on the people and hesitate in inflicting censure and punishment on them are what the world calls attitudes of magnanimity and love. But when a ruler gives charity to the poor and destitute, those with no merit will be rewarded; when he hesitates to inflict punishment, violence and disorder will not cease. In a state where those without merit are rewarded, the people will neither face enemies and fight in battles abroad nor exert their strength in farming and other hard work at home but will rather use their goods and money to bribe those with status and power or do private favours to win good reputations and thereby gain high office and rich emoluments. Therefore, wicked and self-seeking subjects will become more numerous and violent and disorderly persons more overwhelming. Under these circumstances, how long can a state continue without being ruined? (Chapter 14, "Jian-jie-shi chen" p. 74)

[56] King Hui of Wei 魏惠王 asked Bu Pi 卜皮, "You have heard about my reputation. How is it?" Bu Pi replied, "I heard that Your Majesty is kind and magnanimous." The king was happy and said, "So, what do you think I can accomplish?" "Your accomplishment will be the ruin of the state," was the reply. "But," the king protested, "being kind and magnanimous is good behaviour, yet you say it leads to ruin. Why?" In response, Bu Pi said, "A kind person cannot bear suffering; a magnanimous person loves to give charity. A ruler who cannot bear suffering will not punish the guilty; one who loves to give charity will bestow rewards without waiting to see actual achievement. If, in a state, the guilty are not punished, and rewards are bestowed on people without achievements, is it not natural that such a state should fall?" (Chapter 30, "Nei-chu-shuo shang – Qi-shu" p. 169)

[57] The state of Qin was suffering a serious famine. Marquis Ying 應侯 petitioned the king, saying, "In the Five Royal Gardens there is enough grain, vegetables, fruit and nuts to save the people. Please distribute them!" King Zhaoxiang

昭襄王 said, "The law of our state rewards those who are meritorious and punishes those who are guilty. Now to distribute the vegetable and fruit from the Five Gardens is to reward equally people with or without merit. To reward people regardless of whether they have merit is the way leading to disorder. If opening up the Five Gardens causes disorder, it is better to throw away the fruit and vegetable and have order." According to another report, the king said, "To distribute the vegetables and fruit from the Five Gardens to save people is to let those with merit and those without merit fight one another for the food. If those who are saved are to live in disorder, it is better to let them die and keep order in the state. Forget your suggestion, Grand Counsellor." (Chapter 35, "Wai-chu-shuo you-xia" pp. 254–5)

[58] When scholars of the present time talk about government, most of them say, "Give land to the poor and destitute to provide the deprived with some sustenance." Now, if a person, though similar to others yet in a lean year and without alternative income, is alone capable of having enough provisions, he must either have been working very hard or living very frugally. If a person, though similar to others yet in a time not of famine, epidemic diseases or natural or man-made disasters, is alone poor and destitute, he must either have been extravagant or lazy. Those who are extravagant and lazy are, of course, poor; those who are hard-working and frugal are, of course, rich. Now the ruler who taxes the rich to bestow on the poor is robbing the hard-working and frugal to give to the extravagant and lazy. If he wants the people to work hard and be frugal, he cannot have it. (Chapter 50, "Xian-xue" p. 352)

(ii) They make the authorities disrespected and the state ruined

[59] During the reign of Duke Huan of Qi 齊桓公 there was a recluse in the state of Qi named Xiaochen Ji 小臣稷. The duke went to his place three times but never got to see him. The duke said, "I have heard that a commoner cannot move a ruler of a state of ten thousand chariots if he does not think lightly of titles and emoluments, and a ruler with ten thousand chariots cannot successfully court a commoner if he does not practise benevolence and righteousness." So he went again and, at the fifth time, he was granted an audience.

It may be said that Duke Huan did not really know benevolence and righteousness. Now a person may be called benevolent and righteous if he worries about the problems of the world, rushes to render help when there is a crisis in his state, and, in doing so, does not mind taking low positions and performing humiliating chores. Thus, Yi Yin, worrying that the middle kingdom was in chaos, became a cook in order to gain access to Tang; Baili Xi, worrying that the state of Qin was in chaos, became a slave in order to gain access to Duke Mu of Qin. Because they worried about the world and rushed to render help when there was a crisis in a state and did not mind taking low positions and performing humiliating chores, they were called benevolent and righteous.

Now Duke Huan, being a ruler with ten thousand chariots, courted a commoner, hoping that he would help him worry about the problems of the state of

Qi. But Xiaochen would not even see him. This indicates that Xiaochen ignored the needs of the people. A person who ignores the needs of the people cannot be called benevolent and righteous. A benevolent and righteous person will neither forget the rites he ought to observe as a subject nor damage the relative positions of a ruler and a subject.

Within a state, those who attend the court are known as royal servants; those who carry out orders of the government and attend its routine work are known as common subjects. Now Xiaochen was one of the common subjects, and yet he refused what the ruler wanted. Thus, he could not be called benevolent and righteous. Though there was no benevolence and righteousness in Xiaochen's character, Duke Huan nevertheless honoured him! If Xiaochen had wisdom and talents, and yet avoided Duke Huan, he was hiding himself from government service and, for this, he should be sentenced to corporal punishment; if he did not have wisdom and talent, and yet was arrogant and disrespectful towards Duke Huan, he was fraudulent and, for this, he should be sentenced to death. While Xiaochen, because of his conduct, should be sentenced either to corporal punishment or to death, Duke Huan honoured him because he was unable to understand the principle governing the relationship between the ruler and the subjects. Duke Huan was thus teaching the people of the state of Qi the practice of ignoring their superiors and insulting their ruler. This is not the way to govern, and therefore it should be said that Duke Huan did not know benevolence and righteousness. (Chapter 36, "Nan-yi" p. 270)

[60] Zhufu of the state of Zhao 趙主父 sent Li Ci 李疵 to find out whether the small state of Zhongshan was vulnerable to attack. Li Ci reported back, saying, "Zhongshan is conquerable. If Your Highness does not attack now, you will be left behind by Qi and Yan." "Why so?" Zhufu wanted to know. "Because", replied Li Ci, "its ruler reveres people who hide in mountains and caves. He would stop his carriage to talk to scores of scholars living in slums, and he also courts hundreds of commoners with great ceremony." "According to what you just said, he is a worthy ruler. How can I attack him?" Zhufu said. "Not so," said Li Ci, "for, if the ruler respects people hiding in mountains and caves and goes to visit them, then soldiers will be tired of fighting on the battlefields; if the ruler honours scholars and lets them stay in his court, then farmers will be tired of working in their fields. When soldiers are tired of fighting, the army will be weak; when farmers are tired of working, the state will be poor. When a state is poor and its army is weaker than its enemy's, it is unheard of that such a state can avoid ruin. This being the case, why is it not appropriate to attack such a state?" "Very good," said Zhufu, and he raised an army to attack Zhongshan and conquered it. (Chapter 32, "Wai-Chu-shuo zuo-shang" p. 210)

(3) Multiple, confusing ideas and policies

[61] For funeral rites the Mohists wear regular winter garb in winter and regular summer clothes in summer. They make coffins of cheap wood, 3-inch thick, and observe three months of mourning. Regarding their practice as frugal and

restrained, the rulers of the present respect them. In contrast, the Ruists exhaust their family savings for funerals and observe a three-year mourning period until their health is so ruined that they can stand only with canes. Regarding their practice as an act of filial piety, the rulers of the present respect them, too. But, to approve the Mohists' frugality and restraint is to disapprove of the Ruists' extravagance; to approve the Ruists' filial piety is to disapprove of the Mohists' impiety. Now piety and impiety, frugality and extravagance are practised respectively by the Ruists and the Mohists, and the rulers respect them equally . . . Thus the multiple, groundless and confounding theories and practices compete for attention, and the rulers of the present tolerate them all . . . As a result, the people of the world have no established standard for their words and behaviour . . . But ice and burning charcoal cannot remain in the same container for long; winter and summer do not come at the same time; the multiple contradictory teachings cannot be followed to produce order. Now rulers listen to all these theories and observe all these practices. How can there not be disorder? (Chapter 50, "Xian-xue" pp. 351–2)

[62] Where rewards and punishments are not appropriate, the people will have doubts. The people value fame and profit in equal proportion. Where a reward is given to a person who is criticised by the people, it will not be enough to encourage him; where a punishment is imposed upon a person who is praised by the people, it will not be enough to prohibit him. (Chapter 48, "Ba-jing – ting-fa" 八經聽法 p. 337)

[63] In cases where what is censured by the law is preferred by the ruler and what is condemned by the law officers is kept by their superiors, four elements are in contradiction: the law, the private preference, the superiors and the inferiors. If no way can be found to solve it, then, even if there were ten Huangdi 黄帝 around, there can be no order. (Chapter 49, "Wu-du" p. 344)

[64] Zhuozi of Yanling 延陵卓子 was riding in a chariot pulled by a team of beautiful horses with bluish hair resembling pretty pheasant feathers. They were controlled by rein at the front and whip at the back. When they were to go forward, Zhuozi stopped them with the rein and, when they were to go backwards, he stroked them with the whip, and, as a result, they moved sideways. Zaofu 造父 [a famed horse trainer] passed by and cried for the horses, saying, "Since ancient times, when the people were governed in a similar way, the result was the same. Rewards were supposed to encourage people and punishments to prohibit them but, when rewards were followed by disgrace and punishments by plaudits, then people would stand still, not knowing what to do. That practice was what made sages cry." (Chapter 35, "Wai-chu-shuo you-xia" p. 261)

(D) Correct responses

(1) A proper understanding of history and principles of government

[65] In ancient times, men did not have to till the fields because there were enough seeds and fruits in the wild for food; women did not have to weave

because there were enough animal skins for clothing. No one had to toil and yet everyone was adequately provided for. Since the population was small and goods were abundant, the people did not contend, no rich rewards were offered and no harsh punishments administered; the people were orderly by themselves.

Nowadays it is not considered too much for a person to have five sons, and these five sons in turn can have five sons each, so that, before the grandfather dies, he has twenty-five grandchildren. As population grows and goods become scarce, people have to toil and yet have a meagre living. Therefore, they contend and, though rewards are doubled and punishments piled on, disorder cannot be avoided. (Chapter 49, "Wu-du" pp. 339–40)

[66] In great antiquity, when humans were few and animals numerous, people were unable to overcome the birds, beasts, insects, and snakes. Then there appeared a sage who fashioned nests of tree branches to protect people from harm; they were delighted and made him ruler of the world, calling him You-chao-shi (有巢氏 the Nest Builder). People lived on fruits, vegetables, mussels and clams that smelled foul and hurt their stomachs and intestines, and many of them fell ill. Then there appeared another sage who drilled wood and produced fire for cooking thereby enabling people to transform the unsanitary food and avoid illness. People were delighted and made him ruler of the world, calling him Sui-ren-shi (燧人氏 the Fire Maker). In the age of middle antiquity when there was a great flood in the world, Gun 鯀 and Yu 禹 opened up channels for the deluge. In the age of recent antiquity when Jie and Shou ruled in a violent and perverse way, Tang and Wu overthrew them.

Now if anyone were to build nests with tree branches or drill wood for fire in the time of the Xia Dynasty, Gun and Yu would have laughed at him; if anyone were to open channels for water during the Yin or Zhou dynasties, Tang and Wu would have laughed at him. Thus, if people in the present age exalt the ways of Yao, Shun, Yu, Tang, and Wu, the sages of today are certain to laugh at them. (Chapter 49, "Wu-du" p. 339)

[67] When Yao ruled the empire, the thatch of his roof was untrimmed, and his beams were not planed. He ate meals of coarse grain and soup of wild vegetables, wore deerskin in the winter and rough hemp in the summer. Even a lowly gatekeeper of the present is no worse clothed and provided for than he. When Yu ruled the empire, he took pick and shovel in hand to lead his people, working until there was no more down on his thighs or hair on his shins. Even the toil of a slave or prisoner of war of the present is no bitterer than his. Thus, those in ancient times who abdicated and relinquished the rule of the empire were, in a manner of speaking, merely forsaking the life of a gatekeeper and escaping from the toil of a slave, and therefore their handing the empire to someone else is not worthy of much praise. Nowadays, however, after the death of a district magistrate his sons and grandsons are able to go on riding about in carriages for generations, and therefore people prize such offices. Thus, in yielding, people thought lightly about giving up the position of emperor in ancient times but are reluctant to relinquish the post of district magistrate today; this

is because the actual benefits they receive are different. (Chapter 49, "Wu-du" p. 340)

[68] All in the world approve the way of filial piety, fraternal respect, loyalty and obedience but never carefully investigate that way, nor intelligently act according to it. This is the reason why the world is in disorder. Everyone approves the way of Yao and Shun and follows it, and that is why there were those who committed regicide and those who offended their fathers. Yao, Shun, Tang and Wu were those who subverted the right relationship between the ruler and the subject and thus passed wrong lessons down to posterity: Yao was the ruler but made his subject Shun his king; Shun was a subject but made his ruler his subject; Tang and Wu were subjects who murdered their rulers and desecrated their bodies; and yet the world praised them. This is the reason why the world has been in disorder to this day. (Chapter 51, "Zhong-xiao" 忠孝 p. 358)

[69] In the past King Wen of Zhou, located between Feng and Hao, in a fief of 100 *li* square, practised benevolence and righteousness, pacified the western barbarians and eventually became the ruler of the empire. King Yan of Xu, located to the east of the Han River, in a territory of 500 *li* square, also practised benevolence and righteousness. Thirty-six states came with gifts of territory to pay him tribute until King Wen of Jing, fearing for his own safety, called out his troops, attacked Xu, and destroyed it. Thus, King Wen practised benevolence and righteousness and became ruler of the empire but King Yan practised benevolence and righteousness and lost his state. This shows that benevolence and righteousness were useful in the past but not today. Therefore it is said, "When times are different, practice must be different." . . . In great antiquity, rulers resorted to benevolence and righteousness in their competition; in middle antiquity, they applied intelligence and resourcefulness in their struggles; in the present, they use courage and strength in their strife. (Chapter 49, "Wu-du" p. 341)

[70] People of ancient times competed with moral virtue; people of middle antiquity competed with clever schemes; people of today compete with actual strength . . . From these facts it should be clear that abdication, the exaltation of compassion and magnanimity, and the practice of benevolence and righteousness were policies of a wheelbarrow age. To use the tools of a time when human affairs were simple in a time when the affairs are complicated is not what an intelligent person would do. To follow the rules of a time when abdication was practised in a time of great strife is not how a sage would manage the government. (Chapter 47, "Ba-shuo" pp. 326–7)

[71] Since the past and the present have different customs, there should be different measures to respond to the old and the new situations. To use the ways of a generous and lenient government to rule the people of an age of rapid change is like trying to drive a ferocious horse without using reins and whip. This is the misfortune that ignorance invites. (Chapter 49, "Wu-du" p. 342)

(2) An extraordinary leader

[72] Those who do not know the principles of government invariably say, "Do not change what has been established since ancient times and do not alter what has been regarded as normal." Change or not, the sage does not mind, he cares only about what can create order. Therefore, whether that which is ancient and normal should or should not be changed depends on whether it is acceptable. If Yi Yin 伊尹 did not change the old ways of the state of Shang, and Taigong 太公 did not change the old ways of the state of Zhou, Tang 湯 and Wu 武 would not have become kings . . . Now those who found it difficult to change what is ancient are afraid to change what the people have been accustomed to. But not to change what is ancient might be to follow the route to disorder; to accommodate what the people like might be to indulge what the wicked do. The ordinary people are stupid and unable to know what causes disaster. If their superiors are cowardly and incapable of changing course, the government will drift. A great ruler is intelligent enough to know what brings order and resolute enough to enforce what he knows to be right. Therefore, even if his rule antagonises the hearts of the ordinary people, he will carry it out. (Chapter 18, "Nan-mian" 南面 p. 87)

[73] A sage does not practise the ways of antiquity nor abide by a fixed standard; he examines the affairs of the age and designs appropriate responses for them.

There was a farmer in the state of Song in whose field there was a stump. One day a rabbit, racing across the field, bumped into the stump, broke its neck, and died. Thereupon, the farmer laid aside his plough and set up watch beside the stump, hoping that he would get another rabbit in the same way. But he got no more rabbits and, instead, became the laughing stock of Song. Those who think they can take the ways of the ancient kings and use them to govern the people of today are all in the category of stump-watchers! (Chapter 49, "Wu-du" p. 339)

(3) Opportune time and popular support

[74] The factors that enable a clever ruler to accomplish achievements and establish fame are four: the first is the "heavenly time"; the second, "people's hearts"; the third, "ability and tactics", and the fourth, "influential status". When the time is not right, even ten Yao cannot grow one grain in the winter; acting against the hearts of the people, even Meng Fen 孟賁 and Xia Yu 夏育 [two men of the past known for their physical prowess] cannot force people to exhaust their strength. In the right time, a farmer does not have to do much and the grain will grow naturally; when the ruler has the people's hearts with him, he does not have to push them, they will do what is right by themselves; when he applies his tactical ability effectively, he needs not to rush and yet his work will be completed quickly; when he occupies the influential position of the throne, he needs not to push and yet his fame will be established. Thus, it is as water flows and boats float: when a ruler follows the way of nature he can have his endless orders carried out and he is called a bright ruler. (Chapter 28, "Gong-ming" 功名 pp. 154–5)

(4) Special position of power and authority

[75] A person talented, wise and virtuous, but without a high position, will not be able to overcome someone who is unworthy. A plant only 1 foot tall standing on a high mountain can look down on everything 1,000 yards below. As a plant it is not tall but it occupies a high position, being the emperor, Jie was able to control the world not because he was wise and virtuous but because his position was high. As a commoner, Yao could not rectify three families not because he was unworthy but because his position was low. Placed in a boat, an object weighing 1,000 tonnes can float; not being in a boat, an object of a few ounces will sink to the bottom. It is, of course, not that 1,000 tonnes is lighter than a few ounces; whether an object floats or sinks depends on whether it is in a proper position. (Chapter 28, "Gong-ming" 功名 p. 155)

[76] The predominant position of the ruler is his means to overcome the masses. (Chapter 48, "Ba-jing" p. 330)

[77] Shenzi 慎子 said, "A flying dragon floats on clouds and a soaring snake cruises in fog. When clouds are dispersed and the fog evaporates, the dragon and snake are just like ants and earthworms because they have lost their ride. Being in a low position with little power, a virtuous and talented person can be put down by an unworthy one; being in a high position with great power, an unworthy person can dominate the virtuous and talented. As a commoner, Yao could not govern three persons; as the emperor, Jie could cause disorder in the world. From these facts I know that a high position is useful while virtue and wisdom are not worth having. (Chapter 40, "Nan-shi" 難勢 p. 297)

[78] Therefore, where the ruler is good at using his august position, his state is secure; where the ruler does not know how to use his august position, his state is in danger. (Chapter 14, "Jie-jian-shi chen" p. 71)

[79] The ruler's position of power and authority should not be lent to anyone else. If the ruler loses one, the ministers will turn it to one hundred . . . The special position of power and authority of the ruler is like a deep pool. The officials are like the fish. Once the fish gets access to the pool, it can no longer be caught. Once the ruler loses his special position to his officials, he can never regain it. Not wishing to say it straightforwardly, people of ancient times used fish as a metaphor. (Chapter 31, "Nei-chu-shuo xia" p. 179–82)

[80] The special position of power and authority is like the deep pool. It is this position that puts the ruler above the officials. When he loses it, he cannot regain it. When Duke Jian of Qi 齊簡公 lost his position to his minister, Tian Cheng 田成, and when the dukes of Jin 晉公 lost their position to their six high ministers, they lost their states and were murdered. This is why Laozi said, "The fish cannot be let loose in the deep pool." (Chapter 21, "Yu-Lao" 喻老 pp. 116–17)

[81] [In governing the people, the ruler should] rely on his position but not on the people's trust in him. (Chapter 33, "Wai-chu-shuo zuo-xia" p. 216)

(5) Tactics

[82] To the ruler, the state is a chariot and his status is his horse. But, if he does not know the skills of driving, he will be physically exhausted and yet unable to avoid disorder. If he knows the skills, he will enjoy ease and pleasure and yet have the achievements of a true king. (Chapter 35, "Wai-chu-shuo you-xia" p. 259)

[83] Tactics are the means whereby the ruler measures the abilities of people and appoints them to a proper offices, holds accountable according to their titles, exercises power over their life and death, and demands all officials to exert themselves to the best of their abilities. (Chapter 43, "Ding-fa" p. 304)

[84] The way of a bright ruler is to have the intelligent to deliberate thoroughly before he makes a decision so that he will not exhaust his own intelligence. He will let the wise and talented show their abilities and then give them assignments so that he will not exhaust his own abilities. When there is achievement, he will be praised as wise and talented; when there is failure, the subjects will take the blame. Thus, the ruler will never be without good reputation and, though not worthy, he will be the master of the worthies; though not intelligent, he will be the lord of the wise. The subjects will have the hard work but he will own the achievements. This is called the right way of a worthy ruler. (Chapter 5, "Zhu-dao" pp. 18–19)

[85] Huangdi said, "The superiors and the inferiors wage one hundred battles a day." The inferiors conceal their private schemes to test the superiors; the superiors hold the rules and standards to control the inferiors. Therefore, the establishment of rules and standards is the treasure of the ruler; the organisation of partisans and adherents is the treasure of the ministers. The reason why the ministers do not murder the ruler is because their partisans and adherents are not yet organised . . . A ruler following the right way will not empower and enrich his ministers for, when rich and powerful, they will replace him . . . A ruler following the right way will not allow his subjects form partisan factions and thereby cheat him . . . He will repeatedly reduce the power of his ministers like pruning the branches of a tree so as not to let them grow too much and become thicker than the trunk . . . When the branches are thicker than the trunk, the tree will not be able to withstand the spring gale. (Chapter 8, "Yang-quan" pp. 34–5)

[86] [In governing the people, the ruler should] rely on his tactics but not on the people's trust in him. (Chapter 33, "Wai-chu-shuo zuo-xia" p. 216)

[87] In governing the state, a sage has a way that makes people be unable to do anything but love him. He should not rely on people doing what he wants them to do because they love him. He will be in danger if he depends on people doing what he wants for him; he will be safe if he depends on the fact that people can only do what he wants them to do. (Chapter 14, "Jian-jie-shi chen" p. 70)

[88] To tame a crow, its trainer cuts off the feathers at the ends of its wings. As a result, it has to depend on him for food. How can it not be tamed? The same is

true for a bright ruler to control his ministers. He makes it impossible for them not to value his largess and obey his orders. If they cannot but covet his largess and obey his orders, how can they not submit to him? (Chapter 34, "Wai-chu-shuo you-shang" p. 238)

[89] Regarding women in his court, a bright ruler will enjoy their beauty but does not act on their entreaties and grant them their requests. Regarding those close to him, he will use their services but always call their words to account and never allow them to express any uncalled-for opinions. Regarding his uncles, brothers, and great ministers, he, after adopting their words, will make them liable to punishments if what they said turned out to be wrong, and he will never let them make arbitrary recommendations. Regarding things that are pleasurable to him, he will demand to know where they are from and will not allow anyone to present or retract them without his permission, and he will never let the officials speculate on his likes and dislikes. Regarding an act of magnanimity, such as distributing royal largess or opening the treasury and granary to benefit the people, it must be done only under the ruler's order, and the officials will not be allowed to do it as a private favour. Regarding comments officials make on a person, he will investigate the merits they praise and the defects they criticise, checking their allegations against the facts and finding their discrepancies, and, thus, prevent them from commending or discrediting one another. Regarding men of bravery and strength, he will not be niggardly in rewarding their military merit and lenient in punishing their private fights, and, thus, prevent his subjects from acting in their own private interests. Regarding requests from fellow feudal lords, he will grant them if they are lawful but reject them if they are illegal. (Chapter 9, "Ba-jian" p. 38)

[90] What a ruler should employ are seven tactics . . . They are, first, to investigate and compare various points; second, to inflict punishments with certainty and thus make authority clear; third, to bestow rewards faithfully and thus make people do their best; fourth, to listen to the subordinates individually and thus hold the speaker responsible for what is said; fifth, to issue spurious orders and give deceptive assignments; sixth, to ask questions with answers already secretly known; seventh, to say and do what is not really intended. (Chapter 30, "Nei-chu-shuoshang – Qi-shu" p. 158)

[91] The ruler should not reveal his wishes; if he did, his subjects will modify their behaviour to please him. He should not express his opinion; if he did, his subjects will offer their views to support him. Thus it is said, "Get rid of signs of your likes and dislikes, and your subjects will appear as their plain selves." (Chapter 5, "Zhu-dao" 主道 p. 18)

[92] The ruler's way should be invisible; its use should be unintelligible. He should appear purposeless, calm and doing nothing so that he can be in the shadow to observe what is wrong in the light. He will see but will appear not to have seen anything, hear but appear not to have heard anything, and know but appear not to have learned anything. When he hears a statement, he will not make any comment but will compare it with other statements . . . If he

can cover his tracks and hide his intentions, his subjects will not be able to find any clue about how to manipulate him. If he can avoid showing his intelligence and cease demonstrating his abilities, his subjects will not be able to guess what he is going to do. He should keep his objectives to himself and use them as a standard by which to judge the actions of his subjects. He should hold on tightly to the power of rewards and punishments as two handles with which to control his subjects, and thus extinguish any hope and destroy any intention they might have in taking over his position. (Chapter 5, "Zhu-dao" p. 19)

[93] When implementing the established norms, the ruler acts openly like the sky; when employing his subjects, he acts secretly like a ghost. (Chapter 48, "Ba-jing" p. 331)

[94] Duke Ai of Lu asked Confucius: "A popular adage says, 'Not consulting many, one will be bewildered.' Now when I undertook an important task, I deliberated together with many officials, and yet the state is in greater disorder. Why?" Confucius replied, "A bright ruler consults his officials one at a time, letting one official, but not others, know the question. Thus a bright ruler will be up above and all officials will talk straight to him separately. Now if the same question is put to many officials together, they will all say the same thing Jisun 季孫 [the chief minister] says. The entire country speaks with one voice. Your Majesty may ask everyone in the country and yet the state cannot avoid disorder." (Chapter 30, "Nei-chu-shuo shang – Qi-shu" p. 162)

[95] Words and deeds should aim at certain target of utility. If someone sharpens an arrow and shoots it aimlessly, its point always hits something as fine as a piece of a bird's autumn down. But he cannot be called a skilful archer because he does not have a designated target. If a target of 5 inches in diameter is set at a distance of 100 paces away, no one other than Hou Yi 后羿 and Pang Meng 逢蒙[two legendary archers] could always hit the mark. Thus, where there is a established target, the hits by Hou Yi and Pang Meng at a mark 5 inches in diameter is regarded as skilful; whereas, in the absence of a definite target, the hit at a piece of an autumn down is regarded as inept. Now, if in listening to words and observing deeds, one does not use utility as a target, one will find that, though the words are refined and the deeds solid, they are just like arrows shot aimlessly. (Chapter 41, "Wen-bian" 問辯 pp. 301–2)

[96] The way of a bright ruler will not allow an official to present two alternative proposals; he must recommend only one. He will not be allowed to say what he pleases; his words must be verifiable. As a result, fraudulent proposals cannot be presented. (Chapter 48, "Ba-jing" pp. 336–7)

[97] A ruler should clearly understand the tactics of the sage and not follow the arguments popular in the world. He should decide between right and wrong according to the relation between the name and the fact, and examine arguments by comparing and checking them against logic and experience. Then the high officials close to him will know that they cannot get away with deceiving him

. . . and the hundreds of lower officials know that it is unsafe to do wicked deeds. (Chapter 14, "Jian-jie-shi chen" p. 70)

[98] If, after having heard what was presented to him, a ruler does not check it with other arguments, he will not be able to call the speaker to account. If speeches are not put to actual use, false arguments will bewilder the ruler . . . A ruler who knows the way will, after hearing an argument, put it to actual use, and evaluate the result. The evaluation will lead to rewards or punishments. As a result, useless arguments will not be entertained in the court. Office-holders with insufficient knowledge to carry out assignments will be dismissed. An official who exaggerates will be pressed to spell out the details of his statements. When the discrepancy is uncovered, the ruler will be angry. When the result, not being adversely affected by external causes, does not match the statements, the statements are fraudulent, and the fraud will be punished. So every word has its retribution and every argument must be put to actual use. As a result, partisan speeches will not be heard by the ruler. (Chapter 48, "Ba-jing – Can-yan" 參言 p. 336)

[99] A bright ruler ensures that everyone in the world cannot but watch for him and listen for him. Thus he stays in the inner palaces but is aware of everything within the four seas, and none in the world can block his view and deceive him. (Chapter 14, "Jian-jie-shi chen" p. 71)

[100] The right way of the ruler is to make clear to the officials that they can be punished for what they say and punished for what they do not say. If what they say is illogical and groundless they will be punished for saying it; if they are silent in order to avoid responsibility and to keep their positions, they will be punished for not saying it. (Chapter 18, "Nan-mian" p. 86)

[101] The way of the bright ruler is to require the humble expose the wrongdoings of the mighty and punish the inferiors who fail to do so. He will determine the sincerity of a man by checking his words and deeds against many relevant factors, and he will listen widely, barring no channel of information. Thus, the shrewd will not be able to cheat. He will check a person's achievements before giving reward, measure a person's talents before assigning office, and examine the initial plan and observe mistakes in its implementation. He will punish those who have made mistakes and reward those who have accomplishments. As a result, the stupid will not be assigned offices and the shrewd will not dare to cheat. (Chapter 47, "Ba-shuo" p. 325)

[102] Duke Si of Wei 衛嗣公 sent someone as a merchant to go through a customs post. The customs officer made the procedure very difficult. The merchant offered a bribe and was allowed to pass. Then the duke said to the customs officer, "On a certain date a merchant went through your post and gave you a bribe and you let him pass." The customs officer was greatly frightened, thinking the duke clever and observant. (Chapter 30, "Nei-chu-shuo shang – Qi-shu" p. 178)

[103] The method for the ruler to prevent evil schemes is to check the words with the facts. After officials present their arguments, the ruler will give them

assignments and examine the results they produce. If an official's achievement matches his assertions he is to be rewarded; if not, he is to be punished. If what he proposed is great but his achievement falls short, he will be punished. He is not punished for the small achievement but for the mismatch. If his proposal sounds modest but his achievement is great, he will be punished. He is not punished for the great achievement but for the mismatch. (Chapter 7, "Er-bing" 二柄 pp. 27–8)

[104] Officials who are intelligent are promoted step by step to positions of great responsibility. They are to be restrained by the ruler using three measures: *zhi*, *zhen*, and *gu*. *Zhi* is to keep the wife and son of such an official as hostages. *Zhen* is to bestow upon him high rank and rich salary. *Gu* is to check his words and deeds and angrily chastise him when they are inappropriate. A wise official will stop doing wrong when his wife and son are taken hostage. A greedy official will be transformed by the high rank and rich salary. A treacherous one will be subdued by the checks and reprimands. The ruler will lose if he tolerates the official's misconduct and not suppress it. When an official who committed a small wrong is not removed, it will take a great effort to dispatch him. If a punishment is appropriate for the transgression, it should be carried out in public. If the official causes trouble for the government business during his lifetime, or, if his deeds harm the reputation of the state and the ruler, he should be eliminated using poison. Or he should be given to his enemies. This is called getting rid of an evil secretly. (Chapter 48, "Ba-jing" p. 333)

[105] The means by which a bright ruler controls his officials are "two handles", that is all. The "two handles" are penalty and benefaction . . . Penalty is to inflict death and corporal punishment; benefaction is to give rewards and celebrate achievements. As officials fear penalty and welcome benefaction, if the ruler can use penalty and benefaction well, the officials will be fearful of his power and turn to where his benefaction is. (Chapter 7, "Er-bing" p. 26)

[106] A ruler's tactics are what he applies in appointing persons to offices according to their performances on assignments and in checking the substance of a thing against its name. They are used by him in wielding the power of life and death and in examining the abilities of his subjects. (Chapter 43, "Ding-fa" p. 304)

[107] Rewards and punishments are the sharp tools of the state. When they are in the hands of the ruler, he will have control of his subjects; when they are in the hands of the officials, they will overwhelm him. When the ruler indicates that he is to bestow a reward, the officials will subtract a portion from it and give this portion to the recipient as a private favour from them; when the ruler is to impose a punishment the officials will increase the severity to demonstrate their power . . . Therefore it is said, "The sharp tools of the state cannot be revealed to others." (Chapter 21 "Yu-Lao" p. 117)

(6) Law

[108] The bright ruler selects his officials according to law, not his personal preference; he measures their merits according to law, not his personal judgement.

If the ruler personally oversees the hundreds of officials, he will find his day not long enough and his energy not great enough. Moreover, when he uses his eyes, the officials will camouflage their appearance; when he uses his ears, the officials will ornament their voice; when he uses his intelligence, they will make their speech abstruse. Knowing that these three faculties are insufficient, the former kings set aside their own talents and relied on laws and tacties and acted carefully in administering rewards and punishments. (Chapter 6, "You-du" p. 23)
[109] Laws are the great commands promulgated and kept by the government to install firmly in the hearts of the people the prescriptions and prohibitions, and to reward those who obey and to punish those who violate. They are what the officials are to observe. (Chapter 43, "Ding-fa" p. 304)
[110] Law is the rule that the officials have to follow. (Chapter 44, "Shuo-yi" p. 307)
[111] The bright ruler orders his officials never to exercise discretion outside the limit of law and never to do favour within it. Their every move must never be in violation of the law. (Chapter 6, "You-du" 有度 p. 25)

(7) Combination of the three means

[112] Shen Dao 慎到 said, the flying dragon rides on the clouds and the soaring snake cruises in the fog. When the cloud disperses and the fog is burned off, the dragon and the snake are just like earthworms and ants because they lost what they rest on. Thus, if the virtuous and talented are subjected to the unworthy, it is because their power is weak and their position low. If the unworthy are able to subjugate the virtuous and talented, it is because their power is heavy and their position is high. Yao, as a commoner, cannot rule three persons but Jie, as the Son of Heaven, can cause disorder in the whole world. From this I know that power and position are sufficient to rely on; virtue and wisdom are not worth yearning for. (Chapter 40, "Nan-shi" p. 297)
[113] A person responding to Shenzi says: "I do not dispute that a flying dragon and a soaring snake have to rely on clouds and fog but, if you disregard virtue and talent and rely only on a position of power and authority, can you achieve order? I do not see how this can be possible. The dragon and snake are able to ride on clouds and cruise in fog because their abilities are great. Now there are heavy clouds but an earthworm cannot float on them, and there is thick fog but an ant cannot cruise in it. The reason why the ants and earthworms cannot, even though there are heavy clouds and thick fog, is that their abilities are limited. Jie and Shou were placed on the throne to govern the world and given the power and authority of the Son of Heaven, like clouds and fog, for them to ride on. And yet the world could not avoid being plunged into great disorder because their abilities were limited. Moreover, if you maintain that Yao used his position of power and authority to establish order in the world, then I want to ask you how was Yao's position different from that of Jie who used his to cause disorder in the world? In fact, there is no guarantee that the position of power and authority will be used only by the virtuous and talented but not by the unworthy. When it is

used by the virtuous and talented, the world will enjoy order; when it is used by the unworthy, the world will be plunged into disorder. By nature, the virtuous and talented are few, and the unworthy many. Therefore, give the position of power and authority to an average person in this disorderly world of many unworthy people, and the chances of such a person using the position to cause disorder will be far greater than those of a person using the position to establish order . . .

Thus, the position of power and authority can facilitate the establishment of order but can also help create disorder . . . If one speaks only about using the position of power and authority as a means to establish order in the world his knowledge is rather shallow . . .

Now here is a sturdy carriage and a swift horse: if an ordinary servant is to drive them, the result will be laughed at by people; but, if Wang Liang is the driver, they can travel 1,000 *li* a day. Though being the same carriage and horse, they can either travel 1,000 *li* or be laughed at because the skills of the drivers are far apart. Now, if the state is compared to a carriage, the special position of the ruler to a horse, law and order to the reins, and punishments to the whip and spur, and a Yao or a Shun is made the driver, the world will be in order but, if a Jie is to drive, the world will be in disorder. Thus, the effects of a worthy person and an unworthy one are far apart. Now, if one wants to drive fast and far but does not know to employ Wang Liang, if one wants to increase advantages and eliminate harm but does not know to employ worthy and talented men, he has the problem of not knowing this analogy, for Yao and Shun are the Wang Liangs in governing the people." (Chapter 40, "Nan-shi" pp. 297–9)

[114] One may reply to this argument by saying, "While Shenzi maintained that a ruler can rely on his august position for the establishment of order, you insist that there must be virtuous and talented men before good government can be possible. This is not right. For the term 'position' may refer to many things. If it refers to a condition that leads to a result predetermined by nature, then there is no point in talking about using it for any purpose. What I speak of is a condition created by man.

Now you pointed out that, when Yao and Shun had the position, there was order; when Jie and Shou had the position, there was disorder. I do not belittle Yao and Shun, but still order cannot be established by any individual alone. If Yao and Shun were born with the position of power and authority, order was inevitable; even if there were ten persons like Jie and Shou, they could not cause disorder. On the other hand, if Jie and Shou were born with the position of power and authority, disorder was inevitable; even if there were ten persons like Yao and Shun, they could not establish order. Thus, if the conditions are for order, no one can cause disorder; if the conditions are for disorder, no one can establish order. These are the natural conditions, not created by man. But I am talking about conditions created by man . . .

Moreover, Yao and Shun, Jie and Shou would not appear one after another but only once in a thousand generations. The world is thus more often governed by rulers of average quality. The conditions I talk about are those for these average rulers. An average ruler is not as good as Yao or Shun nor as bad as Jie or Shou. If he can embrace the law and hold on to his position of power and authority – the conditions created by man – there will be order; if he disregards the law and loses his position of power and authority, there will be disorder. If we discard the use of power and authority and turn our backs on the law and wait for persons like Yao and Shun to head the government, then there will be one generation of order out of every thousand generations of disorder. If we follow the law and properly use the power and authority and wait for persons like Jie and Shou to cause disorder, then there will be one generation of disorder out of every thousand generations of order . . .

If tools for straightening and bending wood are discarded and instruments for measuring length and roundness are dismissed, even Xi Zhong would not be able to make a single wheel. Similarly, without celebrations and rewards as means of encouragement, and punishments and penalties as means of threat, and the special position of power and authority is given up and the law cast away, Yao or Shun could go from door to door to preach a course, people would argue with him, and he would not be able to govern three families. The usefulness of the special position of a ruler is thus adequately proven and the allegation that, to establish order, it is necessary to wait for virtuous and talented persons is not true. If, for a hundred days, a person declines eating in order to wait for rice and meat, he will die of hunger. Now to wait for a person as virtuous and talented as Yao and Shun to govern the people is like waiting for rice and meat to save the starved.

I think the saying is not right that a sturdy carriage and a swift horse driven by a common slave will only make people laugh but, when driven by Wang Liang, they can travel 1,000 *li* a day. Now if we wait for the good swimmer from the state of Yue to come to rescue people drowning in the Central State, though the person from Yue is good at swimming, the drowning people in the Central State will be beyond salvation before he arrives. To wait for the Wang Liang of the past to drive a horse of today is like the talk of waiting for a person from Yue to rescue the drowning people; the unacceptability is quite clear. If there are a sturdy carriage and good horses, and a station at every 50 *li*, an average coachman can drive fast and far and reach 1,000 *li* a day. Why wait for the Wang Liang of old?

Moreover, in the matter of driving, if the driver is not a Wang Liang, you have to let a common slave ruin it; in the matter of governing, if the ruler is not a Yao or a Shun, you have to let a Jie or a Shou disrupt it. It is like in eating, if the food is not gluten or honey, you have to have bitter vegetables or acrid weeds. These statements are argumentative, using lots of sophisticated words only to make nonsense, and they are arbitrary, offering the choice of two extreme positions. How can they be used to dispute a position that is more in agreement with reason and common sense? Your arguments did not address this point." (Chapter 40, "Nan-shi" pp. 299–301)

[115] An enquirer asked, "Which is more urgently needed by a state – the teachings of Shen Buhai or those of Gongsun Yang?" The answer is, "They do not

comprise a choice. A person will die if he does not have food for ten days. He will also die if he does not have clothes in the bitter cold. If you ask which is more urgently needed by a person, food or clothes, I shall say neither is dispensable, both are necessary to sustain life.

Shen Buhai advocated the use of tactics of control while Gongsun Yang emphasised the use of law . . . If the ruler does not know the tactics of control, there will be problems at the top; if the officials do not follow the law, there will be chaos at the bottom. As means of government, both are indispensable." (Chapter 43, "Ding-fa" p. 304)

[116] The enquirer asked, "Why it is not enough to use only tactics but no law, and it is also not enough to use only law but no tactics?" The answer is: "Shen Buhai was once the chief minister of Marquis Zhao of Han. As a state, Han was originally a part of the state of Jin. Before the laws of the Jin were set aside, new laws of the Han were adopted. Before orders of the previous rulers were rescinded, new orders of the later rulers were issued. Shen Buhai did not straighten the laws and unify the orders. As a result, problems proliferated. Shen Buhai would apply either an old or a new law or order depending on which produced greater advantage to the state. But, when the old and the new laws and orders were in conflict, the wicked officials could argue against Marquis Zhao's decision even though Shen Buhai had taught him to use ingenious tactics. Hence, for seventy years, the state of Han of ten thousand chariots was unable to become hegemonic. The trouble was that, while tactics were used by the ruler, law was not properly applied by the officials.

While governing the state of Qin, Gongsun Yang established the system of denunciation and implication to find the truth and organised every five and ten households into units to inflict collective punishments on every member of the unit for a crime committed by any fellow member. Rewards were generous and certain; punishments heavy and definite. Consequently, the people worked hard without rest and risked danger pursuing enemies without retreat. Therefore, the state became rich and its army strong. But, because the ruler had no tactics to uncover wicked schemes, the wealth and strength of the state benefited only the officials. After the deaths of Duke Xiao and Lord Shang, King Hui ascended to the throne. The laws of Qin had not yet fallen but Zhang Yi betrayed Qin to win favour from the states of Han and Wei. After the death of King Hui, King Wu ascended to the throne. Gan Mao sacrificed the interests of Qin in developing the land of Zhou. After the death of King Wu, King Zhaoxiang ascended to the throne. Marquis Rang crossed Han and Wei to attack Qi. In five years, Qin did not gain a foot of land, and yet he was rewarded the fief of Tao. For eight years, Marquis Ying attacked Han only to secure for himself the fief of Runan. Since then, all those who served Qin have been like Ying and Rang. Thus, when Qin won wars, its great ministers were honoured; when it expanded its territory, private fiefs were established. The reason is because its ruler had no tactics to detect wicked schemes. Though Lord Shang greatly emphasised the use of law, it was turned by the officials to their own advantage. As a result, despite its strength, for several decades Qin did not become an empire. The trouble was that, despite the fact that the officials had strict laws to observe, the ruler had no tactics to control them from above. (Chapter 43, "Ding-fa" pp. 304–5)

[117] The inquirer again asked, "Suppose the ruler applies the tactics of Shenzi and the officials observe the law of Lord Shang, would the result be all right?" This is the reply: "Neither Shenzi's argument for the use of tactics nor Lord Shang's argument for the use of law is perfect. Shenzi said, 'An official should not do anything beyond his duty, and say anything even though he has knowledge of it.' Now, not to do anything beyond one's duty is to act strictly according to one's commission, and that is right. But to be silent about what one knows will make one cover up wrongdoings. When the ruler sees things with the aid of everyone's eyes, his vision is sharper than anyone's; when he listens with the aid of everyone's ears, his hearing is keener than anyone's. If people know something but will not speak, how can the ruler find such help?

The law of Lord Shang says, 'He who beheads an enemy soldier in a foreign war is to be rewarded with one grade in rank. If he wishes to become an official, he will be given an office with a salary of about 500 catties in weight of rice. He who beheads two enemy soldiers is to be rewarded two grades in rank . . .' Thus, the promotion in office and rank matches the merit in beheading enemy soldiers in war. If now there is a law saying, 'He who beheads an enemy soldier is to be made a physician or carpenter,' then no house can be constructed and no illness cured. A carpenter has skilful hands to build things and a physician knows how to prepare drugs. If someone with merit in beheading enemy soldiers is to do either of those jobs, he will not have the abilities. Now, what is required for government work is knowledge and talent. What is required for beheading enemy soldiers is courage and strength. To make a man with courage and strength fill an office that requires knowledge and talent is like making a man with the merit of beheading enemy soldiers serve as a physician or a carpenter. Therefore, it is said, 'In expounding the principles of the use of tactics and law, neither of the two thinkers was perfect.'" (Chapter 43, "Ding-fa" pp. 305–6)

[118] The ruler should make his officials, though wise and talented, unable to act arbitrarily against the law; though virtuous and worthy, not to receive rewards ahead of those who have achievements; though loyal and trusted, not to be exempted from prohibitions prescribed by law. This is called "to demonstrate the absoluteness of the law". (Chapter 18, "Nan-mian" p. 85)

(E) Theory of law

(1) Objectives and functions of law

[119] The sage is careful about what is right and what is wrong, and he thoroughly understands what facilitates order and what causes disorder. Thus, in governing a state, he promulgates correct laws and publicises severe punishments. The purpose is to save the people from disorder, to rid the world of disasters, to prevent the strong from attacking the weak and the majority from oppressing the

minority, to let the old live in peace and the young have a chance to grow, and to make the borders free from conflicts, and, as a result, the ruler and the subjects will have mutual affections, the fathers and sons will be able to take care of one another, and there will be no fear of dying in a battle or being taken prisoner of war. (Chapter 14, "Jie-jian-shi chen" p. 72)

[120] It is therefore said, "Though a skilled carpenter can, using his eyes, see a straight line, he always uses his instruments to make sure of the result; though a highly intelligent person can quickly come up with a proper measure to deal with an affair, he will always compare it with the law of the former kings." (Chapter 6, "You-du" pp. 25–6)

[121] As hammer and anvil are to level the uneven, and a straightening device is to correct the crooked, the law is made by the sage to level the uneven and to correct the crooked. (Chapter 35, "Wai-chu-shuo you-xia" p. 259)

[122] To subdue a tiger without using a cage, to suppress evil without using the law, or to prevent fraud without using a tally will be a trouble for Fen and Yu, and a difficulty for Yao and Shun. Therefore, to construct a cage is not to provide against rats but to enable the weak and timid to subdue a tiger; to establish laws is not to provide against Zeng and Shi but to enable an average ruler to prohibit Robber Zhi. (Chapter 26, "Shou-dao" p. 151)

[123] What the present calls "worthy" is virtuous and truthful behaviour; what it calls "wise" is subtle and sophisticated speech. Such speech is difficult even for the most intelligent to understand. If laws made for the masses are difficult even for the most intelligent to understand, the ordinary people will have no way of understanding them. When there is not enough coarse stuff to fill one's stomach, one will not seek fine grains and meat; where there is not adequate cloth to cover one's body, one will not wait for embroidered silk. In managing the affairs of the world, if the most urgent tasks are not yet finished, the ruler should not work on what is more remote. In the present, what is to be managed is the mundane business of the common people. If the ruler does not use what the ordinary men and women can easily understand but asks them to comprehend what is difficult for the most intelligent, he is doing the opposite of good government. (Chapter 49, "Wu-du" p. 346)

(2) Bases of law

[124] The way to keep a state in peace should be in agreement with nature. People want food when hungry and clothes when cold, they do not need orders from others for doing so. The ancient kings recognised this principle and made laws accordingly. Since the principle is in agreement with nature, the laws were observed willingly by all people subsequently. If a law which orders men who are hungry and cold to stay away from food and clothes, it cannot be enforced even by Fen and Yu; if a law is against nature, it cannot be established. (Chapter 25, "An-wei" p. 147)

[125] In governing the people, the sage will consider what is essential to them but will not simply follow what they desire. His objective is to benefit them. (Chapter 54, "Xin-du" 心度 p. 365)

[126] The people are stupid and incapable of knowing what causes disorder . . . They care much about small profits and are ignorant about great benefits. (Chapter 18, "Nan-mian" p. 87)
[127] The sage who makes laws for a state is inevitably in conflict with the world but in compliance with the Way. Those who know the Way follow it but not the customs; those who do not know the Way follow the customs but not the Way. (Chapter 14, "Jian-jie-shi chen" p. 72)
[128] The ruler should be clever enough to know the path to order and resolute enough to follow it strictly. Therefore, even though he has to go against what the people cherish in their hearts, he will do so and establish order. (Chapter 18, "Nan-mian" p. 87)
[129] Those who are ignorant of the principles of government insist on not changing what is old and not altering what is regular. The sage will not listen to advocates of change or no change. His goal is to establish order. Therefore, to him, whether the old and regular should be changed depends on whether they are conducive to order. (Chapter 18, "Nan-mian" p. 87)

(3) Important characteristics of law

(A) PRAGMATIC

[130] If the ruler makes a law demanding difficult behaviour and punishes those who fail to comply, grievances will grow. (Chapter 27, "Yong-ren" p. 153)
[131] A law that encounters no difficulty and an achivement that has no bad effects do not exist in the world. Thus, where a city of a thousand yards in perimeter is conquered or an army of a hundred thousand men is routed, the attacker loses half his troops. Though armour and weapons are destroyed and soldiers die and are wounded, the attacker will be congratulated for the victory and his gain of land because by calculation he suffers a small harm but gains big profit . . . Therefore, the sage does not seek anything which has no bad effects; rather, he puts his mind to something that is certain to have some good results. (Ch. 47, "Ba-shuo" p. 327)

(B) CONSTANT BUT ADAPTABLE

[132] A state where laws and prohibitions are frequently changed and [conflicting] orders speedily issued is sure to fall. (Chapter 15, "Wang-zheng" 亡徵 p. 79)
[133] It is best for laws to be uniform and constant so that the people can know them. (Chapter 49, "Wu-du" p. 343)
[134] When a mirror is clean and held steady, beauty or ugliness can be revealed; when a scale is properly constructed and held steady, weight can be measured. If the mirror is shaking, the image will not be clear; if the scale is shaking, the correct weight cannot be measured. This is the same for the law. (Chapter 19, "Shi-xie" p. 92)
[135] In governing a large state, if the law is frequently changed, the people will suffer. Thus, a ruler who knows the Way values inaction and is careful about

changing the law. Therefore it is said, "Governing a large state is like cooking a small fish." (Chapter 20, "Jie-Lao" p. 104)

[136] There is no immutable way to govern the people but, as a principle, law should be used to pursue order. When laws are adjusted to the times, there will be order; when government undertakings are in agreement with the age, there can be accomplishments. Thus, when the people are simple, proscriptions can keep them in order; when they are shrewd, penal laws will make them obedient; when the times have changed but laws have not, there will be disorder; when the world is different but laws are not, there will be disasters. Therefore, in governing the people, the sage makes his laws evolve in accordance with the times and his prohibitions adjusted to the conditions of the world. (Chapter 54, "Xin-du" p. 366)

(c) Plain but specific

[137] Where a book is brief, students will debate its meaning; where a law is sketchy, people will have litigations. Therefore, a sage's book always contains careful discussions, and a bright ruler's laws are comprehensive and specific about relevant matters. (Chapter 47, "Ba-shuo" p. 329)

[138] Law is to be written and compiled, deposited in government offices, and promulgated for the common people to know. Therefore, it is best to make law public. When a bright ruler talks about law, all people in the realm, even the humble and uncouth, should be able to hear and understand it. (Chapter 38, "Nan-san" 難三 p. 290)

[139] Law is made for the multitudes of people. If a law is difficult for a highly intelligent person to understand, the common people will have no chance of understanding it. (Chapter 49, "Wu-du" p. 346)

(d) Objective and easy to apply

[140] Laws are reliable; a person's intelligence often leads to mistakes. When the scale is hung, the weight is known; when the compass is used, the roundness is assured. This is the dependable way. A bright ruler makes his people follow this way and consequently, he can be at ease yet have achievements. To discard the compass and rely on one's skill, and to discard the law and rely on one's intelligence is the way that leads to confusion and disorder. (Chapter 19, "Shi-xie" p. 92)

[141] If Yao discarded the law and relied on his personal judgement, he could not put one single state in order; if Xi Zhong 奚仲 [a great wheelwright] rejected the compass and relied on his intuition, he could not make one single wheel; if Wang Er 王爾 [a skilful carpenter] abandoned the ruler and relied on his hunches, he could not correctly determine the right length of things in half the cases. If an average ruler follows the law and a mediocre craftsman holds on to his tools, they can make no mistakes. (Chapter 27, "Yong-ren" p. 152)

(E) FORCEFUL AND EFFECTIVE

[142] To govern the world, it is necessary to be in agreement with people's feelings. Because people have likes and dislikes, rewards and punishments can therefore be useful. Because rewards and punishments are useful, orders and prohibitions can be established and the course of government set. (Chapter 48, "Ba-jing" p. 330)

[143] Without the severe effect of the whip and the forceful restraint of the bridle, even Zaofu 造父 could not subdue a horse; without the position of power and authority and the laws prescribing rewards and punishments, even Yao and Shun could not keep a state in order. (Chapter 14, "Jian-jie-shi chen" p. 74)

[144] In making laws, the sage king makes their rewards enough to encourage people to do good, and their punishments enough to deter people from committing violence. (Chapter 26, "Shou-dao" p. 149)

[145] It is best to make rewards generous and the promise of reward reliable so that the people will care for the rewards; it is best to make punishments severe and the enforcement sure and strict so that the people will be afraid of the punishments. (Chapter 49, "Wu-du" p. 343)

[146] The king of Yue 越王 set fire to his palace, and no one tried to save it. Then he ordered, "In fighting the fire, he who dies will be rewarded as if he died in a battle; he who survives will be rewarded as if he defeated the enemy. For those who do not fight the fire, the punishment will be comparable to that for those who surrendered to the enemy." Thereupon, people covered their bodies with mud, donned wet clothes and charged at the fire, three thousand on its left side and three thousand on its right side. (Chapter 30, "Nei-chu-shuo shang – Qi-shu" p. 171)

[147] The bright ruler offers rewards which can be earned and prescribes punishments which are avoidable. Consequently, the worthy will be encouraged by the rewards . . . and the unworthy will suffer fewer punishments . . . If the ruler institutes difficult requirements and punishes those who fall short of the mark, secret resentment will arise. (Chapter 27, "Yong-ren" pp. 252–3)

[148] The loftiest persons of the world cannot be encouraged with rewards; the meanest persons of the world cannot be restrained by punishments. If, on account of the loftiest persons, rewards are not established, and, on account of the meanest persons, punishments are not instituted, the right way of governing the state and employing the people will be missed. (Chapter 51, "Zhong-xiao" p. 361)

[149] Today, those who do not understand the principles of good government all say, "Heavy punishments do great harm to people. When light punishments are enough to prevent wrongdoing, why resort to heavy punishments?" Such people have not investigated how order is established. Now a wrongdoing which can be prevented by a heavy punishment may not be prevented by a light one. But, if it can be prevented by a light punishment, it certainly can be prevented by a heavy one. Thus, if the authority imposes heavy punishments, all evils will be stopped.

If all evils are stopped, how can heavy punishment do any harm to the people? A punishment is called "heavy" in a case where the gain a wrongdoer makes is small but the punishment the authority imposes on him is great. People will not risk a great punishment to make a small gain; therefore, all evils will stop. A punishment is called "light" in a case where the gain a wrongdoer makes is great but the punishment the authority imposes on him is small. People covet the gain and take lightly the punishment; therefore, evils will not stop. Thus, former sages said, "People do not tumble over a mountain but they do over a small lump of earth." A mountain is big, so people climb with care; a lump of earth is small, so people pay no attention. Now if punishments are made light, they will certainly be ignored by the people. When an offence is committed and no punishment is meted out, it is to drive the nation into disorder and abandon it there. If the offence is then punished, it is like setting up traps to catch the people. Thus, to the people, light punishments are like lumps of earth. Therefore, in governing the people, to lighten the punishments will either cause disorder in the state or be like setting up traps for the people. Now this is, indeed, doing great harm to them. (Chapter 46, "Liu-fan" p. 322)

[150] Scholars all say "Make punishments light!" This way leads to disorder and ruin. For rewards and punishments are for inducing and deterring; if the reward is generous, what the authority wants will be quickly induced; if the punishment is severe, what the authority does not want will be promptly deterred . . . Anyone who wants order must make the rewards generous; anyone who hates disorder must make punishments severe. Those who advocate light punishment have neither enough hate for disorder nor enough desire for order. They are not only incompetent but also unethical. (Chapter 46, "Liu-fan" p. 321)

[151] Moreover, heavy punishments are not meant for the criminal. The law of a bright ruler which prescribes the execution of a murderer is not to correct him because it will be to correct a dead person; to punish a robber is not to correct him because it will be to correct a slave. Thus, it is said, "Make the punishment heavy for one wicked man and the wrongdoers of the entire country will be stopped." This is how order is achieved. Though those who receive the heavy punishments are murderers and robbers, those who are to be warned and frightened are innocent people. Therefore, why should those who desire good government have any doubt of the value of heavy punishments? (Chapter 46, "Liu-fan" pp. 321–2)

[152] In the past, those who were good at keeping the Way of government used what was heavy to prohibit what was light, and what was difficult to stop what was easy. As a result, all men, noble or petty, behaved correctly, and Robber Zhi 盜跖 and Zeng 曾 Shi 史 were equally honest. How do I know this? I know even the greedy robber would not go to the ravine to pick up gold because, if he did, he will not return alive . . . The way a clever ruler makes prohibitions work is to let those like Robber Zhi see the harm they are to suffer in case they wish to grab something they can hardly get . . . When they see this, they become prudent and the world will be just and fair. (Chapter 26, "Shou-dao" p. 150)

[153] According to the law of the Yin Dynasty, those who threw ash into the street were given corporal punishment. Zigong子貢thought it too heavy, and asked Confucius about it. "It was a way of those who knew how to govern", said Confucius, "because throwing ash into the street could harm people and, being harmed, people will be angry and, being angry, they may start a fight and a fight may lead to extensive mutual injuries to the clans involved. As an act which may eventually cause injury to many people, it ought to be punished. Moreover, while to suffer severe punishment is what the people surely hate, to throw ash into the street is what they can easily avoid. To make people do what is easy and help them shun what they hate is the way to lead to good order."(Chapter 30, "Nei-chu-shuo shang – Qi-shu" pp. 166–7)

(F) Absolute and supreme

[154] At present, regarding speeches, a ruler is delighted at the speaker's eloquence but does not look into whether his words are appropriate; regarding activities. he admires the acting person's reputation but does not check whether his actions produce any achievement. That is why, among the multitude of the world, those who make speeches strive for eloquence but do not pay attention to usefulness; as a result, men quoting the early kings and talking about benevolence and righteousness fill up the court but cannot help the government to avoid disorder; men taking action compete to appear lofty but cannot bring about any achievement. (Chapter 49, "Wu-du" pp. 346–7)

[155] Someone asked, "How do contentious arguments originate?" The reply is: "They originate from the ruler's lack of enlightenment." The enquirer further asks, "How is it that, when the ruler is not so enlightened, there will be contentious arguments?" "In a state under a clever ruler," says the respondent, "government orders are the most respected words, and state laws are the best guides for affairs. There cannot be two different sets of words equally respected and two different sets of contradictory actions both lawful. The words and actions which do not conform to law or order must be banned. (Chapter 41, "Wen-bian" p. 301)

[156] Therefore, in the state of a bright ruler, there are no books of learning; law is the only material for instruction. There are no sermons of the former kings; the officials serve as the only teachers. There are no fierce feuds of private swordsmen; cutting off the heads of the enemy is the only deed of valour. Hence, when the people of such a state make a speech, their words must be guided by law; and when they do brave deeds, they do them in the army. Therefore, in times of peace, the state is rich, and, in times of trouble, its armies are strong. These are what are called the capital of a true king. (Chapter 49, "Wu-du" p. 347)

(F) Application and enforcement of law

(1) Pursue relative advantages

[157] Nowadays, all people in the country talk about order and many families keep the laws of Shang Yang and Guan Zhong but the country is getting poorer

because those talking about tilling the land are many but those actually taking up the plough are few. (Chapter 49, "Wu-du" p. 347)

[158] Laws are to regulate undertakings, and undertakings are to seek beneficial results. If, after being established, a law is found to be difficult to enforce, weigh the difficulty against the significance of the undertaking, and enforce it if it will push a significant undertaking to success. If it is anticipated that an undertaking is to have some bad effects, weigh the bad effects against the beneficial results, and go ahead and do it if the beneficial results outnumber the bad effects. A law that encounters no difficulty and an achievement that has no bad effects does not exist in the world . . . Therefore, the sage does not seek anything that has no bad effects; rather, he puts his mind to something that is certain to have some good results. (Chapter 47, "Ba-shuo" p. 327)

(2) Encourage report of wrongdoings

[159] The ruler who knows the way to govern the people prevents evil before it germinates . . . and, by rewarding the reporting of wrongdoings, he prevents it from growing. (Chapter 54, "Xin-du" p. 365)

[160] The best-governed state is good at the task of preventing evil . . . How is small evil to be stopped? It is to make people watch one another in their hidden affairs. How can they be made to watch one another? It is by implicating the persons in the same hamlet in one another's crimes. When a person knows that he can be implicated, it will be natural that he will watch out for fear of not being able to escape unharmed, and the person with an evil scheme will not forget that he is being watched by many. Consequently, everyone will be careful about his own conduct and watch the actions of others and report any wicked secrets. If the informant is not only exempted from collective punishment but also rewarded, and he who fails to denounce an evil act is definitely to suffer such punishment, evil types will be exposed and no evil, however miniscule, will be tolerated. This is the result of encouraging the secret reporting of evil and strict enforcement of collective punishment. (Chapter 55, "Zhi-fen" 制分 pp. 367–8)

[161] A bright ruler makes everyone in the world cannot but watch and listen for him. As a result, while he stays in the innermost court of his palace, everything within the four seas is brightly clear to him, and the world is unable to hoodwink or deceive him . . . In ancient Qin, the officials discarded law for their private interests, and, as a result, the state was in disorder, the army weak, and the ruler humiliated. Lord Shang persuaded Duke Xiao to renovate the law and change the customs by making public justice clear, rewarding the reporting of evil, suppressing trifling undertakings and making fundamental work profitable. At that time, the people of Qin, being accustomed to the old tradition that the guilty could be pardoned and the meritless honoured, took it lightly in violating the new laws. So Lord Shang inflicted severe penalties on the offenders and bestowed generous rewards on the informants. Hence, no culprits were missed and the men who suffered punishments were many, and the people became resentful, and numerous misgivings were reported daily. The duke ignored their complaints and enforced

Lord Shang's laws. Thereafter, the people knew that the guilty were certain to be punished, and informants multiplied. As a result, the people no longer violated the law and punishments became useless; the state was put in order and the army became strong; the territory was expanded and the ruler became honoured. The reason behind all these is that the punishment for concealing crimes was severe and the reward for denouncing transgressions was generous. This is the way to make the world watch and listen on behalf of the ruler. This principle and tactics for ultimate government is very clear, yet the scholars of the world do not know! (Chapter 14, "Jian-jie-shi chen" p. 71)

(3) Conduct hearings

[162] The way to listen to a person making a statement is to look drunk. I will not move my lips to make a quick comment. And when I do, it will sound rather irrelevant. He will himself deviate from his own line and thereby I will know his mistakes. Let what is right and what is wrong come together and show the contradictions. I will not participate in the construction of the narration. Instead, I will stay quiet, inactive and without an opinion; this is the way to ascertain facts. Then I will compare his allegations with those of similar kinds; this is the way to find the truth. After making the comparison, I will analyse the principles and, when the principles are held fast, the varying details will not mislead me to a wrong judgment. (Chapter 8, "Yang-quan" p. 32)
[163] Once two persons were suing each other. Zichan 子產 separated them, keeping them incommunicado, and, after listening to one party, he told the other the opposite of what he had heard. In this way, he learned the truth. (Chapter 30, "Nei-chu-shuo shang – Qi-shu" p. 178)

(4) Make decision

[164] There are six ways to danger . . . The first is "to make cuts within the limits of law". The second is "to grant allowances beyond the limits of law". (Chapter 25, "An-wei" p. 147)
[165] Those in the past who knew the great principles . . . never burden their minds with intelligence and their hearts with private interests. They entrusted law for upholding order and suppressing disorder, and they used the weight and balance to determine what was light and what was heavy. Thus, they never contradict the course of heaven nor hurt the feelings of man. They never blew to part the hair to find small blemishes and never washed away the dirt to investigate what is difficult to see. They never imported something from outside of the line and never pushed something away from inside the line. They were never harsh beyond the boundary of law and never lenient within the boundary of law but observed the established principles and followed self-evident rules. Thus, the punishments they inflicted and the rewards they bestowed were based on reason and law, not on their personal love or hatred. (Chapter 29, "Da-ti" p. 156)
[166] If the ruler discards the regular law and follows his own private opinion, his subjects will decorate themselves with sophistry and skills. When they do so, law

and prohibitions cannot be established, and arbitrary opinions will prevail; the right way of government will be jeopardised. The right way to govern a state is to repudiate what injures law. As a result, those who apply and enforce law will not be confused by their intelligence and skills nor will they be tempted to win good names and high praises. (Chapter 19, "Shi-xie" p. 91)

[167] In the past Shun ordered officials to drain the great flood. One official began working before the order came and achieved some success but Shun had him executed. Once Yu summoned the various feudal lords for an audience in a place named Kuai-ji, when the ruler of Fangfeng 防風 arrived late, Yu had him decapitated. From these facts, that one who went ahead of orders was executed and one who lagged behind orders was beheaded, it is clear that, in the past, to observe orders strictly was a principle held in the foremost respect. (Chapter 19, "Shi-xie" pp. 91–2)

[168] Once, in the past, Marquis Zhao of Han 韓昭侯 was drunk and fell asleep. Seeing the ruler exposed to cold, the keeper of hats put a robe over him. When he awoke, he was glad and asked the attendants about who put the robe over him. They replied that it was the hat-keeper. The ruler punished the keeper of clothes and ordered the hat-keeper to be executed. The reason for punishing the clothes-keeper is that he neglected his duty; the reason for punishing the hat-keeper is that he overstepped his post. It was not that the Marquis did not mind catching cold but considered the harm of an attendant overstepping his post was more serious. Thus, the way a bright ruler employs his subjects is not to let them earn merit by stepping beyond their assigned duties. (Chapter 7, "Er-bing" p. 28)

(5) Use rewards and punishments

(A) MAKE THE SOVEREIGN USE PREROGATIVE

[169] What a bright ruler uses to guide and control his subjects are the two handles – sanctions and magnanimities . . . Sanctions are to order death penalties and corporal punishments; magnanimities are to celebrate and bestow rewards. Because the subjects are fearful of punishments and find profit in rewards, if the ruler can order sanctions and bestow magnanimities by himself, the subjects will be fearful of his power and turn to what is profitable to them . . . Now, if the ruler does not make himself the only source from where the sanctions and magnanimities come and allows his ministers to exercise the power of inflicting punishments and bestowing rewards, then the people of his state will be fearful of his ministers and take the ruler lightly, and eventually turn to the ministers and away from him. What enables a tiger to subdue dogs are its claws and fangs. If a tiger casts aside its claws and fangs and lets dogs use them, it will be subdued by them instead. The ruler uses sanctions and magnanimities to control his ministers. If he casts aside the sanctions and magnanimities and lets them be used by someone else, he will be controlled by that person instead. (Chapter 7, "Er-bing" pp. 26–7)

[170] Tian Chang 田常 asked for, and received, titles and bounties from Duke Jian of Qi 齊簡公, and then he bestowed them on other officials. He used larger

vessels in distributing grain to aid the people. Thus, the duke lost the handle of giving benefits, and Tian Chang used it, and therefore the duke was eventually murdered. Zihan 子罕 said to the ruler of Song, "Since rewards and charities are what the people like, your lordship should bestow them; since executions and punishments are what the people hate, let me, your humble servant, take the responsibility to carry them out. Thus, the Song ruler lost the handle of punishment and Zichan used it, and therefore the Song ruler was ensnared. (Chapter 7, "Er-bing" p. 27)

[171] Zixia 子夏 said, "According to the records of the Chunqiu period, the number of regicides and patricides was in the tens. None of the cases was the outcome of a single day's doing but the result of gradual, accumulative actions. Those who entered into clandestine plots will continue to work on them making them a regular practice; with such practice, they will gain much power and, with great power, they will be able to murder. Therefore, a clever ruler will terminate such persons early. When the signs of Tian Chang doing evil became gradually obvious, the ruler Duke Jian of Qi did not execute him, and Yanzi, instead of recommending any preventive measures, advised the duke to practise benevolence to his people. That was why the duke suffered the calamitous consequences." Therefore Zixia said, "He who is good at holding his position terminates the evil in its bud." (Chapter 34, "Wai-chu-shuo you-shang" pp. 234–5)

[172] In the fifth month of a year, while Jisun 季孫 was chief minister of the state of Lu, and Zilu 子路 was the magistrate of the district of Hou, the state government summoned the people to build a long ditch. During that time, Zilu made gruel with the grain out of his personal emolument and fed the labourers at the crossroads of Wufu. Confucius heard about this and sent Zigong to throw out the food, break the vessels, and tell Zilu, "The ruler of Lu rules the people, why should you feed them?" Greatly angered, Zilu rolled up his sleeves and went to see Confucius and questioned him, "Master, do you dislike me practising benevolence and righteousness? What I have learned from you is benevolence and righteousness. To be benevolent and righteous is to share with the world one's possessions and benefits. Now I feed the people with grain out of my personal emolument, why is it not permissible?" Confucius said, "How rude you are! I thought you understood, but you do not. You are so ignorant of the rites. You feed the people because you care for them but, according to rites, the emperor cares for everyone in the world; a feudal lord cares for those within his territory; a minister cares for those under the supervision of his office; and a gentleman cares for those in his family. Caring for people outside of one's sphere is transgression. Now, since the ruler of Lu rules the people of Lu, your showing your personal care for them is a transgression. Are you not wrong?" Before Confucius finished his speech, a messenger from Jisun arrived criticising him, saying, "Fei 肥 [Jisun's name] summoned the people to do a job, and you, Master, send your disciple to stop it and feed them. Are you trying to rob me my people?" (Chapter 34, "Wai-chu-shuo you-shang" p. 235)

[173] Duke Jing of Qi 齊景公 visited the state of Jin 晉. Right after taking his seat at a drinking party, hosted by Duke Ping of Jin 晉平公 with Maestro Kuang

師曠 in attendance, Duke Jin asked the Maestro, "What do you, Maestro, have to teach me?" The Maestro replied, "All your Highness must do is be beneficial to your people." During the party, much wine was consumed. At the time when Duke Jin was about to leave, he asked again, "What do you, Maestro, have to teach me?" The Maestro replied, "All your Highness must do is be beneficial to your people." When Duke Jin was on his way to the guesthouse, he asked again, "What do you, Maestro, have to teach me?" The Maestro replied, "All your Highness must do is be beneficial to your people." When Duke Jin retired, not quite sober, he understood what Maestro Kuang meant: Prince Wei 公子尾 and Prince Xia 公子夏, two younger brothers of Duke Jin, had much goodwill of the Qi people, and the people liked them. And their families were rich and with high status almost comparable to the court of the duke. It dawned on him that they were the ones to endanger his position. Was it not that the Maestro's advice for him to be beneficial to the people meant that he should compete with his two brothers for the loyalty of the people? Thus, upon returning to Qi, he distributed the grain from the government stores to the poor, and the money from the state treasury to orphans and widows, leaving the stores with no surplus and the treasury no extra funds. Court ladies, with whom he had no amorous relation, were set free to be married, and persons above seventy were granted government aid. By demonstrating his benevolence and distributing his favours in these ways, he competed against his two brothers for the loyalty of the people. After two years, the two brothers escaped abroad – Prince Xia went to the state of Chu, Prince Wei went to the state of Jin. (Chapter 34, "Wai-chu-shuo you-shang" pp. 232–3)

(b) Reward the meritorious and punish the guilty

[174] Order and strength result from enforcing the law; weakness and chaos result from disregarding the law. A ruler who realises this will strictly administer rewards and punishments but not because he is benevolent to his subjects. Titles and emoluments follow achievements; punishments and disciplines follow crimes. Officials who realise this will exhaust their strength and risk their lives in serving the ruler but not because they are loyal to him. (Chapter 35, "Wai-chu-shuo zuo-xia" p. 249)

[175] Marquis Zhao of Han told someone to save his old and worn trousers in storage. Those who waited on him said, "Your Highness is not kind. Even old and worn trousers are saved instead of being given to his attendants." The marquis said, "This is not what you can understand. I heard that, in the case of a bright ruler, a frown or a smile must mean something. He will frown at something that should be frowned at and smile at something that is worthy of a smile. Now a pair of trousers is not a mere frown or smile; there is a great difference. I must wait for someone who has certain achievements to give him the trousers. This is why I had them saved in storage." (Chapter 30, "Nei-chu-shuo shang – Qi-shu" p. 173)

[176] Duke Jing of Qi visited Yanzi 晏子 [a high official] and said, "Your house is small and close to the market. Please let me move your home to the Yu-zhang Garden." Yanzi bowed twice, thanking the duke, but declined the favour, saying,

"My family is poor; we have to go to the market for food in the morning and in the evening. Therefore we cannot live far away from it." The duke laughed and said, "Your people are familiar with the market? Do you know what is expensive and what is cheap?" At that time the duke had made many offences punishable by mutilation, so Yanzi replied, "Wooden feet are expensive, shoes are cheap." "Why?" the duke wondered. "It is because punishments by mutilation are numerous," Yanzi replied. The duke suddenly looked sad and said, "Am I that cruel?" Thereupon, he reduced the punishment for five offences from mutilation to lesser one. One may say that Yanzi was not sincere when he talked about the high price of wooden feet. He only used it as a convenient excuse to request the cessation of excessive punishments. But this is an unfortunate act resulting from ignorance of the tactics of government. If punishments are warranted, it does not matter if they are numerous; if they are not warranted, it does not help if they are few. Instead of reporting the inappropriateness of the punishments, Yanzi criticised their number . . . After an army is defeated, though thousands are executed for retreating, yet it cannot be stopped. Similarly, in an effort to restore order in a situation of chaos, though punishments are made very severe and are widely used and the only fear was that there may not be enough of them, yet evils cannot be eliminated. Now, instead of examining the appropriateness of the punishments, Yanzi argued against their proliferation. How wrong this approach is! Anyone who cares for weeds is to jeopardise the crop; anyone who treats robbers kindly does harm to innocent people. To reduce punishments and practise leniency is to benefit the wicked and harm the good. This is not the way to achieve order. (Chapter 37, "Nan-er" 難二 pp. 273–4)

[177] When severe punishments are given for minor offences, such offences will stop and the major ones will not occur. This is what is called getting rid of punishments by using punishments. If offences are serious but punishments are light, more crimes will occur. This is what is called asking for more punishments by using punishments, and a state following this practice is sure to be ruined. (Chapter 53, "Chi-ling" p. 365)

(c) Use punishments more than rewards

[178] The people of the state of Lu set the refuse in a swamp on fire. The wind was blowing from the north and the fire was fanned southwards, threatening the capital city. Frightened, Duke Ai 哀公 personally took the lead to fight the fire but no one followed him. Instead, everyone went to chase after wild animals escaping from the swamp. The duke summoned Confucius and asked for advice. Confucius said, "Chasing animals is fun and there is no punishment for it; fighting fire is hardship and there is no reward for it. This is why no one fights the fire." "True indeed," said the duke. Then Confucius said, "Now the situation is critical, and there is no time for rewards. Moreover, if everyone who fights the fire is promised a reward, the government will not have enough treasure to keep its promise. Please just use punishment." "Very good," said the duke. Thereupon Confucius issued an order, saying, "Whoever refuses to fight the fire will be

given the punishment comparable to that given to soldiers running away from a battle or surrendering to the enemy; whoever chases after animals will be given the punishment comparable to that given to intruders into the forbidden districts." Before the order was made known to everyone, the fire was extinguished. (Chapter 30, "Nei-chu-shuo shang – Qi-shu" pp. 168–9)

[179] When Zichan, the prime minister of Zheng, was ill and about to die, he talked to You Ji 游吉, saying, "After I am gone, you are sure to govern Zheng. You must be severe with the people. Fire looks harsh, and few people get burnt; water looks harmless, and many drown. You must make your punishments severe so that people will not be hurt by your seeming softheartedness." After Zichan's death, You Ji could not bear to apply severe punishments. Thereupon, young men of Zheng followed one another into robbery and hid in the reed swamp, threatening disaster for Zheng. You Ji personally led an army of chariots to fight them and just defeated them after a battle that lasted a day and a night. Then You Ji sighed sadly, saying, "If I had followed Zichan's advice earlier, I would not have to do this with regret." (Chapter 30, "Nei-chu-shuo shang – Qi-shu" p. 166)

(D) Make rewards and punishments certain

[180] When Yi 羿 was preparing to shoot . . . people from Yue rushed to hold the mark for him. When a young child played with a bow and an arrow, his loving mother hid in her room and closed the door. Thus, when the result was certain, strangers had no fear of Yi; when it is not certain, the loving mother escapes from her young child. (Chapter 23, "Shuo-lin xia" p. 138)

[181] While he was the magistrate of Shangdi in the state of Zhao, Dong Yanyu 董閼于, walking on Shiyi mountain came to a canyon several hundred yards deep with banks as steep as walls. He asked people who lived nearby, "Has anybody ever gone into this canyon?" "No," was the reply. "Has a child or a blind man or a crazy man ever gone into this?" "No." "Has any ox, horse, dog or pig ever gone into this?" "No." Dong Yanyu sighed deeply, saying, "Now I know how to govern. I will grant no pardon to violators of my laws; whoever violates my laws will invariably be punished just like those who enter this canyon will inevitably die; then no one will dare to violate my laws, and, if so, what can prevent me from establishing good government here?" (Chapter 30, "Nei-chu-shuo shang – Qi-shu" pp. 165–6)

[182] Once, in the time of Duke Si of Wei 衛嗣公, a criminal sentenced to hard labour escaped to the neighbouring state of Wei 魏 and became involved in treating the illness of the queen of King Xiang. Having heard about this, Duke Si sent someone with fifty pieces of gold to buy him back. The messenger went five times but the king refused to give up the criminal. Duke Si proposed to give the town named Zuoshi in exchange for the criminal. His ministers and attendants objected, saying, "Is it right to pay for a criminal with a town?" The duke said, "This is not what you can understand. To achieve order, nothing is too small to do; to avoid disorder nothing, is too big to do. If the law is not upheld and punishments are uncertain, it is useless to have ten towns like Zuoshi; if the law

is upheld and punishments certain, it does not hurt even though ten towns like Zuoshi are lost." Having heard this, the king of Wei said, "The duke genuinely wants order. We will be condemned if we do not grant his request." Thereupon, he sent the criminal back without taking either the gold or the town. (Chapter 30, "Nei-chu-shuo shang – Qi-shu" p. 170)

(E) CARRY OUT PUNISHMENTS WITH DUE SPEED

[183] A bright ruler does not hold his anger in suspense. If he does, those being the subject of his anger, will be fearful of punishment and rush to make treasonous plots, and consequently he will be in danger. (Chapter 39, "Nan-si" 難四 p. 293)

(F) APPLY AND ENFORCE LAW UNIFORMLY

[184] According to tales of very ancient times and incidents recorded in *Chunqiu*, those men who violated the laws, committed treason, and carried out major acts of evil invariably followed some eminent and highly placed ministers. And yet, the laws and regulations are usually designed to prevent evil among the humble and lowly people, and penalties usually fell upon them only. Hence, the common people lose hope and are left with no way to air their grievances. (Chapter 17, "Bei-nei" p. 85)

[185] The bright ruler will not let his officials act arbitrarily outside the law or do favour within the law . . . The law does not fawn on the powerful; the straight string does not bend for the crooked. Whatever the law applies to, the wise cannot dispute, nor can the brave defy. In inflicting punishment against wrongdoings, the law does not miss out great ministers; in giving rewards for good deeds, the law does not miss out humble commoners. Thus, for the purpose of correcting the faults of the high and prosecuting the vices of the low, suppressing disorder and rebuking evil, subduing the overbearing and redressing the abused, and eventually making people follow a single appropriate way, nothing is more effective than the law. (Chapter 6, "You-du" pp. 25–6)

[186] Duke Wen of Jin 晉文公 asked Hu Yan 狐偃, "What would be the result when punishments are extremely well administered?" "The punishments will not be circumvented for those who are powerful and related to the ruler. Law will be enforced against those loved by him," was the answer. "Good," said the duke. The next day he ordered a hunting party at Pulu, setting the time for rendezvous at noon, and prescribed that whoever missed the time was to be court marshalled.

A favourite of the duke, named Dianxie 顛頡, came late. When the law enforcement officer asked that he be punished according to the law, the duke was saddened and tearful. The officer said, "Please uphold the law." Thereupon, he broke Dianxie's spine and showed the corpse to the people to demonstrate that the law was faithfully enforced. Thereafter, the people all became fearful, saying, "The ruler loved Dianxie so much and yet he enforced the law against him. What are we? How is the law going to be enforced against us!" (Chapter 34, "Wai-chu-shuo you-shang" p. 247)

[187] The king of Chu sent an urgent summons for the crown prince. According to the law of Chu, carriages were not allowed to approach the Mao Gate of the palace. It was raining and there were puddles in the courtyard, so the crown prince had his carriage driven towards the Mao Gate. The law officer of the Outer Court said, "Carriages are not allowed to approach the Mao Gate. It is against the law." "The king sent me an urgent summons, and I have to avoid the puddles," the crown prince said and continued his approach. The law officer raised a pole-axe, hit the horses and injured the driver. The crown prince went into the palace and cried in the presence of the king, saying, "There were puddles in the court-yard, so I had my carriage driven towards the Mao Gate. The law officer said it was against the law and, with a poleaxe, he hit my horses and injured my driver. I beg Your Majesty to punish him." The king said, "On the one hand, he refused to let down his old master; on the other hand, he declined to succumb to his future master. He is, indeed, a man of principle, and a good official who can uphold my laws." Thereupon the king promoted him two ranks, and opened a rear door to let out the crown prince, warning him, "Don't make the same transgression again." (Chapter 34, "Wai-chu-shuo you-shang" p. 244)

(G) The well-governed state

[188] In a best-governed state, there will be rewards and punishments but they have nothing to do with the ruler's personal feelings of love or anger. The sage will strictly enforce penal law but will not execute in cruel ways; therefore, the wicked will accept their punishments without resentment . . . The ruler can rest in peace and his subjects can be happy with their undertakings; the Way will prevail in the universe and the Virtue last forever. (Chapter 27, "Yong-ren" p. 154)

[189] In a time of absolute peace, the law will be like the morning dew, pure and clear. The people have no grievance at heart and their mouths utter no complaints. Therefore, horses and carriages do not travel long distances wearily, and military banners do not get tangled in great swamps. The ordinary people will not lose their lives at the hands of robbers and invaders, and brave men will not die prematurely in battle. There will be no heroes having their names entered into history books; no bronze will be made to record great military exploits; and, as a result, the chronicle will be left blank. (Chapter 29, "Da-ti" p. 156)

(H) The proper social relationship

[190] Order and strength are created by law; weakness and disorder are caused by love. Because a bright ruler knows this, he makes correct rewards and punishments not because he is benevolent towards his subjects. Titles and emoluments result from merit; sanctions and punishments follow crime. As the subjects know this, they sacrifice their lives and exhaust their strength in government service not because they are loyal to the ruler. When the ruler knows not to be simply benevolent and the subjects know not to be simply loyal, the state can become kingly. (Chapter 35, "Wai-chu-shuo you-xia" p. 249)

[191] Tian Wei 田鮪 taught his son Tian Zhang 田章: "The ruler sells titles and offices; the subjects sell their intelligence and strength. Therefore it is said, 'Rely on oneself but not on others.'" (Chapter 35, "Wai-chu-shuo you-xia" p. 255)
[192] With deep love parents wish their children to be safe and prosperous, yet their instructions are not listened to. The ruler, having no love and benefits for the people, demands their labour and lives, yet his orders are carried out. Knowing this fact, a bright ruler does not keep a heart of love and favour but increases his power and authority by being severe. (Chapter 46, "Liu-fan" p. 320)
[193] When rewards are bestowed on the meritorious, the recipients do not feel grateful towards the ruler personally because they know they have earned the rewards with their contributions; when punishments are inflicted upon the guilty, the victims do not harbour grievance against their superiors because they know the punishments result from their own crimes. (Chapter 38, "Nan-san" p. 285)
[194] Therefore, though the ruler may have a superior intellect, he will not use it on any problem; rather, he will ensure that others know how to address their own situations. Though he may have talents, he will not use them for anything; rather, he will observe how his officials act. Though he may have a brave spirit, he will not show it even in anger; rather, he will let his subjects demonstrate their valour. Thus, by doing away with his own intellect he can have a clear view of all situations; by doing away with his own talents he can have all accomplishments; by doing away with his own bravery he can have all the strength. When the subjects hold on to their jobs, the officials follow their rules, and the ruler employs all of them according to their talents, the situation is called normal. In this situation, the government functions so quietly that its existence is hardly noticeable. (Chapter 5, "Zhu-dao" p. 18)
[195] The subjects should serve their ruler, the son his father, the wife her husband. If they serve well, there will be order in the world; if not, there will be disorder. This is the normal Way of the world which even the enlightened ruler and virtuous and talented ministers cannot change. Hence, even if the ruler is unworthy, his subjects will not dare to encroach on him. (Chapter 51, "Zhong-xiao" p. 358)
[196] A great minister with good moral character honours his ruler; the people with accomplishments want their ruler to have the benefits. This is what happens in a state that has learned the Way. (Chapter 48, Ba-jing" p. 338)
[197] As a minister, a virtuous person faces north and serves his ruler with no two minds. While in the court, he dares not decline a low assignment; while in the army, he dares not avoid danger. He goes along the ruler's way and follows his law. He waits for orders with no opinion of his own and makes no comment on their correctness. Thus, his mouth was never used to utter a word for private interests, and his eyes were never used to look at things of private interests. He lets the ruler have complete control over him. Thus, as a minister, he is like a hand. It is used to care for the head above and the feet below. It never fails to relieve them in extreme cold or heat, and never dares not fight even when a sword as sharp as the famous Moye is thrusting near the body. (Chapter 6, "You-du" p. 23)

[198] Fei Zhong 費仲 tried to persuade King Shou 紂王, saying, "Chang 昌, the earl in the west, is virtuous and talented. The people like him and other feudal lords are attached to him. You cannot afford not to eliminate him. If you do not eliminate him, he is to bring disaster to the Yin Dynasty." "You are talking about a virtuous ruler. How can we eliminate him?" wondered Shou. Fei Zhong replied, "Even though a hat is threadbare, it must be worn on the head; even though the shoes are embroidered, they must be trodden on the ground. Now the earl in the west is a subject, and yet he cultivated his virtue and attracted people towards him. He must be the one who will eventually cause trouble in the empire! A subject should not serve his ruler by making himself virtuous. He must be eliminated. And, moreover, what is wrong if a ruler eliminates a subject?" Shou said, "Benevolence and righteousness are what the ruler uses to educate people. Now, since Chang is benevolent and righteous, it is not right to eliminate him." Fei Zhong offered his advice three times. It was never accepted, and then Yin fell. (Chapter 33, "Wai-chu-shuo zuo-xia" p. 224)

[199] Once Duke Ping of Jin 晉平公 had a feast with his ministers. After having had enough drink, he sighed, saying, "I do not always enjoy being the ruler, except when I speak no one is to disagree." Maestro Kuang 師曠, sitting near the duke, took his lute and hit him. The duke pulled his robe and hastily ducked. The lute hit the wall and damaged it. The duke asked, "Who were you trying to hit, Maestro?" Maestro Kuang said, "Just now a petty, unworthy person next to me said something. I wanted to hit him." "It was me," said the duke. Maestro Kuang sighed deeply, saying, "That was not the kind of remark a ruler should make." Later the attendants asked to plaster and paint the damaged wall. The duke said, "Leave it as it is and let it be a warning to me."

It may be said that Duke Ping lost the right way of a ruler, and Maestro Kuang lost the right way of an official. If the ruler decides that the conduct of an official is wrong, he orders him punished. This is the way how the ruler should treat his officials. If an official disapproves of the conduct of the ruler, he presents his views and, when his good advice is not accepted, he distances himself from the ruler. This is the way how an official should treat his ruler. (Chapter 36, "Nan-yi" p. 269)

[200] [In a well-governed state] a bright ruler does nothing at the top, the myriad officials tremble in terror at the bottom. (Chapter 5, "Zhu-dao" p. 18)

(I) Difficulties

(1) Need for a "bright ruler" and capable officials

[201] No state is permanently strong, nor is a state permanently weak. Where the upholder of law is strong, the state is strong; where the upholder of law is weak, the state is weak. King Zhuang of Jing 荊莊王 annexed twenty-six foreign states and extended his territory by 3,000 *li*. When he died, the state of Jin went into decay. Duke Huan of Qi 齊桓公 annexed thirty foreign states and extended his territory by 3,000 *li*. When he died, the state of Qi went into decay . . . (Chapter 6, "You-du" p. 21)

[202] Duke Ping of Jin 晉平公 asked Shuxiang 叔向, "In the past, Duke Huan of Qi assembled the feudal lords nine times and rectified the empire. I wonder to whom the credits should go – the ministers or the ruler." Shuxiang replied, "Guan Zhong 管仲 was good at cutting patterns, Bin Xuwu 賓胥無 good at sewing, and Xi Peng 隰朋 good at stitching the hem. When the dress is finished, the ruler put it on. All credits belonged to the ministers. What could be claimed by the ruler?"

Maestro Kuang bent over his lute and laughed. "Why are you laughing, Maestro?" asked the duke. "I am laughing at the answer Shuxiang gave you," said the maestro, "The ministers are like cooks. They will make a dish and present it to the ruler. But, if the ruler does not eat it, who dares to force him? Let me use an analogy. The ruler is like the soil; the ministers are like vegetation. Only when the soil is fertile will the vegetation flourish. Therefore all credits are the ruler's. What could be claimed by the ministers?"

It may be said that the answers of both Shuxiang and Maestro Kuang were one-sided. Assembling the feudal lords nine times and rectifying the empire were great feats. The credits belonged neither to the ruler nor to the ministers alone. Formerly, when Gong Zhiqi 宮之奇 was in the state of Yu 虞 and Xi Fuji 僖負羈 was in the state of Cao 曹, though both were intelligent enough to offer proper advice and successfully accomplish the missions assigned to them, yet both Yu and Chao were vanquished. Why? It is because, while there were good ministers, there were no good rulers. On the other hand, when Jian Shu 蹇叔 served in Yu 虞, it was vanquished but, when he served in Qin 秦, it became hegemonic. It was not that he was stupid while in Yu but intelligent while in Qin; it was because in one case there was a good ruler while in the other case there was not. Thus, Shuxiang was wrong in saying all credit belonged to the ministers.

Formerly, Duke Huan had two markets in his palace compound and two hundred quarters in his harem, and he often let his hair down and played with his women. When he got Guan Zhong as his chief minister, he became the greatest of the five hegemonic leaders; after he lost Guan Zhong and got Shu Diao 豎刁, he ended up with an unnatural death, and worms came out of his corpse before he was buried. If the credit belonged not to the minister, how did Duke Huan became a hegemonic leader when he had Guan Zhong? If all credit belonged to the ruler, why when the duke had Shu Diao, there was disorder? Formerly, Duke Wen of Jin was enchanted by his new wife while he was in Qin and forgot his plans to return to his own country. Jiu Fan 咎犯 protested strongly and eventually got him back to Jin. Thus, Duke Huan was able to assemble the feudal lords because of Guan Zhong, and Duke Wen was able to become a hegemonic leader because of Jiu Fan. Therefore, Maestro Kuang was wrong in saying all credit belonged to the ruler.

The fact that the five hegemonic leaders were successful and enjoyed great fame in the world was a result to which the rulers and their ministers had made contributions. This is why the remarks of Shuxiang and Maestro Kuang were both one-sided. (Chapter 37, "Nan-er" pp. 275–6)

(A) Need of a "bright ruler"

[203] Whether the officials will be loyal or fraudulent depends on how the ruler acts. If he is bright and strict, they will be loyal; if he is stupid and weak, they will be fraudulent. To be able to know a plot when it is not yet clear is called bright; to refuse to give pardons is called strict. (Chapter 39, "Nan-si" pp. 292–3)

[204] A bright king does not approve any project that cannot stand close examination. He does not eat anything unusual. He listens to reports of what is afar and watches events of what is close in order to find out the problems within and without. He takes note of mutually agreeing or disagreeing remarks in order to know the partisans. He checks words against deeds in order to find out the truth. He contrasts what follows with what precedes; he upholds the law in governing the masses; and he reviews various points together and compares them. No one will be rewarded by him simply because of luck, and no one dares to violate his rules. He inflicts punishments only on the truly guilty and he gives no pardons. (Chapter 17, "Bei-nei" p. 84)

[205] The armies of three states [Qi, Han, and Wei] approached the Hangu Gorge. The King of Qin talked with Lou Huan 樓緩 saying, "The armies of the three states are deep in our territory. I want to cede the area east of the [Yellow] River to them and ask for peace. How about that?" Lou Huan replied, "Ceding the area east of the River means a big loss; avoiding disaster for the state means a big achievement. This is something to be decided by senior statesmen in the royal family in the royal family. Why doesn't Your Majesty summon Prince Fan 氾 and discuss it with him?" The king summoned Prince Fan and told him about the problem. The prince said, "You might regret it if you asked for peace; you might also regret it if you did not. If Your Majesty cedes the area east of the River and asks for peace, and thereupon the armies of the three states retreat, Your Majesty will certainly say, 'The armies of the three states were about to retreat anyway, and I just gave them three cities!' If Your Majesty does not ask for peace, and the armies of the three states enter the Hangu Gate, then our state will be in great danger, and Your Majesty will regret it deeply, saying, 'This is the result of not giving up the three cities!' Therefore, I say you might regret it if you asked for peace; you might also regret it if you did not." "If I have to regret," said the king, "I would rather regret that three cities are lost in vain than regret when the whole state is in danger. So I have decided to ask for peace." (Chapter 30, "Nei-chu-shuo shang – Qi-shu" p. 174)

[206] I heard that, in ancient times when Bian Que 扁鵲 [a famous physician] treated people's illness, he used a knife to pierce the bones; when a sage saved a state, he gave honest advice that offended the ears. When a bone is pierced, the patient will feel some pain but then he will have the long-term benefit of good health. When the ears are offended, a ruler will feel a little annoyed in his heart but the state will enjoy lasting fortune. Thus, the interest of a seriously ill person is in enduring the pain, and a decisive and forceful ruler will endure annoyance to achieve lasting fortune. (Chapter 25, "An-wei" p. 148)

[207] Yao wanted to cede the world to Shun. Gun 鯀 protested, saying, "It will be disastrous! How can you cede the world to a mere commoner?" Yao did not listen to him; instead, he launched an attack and killed him in the field near the Yu Mountain. Gonggong 共工 again protested, saying, "How can you cede the world to a mere commoner?" Yao did not listen to him either; instead, he launched an attack and sent him into exile in the town of You-zhou. Thereupon, no one dared to protest against the ceding of the world to Shun.

Confucius learned about this and said, "The wisdom of Yao and the talents of Shun were not the most unusual; the decision to eliminate the protesters and the insistence on ceding the world to Shun was the most unusual." In other words, it is most difficult for one not to have doubts about the decision one has made. (Chapter 34, "Wai-chu-shuo you-shang" p. 243)

[208] A ruler who knows the Way does not look for officials of clean conduct. Rather, he works on the tactics by which he will know their activities. (Chapter 47, "Ba-shuo" p. 328)

[209] A bright ruler does not rely on the fact that people will not rebel against him; he relies on the fact that they cannot rebel against him. He does not rely on the fact that people will not cheat him; he relies on the fact that they cannot cheat him. (Chapter 33, "Wai-chu-shuo zuo-xia" p. 221)

[210] The best way for the ruler to act is to be quiet and unassuming. (Chapter 5, "Zhu-dao" p. 20)

[211] The way of a bright ruler is to make the wise deliberate before he decides so that he does not have to exhaust his own wits; to make the talented show their talents before he employs them so that he does not have to exhaust his own talents. When accomplishments are made, the ruler will have the credit; when mistakes are committed, the officials will bear the blame. Thus, the ruler will always have a good name. He may not be talented but he instructs the talented; he may not be wise but he guides the wise. The officials will exert themselves but the ruler will enjoy the success. This is called the proper way of a worthy ruler. (Chapter 5, "Zhu-dao" p. 18)

(2) Need for extraordinary specialists in law and tactics

[212] A wise person who is to apply the tactics of control must be far-sighted and observant. If not, he will not be able to uncover secret schemes. A man dedicated to law must be morally strong and upright. If not, he will not be able to fight evil. (Chapter 11, "Gu-fen" p. 55)

[213] In the case of Hou Ji 后稷, Gao Yao 皋陶, Yi Yin 伊尹 . . . fifteen of them, this was the way they acted as officials: they all got up early and stayed up late, humbled themselves and toiled physically, kept their minds unbiased and their intentions clear, administered justice and managed government affairs, just for the purpose of serving their rulers. They offered good advice, made good laws, and yet dared not brag about their contributions; they succeeded in completing many projects but dared not claim merit. They found no difficulty in sacrificing the interests of their family in order to benefit their states, or risking death in

order to save their rulers. They exalted their rulers as high as the sky and the Tai Mountain, and humbled themselves as low as the valley and the basin . . . Officials like them will have their accomplishments even under disorderly rulers. It is needless to say how much more successful they can be under enlightened ones. They are the helping hands of true kings and hegemonic lords. (Chapter 44, "Shuo-yi" pp. 308–9)

[214] With the help of Yi Yin, Tang, starting from a base of 100 *li* square, became the emperor. With the help of Guan Zhong, Duke Huan of Qi became the first of the five hegemonic lords, assembled the feudal lords nine times, and rectified the empire. With the help of Lord Shang, Duke Xiao of Qin was able to expand his territory and make his army strong. Thus, if a ruler has a truly loyal minister, he will have neither threatening enemies outside his borders nor subversive officials inside his state. The state will enjoy enduring peace and the ruler will leave a great name to posterity. These are the gifts of a truly loyal minister. (Chapter 14, "Jian-jie-shi chen" p. 75)

[215] Xie Hu 解狐 recommended Xing Boliu 邢伯柳 to be the magistrate of Shangdang. Xing Boliu went to thank him, saying, "You have forgiven me for my transgression against you. I am here to express my thanks!" Xie Hu replied, "Recommending you is for the public interest; hating you is because of my private grievance. Go away! I hate you just as before." (Chapter 33, "Wai-chu-shuo zhuo-xia" p. 229)

[216] When Liang Che 梁車 was newly appointed as the magistrate of the district of Ye, his older sister went to visit him, arriving late in the evening when the city gate was closed. She climbed over the wall to get in. Liang Che, enforcing a law against this act, amputated her foot. (Chapter 33, "Wai-chu-shuo zhuo-xia" p. 230)

[217] Those who know the tactics of control are investigative so, when they are employed, they will expose the schemes of the mighty. Those who are dedicated to the law are upright and unbending so, when they are employed, they will correct the evil doings of the mighty. Thus, when those who are to control the wicked and uphold the law are employed, those mighty officials with perfidious schemes and overwhelming power will be ousted. The two types are enemies that cannot coexist. (Chapter 11, "Gu-fen" p. 55)

[218] When a person in a crucial government position takes state affairs into his own hands, people both in and out of the state will be at his service. If the other feudal lords do not pay attention to him, they cannot get what they want from his state; hence, they all praise him. If the other officials do not pay attention to him, they cannot get promotion; hence, they all place themselves at his disposal. If officers in the royal retinue do not pay attention to him, they cannot get close to the ruler; hence, they all cover for him. If academicians do not pay attention to him, they will get meagre salaries and impolite treatment; hence, they eulogise him. These four kinds of helpers are what a perfidious minister uses for self decoration. Such a "heavyweight" will not, because of a sense of loyalty to the ruler, promote anyone who is at odds with himself. The ruler, on the other

hand, cannot bypass the minister's four kinds of helpers to investigate him. As a result, the ruler becomes more hoodwinked, and the minister becomes stronger and more powerful. (Chapter 11, "Gu-fen" p. 55)

[219] On the contrary, advocates of law and tactics of control approaching the ruler are not his close relatives or old acquaintances, and yet they want to change his biased mind with lectures on law and tactics of control, which are opposed to his taste. They are in humble positions and have no partisan support. In a competition for the ruler's favour, those distant to him as opposed to those he trusts and loves have no chance of winning; strangers as opposed to his close relatives or old acquaintances have no chance of winning; those opposed to his taste as opposed to those with the same taste have no chance of winning; the low and humble as opposed to the high and powerful have no chance of winning; and a single voice as opposed to the cacophony of the entire state has no chance of winning. Confronted with the five handicaps, advocates of law and tactics of control are not granted an audience with the ruler for several years. On the other hand, with the five advantages, those in powerful positions speak with the ruler alone in the morning and in the evening. As a result, how can the advocates of law and tactics of control get close to the ruler and how can he come to realise his own problems? Being thus hopelessly handicapped in their capacity and unable to coexist with those in power, how can the advocates of law and tactics of control avoid danger? Those among them who can be falsely accused of crimes are censured with state laws; those who cannot are ended by private assassins. Thus, if the advocates of law and tactics of control who contradict the ruler are not executed through official censure will surely killed by private assassins. (Chapter 11, "Gu-fen" p. 56)

[220] Law and tactics of controlling wicked practices find it difficult to prevail . . . Those around the ruler are not necessarily intelligent. After listening to someone who is intelligent the ruler will discusses that person's remarks with those around him. This is to let the stupid appraise the intelligent. Those around the ruler are not necessarily virtuous. After listening to someone who is virtuous the ruler will discusses that person's behaviour with those around him. This is to make the unworthy evaluate the virtuous. If a wise man's ideas are to be appraised by some fools, and if a virtuous person's conduct is to be evaluated by some scoundrels, then the wise and the virtuous will be ashamed, and the ruler will be deprived of good counsel.

Among those who seek office, the virtuous ones keep themselves clean and upright; the wise ones use their talents to get ahead. A virtuous person will not give bribes in order to work with someone; a wise man will not distort the law in performing government duties. Thus, the virtuous will not try to please those around the ruler; the wise will not allow people to influence the enforcement of law. Those around the ruler certainly are not all as virtuous as Bo Yi 溥疑 [a recluse]. When they fail to receive bribes, good proposals will be suppressed, and vicious slanders will start to clamour. When good proposals are suppressed by those who are close to the ruler, and virtuous behaviour tarnished by slanders, virtuous and wise officials will be dismissed, and the ruler will be hoodwinked. (Chapter 11, "Gu-fen" pp. 58–9)

[221] Tang-xi-gong 堂谿公 talked to Hanzi [Han Fei], "I heard that following the rites and being modest are the ways to preserve oneself, and cultivating one's behaviour and hiding one's wisdom are the ways to fulfil one's wishes. Now, sir, you want to establish new laws and measures, and I think it is dangerous to you personally. How do I prove this? I heard that your point is that Chu became disorderly and its territory shrunken because it did not retain Wu Qi 吳起 [a Legalist and military strategist]; Qin became rich and strong because it employed Lord Shang. Your remarks about the two persons are quite right but, eventually, Wu Qi was dismembered and Lord Shang torn by chariots. The problem was that they did not live in the right times and meet the right rulers. Since whether one lives in the right times and meets the right ruler are unpredictable, misfortune and disaster cannot be readily dismissed. Therefore, to abandon the way of self-preservation and fulfilment and to pursue a course leading to danger is something I think you should not do."

Hanzi said, "Sir, I know what you mean. And I know it is not at all easy to govern the world and put the people in order. The reason I will not follow your very kind advice but insist on doing what I do is that I believe the establishment of the new laws and measures is the right way to benefit the people. I think he who does not escape from the misfortune and disaster which a disorderly ruler or a stupid superior might bring upon him but insists on trying to benefit the people is acting benevolently and wisely. On the contrary, he who escapes from the misfortune and disaster which a disorderly ruler or stupid superior might bring upon him in order to avoid the danger of death, thus seeing only his personal interests but not those of the people, is acting in a despicable way. I cannot stand following that despicable way, nor do I dare to do harm to a pattern of behaviour that is in conformity with benevolence and wisdom. You, sir, have the good intention to do me a favour but, in fact, you have done me great injustice." (Chapter 42, "Wen-tian" p. 303)

Han-fei-zi 韓非子

PART 2
INTERPRETATION

Han Fei 韓非 (280–233 BCE) is the last of the thinkers of the periods we study here. He is regarded as the consummate Legalist theoretician. Preceding him there were many others, including prominently Gongsun Yang, Shen Buhai 申不害 (400–337 BCE) and Shen Dao 慎到 (395–315 BCE), whose ideas he shared and critiqued. According to Sima Qian,[1] all of them studied the philosophy of Huangdi (黃帝 the Yellow Emperor) and Laozi and believed in the law of nature.[2] We have discussed Gongsun Yang. Shen Buhai was employed by Marquis Zhao of Han 韓昭侯 as chief minister and made Han strong and safe; Shen Dao was a member of the Ji-xia 稷下 Royal Academy of Qi but did not hold any office. There were works attributed to them but, in neither case, have substantial parts survived.

Han Fei was a minor aristocrat of Han 韓, once a powerful state then in precipitous decline, repeatedly invaded by neighbours, particularly Qin 秦. He was, for a while, a student of Xunzi but was, apparently, attracted more by the teachings of Laozi and the Legalists. He was never given an important government post. Frustrated, he wrote his ideas down. Someone brought his works to Ying Zheng 嬴政, then the king of Qin, who was greatly impressed by them, announced a strong wish to have Han Fei's service and then launched a military attack on Han to force it to send Han Fei as an envoy to make peace. Han Fei went, completed his mission and stayed, waiting for an opportunity. Meanwhile, fearful of being overshadowed, high officials of Qin plotted against him. One of them, Li Si 李斯, was particularly uneasy because, as a fellow student of Han Fei under Xunzi, he knew Han Fei was much smarter than he. Before the king made up his mind, Li Si pointed out that Han Fei, being an aristocrat of Han, would never be loyal to Qin; rather, if allowed to return home, he, having learned much about Qin during his stay, could do Qin great harm. The king was persuaded and ordered an inquiry. While waiting in custody for a hearing, Han Fei committed suicide using poison courtesy of Li Si. The king realised his mistake and dispatched a messenger to announce a pardon, it was too late.

Han Fei lived in a terrible world. In Gongsun Yang's time there were scores of feudal states; the number was now reduced to seven by incessant, brutal wars. The wars continued among the surviving states and power struggles rampaged inside everyone of them. It was the last stage of the "Warring States Period", when each state struggled for survival, a time Han Fei characterised as *da-zheng zhi shi* (大爭之世 an era of great strife). He was much troubled by this situation and wanted to do something about it. A stutterer, but a good writer, he wrote on many subjects. *Han-fei-zi* 韓非子, the book attributed to him, contains largely his ideas though some parts of it are apparently additions by his admirers. It is a large tome because he reiterated his themes often and used many historical events and some stories and metaphors to illustrate his viewpoints. In addition, he made numerous comments on the ideas of other thinkers, including those of his own School, but particularly, and very critically, those of the Ruists. He was partial to Laozi; therefore, besides generally endorsing many of Laozi's ideas, he devoted two chapters of his book to explain and expound them.

Like Laozi, Han Fei dreamed of the creation of a new world of peace and order under a single sovereign (Laozi's "sage") who, at the pinnacle of power and authority and with clever tactics, would govern according to the laws he makes, applies and enforces. Such a state was later created by Ying Zheng, the first emperor of Qin, largely with the help of Han Fei's lesser fellow student Li Si. Unfortunately, this state was a catastrophe. Why? Were the founders of the empire mainly to blame or was there something wrong with the Legalist theory? Since the theory was consummated by Han Fei, we shall study with care what he stated.

Though its main points are dispersed and repeated through many different chapters, *Han-fei-zi* has an outline that can be discerned after the book has been carefully perused. It starts with an observation of the disorders of his time, proceeds to present a diagnosis of the causes, an examination of the wrong treatments, a suggestion of correct ones and, finally, gives a theory of law, discussing the law's objectives, bases, functions, application, enforcement and results. These steps will be scrutinised and evaluated below.

(A) Symptoms of disorder

(1) Useless and harmful people

In a "time of great strife" a state has to be rich and strong to survive. Like Gongsun Yang, Han Fei saw that the way to this goal is through agriculture and war. The state has to turn its people into farmers and soldiers. They both had a bias against merchants, craftsmen, intellectuals and others whom they considered unproductive (in the narrow sense of raising crops and livestock) and dependent on others for a living. They also dismissed swordsmen who engage in private fights but evade military duties. Han fei characterised them as *xiang-ren* (象人 figurines). Moreover, they thought that the actions of such people are actually harmful to the interests of the state – merchants and craftsmen exploit the farmers, intellectual use sophisticated words to promote their own interests, and swordsmen violate prohibitions. They therefore condemned such people as *du min* (蠹民 woodworm-like people) that erode the state. In addition, Han fei found another type of persons who are disinterested in profit and unafraid of danger and therefore can neither be induced by rewards nor be suppressed by punishments. He called them *bu-ling zhi min* (不令之民 persons irresponsive to government orders) and regarded them similarly useless and detrimental to the state. According to him, these various types of useless and dangerous persons were numerous and contributed significantly to the troubles of his time.

(2) Specious intellectuals and outrageous swindlers

Among the useless people, the intellectuals – scholars, foolish talkers and pleaders – irked Han Fei most. He saw them causing confusion in the minds of gullible rulers, as well as innocent people, about standards and values. He was particularly annoyed by the Ruists and the Mohists. Shortly after the death of Confucius and Mozi, their respective schools split into many sects, each upholding some parts of their teachings and rejecting other parts. This fact prompted Han Fei to ask: since the two masters were no more about 250 years ago, who in his time was able to determine the truth of their teachings? For the same reason, when they talked about the virtues and achievements of Yao and Shun, their statements were even less credible because almost two millennia separated them from the two sage kings. In his view, to make an assertion that is not verifiable is *yu* (愚 stupid) and to act according to such an assertion is *wu* (誣 fraudulent). So he called what the Ruists and Mohists taught *yu-wu zhi xue* (愚誣之學 stupid and fraudulent teachings) and compared it to drawing pictures of ghosts and spirits. Unfortunately, there were many people naive enough to believe in such ideas, including the king of Yan 燕 who employed a person allegedly capable of carving a monkey on the tip of a thorn, and King Xuan of Qi 齊宣王 who kept a pipe player incapable of performing at all alone, and the king of Jin 晉 who believed in an elixir of life. Obviously, Han Fei put many intellectuals of his time in the same company as these swindlers who made a living using artful speeches to deceive people, particularly the rulers. Because the number of such frauds, grand or petty, was very large, when they roamed around practising their shameless trade, the world was in trouble.

(3) Treacherous officials

While useless people enfeeble the state and intellectuals and swindlers exploit it, another type of person will actually ruin it. They are those the ruler loves or respects, including his spouse, close relatives and high ministers. The last group, in particular, can be most dangerous. In one paragraph, Han Fei listed five types of them – those who lavishly use their wealth to buy good reputation; those who richly reward people to change their action; those who form partisan groups, court the shrewd and honour the intellectuals; those who grant leniency and pardon criminals to flaunt their authority; and those who cater to the opinion of the masses, display their personal talents, and make high-sounding speeches to dazzle and awe the people. He called them *wu-jian* (五姦 the five wicked) because they are all trying to usurp the ruler's power. In other paragraphs, he mentioned many more treasonous deeds of evil officials. Here is a few of those and the reasons behind them.

The common objective of evil officials is to obtain personal gains at the expense of the state and the ruler. They do not go into government to serve the public; they serve a ruler who gives them their posts. Since, in most cases, they are not related to the ruler by blood and have no natural affection or loyalty towards him, the relationship is based on *ji-shu* (計數 calculation).

The immediate goal of most officials is to get rich. Where regular emoluments were insufficient, they will embezzle, take bribes and squeeze the people. As a result, the state will become *zhong-bao* (中飽 well-fed in the middle) – the treasury will be empty and the people hungry while the officials become richer every day. This, needless to say, undermines the financial health of the state.

The officials' next goal is to gain more power. Generally they will do everything to please the ruler in order to win his trust and affection. They will serve him in abject obsequious ways, echo his words, implement his orders, observe his expressions, learn his habits and remember his likes and dislikes, so that they can *sian-yi cheng-zhi* (先意承旨 predict his intentions and carry out his wishes before he gives his commands). Specifically they will resort to *ba-shu* (八術 eight tactics). The first three tactics are to bribe the ruler's *tong-chuang* (同床 bedfellows, i.e., wife, concubines and homosexual boys), *zai-pang* (在傍 close attendants) and *fu-xiong* (父兄 senior relatives) for the purpose of using them as spies to get secret information about him and as pleaders to advance the officials' private interests. The fourth tactic is *yang-yang* (養殃 encourage disastrously wanton pursuits) to indulge the ruler in constructing grand palaces and doting on his women and pets and thus corrupt his heart and exhaust his treasure. The fifth tactic is to manipulate *min-meng* (民萌 the common people) to give support to the officials' clandestine agenda. The sixth tactic is to use *liu-xing* (流行 popular arguments) presented by the officials' foreign guests and domestic agents to push their causes and persuade the ruler. The seventh tactic is to create *wei-qiang* (威強 a compelling force) by the officials using private swordsmen to coerce their opponents. The eighth tactic is to ally with *si-fang* (四方 foreign states) to force the ruler to yield to the officials' schemes. In addition, such officials will gang up as partisans, secretly supporting one another but publicly appearing as adversaries and in unison renouncing their real enemies, and thus block the ruler's access to others and have him hoodwinked.

The results such officials produced would be disastrous. An ordinary ruler would be totally isolated and duped by them and give them his total trust and undivided attention, let down his guard and grant what they asked for. Even a clever ruler would find it difficult to remove them because, having applied such tactics, they would be well entrenched in the inner circle of the court. Their relationship with the ruler would be like that of *she* (社 Temple of the Earth) and *she-shu* (社鼠 temple rats) ensconced in the walls or burrowed in the grounds of the temple. When one wanted to flood or smoke out the rats, one would be afraid of damaging the temple.

Consequently, such officials would get what they ultimately wanted – government power. They would, in the absence of orders from the ruler, take government matters in their owns hands and twist the law for their private gain. Then they would force their will upon him and become what Han Fei characterised as *zhong-ren* (重人 mighty men) or *shan-zhu zhi chen* (擅主之臣 officials who control the ruler). Eventually, the head of the gang would have usurped most of the power and authority of the ruler whose throne would be only a few steps away for this official to seize. Han Fei called the members of such a gang *jian-jie-shi chen* (姦劫弑臣 officials who manipulate, ensnare and murder the ruler) and used a long chapter, with this term as its title, to condemn them.

As an example, Han Fei gave us Zihan 子罕, once a chief minister of the state of Song, who asked the ruler to let him do the unpleasant work of making decisions on criminals and administering severe punishments. Eventually, having made the officials, as well as the common people of the state, subjugated to his power, he killed the ruler and took over the government.

Zihan was only a more recent example. There were many other occasions in history where officials carried out evil schemes to strengthen their own positions and depose their rulers. According to Han Fei, from the reign of Zhou Xuan-wang 周宣王 (827–782 BCE) to his time, several tens of states perished, half of them as a result of the rulers being killed by their officials. More surprisingly, he suggested that the tales of Yao abdicating for Shun and Shun abdicating for Yu were false. He believed that, in reality, there was a coup in each case and that the "abdicator" was forced out. And therefore, he said, the establishment of the Shang Dynasty by Tang and that of the Zhou Dynasty by Wu-wang were actually acts of rebellion and regicide.

All those schemes, in which the officials plotted against their ruler, were real to a certain extent. But Han Fei was given to exaggeration and sometimes got himself into trouble. Here is an example. Now, he disputed the story about Yao and Shun abdicating their positions but, in other passages, he said that, in ancient times when rulers had to toil for the people for very meagre rewards, abdication was easy. Besides these contradictory remarks there is another problem. After all, what happened was more than two thousand years before his time and, according to the logic he used in criticising Confucius and Mozi, it could not be verified whether or not abdications or coups happened. But that did not pose a problem for him; his point was that there were perfidious and treasonous officials who cheated their rulers and seized power for themselves thereby producing great disorder before and during his time.

(4) Unwise but wilful rulers

Officials can make trouble only when a ruler is vulnerable because of his own shortcomings which, according to Han Fei, were many, and common to most rulers of his time. In the chapter "*Shi-guo*" (十過 ten mistakes) of his book, he listed ten general ones. In addition, numerous others are mentioned throughout his book: for instance, in the chapter "*An-wei*" (安危 security and danger), he mentioned six ways a ruler would fall; in the chapter *Wang-zheng* (亡徵 signs of ruin), he listed forty-seven circumstances in which a state would perish, among them, thirteen were created by the ruler. In short, many of the rulers were wilful, greedy, licentious, obdurate, arrogant an above all, stupid and naive, unable to comprehend the situation they and their state faced. They often unwisely acted contrary to their own interests. They did not know how to employ the right persons and control the wayward people but were generally duped by a few who were close to them. They were unable to make timely and firm decisions, and could not keep their own plans secret. They did not make correct laws and enforce them faithfully and effectively; rather, they "cut short what is prescribed or stretch beyond what is proscribed", ignoring established procedures and resorting to their personal intelligence which was limited. They were often misinformed and led to believe in wrong principles and methods of government that harmed the people, ruined the state or subverted their own positions. This fault, in particular, was fatal. Han Fei cited two instances where following the ancient rules of benevolence and righteousness resulted in disasters: In one case, wishing to emulate Yao and Shun in abdicating his position to a worthy subject, Kuai 噲, the king of Yan, was murdered by the treasonous minister Zizhi 子之, the intended beneficiary. In another, observing the rules of military engagement of ancient times, when battles were more like war games between gentlemen, Duke Xiang of Song 宋襄公 had his army routed by the troops of Chu 楚 and himself mortally wounded. Han Fei could not help but sneer. He was especially annoyed by the two predominant schools – the Ruists and Mohists – that preached benevolence and righteousness as *the way* to govern. To him it was this general belief of many rulers in this erroneous way, as much as their own personal shortcomings, that produced troubles for the world and tragedies for themselves. They were more miserable than a leper. For them Han Fei had pity but no sympathy.

(B) Causes of disorder

(1) Self interest

Thus, Han Fei found that many problems were produced simply by the misdeeds of intellectuals, officials and rulers, and he offered some obvious explanations. But, by his time, it was fashionable to discuss human nature as a deeper cause for social phenomena. Han Fei had to do so, too. He observed that people have certain biological needs – unlike birds and other animals, people need clothing; unlike "those in Heaven and those grown from earth", people have to fill their stomachs. Therefore, people have a natural inclination to seek gratification and avoid frustration of such needs. From this inclination come common likes and dislikes, and people generally pursue what they like and shun what they dislike. In most people's behaviour this is quite clear. But sometimes people seem to do strange things that no one normally likes to do. For instance, a physician sucks pus out of a patient's abscessed wound; the coffin-maker likes to see people die; labourers toil in the field of their employer who offers good food and high wages to them. Why? It is because there is profit to be made or benefits to be gained. People are naturally preoccupied by self-interest and are therefore calculating in dealing with others. This is also how, in a poor family, parents treat their children: After giving birth to a boy, they congratulate each other; after begetting a girl, they commit infanticide. It is because, while a son will remain in the family and work for it, a daughter will eventually marry out, taking away some of the family property as a dowry. Thus, with the long-term interests of the family in mind, the parents must have cold and calculating hearts.

But self-interest is not the best guide for behaviour because most people are short-sighted, unable to see the future, especially if it requires some sacrifice in the present. Thus, Han Fei said, when Yu was rechanneling the rivers to tame the great flood, the people piled up stones to prevent his work; when Zichan removed barriers between farm plots to improve agricultural productivity, the people of Zheng slandered him. It showed that the intelligence of the common people was as limited as that of infants – when an infant has an abscess, someone has to hold him down and help his mother cut it open to let out the pus and, all the while, he will cry and scream, and struggle against the procedure. All these instances, illustrate that ordinary people are incapable of taking care of themselves. They have to rely on someone cleverer; they have to have government authorities to guide them.

(2) Conflict of interest

More troublesome is the fact that people's interests can be in conflict. Han Fei told a story of a couple praying together: the wife expressed a wish for a very small sum of money; the husband wondered why it was such a pittance and was told by her that, if his wish for more were granted he would use the extra money to buy a concubine. In another paragraph, Han Fei alleged that the queen of a ruler may, after her son is made the crown prince, wish the ruler to die early because she is afraid of being deposed by the king in favour of a younger and prettier woman but, with him dead, she will have the same high status and as much sex as she likes. To make his point more convincing, Han Fei told two anecdotes. First, there was the famous tale of a son reporting his father's crime of stealing a sheep. He was executed because, though rectitudinous in serving the state, he harmed his own father. Second, there was a story about a man who ran away from battles three times, using as an excuse his need to take care of his aging father, was recommended by Confucius because, though being a traitorous subject of the sovereign, he was a filial son. In conclusion, Han Fei exclaimed: "The interests of those in the government and those among the masses are as disparate as this!"

The most serious conflict of interest occurs between the ruler and his ministers. The ruler wants them to obey him and devote themselves to their work; they want to keep their offices and receive government emoluments without much toil and sacrifice. He wants to control them; they like to cheat him. That was why, according to Han Fei, Huangdi 黄帝 said, "The superiors and inferiors fight a hundred battles a day".

(3) Conflict of values

Behind the conflict of interests, Han Fei detected a more fundamental problem – the conflict of values resulting, not only from differences of actual interests, but more from differences in perceptions of what is desirable or repugnant. This conflict was quite noticeable during Han Fei's time between those who knew what he called "the correct way" to govern and those who did not, the latter including many of the rulers and the general public. In one chapter of his book, he listed in one category six types of persons who were against the public interests and yet honoured by the people (for example, those who gave shelter to culprits were criminals accomplices but were praised as "chivalrous and admirable gentlemen") and, in a second category, six types of persons who were for the public interests and yet belittled by the people (for example, those who denounced criminals were supporters of the legal system but were disparaged as "slanderous and despicable scoundrels"). In another chapter, he listed five types of person in the second category (for example, those who disregarded law and violated prohibitions were hailed as "courageous fellows") and nineteen types of person in a third category who were wrongly praised or dismissed by the authorities (for example, on the one hand, praised as "superior men" those whose ideas were grandiose but not practical and whose behaviour was in disagreement with custom; on the other hand, dismissed as "timid" those who were respectful towards the officials and fearful of punishments). In yet another chapter, he listed eight types of behaviour that harmed society and state but were perversely commended by both the people and the authorities: for instance, a person who did private favours to old acquaintances was called a loyal man, and a person who distributed public funds as his private favours was called a benevolent man. But praising such behaviour would have an effect of encouraging the corrupt practice of those in government to gain personal power at the expense of the ruler and the state.

In a society where many of its members' actual interests are in conflict, there will be contention; where their perceived values conflict, there will be discord. The latter makes the situation worse because changing perceptions is far more difficult. When the two conflicts occur at the same time, there will be serious disorder. The world becomes one of "great strife".

(C) Erroneous responses

(1) The basic, critical mistake

Unfortunately, at Han Fei's time, most rulers were themselves confused, unclear about those conflicts and unsure what to do. They often rewarded or punished the wrong persons and thus promoted or inhibited the wrong interests and values. In one chapter of his book, Han Fei pointed out that, because of the rulers' misconceptions and personal biases, sixteen types of person were wrongly rewarded or denied proper recompense. For instance, it was the farmers who would make the state prosper, yet they remained poor while craftsmen and artisans were made rich; it was the soldiers who would help defend the state and expand its territory, yet the orphans of those who died in battle were not adequately provided for and therefore had to beg for food on the streets while the court jesters and entertainers were given carriages and silk dresses; the fertile land and good houses should be used to encourage warriors, yet the families of those whose heads were cut off, bodies split open and bones spread across the battlefield had no shelter and their land was confiscated after the soldiers' deaths, while those whose daughters or younger sisters were pretty and those great ministers with no merit were able to choose the houses and lands offered by the state. Such measures were contrary to the principles of good government. When they are carried out, the state is sure to be weakened and the ruler's position endangered.

(2) Misguided practices of benevolence and righteousness

Why did many rulers make these mistakes? Han Fei thought it was because they were hypnotised by the Ruists and the Mohists who preached benevolence and righteousness as the guiding principles of government, and used the deeds of Yao and Shun as examples to show how these principles could actually work. The Legalists were against these principles, and Han Fei, in particular, repudiated them forcefully, arguing that they are self-contradictory, ineffective, and actually harmful.

(A) They are self-contradictory

To begin with, he said praising Yao and Shun as models of benevolence and righteousness was self-contradictory. He used the fable of the impenetrable shield and the all-penetrating spear to show that Yao and Shun could not exist at the same time to love and correct the people – if Yao were a benevolent and righteous sage ruler, there would be no problems for Shun, a mere subject, to solve; if there was the need for Shun to solve three problems in three years by the force of his personal virtue, Yao could not be a sagacious ruler because he should have transformed the people himself. The argument is tenuous but Han Fei made the point that benevolence and righteousness were not enough for solving social problems.

(b) They are ineffective if not useless

Second, Han Fei argued that benevolence and righteousness are ineffective for government. He pointed out that, if it took Shun a year to solve a single problem, the problems of the world he could solve during his lifetime would be very few. As another example of the ineffectiveness in transforming people, Han Fei referred to Confucius, calling (apparently tongue in cheek) the master "one of the greatest sages of the world", but, in the same breath, adding that, after preaching benevolence and righteousness in many places for many years, he succeeded in converting only seventy persons to be his true disciples. Therefore, one who argues for the government to transform the people by means of benevolence and righteousness has to presume that the ruler can rise to the level of Confucius and that all the ordinary people can become his disciples. The presumption is, of course, a fantasy.

Han Fei was particularly repelled by the allegation of the Ruists and the Mohists that, in the past, sage kings loved their subjects in the way that parents loved their children and, thus, would stop any performance of music at court when someone was to be punished and would shed tears upon learning of an execution. What was implied by this was that there was order under those sage kings because they were benevolent towards the people. Han Fei rejected this argument. First, he said, even in a family with loving parents, children can still be unruly, so that there is thus no definite connection between love and order. Then he pointed out that no love is as great as that of the mother for her son but, when he behaves improperly, she sends him to a teacher for discipline; when he is ill, she dispatches him to a physician for treatment. In the case of a man of bad character, neither the love of his parents nor the advice and admonition of his neighbours and teacher can move him but, when the magistrate comes to enforce the law, he promptly changes his behaviour. Therefore, Han Fei said, the sage kings acted to display their sorrow but did not stop punishments and executions because they knew that doing so would cause disorder. It was pleasant to appear benevolent but it was more important to uphold the law and keep order. Here Han Fei used a metaphor. When children are at play, they use wood and mud for food but, when they are hungry late in the day, they will go home for a real meal. In other words, benevolence is only for show.

(c) They are actually harmful

(i) They make rewards and punishments inappropriate

Thirdly, Han Fei argued that governing according to the principles of benevolence and righteousness actually produces harmful results for the state and the ruler. This is because what the world regards as acts of benevolence and righteousness are to give charity to the poor and destitute, and what the world regards as acts of magnanimity and love are to be compassionate to the people and merciful in punishing them. But, to give charity to the poor and destitute regardless of whether or not they had any merit, will, on the one hand, discourage those who work hard in the fields and those who risk their lives in battle, and, on the other hand, encourage those who avoid farming and fighting. And not to inflict punishment on the guilty will encourage the proliferation of crimes. As a result, the state will be weak and disorderly and finally ruined, and the ruler humiliated and eventually displaced or murdered.

To support his point, Han Fei cited a story about King Zhaoxiang of Qin 秦昭襄王 refusing distribution of the vegetables and fruit in the royal garden to people suffering famine because, among them, some certainly had little merit. Indiscriminately giving charity to people with or without merit would cause disorder. The king would rather let people starve than have disorder. Han Fei apparently approved the king's action and actually went a step further, providing a justification. Ordinarily, all people's conditions are similar. Why in lean years are some, without unusual income, able to have enough provisions? They must have been working very hard or living very frugally. And why, at a time when there are no famine, epidemic diseases or natural or man-made disasters, are some people poor and destitute? They must either have been spendthrift or lazy. It is unfair for the government to tax the well-off to give to the poor. It will be robbing the hard-working and frugal and rewarding the spendthrift and lazy. This is not the right way to govern.

(ii) They make the authorities disrespected and the state ruined

Another harmful effect perceived by Han Fei was that a benevolent ruler would make people lack respect for the authorities and therefore cause disorder. Apparently, he came to this conclusion after observing some contemporary phenomena. First, there were individuals who valued personal freedom and dignity more than public recognition and preferred the lifestyle of the recluse. Second, many people thought that, because of this disinterest in government rewards, a recluse might have unusually wise solutions to government problems. Third, it was not uncommon for ambitious and misguided rulers to seek advice from such men. Fourth, the ruler being courteous to the recluse and humbling himself in their presence were much lauded by many as a sign of the ruler being benevolent and righteous.

Duke Huan of Qi 齊桓公 was one such ruler. According to a report, he repeatedly went to see a recluse named Xiaochen Ji 小臣稷 and was granted an audience only on the fifth visit. It was not clear what advice he received from this commoner. In any case, Han Fei thought the event absurd, and ridiculed the duke for not knowing what benevolence and righteousness really mean and for violating the proper relationship between a ruler and a subject.

In Han Fei's view a benevolent person is one who "worries about the problems of the world, rushes to render help when there is a crisis in his state, and, in doing so, does not mind taking low positions and performing humiliating chores"; and a righteous person is one who never "damages the relative positions of a ruler and a subject, and forgets the rites he ought to observe as a subject in the presence of his ruler". Now Xiaochen Ji refused four times to meet the duke who was eager to seek his advice on state affairs. He was obviously not worried about the problems of the state. And, as a commoner subject, his refusal violated the proper relationship between him and his ruler the duke. For these reasons, he could not be considered either benevolent or righteous and, therefore, should not be honoured by the duke with repeated visits. Instead, he should be punished – if he had wisdom and talent, and avoided the duke, he was hiding himself from government service and he should therefore be sentenced to corporal punishment; if he did not have wisdom and talent, and yet was arrogant and disrespectful towards the duke, he was fraudulent and, for this, he should be sentenced to death. On the other hand, the duke was also at fault. By paying repeated visits to a subject who was neither benevolent nor righteous, and by tolerating repeated rejections, he, too, violated the proper relationship between the ruler and the subject and thus taught his people to disrespect him and government authority. Han Fei was evidently displeased but he did not suggest any measure to be taken against the duke.

Such an event will not only cause disrespect of the government authority but may produce even greater harm. By way of explanation, Han Fei told a story of Zhao Zhu-fu 趙主父 (King Wuling of the state of Zho 趙武靈王) asking Li Ci 李疵, an official, whether Zhongshan 中山, a protectorate of the state of Wei 魏, was vulnerable to attack. Li Ci replied affirmatively. Because, he said, its ruler was fond of recluses and brought tens of them to his court, paid respect to scores of scholars in slums, and treated hundreds of commoners with great courtesy. As such people were honoured and employed, soldiers were tired of fighting and peasants tired of farming, making the state poor and its army weak. In conclusion, Li Ci said, it was unheard of that such a state could survive long. With this information, the king of Zhao attacked and quickly vanquished Zhongshan.

(3) Multiple, confusing rules and policies

Besides holding benevolence and righteousness as the general guiding principle for good government, the Ruists and Mohists preached various other rules of conduct, and many actions carried out according to such rules were promoted by governments during Han Fei's time, which he called *za-fan zhi xing* (雜反之行 conflicting behaviours). For instance, the Ruists advocated elaborate and costly funeral rites and a lengthy mourning period but Mohists insisted on simple burials and a short time for grieving. The rulers respected the Ruist practice as an admirable demonstration of piety and, at the same time, praised the Mohist practice for its frugality. But, as Han Fei pointed out, "ice and burning charcoal cannot remain in the same container for long"; similarly, the two contradictory teachings could not be followed simultaneously without producing chaos. And, making the situation worse, many others, in addition to the Ruists and Mohists, were peddling numerous incompatible ideas which also attracted the attention of some rulers and common people. As there were no longer common standards and unambiguous guidelines for behaviour, everyone was left in confusion and unable to know what to do.

The Legalists alleged that the situation could easily be corrected by the authorities making laws to regulate behaviour and enforcing the laws with rewards and punishments. But, in reality, it was not that simple. By Han Fei's time, every state had lots of laws, many not enforced. Why? Because there are two factors against them: first, the people's feelings and their conceptions of rightness; second, the personal biases of the authorities, particularly the ruler. Where the people generally considered a law inappropriate, it could not be effectively enforced; where the authorities were swayed by their personal prejudices, all laws could be misused. In such cases of conflict between the law and public concepts, and among authorities on different levels, law became empty words rather than concrete standards. Consequently, as Han Fei said, order would be impossible "even if there were ten Huangdi at the top of the government". When a horse is whipped to urge it forward and, at the same time, reined to hold it back, it will jump sideways; when the people face conflicting perceptions of justice and inconsistent application of law they will be perplexed and paralysed or go divergent ways. In either case the result would be the same – confusion and disorder.

(D) Correct responses

Why did the authorities make these erroneous responses? To Han Fei, the answer was simple. Among those who held government power, few were qualified. To begin with, most of them lacked a proper understanding of historical facts and government principles; secondly, they did not know the practical ways and means of government. Therefore, he made an effort to spell out in detail those facts and principles, analyse the ways and means, and instruct how they should be understood and used. His hope was evidently to bring about an extraordinary leader to respond to the chaos of his time and to establish order.

(1) The need of a proper understanding of history and principles of government

According to Han Fei, by his time human history was in its third phase. In the first one – that of great antiquity – people were few and other animals many. There were plenty of seeds and fruit for human consumption but raw food harmed people's health. And there were great floods making their life very difficult. Some sages rose to the challenge: one of them taught people to make nests as shelters against dangerous predators; another invented fire and people learned to cook and avoided illness; and yet others channelled the deluge. These sages were compassionate; they sacrificed their own well-being to improve the conditions of the people. For instance, Yu, while fighting the great flood, toiled so much that not a single strand of hair was left on his legs, and he lived in a shanty and ate meals of coarse grain and soup of wild plants. His labour was no less than that of a slave and his compensation no more than that of a doorman. Gratefully, the people made these sages rulers, and they ruled with benevolence and, because they truly served the people and received little in return, it was easy for them to abdicate their positions in favour of others. This situation changed when the world was more settled and the ruler's power and privileges grew. The practice of abdication ceased, replaced by a system of hereditary succession, and when, one dynasty failed to govern properly, it was overthrown by someone founding a new one. This was how Tang 湯 terminated the Xia 夏 and established the Shang 商; Wu 武 terminated Yin 殷 and established the Zhou 周.

A greater change in the ancient world was caused by the growth of human population. According to Han Fei, the growth followed a simple arithmetical multiplication – a man with five sons will in time have twenty five grandsons, and so on. The natural resources which were enough for a small population in ancient times soon became inadequate. To meet the additional needs, people had to work hard, contend and compete. Now history entered the second phase – that of middle antiquity. At this stage, a ruler had to be not only benevolent and righteous in order to establish himself as a role model for the people but also wise and tactful so that he could make laws to guide the people to behave correctly and make the state rich and strong. As examples, Han Fei gave us King Wen of Zhou 周文王 and King Yan of Xu 徐偃王 – the former, as a ruler of a small state during the late Yin Dynasty, practised benevolence and righteousness, and skilfully pacified the barbarians in the west of his state, and eventually became a true king; the latter, as a feudal lord under King Mu of the Zhou Dynasty 周穆王, also practised benevolence and righteousness but failed to prepare his people against foreign invasion, so his state was vanquished by King Wen of Jing 荊文王.

Two other important factors pushed the times into the third phase – that of Han Fei's time. First, politically, the feudal system established during the Zhou Dynasty was crumbling, weakening the relationship between people at various social levels. Second, economically, the competition for natural resources and manufactured goods became fiercer. Consequently, according to Han Fei, people were more and more freed from the old rules governing mutual intercourse and became more alienated from one another, more solipsistic, greedy, shameless, cunning, ruthless and violent. These changes made benevolence and righteousness as principles of government antiquated and unrealistic. Therefore, rulers of this time had to resort to actual strength in various forms to subdue the unruly and suppress the wicked.

Thus, at different stages, different principles of government must be followed. But Han Fei noted with dismay that many people of his time argued against change and advocated continuation of the old usage of benevolence and righteousness, and some of them even tried to reactivate the ancient practice of sage kings abdicating their positions in favour of worthy subjects. He pointed out that these conservatives were simply accustomed to tradition and intellectually too lazy to contemplate anything new. To a real sage, whether a tradition should be preserved or changed depended on its usefulness. To govern with benevolence and righteousness was an ideal and a policy of a bygone age when things were much simpler – when people used sea shells as sickles and pushed carts for transport. To apply such policies of unsophisticated people in a slow-moving society to the rapidly changing world of ruthless men engaging in ferocious struggles was like, in Han Fei's words, "to drive an untamed horse without using reins and whip". The result, needless to say, would be disastrous.

(2) The need for an extraordinary leader

Such understanding was not common. It takes an extraordinary person, who is intelligent enough to know and resolute enough to use his knowledge, so that "even if his action is against the wishes of the ordinary people he would carry it out". There were such persons, such as Yi Yin 伊尹 (chief minister of Tang 湯, founder of the Shang Dynasty) and Taigong 太公 (that is, Jiang Shang 姜尚, chief minister of Wu 武, founder of the Zhou Dynasty), who overthrew old governments and established new ones. They were revolutionaries condemned by many but praised by Han Fei because they changed the old, moribund ways and saved the people from disaster. He was contemptuous towards those who stupidly stuck with the old practices, comparing them to a stupid farmer who set watch at a tree stump on which a running rabbit had crashed and broken its neck, wishing that he could catch more rabbits this way.

(3) The need of opportune time and popular support

Even an exceptional leader cannot always succeed in making necessary changes. He needs some outside help. First of that, according to Han Fei, is *tian-shi* (天時 heavenly time). He pointed out that, in the winter, ten Yao could not grow one grain. Thus, what he meant was the time in a rather narrow sense – the time of the natural season. It is beyond human control. That is why he often emphasised that the government should use the people for public works only at the right time of the year.

A second kind of help is *ren-xin* (人心 hearts of the people), by which Han Fei meant popular support. Actually, he did not talk much about it. Indeed, it is strange that he, who insisted that a sage ruler would carry out his policies even if they were against the wishes of the ordinary people, would speak about popular support at all. But, of course, as mentioned above, if a policy is against the interests and values of the people and resolutely resisted by them, it cannot be enforced effectively. Han Fei did recognise this but we must not forget that the interests and values he referred to are only those related to human biological needs.

(4) The need of a special position

The third factor that can help a person become an effective ruler is *shi-wei* (勢位 position of power and authority). A person's position gives him certain advantages or disadvantages in his relationship to others: the higher the position, the greater the advantage. When a hereditary feudal system existed, a person's position was fixed by birth, irrespective of his personal qualities. A ruler, being at the top of a state, could command the obedience of the people of his state, even though he was stupid and unworthy; a person without a high position would have rather little influence on others even though he might be wise, virtuous, and talented. To make his point, Han Fei said, as a commoner, Yao could not govern three persons; as the emperor, Jie could cause disorder in the world. Therefore, he argued, the position of the ruler is one of his "means to overcome the masses". Where the ruler is good at using his august position, his state is secure; where the ruler is not, his state is in danger. And, needless to say, the ruler should hold on to his special position firmly and never lend any part of it to anyone, especially his ministers. For, as Han Fei said, "If the ruler loses one, the ministers will turn it to one hundred." To illustrate this danger, Han Fei gave as examples Duke Jian of Qi 齊簡公 who lost his position and his state to Tian Cheng 田成, and the rulers of Jin lost their positions to six ministers and eventually let the state be broken up by three of them. To explain the problem, he quoted Laozi saying: "The fish should not be let loose in a deep pool." It is because, in his own words, "the special position of power and authority of the ruler is like a deep pool. The officials are like the fish. Once the fish gets access to the pool, it can no longer be caught. Once the ruler loses his special position to his officials, he can never regain it."

(5) The ability to use tactics

The fourth factor a ruler must have is *ji-neng* (技能 skill and ability), more simply referred to by Han Fei as *shu* (術 tactics).

We have seen that, in analysing the problems of his time, Han Fei saw as the foremost cause of trouble, the nefarious deeds of those attempting to gain private profits against the interests of the state and the ruler. This realisation incensed him. After spending many paragraphs describing such deeds, he devoted chapter after chapter in preaching that, to counter the corrosive effects of them and to change the situation, the ruler must conduct himself adroitly, and he must use a variety of tactics.

In a chapter named *Qi-shu* (七術 Seven Tactics), Han Fei listed seven important ones: 1. to investigate and compare various propositions presented to him; 2. to inflict punishments with certainty and thus make his authority clear; 3. to bestow rewards faithfully and thus make people to do their best; 4. to listen to his subordinates individually and then hold a speaker responsible for what he says; 5. to issue spurious orders and give deceptive assignments and thus observe how his subjects respond; 6. to ask questions to which the answers are already secretly known to him; and 7 to say and do not what he intends in order to mislead others.

In addition, many other tactics are discussed in other chapters. I have tried here to sort them out and make them easier to understand.

First, Han Fei defined the function of tactics as skills of control. For the ruler, they are those that enable him to control the state and its people, like a charioteer driving his horse and chariot. Second, the purpose of applying tactics is for the ruler to use the strength of his subjects and save his own. A ruler should have the intelligence to deliberate before he makes a decision and let the talented to carry out a task, so that he will not exhaust his own intelligence and ability, and yet get the credit for the achievements. This is, Han Fei said, the normal way of a clever and worthy ruler.

Then there is this question. Why does a ruler have to use tactics? It is because, Han Fei told us, the ruler has interests different from those of his subjects, among whom the shrewd ones always spy on him and cheat him to get more than he ought to give. He has to check on them, to determine their sincerity and measure their ability before appointing them to offices, giving them assignments and rewarding them for their achievements or punishing them for their failures. He cannot assume that they love him and cannot have trust in them. There are, as Huangdi aptly put it, "a hundred battles a day fought between those above and those below". Therefore, the ruler has to reduce the ability of his subjects, particularly that of the high officials, just like clipping the feathers of a bird's wings so that it cannot escape his control, and like pruning the overgrown branches of a tree so that they will not become too heavy and break the trunk in a strong wind. Then he can enjoy their service without being harmed by their treachery, perfidy, betrayal, usurpation, subversion, and murderous attempts.

How is a ruler actually to use the tactics? First of all he should "hide them in his bosom". Han Fei quoted Shen Buhai warning the ruler: "Be careful with your words, for people will know what you think; be careful with your action, for people will follow you." So he advised the ruler not to reveal his wishes and express his opinions, and get rid of any signs of his likes and dislike so that his subjects will appear in their plain selves without trying to flatter, mislead and cheat him. His way should be "invisible" and "unintelligible". He should seem purposeless, calm and inactive so that he can be in the shadow to observe what is in the light. He will see but will appear not to have seen anything, hear but appear not to have heard anything and know but appear not to have learned anything. If he can thus cover his tracks, his subjects will not be able to find any clue of how to manipulate him. In dealing with them he should, Han Fei said, "act secretly like a ghost".

Then the ruler will listen to what is said by his subjects individually and not allow them to corroborate one another's words. Han Fei put this advice in Confucius's mouth, saying "A clever ruler consults his officials one at a time, letting one official but no other know the questions and answers". The officials will not be allowed to *liang-jian* (兩諫 make two alternative proposals) or to make vague, unverifiable statements. Every remark must aim at a certain *di-gou* (的彀 target), and not be just empty talk like shooting an arrow without aiming, so that he can *xun-ming-shi* (循名實 check the statement against logic and facts) and *ding-shi-fei* (定是非 determine the right and wrong). An official who exaggerates will be pressed to spell out the details of his statements so that the discrepancies between the facts and contradictions in logic can be uncovered.

How can the ruler find the facts? He does not see and hear everything but will make the whole world see and hear for him. He not only listens to what people say but also punishes those who withhold a piece of information, and he will encourage everyone, especially those below, to report the evil deeds of those above. After thus learning the facts, he will ask the officials questions to which he already knows the answers to test their honesty.

Then the official making the statements will be assigned the job to carry out what he says, and his achievements will be scrutinised to find out whether there is overachievement or underachievement.

Finally there are two tactics to ensure the effectiveness of all other tactics – in Han Fei's words *san-jie* (三節 three grips) and *er-bing* (二柄 two handles). The first "grip", called *zhi* (質 hostage), is to make a high minister's relatives, wife or sons as guarantor of his good conduct; the second, called *zhen* (鎮 overwhelming), is to make the title and emolument for the official irresistible and pacifying; the third, called *gu* (固 verification and retribution), is to check an official's words and properly reward or punish him depending on whether they are truthful or groundless, in a case where an official has been assigned the task of implementing his own proposals, depending on whether his achievements match his proposals. "If what the official proposed is great but his achievement falls short, he will be punished, not for the small achievement but for the mismatch; if his proposal sounds modest but his achievement is great he will punished, not for the great achievement but for the mismatch."

Thus, in the final analysis, rewards and punishments are, in Han Fei's view, the ultimate means for the control of people. They are the "two handles." They can be prescribed by law and form a part of the law. This will be further discussed later but, when used by the ruler independently to enforce his will, they are tactics. In this sense, they should be held tightly in the hands of the ruler. So Han Fei, in his chapter *Yu-Lao* (喻老 "Explaining *Laozi*"), said, "Rewards and punishments are *bang zhi li-qi* (邦之利器 the sharp tools of the state). When they are in the hands of the ruler, he can control his subjects; when they are in the hands of the officials, they will overwhelm him – when the ruler indicates that he is to bestow a reward, the officials who are actually to distribute them will substrate a portion from it and give this portion to the recipient as a private favour from them; when the ruler is to impose a punishment the officials will increase the severity to demonstrate their power . . . Therefore, it is said, 'The sharp tools of the state cannot be revealed to others.'" If it should not even be revealed to others, needless to say it should not be left to anyone else.

(6) The use of law

Tactics can be a means of control but they alone are not adequate for achieving good government. Han Fei pointed out that there must be laws. In ancient times, there was an argument against the need for law, at least for written, promulgated law. We have seen earlier Shuxiang 叔向 expressly said so and Confucius implicitly supported this view. But, in due course, the need became obvious and all states adopted and publicised their laws. We shall discuss in some detail law's many attributes but here we shall only point out that Han Fei considered law as another means for the control of the people. It is used as an objective standard to measure their talents and shortcomings, merits and mistakes, and decide how to respond. It is easy to use and can produce accurate results. It is effective because, unlike tactics which should be kept secret, it is in the open, with the "two handles" clearly incorporated in it – in Han Fei's words, it is "the great command promulgated and kept by the government to install firmly in the hearts of the people the prescriptions and proscriptions, and to reward those who obey and punish those who violate". Moreover, it has another advantage: it can be widely applied and enforced, not by the ruler alone but also by his officials as his agents who are themselves subjected to strict control by him and, as Han Fei stressed, never allowed to "exercise discretion outside the limit of the law, or do favours within it".

(7) Combined use of position, tactics and law

Among the various factors or means for a ruler "correctly" to respond to the situation of a world in great strife and govern his state well, Shen Buhai stressed the tactics, Gongsun Yang the law and Shen Dao the ruler's special status. Apparently, in Han Fei's time, there was a debate about which means was more effective. In his book, he resorted to an imaginary conversation between him and "a guest" and an "enquirer" to address this issue.

At the outset, he restated Shen Dao's position on *shi*, comparing it to the clouds and the fog on which flying dragons and soaring snakes ride and cruise, and arguing that, when the clouds disperse and the fog is burned off, the dragons and snakes will be just like earthworms and ants. A person is no different. One with a position of power and authority can rule others; one without will be ruled by others. The importance of *shi* should thus be obvious.

Then Han Fei presented his guest's refutation of Shen Dao's argument. First the guest acknowledged that it is crucial for a person to have *shi* to have his commands carried out, and therefore, as a commoner, even Yao could not rule three persons. Then he argued that to be in such a special position will not automatically make a person a good ruler because the position has no orientation of its value in itself and therefore can enable its holder to do either good or evil – a Yao in the special position can bring order to the world; a Jie in the special position can cause disorder. Thus, whether or not the special position can help establish order depends on whether there is a virtuous and talented person. Since, as a matter of fact, persons of great virtue and talent are fewer than those who are mediocre or worse, and there is no way to ensure that the special position goes to the virtuous and talented, the chances are greater that it will be occupied by the less worthy. Therefore, this guest said, "If one speaks only about using the position of power and authority as a means to establish order in the world, his knowledge is rather shallow." To illustrate his point he used an analogy: a horse and carriage will perform poorly in the hands of a common servant but can travel 1,000 *li* a day when driven by Wang Liang 王良, a skilful driver in the past.

We are not told who this "guest" was. But he was obviously arguing for a view held by the Ruists and the Mohists that good government can be achieved only by good men. It compelled Han Fei to mount a lengthy and spirited rebuttal. First, he went to Shen Dao's defence, pointing out that the term *shi* can have multiple connotations – besides a special position of power and authority, it can denote a situation beyond human control. For instance, if a Yao or a Shun is born in the special position of power and authority, even if at his time ten Jies or Shous exist, there can be no disorder. This is because the situation is preconditioned for order. It will also be true if a Jie or a Shou is born in the special position of power and authority. Under him there can be no order even if there are ten Yaos or Shuns around. In either case, the precondition of a particular type of person occupying a special position is a coincidence that happens purely by chance. It is not an arrangement that man can make; it is *zi-ran zhi shi* (自然之勢 a situation created by natural forces) and thus immune from human interference, no matter how good or bad a person is who wants to have any effect on it.

But Han Fei did not simply endorse Shen Dao. He was arguing against both extreme views – one insisting on the overwhelming importance of the special position and the other on that of exceptional men. He quoted a metaphor of the all-piercing spear versus the impenetrable shield. Such absolutes cannot be in use at the same time. But this argument has a flaw. Unlike the cloud and fog which exist independently of the flying dragon and soaring snake, a truly extraordinary person can create the extraordinary position he needs. Han Fei admitted this. We remember he said that it took such persons to change the principles of government in accordance with the changing times. They were the founders of new dynasties.

Thus, Han Fei's own logic would push him to give greater weight to extraordinary men but, knowing that such men can be either good or bad, he discontinued this line of thought and twisted it to emphasise that, to achieve good government, extraordinary men are unnecessary. He pointed out that such men are rare: if a Yao, a Shun, a Jie or a Shou appears as a ruler once in a thousand generations, such appearances will be considered frequent. Between two appearances, there will be generation upon generation of ordinary rulers. Thus, what he talked about is a situation created not by exceptional rulers. What he talked about is a situation that is *ren zhi suo de-she* (人之所得設 what man can manage); it is not extreme but *zhong* (中 in the middle). In such a situation, the ruler is not as good as Yao and Shun nor as bad as Jie and Shou. If he embraces the law and holds on to his special position of power and authority, there will be order; if he discards the law and loses his special position, there will be disorder. This situation, Han Fei insisted, is more realistic and preferable. For if a state, with rulers who discard the law and lose their special positions, waits for a Yao or a Shun to establish order, it will have one generation of order in a thousand generations of disorder. If a state, with rulers who embrace the law and hold on to their special positions, waits until a Jie or Shou causes disorder, it will suffer one generation of disorder out of a thousand generations of order.

In Han Fei's view, the law and the special position are like tools for straightening or bending wood and instruments for measuring length and roundness. If such tools and instruments are not used, even Xi Zhong 奚仲, a famed wheelwright of the past, could not make a single wheel. If the law and the special position are discarded, a Yao or a Shun may go door to door to preach a course of action but people will argue with him, and he will not be able to rule three families. Thus, Han Fei said, the usefulness of the special position of a ruler is evident and the allegation that, to establish order, it is necessary to have a virtuous and talented ruler is not true.

To illustrate his point, Han Fei used another metaphor: a person who refuses to eat for a hundred days while waiting for gourmet food is sure to die of hunger. To wait for a person as worthy as Yao or Shun to rule the people of today is just like that. If that metaphor is not enough, Han Fei invoked yet another: if people in Zhong-guo (中國 the middle country) are drowning and they have to wait for good swimmers from the southern state of Yue 越 to come to their rescue, they will have died before the swimmers arrive.

As to the saying that a horse and carriage driven by a common servant will be laughed at by people but, driven by Wang Liang, will travel 1,000 *li* a day, Han Fei could not agree. He pointed out that, if on a road, there is a relay station every 50 *li*, the carriage and horses driven by average coachmen can reach 1,000 *li* a day as well. The point he wanted to make is again that, with special position and law, an average ruler can achieve good government.

More directly, Han Fei pointed to a flaw in the argument of his guest: it offers only a choice between two extremes – in driving, the driver is either an extremely inept common servant or an extremely skilled person as Wang Liang, and, in governing, the ruler is either an extremely virtuous and talented sage like Yao and Shun or an extremely cruel and debauched tyrant like Jie or Shou. It is like in eating, if one cannot have honey one must therefore chew bitter weeds. This is arbitrary and absurd because, between the extremes, there can be other choices neither as good nor as bad.

Having repudiated the notion of superior men as a prerequisite for good government in ordinary times, Han Fei went on to address the relative importance of the ruler's tactics and the state law. He made another "enquirer" ask the question, and he in reply said that both are essential – food and clothes are both necessary for a person to survive. According to him, "If the ruler does not know the tactics of control there will be problems at the top; if the officials do not follow the law, there will be chaos at the bottom."

Then the enquirer asked why the use of only one of these means is not enough. Han Fei explained with historical facts: when Marquis Zhao of Han 韓昭侯 was the ruler and Shen Buhai the chief minister, the state, formerly a feudal subdivision of the state of Jin 晉, had many old Jin laws and many new Han laws. Shen Buhai did not try to make those laws consistent but simply taught the marquis to rely on tactics and to use whichever law was advantageous. When old and new laws conflict and evil officials argued against the marquis's decision, he was lost, and the state, despite its ten thousand chariots never achieved hegemony. Thus, tactics alone, no matter how ingenious, were not enough.

On the other hand, while governing the state of Qin, Gongsun Yang made many laws and enforced them rigorously. As a result, the state became rich and strong. But, after his time, the rulers of Qin did not know the tactics to use to control their officials and, consequently, for decades while the laws were still in place, the wealth and strength of the state were squandered or stolen by the officials, and Qin did not become an empire. This proved that law alone, no matter how comprehensive, was not enough.

The enquirer asked further, "Suppose the ruler applies the tactics of Shen Buhai, and the officials observe the laws of Lord Shang, would the result be all right?" Han Fei's answer was qualified because he thought the tactics advocated by Shen Buhai and the laws made by Lord Shang were imperfect. For instance, one of Shen Buhai's tactics was to prohibit an official from doing anything beyond his duties and saying anything that is of no concern to his office. Han Fei pointed out that, while the first prohibition is fine, the second will block the flow of information to the ruler and keep him in the dark, unable to learn about any intrigues against him and the state. A clever ruler, according to Han Fei, will punish officials who make overstatements, understatements and groundless ones, and will also punish those who do not divulge their knowledge of anything that might be harmful to the ruler and the state.

Gongsun Yang's laws also have problems. For instance, one of them prescribes that a soldier who beheaded an enemy will be given a rise in rank and, if he wishes to work in the government, he can be made an official with a salary of 50 catties of rice, and that the reward will be increased if he killed more enemies. That law is inappropriate, Han Fei said. It is like making the soldier a physician or carpenter. The ability to cure illness, build a house or perform government functions is different from that of killing enemies. A soldier who can kill in battles will, as an official, not know what to do with the people who are not his enemies.

It is interesting that, after placing great emphasis on the usefulness of tactics, Han Fei admitted that it has limits. And his criticism of Gongsun Yang's law, though inappropriate (a brave soldier may not be made a physician or carpenter but can rightly be appointed a military officer) apparently implies that law is not just the ruler's command; there is something beyond his will that should be used to judge its value, a view, as we shall see, Han Fei rejected.

Evidently, Han Fei thought this lengthy "discussion" between him and his "guest" and "enquirer" was necessary. He accepted the positions of Shen Dao, Shen Buhai and Gongsun Yang but saw some defects in each case and was compelled to fix them before constructing his own theory which is in serious disagreement with theories of most other schools of his time. To fight his adversaries he had to fix the weak positions of his fellow Legalists and present a stronger one of his own.

(E) Theory of law

Han Fei's position is at least more comprehensive than that of the other Legalists. His theory touches on law's functions and objectives, its origin and bases, its distinctive characteristics and its application and enforcement.

(1) Objectives and functions

All Legalists were pragmatic. Gongsun Yang saw a very narrow objective of law – to make the state rich and strong. As we shall see, Han Fei's utopia is more attractive but, when not dreaming about it (that being most of the time), he also focused on the immediate, rather limited objectives which he said were to save the people from disorder, to rid the world of disasters, to prevent the strong from attacking the weak and the majority from oppressing the minority, to allow the old live in peace and the young have a chance to grow, and to make borders free from conflicts. These are broader than Gongsun Yang's objectives, but not much. It is because, like Gongsun Yang, Han Fei was not concerned about making all people better but only about deterring some people from doing harm. In his words, "In managing the affairs of the world, if the most urgent tasks are not yet finished, the ruler should not work on what is more remote." Law is not made for the virtuous, such as Zeng Shen 曾參 and Shi Yu 史魚 (two men of the past known for their filial piety and righteousness), but for the ruler to suppress miscreants such as Robber Zhi 盜跖 (a legendary leader of a robber band). People of integrity need no artificial law but, without law, it would be difficult even for very powerful men, such as Meng Fen 孟賁 and Xia Yu 夏育 of old, to keep the unscrupulous, depraved and aggressive from disrupting order.

Thus, law has two basic functions – a positive one to establish standards and a negative one to suppress disorder. It is used as an instrument to measure behaviour, like the compass and the scales to determine roundness and weight, which are valued because they are reliable and easy to use. And it is used as equipment to impose restrictions, such as a cage to confine a tiger, which is valued because it is effective. These functions were commonly recognised by all Legalists. They are basically passive, judging people as they are and restraining them. Han Fei pointed out an active function – to force people to become what the ruler wants them to be, like *zhui-duan* (椎鍛 hammer and anvil) and *beng-qing* (榜檠 timber-bending device) that are used to make materials into what the craftsman wants them to be. This function is of crucial importance. It makes law conceptually and practically a more powerful means for the ruler to intrude into people's lives and force changes. This function cannot be overemphasised. It dramatically distinguishes law from other norms which, as a rule, merely post some ideals for people voluntarily to pursue.

(2) Bases

On what bases are laws to be made so that they can have those functions and realise their objectives? All ancient Chinese thinkers exalted *dao*, the Way, as the most fundamental, but none spelled out what exactly it is. When pressed for an answer, the Ruists talked about people's needs, feelings, aspirations, and *li* (理 reason) which, to them, is an attribute of human nature. As a student of Xunzi, Han Fei paid some lip service to *li* but he was more an admirer of Laozi and said that law should be in agreement with *tian-li* (天理 Heavenly reason). By this term, however, he did not mean anything profoundly transcendental and metaphysical but only some very simple principles of nature as when a hungry person needs food and a cold one needs clothes. He pointed out that law should be in agreement with this "nature", not against it, but said little more. No argument in his book supports any belief that there is something above artificial laws by which they are to be judged and about which the common people are capable of knowing. He said that, in making law, a sage will consider what is "essential" to the people but, in the same breath, he added that the sage will not simply follow what they desire because they are stupid, incapable of knowing what is truly good or bad for them, and therefore are careful only about small profits but ignorant about great benefits. Therefore, law should be based on what is the right way to benefit the people, not on their desires. A ruler should be astute enough to know this way and resolute enough to follow it. As a result, the law he makes may be against the people's wishes and "in conflict with the world", but will establish order which is the greatest benefit to the people. Thus, in practice, the ruler should make laws as he sees fit. They are simply his handiwork and, if they seem to be arbitrary to the common people, so be it.

Another commonly recognised basis of law is established practices known as custom or tradition. As a law reformer, Gongsun Yang generally maintained that, when the circumstances change, law should change but ordinary people are short-sighted, bound by tradition. A far-sighted law-maker should disregard tradition and make new laws to meet new needs. Han Fei agreed, saying that, whether a tradition can be preserved, depends on whether it is useful for the present, and the decision is to be made by the law-maker whose objective is to "establish order" and thereby "to benefit the people" in the long run.

(3) Important characteristics

Because of the functions and the objectives it wants people to pursue, law has certain special characteristics which distinguish it from other norms. Han Fei alluded to many. Six of them are readily discernible in his book, including being pragmatic, constant and yet flexible, specific, definitive, easy to know and observe, easy to apply, forceful and effective in bringing about the desired results, and superior to other norms.

(A) Pragmatic

First, as law is to require people to do or avoid certain acts, it must be pragmatic. The acts must be practically doable or avoidable. Needless to say, a law cannot command people to perform miracles; a law that requires people to do a very difficult task and punishes them for not accomplishing it will not be effective, and it will make them resentful and rebellious.

Instead, a law should aim at what is achievable. The result may not be perfect but there is no such thing in the world as a perfect law. It always has some undesirable side effects. Therefore, Han Fei said, in making a law, a sage weighs its benefits and disadvantages. If the benefits outweigh the disadvantages, he will enact it.

(B) Steady but adaptable

Second, related to this pragmatism, law has another necessary character – to be steady but adaptable to changing circumstances. Under normal conditions, law should remain consistent and constant, otherwise people will find it perplexing and unreliable. As Han Fei said, when a mirror shakes, one cannot see a clear image; when a scale is unsteady, one cannot get a correct weight; when laws and prohibitions frequently change and numerous orders are issued, people will be troubled and the state chaotic. Therefore, a ruler who knows the right way to govern values inaction and tranquillity. When a law is made, it should not be changed simply because of some criticism. This is why Laozi famously said, "To govern a big state is like cooking a small fish." And Han Fei in his chapter "Jie–Lao" (解老 deconstructing *Laozi*) explained: If it is much stirred it will be shredded.

But, while law is to be constant, it should never become petrified; it should change when circumstances change. As mentioned above, Han Fei thought little about established practices and was repelled by those "who do not know the principles of government" and argue against changing tradition. To him, law is in the same position – whether a law of the past should be preserved or changed depends on its usefulness to the present. A ruler clever enough to know the right principles of government should decide to change the law when necessary and rigorously enforce the new law even though it is against the wishes of the ordinary people.

(C) Plain but specific

Third, in Han Fei's view, the most serious trouble with other norms is that they are largely vague principles susceptible to different interpretations that often contradict. Law should be different, it should be specific. He made this point clear by an analogy: when a book is sketchy, students will debate its contents and meaning; therefore a sage's book always includes detailed discussions. When a law is broad and general, people will get involved in litigation; therefore, the law of a bright ruler must have specific rules for relevant matters.

Then it is necessary to have laws spelled out in plain written language, deposited in government institutions and promulgated publicly for the ordinary people to learn. If a law is in abstruse words, difficult even for the highly intelligent to comprehend, it will not be understood by ordinary people and will not be observed by them.

(D) Objective and easy to apply

Fourth, law should be easy to apply. It should be an objective standard like a measuring instrument that is simple to use. When a scale is hung, the correct weight is revealed; when a compass is applied, a circle of perfect roundness can be drawn. This is the sure way to produce correct results. If, instead of such instruments, one resorts to personal intelligence in making decisions, one will inevitably cause confusion and disorder; this is because, even for a person of great intellect, using it in making decisions is difficult. Without the easily used compass, a skilled wheelwright cannot make a good wheel; without readily applicable law, even Yao cannot rule three persons. But a clumsy craftsman using the proper instrument and an average ruler applying the proper laws can always avoid mistakes.

(E) Forceful and effective

Fifth, law should be forceful to bring about the desired results. Most other norms are advisory in nature, relying on education and persuasion to make people follow voluntarily. Some such norms have deep roots in human reason and feelings, and therefore, appealing to them can cause a resonance but the consequence is not certain. Law is different. It can be arbitrary and difficult to elicit a sympathetic response. Therefore, it can only be imposed upon people and it should be coercive; as Han Fei said, it should be like the hammer and the anvil. How can it be so forceful? Because it is backed by the power of the state. What does the state do? This brought a protracted answer from Han Fei.

To begin with, he pointed out that, generally, people love profit and hate loss. Government can therefore use reward and punishment to encourage or prohibit certain behaviours. For this reason, law should include in its provisions these "two handles". They will make people obedient as a whip and bridle will make a horse obey. For quick and dramatic effects, rewards should be generous and punishments severe. To illustrate this point, Han Fei told a story where the king of the state of Yue set his own palace on fire, and ordered that those who fought the fire and died were to be rewarded as if they had died in a battle; those who fought and survived were to be rewarded as if they had defeated the enemy; but, on the other hand, those who did not fight the fire were to be punished as if they surrendered to the enemy. Immediately, people covered their bodies with mud and wet clothes and rushed towards the fire, three thousand on its left side, three thousand on its right side.

But there are limits. First, Han Fei said, "The bright ruler offers rewards that can be earned, and prescribes punishments that are avoidable." If an act is too difficult to do or avoid, rewards and punishments will have no effect, regardless of how generous or severe they are. Indeed, there can be such situations. We remember Mencius said that it is impossible for anyone to carry Mount Tai under his arm and stride across the North Sea, and Xunzi said that, when the army is being routed, the law against desertion is not enforceable.

Han Fei also recognised that rewards and punishments are ineffective in cases involving extraordinary people. To *tian-xia tai-shang zhi shi* (天下太上之士 the loftiest persons of the world) no reward is great enough to nudge them; to *tian-xia tai-xia zhi shi* (天下太下之士 the meanest person of the world) no punishment is harsh enough to prevent them. But, of course, rewards and punishments are not established for them but for the ordinary people. In Han Fei's words, "If on account of the loftiest persons, rewards are not established, and on account of the meanest persons, punishments are not instituted, the right way of governing the state and employing the people is missed."

While Han Fei accepted that rewards and punishments are both useful, he, like Gongsun Yang, placed greater emphasis on punishment and argued that law should have more punitive provisions. It is because they both were paranoid about disorder and believed that punishments are more effective in deterring disruptive acts. Moreover, they believed that the effectiveness increases when punishments are made severe. This idea was not widely accepted. The Ruists hailing benevolence and the Mohists advocating universal love were adamantly against harsh punishments, arguing that the severity of punishment should be proportionate to the seriousness of crime, and that, if light punishment is enough to deter, a severe one just harms people needlessly. The Legalists thought this argument fallacious and conducive to disaster.

To begin with, they pointed out that humans are calculating. In deciding whether to do an act, they will assess the gain they may have against the loss they may suffer. If the gain is more than the loss, many will decide to do it; if the two are of about equal value, some will take a chance; if the loss is overwhelmingly greater than the possible gain, few will run the risk. We may remember a story in *Zhuangzi* where a person was asked whether he would take the world if he was to lose a hand as a price and the answer was negative. Han Fei made the same point saying that even a robber would not risk going to the bottom of a canyon to fetch gold and become trapped there.

He then made another point: small penalties will not catch people's attention. He started this argument by quoting some "former sage's adage" *bu-zhi-yu-shan er zhi-yu-die* (不躓於山而躓於垤 people do not tumble over a mountain but they do over a small lump of earth). And then he gave his own explanation: "A mountain is big, so people climb with care; a lump of earth is small, so people walk towards it paying no attention. If punishments are light they will certainly be ignored."

With these reasons he proposed to make punishments for all offences, regardless of their seriousness, overwhelmingly severe, and alleged that, if a punishment can deter a serious crime, it certainly can deter a lesser one, but not vice versa.

Further, he explained why, if punishments match crimes, especially if a light punishment is prescribed for a minor offence, the result will be disastrous. It is because criminals are not always caught and many people will be tempted to try their luck. If law enforcement is made effective to catch such persons, it is to entrap them. This practice, in Han Fei's view, is truly doing great harm to people. Thus, he said, those who cried "Make punishment light!", arguing that harsh punishments were unnecessarily harming the people, were "not only incompetent but unethical". On the contrary, when a punishment is made severe for an evil man, many ordinary people, who may be contemplating a wrong act, will be stopped. Thus, when a relatively small number of bad elements are harshly punished, the great majority of innocent men are frightened and kept away from wrongdoing, and never get caught and punished. This, to Han Fei, is true benevolence.

Han Fei elaborated further on this point, arguing that severe punishments are not meant to affect the criminal because to execute a murderer will not have any corrective effect on him when he is dead; nor will a punishment on a robber have much effect on him as he is to be made a slave under permanent control. The real purpose of inflicting punishments is to warn and frighten the innocent people and deter them from committing crimes.

Therefore, he said, "In the past those who were good at keeping the Way of government used what was heavy to prohibit what was light . . . As a result, all persons, noble and petty, behaved correctly." This is the way leading to order. "How can those who desire good government have any doubt of the value of severe punishments?", Han Fei demanded.

In case some people still do, Han Fei made an appeal to an authority with which they could not dispute – Confucius. He told them a story of the Master supporting the Yin Dynasty law prescribing amputation of the hand of anyone throwing ash into the street. According to him, Confucius said, "Because throwing ash into the street could harm people; being harmed, people will be angry; being angry, they may start a fight, and a fight may lead to extensive mutual injuries to the clans involved. As an act which may eventually cause injury to many people, it ought to be punished. Moreover, while to suffer severe punishment is what the people surely hate, to throw ash into the street is what they can easily avoid. To make people do what is easy and help them shun what they hate is the way to lead to good order."

(F) Absolute

Sixth, and finally, law should be regarded as absolute and held as the supreme, if not the only, norm. This characteristic of law is particularly emphasised by the Legalists.

Han Fei, like Gongsun Yang, was aware of the existence of many other norms that compete with law for authority, and he alleged that this fact was one of the main causes of disorder during their time. They both advocated rejecting the useless and harmful norms hailed by the Ruists and the Mohists. We have seen how Han Fei discredited those norms. He further denounced those who perorate them. In his words, "Men quoting the early kings and talking about benevolence and righteousness fill up the court but cannot help the government avoid disorder." The reason is not only because they are empty words but also because they are self-contradictory and cause contentious arguments. Therefore, law must be made the only subject of study and discourse. In his words, "The government orders are the most respected words, and state laws are the best guides for affairs. There can be no two different sets of words equally respected, and no two different sets of contradictory actions both lawful. The words and actions that do not conform to law must be banned." Therefore "in the state of a bright ruler there are no books of learning; law supplies the only instruction.

There are no sermons of the former kings; the officials serve as the only teacher . . . and, hence, when the people of such a state make speeches, they say nothing that is in contradiction to the law." In other words, law is not something to be argued about. Any discourse on law, probing its objectives, functions, and attributes, is profitable only to produce confusion. Instead, law must be received at its face value, its words considered self-explanatory, its meaning self-evident. No interpretation is needed, none that contradicts the obvious connotation or even suggests an implication should be allowed. The provisions, in their unadulterated form, should be held as the sole commands and the absolute standards. Thus, law should not only be the only norm in practice but conceptually be a sacrosanct one above intellectual investigation and critique. This is an extreme position implied in Han Fei's theory.

(F) Application and enforcement of law

That extreme position, though implicit, can be detected in Han Fei's words. In one paragraph, he dismissed those who indulged in empty discussions, even about the laws adopted by Gongsun Yang and Guan Zhong 管仲. According to him, in his time many people kept copies of those laws and presumably discussed them but the country was getting poorer because people just talked but did not actually observe the laws.

Therefore Han Fei placed great emphasis on the application and enforcement of law, discussing in some detail the judicial process. At various procedural steps, he alluded to a principle in his theory, and then gave some common-sense explanations to make it more understandable, or some more detailed practical advice on how it should be realised, or some everyday experience or historical anecdotes as examples to prove its practicality and benefits. Thus, though some parts in the following may seem to be repeating what has been stated above, they make clearer a unique aspect or dimension of his theory and are therefore worth the recapitulation and further explanation.

(1) Pursue relative advantages

As mentioned earlier, Han Fei admitted that no law can be perfect in its design, and, in applying and enforcing an imperfect law, some undesirable side effects may be inevitable. Thus, the first guiding principle is to compare the expected achievement with the possible side effects and pursue the relative advantage. In any undertaking, one has to endure some small harm in order to gain a great benefit. This was how Han Fei put it: "He who washes hair will lose some of it; he who cures a wound removes some blood and flesh; he who sees the harm of such undertakings and gives them up is a man of no consequence . . . Therefore, the sage does not seek anything that has no bad effects; rather, he puts his mind to something that is certain to have some good results."

(2) Encourage report of wrongdoings

In administering justice, it is of vital importance to detect and deter violation. Since law-enforcement resources are limited, the best way to carry out these tasks is to make the whole population watch on behalf of the authorities and report crimes – better still, the small signs of anyone about to commit a crime. But, to spy on others and expose their action, design or intention are normally frowned upon and possibly dangerous. How can the government make people do it? The Legalists suggested the use of rewards and punishments. A person can be made to report crimes if he will be punished for the offences of others related or close to him. Han Fei said, "When a person knows that he can be implicated, it will be natural that he will watch out for fear of not being able to escape unharmed, and the person with an evil scheme will not forget that he is being watched by many." The effect will be greater if, in addition to collective punishment, special rewards are bestowed on the informant. Again in Han Fei's words, "If the informant is not only exempted from collective punishment but also rewarded . . . Evil types will be exposed, and no villainy, however minute, will be tolerated."

As a proof of the effectiveness of these measures, Han Fei pointed to the success achieved by Gongsun Yang who organised the people into units of five and ten families and held members of each unit responsible for the wrongdoings of one another. His laws offered those who reported evil acts or schemes the same rewards as for decapitating enemy soldiers, and inflicted on those who failed to report such acts or schemes the same punishments as for surrendering to the enemy. "As a result," according to Han Fei, "the people no longer violated law and punishments became useless."

(3) Conduct hearings

Besides relying on the informants' reports, the authorities should discover the truth at hearings. Being an enthusiast of tactics, Han Fei had some practical advice on how to do this. The most crucial tactic was that, in listening to a presentation, the listener should stay quiet and inactive, certainly not make any comment, nor even to move his lips or show any sign of an opinion or an emotion and thus participate in the construction of a story. He should look drunk and, if he makes any sound or movement, it should be obviously irrelevant so that the speaker will continue to speak and will be unable to adjust his remarks according to what he guesses to be the listener's reaction. While the speaker is making his speech, the listener should carefully detect the various lines in the narrative, analyse them, find their inconsistencies and contradictions, if any, and compare the allegations with what are known as facts.

This is, of course, just more detailed advice on how to listen to people in general. He mentioned a special tactic in conducting criminal hearings. It was used by Zichan 子產 who separated the litigants and, after listening to one party, he told the other the opposite of what he had heard. In this way, Han Fei said, Zichan was always successful in finding the truth.

(4) Make decision

Having finished the hearing, the judge is to make a decision. At this point, he should, Han Fei stressed, set aside his own opinion because, even a clever man relying only on his personal judgement, will inevitably make mistakes. He should, instead, apply the law that sets up standards and use it as an instrument to determine correctness. The application of law must be faithful, and its coverage should not be stretched or shrunk. No strenuous efforts should be made to reveal its implications, "like blowing to part the hair to find small blemishes". "The clear, self-evident meaning of a law must be upheld or there will be disorder. Thus, in his chapter *An-wei* (安危 security and danger), Han Fei said, "There are six ways to danger . . . The first is to make cuts within the limits of law and the second is to grant allowances beyond the limits of law."

In Han Fei's view, applying law faithfully has three other benefits: first, the judge will not be overworked. A man's intelligence is limited; thus, to use it in deciding cases, a judge will soon become exhausted and make mistakes; to use law faithfully is much easier and safer. Second, the people involved in litigation will be inhibited from making extra-legal arguments about morality and values not sanctioned by law. This will greatly simplify the trial, reduce arbitrariness in the decision-making, increase the consistency and credibility of the judicial process, and enhance the authority of the law. Third, and perhaps most important, when law is used as an objective standard, it will, in Han Fei's words, "never contradict the course of Heaven nor hurt the feelings of man".

These benefits of faithful application of law were well recognised by sages and effective rulers of the past. According to Han Fei, Shun executed officials who started draining the flood before receiving his order, even though they achieved some success. Yu decapitated Fangfeng 防風, a tribal chief who came late to a meeting. These events illustrated that the great sages applied law faithfully. In another story, Marquis Zhao of Han 韓昭侯 punished both the hat-keeper who, fearing that the marquis might catch cold while taking a nap, covered him with a robe, and the clothes-keeper who failed to do so, because the former overstepped his post and the latter fell short of his. Han Fei gave this example to praise the marquis for strictly enforcing the law and not allowing himself any discretion.

(5) Use rewards and punishments

Law, unlike other norms, has the advantage of being backed by the power and authority of the government and therefore has the force of a hammer and an anvil. The actual means the government uses to enforce law are rewards and punishments – the "two handles" of control. As they can affect the lives of the people and the fate of the state, they must be used with care.

(A) MAKE USE OF THE LAW A SOVEREIGN'S PREROGATIVE

Han Fei particularly stressed that the "two handles" must be held only in the hands of the ruler. If this sovereign prerogative is usurped by someone, that person will erode the ruler's authority, take over the government, and have him deposed, even murdered. Thus, the "two handles" are like the fangs and claws of a tiger – with them the tiger can subdue dogs; without them it will be subdued by dogs. Han Fei used the metaphor to explain many historical events. Among them two were mentioned repeatedly: The ruler of the state of Song let Zihan 子罕exercise the prerogative of inflicting punishments and was consequently killed by the treasonous minister. Duke Jian of Qi let Tian Chang 田常 bestow government titles and emoluments to officials and distribute aid to people as private favours. Eventually, Tian Chang committed regicide and took over the government of Qi. Such evil deeds were numerous in Han Fei's time and before. He quoted Zixia 子夏, a disciple of Confucius, saying that none of these cases was the outcome of a single day's doing but the result of gradual, accumulative action . . . Therefore an intelligent ruler should terminate such schemers early on.

It is easy to understand that a ruler who does not have the power and authority to punish will lose; it is less clear that one whose exclusive right to give rewards is usurped will also fail. Therefore, Han Fei told the story of Confucius stopping Zilu 子路, a disciple serving as the magistrate of a district in the state of Lu, from using his own funds to provide food for the labourers working on a government project. According to him, Confucius said that the rites allow only the ruler of a state to care for its people and command their allegiance. Anyone else who gave people private favours was infringing on this royal prerogative and depriving the ruler of some of his power and authority. To illustrate this result, Han Fei told another story where Duke Jing of Qi 齊景公 competed against his two brothers for the loyalty of the people and won by giving them more benefits than his brothers could afford.

(b) Reward the meritorious and punish the guilty

To be effective, rewards and punishments must, according to Han Fei, be *dang* (當 matching). The word can mean matching in degree (the value of a reward matching the significance of an achievement; the severity of a punishment matching the seriousness of a crime), or matching in a broad, unspecific sense (reward for merit; punishment against misconduct). Han Fei used it only in the second sense. To him, if an act is proscribed as a crime, it is "warranted" to be punished; if the effect of an act is recognised as an achievement, it is "warranted" to be rewarded. The value of rewards and the severity of punishments are different matters.

It is easy to see that rewards should be given only to those who are meritorious. To make this point clear, Han Fei told a story of Marquis Zhao of Han 韓昭侯 having his threadbare trousers saved for those who had achievements worthy of his favour. Han Fei apparently thought that was a correct measure for a "bright ruler". But this principle can have unfortunate results when pushed to its logical extreme, as we have mentioned above that, when there was a famine in the state of Qin, King Zhaoxiang 昭襄王 refused a request to let the starving people have fruit and other foodstuffs from the royal gardens. That decision, however, was obviously endorsed by Han Fei with admiration.

It is less easy to comprehend Han Fei's position that, in a criminal case, a crime warrants punishment but the two need not match in degree – he supported prescribing severe penalties against minor offences. We have seen his justification for this position. Now we find that he also rejected the suggestion of other thinkers that decriminalisation of minor wrongdoings could help avoid punishing large numbers of people. In his view, a state can proscribe many acts as crimes and punish everyone who violates the prohibition. This point was made clear by him in a story where Yanzi 晏子, a high minister of the state of Qi reported to Duke Jing of Qi 齊景公 that, in their time, wooden feet were more expensive than shoes because so many people committed crimes punishable by amputation of a foot. In response, the duke reduced the punishment for five offences from amputation to lesser types. Both Yanzi's report and the duke's response were criticised by Han Fei: the idea of intending to reduce the number of people having feet amputated was misguided. For, if the punishment was inflicted only on the guilty, it did not matter how many of them were to suffer it. It would be different in a case where an army was routed and the soldiers retreated in chaos. They should not be punished because their act was not proscribed as a crime.

The duke's action was criticised as counterproductive because, if an offence is to be deterred, lessening its punishment will not have that effect but, rather, increase the number of persons committing it. In punishing such persons, the ruler should show no mercy, because, "Anyone who cares for weeds will jeopardise the crop; anyone who treats robbers kindly does harm to innocent people. To reduce punishments and practise leniency is to benefit the wicked and harm the good. This is not the way to achieve order." The right way, according to Han Fei, is to inflict severe punishments on culprits of minor offences so that minor offences will cease and major ones will not occur. This way of *yi-xing qu-xing* (以刑去刑 using punishments to get rid of punishments) was the right way to achieve lasting order; it had been used by former sage rulers with great success.

(c) Use punishments more than rewards

While rewards and punishments are meant to induce and deter certain acts, where an act can be encouraged by a reward or compelled by punishment, punishment is to be preferred. We remember Gongsun Yang said that, in a well-governed state, punishments were used ten times more frequently than rewards. Han Fei endorsed this line because, he said, reward is more costly and less effective. To make this point, he told another story, making Confucius speak for him. During the time of Duke Ai of Lu 魯哀公, when Confucius was the Minister of Justice, a fire broke out near the royal palace. The duke personally took the lead in fighting it but none of the people followed him. He asked Confucius what to do. Confucius suggested that he should make use of punishment because the situation was critical, allowing no time for rewards, and, moreover, if everyone who fought the fire was to be rewarded, the government would not have enough treasure to be able to keep its promise. The suggestion was accepted and Confucius gave the order: "Whoever refuses to fight the fire will be given the punishment comparable to that inflicted on soldiers running away from a battle or surrendering to the enemy." Before the order was made known to everyone, the fire had been extinguished. This was one rare example where Han Fei approved Confucius's action because it is in agreement with his emphasis on the greater usefulness of punishment.

As another example, when Zichan was ill, he told You Ji 游吉, his expected successor as chief minister of the state of Zheng, to be severe with the people so that they will not easily violate the law and be punished, saying, "Fire looks harsh, but few people are burnt; water looks harmless, but many drown". Later, as chief minister, You Ji could not bear to use severe punishments for minor transgressions. In consequence, young men of Zheng joined robber bands in a swamp area and threatened disaster for the state. You Ji had to lead an army of chariots to fight them and barely defeated them after a battle of a day and a night. With deep regret, he said, "Had I followed Zichan's advice, I would not have to do this."

(d) Make rewards and punishments certain

To be effective, rewards and punishments must be certain – sure to follow the encouraged or prohibited acts – otherwise the people will have doubts and hesitate to do what is encouraged or take a chance in doing what is prohibited. When the great archer shoots, people love to hold the target for him; when a child plays with bow and arrow, his loving mother hides behind closed doors. Han Fei particularly stressed that, when punishment is made certain, it will become unnecessary because no one will violate the law. For instance, he said when Dong Yanyu 董闕于, a magistrate of a district where there was a deep canyon, after learning that no one ever descended into it, declared that he was to enforce his law so rigorously so that everyone would know that a harsh punishment would inevitably follow a violation and, as a result, no one would dare to violate any of his prohibitions.

As another example, a criminal sentenced to hard labour in the state of Wei 衛 escaped to the neighbouring state of Wei 魏. Duke Si of Wei 衛嗣公 offered to cede a town named Zuoshi 左氏 in order to have the criminal extradited. When his ministers objected to the exchange of a town for a mere criminal he told them, "This is not what you can understand. For achieving order, nothing is too small to do; for avoiding disorder nothing is too big to do. If the law is not enforced and punishment avoidable, it is useless to have ten towns like Zuoshi; if the law is upheld and punishment certain, it does not hurt even though ten towns like Zuoshi are lost."

(e) Carry out punishments with due speed

Once it is decided that a person is guilty, the ruler must not hold this decision in suspense; the punishment must be carried out expeditiously or there can be unpredictable consequences. Han Fei gave many examples where a ruler who failed to punish his evil officials was eventually replaced or even murdered by them. Besides giving examples, Han Fei added weight to his point by appealing to the authority of Zixia 子夏, a prominent diciple of Confucius. As mentioned above, Zixia emphasised that, when an evil plot is detected, it should be nipped in the bud immediately.

(F) Apply and enforce law uniformly

A reward or a punishment will be more acceptable to the people if it is applied equally to everyone, regardless of the status of the recipient. But alas! Han Fei noted that, according to ancient stories and historical records, all those who committed serious crimes and carried out evil schemes were lofty officials and their followers, and yet the law was used to crack down only on the humble and lowly people. As a result, they had no hope and nowhere to air their grievances. A bright ruler should correct this tradition: he should not let officials act arbitrarily but demand that they apply and enforce the law strictly and uniformly on everyone: "In inflicting punishment against wrongdoings, the great ministers should not be spared; in bestowing rewards for good deeds, the humble commoners should not be ignored," Han Fei said, and again he cited approvingly some historical events. In one case, Duke Wen of Jin 晉文公 ordered the execution of one of his favourite officials who came late to a hunting party; in another case, the crown prince of Chu, being urgently summoned by King Zhuang 莊王, had his carriage driven inside the south gate of the royal palace in violation of a law. The palace guard stopped him, hit his horse and damaged his carriage. Instead of punishing the guard, as the crown prince begged, the king rewarded the guard for upholding the law, giving him a promotion of two ranks.

While the principle of equal application of law sounds ideal, there is, however, a glaring problem – law is not really applicable to all. The ruler is never mentioned and is evidently above the law, and, to a lesser degree, the crown prince was also exempted. In the case of the crown prince of Chu he was allowed to go through a back door. This problem poisoned the judicial system, making a mockery of the rule Han Fei advocated because the ruler, as the ultimate lawmaker and enforcer, can always make exceptions to the rule.

(G) The well-governed state

What would a state be like if its ruler followed Han Fai's advice? How do people live and interact? Han Fei had some ideas. We have mentioned that he said, in effect, that the measures he suggested will save the people from disorder, rid the world of disasters, prevent the strong from attacking the weak and the majority from oppressing the minority, let the old live in peace and the young have a chance to grow, and make borders free from conflicts and, as a result, the ruler and his subjects will have mutual affection, the fathers and sons will be able to take care of each other, and there will be no fear of dying in a battle or of being taken prisoner of war. This is a much broader view than that of Gongsun Yang who focused only on making the state rich and strong. Indeed, Han Fei was more optimistic. In another passage, he described what he called *zhi-an zhi shi* (至安之世 a world of absolute peace) showing a more rosy picture:

> In a time of absolute peace the law will be like the morning dew, pure and simple. The people have no grievance at heart and their mouths utter no complaints. Therefore horses and carriages do not wearily travel long distances, and military banners do not get tangled in great swamps. The ordinary people will not lose their lives at the hands of robbers and invaders, and brave men will not be killed in battle. There will be no heroes having their names entered into history books, no bronze will be made to record great military exploits, and, as a result, the chronicle will be left blank.

This sounds almost poetic. How can such a utopia emerge from the cold, calculating mind of a Legalist? I imagine what actually appears in his mind is more or less like a machine, well designed and oiled. There are no obstructions or detractions from within and without – no books of learning, no talks about other norms: law provides the only instruction and people speak and do nothing that is in contradiction to law – every person acts like a part of this machine and functions perfectly according to the role assigned to him, and the whole thing runs by itself according to the law made by the ruler. There is no need for special persons as operators. Because everyone is so perfectly co-ordinated with others, society will function smoothly and efficiently and there will be no shortfalls, no unmet needs, no competition, no contention, no crimes, no conflicts, no war. Everyone will live happily in peace. In case some glitch develops and some measure is needed to correct it, the correction, in the form of rewards and punishments, will be administered automatically according to law, neither as a favour nor in anger by the authorities, and therefore those who receive rewards feel no gratitude and those who suffer punishments harbour no resentment. All is impersonal, all will return to order.

Sometimes, Han Fei seems quite elated by this prospect. In one paragraph, he said that, in his ideal state where law is completely effective, "the ruler can rest in peace and his subjects can be happy with their undertakings; the Way will prevail in the universe and the Virtue last forever". Here, we must note, he used *dao* (道 the Way) and *de* (德 the Virtue) in a rather transcendental and metaphysical sense denoting not merely an earthly order but a celestial one. We have seen "the Way" and "the Virtue" being discussed a lot by other thinkers of ancient China but not much by the Legalists. Han Fei was an exception. It was because he admired Laozi. In the statement quoted above, he obviously used *dao* and *de* in line with Laozi's ideas, and thus seemingly incongruent with his own emphasis on a world order solely dependent on artificial law. When talking about ideals, anyone can be romantic but then perhaps Han Fei really believed that law could be made perfect and effective.

(H) The proper social relationship

The world of absolute peace is quite attractive but it is rather bleak: in it we see only order and security. Generally, how do people behave and interact in an ideal state? The Ruists said that people should act in accordance with rites and have harmonious relationships; the true Primitivists, such as Zhuangzi, said they should be free and follow the way of nature; Laozi said much about government non-interference but actually wanted people to be manipulated by an invisible hand of a sage to live like sheep; the Mohists said they should bound tightly together by universal love; the Legalists liked Laozi's idea but were less subtle; they advocated using brutal law to coerce people into staying in line.

The reason why the Legalists focused on order is that they had a morbid fear of disorder. In the time of "great strife", Han Fei was more painfully aware that disorder was the greatest threat to the survival of society and its individual members. He believed that order can be established only under a single authority which allows no dissension from its law. His position on human relationship is predetermined by this state of mind and belief.

Like all Legalists, he paid special attention to the relationship between the ruler and the ruled. Deep down he had a very low regard for the ordinary people, and he insisted that they are incapable of regulating their own affairs and therefore have to have a ruler. He keeps them from competing violently for resources and imposed order on them in their efforts to meet their needs and live together in peace. In return, they support him as their master and do his bidding. Thus, the relationship between the ruler and his subjects is quite simple: he directs; they obey. This view is shared by most other thinkers except Zhuangzi, the anarchist. But there are significant differences. First, while the Ruists, the Mohists and, to a lesser extent, Laozi insisted that the ruler is to lead and the people are to follow, the Legalists, particularly Han Fei, maintained that the ruler is only to give commands. To lead is difficult, requiring a lot of thinking, planning, actual work and tremendous self-discipline. To direct is relatively easy: the ruler need only make and enforce laws, in both cases with the help of officials. He need not exhaust his own intelligence and strength.

Second, while the Ruists and the Mohists asserted that the ruler leads the people because he loves them, Han Fei thought that idea ridiculous. According to him, the ruler simply hates disorder and perhaps also the destruction it brings. To restore order, he need not, indeed should not, be emotionally involved. In making law, he should bear in mind the long-term interests of the state and dismiss the desires of the people, and, in applying and enforcing law, he should be cool and rational, consider only the provisions of a relevant law, and ignore his personal feelings. Rewards come from the state to encourage achievements, not from him to show his love; punishments are to demonstrate societal condemnation of wrongdoers not to vent his anger.

How are the people to treat the ruler? According to Han Fei, they should be absolutely obedient. But they do not look up to the ruler as their model or even as their shepherd but simply subject themselves to his law and try their best to win the rewards and avoid the punishments it prescribes. They do not do this for the ruler. As Han Fei pointed out, when they receive a reward, they are not grateful to him because they know they have earned it, and, when they suffer a punishment, they do not resent him because they know they deserve it.

Thus, the relationship between the ruler and the people, in general, is impersonal. According to law, he demands their service; according to law, they receive rewards and punishments through him. There is no emotional connection – he has no love for them; they have no loyalty to him – but only calculation. The result will be perfection. In Han Fei's words, "When the ruler knows not to be just benevolent and the subjects know not to be just loyal, the state can become kingly," and yet "the government functions so quietly that its existence is hardly noticeable".

The relationship between the ruler and the officials is more complicated. We have seen that Han Fei blamed wicked officials as the main causes of disorder; therefore the ruler must control them effectively. He should treat them as his animals – training them like birds and horses. Being so treated, an official would become good or, rather, just servile. Good officials, according to Han Fei, honour their ruler and do their best on his behalf. This, he said, is "what happens in a state that has learned the Way". Because good officials want to serve their ruler well, they are not only without private interests but also without minds of their own. They are like a hand, Han Fei said, that "is used to protect the head above and feet below, never failing to relieve them in extreme cold or heat, and never daring to avoid a fight even when a sharp sword is thrusting near the body".

Thus the relationship is one-sided. The official should always be loyal and submissive whether or not the ruler is worthy. There can be no reciprocity because the ruler and the officials belong to two different classes. To support this point, Han Fei quoted Fei Zhong 費仲, an official under King Shou 紂王 of the Yin Dynasty, who compared the ruler to a hat and the officials to a pair of shoes, saying, "Even though a hat is threadbare, it must be worn on the head; even though the shoes are embroidered they must be trodden under the feet."

Carrying this argument of different positions to its extreme, Fei Zhong advised King Zhou to eliminate Chang 昌, the ruler of the state of Zhou, who was practising benevolence and winning the allegiance of many other feudal lords, as well as the common people, and thus threatening the position of the king. When the king demurred, Fei Zhong asked, "What is wrong if a ruler eliminates a subject?"

If a ruler can eliminate a feudal lord who poses a potential threat, it goes without saying that he can punish anyone who actually offended him. Han Fei made this point in a story where Duke Ping of Jin 晉平公, after having had enough wine, said, "I do not always enjoy being the ruler, except that when I speak no one disagrees". Maestro Kuang 師曠, sitting near the duke, took his lute and hit him, criticising his remark as unfitting for a ruler. The duke was embarrassed and implicitly accepted the criticism. Han Fei thought it outrageous that an official could attack the person of the ruler with impunity. The offender should be severely punished lest treasonous acts should proliferate. What if an official does have a view different from that of the ruler? Han Fei made a concession here: he should present it and, if it is rejected, he should distance himself from the ruler. This, Han Fei said, is the way an official should treat his ruler. But, in view of his theory as a whole, Han Fei must have made this concession rather reluctantly.

Han Fei said that, in a well-governed state, the ruler can rest in peace and his subjects can be happy with their undertakings. But here is another statement of his: in such a state "a clever ruler rests in peace at the top, the myriad officials tremble in terror at the bottom". So the ordinary people and the officials fared differently under a astute ruler.

In addition to the relationship between the ruler and the people, other thinkers also discussed that between the father and the son. Han Fei did so, too, and he went a step further to prescribe the relationship between husband and wife. He said that the son should submit to the father and the wife to the husband, just as the people did to the ruler. This, according to him, is *tian-xia zhi chang-dao* (天下之常道 the Normal Way of the world) and, "if they (the subjects, the sons, and the wives) are obedient the world will be in order; if not the world will be in disorder". This idea, probably shared by many Legalists, was first articulated by Han Fei. Later it was hailed by supporters as arch principles for Chinese society, called *san-gang* (三綱 three essential strands of the social fabric) and used to justify all kinds of authoritarian measures. But, by a twist, it was attributed to the Ruists. This is profane because, as we have seen earlier, one of the most remarkable Ruist teachings is: "Follow the Way but not the mere command of the ruler; observe righteousness not merely the order of the father."

(I) Difficulties

(1) Need for a "bright ruler" and capable officials

Han Fei was ambitious in constructing a theory to support what he believed to be feasible measures to deal with the problems of a world in "great strife". But his theory is itself problematic. Apart from some of his questionable ideas, which we have briefly mentioned above, there is a practical difficulty – the need for specially qualified persons to implement his theory including, especially, a clever ruler and some particularly capable and dedicated law officials. In two lengthy paragraphs, Han Fei pointed out that, to make a state strong and victorious, both these types of extraordinary persons are necessary. But, in many other paragraphs, he made it clear that a clever ruler is more crucial.

(A) Need for a bright ruler

We remember that Han Fei insisted that it takes only a *zhong-zhu* (中主 average ruler) to uphold law. A careful study of his theory reveals that, in the end, he actually acknowledged the need for a *ming-zhu* (明主 bright ruler). A "bright ruler", in Han Fei's parlance, is a very intelligent person. We have heard him saying, "Intelligence is the ability to know a thing before it is fully developed." This definition is quite unusual; only Laozi said something similar. According to Han Fei, extraordinary intelligence is necessary for a ruler because he needs to be able to see the long-term, real interests of a state and, more importantly, to overcome treacherous officials who fight him a hundred battles a day. In Han Fei's words, "Whether the officials will be honest or fraudulent depends on how the ruler is. If he is clever they will be honest; if he is stupid they will be fraudulent. To be able to know a plot when it is not yet clear is called bright." In addition to being unusually intelligent, a ruler has to have the ability and skill to observe and listen carefully to all things near and far, to compare what he sees and hears, to check them against the facts to find the truth, and, finally, he has to have the wisdom and will to make a decision which can be right or wrong but cannot be avoided. Thus, for instance, when the armies of Qi 齊, Wei 魏 and Han 韓 approached the Hangu Gorge 函谷關, the route leading to the capital of Qin 秦, its king had to rely on no one's opinion but his own to decide whether to resist or to seek peace.

After a decision is made, it must be carried through. A bright ruler will do so in spite of difficulties. As a good surgeon, named Bian Que 扁鵲 would use a knife to cut the flesh and pierce the bones to cure a disease, a ruler should enforce tough decisions to restore order, even if they offend the people. To support his argument, Han Fei gave an uncommon interpretation of a legendary event – Yao's abdication in favour of Shun. According to him, when Yao made the decision to abdicate, two high officials, Gun 鯀 and Gonggong 共工, objected. Yao killed Gun and exiled Gonggong, and carried through his decision. (In many ancient tales, the two officials were punished for failing to tame the great flood of Yao's time.)

After his narration, Han Fei reported that Confucius, impressed by Yao's acts, said, "The wisdom of Yao and the talents of Shun were not the most unusual; Yao's decision to eliminate the protesters and the insistence on ceding the world to Shun was the most unusual." Obviously, the point that Han Fei wanted to make is that a bright ruler must not have doubts about his own decision and must implement it resolutely.

To implement a decision, the ruler has to be tactful. He must have his subjects, particularly the high officials, absolutely under his control. Since they all want to pursue their private interests, Han Fei said, "A ruler who knows the Way does not look for officials of clean conduct. Rather, he works on the tactics by which he will uncover their evils." And, to make this more explicit, Han Fei further said, "A clever ruler does not rely on the fact that people will not rebel against him; he relies on the fact that they cannot rebel against him. He does not rely on the fact that people will not cheat him; he relies on the fact that they cannot cheat him."

How is the clever ruler to achieve this? The best way for him to act is to be "quiet and unassuming". He should use the talents and labour of his subjects, and reward or punish them according to their accomplishments. This is the outcome of a ruler's use of clever tactics: "He may not be talented, but he instructs the talented; he may not be wise, but he guides the wise. The officials will exert themselves, but the ruler will enjoy the success." This, Han Fei said, is "the proper way of a bright ruler". Such a ruler is nothing short of Laozi's "Sage", a demigod. Where can we find him?

(2) Need for extraordinary specialists in law and tactics

Even if a bright ruler can be found, he cannot be successful if he acts alone or is surrounded by incapable or wicked people, including his "bed fellows" and treasonous officials. He needs some extraordinary *fa-shu zhi shi* (法術之士 specialists in law and tactics) as his assistants.

Such a specialist is one to uphold law. Because law is in the interest of the public and the state and against the private interests of the devious individuals, particularly corrupt officials, the law specialist must be morally strong and upright, or he will not be able to fight evil, and he must be far-sighted and observant, or he will not be able to uncover secret schemes. He must keep his mind unbiased and his intentions totally unselfish. He must devote himself to the public good and, in doing so, he must not be swayed by his personal feelings and wishes. He must work hard to accomplish government projects but never claim credit for himself; instead, he should give it to the ruler. He should exalt him "as high as the heaven and the Tai Mountain" and humble himself "as low as the valley and the basin and, if necessary, he should risk death to save him". As examples of such officials, Han Fei mentioned many famous ones of the past including Hou Ji 后稷, Gao Yao 皋陶, Yi Yin 伊尹, Guan Zhong 管仲 and Gongsun Yang – those who helped to found new dynasties and make their rulers true kings or hegemons. In addition, two lesser officials were given as examples of their commendable behaviour. In one case, Xie Hu 解狐 recommended his enemy Xing Boliu 邢伯柳 for the post of a magistrate. In another Liang Che 梁車, as a magistrate, ordered the amputation of his older sister's foot for the offence of entering his city unlawfully.

But not every person with such qualifications can accomplish what he aspires to. This is because he will be fighting those close to the ruler whom Han Fei called *dang-tu zhi chen* (當途之臣 officials in power), *gui-zhong zhi chen* (貴重之臣 high and mighty officials) or simply *zhong-ren* (重人 the mighty persons). When appointed to an office, this person, being a specialist in law and tactics, wants to uphold the law, expose the evil schemes of the mighty and oust them. But they have the ears of the ruler and, thus, overwhelming power. Hence, he and they are enemies by nature and cannot coexist, and the result of the struggle is normally in their favour. Only in a very exceptional case can such a person prevail, like Gongsun Yang who had the good fortune of having the support of the astute ruler Duke Xiao of Qin. But. as pointed out by Tang-xi-gong 堂谿公, a recluse, in a conversation with Han Fei, even in such a case, the end for the selfless enforcer of law was tragic: having stepped on the toes of many mighty officials and aristocrats, Gongsun Yang was killed, his body torn by chariots. After reminding Han Fei of this and some other similar events, Tang-xi-gong advised him to stop playing the role of a specialist in law and tactics. But Han Fei was undaunted. Instead, he gave a long speech expressing his ambition, ideals and determination:

> Sir, I know what you mean. And I know it is not at all easy to govern the world and put the people in order. The reason I will not follow your very kind advice but insist on doing what I do is that I believe the establishment of the new laws and measures is the right way to benefit the people. I think he who does not escape from the misfortune and disaster which a disorderly ruler or a stupid superior might bring upon him but insists on trying to benefit the people is acting benevolently and wisely. On the contrary, he who escapes from the misfortune and disaster which a disorderly ruler or stupid superior might bring upon him in order to avoid the danger of death, thus seeing only his personal interests but not those of the people, is acting in a despicable way. I cannot stand to follow that despicable way, nor do I dare to do harm to a pattern of behaviour that is in conformity with benevolence and wisdom. You, sir, have the good intention to do me a favour but, in fact, you have done me great injustice.

The conversation was probably imaginary (because the speakers were not contemporaries) but the words attributed to Han Fei were moving. They might reflect the hearts and minds of people like him who, though misguided, earnestly wished to change the existing situation of chaos and misery, dominated by inept rulers and treacherous officials, to one of order for the benefit of the helpless common people. The trouble, of course, is that persons like him are rare and their chances of working together with a bright ruler are rarer still. As a result, the utopia Han Fei talked about is just that, a utopia.

Though the difficulty Han Fei lamented most was real, his theory was largely implemented first by his intellectual forerunner Gongsun Yang, then by his lesser fellow pupil Li Si, the former being trusted by Duke Xiao, the latter by King Zheng of Qin 秦王政, eventually the first emperor of the Qin Dynasty. While they succeeded in making the weak state of Qin strong and then unified China, the long-term effect of Han Fei's theory was, alas, disastrous. It will be discussed later. For now, only a brief review of some of the problems inherent in the theory will be attempted below.

The root of Han Fei's problem is in the fact that, being traumatised by the brutal struggles between the warring states of his time and frustrated by his personal experience of being an aristocrat kept in political limbo, he saw history and his contemporary world with jaundiced eyes. He had an agenda and tried to justify it. The effort was strained, and sometimes he contradicted himself.

His problems begin with his perception of human nature. All characterisations of "human nature" are hypothetical, reflecting the view of the proponent. One who is serious about his view is tempted to "prove" it with supporting "facts", and then extrapolate without providing further evidence. Mencius, Xunzi and many others did exactly that. Han Fei was no exception. But his view that human nature is cold and calculating was not new. Zhuangzi's theory emphasising *baozhen* (葆真 preserving one's true, innocent self) has a solipsistic streak which was made notorious by Yang Zhu who emphasised the self as the very basis of all values. Han Fei shared this view with them. But, while Zhuangzi warned against interfering with others and Yang Zhu did not want to take over the world for his own benefit, Han Fei stressed that any means can be justified for one's own survival. If it happens to be detrimental to others, so be it.

To illustrate his point, he gave several examples as evidence, including regicide by queens and female infanticide by parents. He used them not only to support the view that human nature is selfish but also to deny love, even that of a mother for her son, as a common human emotion that can make people transcend personal interests. But regicide and female infanticide, though they happened, were not regularly practised. At best, they show that people can be egregious (a commonsensical point) but they are not enough to prove that human nature is bad. Here is a serious flaw in Han Fei's methodology – using a small number of exceptional cases to support a general conclusion.

His conclusion also goes against facts. History actually validates an opposite view: most people were not overly calculating and selfish but quite capable of being compassionate and altruistic, even under very difficult circumstances. That was how mankind has survived natural and human-made catastrophes.

Han Fei's view of human nature also has pernicious practical consequences. If extreme selfishness was identified as the central problem, there can be two possible solutions. One was to ameliorate it by education introducing the value of altruism. That was what Xunzi did. The other solution, adopted by Han Fei, was to allow one's self-interest to fight against everyone else's. The former approach can result in tolerance, at least; the latter will inevitably cause endless struggles, particularly between the ruler and his subjects. The struggles can be avoided only if the ruler can defeat all those who might challenge him. This urged Han Fei to advocate the concentration of power in the hands of the ruler.

According to Han Fei, the ruler can become all-powerful by using three means – his special position, certain tactics, and law. Though they are all necessary, Han Fei's emphasis was on tactics. Of course, in governing a state, a ruler has to be tactical. The Ruists and the Mohists advised the ruler to be decent and trustworthy, righteous and benevolent, and thus to make himself a model for all his people. Han Fei dismissed that approach as ineffective, even fraudulent. But, using the sort of tactics he suggested to the ruler, which are, in many cases ,mean-spirited, cruel, and unethical, treating people as enemies, or worse still, as non-human objects, would inevitably invite others to reciprocate in kind. That is not a way to achieve peace and order, and certainly not to make the ruler's job easy – he will never relax but forever be kept on high alert to fight his own people.

But Han Fei insisted that this result can be avoided by the ruler upholding the law. This is strange because, to him, law is just a tool which has to be used by the ruler tactically. Even if we ignore this problem, we shall still find his theory of law flawed.

First of all, there is the problem concerning the basis of law. To most thinkers, there are things higher or more fundamental than law, on which it should be based. Han Fei recognised none. Occasionally, he alluded to *dao* (道) or *tian-dao*

(天道) but never spelled out what it was. He did not value the wisdom of past sages, such as Yao, Shun, Confucius and Mozi. He particularly despised their teachings of moral principles, such as benevolence and righteousness, comparing them to children's playthings and blaming them as causes of disorder. He dismissed custom and tradition because they are largely outdated and often harmful when followed in new circumstances. He recognised "human nature" but defined it only in terms of physical and biological needs. He denied the significance of human feelings which he thought can be manipulated, anyway. He did not admit that a society can have common ideals and aspirations because he thought that ordinary people are stupid and selfish. He, of course, could not maintain that law can be unreasonable but, by equating law with measuring instruments – in most instances arbitrary contraptions – he obviously did not stress the essential importance of reason as a basis of law.

So on what grounds should law be based? In Han Fei's time, the law-maker was the ruler of a state. Others could give him advice but decisions were his alone. Han Fei accepted this fact and held that law is merely the command of the ruler. It has no other basis than the ruler's will. If so, is it necessary to have a good ruler to make good laws? To Han Fei this question was not meaningful. He would probably admit that a law can be fatally defective if it is logically self-contradictory and therefore self-defeating, or if it prescribes something impossible for humans to do. Otherwise, to him, a law is not intrinsically good or bad because there are no standards existing above law by which it can be judged. It may only be viewed as successful or unsuccessful after it is enforced. But this view evidently contradicts ordinary people's common sense and shared experience.

The second major problem with Han Fei's theory of law is that he saw laws as mechanical tools. Like Gongsun Yang and other Legalists, he compared law to measuring instruments but the comparisons is inappropriate. Xunzi made the same comparisons but stressed that a law cannot be applied and enforced mechanically because its meaning is not always clear, there is always a need of interpretation, and, for this purpose, it is necessary to look into the backgrounds, objectives, and underlying principles ("the spirit") of the law. Han Fei should have learned this from his teacher but, apparently, he deliberately ignored this lesson and went on to push the comparison to the extreme, asserting that law can be applied almost mindlessly.

Han Fei further compared law to the hammer and anvil – tools to beat things into particular shapes. This comparison was his innovation and was even more troublesome. It requires two presumptions: first, the existence of a standard against which a thing can be determined as correct or incorrect; and second, the infinite malleability of human behaviour. But whence the standard? Han Fei's answer must be that it comes from the ruler. He did not go to the extreme of asserting that the ruler can be totally whimsical, but he denied anything above the ruler's will as the basis of law and he did say that, in making law, the ruler does not have to heed the wishes of the people because they are too stupid. Next, how mouldable are people? He asserted that people can be forced by the ruler's "two handles", but admitted that rewards can be too costly, and therefore more punishments should be used. Moreover, he suggested that heavy punishments for minor offences can deter crimes and eventually make punishments unnecessary. This is disingenuous because, knowing such a policy, a truly wicked and calculating criminal will find it profitable to commit more serious offences to maximise his possible gains at the same risk and cost, and thus, if implemented, such a policy can have the opposite effect. Moreover, since the heaviest possible punishment is death, Han Fei, though being an admirer of Laozi, obviously forgot what the master said: "When a person is no longer afraid of death, how can the death penalty be used to frighten him?"

Another way to make enforcement of law easy, Han Fei suggested, was to encourage and compel the reporting of actual or potential violations. Gongsun Yang had implemented this policy and we have discussed its results. It is regrettable that all Legalists fell into this trap. As society becomes more tightly organised, the results produced by this strategy become more tragic. Unfortunately this became true in later periods in China and other parts of the world.

Han Fei's emphasis on applying law uniformly on everyone regardless of their social status was remarkable but deceptive. By everyone, he meant all the people apart from the ruler. In theory, the ruler can be included but how in practice this idea is to be realised is a different question. Other thinkers of ancient China had invented the idea that the ruler was below some transcendental or metaphysical authority which they vaguely called the "Heaven" or the "Way" but, to different degrees, equated it to the will of the people. Han Fei found such thinking preposterous and subversive. The ruler, being "brightar" than the people, should not be subject to them, and, being the maker as well as the ultimate enforcer of law, cannot be bound by it. To apply law to him is not only impractical but also illogical. If the ruler is excluded, what about his heir apparent? In Han Fei's story, the crown prince of Chu, after breaking a law, was allowed to go through a back door of the palace. It demonstrates that the exemption could be extended. But where does it end? While Han Fei apparently criticised the practice of exempting the privileged, he forgot that the problem was rooted in his theory of putting the ruler beyond the reach of law.

In addition, Han Fei's theory of law has two more fundamental flaws. First, his assertion that law should be the only norm and his condemnation of all other norms; second, his justification of rule by law. It is a fact that no society has ever existed with law as the only norm, or even the highest norm. This point is so evident that no further elaboration is needed. The sole reason Han Fei was in favour of rule by law is that it makes government easy – even an average ruler can do it. But this is naive. If law is a tool, it has to be used by skilled people for an acceptable purpose. Han Fei should recall what Xunzi had said: a treacherous person can always misuse or abuse tools, and therefore, "tools are the last means for good government; virtuous persons are the source of it". Indeed, in the end, Han Fei actually conceded that to implement his theory, a "clever ruler" is necessary. Thus, his protestations notwithstanding, Han Fei's emphasis on law is perhaps only a camouflage. His rule by law is actually rule by an extraordinary man – a dictator.

It follows that the ruler's relationship with the people is unequal – the ruler is the "hat", the people the "shoes". He cannot let them all perish and thus deprive himself of their service but, in treating individuals, he has complete freedom, even to the extent of terminating their lives without giving a reason. Han Fei's advocacy of unconditional obedience of the son to the father and the wife to the husband, just as the subjects to the ruler, extending subjugation in the political arena to domestic circumstances, is particularly sinister, causing untold suffering to children and women.

The political relationship, advocated by Han Fei as the bedrock of order, is, in fact, inherently unstable and dangerous. It lasts only while the ruler has the ability to control the people and keep them in subsistence. He has to be constantly on his guard or the oppressed people will secretly plot or openly rebel against him. Xunzi aptly compared the people to the water and the ruler to a boat, and pointed out that, while water can bear up boats, it can also capsize them. Apparently, Han Fei did not accept this lesson. But it seems he was aware of the problem and that is why he used so much space in his book to teach the ruler how to maintain the unequal relationship in various ways, and more importantly, having a completely amoral mindset, an ice-cold heart, and a pair of ruthless iron hands to suppress all opposition, not only in action and word, but also in the minds of everyone. Laws are the only things people can have in their minds, and the ruler is the LAW.

Finally, Han Fei's theory has a narrow and short-sighted vision for society and is therefore demeaning to humanity. He was frightened by "the world of great strife" and yearned for peace and order. His ideal world was largely a peaceful one. Everything will be in order if it is regulated by law; everyone will stay in a place designated by law and act according to law – mainly, to produce wealth, to fight aggression and to prevent crime. Because few other pursuits are allowed, there is little for people to learn and undertake. There is nothing to inspire them and they have no aspirations. They are thus turned into simpletons who live a life of absolute calm, platitude, monotony and stagnation, with impersonal, cold relationships devoid of love, hatred, compassion or any other passion. There will be no strife, no excitement, no change, and no future, just the everlasting present of peace and order. Is this peaceful world better than the chaotic one of Han Fei's time? What is the purpose of life? Is it more worthwhile to languish in a pool of still water than to struggle in a sea of turbulent waves? And are these the only alternatives? Can humans live in a world where they are neither predators and prey nor ants and bees?

Thus Han Fei's ideas are problematic. He was a failed man of action masquerading as a thinker. Though being characterised as a Legalist, he was actually a tactician. That is why he spent so much space (over 60 per cent according to my rough estimation) of his book discussing tactics. Sima Qian grouped him with Laozi and Shen Buhai in one biography because they had some essential traits in common: namely, a belief in *dao-de* (道德 rules of nature). Such a believer is an amoral person who sees every human action as a tactical move. We have seen that Shen Buhai thought so. We found that Laozi also emphasized tactics in dealing with people and was often mentioned together with Huangdi, the primary and consummate tactician. Han Fei was, at best, a legal tactician who would use law as a tool to enable the ruler to control the people. Thus, his theory naturally leads to dictatorship and despotism. This course was followed later in Chinese history when his theory was put into practice. In several chapters of his book, he complained about his personal misfortune of not having the rulers of his time taking his advice but it was more unfortunate that for over 2,000 years China suffered largely because of his theory.

Notes

1. Sima Qian wrote only a few lines about Shen Buhai and Shen Dao, and only a short biography of Han Fei. See *Shi-ji*, vol. 63, Chapter 3, pp. 2146–56; vol. 74, Chapter 14, p. 2347.
2. Sima Qian characterised this philosophy and belief as *Huang-Lao Dao-de zhi shu* (黄老道德之術 the Way of Huangdi and Laozi) implying that they are sophistic, devious, beguiling, pragmatic and devoid of human feelings.

Epilogue

Having studied the eight thinkers' theories, we shall now take a look at their effects. In the preface, a number of jurisprudential and philosophical questions were raised. Assuming that the more comprehensive a thinker was in providing articulate and reasoned answers, the more influential he would be, I kept those questions in mind and paid attention to what the thinkers said directly or indirectly in response. In this epilogue I shall try to show their influence: on one another; on thinkers, rulers and the common people of later times; and finally on the development of China's legal system.

(A) The thinkers interacting with one another

The eight thinkers have been presented chronologically but many of their ideas had been in existence long before[1] and, therefore, though an earlier thinker could not actually interact with the later ones, he could discuss ancient ideas.

It is likely that, in very ancient times, people already had two distinctive attitudes towards human life: some held the view that it was unique, and a belief that humans had the ability to make it better, and they actually tried to make it so. Others had doubts about human ability, and were less ready to strive for specific goals but preferred to live in harmony with their circumstances. Confucius was a representative of the former camp. Before him, there were the legendary persons who first developed civilisation by inventing fire, domesticating animals, developing agriculture, making the physical environment more suitable for human life, followed by Yao, Shun, Yu, Tang and others who established social institutions which, according to Confucius, were almost perfected by the Duke of Zhou, and he saw himself standing on the shoulders of these giants in order to carry on their mission in preserving and furthering what they had achieved.[2] After his death, many thinkers entered this camp. Apart from his followers, the Ruists, there were the Mohists and the Legalists. In the other camp there were fewer prominent figures because most of those who lacked the will or ability to change their lives were just dragged along by those who did. Only when the movement was plagued by unfamiliar problems, and the vanguards were at a loss, were the followers' doubts expressed. Their views were articulated by Zhuangzi but, before him, there were some who appeared as recluses, and there was Laozi who shared some of their ideas. After the country came under the control of the Qin, few emerged genuinely to advance Zhuangzi's theory further.

Though firmly convinced of his mission, Confucius was, on a number of occasions, puzzled by those from the other camp. It is reported in *Lun-yu* that some recluses thought he was vain and his efforts hopeless, and advised him to abandon his efforts to change the world.[3] Then there was Laozi, who shared this view, asserting that the world was like a sacred vessel to which nothing could be done, and anyone who tried would ruin it.[4] According to his biographer, Sima Qian, he disliked Confucius's self-righteousness and told him to go along with the trend of the world and not be critical of others. Moreover, he advised Confucius to conceal his opinion like a shrewd merchant hiding his wares as if he lacked any and, like an ambitious person, making himself seem stupid.[5]

The more sophisticated versions of these views were constructed later by Zhuangzi. He saw everything in relative terms, existing ephemerally and turning to its opposite phase in endless cycles.[6] Nothing is of permanent value; human life has no purpose; all efforts to seek one are meaningless. Therefore, he invented the story of "Ran-wang" (讓王 to give up the throne) and "Dao Zhi" (盗跖 Robber Zhi): the former to expose the devious acts of some power-holders giving their government to virtuous persons but actually to demand their submission;[7] the latter to point out the hypocrisy of those, like Confucius, who preposterously asserted that they had cures for social ills.[8]

Confucius was able to respond to some of his critics directly. It is reported that, after the audience with Laozi, he compared the elusive mystic to a dragon whose thinking and behaviour were incomprehensible. This may sound like a compliment but, actually, it implied that Laozi was of a species entirely different from ordinary humans.[9] On another occasion, when he heard a recluse Jienie 桀溺 advising him to escape the world, he said he was unable to live outside human society with birds and beasts.[10] It can be interpreted that he considered the recluse also not quite human. What prompted him to make such remarks? It was because he believed that human life was different from that of other species. Humans had norms that govern their personal behaviour and their relationships with one another. Such norms were of crucial importance; disregarding them would make humans indistinguishable from other animals.[11]

But why do humans have norms and obey them? What are norms for? Does human life have a purpose other than living and reproducing like all species do? Does it have a special goal? If so, what is it? These were questions raised by thinkers such as Zhuangzi. Confucius did not directly discuss them but, evidently, he believed that humans are unique and that a human's life, though short, has an objective which is to develop the intellectual and moral potential in individuals and make society more prosperous, rational, just and harmonious. We may imagine that, to him, it was rather strange that some people would argue against human life having any meaning because making such a nihilist argument would be a meaningless act in itself.

Besides the recluses and the nihilists, Confucius faced some criticisms also from those in his own camp who shared with him the aspiration of guiding society to certain goals. First, it was Laozi in the story told by Sima Qian. Despite his warning against Confucius's effort to change the world, his other advice for Confucius was puzzling. Why should a learned man, dedicated to doing something he believed to be worthy, appear stupid and lacking any opinion or ambition? It could mean only that this was a camouflage to make the people drop their guard and follow him without suspicion, just like a shrewd merchant who, after winning the trust of people, could induce them to buy anything from him sight unseen. This trickery, known as *Huang-Lao shu* (黃老術 tactics of Huangdi 黃帝 and Laozi), was rejected by Confucius whose honesty and straightforwardness were well recorded; for instance, when he once made a tongue-in-cheek remark, he promptly apologised;[12] and, when he had the power to do something, he did it openly without resorting to any disguise.[13]

Among the more sincere critics in Confucius's own camp were Zichan and Yan Ying 晏嬰. The former, we remember, emphasised his pressing responsibility of solving immediate, practical problems, implicitly criticising Shuxiang who advocated applying moral principles before law. Confucius's reaction, though not direct, was his famous statement: "Guide the people by orders, keep them in line with punishments, they may avoid getting caught but will have no sense of shame. Guide them by virtue, keep them in line with the rites, they will know shame and be rectified." The latter, a senior minister of the state of Qi, hearing that the ruler was to bestow a fief on Confucius, objected, pointing out that he was impractical and that honouring him would invite the people to indulge in useless pursuits.[14] There is no record of Confucius's response. But this criticism, though rather common, was in contradiction to reports of Confucius's success in interstate affairs and domestic administration.[15]

Thus, the interaction among the early thinkers seems to have been rather limited. Of course, we have few records of it; but another reason was that many of the issues debated by later thinkers had not yet been brought into focus. They included what human nature is, what ability humans have, what would happen if humans were left alone, what did happen in history, what should humans do for the future, and what would be their prospects.

These issues did not go unnoticed by the early thinkers. Confucius characterised the human nature of all people as similar and malleable. He did not speculate on what the primitive world was like but considered that, at the time of the Zhou Dynasty, the world was more civilised than during previous periods, thus revealing a progressive view of history and a belief in the human capability of making progress. The recluses seemed to think otherwise. Zhuangzi imagined an idyllic past, stressed the limits of human potential and blamed human meddling with nature as the causes of all social problems. Laozi shared some of these ideas but, as an activist, he alleged that a superhuman sage could use some mysterious power to make people stupid, prevent their wrong moves, arrest the development of history, return to a tolerant past, and remain there. Though these three thinkers had those ideas, they did not explicitly make them the starting points of their respective theories. Mozi painted a clearer picture of history. It started in chaos because everyone had different opinions and no one had the ability to solve the problem until Heaven sent its Son to unify the opinions and impose order. To continue the order, it was necessary to establish an indestructible political structure headed by an absolute ruler and supported by a system of control over the populace that can detect deviant opinions effectively and weed them out. Therefore, he disagreed with the idea of an idyllic past. He also objected to Confucius's emphasis on rites and music because of his perception of human nature, ability and history. It was not because rites and music were not good and enjoyable but, at his time, they were luxuries only the elite could enjoy; when the well-being of the people was generally improved, it would be acceptable for them all to observe rites and enjoy music. His advocacy of universal love was an objection to Confucius's proposition of an ethics supporting graded treatments to people of different distances from one's own bloodline. This was because he believed that the inclination of a person to distinguish those close to him from those farther away, and more generally, to distinguish himself from all his fellow men, was the root of all social problems.

By Mencius's time, discussion of human nature, the state of nature, and the historical development of human society became more fashionable, and interactions among the thinkers increased. A rather commonsensical view, such as that of Confucius, was held by Gaozi 告子. Mencius disputed it and alleged that humans are, by nature, good and have feelings of compassion in common, as well as the ability to recognise virtue, and are thus capable of making great achievements – every person can become a Yao or a Shun, and human society, as a whole, can have peace and prosperity. But humans can become bad as a result of bad influence from outside. Why there were such influences Mencius did not explain. His purpose was to refute the dismal view of human ability held by Zhuangzi and the recluses, and Mozi's idea that people necessarily have different and conflicting opinions. It was also to repudiate the Legalist argument of an absolute need for external rule – law made by political authorities – to keep people in order. Mencius's view of the state of nature was not pleasant, however. In the time of Yao, he said, the world was still inundated by a great flood, overcrowded with vegetation, infested with wild animals, there were no crops for people to eat, and fierce birds and beasts preyed on humans.[16] This view was a blow to the theories of Laozi and Zhuangzi which began with the premise that the state of nature was idyllic so that, when people were left alone, their lives were carefree and happy. Contrary to their assertion that paradise was lost because humans with inadequate ability meddled with it, Mencius pointed out that it was the wise and selfless efforts of persons such as Yao and Yu who saved people from catastrophes, ensured their survival and ameliorated their harsh lots.

Xunzi did not speculate about what the state of nature was like but asserted that humans were, by nature, "bad". He "proved" this assertion by pointing out that, when hungry, people want food; when cold, they need clothes; and, when people did not have the ability to acquire or produce enough materials to meet their needs, they would fight, the strong would exploit the weak, the majority oppress the minority, and then the world fell into chaos and life became miserable. This was, of course, another way to disprove Zhuangzi. It was also a revision of Mencius. Because human nature was bad, norms could not spontaneously germinate from the human heart. Humans had to be taught and disciplined. This led Xunzi to argue for external authority and rules. But he believed that, with good education and enough self-discipline, anyone could become as good as a Yu. He conceded the need for law but argued powerfully against its automatic and independent use. He finally justified the rule of a good human, not law.

The Legalists held the same view that man was by nature bad in the sense of being egocentric and selfish. Therefore, according to Gongsun Yang, human history went through three stages – *qin-qin* (親親 caring only for one's relatives), *shang-xian* (上賢 respecting the capable) and *li-jun* (立君 establishing the ruler) – proving that people had limited ability to live in peace by themselves; they needed outside authority to keep them in order. Han Fei also held the view that people fought fiercely among themselves for stupid, short-sighted self-interest, and could be saved only by intelligent rulers. Both thinkers stressed this defect in human nature, not only to justify their support for dictatorial political power but also to repudiate others who were against it, including Zhuangzi, Mencius and even Xunzi who, though having a similarly low regard for human nature, still believed that humanity could be made good and capable by education. To Gongsun Yang and Han Fei, that was wishful thinking. They argued that people could be enticed only by rewards and prohibited only by punishments, and, to gain these results, the ruler had to use authority, tactics and law to force people to follow him. They vilified the other thinkers, calling them parasites, and advocated the suppression of their wrong ideas which damaged the interests of the state and its ruler. But their own ideas were seriously skewed and roundly criticised. Confucius and Xunzi pointed out the inadequacy of law. Zhuangzi condemned all law that restricted freedom. Laozi, though supportive of the advocacy of the use of political authority and tactics, said famously that where there were more laws there were more crimes. Mozi's ideas were largely in agreement with those of the Legalists but he emphasised the will of Heaven as the ultimate standard and thus, at least in theory, objected to making artificial law and human authority supreme.

While mutual criticisms were many and often pertinent, what influence had they on their targets? Confucius, with strict intellectual honesty and moral decency, was capable of listening to his detractors and sympathetic to their feelings, and, probably in a particularly dispirited moment, lamenting that the Way was not prevailing, said he was to ride a raft and float to the sea – to become a recluse.[17] He also conceded that law, though being a low norm, could not be dispensed with. This point was shared by Xunzi. The same cannot be said about other thinkers. They were more adamant about their respective views and disparaging of those of their rivals – as we have seen, Mozi basically regarded the Ruists as rotten elitists, callous about the sufferings of the common people. Mencius rebuked more savagely, calling Mozi and Yang Zhu, the precursor of Zhuang, beasts. The worst of them all in this respect were the Legalists who degraded the other thinkers to the level of a louse.

What really made the thinkers so uncompromising was the future they respectively wished to see. Zhuangzi saw no special meaning in human endeavours and wanted people to return to a state of the nature of his dream where everyone is left alone and carefree. The three Ruists' vision was of a society of morally perfect individuals with natural bonds of mutual care and respect willingly participating in joint ventures to advance civilisation. Laozi wished to have people pacified, living forever in a small state with minimal necessary conveniences. Mozi in effect endorsed this vision, hoping to have authoritarian social control and complete individual obedience to the ruler in securing more materials to meet the most basic needs of the masses. The Legalists argued further in this direction, visualising a society with a ruler holding absolute power and all the subjects trembling at his feet and doing his bidding to make the state rich, strong and invincible. Thus, while their details vary, the theories of the eight thinkers differ in fundamental ways regarding the status of the individual in society. From this point of view, we can see that Zhuangzi, the Ruists, Mozi, Laozi and the Legalists moving from one pole of individual solipsism to the opposite one of social collectivism. The two ideas were so extreme it was impossible for their advocates to compromise. But what is the likelihood of either theory being implemented completely? An individual human being living by himself easily and happily is practically improbable. On the other hand, a society of absolute regimentation will force people to live like ants and bees, a way of life few can endure for long. And, in neither case, is there a future. Time would stand still and everyone would be running in circles. Is either scenario worthwhile? Is the position of the Ruists more balanced? In Chinese history, what actually happened in the millennia after the eight thinkers?

(B) Further developments

The ideas of the eight thinkers were further developed later by intellectuals and those in government – the former to seek theoretical perfection; the latter to justify their hold on political power. They influenced each other mutually, sometimes beneficially, sometimes detrimentally. This interaction produced significant results in the thinking and actions of both groups and the common people that naturally affected the evolution of the legal system, our focus of attention.

(1) The efforts of the intellectuals

Initially, most of the intellectuals were disciples and followers of the eight thinkers but the best of them soon began to develop their masters' ideas further. After the Warring States Period, when many schools blossomed, a new trend emerged in the Qin and the early Han. Some material about well-known figures of the past was collected and published in their names; for instance, *Guanzi* 管子 and *Yanzi* 晏子, showing a mixture of the theories of different schools.[18] A more remarkable effort to harmonise the various theories was made by a group of ghostwriters for Lü Buwei 呂不韋, a chief minister under Ying Zheng 嬴政, the king of Qin and later the first emperor of the Qin Dynasty. They came up with a huge book, *Lü-shi chun-qiu* 呂氏春秋, which was based mainly on the Ruist principles but also included some ideas of many other schools, particularly the one emphasising *yin-yang wu-xing* (陰陽五行 the female, male and five other primordial elements – metal, wood, water, fire and earth – that supposedly affected everything).[19] In the early Han, more such books were compiled, among them two were famous – *Huai-nan-zi* 淮南子 and *Chun-qiu fan-lu* 春秋繁露. The former was a collective work of many scholars sponsored by Liu An 劉安, the Prince of Huai-nan 淮南王. It mixed the Ruist and the Daoist theories.[20] The latter, by Dong Zhongshu 董仲舒, a renowned scholar, expounded on the Ruist principles and interpreted history to show *tian-ren xiang-ying* (天人相應 interaction between Heaven and humanity) according to the theory of *Yin-yang wu-xing*.[21]

This trend continued and produced several works that more evidently affected China's political, legal, economic and cultural developments: among them the most prominent ones include *Li-ji* 禮記,[22] *Zhou-guan* (周官 rites of the Zhou),[23] *Yan-tie lun* (鹽鐵論 "The Salt and Iron Debate")[24] and *Bai-hu tong-yi* (白虎通義 the White Tiger Hall Conference Symposium).[25] In addition, there were many works by erudite scholars that annotated legal statutes in tens of thousands of words, many in accordance with the Ruist and Daoist principles.[26]

There was a number of reasons why intellectuals were persuaded to make these efforts. First, it was psychological. By their time, China, after more than five centuries of disorder caused by warring feudal lords, was finally united under one single political authority. They naturally felt a need to create an all-embracing theory to reflect this new reality. Second, though intellectually distinctive from one another, the ideas of the various schools were not completely irreconcilable. Now that the great disputing masters who took extreme positions were gone, people could more calmly appraise their views and find common ground. Third, in dealing practically with concrete problems, the intellectuals of the Han found it difficult to stick to one set of principles but convenient to apply the ideas of the various schools which were suitable to the circumstances in individual cases – if they could manage to explain away the conflicts.

Though impressive, this effort to synthesise the theories of various schools left out one of them. It was that of the Mozi. After Mozi's death, his disciples continued for a while during the Warring States Period to practise his doctrines but, since the Qin, they became silent and invisible and, in the subsequent two millennia, very few intellectuals did much serious study of his theory.[27] Here are some of the more readily understandable reasons. First, his theory was seriously at odds with those of other schools – the idea of universal love contradicts the Ruist view of a hierarchical society based on different degrees of blood relationship among people, in which a person should love his relatives more and strangers less; the emphasis on tight political and social organisation was certainly anathema to Zhuangzi; and the assertion that even the supreme ruler of a state is subject to the will of Heaven was unacceptable to the Legalists. Second, ironically because his theory does have some points similar to those of the Ruists, the Legalists and Laozi, it was easy for those who had only some superficial understanding of it to ignore it. Third, the more profound parts of his theory, those about logic, ontology, epistemology, science, technology and metaphysics, were too sophisticated and abstract for most intellectuals of later times who were more deeply concerned with social and ethical problems. Fourth, in practice, his insistence on frugality and asceticism was too much for ordinary mortals, especially those intellectuals who were activists in world affairs and aspirants to worldly rewards. Fifth, as champions of the masses against their oppressors, the Mohists shared with them the mentality and behaviour of the members of a fighting unit which requires personal bravery, strong discipline and selfless dedication to a cause. They were very different from the intellectuals who were usually more effete, individualistic and self-seeking. Finally, but perhaps most importantly, because of their sympathy with the common people, they posed a challenge to the established political order and therefore often provoked suppression from it. This will be discussed in the next section.

The focus on classical philosophy was lessened when Buddhism was introduced to China in the first century CE. Intellectuals were attracted by it, absorbing some of its ideas which they perceived as agreeing with those of the classical Chinese thinkers, and rejecting some that they found unacceptable. Those which they took on board were chiefly: 1. a negative view of worldly authority that caused some intellectuals in the Jin 晉 and later dynasties to develop a passive, anti-establishment thinking and lifestyle that echoed Zhuangzi;[28] 2. a creed of *yin-guo bao-ying* (因果報應 delicate causes and effects and divine retribution) that was compatible with the ancient Chinese faith in gods and spirits, and the idea of interaction between Heaven and man;[29] 3. an emphasis on cultivating personal virtues to reach nirvana which was, of course, one of the most important parts of the teachings of Confucius, Mencius and Xunzi, though they did not have a specific image of the Buddhist transcendental state of human existence; and 4. the *yin-ming* theory (因明學 Hetuvidyā, a type of logic) and *xing-er-shang xue* (形而上學 metaphysics) that recall some theories of Mozi and *ming-jia* (名家 logicians).[30]

What were rejected were mainly: 1. a denial of filial duties and political loyalty – the Buddhist idea of a person abandoning his or her family, and leaving the parents and elders unattended, was anathema to Chinese of every conviction;[31] and 2. an other-worldly outlook and a dismissive view of human achievements – though the latter was, to a lesser degree, shared by Zhuangzi, both were repugnant to most Chinese intellectuals who, under the influence of the other classical thinkers, took upon themselves the task to search for a proper way for this world and the obligation to improve its conditions.

Thus, in short, Buddhism did not cause a fundamental change in the traditional Chinese philosophical system. Instead, it induced a rational and ethical reaction against a foreign challenge. This effort blossomed during the Song and the Ming periods into a school of thought known as *li-xue* (理學 the study of reason) or *dao-xue* (道學 the study of the Way). It starts with an examination of the questions concerning human nature and the meaning of existence of all things. These points were broached by Confucius and Xunzi but discussed more by Mencius, Laozi, Zhuangzi and Mozi. Their discussions shared a common element that was introspective, transcendental, metaphysical and speculative. This element was even more conspicuous in the thought of the Song and Ming scholars obviously because of the influence of Buddhism. They enriched the classical Ruist philosophy but were quite different from it in a crucial aspect: many of them were concerned less about finding a way to guide the world than about discovering a route for personal perfection or salvation. In this sense, it was called *xin-ru-xue* (新儒學 Neo-Confucianism) and criticised as an adulteration of the genuine Ruist theory by intellectuals of the Qing who made great efforts to rediscover the authentic meaning of many classical works.[32] Many of the criticisms were pertinent but it is not for us to examine them here. What attracts our attention is that neither the "Neo-Confucians" nor the Qing scholars of philology and exegetical analysis said much about law, and that both groups upheld the principle of *san-gang* (三綱 subjugation of the subjects to the ruler, the son to the father and the wife to the husband), a Legalist doctrine that first appeared in *Han-fei-zi*.[33] For these reasons, they did not have much to contribute to the development of judicial theories.

Apart from the eminent defenders and developers of Chinese culture, there were, unfortunately, many whom Confucius dismissed as *xiao-ren ru* (小人儒 petty Ruists) who, misled by some of the more defective ideas of the other thinkers and their followers, and blinded by their own petty private interests, sold their souls to those in power, flattering them and carrying out their commands, in total disregard of personal integrity, let alone higher principles. They contributed nothing of worth to the development of the classical theories but demonstrated the worst aspects of some doctrines of other schools, distorted Ruist ideas and did much harm to China, particularly, as it will become clear in the following discussion, its legal system.

Among such "Ruists", Dong Zhongshu was a regrettable example. Erudite, and particularly well versed in the Ruist Classics, he was famous for the so-called *tian-ren san-ce* (天人三策 three essays on Heaven and man) responding to three questions Emperor Wu gave to scholars in an imperial inquiry. He argued strongly for the Ruist principles, criticised the ideas of the other schools and, in effect, suggested their suppression. Like most thinkers of his time, he was appalled by the dreadful chaos and wars of the recent past – the Warring State Period and the long years of ferocious struggles before and after the establishment of the Qin Empire – and supported national unification under a single political authority. We may recall that Mencius, when asked how the world might be settled, said *ding yu yi* (定於一 when it was unified). He did not elaborate about what kind of leadership the unification should be under but, judging by his theory as a whole, it is safe to assume that he would have wanted political authority to be in the hands of benevolent rulers. He would have rejected a dictator and insisted on a certain reciprocity in the relationship between the ruler and the subjects. This was, of course, also what Confucius and Xunzi held in common. But it was not the position of Dong Zhongshu who discarded it in favour of the Legalist doctrine *San-gang*. Though as a Ruist, he knew political power must be properly restrained, he did not dare to say so straightforwardly. Instead, he resorted to the Mohist doctrine that rulers should be under the control of Heaven, and created a new term for this idea of mutual influence between Heaven and man. According to him, a ruler's actions would bring about a reaction from Heaven which would either reward or punish him. It is a rather feeble attempt to warn against abuse of power but, in early Han, a philosophy known as *yin-yang wu-xing-shuo* (陰陽五行說) was quite popular. Confucius, Mencius and Xunzi would certainly have dismissed it but Dong Zhongshu, lacking their intellectual honesty and moral courage, took shelter under the superstitious ideas of mythical retribution. When the temple of the founding emperor of Han caught fire, he insinuated that it was a Heavenly warning against misdeeds of those in power at his time. Angered by this implicit criticism of his behaviour, Emperor Wu called for a trial and Dong was sentenced to death, only to be spared by a special pardon. After that, he was subdued, never talking about Heaven–human interaction again.[34]

Later on, intellectuals of far less integrity than Dong, more shamelessly sang the praises of concentrating power in the hands of the emperor. Besides the Legalists, many so called Ruists slyly joined their ranks. Here are two prominent examples: Han Yu 韓愈 of the Tang Dynasty, who claimed to be the one who upheld the tradition established by Yao, Shun, Tang, Wu, Duke Zhou and Confucius, objected to Confucius's teaching of *jun, jun; chen, chen* (君, 君; 臣, 臣 A ruler should be a proper ruler, then a subject will be a proper subject) and Mencius's justification for Tang and Wu leading revolutions against Xia Jie and Shang Shou respectively, saying that the ruler was to give orders and the subjects were to obey or be executed.[35] Another example was Sima Guang 司馬光, a chief minister and widely acclaimed "Ruist" of the Song Dynasty. In his words, "the different positions of the ruler and the subjects are as unalterable as those of the sky and the earth", and, in their relationship with the ruler, the only thing the subjects could do was to keep his obligations and die for him.[36] It was an almost exact reiteration of Han Fei's ideas about the relationship between the ruler and the subjects[37] but, coming from a Ruist distorting the genuine position of the founders of the school, it had a far more pernicious effect on the political and legal systems.

(2) Intervention by the rulers

Most rulers were not intellectuals but could manipulate those who were and thus influence the development of theories. We have seen the most strident example of blatant intervention in the first emperor's fierce implementation of the Legalist doctrines in burning certain books and actually burying some Ruist scholars. Liu Bang 劉邦, the founder of the Han Dynasty, was disdainful of intellectuals, particularly the Ruists. When advised to pay more attention to the Ruist principles, he indignantly retorted that, having gained control of the world while on horseback using military force, he had no use of them. Lu Jia 陸賈, a Ruist who proffered the advice, famously asked whether he could rule the world from horseback. Immediately, Liu Bang realised his own naivety and saw the need of, over many things, rules – not only the three simple rules he had pronounced upon breaking into the capital of the Qin to keep minimum order among the people, namely: those who commit murder are to be executed; those who maim or rob to be given appropriate punishments respectively;[38] but more elaborate ones that could keep his government functioning. Promptly, he ordered Shusun Tong 叔孫通, another Ruist, to draft a set of rites that *he could practise*.[39] Without going into the details, it is enough to say that these rites were to establish a political system with the emperor at the top holding absolute power, quite different from the rites the classical Ruists praised which established proper behavioural standards for the ruler and the subjects respectively.

Liu Bang's successors – Emperor Hui 惠帝 (194–188 BCE), Empress Lü 呂后 (187–180), Emperor Wen 文帝 (179–157) and Emperor Jing 景帝 (156–141) – applied the Daoist theory of not doing much so that the people could recuperate from the wars. Emperor Wu 武帝 (140–87) became politically active and found a perfect justification for his own absolute power in Han Fei's idea of *san-gang* 三綱 which, thanks to the misguided Dong Zhongshu, was, as stated above, turned into a Ruist dogma. He therefore exalted the adulterated Ruist school and suppressed the others.[40] But, in practice, he was aware of the shortcomings of the Ruists and did not entrust his government to them. As an illustration, here is an interesting though sad story. In the early Han the *xiong-nu* (匈奴 the Huns) repeatedly invaded China. Being very weak after the revolution against the Qin and the many years of civil war, the Han government adopted a policy of appeasement. During the reign of Emperor Wu, the Huns again threatened and the imperial court was divided between hawks, headed by Zhang Tang 張湯, a Legalist minister, and doves, represented by Di Shan 狄山, a Ruist *bo-shi* (博士 Doctor of Classical Studies). Zhang Tang called Di Shan ignorant and a coward; Di Shan accused Zhang Tang of false loyalty, implying that he was a mere flatterer of the emperor who was determined to repulse the Huns. Annoyed, the emperor asked Di Shan whether he could defend a county against the aggressors. Di Shan said no. What about a district? No, again. What about a frontier station? Fearing another negative answer would bring down imperial wrath upon him, Di Shan said yes. He was sent to such a station on the border. Shortly, the Huns came, decapitated him and went away with his head.[41] It was unfair to dispatch a scholar to man a military post but the story was used, quite probably with a bit of *Schadenfreude*, by the Legalists and their supporters as a proof of Ruists' inability to handle practical problems.

Emperor Wu's cherry-picking different theories to deal with different problems was followed by practically all rulers of subsequent times. This was epitomised in a famous remark of Emperor Xuan 宣帝 (73–49), the great grandson of Emperor Wu and an effective, authoritarian ruler. Asked by his crown prince, subsequently Emperor Yuan 元帝 (48–33), to employ more Ruists and implement benevolent rules, he was vexed and asserted: "The House of Han has an established policy of using principles of both *wang* (王the true kings) and *ba* (霸 the hegemons) [namely principles of both the Ruists and the Legalists] in governing the empire," and then expressed a fear that the crown prince would ruin the dynasty.[42]

Various other theories were allowed or used in politics. When Wang Mang 王莽, a powerful, treasonous minister of the late Western Han, was preparing to usurp the throne, he encouraged the *yin-yang wu-xing* school to use *chen-wei* (讖緯 omens and oracles of hidden meaning in the Classics) to justify a treacherous, though peaceful, regime change.[43]

Buddhism was also made use of by the rulers. Some of them were probably genuine believers but most found it helpful in pacifying the masses, especially during periods when China was experiencing political or economic difficulties. But, when the Buddhist establishment and its practices interfered with government policies, particularly those concerning land taxation and compulsory corvée or military service, the rulers promptly cracked down.[44] The government imposed a limit on the numbers of persons who could become monks and nuns by requiring them to apply for ordainment certificates from the Ministry of Rites. A law was introduced into the Tang Code against unauthorised ordainment, prescribing punishments for those involved.[45] The law was inherited and tightened in later dynasties, extending punishments to those who built new temples and monasteries.[46] In addition, a Tang law extended the application of provisions governing family relationships to those between the monks/nuns and their masters and fellow converts;[47] a Tang imperial edict requires monks and nuns to worship their parents and ancestors and keep the same relationships with other family members;[48] and this edict was made law in the Ming and the Qing codes.[49] These laws attacked a very basic Buddhist command that monks and nuns sever their ties to their families, and that converts in general separate themselves from the mundane world as much as possible. The clear purpose of the laws was to suppress Buddhism as a potential challenge to government authority which, as we have analysed, was based on the values and structure of the family.

In the late Eastern Han, when Buddhism was introduced, an indigenous folk religion emerged independently. At the time, China was again in great chaos. The common people organised many self-help groups, known as *Wu-dou-mi-dao* 五斗米道, *Tian-shi-dao* 天師道, *Tai-ping-dao* 太平道, and so on. Realising the need for an ideology and doctrines to bind their members, they mixed the ancient Chinese belief in gods and spirits, the tales of Huangdi 黄帝 and Laozi, and the theory of *yin-yang wu-xing* to form a cult later generally called *Dao-jiao* (道教 the Dao religion).[50] It was not a serious intellectual endeavour but attracted large numbers of the oppressed and exploited. Its relationship with the government was complicated: sometimes hostile; sometimes co-operative. At the end of the Sui Dynasty (605–617 CE) Li Yuan 李渊, one of the rebels, was told by a Daoist priest that he was to succeed. After establishing the Tang Dynasty in 618, he praised Dao-jiao more than "Kong-jiao" (孔教 teachings of Confucius) and Buddhism, and, through the dynasty, his successors, making the ludicrous claim that they were the descendants of Li Dan 李聃 – Laozi – the Sage, used Dao-jiao as a fanciful ornament to the regime and another way in which to divert people's attention from the hardships of their daily lives.[51] But, when it interfered with government work, the converts were given the same treatment as Buddhist monks and nuns. Some opportunist intellectuals tried to create a respectable Daoist religious philosophy but never quite succeeded.[52]

Eventually, finding the *san-gang* idea supporting their hold on political power particularly effective, rulers in the Tang made the Ruist theory the orthodoxy through the civil examination system that gave the highest honours only to those who had answered well the test questions based on the Ruist Classics. But, even after this development, the rulers continued to meddle. Zhu Yuanzhang 朱元璋, the founder of the Ming Dynasty (1368–1643) and a Buddhist monk in youth, learned enough *Mencius* to order some eighty-five passages deleted from it because of their incompatibility with the absolute political power he exercised.[53] In the Qing, besides conducting a brutal literary inquisition to persecute those with rebellious ideas against the Manchus, the Yongzheng emperor 雍正帝 (r 1723–1735) wrote a book, *Da-yi jue-mi-lu* (大義覺迷錄 the great truth awakening the misconceived), citing Ruist Classics to justify the Manchus' rule. But it was soon banned by his son, the Qianlong emperor 乾隆帝 (r 1736–1795), for many reasons, among which an implicit one was his father's unorthodox interpretation of the Classics.[54]

Thus the rulers often intervened in the development of the classical theories, making them more in favour of the concentration of power, and they often won. In one instance, Li Shimin 李世民, the second emperor (r 627–683) of the Tang, who disliked Confucius's admonition of *jun, jun; chen, chen* declared blatantly: "Though a ruler is not a proper ruler, the subjects cannot be disobedient subjects".[55] Thus, he was once more driving bluntly into the minds of the common people the Legalist dogma that their subjugation by the ruler was absolute.

Rulers could be beneficially influenced by intellectuals, become wise and make remarkable achievements. But such examples were few. Most rulers who inherited the throne, being conscious of their special position and surrounded most of the time by subservient maids and eunuchs, and thus largely out of touch with the outside world, were often narrow-minded, short-sighted, arrogant, and wilful. Many a dynasty since the Han had the practice of appointing one or two learned scholars, usually Ruists, as tutors to the heir apparent but having, at best, only a few moments a day with the student who was to be their ruler, the tutors had rather limited influence on them.

While knowing the advantages of applying a mixture of theories in government, the rulers never saw much use for the ideas of Mozi. In fact, they often suppressed them. The reasons were many. To begin with, the rulers could not abide by his advice against the extravagant lifestyle in which they all indulged. But that is superficial. More importantly, they could not accept the Mohist organisations and rules. During his lifetime, Mozi had hundreds of disciples who would, under his order, risk their lives in defence against aggressive wars. After his death, they chose leaders known as *ju-zi* (鉅子 Grand Masters) as his successors and would happily die for one for a cause he espoused.[56] They also had their own "laws" and would enforce them independently of state laws. As an example, in the Warring States Period, when a Mohist *ju-zi* named Fu Tun 腹 䵍 was in the state of Qin, his son killed someone and was sentenced to death. King Hui 秦惠王 said to him, "Sir, you are in advanced age, I have ordered the officials not to execute your only son. Please, Sir, in this case let me have it my way." Fu Tun replied, "The law of the Mohists says one who commits murder is to die and one who maims is to be punished. This is how to prevent murder and mayhem . . . Though Your Majesty had shown great kindness to me by waiving the execution, I cannot fail to enforce the Mohist law." Thus, he declined the pardon and executed his son.[57] It is easy to see that such organisations and laws of the Mohists could be troublesome to a country, especially one under a strong unified government. That was why, since the Qin, the Mohists had been watched over by the political authorities. No organisation known as Mohist was formed and few individuals followed Mohist practices. The school seemed just to disappear. But, as we shall see, now and then there have been some exceptional individuals motivated by the noble spirit of Mohism.

(3) The combined effects on the character of the Chinese people

What the intellectuals and the government did produced numerous effects. Besides those on the legal system that are to be discussed later, it is worth mentioning briefly here the influences on the people's character which, of course, affects everything.

Because of the intellectuals' efforts to make theories more practical, distinctions among the various schools were blurred. Most intellectuals of later times were no longer purists of any particular school but hybrids of many and, before long after the Han, all of them were generally called *ru-zhe* (儒者 Ruists) although, having been exposed to various other theories, they were a far cry from the originals and differed from one another. Many of them would have been criticised by Confucius as *xiao-ren ru* or condemned by Gongsun Yang or Han Fei as *liu-shi* (六蝨 various parasites) or *jian-ji-shi chen* (姦劫弑臣 disloyal and treasonous subjects) who would, to obtain some personal gain, delude the people, support corrupt rulers and abuse power. But the best of the latter-day

"Ruists" retained many superior characters hailed by different schools: attributes of Confucius's *jun-zi ru* 君子儒; Mencius's *da-zhang-fu* 大丈夫; Xunzi's *da-ru* 大儒; Laozi's good sage who "helps things grow but never possesses them and, after making achievements, retires without claiming credit"; Zhuangzi's *jun-zi* 君子 who "reluctantly ruled the world"; and even the *fa-shu zhi shi* 法術之士, described by Han Fei in his conversation with Tang-xi-gong 堂谿公, who would risk their lives for the good of the state. Indeed, in Chinese history, there were many intellectuals with such characters. Some of them, as we shall see, stood up for their principles and helped to guide and protect the development of various aspects of Chinese culture, especially the political and legal systems.

Mozi's theory was attacked by Mencius and his practices disliked by the political authorities. As a result, Mohist influence on people became inconspicuous. Much of the Mohist knowledge about science and technology was ignored by the latter-day "Ruists", leaving these fields to less educated craftsmen. It is regrettable. But some of the Mohist emphasis on selfless dedication to a cause, personal courage, loyalty to comrades, resistance to oppression and sympathy towards underdogs was retained by some people. The best of them were like Yue Fei 岳飛 who fearlessly campaigned against aggressors from abroad and traitors at home,[58] and the idealistic revolutionaries who sacrificed their lives to fight against nefarious, self-serving regimes and save the people from subjugation and destruction. The lesser ones became *xia-shi* (俠士 paladins) who individually fought against injustice or joined organisations such as the one depicted in the novel *Shui-hu-zhuan* (水滸傳 *Tales of the Marsh*)[59] that robbed the rich to give to the poor, defeated the overbearing to save the downtrodden, and, above all, challenged the corrupt judicial system. They were often tragic heroes but they gave the people in desperate situations the moral strength to withstand injustice and preserve their integrity. China survived numerous misfortunes and disasters (including dreadful abuses of the judicial power such as that which killed Yue Fei) to a large part because of this Mohist spirit.

(C) Influences on the legal system

(1) The early development

In a broad, rudimentary sense, the legal system predated the eight thinkers. Surely, detailed rules must have been well developed when Yu led the people in taming the great floods. The rules of the Zhou Dynasty known as "Rites of the Zhou" were amazingly comprehensive.[60] It was the misuse or lack of use of those rules that caused the decline and fall of the Zhou feudal system and induced thinking men to engage in an intensive search for a way out of the chaos. After constructing their theories, most of them approached those in power, trying to gain opportunities for the realisation of their ideas. We take here a very brief look at the results of their efforts.

Among the eight thinkers, Confucius addressed important jurisprudential and philosophical questions most rationally. It was reported that, only seven days after assuming the office of acting chief minister, he ordered the execution of a notorious person named Shaozheng Mao 少正卯, apparently without proper trial.[61] But that was certainly an exaggeration, for he always stressed that enforcement of law must be preceded by thorough moral education for the general public. Many people evidently admired him for his theory but found its emphasis on perfecting the human individual as the starting point of a long process to achieve order, prosperity and continuous development of higher and finer civilisation too abstract, difficult and, above all, painfully slow. Being pressed by the need to make quick fixes to urgent problems at hand, those in the government thought his suggestions impractical. Therefore, despite his enthusiasm for politics, he served in the government of a small state very briefly, leaving rather transient effects on his contemporary world. He had numerous disciples: many of them learned from him well and carried out his teachings in various ways successfully.[62] Thus, his influence became more obvious rather later than his own lifetime.

Mencius was even less practical. His theory was largely ignored by men of action not only because it started with some questionable assumptions about human nature, and developed with some extended logic, but, more importantly, because it suggested few concrete measures for government to act upon. In addition, his claim to moral superiority over those in government undoubtedly alienated them, and his apparent lack of compunction in accepting lavish gifts from them earned him some derision. His behaviour reflected a heightened sense of self-esteem of intellectuals but his argumentative words and some bizarre antics actually caused more damage to their image. His emphasis on people's will as the basis of government was an important contribution to jurisprudence but it was cast aside by all rulers because of his statements supporting popular uprisings against abuse of government power.

Xunzi knew the importance of law but regarded it as less important than rites. He compared law to measuring devices but pointed out that they could be misused. He argued for the rule of good men but raised the standards too high for ordinary mortals to meet. The rulers of his time must have been confused and did not find enough reason to trust him with important office. And they certainly could not appreciate his assertions that the people should follow the Way, not just the orders of the ruler, and that, while the people could support the government, they could also overthrow it.

In short, it was the position of these three thinkers that there was something above law and its makers and enforcers that brought them the disfavour of the political establishment and diminished their influence on it and on the legal system it controlled.

Mozi supported strong government. In effect, he argued for dictatorship and supremacy of law by which he meant the ruler's command. Presumably, rulers ought to have embraced his theory but they did not. It was because of his idea that, even an emperor has to obey the will of Heaven, and Heaven loves the people. This was an ingenious way to say that the emperor was there to serve the people. It posed a restriction, though mystical, on discretionary power. That was anathema to most rulers. As a corollary, he argued against war because it would enhance the power of the ruler and harm the people. That was another point which was distasteful to the more powerful rulers of his time who were hell-bent on conquering the world. More importantly, his theory was close to a theology, and his disciples were quite like followers of a cult. This made the rulers very uneasy. They did not persecute him but kept him at arm's length. His influence on them was thus negligible. Some small states, being victims of aggression, welcomed him but offered him no opportunity to realise his ideals.

Neither Confucius nor Mozi entertained any doubt about the meaning of human life, and apparently thought it should have certain objectives. But there were always those who had questions. Among them, Zhuangzi was the most articulate. He regarded such ideas as illusions and maintained that people should exist just like any other living or inanimate things according to the law of nature. All artefacts, including norms and institutions, should be discarded. This was not the way to endear him to a government obsessed with power. Some of them might find him amusing but none paid him much attention.

Zhuangzi and Laozi were grouped together but, as we have seen, there were differences between them. Unlike Zhuangzi, Laozi did not want to let people have freedom; he wanted them strictly controlled by a ruler using deceptive tactics, some of them in the guise of laws of nature. The ruler's agenda should not be known by the people. He was, in Laozi's mind, a "true Sage" but, in reality, he was an autocrat. This theory was put into practice by most rulers of Laozi's time, some openly, many secretly.

Laozi's theory was wholeheartedly accepted and further expounded by the Legalists. They rightly saw the need for tactics in fighting political battles between the ruler and the perfidious officials but they put more emphasis on law. In enforcing law, they advocated the use of brute force like that of the hammer and anvil. The people were not only to be made docile in a simple little state of Laozi's choice but more to be forged into tools and weapons useful to a big one to achieve its goals of becoming richer, stronger and victorious over its rivals.

Naturally, this theory was welcomed by those with government responsibilities. A modest version of it could be detected in the policies of Guan Zhong and Zichan who were regarded as the forerunners of the Legalists. Gongsun Yang developed and implemented the theory with vigour. Ruthless and brutal, he succeeded in establishing order in the state of Qin and making it triumphant in many aggressive wars. Han Fei further improved the theory, which was largely carried out by Ying Zheng 嬴政, first as King of Qin (r 246–222), later as the first emperor of the Qin Dynasty (r 221–210).

(2) Influences on the legal systems of later times

Regarding the eight thinkers' influences on Chinese legal systems in later times, I shall present my observations in broad terms and use some significant, well-known historical events to illustrate my points.

Under the first emperor of the Qin, China established a unified legal system. Over the next twenty-one centuries, until the end of the Qing Dynasty, it developed continuously without serious disruption or fundamental change. This development involved five groups of people – the emperors who were the ultimate law-makers and final judges; the high officials who assisted the emperor; the law specialists who carried out the basic law-making and decision-making work; the ordinary people who were affected by the system; and many intellectuals who did not actively serve in the government but helped expound and implement the theories of the eight thinkers relevant to the legal system. Unlike the original thinkers, who had to distinguish between one another, people of later times found something they liked in some of the theories, kept in mind a blend of them, and picked those parts which supported their pursuit of different objectives. Such practice caused inconsistencies in many people's behaviour and some divergent developments of the legal system.

(A) Law-makers and law-making

Who was to make law? What qualifications should law-makers have? How were they to make law? By the time of the eight thinkers, the first question already had a definitive answer. It was the political elites headed by a state ruler. The answer to the second question was never clear. The thinkers mentioned far-sightedness, understanding of human feelings, the ability to identify and analyse important social problems, and the wisdom to solve them but, in reality, it was mainly the possession of political power. As to the third question, it was well known that, in practice, the law-makers always chose an ideology and a procedure that suited their own agendas. This point was made clear by the admonition Emperor Xuan of the Han 漢宣帝 (r 73–49 BCE) gave his crown prince, mentioned above, that the House of Han had a system which mixed the ways of benevolent kings and forceful hegemons, never relying only on moral teachings. In other words, theories of the various thinkers should be used selectively. It is especially revealing that the emperor made this statement in spite of the fact that his great grandfather, Emperor Wu 武帝, allegedly exalted Ruist teachings above all other theories.

As a rule, the kind of laws which should be adopted depends on the social situations – lenient ones when society is exhausted and recuperating, harsh ones when it is restive and disorderly.[63] Thus, after prolonged civil wars, the first four emperors of the Han abolished the draconian laws of the Qin and adopted simple and beneficent ones to let the people have more than half a century to recover in peace. Then, when the country prospered and the people became more adventurous, Emperor Wu began numerous ambitious domestic projects and military campaigns against enemies on China's borders. To facilitate these efforts he brought in many strict laws.[64] Once adopted, such laws were difficult to rescind. Eventually, a revolution or coup would bring about a new regime and reform of the law. These experiences were repeated as China went through her dynastic cycles.

The personal character of an emperor always mattered. That was why, in the same dynasty, some emperors made beneficent laws, others harsh ones. For example, Emperor Wen 漢文帝 (r 179–157 BCE) abolished punishments involving mutilation;[65] Emperor Wu adopted laws imposing collective responsibilities on people for many acts previously not proscribed.[66] Thus, laws reflected the emperor's inclinations. No wonder Du Zhou 杜周, a chief judge during Emperor Wu's reign, in response to criticism that he ignored established laws, retorted: "Whence comes the law? What were desired by a former ruler became statutes; those by a later one are made substatutes. Law is thus nothing but that which is approved by a ruler."[67] This definition of law was uncommon but, at that time, quite realistic. Fortunately, it was not generally accepted and what emperors desired did not always become law. For instance, in later times, many emperors wanted to revive the punishments of mutilation but cancelled their orders because of strong arguments against them.[68]

More commonly, new laws were made according to a routine. When a problem arose, the emperor would order the high officials to deliberate and suggest a solution or, occasionally, the officials themselves might take the initiative. If approved, the suggested measure could be made law. In the Tang Dynasty, a more elaborate procedure was introduced. One government office would prepare a draft and another office would check it against existing laws to see whether there was any conflict or redundancy. If there was none, the draft would be sent to a third office for a final review and, if it found something wrong, it could withhold the imperial decree authorising the law's enactment.[69]

This experiment with careful law-making was exceptional and short-lived.[70] Indeed, since the feudal system was basically abolished in the Qin, political power continued to concentrate, causing the law-making process to be more and more dictatorial. Emperor Huizong of the Northern Song Dynasty 北宋徽宗 (r 1101–1125), for instance, made numerous laws known as *yu-bi* (御筆 edicts in the emperor's handwriting).[71] Later, during the reign of Emperor Gaozong of the Southern Song Dynasty 南宋高宗 (r 1127–1162), chief minister Qin Hui 秦檜 issued thousands of *du-tang pi-zhuang, zhi-hui* (都堂批狀、指揮 rescripts and orders from the chief minister's office) with the effect of law.[72] The worst culprit of wilful law-making was Emperor Tai-zu, founder of the Ming Dynasty 明太祖 (r 1368–1398), who, in 1385–1387, issued four volumes of *da-gao* (大誥 grand instructions) consisting of hundreds of the most horrifying criminal provisions[73] before he promulgated the Ming criminal code in 1397 which was based on the more rational and lenient Tang Code.

Why were emperors permitted to exercise such absolute power in making laws? It was often said that because people were influenced by Ruist ideology, they supported authoritarian rule. This is only partly correct. Confucius taught his disciples to be deferential to the authorities but to challenge them when they were wrong. Mencius encouraged people to speak with contempt to those in power. By Xunzi's time, the government had become more oppressive but he still advocated the principle of following the Way, not just the orders of a ruler. As stated earlier, it was Dong Zhongshu who endorsed the Legalist *san-gang*, and then countless more shameless intellectuals of later times who, wishing to ingratiate themselves with the power-holders, further distorted the classical Ruist teachings.

The Mohists were also accomplices because they supported the concentration of political power. But they, at least in theory, insisted that even the Son of Heaven had to obey the will of Heaven which was manifested in its love of the common people. The true culprits of authoritarianism were Laozi and the Legalists who all alleged that the world could be ruled only by a sage (or a miraculous Legalist "average ruler"). A sage was necessarily authoritarian so that no one could disobey him. This idea was stolen by emperors of later times who proclaimed themselves sages and, moreover, claimed to have the Mandate of Heaven with which to govern.[74] Periodically, this claim was challenged by rebels but not by the intellectuals who were either cowed by the government or aspired to get into it. As a result, law in traditional China remained a product of government authorities and no effective measures to prevent abuse of the law-making power were developed.

(B) Objectives of law

What is law for? In ancient China, when law was considered a norm clearly distinguishable from moral principles, rites, custom and rules governing political, economic, military and communal activities, the answer was clear. It was specifically to spell out crimes that should be prohibited and to prescribe punishments. When society became more complex and social problems more complicated, law took over many of the functions of other norms and rules because it could be more readily recognised and enforced more effectively through government power. That was why Zichan promulgated detailed laws. When law was used to deal with various social problems, it was no longer used simply to deter and punish offences and provide expedient short-term remedies which could, in the long run, be harmful. Law was to guide society to achieve certain objectives. What were the objectives and what should they be?

(i) Political objectives

Political objectives were salient. Among them, the most obvious were generally to protect the government from internal and external threats, and, more specifically, to uphold the prerogatives and privileges of those in power. Zhuangzi, of course, rejected these but they were, to different degrees, recognised by all other thinkers. Since ancient times, various laws and extrajudicial measures had been enacted to punish rebels, traitors and plotters of coups. It was declared in the proclamations of ancient rulers that these offenders' bloodlines were to be exterminated.[75] After founding the Han Dynasty, Liu Bang purged most of those who helped him establish his regime on trumped-up charges of treason or rebellion.[76] In later times, more specific laws were adopted to punish political offences. Among the *shi-e* (十惡 ten most abominable crimes) listed in the Tang Code, five were against the political establishment: rebellion, harming the imperial person, treason, disrespect of the throne, and killing officials above a certain rank or the head of a local government.[77] In addition, the code had numerous other provisions protecting government personnel, property and function, all prescribing severe punishments. In particularly serious cases, collective responsibility was imposed upon those implicated.[78] Gongsun Yang adopted such laws and used them widely. In the early Han, this punishment, known as *zu-zhu* (族誅 termination of the clan), was banned except for revolution and in treason cases.[79] Its use and abuse were common when the government felt challenged or the emperor personally threatened. Emperor Wu of the Han charged many persons, including the crown prince, who were suspected of using witchcraft against him, and had thousands of them executed.[80]

A cruel measure, connected to persecution of political offenders, was a requirement that people report such offences. We have seen that Confucius strongly objected to the practice of reporting crimes committed by close relatives. The Legalists required everyone to report crimes by others. The Tang Code had a specific provision punishing those who withheld information about rebellion, treason and action against the imperial person or shrines.[81] Empress Wu 武后 (684–704) allowed the circulation of a book known as *Gao-mi luo-zhi jing* (告密羅織經 guides for reporting secret crimes and entrapping suspects) and the use of ten terrifying types of torture on persons suspected of treason – the ninth and the tenth would make a victim "beg for a quick death for himself and the extermination of his entire family". Numerous persons suspected of objecting to the empress's usurpation of the Tang throne were persecuted.[82]

A more infamous case alluded to briefly earlier was the murder of Yue Fei 岳飛, a general of the early Southern Song Dynasty, by Qin Hui 秦檜, then the chief minister. After Emperor Qin 欽宗 (r 1126), the last emperor of the Northern Song Dynasty was captured by the Tartar state of Jin in northern China, his son ascended the throne in the south as Emperor Gaozong 高宗 (r 1127–1162) of the Southern Song Dynasty. Qin Hui, knowing that Gaozong had no intention to fight the Jin, retrieve his father and lose his own throne, falsely accused Yue Fei, who was campaigning victoriously against the Jin, of treason, conducted spurious trials, and, obviously with the emperor's tacit consent, had Yue Fei murdered in prison.[83]

Besides those who posed apparent threats to the central authority, there was another group considered to be potentially dangerous. During the Warring States Period, many aristocrats had large numbers of intellectuals as guests who helped them in their struggle to stay in power. As mentioned earlier, in the early years of Ying Zheng as king of Qin Lü Buwei, the chief minister sheltered three thousand such guests and had them compile a large book, *Lü-shi chun-qiu*. It combined the principles of the Ruists, the Daoists and the Mohists, emphasising particularly those of the Ruists and implicitly critical of the first emperor's unflinching implementation of the theories and practices of the Legalists. Fearing Lü's possible treasonous plots, the king exiled him in 235 BCE. He committed suicide and all his guests were severely punished.[84]

Then, in 213 BCE, Ying Zheng, now the first emperor of the Qin, ordered the burning of works of various schools and made discussion of those works a crime *yi-gu fei-jin* (以古非今 using the past to criticise the present), punishable by death, and, in the following year, buried alive more than 460 scholars who slandered him and *wei yao-yan yi-luan qian-shou* (為妖言以亂黔首 making heretical speeches to confuse the common people).[85]

This persecution of intellectuals who showed any sign of disobedience to the emperors became an established practice in later dynasties. After an alleged rebellion led by his uncle Liu An 劉安 was suppressed, Emperor Wu persecuted Liu An's followers, including hundreds of intellectuals who participated in writing the book *Huai-nan-zi* 淮南子, which was suspected of criticising government policies, and banned as *yao-yan* 妖言.[86]

Banning certain books and conducting literary inquisitions became frequent practices in the following dynasties. We have mentioned that Emperor Tai-zu of the Ming Dynasty ordered some eighty-five passages of *Mengzi* deleted because they were against dictatorial political power. In his "Grand Instructions", there is a provision making those who refused his appointments a crime punishable by death.[87]

But the most flagrant persecution of the intellectuals was committed by the Manchus in the early Qing Dynasty. Fearful of the resentment of the conquered Han majority, a campaign known as *wen-zi-yu* (文字獄 literary inquisition) was launched to purge anyone who did not support the new regime. A few who wrote, copied, kept or disseminated works considered critical of the Manchus and their policies were charged with treason. In each of several hundred cases, countless people were implicated and executed, including not only the offender's own family and his mother's and his wife's families but also neighbours and those responsible for local security, and even his teachers and students and their families.[88]

A greater fear for the ruler was, as Han Fei pointed out, the people, especially the officials and intellectuals, ganging up and opposing him. The opposition could be against some measures of rather minor importance but the fact that several people acted together set alarm bells ringing. They would be branded as *peng-dang* (朋黨 partisans) and suppressed. It happened many times in history and the events, called *dang-huo* (黨禍 partisan calamities) often implicated many innocent persons.[89] Unsatisfied by such ruthless suppression, after the offence, some rulers published severe warnings against officials forming *peng-dang*. The Yongzheng emperor of the Qing 清雍正帝 (r 1723–1735) promulgated one called *Peng-dang lun* (朋黨論 "On Partisanship") in 1724.[90] Thereafter, public opposition to the positions of those in control of the government was effectively silenced. The intellectuals, as well as the ordinary people, were isolated. Every person was kept in a solitary position; each could have his opinion but was not allowed to express it jointly with others. Officials, in particular, had to live a rather isolated life just as Xunzi observed in the Qin state he visited.

All these cases clearly show that, after a political structure had been established, those in control of it were determined to protect their privileges and, to that end, created special laws and enforced them with special instruments and procedures or forced the regular judicial system to act under their orders. When political power became more concentrated, this use of the law became more ruthless.

Law, of course, can also be used to support other types of political structures that prevent unhealthy concentration of power and protect the politically weak. But this did not happened in traditional China. As we shall see, in every period, there were large numbers of administrative laws but they were for the control of the bureaucracy, designed to reinforce power concentrated at the centre, not to divide or restrain it.

(ii) State security objective

The said political objective was often tied up with state security. Therefore, again with the exception of Zhuangzi and perhaps to a lesser degree Laozi, the other thinkers all emphasised strengthening state security as an important objective, and suggested various measures and laws to achieve it. In addition, these thinkers shared a desire that China would be unified at some point so that the security of the different states would no longer be a problem. This wish was realised by the first emperor of the Qin. But, immediately, he faced two challenges: to maintain the internal and external security of the new union. For the first, he abolished the feudal system and placed the entire country under the rule of central government. He enacted laws to standardise things in common usage, including instruments of measurement, the widths of public roads, and the written language. More significantly, he bestowed upon himself the title "The First Emperor", thus deliberately trying to establish a new political reality, namely, that the nation would be governed forever as a unified state by an eternal dynasty. To instil this idea into the minds of the people he travelled far and wide around the country as its sole ruler and the symbol of its unity.[91] His actions were criticised both during his reign and later but they did strengthen the ideal held by most ancient and later thinkers, and helped the Chinese people believe that, despite many periods of division, China would always reunite and become whole again.

The second task was to defend unified China against threats from outside. Many of the First Emperor's journeys were to potentially troubled borders to show off the power of the dynasty. But the main threat was from the Huns, a nomadic nation who roamed in the Mongolian steppes and incessantly ravaged the agricultural Chinese north. A mere visit there by the emperor was not enough to overawe them and keep them away. He put much of his army there under the command of his crown prince and one of his best generals. They connected the fortresses and defence lines of the former northern states and built the Great Wall, and, during his reign, the Huns were held at bay.

In the early Han, when the country was ruined by prolonged, large-scale civil wars, the Huns resurged and repeatedly invaded. The Han government appeased the aggressors by sending them court ladies and treasures as tributes. A generation later, when the country had become rich and strong, Emperor Wu decided to avenge the humiliation. In the forty-four years from 134 to 90 BCE, he launched more than ten major military campaigns, each involving many hundreds of thousands of soldiers, and eventually defeated the Huns and subdued many small states in what is now known as Xinjiang. In addition, China conquered Korea, Vietnam and areas adjacent to Tibet, and thereby imposed peace and order on all borders of the Han Empire.[92]

But the victories were enormously costly. Government coffers were emptied and people plunged into poverty. To continue the struggle, new laws were adopted from the middle of Emperor Wu's reign to impose a poll tax on everyone from fifteen to fifty-six years of age, a duty on all vehicles and ships, and a levy on all merchandise. And, to deter tax evasion, a law required people to report violators, especially deceitful merchants. More importantly, four new measures were initiated: two state monopolies (one of production of iron and salt, the other of distillation of spirits) and two price-control strategies (one requiring areas that had surplus of certain goods to send them as tribute to the government to be distributed to areas short of them; the other ordering local government to purchase goods when they were cheap at a higher price and to sell them when they are dear at a lower price).[93]

Of the early campaigns, the objective of national defence was clear and, for that objective, the military and economic measures were accepted by the people. But, when defence turned into offence in order to secure long-term peace at the borders and the costs mounted, people began to wonder about the direction of the country. Six years after Emperor Wu's death, his heir Emperor Zhao 昭帝 (r 86–74 BCE) ordered a review. Several high government officials, including the chief minister, the censor and the treasurer, and over sixty *wen-xue* (scholars) and *xian-liang* ("worthies", that is, persons known for their virtue) selected from various parts of the empire, were brought to a conference to re-evaluate the various government policies. The officials argued that the campaigns were to defend and extend China's borders in order to protect its people and culture, and the economic measures were necessary to finance the campaigns. The scholars and the worthies disputed these objectives, arguing that China's security could be better achieved by winning over the Huns and others on the borders by means of the superior Chinese culture. In Confucius's words: *yuan-ren bu-fu ze xiu wen-de yi lai zhi* (遠人不服則修文德以來之 when far away people are disobedient, cultivate civic virtues to attract and convert them).[94] More strongly, they maintained that it was more important to improve the well-being of the people; if that objective was ignored, all the military victories would be pyrrhic. This debate, later known as *Yan-tie lun* (鹽鐵論 "The Salt and Iron Debate"), lasted five months but no common ground was found. Finally, the emperor decided to abolish the state monopoly of the distillation of spirits but to keep all the other measures; obviously because of the desperate needs of the military campaigns, the government had to collect as much revenue as possible.[95] Here again, we hear the echo of the opposing opinions of Zichan and Shuxiang: one that expedient action must be taken to tackle the urgent problems of the present; the other that the long-term interests of society should not be sacrificed for immediate gain. In fact, these opinions are not necessarily in conflict but they have been the subject of perennial debate since then.

Apparently the scholars and the worthies, by then most of them Ruists, lost that round. And, in later times, when national security and people's welfare were in conflict, the government usually favoured the former. Only the Southern Song Dynasty (1127–1279) seemed to have adopted a different approach. Instead of fighting the Tartar invaders from the north, the government decided to appease them with tributary gifts of vast value. To meet this need, orders were issued, on the one hand, to suppress border adventurism and, on the other, to stimulate the domestic economy.[96] The policy worked – peace was preserved, the economy grew, cultural achievements soared and society became more civilised – but the policy was fundamentally flawed, merely to win a breathing space for a short time. The people lived in humiliation, and the state, with its military preparedness neglected, was easily conquered by the Mongols.

To help achieve the national security objectives, laws were adopted and administered by special government agencies. In the early dynasties, the central government had only two principal departments – the military and the civilian, the former headed by *da-si-ma*, *da-jiang-jun* (大司馬, 大將軍 the grand general), the latter by *cheng-xiang* (丞相 the chief minister). Since the Tang, regular military affairs were placed under the *Bing-bu* (兵部 Ministry of Military Affairs) to maintain the armed forces and prepare for military campaigns. It issued several sets of laws for conscription and the training of soldiers, selection and appointment of officers and rewarding and disciplining them. It is worth noting that, besides *Bing-bu*, there were five ministries, namely, *Li-bu* (吏部 Ministry of Civil Affairs), *Li-bu* (禮部 Ministry of Rites), *Hu-bu* (戶部 Ministry of Home Affairs), *Xing-bu* (刑部 Ministry of Justice), and *Gong-bu* (工部 Ministry of Public Works), all civilian. The emergence of these agencies reflected two realities: first, that government functions had multiplied, and the old saying "The great affairs of the state are only the worship ceremonies and the military"[97] was no longer true. Second, that national defence became an objective of lesser priority. The last fact was created partly because the major threat to China, the Huns, had been checked during the Han Dynasty and had turned their aggression more towards the West. But the general degradation of the military establishment was undoubtedly pushed by the Ruists, stressing this fact and the waste and futility of military campaigns, as those in "the iron and salt discussion" did. It was true that this development saved resources and energy, and improved the welfare of the ordinary people. But the costs were terrible. Owing to the neglect of military preparedness and tardy enforcement of laws controlling the armed forces, China became weak and was harassed by other foreigners – the Song Dynasty was first reduced to a tributary state of the Jin and then conquered by the Mongols; the Ming Dynasty was vanquished by the Manchus; and Qing China was partly colonised by Western and Japanese powers.

(III) Economic objective

In addition to protecting the political system and strengthening state security, many laws were made to regulate the economy. The two major problems to be addressed were the production and distribution of wealth. Zhuangzi, obviously believing that there were enough resources for everyone, was not troubled. Laozi was not so romantic but had little to say. Confucius recognised the need to increase production as a precondition for further social development but he saw low productivity as a lesser worry than inequitable distribution.[98] Mencius suggested that people should have certain means to provide for themselves and he was aware of the importance of commerce. Mozi, appalled at the exploitation of the common people by the aristocrats, demanded increasing production of necessary goods and curbing wasteful living but did not suggest definite measures. The Legalists' discussion was more detailed. They subscribed to the traditional view that agriculture was the primary source of wealth and wanted the people to be bound to the land and to cultivate it. They allowed handcrafts but disparaged work on fine, but useless, artefacts, and, failing to see the importance of commerce, they suppressed the merchant class. The influence of their views on the legal system was evident. We have seen Gongsun Yang's pro-agriculture and anti-commerce laws. Similar laws and orders were numerous in later times but never effective.[99] There was a vast number of laws regulating the production and distribution of resources administered by various government agencies but a paucity of rules governing private business.[100] A close look at the laws governing economical and financial matters administered by *hu-bu* (the Ministry of Home Affairs) since the Tang reveals that, apart from those concerning the use of land, land tax, inheritance, salt-making, currency, customs, and transport, only a very small number of provisions were to regulate contracts, debts, credit, and trust.[101]

A more serious problem concerned the distribution of crucial resources. After private ownership of land appeared in the Han Dynasty, it was left largely unregulated. The Legalists said little about it, and the governments of later times were unsure what to do. The early Han prohibition against ownership of land by merchants was never effectively enforced, and no law was adopted later to keep land from being grabbed by a few. The problem was aggravated by the rules of inheritance, according to which the estate of a deceased person was to be divided equally among his sons conceived by his wife, concubines and housemaids. Even his illegitimate sons, born to women outside of his household, could inherit half of a legitimate son's share.[102] In due course, a piece of land left by its owner would be divided into plots too small for profitable use, and his descendants had to sell them. Those with money, usually the powerful officials and rich merchants, would acquire them piece by piece and become big landlords, reducing the landless to being bond peasants or servants or paupers.

The laws oppressing the merchant class were another problem. To begin with, they were ill-conceived. As agents of distribution of materials and goods, the merchants provided a necessary service; the laws discriminating against them drove up their operating costs but, in response, the merchants simply raised the prices of their goods and became richer. While they were forbidden from certain lifestyles, no law imposed progressive tax on their wealth. And, when the government had financial difficulties, many of them were encouraged to purchase titles or offices, and some, who were guilty of crimes, were allowed to redeem their punishments by payments to the government.[103] Such measures were invariably recommended by persons with arguments similar to those of the Legalist officials and opposed by the Ruist scholars in "the salt and iron debate". Implementing them was, as a proverb says: *yin-zhen zhi-ke* (飲鴆止渴 drinking hemlock to quench thirst).

The Legalists' ideas and measures to disparage, or even suppress, artisans from making clever but impractical objects had the damaging effect of impeding technical innovation. On this, the other thinkers shared some of the blame. Luckily, the Chinese people's ingenuity was not totally smothered and they made significant contributions to science and technology. But no law was made to give an innovator the exclusive right to his intellectual property, and this fact raised no objection – scholars, even novelists and playwrights, felt honoured to find their works reproduced, and artisans were usually employed by aristocrats and the idle rich and never produced in quantity anyway. Most people shared a traditional belief that intellectual properties were to be enjoyed by all as a part of common human heritage. An inventor of ideas, useful objects or procedures was left to his own devices to keep them from being copied, and was often despised for doing so in order to gain profit. But an innovation may require enormous investment of time and other resources. If this fact is ignored, and no material compensation is assured, it will eventually have adverse effects on innovation. But this prospect did not bother the intellectuals whose main interests were in perfecting personal virtue and serving in the government.

(iv) Social objective

At the time of the eight thinkers, Chinese society had long been agricultural. With only primitive tools, people had to toil in groups. The most natural groups were formed by persons who had blood or marriage ties or who lived in close proximity, and therefore families and villages became the basic building blocks of society. When people engaged in other legitimate activities, they formed other types of groups. Though they might have different interests, they would fit into the existing social structure and, together, pursue the same general objectives.

The easiest and surest way to study this general objective is to scrutinise those two basic groups – family and local community. In both cases, we find that, generally, the members need mutual care and support and, particularly, guidance for the young. These needs gave rise to an organising principle – respect for the seniors and care for the juniors – and a hierarchical structure, with the seniors occupying the higher levels and the juniors the lower ones. These facts must have been evident to the thinkers but, strangely, only the Ruists discussed it. Zhuangzi did not think much about society because life was ephemeral, almost surreal.

Laozi, Mozi and the Legalists all wanted people to submit to an authority outside of the family and local community – a sage in Laozi's case, a *ju-zi* (鉅子 great leader) in Mozi's, and the supreme ruler of the state in the case of the Legalists.

The Ruists acknowledged that society as a whole needed leaders but stressed that the very basic cohesive element to keep society together was filial piety which could be transformed into virtues governing all human relationships – love, trust, loyalty, sympathy, compassion and so on. This idea was preached by Confucius and his disciples but largely ignored by the rulers of their time – many of them usurped their fathers' positions, and even murdered them. The first emperor of the Qin exiled his mother, accusing her of licentious conduct but, one day, it dawned on him that, if he claimed to be the father figure of the nation, Ruist teaching could help make the people his "filial children" and loyal subjects. So he brought back his mother and went on extensive tours across the country extolling filial piety and ordering measures to promote it.[104] The lesson was learned well by the rulers of the Han Dynasty who pronounced that they would *yi xiao zhi tian-xia* (以孝治天下 to govern the world according to the principle of filial piety) and included the character *xiao*孝in their official titles – for instance Emperor Xiaowen 孝文皇帝, Emperor Xiaowu 孝武皇帝.

More importantly, the Ruists managed to have *bu-xiao* (不孝 not being filial) listed in the criminal code as one of *shi-e* (十惡 ten most abominable crimes) liable to the most severe punishments. Specifically, a person could be punished for failing to provide for his parents and grandparents, leaving them unattended, disobeying their orders, accusing them of crimes, cursing them, injuring them, establishing a household separate from theirs, marrying during the prescribed period of mourning their death.[105] In addition, the Ruists also helped introduce many statutes that upheld the hierarchy in families and clans, prescribing punishments against disobedient juniors and inferiors.[106]

Furthermore the Ruists helped draft norms known as *jia-xun* (家訓 family teachings) and *zu-gui* (族規 clan rules)[107] prescribing detailed regulations for a member to develop himself and to interact with other members and outsiders, and for the family or clan to manage its property. Besides such prescriptions, these norms included articles spelling out rewards and punishments, and some of the latter could be quite severe. Other Ruists were more ambitious. In the Song Dynasty, Fan Zhongyan 范仲淹, a high official, created *yi-zhuang* (義莊 charity farms) to provide material help for the needy in his greatly extended clan.[108] Lü Dafang 呂大防, another high official, drafted a *xiang-yue* (鄉約 village covenant) for his home district to help maintain order, promote education and provide for the poor.[109] These rules were widely imitated in later times. A common provision in practically all these rules commanded people to abide by the law and avoid litigation. This made the rules acceptable to the government. In many cases, local authorities were quite willing to help enforce them.

Besides these rules for specific groups, many officials, especially those of local government, published their own advice for people in general. Even many emperors joined in the preaching. We have mentioned that the first emperor of the Qin did it. The Kangxi Emperor 康熙帝 (r 1662–1722), the second of the Qing, promulgated a sixteen-point imperial edict instructing people to behave correctly. Among them, most noticeable were Point Number One (to observe filial piety and brotherly love), Point Number Three (to achieve harmony in the local community and avoid litigation) and Point Number Eight (to learn law and deter the wicked). The other points told people to acquire education, engage in agriculture, pay taxes, help maintain order and be generally virtuous. In 1724, the Yongzheng emperor published a book entitled *Sheng-yu guang-xun* (聖諭廣訓 *Annotations to the Sacred Imperial Instructions*) to expound on his father's edict, and ordered that the book be read by officials and village elders to the general public all over the empire twice a month on the first and the fifteenth days.[110]

Thus, the primary objective of the families and local communities was to keep order. It is safe to assume that it was also a common objective of other social groups, such as schools, guilds, professional associations, religious organisations, and so on. Together, these groups formed a civil society. It was vibrant and harmonious, helped the government in preserving peace and performed some functions the government ignored, and also won from it some autonomy. A member of this society would be well indoctrinated by its various rules and would be civilised.

This society was tightly knit and stratified, forming a pyramidal hierarchy. There were rules specifically for people at each level and rules governing the relationship between those on different levels. The latter set of rules was mostly one-directional: for instance, those prescribing filial piety and respect for the seniors did not have a corresponding one spelling out how parents and seniors should act towards children and juniors. The relative responsibilities and obligations of the rulers and the people were not clearly stipulated. Apparently, Laozi, Mozi and the Legalists found nothing wrong with this fact. It was generally believed that the Ruists accepted the one-sided rules governing the family relationships. But those were the *xiao-ren ru* (小人儒 petty Ruists) who failed to follow Confucius's teaching of *fu, fu*; *zi, zi*; in other words, each person should act properly in his role and there should be reciprocity. Thus, superficial order and harmony were not the objectives Confucius thought society should pursue. Mencius and Xunzi share with him the same view but the later Ruists failed him because they were cowed by concentrated political power and tried only to fend it off a little and preserve some peace and harmony among people at the lower level of the social strata.

What kind of society did the true Ruists wish to have? We have seen a grand vision of *da-tong* (大同 great harmony) and a lesser one of *xiao-kang* (小康 modest prosperity) reportedly presented by Confucius. In a rather short passage he placed two stages of societal development in contrast, pointing out that in personal cultivation and social relations, people at the earlier stage emphasised trustworthiness and civility, cared about one another generally and helped everyone to live well and properly develop his potentials. In managing communal affairs they selected the virtuous and capable and trusted them with government responsibilities. For the well-being of everyone they worked hard to produce goods and distributed them widely, taking particular care of the needs of the less fortunate.

People were self-disciplined and compassionate, and society was peaceful and harmonious. At the later stage a person worked largely for himself and those close to him, and passed his positions and possessions only to his descendants. Inevitably he competed with others and therefore there were schemes, struggles and wars. Many institutions and rules were created to guide and constrain people and punish those who strayed, but only the sage kings barely succeeded in keeping order, and society was tense. Why the difference? Confucius mentioned a reason: at the first stage society existed for the public interests of the whole community (為公 *wei-gong*); at the second stage it did so for the private interests of the individual families (為家 *wi-jia*).

Da-tong had been widely hailed in China as the ultimate objective of society; *xiao-kang* as a lower but perhaps more feasible one. But unfortunately neither had been effectively pursued since Yu established the system of hereditary political succession over three millennia ago.

Apart from practical difficulties there are some theoretical problems with the idea of *da-tong*. According to Confucius's description, in this situation there were no man-made norms. He said people followed *da-dao* (大道 the Great Way), but he did not spell out what it was. Mencius said it could be found in people's hearts but Xunzi disagreed. If a norm is not readily known or knowable it cannot be easily observed, therefore *da-tong* remains a mirage. The idea of *xiao-kang* is also problematic. To reach this goal it is necessary to have extraordinary leaders. Confucius mentioned only six ancient sage kings in this category. In later Chinese history no ruler was their equal.

The Ruist society is hierarchical, in which each individual is assigned to a specific position and required to behave according to a specific set of rules. If the assignments and requirements are arbitrary and rigid, such a society could become authoritarian and stagnant, as China had largely been in the past since the Qin. But, as we have discussed at length, that was not what the true Ruists envisioned. What they wished to see was actually the opposite; it is regrettable that their original ideas were later corrupted by lesser men. Nevertheless, the vision of *da-tong*, idealistic certainly, is worth striving for, not only by the Chinese but by all humanity.

(v) Cultural objective

All species need life-sustaining materials and security, but humans apparently want more. This desire manifested itself in primitive cave paintings and in the decorative objects made in great antiquity for no obvious practical use, showing that people had interests in things beyond those which were necessary to meet their physical needs, and they wanted to enjoy them; they had feelings and dreams and wanted to express them; and, above all, they were curious about what was strange and wanted to understand it. As a result, they created culture. Zhuangzi did not think much about it. Laozi recognised only some of its rudimentary aspects. Mozi and the Legalists actually disproved of high culture: the former regarded it as an excuse for the exploitation of poor ordinary people; the latter thought it retarded the effort to enrich and strengthen the state in a world of great struggles. Only the Ruists appreciated it. Confucius was asked what the authorities should do after having enabled people to prosper. "Let them have education," he said.[111] It may not sound profound since education was also encouraged by other thinkers, except for Laozi who wanted people to be kept in ignorance and Zhuangzi who wanted people to be natural, unspoiled.

What kind of education should the people have? Mozi wanted it be technical, teaching people the various skills for the production of material goods. The Legalists wanted to ban all learning except that of law but, according to Gongsun Yang, this legal education was only to learn the plain contents of the statutes, with no further delving. Confucius had in mind something much broader. At his time, an advanced student was taught the Classics (chiefly *The Book of Historical Documents*, and *The Book of Odes*), histories of the various states and *liu-yi* (六藝 the Six Arts), namely rites, music, calligraphy, charioteering, archery and mathematics. In the following centuries, many great academics, poets, dramatists, playwrights, painters, calligraphers, musicians and experts in the martial arts appeared and were adored and honoured. But, to the Ruists, the finest product of education was a good man who would be called a *jun-zi* (君子 noble man) by Confucius, a *da-zhang-fu* (大丈夫 great man) by Mencius or a *cheng-ren* (成人 an accomplished man) by Xunzi. What kind of a man is he? According to Confucius, he will abide by the rites and improve himself. He will not impose on others what he does not want to receive from them. More importantly, while he wishes to stand up and accomplish what he desires, he wants to help others do the same. Mencius's great man will keep himself upright and follow the Way. When he has the opportunity, he will lead the people to it, otherwise he will walk it alone. Wealth and high position will not make him indulgent; poverty and humble status will not make him unsteady; authority and force will not make him yield. Xunzi described in more detail his accomplished man: "Accomplishment" means having a grasp of what is truly worthy in a human being – rectitude, honesty, self-restraint, respect for others, tolerance, trust, loyalty, sympathy, compassion, generosity, love, benevolence, altruism, sacrifice for justice, and, above all, knowledge of the Way. An accomplished man will correct himself and help others; he will be the first to tackle difficulties and the last to claim rewards; he is not averse to profit but will never do anything improper to gain it; he is not adventurous but never fears death in pursuit of justice; he is not cowed by power and authority, not intimidated by the masses, and not even moved by an opportunity to govern the world if the offer is unjust; he will act according to his principles and is indifferent to outside attractions; he can go anywhere in the world and be respected and trusted, and can change others, even the barbarians.

In short, unlike the nihilist Zhuangzi who dismissed culture, the cynical Laozi who would keep people in ignorance, the narrow-minded Mozi who wanted people to learn only skills that help increase production of basic materials for subsistence, and the authoritarian Legalists who limited learning to law, the Ruists believed that mankind could have a meaningful existence which would become more and more satisfying, physically, emotionally, intellectually and spiritually. It would have culture; it would be fine and beautiful. Therefore, the Ruists made it a higher objective for society to pursue after it had achieved the more basic ones of meeting the needs of survival and security.

While other thinkers more or less ignored this objective, it was, fortunately, valued by many governing elites. Duke Zhou reportedly created the rites of the Zhou Dynasty which Confucius admired as the zenith of cultural development up to his time. To implement the rites, the Zhou established in the government a number of special offices which were inherited by later dynasties. The Qin was a dark period but the founding emperor of the Han ordered a new set of rites for his court and, soon, interest in classical culture was revived. People were encouraged to bring out written works of all kinds that had been banned under the Qin. Many scholars studied them and taught them to thousands of students. Emperor Wu, who favoured the Ruists and was reputed to *du-zun ru-shu* (獨尊儒術 exalt the Ruist teachings exclusively), created a *tai-xue* (太學 imperial university) in the capital for advanced study of Confucius's teachings. Shortly thereafter, every local government established public colleges, and private primary schools sprang up in every village. Though Emperor Xuan said the House of Han used mixed theories, his son, Emperor Yuan, was a more genuine Ruist and, since then, the Ruist ideals have been the main cultural objectives of China.

The Tang Dynasty added a research institute, named the *Han-lin-yuan* (翰林院 Imperial Academy), for hundreds of scholars, and combined several offices in charge of education into the *Li-bu* (禮部 Ministry of Rites). It also introduced an examination system to qualify persons who aspired to government appointment. The most critical tests were about the Ruist canons and this became a tradition until the very end of the Qing Dynasty.[112] In a society where commerce and industry were disparaged, and honour, authority, privilege and financial rewards came with government office, the tests and appointments became a powerful incentive for people to become "Ruists".

In different periods there were varying numbers of people in the Imperial University, the Imperial Academy and the various government offices but, roughly, they amounted to a few tens of thousands, and there were thousands upon thousands more who wanted to get in. They created an atmosphere that induced people to take education seriously and to believe that knowledge had a value in itself. This inevitably led some people to learn more than just the Ruist teachings. Thus, since the Han, there have been many who were interested in the various humanities and science subjects. To cater for their needs, many *shu-yuan* (書院 private academies) were established by distinguished scholars, some of them with local government support.

Consequently a very large group of educated people, in and out of government, came into being. They formed a class, the literati, who generally valued learning, loved fine arts, observed rites, cultivated a high self-expectation, and harboured an ambition to help enlighten the world. They gave society an important objective – to cherish culture and improve it. For these developments, a great number of laws were adopted and, judging by the fact that for over two millennia China led the cultural development in East Asia to remarkable heights, the legal system that supported this effort must have worked reasonably well.

The intellectuals were not all Ruists. Many found the teachings of Zhuangzi and some parts of Laozi and the Buddha enlightening, and devoted much of their lives to expounding them, making great contribution to Daoism and Buddhism, another two pillars of Chinese culture. But they were never recognised as the major cultural objectives of China. It was because, as religious organisations, both had some difficulties with the government arising from their ostensible desire to exist outside its control with objectives not in conformity with what is prescribed. They thus posed a challenge to the political authorities. As alluded to earlier, since the late Eastern Han, a Daoist cult known as *Wu-dou-mi-dao* (五斗米道 the Five-peck-rice Way) repeatedly led rebellions.[113] In the fifth, sixth, ninth and tenth centuries, governments of various dynasties suppressed Buddhist sects for political reasons.[114] Despite these events, the two religions were allowed to exist because many people needed them as psychological crutches and practical shelters. But knowing that, in the past, every rebellion or revolution always had some religious instigation, incitement and support, and seeing all religious groups as competitors for power and influence, the government was ever fearful and vigilant about them, and, as briefly mentioned earlier, placed them under close surveillance and strict control and made many laws for these purposes and enforced them strictly. Aggressive proselytising was discouraged, establishment of temples needed government permission, the life of adherents was minutely regulated and their political activities absolutely prohibited.[115]

A more basic reason why neither Daoism nor Buddhism, nor for that matter any religion, was made a major cultural objective is that they are in conflict with Confucius's teachings. Confucius believed that the result of an event is determined by numerous factors: the more factors a person controls, the more successful he will be in achieving a certain result. When he fails, it is not that some critical factors are controlled by superbeings with a will against him. That was why Confucius was characterised by his contemporaries as someone who would try things that were seemingly impossible and why he studiously refused to concern himself with the supernatural. He advised people to do their utmost and, when the result was disappointing, not to justify it as preordained by a superbeing and shrink from their own responsibility. Thus, his teachings do not comprise a religion but have many sound guiding principles for human behaviour which are shared by many religions. Unlike religious dogmas, which supposedly come from divine origins, his principles are based on human relationships, proven valid by human experience and therefore more appealing to rational minds. Thus, those who accept his teachings are not simply believers in his dogma but his students whom he would encourage to examine his words, raise questions and arrive at their own conclusions. It is therefore a philosophy for positive human endeavour. Compared to it, any religion seems escapist and is therefore rejected by the majority of Chinese who had faith in human ability and respect for the dignity of the individual. It is true that many thinking Chinese found it interesting to study religion as a philosophy, and a number of them in the seventh century mixed Daoism and Buddhism and founded *chan-zong* (禪宗 the Zen sect).[116] Zen achieved wide popularity in China and East Asia but never became the mainstream of Chinese culture.

Another aspect of culture was also retarded, though not intentionally by the government. This was the study of law. In the Han there were many scholars who studied and taught law and attracted hundreds of students.[117] But enthusiasm for legal education soon waned, undoubtedly because, compared with the Ruist canons, the law was considered narrow and technical. Centuries later, during the reign of Emperor Ming of the Wei Dynasty 魏明帝 (r 227–239), the post of *lü-bo-shi* (律博士 Doctor of Law) was first established at the Imperial Academy but it did not enjoy much prestige or popularity and, in the Yuan Dynasty, this post was abolished.[118] Since the Tang, law was one of the civil examination tests but was never taken seriously by examiners and students. The test questions were usually broad and the answers could be based on common sense and Ruist principles rather than on solid legal knowledge.[119] The lack of serious studies of law led to the stagnation of this discipline. The development of jurisprudence was never made a valued cultural objective. Therefore, in late Qing, the legal system seemed backward in the eyes of the Western powers which had recently undergone significant law reform. This was rather unfortunate.

(vi) Governmental objectives

Finally, an objective of government is to maintain itself functioning properly and efficiently. For this purpose, many laws and practices are adopted. This was manifested in the work *Zhou-guan* (周官 *The Offices of the Zhou*) where numerous government agencies, which supposedly existed in the Zhou Dynasty, were listed with detailed descriptions of their responsibilities.[120] In later dynasties, countless laws were made to create government offices and regulate their work.[121] In the Qing there were about thirty central government offices, twenty provinces and special regions, hundreds of circuits and prefectures, and over a thousand districts, all administered by civil officials. *The Compendium of Qing Laws* includes thousands of statutes, substatutes, regulations, ordinances, imperial edicts, and judicial precedents spelling out the structures and functions of these agencies.[122] Then there were several sets of laws specifically to guide the proper operation of various government offices, particularly those administered by *Li-bu* (吏部 Ministry of Civil Service), establishing standards and procedures for appointment of all civil officials, defining each official's responsibilities, evaluating his performance, promoting, demoting, dismissing, rewarding, disciplining him or referring a criminal case to *Xing-bu* (刑部 Ministry of Criminal Affairs) for punishment; those administered by *Bing-bu* (兵部 Ministry of Military Affairs), did the same for military officers; and those administered by the *Du-cha-yuan* (都察院 Grand Censorate), stipulated the procedural rules for the censors to impeach all officials and officers.[123] These laws, and their equivalents in all the previous dynasties, were administrative in nature and were of great importance because tens of thousands of officials and officers, working in a very large territory on a myriad of tasks, had to be placed under the effective control of the central government. Throughout most periods of Chinese history, the civilian part of the governing machine performed reasonably well, though many officials were corrupt and abusive. The military was more corrupt and often incompetent but not many large-scale uprisings led by officers occurred. This fact indicates that governmental objectives had been largely achieved.

While such administrative control over officials and officers was necessary, it was not emphasised by the thinkers except Mozi and the Legalists. Mozi proposed a bureaucratic hierarchy in which an official was strictly to follow the commands of an immediate superior and thus the entire bureaucracy would follow the command of the Son of Heaven. The way to help achieve this was to demand that everyone in the country should report disobedience. The Legalists adopted this idea and carried it out with rigour. Gongsun Yang punished aristocrats who resisted his orders. Han Fei suggested to rulers various tactics with which to spy on possibly disloyal officials. In later times, as mentioned above, multitudes of laws were made to keep officials under control. In the Qing, an official was constantly under surveillance and could be disciplined or punished for so many acts proscribed by the *Li-bu chu-fen ze-li* (吏部處分則例 disciplinary rules and precedents of the Ministry of Civil Affairs) that he was said to be like a glass partition which could be shattered by a slight touch of the hand.[124]

This system of control had a drawback: it inhibited initiative. Fearing that any unorthodoxy would bring impeachment, officials stuck to the well-trodden path even though it might lead to impasse or even disaster. This caused stagnation, even paralysis, a phenomenon often seen in traditional Chinese government.

(c) Bases of law

Having looked at the objectives of the traditional legal system, we now turn our attention to law itself. First, on what bases should law be made? The Legalists argued for the wisdom of a sage ruler; the Daoists the law of nature; Mozi divine will; the Ruists morality and custom. Throughout history these ideas competed. But most people of later times took a more common-sense view, believing that law should be based on *tian-li* (天理 natural reason) and *ren-qing* (人情 human feelings) and say *fa-lü bu-wai ren-qing* (法律不外人情 Law is not beyond human feelings). Some rulers also had this view. Emperor Jing of the Han Dynasty 漢景帝 (r 156–141 BCE) decreed that a decision should be revised if, though in accordance with a law, it violated human feelings.[125] According to an edict of Emperor Tai-zong of the Tang Dynasty 唐太宗 (r 627–649) to judicial officials, the way to administer criminal justice was to find a reasonable resolution before making a decision in law.[126] Emperor Tai-zu of the Ming Dynasty 明太祖 (r 1368–1402) ordered that, in deciding cases where persons in any of the five closest relationships (ruler/subject, parent/child, husband/wife, brothers and friends) were involved, regular law should be modified, yielding to reason and human feelings.[127] Because of such imperial instructions, many statutes were adopted through the dynasties providing sympathetic treatment towards minors, seniors, women and the infirm.

A more troublesome problem was raised in cases of revenge killing (復仇 *fu-chou*). Such killings were common in ancient China. How did people feel about them? How should they be handled? A number of such cases were reported in the *Chun-qiu*, some attracting praise, others censure. In one instance, the *Gongyang zhuan* (公羊傳 *Commentary on Chun-qiu* by Gongyang) states that a son is not a son if he does not take revenge on his father's killer; in another instance, it asserts that, where the father is not given a death sentence and is wrongly killed, the son can avenge the death but, where the father is liable, the son should not.[128] During the Han Dynasty, there were cases where the avengers were sentenced to death and then pardoned.[129] The Wei Dynasty (220–264) prohibited revenge killing but the law was not accepted in later times.[130] These facts demonstrated a conflict between Ruist and Legalist thinking.

During the Tang Dynasty a debate broke out over two cases. In the reign of Empress Wu, a man was killed by the order of a magistrate. The man's son murdered the magistrate and surrendered himself to the authorities. An official, named Chen Ziang 陳子昂, suggested that the son be executed according to the law and honoured posthumously for his filial piety.[131]

The suggestion was accepted but, more than a century later, another official, Liu Zongyuan 柳宗元, exposed its irrationality of the suggestion and argued that the murderer should be either executed if the father was put to death lawfully or honoured if his father was wrongfully killed.[132] In 811, again a man murdered his father's killer and surrendered. Emperor Xian-zong 唐憲宗 (r 806–820) ordered a conference of high officials to deliberate on a decision. One of them, Han Yu 韓愈, pointed out that, while the classical canons and historical records were inconsistent, the law was conspicuously silent. He then argued that it was not that the law overlooked the problem; it was rather that, if it prohibited revenge killing, it would break the heart of a grieving son and ignore the teaching of the early kings about filial piety. But, if the law explicitly permitted revenge killing, people would use the law to justify murder, and there would be no way to stop such killings. The reason behind the absence of a provision against repeated revenge killings, Han Yu maintained, was to require regular judicial officials to sentence a killer according to the existing law proscribing murder, and let higher officials deliberate on whether a special act of mercy, in the form of an imperial pardon, could be considered. Thus, Han Yu did not recommend a substantive law solution to the problem but a procedural one. It relieved judicial officials of the responsibility of making a satisfactory decision and shifted it to others who, Han Yu suggested at the end of his argument, should be those in the chief minister's office with a deep understanding of high principles and human feelings.[133]

It is obvious that none of the three officials was clear in his own mind how the conflict between faithful application of law and careful consideration of human feelings should be solved. Chen's solution was most muddled; Liu made application of law contingent on certain facts, which could be difficult to ascertain; Han's suggestion only went a step further in the judicial process and left the outcome in the dark just as before.

While thinkers could debate, those with judicial responsibilities had to act. They found Han's suggestion the easiest to follow. Once it was accepted, requests for special consideration by high authorities were not limited to revenge killings but allowed in many other cases where strict application of law was questionable. The procedure was inevitably overused as judicial officials found it safer to kick the problem upstairs. In some periods, the practice was more restricted but never abandoned. In fact, many emperors indulged in giving special reviews of serious cases and, in the Ming and Qing dynasties, laws were adopted that made such reviews mandatory in all capital cases.

This development, though unsatisfactory, was a Ruist success in their efforts to soften the harsh effects of the Legalist theory. The classical canons, *Chun-qiu*, *Li-ji* and *Zhou-li*, cited by the three Tang officials were all Ruist works, and the officials were all famous Ruists.

(D) Proliferation of laws and its remedies

A conspicuous feature of the development of the Chinese legal system was the rapid proliferation of laws. As the king of the state of Qin, Ying Zheng inherited many laws and made many more. Qin documents, unearthed by recent archaeological projects, show an astonishing array of statutes of his time regulating in amazingly detailed ways people's everyday lives: for instance, when and under what condition a peasant was allowed to borrow farm tools and other objects from the local government.[134] As the First Emperor, Ying Zheng initiated numerous new nation-building measures mentioned earlier. In addition, he took unusual steps in establishing a social order that was to his liking, including punishing men engaging in petty commerce or marrying into wives' families, by sending them into battle or building huge new palaces and the Great Wall and other public works alongside convicts and slaves hundreds of thousands in number.[135] For all these, and other measures, laws were needed and, to ensure complete control of the people, he wanted to make law not just the supreme norm but the only one. In 213, the eighth year after ascending the imperial throne, he approved a proposal of Li Si 李斯, the chief minister, to ban the *si-xue* (私學 private learning) of scholars who hailed the principles and practices of the past and criticised his government, to burn the historical records of all states other than the Qin and copies of *Shang-shu* and *Shi-jing* kept in private collections, to execute those who discussed these two works and to encourage the learning of law from the officials.[136]

It is clear that the First Emperor was influenced by the Legalists. It was their knee-jerk reaction to a problem: slap it with a law. But his multitude of laws did not help uphold his empire for long. In fact, during his reign, crime increased, forcing him to hear cases during the day and write decisions in the night, dispensing cruel sentences that made convicts overfilled the prisons, and those to be sent into exile and hard labour formed endless lines on the road. Soon after his death, large-scale rebellions broke out. His son carried on the dreadful rule for less than three years, issuing ever more laws and inflicting harsher punishments, and then the dynasty was toppled. It was unfortunate that neither of them had learned from Laozi that, where there are more laws, there will be more crimes, and when people are no longer afraid of death, the death penalty will cease to be a deterrent.

Most Qin laws were abolished by Liu Bang who replaced them with only three simple principles — those who murdered were to die and those who maimed or robbed were to be appropriately punished. His example was followed by founders of all subsequent dynasties who gained the throne after devastating wars. For instance, the first emperor of the Tang Dynasty (618–906) abolished the criminal code of the Sui Dynasty (581–617) and promulgated only twelve provisions punishing murderers, armed robbers, deserters, and rebels.[137] But those simple rules were not enough. When the government wanted to have more control over the people, it increased the number of laws and relied on them in disregard of other norms. Thus, shortly after proclaiming himself emperor, Liu Bang ordered the creation of a set of rites and a penal code. The code was still relatively simple, consisting of nine chapters of *lü* (律 statutes). But we note that it rapidly ballooned. In the following dynasties, the number of statutes remained more or less the same but numerous substatutes, known as *ling* 令, *ge* 格, *shi* 式, *zhang-cheng* 章程, *ze-li* 則例, and so on, were added to supplement, explain, or even substitute the statutes. Often, a specific substatute was adopted for a particular time, place or case. Moreover, countless judicial precedents, known as *jue-shi-bi* 決事比 or *shi-li* 事例, were made binding. The last edition of *Da Qing Hui-dian Shi-li* (大清會典事例 *The Compendium of the Qing Laws and Precedents*), published in 1899, recorded innumerable laws, precedents and imperial edicts, filling 1,220 volumes, each with hundreds of pages.[138]

In addition to the laws promulgated by the central government, lower authorities, from provincial governors to district magistrates, regularly issued regulations and ordinances to adapt the statutes and substatutes for application in the areas concerned and, in some cases, to fill gaps left by the imperial laws or to deal with special local problems. Such bylaws were voluminous. As an example, *Xi-jiang zheng-yao* 西江政要, a late nineteenth-century compilation of the ordinances of Jiangxi province, one of the smallest, has 131 volumes, totalling over 4,300 pages.[139]

Many efforts were made to address this problem of proliferation. First, laws were frequently pruned to get rid of redundant ones. Second, laws were periodically codified. Codification was a process by which laws were organised into a theoretical and practical system. In this process, the codifiers would scrutinise each existing law to find its rationale and justification and then fit related laws into a coherent structure. As a result, the number of laws which were included was significantly reduced. The first known codification was accomplished by Li Kui 李悝 (455–395 BCE), a minister of the state of Wei 魏, who selected from a large number of laws of the various states of the Chun-qiu and the Warring States periods certain significant ones and organised them into a work known as

Fa-jing (法經 *Canon of Law*) consisting of only six chapters, on robbery, mayhem, various other crimes, arrest, trial, and assessment of punishments.[140] After that the laws were periodically codified. The total number of basic statutes was only five hundred in both the Tang and the Song codes, 606 in the Ming Code, and 436 in the Qing Code.[141] But, after each codification, substatutes in various names were immediately adopted and soon exploded into tens of thousands, though they were supposed only to make the statutes clearer and were mostly deleted in the next codification. Thus, the pruning and codification had to be repeated periodically.

(E) Inadequacy of law and its remedies

The proliferation of law was astounding, yet laws were never adequate. There are two reasons for this, one peculiar to the Chinese legal system, the other more common. In China, law was considered to be a low norm primarily to proscribe antisocial and politically incorrect activities. Regulation of ordinary interactions between people was left to rites, custom and rules made by the people of various civil groups, that were believed to have deeper roots in human feelings, reason and shared experience. A very small number of rules, governing family relations and property, were turned into laws because violation of them could be seriously disruptive to the social order and therefore liable to criminal punishment, but there was not a body of comprehensive laws governing civil matters.

The other, more common reason for the inadequacy of law is jurisprudential. To be effective, law should be neither too general nor too specific. When too general, like Liu Bang's three principles, many things are left unregulated; when too specific, like the laws of later times, people will have difficulty in knowing and observing them. In the latter instance, law can be inadequate because a very specific law will be inapplicable to a case where the facts are slightly different from those for which the law was made and, needless to say, no law-maker can foresee all possible situations that need to be regulated. This problem was recognised in ancient times. In *Shang-shu* there is a chapter "Lü-xing" (呂刑 The Penal Law of Lord Lü) about criminal justice of the Zhou Dynasty. It pointed out that there were many crimes of a similar nature liable to various types and degrees of punishment, and then suggested *shang-xia bi-zui* (上下比罪 to compare the heavier and lighter punishments): when a punishment is too heavy for a crime, it should be reduced; when a punishment is too light for a crime, it should be increased.[142] Li Kui in *Fa-jing* included a chapter "Ju-lü" (具律 rules for application of law) which was, in later dynasties, renamed "Ming-li" (名例 terms and examples). It more specifically included a provision allowing judges to compare a case at hand, which was not clearly governed by a law, with a similar case that was, and make an appropriate decision.[143] But this rule did not really solve the problem because the comparison could be very difficult. Therefore, in the time of Emperor Wu of the Han, many difficult cases were sent by the emperor to Dong Zhongshu for an opinion. Dong did not bother to make any comparison but suggested decisions based on principles he found in the Classics, particularly *Chun-qiu* which was supposedly the annals of the state of Lu, but, in it, major historical events were not reported straightforwardly as facts but stated as what should be seen in the point of view of its editor – Confucius. Thus, initially, a syllabus Confucius used to teach the moral lessons he found in history was now used by Dong to justify his decision on concrete cases. In many instances, where applicable laws were non-existent or inequitable, his opinions were reasonable and well received.[144] This practice of resorting to higher principles in addressing the inadequacy or defects of law was often used in later times. Many judges were proud of being able to do so but it made decisions unpredictable because the Classics were inconsistent and even a single text was open to different interpretations. This, of course, invited severe criticism from the Legalists.

More troublesome than actual inadequacy was a perceived one. In this view, even where there was an apparently relevant law, it could never be readily used in making a correct decision. This view was more or less shared by most thinkers except the Legalists. We recall Shuxiang held this view and Zichan disagreed. A very serious debate over how faithfully law should be observed took place during the reign of Emperor Wu of the Western Jin Dynasty 晉武帝 (r 265–289). Zhang Fei 張斐, an official in charge of legal education, argued that, while the *li* (理 reasons) on which cases were to be decided could be very complicated and profound, law could reflect them only in rather simple ways. Therefore, in deciding a case, a judge could not just look at the letter of the law; he had to consider the facts and circumstances in fine detail and ponder the reasons that should be followed before determining whether and how a law could be applied.[145] This argument, an echo of Shuxiang's criticism of Zichan's attempt to make law a readily useable objective tool in making judicial decisions, justified the decision-maker's discretionary power. It was welcomed by judges of the time, and they produced widely divergent decisions. It was also favoured by Emperor Hui 惠帝 (r 290–306) who loved making ad hoc decisions himself that were *qu-dang* (曲當 perfectly fitting) to the facts and circumstances.[146]

Many high officials objected, however. Pei Wei 裴頠, a minister, argued that, indeed, because laws were limited in number, there were instances where profound reasoning had to be resorted to in deciding exceptional cases but this should not be made a regular practice.[147] Liu Song 劉頌, another minister, pointed out that, as a principle, *kan-ren she-jiao* (看人設教 observe a person and devise a lesson specifically for him) was fine but it was the job of a law-maker. If it was followed by judges, their decisions could differ widely, giving people inconsistent, even conflicting, directions. Further, while some ad hoc decisions might be equitable, more could be prejudicial. Therefore, he suggested that: 1. in a case where there was a relevant law, the judge must apply it; 2. in the absence of such a law, the judge should decide according to a general principle in *Ming-li*; 3. if no general principle was available, the case should be dismissed outright; 4. where a law could be construed in different ways, law officials in the central government should debate it within the framework of the legal system as a whole but not outside of it, making extralegal arguments, and their opinions should then be reviewed by the ministers before recommending a solution to the emperor who could take into consideration other factors important to society and the state and, if necessary, make a *fei-chang zhi duan* (非常之斷 extraordinary decision).[148]

These suggestions were ignored but the question was raised again in the Eastern Jin Dynasty during the reign of Emperor Yuan 晉元帝 (r 317–322) by another official, Xiong Yuan 熊遠, who rebuked Zhang Fei's argument and stated that, theoretically, law did not reflect *miao-dao* (妙道 abstruse, esoteric principles) which could be construed in different, sophisticated ways; rather, it was *cu-shu* (粗術 rough, broad measures) based on common characteristics of things to make them conform to some general rules. Therefore, one who made strenuous efforts to reach a decision that fitted a case was not applying law, he was deciding in disregard of it. Xiong Yuan then pointed out that, practically, when there were too many such decisions by high authorities, the lower judges would be confused, not knowing which one to follow. They would repeatedly request instructions from above and, as a result, leave many cases not adjudicated. For this reason, he went a step further, suggesting that all officials should apply law faithfully; only the emperor was to *kai-sai sui-yi* (開塞隨宜 clear up obstructions and follow what is appropriate) and *quan-dao zhi-wu* (權道制物 consider the Way in regulating things).[149] In short, he recognised the fact that, in some circumstances, laws could be inadequate, and he sensibly conceded that someone had to make up the deficit. Who would be the right person? Xiong Yuan could think of none other than the emperor. Regrettably, his arguments gave further support for the dictatorial power of the throne but, to him and all other intellectuals employed by the government, an independent judiciary was unthinkable. We recall that, hundreds of years later in the Tang Dynasty, this debate was renewed in revenge killing cases. It shows that the issue had still not been settled. But Han Yu's suggestion, which was basically the same as Xiong Yuan's, was, in later times, more generally followed, and it was turned into law in the Ming and the Qing dynasties such that all capital cases had finally to be decided by the emperor.

It was not a satisfactory solution. Realising this, some people took a different approach. They tried to solve as many as possible of the problems affecting their lives not dealt with or unsatisfactorily dealt with by law. Since ancient times, they had created many rules for the family, the village, and various other social groups. Together with local customs, these rules regulated problems arising from relationships between people (marriage, divorce, inheritance, interactions between men and women, senior and junior, superior and inferior . . .) and from people's relationship with property (ownership, sale, purchase, mortgage, lease, loan, debt, interest. . .). Most of these rules had been created with the help of learned men, many of them Ruists. As long as these rules did not conflict with law, they were tolerated, even supported by the government because the help offered by these organisations in maintaining order lessened the workload of the authorities. This was important because, despite its ambitions, the traditional Chinese government was small, with inadequate manpower and resources to exercise complete control over society.[150] The rules of the various social groups were generally well implemented. Many such groups solved internal disputes without litigation, and helped maintain local peace and order for hundreds of years. This fact proved that law was never the only norm. The other norms, based on ideas and ideals of Ruists and other thinkers, worked far more comprehensively and effectively, creating a civil society alongside the government. While governments came and went, this society remained largely unchanged and functioned well enough so that China, despite its periodic convulsions, has been in existence arguably as the longest surviving civilisation of distinction on earth.

(F) Implementation of law

The actual implementation of law was never easy, and the judicial process was always complicated. When there was a breach of a law, the first problem was to determine the facts. The authorities welcomed the reporting of crimes. Gongsun Yang made this a legal responsibility for everyone. It was an onerous burden and would cause general distrust. Confucius maintained that close relatives should be allowed to conceal each other's offences. In the early Han Dynasty, a law it inherited from the Qin Dynasty, punishing neighbours as well as relatives who failed to report, was abolished except in cases of crimes against the state or the throne. Unfortunately, this exception was often used to implicate hundreds of thousands of innocent people in campaigns against political enemies of a new regime, such as the Han under Emperor Gaozu, the Tang under Empress Wu and the Ming under Emperor Taizu.

The second but more serious problem was to decide who was to conduct the trial and how. Since ancient times, China had had officials in the central government who specialised in hearing criminal cases. In a feudal state, or a district directly under the control of the central government, the chief executive official doubled as the judge. The sovereign ruler, attracted to an extraordinary case, might intervene and make the final decision. Many rulers loved this prerogative and abused it. The first emperor of Qin was an egregious example. Another was Emperor Taizong of the Song 宋太宗 (r 976–997). When it was suggested that a monarch should not be involved in making small criminal decisions, he disagreed, saying that, if he refrained from reviewing small cases, problems below would not be corrected. Once, believing a judge had made a mistake, he declared: "We regret not being able to hear all cases from all parts of the empire!"[151] Even Emperor Tai-zong of the Tang 唐太宗 (r 627–649), widely admired for his enlightened and benevolent rule, ordered the execution of Zhang Yungu 張蘊古, a judge, whom he thought guilty of distorting the law. Shortly afterwards, he discovered his mistake and, with profound remorse, initiated the procedure of *san-fu-zou* (三覆奏 reporting a death sentence three times for imperial reconsideration before it is finalised). This procedure was institutionalised in the Qing Dynasty.[152]

Such immediate interventions were exceptional. More commonly, an emperor would make a decision only after a case had been reviewed by high judicial officials. In a famous Northern Song Dynasty example, a woman named A Yun 阿云 surrendered herself after learning that her failed attempt to kill her fiancé had been exposed. Emperor Shenzong 神宗 (r 1068–1085) repeatedly ordered her death sentence reviewed by the central judicial officials, censors, ministers and grand counsellors, and, following their different and conflicting recommendations, changed relevant laws twice before finally, in 1070, making a personal decision to reduce the woman's sentence. But sixteen years later, in 1085, the case was reopened and debated. Eventually Emperor Zhezong 哲宗 (r 1086–1100) reversed the decision and rescinded the reduction.[153]

Some emperors used as an excuse for their intervention the negligence of high officials in carrying out their judicial responsibilities. As early as the Han Dynasty, there were reports that high officials often left their work to their subordinates, clerks and private assistants.[154] Indeed, there were reasons supporting the reports. First, there were just too many laws for an ordinary person to grasp. Second, after the collapse of the Qin Dynasty, study of law went out of fashion and the situation was aggravated by the examination system begun in the Tang Dynasty. Third, at every level of government, its head had executive, military as well as judicial responsibilities, and the first two were generally considered more important.

To help the overburdened officials, a group of specialists emerged. They were intellectuals who had failed to get formal government appointments. As an alternative, they studied law and sought employment as clerks and private secretaries assisting officials to keep records and use them in drafting legal opinions and decisions.[155] Though thus being significant participants of the judicial process, they were generally belittled for not being versed in the Classics, for being narrow-minded and short-sighted, capable of noticing *dao-zhui zhi mo* (刀錐之末 the finest points of law) but *bu-shi da-ti* (不識大體 unable to comprehend the great principles of government). More specifically, they were accused of abusing their expertise in law by choosing or disregarding certain provisions or precedents in order to bring about the results they preferred. Studies of Chinese legal history show that there were, indeed, cases improperly handled in this way by such law specialists.[156] Attempting to solve this problem, many an emperor ordered heads of regional governments regularly to review all cases decided by lower judges, report their decisions to the central judiciary, and send all capital cases to him for final decision. But such orders were meaningless as long as the above-listed causes for official negligence were not actually addressed.

The trouble with emperors intervening in the judicial process was compounded where they doubled as prosecutors. In every dynasty, there were cases known as *Zhao-yu* (詔獄 trials ordered by the throne), most of them against political offenders. The founding emperors of the Han and the Ming dynasties had practically all their revolutionary comrades tried and executed. In such cases, most trial judges could hardly challenge the emperor's position but do as Du Zhou 杜周 did. In cases without major political implications, however, there were some extraordinary judges, such as Zhang Shizhi 張釋之, who refused the instruction of Emperor Wen of the Western Han to punish severely a person who unintentionally scared the horse the Emperor was riding. In an especially interesting case, a slave of Princess Hu-yang 湖陽公主, a sister of Emperor Guangwu of the Eastern Han 東漢光武帝 (r. 25–57), murdered a person in broad daylight and was given shelter by the princess. One day, when the princess came out of her palace with the slave in the retinue, Dong Xuan 董宣, the magistrate of the capital city, stopped the procession, upbraided the princess for her wrongdoing, arrested the slave and executed him on the spot. After the emperor, in a fury, ordered his death, Dong Xuan smashed his head against a pillar in the presence of the emperor and the princess in an effort to commit suicide but was saved by court attendants. He was then ordered to apologise to the princess but he refused. When the attendants forced him to kneel and pressed his head down to kowtow, he pushed his upper torso up with his hands on the ground, his arms straight and his head unbowed. The princess sneered at her brother, pointing out that, as a warrior, he had killed countless enemies in battles but, as emperor, he was unable to subdue a mere magistrate. The emperor laughed, saying that an emperor was different from a warrior, and told the attendants to let the *qiang-xiang ling* (強項令 the stiff-necked magistrate) go.[157] This story was widely circulated and repeatedly told throughout later periods. It was because such a case of a judicial official standing up against the power of an emperor intervening in a criminal case was extremely rare.

In later times, the emperors, with more and more power concentrated in their hands, were more authoritarian. During the Song Dynasty, some officials apparently refused to implement Emperor Huizong's *yu-bi* on the grounds that they conflicted with established laws. Incensed, he issued an order condemning them for *da-bu-gong* (大不恭 great disrespect to the throne),[158] one of *shi-e* crimes punishable by death. In the Ming Dynasty, some intellectuals, who objected to Emperor Taizu's *da-gao*, disfigured themselves to avoid serving in his government. In response, the irate monarch enacted a law imposing death on all intellectuals who refused his appointments.

While ordinary judges were subservient to the imperial will, many of them abused their judicial power independently. According to observers, numerous judicial officials through the dynasties were guilty of this offence. Gongsun Yang was notorious and many judges of later times were known as *ku-li* (酷吏 cruel officials). Generally, lower officials tended to give harsher sentences because, by law, judges would be punished for wrong decisions and, in practice, the punishment for being too lenient was much more severe than that for being too harsh,[159] although there were well-recognised principles against this practice,[160] and a law in the Tang Code that sanctioned exactly the opposite.[161] Why were many judges so vicious and cruel? According to a Tang observer, it was not that they were by nature merciless or enjoyed hurting people, they were merely following the examples of those above in order to save themselves.[162]

Then, were emperors and high officials cruel by nature? Some probably were; more were brutalised by absolute power. How could they justify their actions? The only theory they could use was that of the Legalists. Gongsun Yang saw nothing wrong with harsh punishments because, he said, a correct ruler should regard all subjects as *jian-min* (姦民 wicked people). Many particularly cruel emperors and officials must have shared this view with him. In fact, because of this view, torture to extract confession from suspects was legalised and specific instruments of torture were prescribed by law. When torture was allowed, its abuse was inevitable. A *ku-li* won his sobriquet mainly because he inflicted torture and extraordinary punishments. But he would seem benign in comparison to some emperors whose ill-temper knew no bounds. Many of them ordered *peng* (烹 boiling), *yao-zhan* (腰斬 sever at the waist), *ling-chi* (凌遲 slow death by multiple cuts) for those they convicted. While giving an audience, Emperor Wen of the Sui Dynasty 隋文帝 (r 589–604) and Emperor Taizu of the Ming Dynasty often ordered high officials stripped and beaten for minor offences, killing many of them right in the imperial court.[163] Even the much admired Emperor Taizong of the Tang Dynasty had Lu Zushang 盧祖尚, a provincial governor, beheaded in the court for disobeying an imperial decree.[164] Atrocities such as these were not committed even by the First Emperor of the Qin. The only explanation was that further concentration of power in later times corrupted even the best rulers. But Han Fei did say that, when a ruler executes a subject, there is no need for justification. Above all, he, like Gongsun Yang, had a grander argument: severe punishments against minor offences would effectively deter all offences and eventually make punishment unnecessary. In his more animated language: people stumble over a lump of earth but never over a mountain.

But, in good conscience, one, even a strict adherent to Legalist theories, has to admit that laws can be misapplied and wrongly enforced. Traditionally, there was a number of remedies. First of all, serious cases were routinely reviewed by higher officials. In the Han Dynasty, cases of prisoners awaiting execution were periodically re-examined in a process known as *lu-qiu* (錄囚 checking the records of prisoners) in order finally to decide whether the sentences should be carried out. The practice continued throughout later dynasties and, in the Qing, it was institutionalised and called *qiu-shen* (秋審 autumn assizes) because it was conducted in the autumn. A decision reached by an assembly of practically all the high officials in the central government confirming a death sentence would then be presented to the emperor on three different days for the imperial act of *gou* (勾checking off). If the prisoner was not checked off for execution, he was to remain in prison until the next autumn assizes.[165]

Besides the automatic reviews, a case could be appealed. In theory, a dissatisfied party should appeal to the immediate superior of the trial judge and then to the officials at higher levels of the judicial structure but, in practice, people often went immediately to higher authorities in acts known as *yue-su* (越訴 an appeal skipping the proper steps). In some extreme cases, some would do *jing-kong* (京控appealing to the judicial offices in the capital), *kou-hun* (叩閽 knocking on the palace door) and *ying-che-jia* (迎車駕 greeting the imperial carriage) to file their appeals. Such a case would normally be referred to a superior official for complete retrial, and the result could be appealed again until a final decision was made by the emperor.[166]

When a superior official found the decision of a subordinate incorrect, he could amend it or, in a criminal case, rescind it and set the convict free, or deliver a sentence heavier or lighter than the original. His decision, again, would be reviewed and could be appealed.

When the emperor disapproved of a decision in a serious criminal case, he could exercise the imperial prerogative of commuting the sentence or pardoning the convict. This practice was generally accepted in cases where strict application of rigid laws placed the decisions in conflict with reason and human feelings. We have seen this in cases of revenge killings. In addition, since ancient times, a criminal could be pardoned or granted commutation if his offence was committed owing to a mistake or some unfortunate circumstances on the grounds that he did not do it intentionally. In the early Zhou, pardons began to be regularly granted to offenders who were very young, very old, mentally retarded or physically disabled, on the assumption that they were incapable of making correct judgements and therefore lacked criminal intent or ability to carry out the criminal act.[167] In later times, when law became more rigid, prescribing commutation of the death penalty for everyone guilty of murder, even in cases of *xi-sha* (戲殺 killing of a playmate in a game), *wu-sha* (誤殺 killing a bystander in a fight) and *shan-sha* (擅殺 unauthorised killing of a criminal) was more frequently granted. A person convicted of such a crime would be given a *xu-ni si-zui* (虛擬死罪 nominal death penalty) and kept in prison for years before his sentence was routinely reduced to exile.[168]

Besides commutations and pardons granted to individuals, there were general amnesties which were of an entirely different nature. Amnesty exonerated all convicts and stopped the prosecution of an act committed before it was pronounced a crime. Instead of being a remedy for an inequity in the law or a mistake in the judicial process, it was a personal favour from the emperor conventionally given on special occasions, such as the establishment of a new dynasty, the death of an emperor, the crowning of a new emperor, the birth of a crown prince, the birthday of the emperor or the empress or the empress dowager, a victorious military campaign, a natural disaster such as an earthquake, an appearance of an unusual phenomenon such as a solar eclipse or a gathering of certain rare birds in the imperial court, and so on. In 231 years, the Western Han Dynasty granted ninety-nine amnesties, fewer than one every two years. Emperor Hui of the Northern Song Dynasty issued seventy-seven in twenty-five years. Emperor Gaozong of the Southern Song Dynasty announced four in a single year, 1194.[169] Some dynasties were more conservative, but none avoided this practice.

How was the practice justified? It seemed that, after an extended period of disorder resulting from natural or man-made disasters that pulled asunder social fabrics and forced ordinary people into activities that could not be simply judged as lawful or unlawful, an amnesty was an acceptable way to wipe the slate clean and enable the people to start afresh. In ordinary times, a general amnesty would not have that effect. Rather, it disrupted the judicial process. Frequent and frivolous amnesties caused even greater harm. There would be a belief that criminals would not be brought to justice, and, if they were, their punishments would soon be commuted. Crimes would proliferate and recidivism rise. The judicial system would be paralysed and made a mockery.[170]

Why did the judicial system inflict such injury on to itself? It might have some genuine doubt about its own ability to achieve justice. But, to erase its own work entirely was certainly not the right way to improve it. The true reason was beyond that. It was arrogance on the part of the emperors who identified their personal interests with that of the state or, rather, made them superior. And they sometimes acted under the misconception that an amnesty was a demonstration of their benevolence towards the people. All these were expressed in high-sounding words with Ruist flavour. But those who drafted amnesty announcements obviously forgot that Confucius advocated only *she xiao-guo* (赦小過 forgive the small mistakes) and never supported unreasonable clemency.[171]

(G) "CONFUCIANISATION" OF THE LEGAL SYSTEM

From the brief analysis above, we can see that the followers of the eight classical thinkers competed for influence on the legal system. The head of the system, the sovereign ruler, had interests of his own which were basically to concentrate more power in his own hands and to strengthen his control over everyone else. It was up to him to choose the measures and theories that he thought would advance his agenda, and he usually found those suggested by the Legalists more effective in addressing immediate problems. But he also found it useful to practise the Daoist restraint on overaction after the country had suffered devastating wars, and even to perform the Mohist gesture of personally tilling farmland and living a frugal lifestyle when the country was recovering from those devastations. When order was restored and the economy rejuvenated, he discovered the utility of rites and paid lip service to Ruist teachings. Many, who would have been branded by Confucius as *xiao-ren ru*, rose to ingratiate themselves with the ruler by providing justifications for his actions which could be quite contrary to genuine Ruist principles. There were, as we mentioned, some *jun-zi ru* who heroically tried to restrain absolute power but many of them, realising that such efforts produced only transient results, decided to take a different approach. When Emperor Xuan of the Han Dynasty conscientiously tried to revamp the judicial system by appointing upright men to the highest tribunal and by personally reviewing serious cases, Zheng Chang 鄭昌, a provincial governor, pointed out in a memo that such measures could yield only some temporary, superficial improvements. For long-lasting, fundamental results, the law had to be improved.[172] This was the approach adopted by law-makers of later dynasties when the Ruist and the Legalist ideas increasingly mixed.

This approach consisted of several steps. First the law-makers identified the problems in the legal system, including proliferation of laws, arbitrariness of judicial decisions, and cruel punishments. Second, they argued against certain points in Legalist theory as the causes of those problems. Third, they suggested measures to fix some of them – revising some old laws, proposing some new ones and suggesting certain institutional and practical changes. Finally, and most importantly, after having convinced some more reasonable rulers, they had themselves appointed as members of codification commissions.

In ancient times laws were made known to people (at least those with government functions), and became publicised from 563 BCE when Zichan cast the law of the state of Zheng in bronze. But most of the laws made before the Tang Dynasty were lost.[173] Only the *Tang lü* (唐律 the Tang [basically criminal] laws) and *Tang liu dian* (唐六典 Tang administrative laws) survived *in toto*. The makers of these laws were men of action who helped establish the Tang Dynasty, together with erudite scholars. Their products became models for all later codes. The *Tang lü*, in particular, was hailed as an extraordinary achievement. Many of its features are remarkable. To begin with, the code's very first article prescribes only five lawful punishments – beating with light or heavy bamboo rods, penal servitude, banishment, and death. The implication is that all other punishments are not legal.

Second, some practices and principles, though they existed earlier, were regularised and spelled out explicitly. They included sending up to the throne for special consideration cases involving those known for their great virtue, talent, public achievements and those of particular aristocratic status; granting leniency for the old, the young, the infirm, and offenders who voluntarily surrendered; punishing persons guilty of multiple crimes only for the most serious one.[174]

Third, a host of procedural measures were created or emphasised, including: 1. a requirement that ordinary complaints be presented to the local authorities with an exception allowing those who suffered grave injustice for which no regular remedies were obviously available to bring their cases directly to the throne;[175] 2. a prohibition against anonymous accusation;[176] 3. provisions prescribing punishments against groundless accusations;[177] 4. provisions permitting mutual concealment of crimes other than rebellion and treason committed by close relatives and household members;[178] 5. a prohibition against requiring such persons to testify against each other;[179] 6. a command that judges consider thoroughly the facts, circumstances, reasons and human feelings involved in a case;[180] 7. a prohibition against judges probing into issues not specifically raised in a criminal complaint;[181] 8. a prohibition against requiring the very old [over eighty], the very young [under ten] and those seriously disabled or ill to give testimony;[182] 9. a requirement that judges hearing a case as a panel reach an agreement before ordering inquisitorial torture;[183] 10. a provision against using torture on the old [over seventy], the young [under fifteen] and the physically or mentally handicapped to obtain confession, allowing their cases be decided on the basis of multiple testimonies of witnesses;[184] 11. a prohibition against torturing pregnant women;[185] 12. provisions limiting torture on a suspect up to three times and two hundred blows of the bamboo rod, allowing the suspect to be released on bail if, after receiving the maximum torture, he still did not admit his guilt, and inflicting the same degree of torture on the complainant unless he was a victim of robbery or a relative of a murder victim;[186] 13. an authorisation for dismissal of a case where there was conflicting evidence, or for a replacement of the punishment with monetary redemption;[187] 14. a requirement of citing a specific law in a criminal decision;[188] 15. a provision prescribing punishments against law-enforcement officers coaching prisoners to recant their confession;[189] 16. permission for a judge in a criminal case, where there was no clearly applicable law, to use a law governing similar cases as reference in determining whether to impose on the defendant in the case at hand a punishment heavier or lighter than the punishment prescribed by that law;[190] 17. an allowance for high officials reviewing a case, where an applicable law was susceptible to different constructions, to state their different opinions separately;[191] 18. a demand that the tribunal obtain statements from both parties accepting its sentence;[192] 19. provisions on how punishments were to be executed;[193] 20. a set of rules prescribing in detail how cases of varying seriousness were to be decided and reviewed;[194] 21. a set of rules for delivery of prisoners to the reviewing offices;[195] and 22. provisions prescribing punishments against judicial officials who violated these procedural measures and made wrong decisions.[196] These provisions were obviously to guard against using criminal procedure to abuse those involved and to protect the innocent from being wrongly convicted. They evidently reflect a more rational and compassionate policy.

Though impressive, those measures were not all Tang innovations. Many of them were recognised in the past; for instance: the rule governing the trial; the making of a decision; and execution of punishments, including the famous principle of "rather than killing an innocent man, it is better to let a criminal go free", were recorded in *Shang-shu*.[197] *Zhou-li*, a work well known in the late Han, though not necessarily an authentic record of Zhou institutions, reports many procedural rules, some of them, such as those prescribing *wu-ting* (五聽 five methods of hearing a case), *san-ci* (三刺 three consultations before making final decisions), were even more detailed than those in the Tang code.[198] This fact indicates that the Tang procedural law was much influenced by the Ruist tradition in dramatic contradiction to the Legalist one which, as we may recall, required public denouncement or secret reporting of wrongdoing, denied mutual concealment of crimes by relatives, prescribed heavy punishment for minor offences, and logically allowed, though not explicitly prescribed, inquisitional torture. It was reported that Gongsun Yang, once as a judge reviewing criminal cases by the Wei River, ordered the execution of seven hundred prisoners in a single day, turning the water red.[199] The procedure he followed could not have been very strict or compassionate.

Finally there are some thirty provisions in the Tang Code that protect family values and punish offences committed by family juniors and inferiors against family seniors and superiors.[200] They, together with the few provisions mentioned above which bestow leniency to the elderly, and so on , were obviously introduced by the Ruists. Since the code had 502 provisions, the Ruist additions were small in number. Most other provisions were to maintain general public order and support government authority, an objective accepted by the Ruists and most thinkers except Zhuangzi. Such provisions must, in principle, have been in existence earlier. Indeed, though the laws of the Qin and earlier times have been largely lost, as have those of later periods prior to the Tang, yet many of the Tang provisions could be traced to remnants of some laws of the previous dynasties and to norms, particularly the rites practised since the Zhou. The emphasis on filial piety, for instance, was conspicuous in the Ruist Classics *Zhou-li* and *Li-ji*.

This fact prompted the prominent legal historian, Qu Tongzu 瞿同祖, to call the movement starting in the Han "the Confucianisation" of Chinese law.[201] But it must be pointed out that Confucius, Mencius and Xunzi all insisted on a certain reciprocity between people of different stations. It was the Legalists who advocated a one-sided relationship between people of senior/superior and the junior/inferior status. And it was Dong Zhongshu and other intellectuals who were effectively suppressed by the highly concentrated political power that supported the pernicious idea of *san-gang*. They were not true Confucians but petty Ruists.

And, besides, the Tang did not really transform the traditional substantive criminal laws according to Confucian ideology. Though the Tang Code outlawed cruel and unusual punishments, many of them were, in fact, allowed in practice, and the minimum punishment of beating with *chi* (笞 "the light bamboo rod") could easily cause death. Many offences were still liable to capital punishment, and collective penalty was sanctioned against political crimes and some other offences.[202] It is because of these facts that Shen Jiaben 沈家本, the Commissioner of Law Reform at the end of the Qing Dynasty, submitted a memo suggesting the abrogation of such laws which the Qing had inherited from the Tang.[203]

The truly significant achievement of the Tang codifiers was their effort to make all provisions in the code more in agreement with reason and human feelings. To this end, they produced a remarkable volume, *Tang-lü Shu-yi* (唐律疏議 Annotations to the Tang statutes). It explained the language of every provision and provided examples of its acceptable application, making the code an easily understandable and largely rational document. But, in some instances, the explanations could be rather tortuous because they were to justify arbitrary laws.

The best result of the rationalisation is seen in the procedural laws which were less subject to political considerations and ideological strictures but more to seek effectiveness in determining truth and in carrying out the fair and effective implementation of law. The effort to achieve these results had been in progress since ancient times but the Tang codifiers succeeded to a remarkable degree. As mentioned, many of the procedural rules institutionalised in the Tang Code are reasonable and humane, reflecting true Confucian ideas and rejecting the Legalist ones. But, even in this aspect, there are problems. The most damaging is the allowance of torture as a means to extract confession. Since ancient times there has been the saying, *san-mu zhi-xia he qiu bu-de* (三木之下何求不得 what statements cannot be obtained from a person under torture?)[204] Despite the many precautions the Tang Code prescribed, torture was apt to be misused or abused, not only by especially wayward officials recorded in the *ku-li-zhuan* (酷吏傳 biographies of cruel officials) but also by countless ordinary ones as reported by many observers.

It is therefore fair to say that the Tang codifiers, as well as those before and after them, did try to improve the legal system. They did not truly "Confucianise" it but many of them, being Ruists, only "Ruified" it, bringing into it some less significant Confucian ideas. The reasons are many, mainly as mentioned earlier, because the intellectuals who assisted the development of the legal system were suppressed by the increasingly concentrated political power which insisted on its prerogatives and privileges, discouraged legal education and research, burdened the law officials with non-legal responsibilities, and, most ironically, perverted the judicial process by instituting multiple reviews, giving those at the top the final say in too many cases.

(D) Recent situation

Thus the legal system became increasingly petrified and, finally, a more drastic reform was forced upon the Qing government by foreign powers which, after invading China, establishing colonies and seizing consular jurisdiction for their expatriates, demanded reform of the Chinese legal system to bring it in alignment with theirs as a condition for them giving up extraterritorial privileges.

The initial response from China was reluctant and superficial, mainly to address problems raised by the Western powers which, at that time, were mostly concerned with their commercial and missionary interests in China. In its haste to remove the consular jurisdiction, the Qing government repealed a few laws and bestowed upon the foreign powers a number of favourable concessions.[205] But such moves proved ineffective, and soon, a number of intellectuals in and out of the government began a more comprehensive review of traditional laws, institutions, practices and political and legal culture as a whole, and suggested various changes. The more conservative among them insisted on a principle of *zhong-xue wei-ti, xi-xue wei-yong* (中學為体, 西學為用 keeping Chinese culture as a basis, using Western culture as tools); the more radical ones argued for *quan-pan xi-hua* (全盤西化 total Westernisation). There is no evidence, however, that either group had sufficient knowledge of the West.

With assistance chiefly from Japanese legal scholars, the reformers managed to draft a new criminal code and several other laws, even including a constitution. But, before they had a chance to implement them, the Manchu Dynasty was toppled by the 1911 revolution. The Nationalists founded the Republic of China but, immediately, the country was embroiled in armed conflicts among the revolutionaries and warlords. The Nationalists prevailed in 1930 but soon Japan invaded and the Communists rebelled. After nearly half a century of bloody conflict and turmoil, the Nationalists were driven to Taiwan and the Communists established the People's Republic of China in 1949.

The Nationalists and the Communists both expressed their intention of creating a "new" China. They constructed different political systems based on Western models. Sun Wen 孫文 (alias Sun Yetsen 孫逸仙), the founder of the Nationalist Party and "the Father of the Republic of China", had traditional Chinese and Western educations and was evidently more knowledgeable of both cultures. His plans for the country, though revolutionary, were rational but there was never an opportunity for them to be implemented before the Nationalists were defeated by the Communists and moved to Taiwan in 1948. They brought with them the laws they made earlier but ruled the island under martial law for nearly four decades (1949–1987). Thereafter, the old laws have been revised and new laws made through a more democratic legislative process, taking into consideration both the Chinese tradition and the modern situation. The Communists saw little value in traditional Chinese culture and tried brutally to uproot it and change the country according to ideas advocated by Marx and Lenin. For a considerable period of time, the People's Republic of China was governed by orders issued from the Communist Party but soon laws proliferated. Recently, the government tried to stimulate nationalistic fervour by touting Confucianism, obviously a version advocated by the later Ruists.

(E) Summary, evaluation and suggestions

This study of the classic thinkers tries to show that they addressed many of the jurisprudential and philosophical issues raised in the preface and made remarkable contributions to both fields but also left us with a number of questions. I study them because of a belief that there is a lack of understanding of them which has impeded China's effort to develop a modern legal system. Here, I will first present a summary of my understanding of the Chinese legal tradition, initially articulated by these thinkers and developed by various people of later times, and a crude evaluation of some features of this tradition, and then offer some suggestions. As the summary will repeat what I have already stated earlier, I shall make it very brief. The evaluation and suggestions are, of course, made in the light of the present and from my own point of view.

The classic thinkers roughly fell into two camps, one positive the other negative about human ability and civilisation. Zhuangzi was the representative of the negative camp. His view that everything has a value in itself is remarkable. It promotes respect for the individual and puts an emphasis on freedom and tolerance. But his assertion that everything is relative leads to the conclusion that all human efforts are meaningless and invites some serious questions. An adherent to his theory may not care much about most things, including life and death, but what about illness and pain? Would he simply ignore these or would he hope that medicine could cure and alleviate them? What if he sees a child about to fall into a well? Would he be shocked and rush to its rescue? If medicine is desirable, wouldn't it be also true for other human inventions that could make life more tolerable? If sympathy is natural, wouldn't moral principles guiding human attitude and behaviour be useful? And besides individual human experience, was not human history a testimony of collective efforts to improve human life (though often being misguided and producing unfortunate results)? Mencius pointed out that each individual needed hundreds of others to provide for his basic needs. Could Zhuangzi deny this fact and honestly believe that humans can live like wild deer in a state of nature? If not, how could he sincerely propose the abolition of all artefacts, including the law? He, like the recluses, did not recognise these questions. But how could many ordinary people do so? It was apparently because of his silence on these questions that not many people were able to heed his advice of living an independent, free life, resisting power, wealth and other worldly attractions.

Laozi was problematic. Sima Qian was unable to pinpoint a particular person as Laozi. In *Laozi* there are at least two voices speaking, both using abstruse language, some similar to that of Zhuangzi, which is why a casual reader might easily think they are in the same school. But peruse the work more carefully and one finds that a larger portion of it shows a different and more dominant theme. It starts from a dismal regard for the ordinary people, believing that they could not live freely and happily in a state of nature. This Laozi thought that the chaos of his time was caused by them using their low intelligence. He disliked civilisation and wanted people to go back to a "small state" to live in peace. But that state was not devoid of artefacts; people would still keep many (carts, boats, and so on) but would not make use of them. Why would people refrain from using means that would enable them to make life easier? After civilisation had begun, could its progress be arrested, let alone reversed? Wasn't the "small state" a rather arbitrary stage in the course of social evolution? If so, then there is a problem in Laozi's theory. Why did he not, as Zhuangzi did, tell people to go all the way to a state of nature where they would live just like other animals? He dismissed human norms and exalted the law of nature, but what was that law? And why had people disobeyed it and fallen from a state of nature? He said it would take a true sage to get people to the "small state" but from where would such a sage emerge? He intimated that the sage would make people ignorant, lead them like sheep and, when they showed any sign of free will, promptly suppress it, but finally he stressed ruling without much ado. Wasn't all this talk preposterous? The ordinary people could not possibly follow his advice; it was welcomed by those who wanted to control them. He was thus, in fact, an activist, an advocator of dictatorial power poorly disguised as a nihilist, anarchist or primitivist.

Openly in the positive camp were all the other thinkers. The more blatant ones were Mozi and the Legalists. Mozi thought humans had free will and were wilful and therefore, when left alone, they would have different and conflicting opinions and would thereby cause disorder. He was sympathetic to the ordinary people who, in his view, were oppressed and exploited by those in power. Yet he alleged that, to escape from chaos, the people had to obey orders issued from a single source – a supreme ruler he called the Son of Heaven. Fearing abuse of power at the top, he argued that the ruler had to obey the will of Heaven. But what was it? He said that it was to help make the lives of the masses less harsh. Obviously, because he thought there were not enough resources to meet their basic needs, he wanted everyone to work extremely hard, live frugally and shun luxury, including rites and music. But could people endure this regime and what if they lapsed? He insisted that endure they must and, to ensure against lapses, everyone should spy on everyone else. But would this not cause universal suspicion, tear the social fabric asunder and make effective co-operation difficult if not impossible? And then if, by working hard and living in austerity, people succeeded in avoiding want, what did they have to look forward to in the future? He did not say. He argued for universal love, believing that it could help produce harmony. This is a teaching quite common to many religions, expressing a worthy feeling of compassion. But could anyone really ignore the distinction between one close to him and a complete stranger? If he could, wouldn't it be true that he actually loved no one, as was implied by Mencius when he likened Mozi to a beast? For these reasons, few, apart from a small number of true believers in his time, followed his ideas and ideals.

The Legalists were unashamed activists. They had a conviction that humans could control their own destiny. They pointed out that humans had to live in society according to certain rules and that, as society evolved because of changing conditions in itself (population growth being a crucial one) and in the environment, rules had to change accordingly. They acknowledged that rites had worked in the past but law had become more effective and necessary in their times and would be even more so in the future. They made significant contributions to jurisprudence in discussing what the law's bases and functions were, and how it should be made and enforced. But their theory had many problems. First, more than Laozi, they despised the common people whom they considered selfish and stupid. They, like Laozi, maintained that it was the fault of such people that the world fell into disorder and they could only be rescued by someone far superior to themselves. He was to overcome them with power, control them with tactics, and use laws as a hammer and anvil to beat them into tools to achieve his goals which were mainly to make the state rich and strong (and himself supreme). To achieve these goals the people have to be regimented, disciplined and driven to hard work; and, to prevent disobedience, they were required to report transgressions, and offenders were to be punished harshly. But what would people's lives be like after the state had become rich and strong? The Legalists offered no answer. Other problems in their theory include: 1. their insistence that law should not be the supreme, but the sole type of norm; 2. their assertion that law was merely the command of the sovereign, which could be applied automatically as an objective instrument to produce correct results, and enforced by punishments whose severity need not be proportional to the seriousness of the offence; and 3. their hypocrisy in maintaining equality under the law. Many of the Legalists' positions were roundly criticised by their contemporaries, most pointedly by Xunzi, the teacher of the prominent Legalists, Han Fei and Li Si. Nevertheless, their theory was welcomed by power-holders and became predominant.

Thus, here is a general and fair observation. Each of the theories mentioned above contains some truth and shows some wisdom. When their basic ideas and ideals are presented in moderate terms, they are reasonable and acceptable to many but, when pushed to the limit, they can appear perverse, erratic, unjustifiable, and even absurd. The reason behind such pushing was the desire of each of those more emotionally involved thinkers to distinguish himself and rebut the others.

The Ruists were under less pressure to do that. Confucius certainly was not. He was, by nature, "even-tempered, kind, respectful, modest and yielding"[206] and, indeed, we find in *Lun-yu* that he never took an extreme position. Mencius and Xunzi went too far in arguing that human nature was good and bad respectively;

Confucius said only that human nature was similar in all humans but could differ in individuals owing to different influences. Mencius called those who refused to recognise proper relationships between people "birds and beasts" but Confucius was never polemical, and Xunzi was also moderate. Generally, the three masters affirmed the value of the individual, society and civilisation, and pointed out realistic ways for the individual to develop his potential and help improve social conditions and civilisation. But they also had problems. Were their ideas and ideals too abstract, high-minded, and thus difficult to realise? Many of their contemporaries apparently thought so and, indeed, because they insisted on addressing very fundamental human issues before tackling specific tasks, their achievements in government were modest. A second problem with their theory arises from their relative, circumstantial ethics. The correct answer to the right or wrong of an action has to be determined by a standard particularly appropriate for the circumstances. Such a standard could be too profound for ordinary people to understand, and this requirement often caused bewilderment. A third problem relates to actual implementation of their ideas – they emphasised the rule of good men. Though, unlike the sage in Laozi's sense or the "average ruler" in Han Fei's parlance, their "good men" were not born as such but were products of a good education, such products were nevertheless not easy to come by. And what amounted to a good education was itself questionable. Confucius emphasised that it was based on the best of the civilisations before his time and capable of evolving alongside changing conditions; Mencius was somewhat metaphysical and mythical, arguing that goodness was inherent in human nature but he still warned people to learn how to ward off evil influences; Xunzi was less optimistic and emphasised rigorous learning and strict self-improvement. But this kind of education was not widely available to ordinary people, and even for those who had access to it, its effects were uncertain. For instance, rites were held as a crucial part of good education, because they could create a right atmosphere that could induce a right mood in which a right conduct could be produced. Therefore, rites were not mere formalities, but, evidently, the Ruist masters were unsuccessful in making this lesson clear enough, and most people, even many who were educated, missed the point. Similarly, they failed to make people see the crucial reciprocity in correct relationships between persons of different social status. Confucius's deference to the authorities was misinterpreted as obsequious servility; Mencius's teaching for people to stand up to those in power and Xunzi's advice for people to follow the Way, not merely the orders of the superiors, were thought impractical. For these reasons, their influence on the people of their times was not as great as they wished it to be.

After the time of the classic thinkers, China was unified under the Qin. Two new elements emerged that seriously affected the evolution of China's civilisation, particularly the legal system: first, the mixing of the theories of the classic thinkers; second, the more blatant interference by the rulers in the use and development of those theories.

The mixing of the theories reflected a psychological and intellectual need to explain the unification. Unfortunately, in addition to the theories of the eight thinkers which were mostly rational, many other ideas of a mystical and superstitious nature were brought in, among them most prominently the belief in *yin-yang wu-xing*, which, initially used as a conceptual tool to curb arbitrary power, was perverted and became a support for the Legalist idea of *san-gang* that adulterated classical Ruism and justified authoritarian rule. This belief also corrupted the ideas of Zhuangzi and the classic recluses and provided a cover for the pseudo-nihilist ideas and behaviour of intellectuals of the Wei and Jin dynasties, giving them a pretext by which to escape social responsibility. Further, this belief facilitated the creation of the Daoist religion and helped the spread of Buddhism. They, in turn, inspired *li-xue* or *dao-xue* of the Song and the Ming dynasties that largely turned the intellectuals inward-looking, avoiding ventures into the outside world to improve it.

But the greatest influence on the development of the theories and their implementation came from the power-holders of the Qin and subsequent dynasties. Besides their sheer will and actual power, they had the assistance of the intellectuals who, unlike farmers, craftsmen and merchants, did not engage in activities that made available materials to meet physical needs, and therefore had to be employed by those who had the resources and were willing to pay them for their services which were basically to manage the productivity and distribution of such materials. Since there was not much private business in early China, the management was basically a function of the government, and thus the intellectuals were all seeking government employment. In the time of the eight thinkers, when feudalism was still functioning, an intellectual could find many more-or-less independent regimes to offer him jobs. But, when the country was unified, intellectuals received offers only from a single source – the imperial government. As the choices became severely limited, the intellectuals had to compete for the favour of the emperor, the ultimate employer. When he was intelligent, fair and benevolent, they could do good deeds; when he was not, they, by and large, had to submit to his whims. This was how the emperors largely dictated government affairs, including, of course, the operation of the legal system, and influenced the theories justifying their actions.

Imperial influence was not absolute or entirely egocentric. After all, the interests of the emperor could not be completely in conflict with those of his subjects. Thus, when not insane, no emperor would want to harm himself by letting his desires run wild and destroy his own power base; he had to accept certain rules that kept society in order and, to a large extent, abide by them. For this reason, the people, especially the intellectuals, did have some influence on him. First, they helped formulate the rules – the various norms, including laws; second, they formed a formidable bureaucracy, purportedly to implement the laws, but which developed a weight of its own that even the emperor could not easily sway; third, perhaps most importantly, they created the civil society which effectively limited intrusion of government power into large areas of ordinary people's private lives in which the emperor had no direct interest.

Thus, the eight thinkers helped people consider many questions which were not merely abstract and academic but actually affected their lives. Their theories, and the further developments of those theories in later times, guided the evolution of many aspects of Chinese institutions and practices, including the legal system. This system, together with civil organisations, worked reasonably well for over two millennia. But, in the later part of the nineteenth century, many of the system's long-recognised shortcomings, such as cruel and unusual punishments, torture, political interference in the judicial process, and ineffective implementation of many laws prohibiting such practices, were brought into a light cast by the West which only quite recently had emerged from similar, or worse, conditions and now stood on an apparent moral high ground, condemning them in China and, by force, imposed extraterritorial consular jurisdiction on her. Thus, another new element was injected into the situation and caused dramatic changes to China, firstly, and most conspicuously, to its legal system.

Reform of the legal system was initiated by many since the late Qing and actually attempted by the Nationalists and the Communists. For a long time, the effort was mainly to emulate the West. Now that more than a century has passed, some people may ask how successful this effort has been, but the question is rather outdated. It is true that, being ahead of the rest of the world in facing new problems and trying to solve them, the West still has experience worth learning from but the whole world is changing fast. Every country is in a new situation of its own, in some aspects similar to those of the West, in others quite different. Therefore, all countries, including those in the West, constantly have to "modernise".

Since the late Qing, China has been trying to modernise its traditional legal system mainly by introducing into it many ideas and practices of the West. The effort has not been entirely successful because, as I said, not enough attention has been paid to China's legal tradition. Here are some of its aspects that I think should be carefully considered, including those concerning the objectives of society, the nature and function of law, the making and enforcement of law, the exercise of power, and social relationships. Though they have been discussed earlier, I want to recapitulate them here so that I can suggest that some of them should be emphasised and some others dismissed so that further development of China's legal system can be more successful.

First, regarding objectives for society, the classic thinkers had several ideas. Zhuangzi would like to have a world of complete freedom for everyone as it would be in the state of nature of his imagination. Laozi hoped to have a small state in which people would exercise extreme self-denial. To reach their objectives both thinkers saw the ultimate necessity of the elimination of human intelligence. That was unrealistic. The Legalists wanted to make the state rich and strong, Mozi wished to have a state where the ruler would observe the will of Heaven and promote the basic interests of the ordinary people. Both ideas were short-sighted and unacceptable as the attempt to reach those objectives would make people to live like ants and bees. The Ruists were more rational and had a deep understanding of human needs and feelings. They suggested *da-tong* 大同 as the final objective and *xiao-kang* 小康 as an intermediate one. The beauty of *xiao-kang* is that it is reasonable and achievable, and what makes *da-tong* admirable and inspiring is that it visualises not only peace among all humans, and between them and their environment, but also opportunities for every person to realise his potential and help others achieve their aspirations and thus make society as a whole prosperous and harmonious, and human life enjoyable and meaningful. A society with such objectives will be different from one that, on the one hand, focuses on either the individual or the collective, overemphasises the material gain and pursues superficial equality; and that, on the other hand, acquiesces in exclusivity based on race, creed, sex, work, physical or mental ability, and many other artificial differences. The Ruist ideal society is all-embracing and it values diversity in all forms. It even tolerates ideas contrary to its objectives, as long as they are not meant to destroy society itself. To realise the Ruist objectives is not easy but it is worth trying – for China and, indeed, for all nations.

Second, regarding the nature and function of law, Zhuangzi insisted on the law of nature but society needs norms which, as the other classic thinkers pointed out, are artificially made for humans only. Social norms can be of different kinds, including moral precepts, religious doctrines, customs and law. The Legalists insisted that law should be the only social norm. This position was in conflict with common sense as well as with the positions of all other thinkers. The more generally accepted view was that society needed many types of norms and that they form a hierarchy with law at the bottom because it was only to establish a set of minimum standards and to prescribe punishments against behaviours that fell below those standards and harmed society. Law was, thus, basically criminal in nature; many civil matters, such as entering into an ordinary contract, were not regulated by law but by custom or rules created by local communities and non-governmental organisations. This narrow scope of law, and the fact that law was made by holders of political power and therefore often biased, caused a certain degree of disregard for it. Such a result was unfortunate. A new attitude is now necessary because the many rapid changes in society are making custom, and rules of traditional social organisations less and less adequate, and law has to regulate more activities. Nevertheless, it must be emphasised that law can never be comprehensive; a legal system should always allow as many aspects of people's lives be governed by other norms. This is especially true for a country such as China with a large territory and a large number of different ethnic groups.

Law cannot be the only norm, nor can it be supreme. Mozi argued that it should be based on the will of Heaven but he did not tell us how that will was revealed and made known to the public. Without a supernatural origin, law itself cannot justify itself. It could be made supreme only by government power. Laozi's "sage" might lead the people along the "Way" which he derived from law of nature but people did not understand what he meant and therefore he elicited no natural respect from them; the sage had to have the "nameless primordial substance" to suppress the disobedient. The Legalists' "bright ruler" could make law to manipulate people but he, too, had to use harsh punishments to force their submission. The rulers of later periods could make their command law but it might not command people's loyalty. This point was clear to Confucius who argued that law must be based on reason, human feelings and social experience. He realised that only the virtuous could make good law and therefore preached that the law-makers should rectify themselves. Mencius scolded law-makers who lacked virtue. Xunzi was more practical. He suggested detailed rules to train men to be good law-makers and argued that good men were the source of good law. Because of these emphases, the three Ruist masters had been accused of advocating the rule of men but this is a misunderstanding; they never dismissed the need for good law; they only indirectly maintained that men who lacked virtue, knowledge and wisdom could not make good law and elevate it as the supreme norm.

There were also serious misunderstandings of certain ideas of the classic Legalists. First, though they wanted to make law the only, or the supreme, norm, they did point out that law had to be based on human nature which, according to them, was selfish and calculating, and that law could not ask people to do something humanly impossible. Thus, they did not simply maintain that a ruler could make a law whatever he fancied. It was Du Zhou 杜周, a shameless, unprincipled law official of the Han Dynasty, who advocated the opposite but that was not a genuine Legalist position. Rather, the classic Legalists recognised that, in order to earn the respect of the people, law had to have certain characteristics, including clarity in its language, consistency in its contents, feasibility of what it demands, flexibility in coping with changing circumstances, and equality in its treatment of all people. If these conditions were followed by a law-maker, his law would not be completely arbitrary. Thus, to the Ruists and the Legalists, neither the rule of law nor the rule of men was acceptable. In essence, the Ruists wanted the rule of good men with good law; the Legalists wanted the rule of good law made by wise men and administered by "average rulers" abided by such law. This should be the preferred position of China's legal system in the future.

A second misunderstanding about the Legalists is that they supported the idea of equality under the law. It is true that, unlike the Ruists who openly maintained that law should treat people of different social stations differently, the classic Legalists did generally argue that law should be equally applied to everyone, but that was only an ideal; in practice, they accepted that the ruler and certain persons close to him were above the law. In any event, since they held the ruler to be the ultimate law-maker, they had to admit that he had the power to change existing laws and make retroactive laws and therefore stay above the law. Thus, equality under the law was never a legacy of traditional Chinese legal theories and practices. Now, it is without question to all who believe in human dignity that this equality should be established in China's new legal system. But to this rule there have always been exceptions based on unusual conditions and circumstances a particular person or matter is in. Therefore, a more general rule of dispensing justice, stated in the Ruist canon *Shang-shu* 尚書, *wei-qi fei-qi you-lun you-yao* (惟齊非齊, 有倫有要 seek equality but not uniformity, allow variations while observing the principles),[207] is worth preserving.

Third, regarding application and enforcement of law, the classic Ruists and Legalists agreed that to find truth, hearings and investigation must be conducted with care and skill. But the Ruists insistence that education must precede these procedures was rejected by the Legalists who found it too slow and believed that those under pressure to solve urgent problems did not have the luxury of the time that educators could have. These conflicting positions were first and most eloquently expressed in the arguments between the idealist Shuxiang 叔向 and the pragmatist Zichan 子產. It is worth noticing that Zichan did not deny the importance of education in moral principles and the rites, and asserted, as Han Fei did, that law should be the sole subject of education.

There was a more serious disagreement between the Legalists and other thinkers on how law should be applied. Laozi and Zhuangzi did not think application of artificial law worthwhile; they argued that such law should be discarded. The Ruists acknowledged that, where there was a clear law, it should be applied; where a law was ambiguous or there was no law, a decision should be based on higher principles, a position repudiated by the Legalists. This dispute was settled during the Jin Dynasty by requiring the lower judicial officials to apply law strictly, letting the higher officials, in reviewing difficult cases where a law was not very clear, consider moral principles, and giving the emperor the authority to make the final decision. It was not a satisfactory solution, because emperors were not necessarily qualified to make fair judgments, but then judicial process has to have some kind of finality. For this reason, the new legal system of China should perhaps entrust the power to finalise legal disputes to a body of legal experts. But, if a dispute is of a political nature, it would be better left to the law-makers to solve in accordance with the strong mores of an educated majority of the time.

In enforcement of law, the Legalists relied on rewards and punishments, and they argued that, to deter violations, punishments should be harsher than most people would think appropriate. But this position is morally wrong and likely to produce results contrary to its objectives. It should be rejected. The other pernicious Legalist demand, of everyone reporting wrongdoings of others, was also deeply harmful to society and was condemned by the Ruists but enforced by many regimes. It should have no place in China's new legal system.

Another regrettable aspect of the traditional legal system is that, though there were detailed procedural laws, they were not observed faithfully. Instead, torture was allowed to save judicial officials from difficult and time-consuming efforts to find truth, and redundant and pro forma reviews were conducted to give an impression of making careful final decisions. Both the Ruists and the Legalists were responsible for these problems. Their legacy in this respect should be disregarded.

Fourth, regarding the concentration and abuse of power, no satisfactory solution was suggested and practised in traditional China. After the breakdown of the Zhou Dynasty feudal system, political power became concentrated. This development was openly encouraged by the Legalists and acquiesced to by all other thinkers except Zhuangzi. Mencius's belief that the chaotic world of many power centres of his time could be settled only when it was unified and placed under a single government was shared by most of his contemporaries. But, when power was more concentrated, its abuse became more difficult to prevent. Since the Han Dynasty, intellectuals had tried to restrain the abuse conceptually with superstitious or pseudoscientific theories, and failed dismally. Practical men invented institutions and bureaucracies to confine imperial power and failed, too, because the emperors soon learned, on the one hand, to take advantage of the ideologies by creating something like a theology with them as its ultimate beneficiaries, and, on the other hand, to control the bureaucracy by increasing its branches and thus limiting their responsibilities and diminishing their authority. These schemes were helped by the Legalists and petty Ruists advocating *san-gang* which produced egregious consequences that poisoned traditional Chinese society. They must be stopped. First of all, no one should be allowed to seize power by force and pass it on to someone of his choice. To give government posts to persons publicly recognised as *xian-neng* (賢能 worthy and able) was an idea that is not alien to the Chinese. Supposedly Yao and Shun were chosen by tribal leaders, and, in the Han and the Jin dynasties, there was a procedure known as *xiang-ju li-xuan* (鄉舉里選 local communities selecting and recommending candidates for government appointments). But it was suspended during a period of disorder thereafter and then replaced by the civil examination system starting in the Tang Dynasty. In addition, various methods of discerning public opinion were used in the past, including investigations by censors and scholars of the Imperial Academy and canvassing the opinions of the gentry by local and regional authorities. For a while, during the Tang, an arrangement was put into practice to divide the central government into several branches that put checks on one another and, together, prevented the promulgation of improper laws and imperial orders. Such procedures and arrangements made it conceptually not difficult for the Chinese to accept Western representative democracy. It is not without problems but now China has the benefit of learning from the experience of the West and it is to be hoped the country can avoid their mistakes and achieve better results.

Another strategy against abuse of power that has proven effective in the West is to make the judiciary independent and give it the authority to review actions of other branches of government as well as those of the people in general. China never had this strategy. Though in most dynasties there were judicial officials at most levels of government, they were always a rank or two below the head of that government. In serious cases, decisions were made jointly by them, and the ultimate judicial power rested with the emperor. The result was far from satisfactory. The Western strategy is worth adopting. But, of course, judicial power can be misused, even abused. Apart from confining it with strict laws, a traditional Chinese method can be applied. This is to take away from the judiciary some of its functions and give them to civil society – let many problems which do not involve violence be handled by communities and non-governmental organisations using mediation and arbitration and, perhaps, other more innovative methods. This was probably what Confucius had in mind when he said that, if he had his way, he, as a magistrate, would like to keep litigation from arising under his watch. That may be too much to hope for but limiting the power of the judiciary by reducing the type and number of cases tried by it – a tactic known as *fu-di chou-xin* (釜底抽薪 pulling fuel logs out of a fire beneath a wok) practised by the Chinese especially effectively since Song times – should be applied as much as possible.

Fifth, regarding relationships between the government and the people, Zhuangzi wanted the government authorities to be like high boughs on tall trees and the people like wild deer roaming happily below. That was, regrettably, too fanciful an image. Other thinkers recognised that government and the people had to interact. What should the relationship be like? Mozi wanted the people be strictly regimented in a rigid hierarchical state. Laozi said the sage would treat the people like children or, indeed, like infants. The Legalists advocated *san-gang* to make the people subservient to the ruler. These ideas produced, in many people, two contradictory attitudes towards the authorities – awe and resentment – one made them submissive and dependent, the other induced them to cheat the government without shame, secretly subvert its orders and eventually openly rebel against it. Only the Ruists wanted to see a healthy reciprocal relationship. They did not have an idea of universal human rights but stressed, generally, that *human beings should treat one another as human beings* (the essence of Confucius's primary moral principle *ren* 仁; in his words, one should not do to another anything one would not wish to have done to oneself by others, and one who wishes to reach one's own goals should help others to reach theirs). More specifically, a person in a particular social station should behave in a way that is worthy of it – a ruler should act as a correct ruler, a subject a correct subject. While a subject should be loyal to a correct ruler, the ruler should be benevolent to the correct subjects. This kind of relationship should make society stable and vibrant but, unfortunately, by Confucius's time, those in power had already rejected it. When, after the Qin, political power became more concentrated, most people, being suppressed by the government authorities, did indeed become as submissive as children, while many others shied from government service and social responsibilities, and some turned to rebellion and revolution. That is why, more than two millennia ago, China repeatedly experienced alternating periods of docility and violent convulsions. To escape from this circle, the relationship between the people and the government should be better balanced in accordance with the principle spelled out by the classic Ruists, and, to protect this relationship, the legal system and other institutions should be established to enable the government to function properly and the people to live in peace and realise their aspirations within the boundaries of reasonable laws, not like wild deer under tall trees but like those in a utopia described by a different "Laozi" where the government truly does not do much to control the people and they only vaguely know that it exists.

The task of constructing a new legal system for China's future is a colossal and difficult one. It will take countless people to study more thoroughly China's legal tradition and the relevant ideas and practices of other countries, and to deliberate more carefully about China's objectives before working out the details of her new legal system. Because circumstances continue to change, this task will be open-ended. The classic thinkers had done their part in search of a way out of their troubled world; those of us who have similar ambitions have to continue searching for ways leading to a future better than that which China has today.

Notes

1. Confucius said he *shu er bu-zuo* (述而不作 restate but not create). See Liu Baonan劉寶楠, *Lun-yu Zheng-yi* 論語正義 Chapter 7 "Shu-er" 述而 p. 134. That was largely true with Laozi. The work attributed to him was evidently completed much later than his time, mixing many conflicting points of earlier thinkers, including those of the ancient recluses and political strategists.
2. Confucius was candid on this point. Once, being mistaken as Yang Hu 陽虎, an official who had abused the people of a place called Kuang 匡, Confucius was attacked by them. In danger, he said calmly, "King Wen 文王 is gone. Is the responsibility of continuing the development of civilisation resting on me? . . . If Heaven is not to terminate civilisation what harm can the Kuang people do me?" See Liu Baonan, *supra*, Chapter 9 "Zi-han" 子罕 p. 176.
3. Their views, showing a very different attitude towards life, are summarised here. 1. Weisheng Mo 微生畝 said to Confucius, "Qiu [丘Confucius's name], why are you so restless and in such a hurry? Are you trying to demonstrate your talent in making sophisticated arguments?" (See Liu Baonan, *supra*, Chapter 14 "Xian-wen" 憲問 p. 320). 2. The gatekeeper of Shimen 石門 of the capital of the state of Lu called Confucius "the man who does what he knows is impossible" (ibid., p. 325). 3. When Confucius was once playing a stone instrument, an unnamed person who, carrying a bamboo basket, passed by, stopped and listened and then commented that the player must be very stubborn (ibid.). 4. Jieyu 接輿, a "mad man from the state of Chu" sang a song lamenting Confucius's failure to understand that, for him, what had passed was gone but what was to come was worth saving, and that anyone who engaged in politics wishing to cause change in the current situation was doomed (ibid., Chapter 18 "Weizi" 微子 p. 390). 5. Jieni 桀溺 told Zilu 子路, a disciple of Confucius, that the world was in chaos and no one could change it; thus; rather than follow one who avoided bad people, it was better to follow one who avoided this chaotic world altogether (ibid., pp. 391–2). 6. Once, on a trip, Zilu fell behind Confucius and met an elderly man carrying a hoe; he asked whether the man had seen the master. The man said, "You apparently have never toiled with your limbs and are incapable of distinguishing one kind of grain from another. Who is your master?" It was, of course, a criticism of Confucius as someone of no practical skills but only useless ideas (ibid., pp. 393–4).
4. Wei Yuan 魏源, *Laozi ben-yi* 老子本義 Chapter 25, p. 23.
5. Sima Qian 司馬遷, *Shi-ji* 史記, Chapter 47 "Kong-zi shi-jia" 孔子世家 p. 1909; Chapter 63 "Laozi Han Fei lie-zhuan" 老子韓非列傳 p. 2140.
6. Zhuangzi argued that human life results from the concentration of *qi* (氣 vital energy) and death is the dissipation of *qi*. As this *qi* perpetually concentrates and dissipates, life always ends in death and death is the beginning of life. See Guo Qingfan, *Zhuangzi ji-shi* 莊子集釋, Chapter 22 "Zhi-bei-you" 知北遊 p. 320.
7. In *Zhuangzi* there are five such stories. First, Shun 舜 offered the government to Shan Juan 善卷 who declined, saying he was happy as a mere farmer, and then escaped into the mountains; second Shun offered the government to *Shi-hu zhi nong* (石戶之農

a peasant of Shi-hu) who also declined and, with his wife and son, escaped into the sea and never returned; third, Shun offered the government to his friend Beiren Wuze (北人無擇 the hapless northerner) who, disgusted by the offer, jumped to his death in a deep pool of clear, cold water; fourth, Tang 湯, after vanquishing the Xia Dynasty, offered the government to Bie Sui 卞隨 who, feeling insulted, drowned himself in the River Chou; fifth, Tang offered the government to Mao Guang 瞀光 who, also feeling insulted, held a large lump of stone and drowned himself in the River Lu. See Guo Qingfan, *supra*, Chapter 28 "Ran-wang" 讓王 pp. 414–15, 423–4.

8. Robber Zhi accused Confucius of never engaging in any productive activity, but talked preposterously about deeds of the ancient sages to criticise current affairs, and yet wishing to win high office and rich remuneration but failed because nothing he asserted was true. After the interview, Confucius left absolutely shaken. Three times he failed to grasp the reins to climb on to his carriage; then he leaned on its guard bar, head bowed, face ashen, eyes dazed, and unable to breathe. See Guo Qingfan, *supra*, Chapter 29 "Dao Zhi" 盜跖 pp. 426–33.
9. This is what Confucius reportedly said after the interview: "Birds, I know, can fly; fish, I know, can swim; beasts, I know, can run. In order to catch them I can make nets for those that run, line and hook for those that swim, tethered arrow for those that fly. As to a dragon, I cannot know how it rides on wind and cloud and ascend to the sky. Today, I saw Laozi. Is he like a dragon?" See Sima Qian, *supra*, Chapter 63 "Laozi Han Fei lie-zhuan" 老子韓非列傳 p. 2140.
10. See Liu Baonan, *supra*, Chapter 18 "Weizi" 微子 pp. 392–3.
11. This point was made clear by Zilu 子路, who commented on Jieni's advice of escaping from the world, saying, to disregard *da-lun* (大倫 great relationships between seniors and juniors, and between the ruler and the subjects) only to preserve one's own integrity was not right. See ibid., p. 395.
12. The Confucius in *Lun-yu* was a rather serious man. The only occasion he joked was when he arrived at Wu-cheng 武城, a district governed by his disciple Ziyou 子游, and heard people reading poems and playing music. He smiled and said, "It is unnecessary to kill a chicken with a knife used for butchering an ox." Ziyou protested, saying that he had heard from the Master that, when ordinary people have learned the Way, they become easy to govern. Confucius promptly conceded that Ziyou was right and admitted his previous remark was only to tease him. See Liu Baonan, *supra*, Chapter 17 "Yang Huo" 陽貨 p. 369.
13. In 497 BCE, as the Minister of Justice of the state of Lu, Confucius suggested and then proceeded to reduce the high city walls of three powerful aristocrats to prevent them from harbouring private armies against the ruler, Duke Ding 魯定公. The three aristocrats united and defeated Confucius's plan and eventually caused him to resign. See Sima Qian, *supra*, Chapter 47 "Kong-zi shi-jia" 孔子世家 p. 1916.
14. Sima Qian, *supra*, Chapter 47, p. 1911.
15. It was reported that, in a meeting between the rulers of Lu and Qi, Confucius, as the diplomatic assistant of the Duke of Lu, bravely repelled the humiliating treatments planned by Qi and succeeded in retrieving a piece of land Qi seized from Lu. And later, as the acting chief minister for only three months, he established such good order in the state of Lu that people became completely honest – they would not unjustly raise prices of merchandise or pick up what was left in the street and appropriate it – and travellers from abroad found the government functionaries properly at work to address their problems and thus felt quite at home. See ibid., pp. 1915–16, 1917.
16. Jiao Xun 焦循 Jiao Hu 焦琥, *Mengzi Zheng-yi* 孟子正義, Chapter 5 "Teng Wen-gong shang" 滕文公上 p. 219.

17. Liu Baonan, *Lun-yu zheng-yi* 論語正義 Chapter 5 "Gongye Chang" 公冶長 p. 90.
18. The two works were attributed respectively to Guan Zhong 管仲 (c.719–648 BCE), a chief minister of the state of Qi, and Yan Ying 晏嬰 (c.578–500), another chief minister of the same state. See Luo Genze 羅根澤, *Guanzi tan-yuan* 管子探源; Wu Zeyu 吳則虞, *Yanzi chun-qiu ji-shi* 晏子春秋集釋. But Guan Zhong and Yan Ying preceded the rise of the various schools.
19. See Sima Qian, *supra*, Chapter 85 "Lü Buwei lie-zhuan" 呂不韋列傳 p. 2510; Chen Qiyou 陳奇猷, *Lü-shi-chun-qiu jiao-shi* 呂氏春秋校釋.
20. Gao You 高誘, *Huai-nan-zi zhu* 淮南子注.
21. Lin Shu 林曙, *Chun-qiu fan-lu zhu* 春秋繁露注
22. Sun Xidan, *Li-ji ji-jie* 禮記集解; Wang Pinzhen 王聘珍, *Da Dai li-ji jie-gu* 大戴禮記解詁. These works explain the *raison d'être* of the rites.
23. The work is also known as *Zhou-li* 周禮. It first appeared in late Western Han, describing in detail the government institutions of the Zhou, but is generally believed to be a creation of Liu Xin 劉歆 though he probably had access to some relevant ancient materials existent at his time. See Zheng Yuan 鄭元 and Jia Gongyan 賈公彥, *Zhou-li zhu-shu* 周禮注疏; Sun Yirang 孫詒讓, *Zhou-li zheng-yi* 周禮正義. What was described was used in later times as an ideal for construction of government institutions.
24. Huan Kuan 桓寬, *Yan-tie lun* 鹽鐵論. Its significance will be discussed further in a later section of this epilogue.
25. The conference was convened in 79 CE under the order of Emperor Zhang of the Eastern Han 東漢章帝. Numerous high officials and scholars participated in an effort to reach an orthodox interpretation of the Ruist Classics, but Ban Gu's transcript shows that many ideas of other schools, such as the determinism of *Yin-yang wu-xing* and the *san-gang* 三綱 of the Legalists, were used in the "interpretations".
26. See Fang Xuanling 房玄齡 et al., *Jin-shu* 晉書 Chapter 30 "Xing-fa-zhi" 刑法志 p. 923; Yang Honglie 楊鴻烈, *Zhong-guo fa-lü fa-da-shi* 中國法律發達史 pp. 160, 193–4. Unfortunately most of such works were lost.
27. The few works include one on Mozi's logic, epistemology, methodology and metaphysics by Lu Sheng 魯勝 (c.250–320). The work was lost; only its preface "Mo-bian-zhu xu" 墨辯註序 of about three hundred words appears in Fang Xuanling 房玄齡 et al., *Jin-shu* 晉書 collected in *Er-shi-si shi* 二十四史 vol. 4, pp. 2433–4. Another one, "Du Mozi" 讀墨子, by Han Yu 韓愈, was not a serious study of *Mozi* but an attempt to show that it is basically in agreement with the Ruist principles. See Ma Qichang 馬其昶, *Han Changli wen-ji jiao-zhu* 韓昌黎文集校注, vol. 1, pp. 22–3.
28. Their philosophy was known as *Xuan-xue* 玄學. A famous group of them was called *zhu-lin qi-xian* (竹林七賢 seven worthies in the bamboo forest, namely Ji Kang 嵇康, Ruan Ji 阮籍, Shan Tao 山濤, Xiang Xiu 向秀, Liu Ling 劉伶, Wang Rong 王戎 and Ruan Xian 阮咸). See their respective biographies in Fang Xuanling 房玄齡 et al., *Jin-shu* 晉書.
29. The theory, articulated by Dong Zhongshu, had its roots in the ancient Chinese belief in Heaven. Though Confucius and Xunzi wanted people to focus on this world, they did not deny the existence of supernatural forces. This belief was famously restated in *Tai-shang gan-ying pian* 太上感應篇, a book that first appeared during the late Han Dynasty, probably penned by a Daoist but quoted many other thinkers and included anecdotal tales of earlier times to prove divine retribution. See Hui Dong 惠棟, ed. *Tai-shang gan-ying pian* 太上感應篇.
30. For brief surveys of the theories of Mozi and the others, who were more commonly

known as Logicians, see Mou Zongsan 牟宗三, *Ming-jia yu Xunzi* 名家與荀子; Sun Zhongyuan 孫中原, *Mo-xue tong-lun* 墨學通論; He Qimin 何啟民, *Gongsun Long yu Gongsun-long-zi* 公孫龍與公孫龍子.

31. This point was eloquently emphasised by Fu Yi 傅奕 (555–639) and Han Yu 韓愈 (768–824), two eminent scholar-officials of the Tang Dynasty. See their famous memoirs on this point in Liu Xu, 劉昫, *Jiu-Tang shu* 舊唐書, Chapter 79 "Fu Yi zhuan" 傅奕傳 pp. 2715–19 and ibid., Chapter 161 "Han Yu zhuan" 韓愈傳 pp. 4198–201.
32. Numerous works of *li-xue* scholars are available. For a brief survey see Feng Youlan 馮友蘭, *Zhong-guo zhe-xue-shi* 中國哲學史. For a sample of criticism of this school see Yan Yuan 顏元, *Yan Xi zhai nian-pu* 顏習齋年譜 and *Xi-zhai ji-yu* 習齋記餘.
33. See Wang Xianshen 王先慎, *Han-fei-zi ji-jie* 韓非子集解. It is often quoted that Cheng Yi 程頤, a prominent "Neo-Confucian", notoriously said *e-si shi xiao, shi-jie shi da* (餓死事小, 失節事大 For a widow it is a minor matter to die of hunger but a grave matter to lose her dedication to her deceased husband.) See Cheng Hao 程顥 and Cheng Yi, *Er Cheng Quan-shu* "Yi-shu" 二程 全書 "遺書" vol. 22, leaf 5b. This admonition was later interpreted to cover the relationship between a subject and his ruler. As far as I know, no Qing scholar challenged the idea of *san-gang* in writing.
34. See Ban Gu, *supra*, Chapter 56, pp. 2495–526.
35. See Han Yu, *supra*, "Yuan-dao" 原道.
36. See Sima Guang, *Zi-zhi tong-jian* 資治通鑑 vol. 1 "Zhou-ji, Wei-lie wang er-shi-san nian" 周紀威烈王二十三年 p. 3.)
37. Particularly his comparison of the ruler to the hat and the subjects to the shoes and his apparent endorsement of the advice Fei Zhong 費仲 gave to King Shou of Shang 商紂王: *Zhu er zhu chen, yan-you guo* (主而誅臣焉有過 What is wrong for a ruler to execute a subject?). See Wang Xianshen 王先慎, *Han-fei-zi ji-jie* 韓非子集解, Wai-chu-shuo zuo-xia" 外儲說左下 p. 224.
38. See Sima Qian, *supra*, Chapter 8, "Gao-zhu ben-ji" 高祖本紀, p. 362.
39. See ibid, Chapter 97 "Lu Jia lie-zhuan" 陸賈列傳 p. 2699; Chapter 99 "Shusun Tong lie-zhuan" 叔孫通列傳 p. 2722.
40. See ibid., Chapter 6 "Wu-di ji" 武帝紀 pp. 155–6, 212; Chapter 56 "Dong Zhongshu zhuan" 董仲書傳 p. 2526.
4.1 See Ban Gu 班固, *Han-shu* 漢書 Chapter 59 "Zhang Tang zhuan" 張湯傳 pp. 2641–2.
4.2 See Ban Gu, *supra*, Chapter 9 "Yuan-di ji" 元帝紀 p. 277.
43. See Zhong Zhaopeng 鍾肇鵬, *Chen-wei lun-lüe* 讖緯論略. Wang Mang succeeded in forcing an infant emperor Ruzi Ying 孺子嬰 to abdicate in his favour in 9 CE and established a new regime called *Xin* 新 that lasted thirteen years (9–22 CE).
44. During the reigns of Emperor Taiwu of the Northern Wei 北魏太武帝 (r 424–451), Emperor Wu of the Northern Zhou 北周武帝 (r 561–577), Emperor Wu of the Tang 唐武宗 (r 841–846) and Emperor Shi-zong of the Late Zhou 後周世宗 (r 944–959), Buddhism was suppressed because of their personal disbelief in the religion and their thinking that Buddhists tried to avoid government conscription and Buddhist temples occupied too much land exempted from taxation. See the biographies of the four emperors in Li Yanshou 李延壽 *Bei-shi* 北史, Liu Xu, *supra* and Xue Juzheng 薛居正 *Jiu Wu-dai-shi* 舊五代史.
45. They included the monk/nun, the person who performed the rites of ordainment, the head of the family of the monk/nun, the clerk for household registration who deleted the name of the monk/nun from the registrar, their superiors in the district government who were aware of the violation, and the superintendent of temples and monasteries which took in the monk/nun. The punishment against unlawful

ordainment of a single monk/nun ranged from 100 blows of the heavy bamboo to one year of penal servitude. For every additional violation, an additional punishment would be inflicted. See Zhangsun Wuji 長孫無忌 et al., *Tang-lü shu-yi* 唐律疏議, "Si-ru-dao" 私入道pp. 235–6

46. See *Ming-lü ji-jie fu-li* 明律集解附例, "Si-chuang an-yuan ji si-do seng-dao" 私創庵院及私度僧道 Chapter 4, p. 549; *Da-Qing lü-li* 大清律例, Chapter 8, pp. 194–5.
47. See Zhangsun Wuji, *supra*, "Cheng dao-shi nü-guan" 稱道士女冠 pp. 143–5.
48. See Xue Yunsheng 薛允升, *Tang-Ming-lü he-bian* 唐明律合編, Chapter 9, leaves 30b–31a.
49. See *Ming-lü ji-jie fu-li, supra*, "Seng-dao bai-fu-mu" 僧道拜父母, Chapter 4, p. 975; *Da-Qing lü-li, supra*, Chapter 17, p. 293.
50. For the deeds of Zhang Daoling 張道陵, his son Zhang Heng 張衡 and grandson Zhang Lu 張魯, the three more famous founders of the Dao sects, see Fan Ye 范曄, *Hou-Han-shu* 後漢書 Chapter 75 "Liu Yan zhuan" 劉焉傳 pp. 2432–6; Chen Shou 陳壽, *San-guo zhi* 三國志 Chapter 8 "Zhang Lu zhuan" 張魯傳 pp. 263–5.
51. See Liu Xu 劉煦 et al., *Jiu-Tang-shu* 舊唐書 Chapter 1 "Gao-zu ben-ji" 高祖本紀 pp. 2, 3; Chapter 192 "Wang Yuanzhi zhuan" 王遠知傳 p. 5125. Lu Xinyuan 陸心源, *Tang-wen shi-yi* 唐文拾遺 "Xian Lao hou Shi zhao" 先老後釋詔 vol. 1, leaf 2a ; Du Guangting 杜光庭, *Li-dai chong-dao-ji* 歷代崇道記.
52. Their works, together with those written before and after, were collected in 5,485 volumes, and were known as *Dao-zang* (道藏 canons of the Dao). See Zhang Yuchu 張宇初, et al., *Zheng-tong dao-zang* 正統道藏.
53. See Liu Sanwu 劉三吾, *Mengzi jie-wen* 孟子節文; Yang Bojun 楊伯峻, *Mengzi yi-zhu* 孟子譯注.
54. See Qing Shi-zong 清世宗, *Da-yi-jue-mi-lu* 大義覺迷錄.
55. In Chinese, *jun sui bu jun, chen bu ke-yi bu chen* 君雖不君, 臣不可以不臣. See Liu Xu, *supra*, Chapter 2 "Tai-zong ben-ji shang" 太宗本紀上 p. 34.
56. For a fair evaluation of the characters of Mozi and some of the "Grand Masters", and their contribution to Chinese culture, see Guo Qingfan, *supra*, Chapter 33 "Tian-xia" 天下 pp. 464–7.
57. See Bi Yuan, *supra*, Chapter 1 "Meng-chun-ji – Qu-si" 孟春紀 – 去私 pp. 10–11.
58. Yue Fei was a national hero who led many successful campaigns against the Jin (金 a dynasty [1115–1234] established by the Jurchen Tartars in north China) in order to recover the territory of the Northern Song Dynasty (960–1126) but was only half-heartedly supported by the government of the Southern Song (1127–1278) and was finally executed under trumped-up charges. His righteousness, bravery, loyalty to the country and personal sacrifice for its interests were eternally admired by the Chinese people. See Tuo Tuo 脫脫, et al., *Song-shi* 宋史 collected in *Er-shi-si shi* 二十四史 vol. 16, Chapter 365 "Yue Fei lie-zhuan" 岳飛列傳 pp. 11375–98).
59. See Shi Naian 施耐庵, *Shui-hu-zhuan* 水滸傳; Pearl S. Buck, *All Men are Brothers* (New York: Grove Press, 1957); Sidney A. Shapiro, *Outlaws of the Marsh* (Wai-wen chu-ban-she 外文出版社 Beijing: 1999).
60. Though the book *Zhou-li* 周禮 appeared much later, it recorded many of the rules which were mentioned in earlier works such as *Shang-shu* 尚書, *Zuo-zhuan* 左傳, *Guo-yu* 國語 and those attributed to the eight thinkers discussed here.
61. The story was first reported in *Xunzi*. See Wang Xianqian 王先謙, *Xuzi Ji-jie* 荀子集解, Chapter 28 "You-zuo" 宥坐, pp. 341–2.
62. It was often said that Confucius had *san-qian* (三千 three thousand) disciples. But that was only to emphasise the size of his student body. In ancient times, the word

san was often used figuratively to mean many, as in *bu-xiao you-san wu-hou wei-da* (不孝有三, 無後為大 There are many violations of the filial piety but none is more serious than not producing an heir). According to Sima Qian, among the multitude of Confucius's disciples, seventy-two were well versed in all *liu-yi* (六藝 the six arts of rites, music, poetry, history, writing and mathematics). Many of them served in governments with distinction; some were successful in other fields. Zigong 子貢, for instance, became a very prosperous businessman. See Sima Qian, *supra*, Chapter 47 "Kong-zi shi-jia" 孔子世家 p. 1938; Chapter 67 "Zhongni di-zi lie-zhuan" 仲尼弟子列傳 pp. 2185–226.

63. This view, *xing-fa shi-qing shi-zhong* (刑罰世輕世重 punishments should sometimes be heavy and sometimes light) first appeared in *Shu-jing* 書經. See Kong Yingda 孔穎達, *Shang-shu zhu-shu* 尚書注疏, Chapter 29 "Lü-xing" 呂刑 leaf 30b. It was made clearer by a statement in *Zhou-li* 周禮: *xing xin-guo yong qing-dian, xing ping-guo yong zhong-dian, xing luan-guo yong zhong-dian* (刑新國用輕典, 刑平國用中典, 刑亂國用重典 to govern a newly established state, use laws prescribing light punishments; to govern a state in peace, use laws prescribing punishments proportionate to the seriousness of offences; to govern a state in disorder, use laws prescribing heavy punishments). See Zheng Yuan 鄭元 and Jia Gongyan 賈公彥, *Zhou-li zhu-shu* 周禮注疏, Chapter 34 "Qiu-guan da-si-kou" 秋官大司寇, leaves 13–13b.
64. As mentioned earlier, it was reported that, when Liu Bang 劉邦, the founder of the Han Dynasty, first entered the state of Qin he had vanquished, he proclaimed in lieu of the myriad of Qin laws only three simple rules. Then more laws were added. In the time of Emperor Wu (r 140–87 BCE) statutes numbered 359 chapters, in which 409 provisions prescribed the death penalty for 1,812 offences, and, in addition, 13,472 capital-case decisions were sanctioned as precedents. Documents recording these statutes and precedents filled the government depository; even those in charge of them could not find them all. See Ban Gu, *supra*, Chapter 23 "Xing-fa-zhi" 刑法志 p. 1101.
65. See ibid., pp. 1097–8.
66. See ibid., p. 1101.
67. See Ban Gu, *supra*, Chapter 60 "Du Zhou zhuan" 杜周傳 p. 2659.
68. Several punishments involving mutilation were used in ancient China rather readily. They included tattooing, cutting off the nose, amputating the foot, and castration. In 107 BCE Emperor Wen of the Han 漢文帝 abolished the first three. (See Ban Gu, *Han-shu* "Xing-fa-zhi *supra*, pp. 1097–8.) In 39 CE Emperor Guangwu of the Eastern Han 東漢光武帝 wanted to reinstitute such punishments but was dissuaded from doing so by Du Lin 杜林, a prominent Ruist official. (See Fan Ye, *supra*, Chapter 27 "Du Lin zhuan" 杜林傳 pp. 937–8.) In 189, during the reign of Emperor Xian of late Han 漢獻帝 (r 189–219) a second attempt was made and again dismissed because of objections by Ruist officials. (See ibid., Chapter 49 "Zhong Changtong zhuan" 仲長統傳 p. 1652; ibid., Chapter 70 "Kong Rong zhuan" 孔融傳 pp. 2266–7.) The third and last time, when a serious attempt was made in 220 during the reign of Emperor Wen of the Wei Dynasty 魏文帝, almost a hundred officials participated in the debate and finally the attempt was defeated and the subject finally put to rest. (See Chen Shou, *supra*, Chapter 13 "Zhong Yao zhuan" 鍾繇傳 pp. 397–8.) Punishments involving mutilation were excluded from *wu-xing* (五刑 the five officially sanctioned punishments) listed in the Tang Code but, in practice, there were instances of violations and, during the Qing, tattooing was reinstituted.
69. For a detailed analysis of this system see Sa Mengwu 薩孟武, *Zhong-guo she-hui zheng-zhi shi* 中國社會政治史 vol. 3, pp. 278–93.
70. This was because, by the time of the Tang, the emperor had long been established

as the ultimate ruler. The separation of the legislative power worked only when he allowed it. He could always appoint those who supported him to any of the three offices and dismiss those who did not. Shortly, favoured officials were allowed to serve in more than one of the three offices and, eventually, the three were, in fact, merged. See ibid.

71. See Tuo Tuo 脫脫, et al., *Song-shi* 宋史 Chapter 22 "Hui-zong ben-ji" 徽宗本紀 p. 414; Chapter 199 "Xing-fa-zhi yi" 刑法志一 p. 4965; Chapter 200 "Xing-fa-zhi er" 刑法志二 p. 4991.
72. See ibid., Chapter 199, p. 4965.
73. Yang Yifan 楊一凡, *Ming da-gao yan-jiu* 明大誥研究.
74. Originally, the term *sheng-ren* (聖人 sage) referred to a wise and knowledgeable person. Many in ancient China were called sages. By the time of the Warring States Period, when the *shi* 士 class became prominent, the term gained a moral meaning and was used for someone who was highly ethical as well as exceptionally wise. Many thinkers labelled legendary rulers of the past as *sheng-wang* (聖王 sage kings) and thus gave the term a political meaning. The first emperor of the Qin Dynasty bestowed on himself the title *huang-di* 皇帝, making himself above all those rulers, and, in numerous proclamations, characterising his political measures as *sheng-zhi* (聖治 sagacious rule). In ancient times, when people believed in gods and spirits, rulers often claimed to be their agents. When the ideas of Heaven and its mandate emerged, people thought the good sage kings all had mandates from Heaven, giving the term "sage king" an additional transcendental meaning. Then, all rulers, including, as we have mentioned, the debauched Shou, the last ruler of the Yin Dynasty, claimed to have the mandate. In later dynasties, all founders were said to have mythical births as a proof of their mandate. Such myth-making became viral and created a school known as *chen-wei zhi xue* (讖緯之學 study of omens and hidden meanings in the Classics) which, in large part, tried to give Heaven's mandate to reigning emperors. The efforts to eulogise the emperors as sages to justify their rule never ended throughout Chinese history. For a detailed analysis, see Wang Wenliang 王文亮, *Zhong-guo sheng-ren lun* 中國聖人論 pp. 4–14, 215–80.
75. See, for instance, Kong Yingda, *Shang-shu zhu-shu* 尚書注疏 Chapter 9 "Pan-geng zhong" 盤庚中 pp. 130–3; Chapter 17 "Duo-fang" 多方 pp. 254–9.
76. Sima Qian, *supra*, Chapter 8 "Gao-zu ben-ji" 高祖本紀 pp. 382–94; Chapter 9 "Lü Tai-hou ben-ji" 呂太后本紀 p. 396.
77. Zhangsun Wuji, *supra*, pp. 6–16.
78. See for instance, ibid., Chapter 7 "Wei-jin" 衛禁 pp. 149–79; Chapters 9–10 "Zhi-zhi" 職制 p. 230; Chapter 15 "Jiu-ku" 廄庫 pp. 275–97; Chapter 16 "Shan-xing" 擅興 pp. 298–320; Chapter 17 "Zei-dao" 賊盜 pp. 321–3, 325, 326; Chapter 21 "Dou-song" 鬥訟 pp. 395, 396, 398, 399.
79. In the Qin, this punishment was inflicted on three groups of persons related to offenders of all serious crimes – those related to his father, his mother and his wife. In 187 BCE Empress Lü 呂后, Liu Bang's wife, banned the the punishment. Her order was reaffirmed and broadened in 178 by Emperor Wen 文帝 but soon the punishment was reinstituted against those who committed rebellion, treason and attack on the imperial person. See Ban Gu, *supra*, Chapter 23 "Xing-fa-zhi" 刑法志 pp. 1104–5. This limited form of collective punishment was listed in the Tang Code. See Zhangsun Wuji, *supra*, Chapter 17 "Zei-dao" 賊盜 pp. 321–2, 325–6.
80. See Ban Gu, *supra*, Chapter 6 "Wu-di ji" 武帝紀 pp. 208–209; Chapter 63 "Wu wu zi zhuan" 武五子傳 pp. 2741–9.

81. Zhangsun Wuji, *supra*, pp. 427–8.
82. Liu Xu, et al., *supra*, Chapter 50 "Xing-fa-zhi" 刑法志 pp. 2143–4.
83. Tuo Tuo, *supra*, Chapter 365 "Yue Fei" 岳飛 pp. 11375–98.
84. Sima Qian, *supra*, Chapter 85 "Lü Buwei lie-zhuan" 呂不韋列傳 pp. 2505–14; Chapter 6 "Qin-shi-huang ben-ji" 秦始皇本紀 p. 231.
85. Sima Qian, *supra*, Chapter 6 "Qin-shi-huang ben-ji" 秦始皇本紀 pp. 255, 258.
86. Ibid., Chapter 118 "Huai-nan Heng-shan lie-zhuan" 淮南衡山列傳 pp. 3082–94; Chapter 30 "Ping-zhun-shu" 平準書 p. 1424.
87. The emperor created a name for the crime: *huan-zhong shi-da-fu bu-wei jun-yong* 寰中士大夫不為君用, see Yang Yifan, *supra*, pp. 385–7, 390–1.
88. See *Guo-li gu-gong bo-wu-yuan* 國立故宮博物院 ed., *Qing-dai wen-zi-yu dang* 清代文字獄檔.
89. In many cases the "partisans" were simply dismissed from government. See, for instance, Tuo Tuo, *supra*, Chapter 319 "Ouyang Xiu zhuan" 歐陽脩傳 pp. 10375–9. The most serious *dang-huo* took place during the Ming Dynasty. It began soon after Emperor Shi-zong 世宗 (r 1506–1521) succeeded his cousin, Emperor Wu-zong 武宗 (r 1506–1521). One day, more than 220 officials from various departments of the central government knelt in front of the imperial audience hall and cried against the emperor's intention to honour his father as an emperor. He ordered eighty-six of them to be suspended from office, 134 imprisoned pending trial, and many beaten straight away in the court, resulting in sixteen deaths. Thereafter, many intellectuals formed a party known as *Dong-lin dang* 東林黨 opposing many government policies. Many of its members were persecuted but it persisted for more than a century. After the establishment of the Qing, its members resisted the Manchu rule and were massacred under the literary inquisition.
90. See Kungang, *supra*, Chapter 389 "Li-bu, xue-xiao, xun-shi gui-tiao" 禮部學校訓士規條 leaves 4b–8b (pp. 10229–31).
91. There was a debate about whether the feudal system should be abolished, and there were even-handed descriptions of the emperor's achievements and his faults and quotations of his proclamations intended to indoctrinate the people about a new mindset and behaviour in a unified country. See Sima Qian, *supra*, Chapter 6 "Qin-shi-huang ben-ji" pp. 235–63.
92. See Ban Gu, *supra*, Chapter 6 "Wu-di ji" 武帝紀.
93. See ibid., Chapter 24 "Shi-huo-zhi" 食貨志 pp. 1141–2.
94. Liu Baonan, *supra*, Chapter 16 "Ji-shi" 季氏 p. 352.
95. Ban Gu, *supra*, Chapter 7 "Zhao-di ji" 昭帝紀 pp. 223–4. Huan Kuan, *supra*.
96. Many of the orders of Emperor Gao-zong 高宗 and chief minister Qin Hui 秦檜, the architects of the appeasement policies, were collected together as laws. See Tuo Tuo, *supra*, Chapter 199 "Xing-fa-zhi yi" 刑法志一 p. 4965. For economic measures, see ibid., Chapters 173–86 "Shi-huo-zhi" 食貨志.
97. *Guo-zhi da-shi zai-si yu-rong* 國之大事在祀與戎 See Yang Bojun, *Chu-qiu Zuo-zhuan zhu*, "Cheng-gong shi-sannian" 成公十三年 p. 861.
98. In his words, "Those who head a state or a family should worry not about scarcity of resources but about inequitable distribution; not about poverty but about people not at peace with what they have." See Liu Baonan, *supra*, Chapter 16, "Ji-shi" 季氏 p. 352.
99. Liu Bang, the founder of the Han Dynasty, prohibited merchants from wearing silk and riding in carriages, and imposed heavy taxes on them. Later laws banned them and their descendants from taking government offices and owning land, and imposed on them numerous types of taxes and levies. In addition, governments of

later periods instituted various measures to prevent merchants from certain trades and the practice of hoarding and price manipulation. But such measures were never seriously enforced to begin with and many were soon shelved. By the time of Emperor Wu, Dong Zhongshu already pointed out that, though the laws were harsh, the merchants continued to prosper, lived in outrageous extravagance and exercised great influence on the government. See Sima Qian, *supra*, Chapter 30 "Ping-zhun-shu" 平準書 pp. 1418, 1422–3; Ban Gu, *supra*, Chapter 24 "Shi-huo zhi" 食貨志" pp. 1132–4, 1142, 1144, 1153, 1165–6, 1176, 1186.

100. For economic laws implemented by government offices, see Sima Qian, *supra*, Chapter 30 "Ping-zhun-shu" and the "Shi-huo-zhi" 食貨志 in the official histories of the other major dynasties.
101. See Zhangsun Wuji, *supra*, pp. 484–5.
102. See ibid., pp. 241–2. The Qing code made this rule more explicit. See Kungang 崑岡 et al., eds, *Qin-ding da-Qing hui-dian shi-li* 欽定大清會典事例, Chapter 753 "Hu-bu hu-lü hu-yi bei-you si-shan-yong cai" 戶部戶律戶役卑幼私擅用財 pp. 17b–18.
103. This practice started in the early Han, see Sima Qian, *supra*, Chapter 30 "Ping-zhun-shu" pp. 1418, 1422–3. It continued largely throughout the later dynasties.
104. See Sima Qian, *supra*, Chapter 6 "Qin-shi-huang ben-ji".
105. See Zhangsun Wuji, *supra*, pp. 12–14. The same provisions occurred in slightly different language in the criminal codes of the subsequent dynasties.
106. The punishment for a crime committed by a family junior or inferior against a family senior or superior was heavier than that for the same crime committed by a family senior or superior against a family junior or inferior. For instances, see ibid., pp. 401–7, 410–16.
107. For a collection of some of the more famous family and clan rules see Xu Zi 徐梓 ed. *Jia-xun – fu zu de ding-ning* 家訓- 父祖的叮嚀.
108. See Tuo Tuo, Chapter 314 "Fan Zhongyan" 范仲淹 p. 10276, "Fan Chunren" 范純仁 p. 10293.
109. See ibid., *supra*, Chapter 340 "Lü Dafang" 吕大防 p. 20844.
110. Yinzhen 胤禎, *Sheng-yu guang-xun* 聖諭廣訓 (1724). For a complete version of the sixteen admonitions and annotations, and imperial orders for regular public readings see Kun-gang, *supra*, Chapter 397 "Li-bu feng-jiao jiang-yue yi" 禮部風教講約一 1–32b (pp. 10332–47)
111. Liu Baonan, *supra*, Chapter 13 "Zilu" 子路 p. 287.
112. For a concise discussion of this system, see Zhang Weiren 張偉仁, *Mo-jing– fa-xue jiao-yu lun-wen ji*" 磨鏡—法學教育論文集 Chapter 1 "Qing-dai de fa-lü jiao-yu" 清代的法律教育 pp. 1–93.
113. See Ren Jiyu 任繼愈, *Zhong-guo dao-jiao-shi* 中國道教史.
114. See Tang Yongtong 湯用彤, *Han Wei liang-Jin Nan-Bei-chao fo jiao shi* 漢魏兩晉南北朝佛教史.
115. As mentioned earlier, ordainment of Buddhist and Daoist monks and nuns had to be authorised by local officials in charge of religious affairs. In later dynasties, the control was increasingly tightened. In the Qing, the number of religious temples and the number of monks and nuns of each temple were prescribed by law, every aspect of their lives was strictly regulated, and violations were severely punished. See Kun-gang, *supra*, Chapter 501, "Li-bu fang-ji seng-dao, la-ma jin-li, zheng-yi zhen-ren shi-li" 禮部方伎僧道喇嘛禁例正一真人事例 1b–31 (pp. 11735–50).
116. See Shi Yinshun釋印順, *Zhong-guo chan-zong shi* 中國禪宗史.

117. See Fang Xuanling 房玄齡 et al., *supra*, Chapter 30 "Xing-fa-zhi" 刑法志 p. 923; Xiao Zixian 蕭子顯, *Nan-Qi-shu*, 南齊書 Chapter 28 "Cai Zusi lie-zhuan" 崔祖思列傳 p. 519.
118. See Chen Shou 陳壽, *San-guo zhi* 三國志 Chapter 21 "Wei-shu Wei Ji lie-zhuan" 魏書魏覬列傳 p. 611. In the Yuan Dynasty, which had a rather different bureaucracy, this post was not established.
119. See Zhang Weiren, *supra*.
120. The work is also known as *Zhou-li* 周禮. See Zheng Yuan 鄭元, Jia Gongyan 賈公彥, *Zhou-li zhu-shu* 周禮注疏; Sun Yirang 孫貽讓, *Zhou-li zheng-yi* 周禮正義.
121. Most major dynasties compiled such laws in the form of compendiums known as *hui-dian* 會典 or *hui-yao* 會要. For instance, *Tang liu-dian* 唐六典, *Song hui-yao* 宋會要 and *Qing hui-dian* 清會典. For some examples of such compilations see Zhang Weiren 張偉仁 *Zhong-guo fa-zhi-shi shu-mu* 中國法制史書目 vol. 1 pp. 577–99.
122. See Kungang, *Da Qing hui-dian* 大清會典.
123. For the titles of some important compilations of these laws and brief introductions to each title see Zhang Weiren, *supra*, *Zhong-guo fa-zhi-shi shu-mu*, vol. 1, pp. 56–90.
124. See Wang Huizu 汪輝祖, *Xue-zhi yi-shuo* 學治臆說 vol. 2, p. 23.
125. Ban Gu, *supra*, Chapter 5 "Jing-di ji" 景帝紀 p. 148, Chapter 23 "Xing-fa zhi" p. 1106.
126. See Liu Xu, *supra*, Chapter 50, p. 2136.
127. See Zhang Tingyu 張廷玉 et al., *Ming-shi* 明史 Chapter 93 "Xing-fa-zhi" 刑法志 p. 2283.
128. See He Xiu 何休, *Chun-qiu Gongyang zhu-shu* 春秋公羊註疏 Chapter 3 "Lu Yin-gong shi-yi nian" 魯隱公十一年 leaves 16b–17b (pp. 41–2), Chapter 6 "Lu Zhuang-gong si nian" 魯莊公四年 leaves 10b–13b (pp. 76–8), Chapter 7 "Lu Zhuang-gong jiu nian" 魯莊公九年 leaves 5a–6a (p. 57), Chapter 25 "Lu Ding-gong si nian" 魯定公四年 leaves 14b–16b (pp. 320–1).
129. During the reign of Han Zhang-di 漢章帝 (76–88) this practice was sanctioned by the emperor and a suggestion was made to turn it into a law called *qing-wu fa* (輕侮法 law against insult) but that suggestion was dismissed. See Fan Ye, *supra*, Chapter 44 "Zhang Min lie-zhuan" 張敏列傳 pp. 1502–4.
130. See Chen Shou, *supra*, Chapter 2 "Wei Wen-di ji" 魏文帝紀 p. 82.
131. See Liu Xu, *supra*, Chapter 190b "Wen-yuan zhong, Chen Ziang" 文苑中, 陳子昂 p. 5024.
132. Liu Zongyuan 柳宗元, *Liu Zongyuan ji* 柳宗元集 Chapter 4 "Bo fu-chou-yi" 駁復讎議 pp. 102–5.
133. Liu Xu, *supra*, Chapter 50 "Xing-fa-zhi" 刑法志 pp. 2153–4.
134. See *Shui-hu-di Qin-mu zhu-jian zheng-li xiao-zu* 睡虎地秦墓竹簡整理小組, ed., *Shui-hu-di Qin-mu zhu-jian* 睡虎地秦墓竹簡 "Qin-lü shi-ba zhong" 秦律十八種 pp. 316, 340–1, 351–2.
135. See Sima Qian, *supra*, Chapter 6 "Qin Shi-huang ben-ji) pp. 253, 256, 262.
136. Ibid., pp. 255, 258.
137. See Liu Xu, *supra*, Chapter 50 "Xing-fa zhi" 刑法志 p. 2133.
138. See Kun-gang, *supra*.
139. See *Jiang-xi an-cha-si* 江西按察司 ed., *Xi-jiang zheng-yao* 西江政要.
140. See Zhangsun Wuji, *supra*, pp. 2, 26.
141. See Zhangsun Wuji, *supra*; Dou Yi 竇儀 et al., eds *Song xing-tong* 宋刑統; *Ming lü ji-jie fu-li* 明律集解附例 (1906); *Da Qing lü-li* 大清律例.
142. See Kong Yingda, *supra*, Chapter 19 "Lü-xing" 呂刑 leaves 27a–30b (pp. 301–2).

143. See Zhangsun Wuji, *supra*, p. 36, Chapter 6 "Ming-li, duan-zui wu-zheng-tiao" 名例斷罪無正條 p. 134.
144. See Ban Gu, *supra*, Chapter 56 "Dong Zhongshu zhuan" 董仲書傳 p. 2525. For examples of some cases Dong decided, see Cheng Shude 程樹德, *Jiu-chao lü-kao* 九朝律考 vol. 1, Chapter 7 "Chun-qiu jue-yu kao" 春秋決獄考 pp. 197–212.
145. See Fang Xuanling, *supra*, Chapter 30 "Xing-fa-zhi" 刑法志 pp. 928–31.
146. See ibid., p. 935; ibid., Chapter 46 "Liu Song lie-zhuan" 劉頌列傳 p. 1302.
147. Ibid., Chapter 30 "Xing-fa-zhi" pp. 933–5
148. Ibid., pp. 935–8.
149. Ibid., pp. 938–9.
150. In the eighteenth and nineteenth centuries, the Qing Empire, about a third larger than the United States today, was divided into over a thousand basic geographical units. A typical unit, with a population up to a few hundred thousand people, had only a magistrate assisted by a regular staff of about a hundred, including subordinate officials, clerks and runners or policemen. The central government had some twenty departments, each with fewer than ten high officials and scores of subordinates and clerks. The governments of other periods were of more or less the same size.
151. Tuo Tuo, *supra*, Chapter 199 "Xing-fa-zhi yi" 刑法志一 pp. 4969–70.
152. See Liu Xu, *supra*, Chapter 50 "Xing-fa-zhi" 刑法志 pp. 2139–40.
153. Tuo Tuo, *supra*, Chapter 201 "Xing-fa-zhi san" 刑法志三 pp. 5006–7; Chapter 330 "Xu Zun" 許遵 pp. 10627–8.
154. See Ban Gu, *supra*, Chapter 23 "Xing-fa-zhi san" p. 1101; Tuo Tuo, *supra*, Chapter 199 "Xing-fa-zhi yi" 刑法志一 pp. 4968, 4970, Chapter 200 "Xing-fa-zhi er" 刑法志二 p. 4996.
155. For a brief discussion of the rise of clerks and private secretaries see Zhang Weiren, "*Mo-jing – fa-xue jiao-yu lun-wen ji*" pp. 1–85.
156. See Ban Gu, *supra*, Chapter 23 "Xing-fa-zhi san" p. 1101; Liu Xu, *supra*, Chapter 50 "Xing-fa zhi san" pp. 2134–5, 2146–7; Tuo Tuo, *supra*, Chapter 200 "Xing-fa-zhi er" 刑法志二 p. 4994.
157. See Fan Ye, *supra*, Chapter 77 "Ku-li-zhuan Dong Xuan" 酷吏傳董宣 pp. 2489–90.
158. See Tuo Tuo, *supra*, Chapter 200 "Xing-fa-zhi er" pp. 4990–1.
159. Ban Gu, *supra*, Chapter23 "Xing-fa-zhi" p. 1101; Liu Xu, *supra*, Chapter 50 "Xing-fa zhi" p. 2140.
160. The principles recorded in *Shang-shu* 尚書 read: *Zui yi wei qing* (罪疑惟輕 when there is doubt about the seriousness of a person's crime, he should be given a lighter punishment) and *yu-qi sha bu-gu ning-shi bu-jing* (與其殺不辜寧失不經 rather than executing an innocent person, it is less wrong to free a guilty one). See Kong Yingda, *supra*, Chapter 4 "Da Yu mo" 大禹謨 leaves 7a–7b (p. 55).
161. The provision was against a judge who wrongfully *shi ru* (失入convicting an innocent person or giving a criminal a sentence more severe than it should be) or *shi-chu* (失出 letting a criminal go free or giving him a sentence lighter than it should be). In the case of *shi ru* the judge was to receive the full punishment he gave the innocent person or a punishment three degrees less severe than the punishment he gave the criminal. In the case of *shi chu* the judge was to receive the full punishment against the criminal he wrongly freed or a punishment three degrees less than the punishment he gave the criminal. See Zhangsun Wuji, *supra*, "Guan-si chu ru ren zui" 官司出入人罪 pp. 562–7.
162. See a memo of Chen Ziang 陳子昂 in Liu Xu, *supra*, Chapter 50 "Xing-fa-zhi" pp. 2176–7.

163. See Wei Zheng 魏徵, *Sui-shu* 隋書 Chapter 25 "Xing-fa-zhi" 刑法志 p. 713; Zhang Tingyu 張廷玉, *Ming-shi* 明史 Chapter 95 "Xing-fa-zhi san" 刑法志三 pp. 2329–30.
164. See Liu Xu, *supra*, Chapter 50 "Xing-fa zhi" p. 2139.
165. For a brief account of this procedure see Zhao Erxun 趙爾巽, et al., *Qing-shi gao* 清史稿 Chapter 144 "Xing-fa-zhi san" 刑法志三 pp. 4206–11.
166. See ibid., p. 4212.
167. See Zheng Yuan 鄭元, Jia Gongyan 賈公彥, *Zhou-li zhu-shu* 周禮注疏 Chapter 36, leaf 3a.
168. See Shen Jiaben 沈家本, *Shen Jiyi xian-sheng yi-shu jia-bian* 沈寄簃先生遺書甲編 "Xu-ni si-zui gai-wei liu tu zhe" 虛擬死罪改為流徒摺 vol. 2, pp. 882–3.
169. See ibid., "She kao" 赦考 vol. 1, pp. 230–330; Chen Menglei 陳夢雷 ed., *Gu-jin tu-shu ji-cheng* 古今圖書集成 vol. 165 "She you bu" 赦宥部 pp. 1844–52, 1981–3; Tuo Tuo, *supra*, Chapter 201 "Xing-fa-zhi san" p. 5028.
170. See Shen Jiaben, *supra*, "She kao – lun she" 赦考 – 論赦 vol. 1, pp. 336–51.
171. Liu Baonan, *supra*, Chapter 13 "Zilu" 子路 p. 280.
172. See Ban Gu, *supra*, Chapter 50 "Xing-fa zhi" p. 1102.
173. For remnants of some of the pre-Tang laws see Cheng Shude, *supra* and Yang Honglie 楊鴻烈, *Zhong-guo fa-lü fa-da shi* 中國法律發達史.
174. Zhangsun Wuji, *supra*, pp. 16–32, 80–6, 101–5, 123–30 .
175. Ibid., pp. 441–2, 447.
176. Ibid., p. 439.
177. Ibid., pp. 444–5.
178. Ibid., p. 130.
179. Ibid., p. 551.
180. Ibid., p. 553.
181. Ibid., p. 555.
182. Ibid., p. 551.
183. Ibid., p. 552.
184. Ibid., p. 550.
185. Ibid. pp. 550, 552–3, 570.
186. Ibid., pp. 552–4.
187. Ibid., p. 132.
188. Ibid., p. 561.
189. Ibid., p. 548.
190. Ibid., p. 134
191. Ibid., p. 575.
192. Ibid., p. 568.
193. Ibid., pp. 557–60.
194. Ibid., pp. 561–2.
195. Ibid., pp. 555, 556.
196. Ibid., pp. 562–6.
197. See Kong Yingda, *supra*, Chapter 19 "Lü-xing" 呂刑.
198. See Zheng Yuan, Jia Gongyan, *supra*, Chapter 34 "Qiu-guan da-si-kou" 秋官大司寇 leaves 13a–18a, Chapter 35 "Qiu-guan xiao-si-kou" 秋官小司寇 leaves 1a–9a.
199. See Sima Qian, *supra*, Chapter 68 "Shang-jun lie-zhuan" 商君列傳 p. 2230.
200. Ibid., pp. 69, 72, 130, 236, 237, 241, 257, 258, 262, 267, 268, 327, 328, 333, 365, 366, 372, 409, 410, 411, 413–22, 435–7, 472. Generally, they prescribe unequal treatments to family members of different status – an offence committed by a junior or inferior against a senior or superior is punished more severely than the same offence committed by a senior or superior against a junior or inferior.

201. Qu Tongzu, *Law and Society in Traditional China*, pp. 274–9.
202. For instance, in the case of murdering three innocent persons of the same family and the case of murdering a person and dismembering the corpse, the culprit was to be decapitated and his wife and children exiled to a place 2,000 *li* away. See Zhangsun Wuji, *supra*, p. 332. As another example, if a person raised or taught others to raise *gu* (蠱 poisonous insects or animals) that could cause death or unspeakable pain to a victim, he was to be strangled, and all those who lived with him in the same household, though unaware of the fact, were to be exiled to a place 3,000 *li* away. See ibid., p. 337.
203. Shen Jiaben, "Shan-chu lü-li nei zhong-fa zhe" 刪除律例內重法摺 in Shen Jiaben, *supra*, vol. 2, pp. 880–3.
204. Originally, *san-mu* referred to a particular form of torture pressing the thighs of a victim between three wooden bars. The term came to be used to mean torture of all kinds.
205. See G. W. Keeton, *The Development of Extraterritoriality in China* (New York: Howard Fertig, 1969); Immanuel Hsu, *China's Entrance into the Family of Nations* (Cambridge, MA: Harvard University Press, 1960).
206. In Chinese wen liang gong jian rang 溫良恭簡讓. This was how his disciple Zigong 子貢 described him. See Liu Baonan, *supra*, Chapter 1, "Xue-er" 學而, p. 14.
207. Kong Yingda 孔穎達, *Shang-shu zhu-shu* 尚書注疏 Chapter 29 "Lü-xing" 呂刑 leaf 30b.

Bibliography

Ban Gu 班固, *Bai-hu tong-yi* 白虎通義 (Yi-wen ying-shu-guan 藝文印書館, Taipei, 1970).

Ban Gu 班固, *Han-shu* 漢書 collected in *Er-shi-si shi* 二十四史 vol. 1 (Zhong-hua shu-ju 中華書局, Beijing, 1997).

Bi Yuan畢沅, *Lü-shi chun-qiu xin jiao-zheng* 呂氏春秋新校正 collected in *Xin-bian zhu-zi ji-cheng* 新編諸子集成 vol. 7 (Shi-jie shu-ju 世界書局, Taipei, 1978).

Chen Menglei 陳夢雷 ed., *Gu-jin tu-shu ji-cheng* 古今圖書集成 vols 75–6 "Xiang-xing-dian" 祥刑典 (Ding-wen shu-ju 鼎文書局, Taipei, 1976).

Chen Qiyou 陳奇猷, *Lü-shi chun-qiu jiao-shi* 呂氏春秋校釋 (Hua-zheng shu-ju 華正書局, Taipei, 1985).

Chen Shou 陳壽, *San-guo zhi* 三國志 collected in *Er-shi-si shi* 二十四史 vol. 3 (Zhong-hua shu-ju中華書局, Beijing, 1997).

Cheng Hao 程顥 and Cheng Yi 程頤, *Er Cheng Quan-shu* "Yi-shu" 二程 全書 "遺書" (Taiwan Shang-wu yin-shu-guan 台灣商務印書館, Taipei, 1983).

Cheng Shude 程樹德, *Jiu-chao lü-kao* 九朝律考 (Taiwan shang-wu yin-shu-guan 台灣商務印書館, Taipei, 1965).

Da Qing lü-li 大清律例 (Tian-jin gu-ji chu-ban-she 天津古籍出版社 Tianjin, 1993).

Dai Wang 戴望, *Guanzi jiao-zheng* 管子校正 collected in *Xin-bian zhu-zi ji-cheng* 新編諸子集成 vol. 5 (Shi-jie shu-ju 世界書局, Taipei, 1978).

Dou Yi 竇儀 et al., ed. *Song xing-tong* 宋刑統 (Zhong-hua shu-ju 中華書局 Beijing, 1984).

Du Guangting 杜光庭, *Li-dai chong-dao-ji* 歷代崇道記 (Shang-wu yin-shu-guan 商務印書館, Shanghai, 1923–1926).

Dubs, Homer H., *The Works of Hsuntze* (Arthur Probsthain, London, 1928).

Duyvendak, J. J. L., *The Book of Lord Shang* (University of Chicago Press, Chicago, 1963).

Fan Ye 范曄, *Hou-Han-shu* 後漢書 collected in *Er-shi-si shi* 二十四史 v. 3 (Zhong-hua shu-ju 中華書局, Beijing, 1997).

Fang Shouchu 方授楚, *Mo-xue yuan-liu* 墨學源流 (Taiwan zhong-hua shu-ju 臺灣中華書局, Taipei, 1979).

Fang Xuanling 房玄齡 et al., *Jin-shu* 晉書 collected in *Er-shi-si shi* 二十四史 vol. 4 (Zhong-hua shu-ju 中華書局, Beijing, 1997).

Feng Youlan 馮友蘭, *Zhong-guo zhe-xue-shi* 中國哲學史 (Taiwan Shang-wu yin-shu-guan 臺灣商務印書館, Taipei, 1994).

Gao Shiqi 高士奇, *Zuo-zhuan ji-shi ben-mo* 左傳紀事本末 (Li-ren shu-ju 里仁書局, Taipei, 1980).

Gao You 高誘, *Huai-nan-zi zhu* 淮南子注 collected in *Xin-bian zhu-zi ji-cheng* 新編諸子集成 v. 7 (Shi-jie shu-ju 世界書局, Taipei, 1978).

Guo Jingyun 郭靜云, *Xia Shang Zhou – Cong Shen-hua dao shi-shi* 夏商周— 從神話到史實 (Shanghai gu-ji chu-ban-she 上海古籍出版社, Shanghai, 2013).

Guo-li gu-gong bo-wu-yuan 國立故宮博物院 ed., *Qing-dai wen-zi-yu dang* 清代文字獄檔 collected in *Zhong-hua wen*-shi cong-shu di shi-er ji 中華文史叢書第十二輯 (Taiwan hua-wen-shu-ju 台灣華文書局, Taipei 台北, undated).

Guo Moruo 郭沫若 *Shi pi-pan shu* 十批判書 (Qun-yi chu-ban-she 群益出版社, Taipei, 1948).

Guo Qingfan 郭慶藩, *Zhuangzi ji-shi* 莊子集釋 collected in *Xin-bian zhu-zi ji-cheng* 新編諸子集成 vol. 7 (Shi-jie shu-ju 世界書局, Taipei, 1978).

Han Yu 韓愈, *Han Changli wen-ji* 韓昌黎文集 (Tai-bei shi-jie shu-ju 台北世界書局, 1960).

He Qimin 何啟民, *Gongsun Long yu Gongsun-long-zi* 公孫龍與公孫龍子 (Xue-sheng shu-ju 學生書局, Taipei, 1988).

Huan Kuan 桓寬, *Yan-tie lun* 鹽鐵論 collected in *Xin-bian zhu-zi ji-cheng* 新編諸子集成 vol. 2. (Shi-jie shu-ju 世界書局, Taipei, 1978).

Huang Jinxin 黃進興, *You-ru sheng-yu* 優入聖域 (Yun-chen 允晨, Taipei, 1994).

Hui Dong 惠棟, ed. *Tai-shang gan-ying pian* 太上感應篇 (1866).

Jiang-xi an-cha-si 江西按察司 ed, *Xi-jiang zheng-yao* 西江政要 (1875–1908).

Jiao Xun 焦循 Jiao Hu 焦琥, *Mengzi Zheng-yi* 孟子正義 collected in *Xin-bian zhu-zi ji-cheng* 新編諸子集成 vol. 1 (Shi-jie shu-ju 世界書局, Taipei, 1978).

Kong Yingda 孔穎達, *Shang-shu zhu-shu* 尚書注疏 collected in *Shi-san jing zhu-shu* 十三經注疏 (Yi-wen yin-shu-guan 藝文印書館, Taipei, 1965).

Kungang 崑岡 et al., ed. *Qin-ding da-Qing hui-dian shi-li* 欽定大清會典事例 (Qi-wen chu-ban-she 啟文出版社, Taipei, 1963).

Lau, D. C., *Tao Te Ching* (Penguin Books, London, 1963).

Lau, D. C., *Mencius* (Penguin Books, London, 1970).

Lau, D. C., *The Analects* (Penguin Books, London, 1979).

Legge, James, *The Chinese Classics* (Hong Kong University Press, Hong Kong, 1960).

Legge, James, *The Tao Teh King* (Ch'eng-wen Publishing Co., Taipei, 1969).

Legge, James, *The Writings of Chauang-tzu* (Ace Books, New York, 1971).

Li Junming 李均明：*Qin Han jian-du wen-shu fen-lei ji jie* 秦漢簡牘文書分類輯解 (Beijing Wen-wu chu-ban-she 北京文物出版社, Beijing, 2009).

Li Yanshou 李延壽 *Bei-shi*北史 collected in *Er-shi-si shi* 二十四史 vols 8–9 (Zhong-hua shu-ju 中華書局, Beijing, 1997).

Lin Qingzhang 林慶彰, Li Xueqin 李學勤, et al, *Xin chu-tu wen-xian yu xian Qin si-xiang chong-gou* 新出土文獻與先秦思想重構 (Taiwan Shu-fang, 台灣書房, Taipei, 2007).

Lin Shu 林曙, *Chun-qiu fan-lu zhu* 春秋繁露注 (Tai-bei shi-jie shu-ju 台北世界書局, Taipei, 1958).

Liu Baonan 劉寶楠, *Lun-yu Zheng-yi* 論語正義 collected in *Xin-bian zhu-zi ji-cheng* 新編諸子集成 vol. 1 (Shi-jie shu-ju 世界書局, Taipei, 1978).

Liu Sanwu 劉三吾, *Mengzi jie-wen* 孟子節文 collected in Beijing tu-shu-guan gu-ji zhen-ben cong-kan 北京圖書館古籍珍本叢刊 (Shu-mu wen-xian chu-ban she 書目文獻出版社, Beijing, 1988).

Liu Xiang 劉向, *Zhan-guo ce* 戰國策 (Li-ren shu-ju 里仁書局, Taipei, 1982).

Liu Xu 劉煦 et al., *Jiu-Tang-shu* 舊唐書 collected in *Er-shi-si shi* 二十四史 vols 11–12 (Zhong-hua shu-ju 中華書局, Beijing, 1997).

Liu Zongyuan 柳宗元, *Liu Zongyuan ji*柳宗元集 (Zhong-hua shu-ju 北京中華書局, Beijing, 1979).

Lu Xinyuan 陸心源, *Tang-wen shi-yi* 唐文拾遺 v.1 "Xian Lao hou Shi zhao" 先老後釋詔 (Wen-hai chu-ban-she 文海出版社, Nanjing, 1962).

Luo Genze 羅根澤, *Guanzi tan-yuan* 管子探源 (Li-ren shu-ju 里仁書局, Taipei, 1981).

Ma Qichang 馬其昶, *Han Changli wen-ji jiao-zhu* 韓昌黎文集校注 (Shi-jie shu-ju 世界書局, Taipei, 1960).

Mei, Yi-pao, *The Works of Motze* (Confucius Publishing Co., Taipei, 1929).

Ming-lü ji-jie fu-li 明律集解附例 (Cheng-wen chu-ban-she 成文出版社, Taipei, 1969).

Mou Zongsan 牟宗三, *Ming-jia yu Xunzi* 名家與荀子 (Xue-sheng shu-ju 學生書局, Taipei, 1982).

Qing Shi-zong 清世宗, *Da-yi jue-mi-lu* 大義覺迷錄 (Jing-hua chu-ban-she 京華出版社, Beijing, 2001).

Qu Tongzu 瞿同祖, *Law and Society in Traditional China* (Mouton, The Hague, 1965).

Qu Tongzu, *Zhong-guo fa-lü yu zhong-guo she-hui* 中國法律與中國社會 (Li-ren shu-ju 里仁書局, Taipei, 1982).

Qu Wanli 屈萬里, *Shi-jing quan-shi* 詩經詮釋 (Lian-jing chu-ban-she 聯經出版社, Taipei, 1983).

Ren Jiyu 任繼愈, *Zhong-guo dao-jiao-shi* 中國道教史 (Taipei Gui-guan 台北桂冠, Taipei, 1991).

Sa Mengwu 薩孟武, *Zhong-guo she-hui zheng-zhi shi* 中國社會政治史 (San-min shu-ju 三民書局, Taipei, 2003).

Shen Jiaben 沈家本, *Shen Jiyi xian-sheng yi-shu jia-bian* 沈寄簃先生遺書甲編 (Wen-hai chu-ban-she 文海出版社, Taipei, 1964).

Shi Naian 施耐庵, *Shui-hu-zhuan* 水滸傳 (Zhong-hua shu-ju 中華書局, Beijing, 1990).

Shi Yinshun 釋印順, *Zhong-guo chan-zong shi* 中國禪宗史 (Zheng-wen chu-ban-she 正聞出版社, Taipei, 1989).

Shui-hu-di Qin-mu zhu-jian zheng-li xiao-zu 睡虎地秦墓竹簡整理小組, ed., *Shui-hu-di Qin-mu zhu-jian* 睡虎地秦墓竹簡 (Li-ren shu-ju 里仁書局, Taipei, 1981).

Sima Guang 司馬光, *Zi-zhi tong-jian* 資治通鑑 (Hua-shi chu-ban-she 華世出版社, Taipei, 1987).

Sima Qian 司馬遷, *Shi-ji* 史記 collected in *Er-shi-si shi* 二十四史 vol. 1 (Zhong-hua shu-ju 中華書局, Beijing, 1997).

Sun Xidan 孫希旦, *Li-ji ji-jie* 禮記集解 (Zhong-hua shu-ju 中華書局, Beijing, 1995).

Sun Yi-rang 孫詒讓, *Mo-zi jian-gu* 墨子閒詁 collected in *Xin-bian zhu-zi ji-cheng* 新編諸子集成 vol. 6 (Shi-jie shu-ju 世界書局, Taipei, 1978).

Sun Zhongyuan 孫中原, *Mo-xue tong-lun* 墨學通論 (Liaoning Jiao-yu chu-ban-she 遼寧教育出版社, Shenyang, 1995).

Tang Yongtong 湯用彤, *Han Wei liang Jin Nan Bei chao fo jiao shi* 漢魏兩晉南北朝佛教史 (Beijing da-xue chu-ban-she 北京大學出版社, Beijing, 1997).

Tuo Tuo 脫脫, et al., *Song-shi* 宋史 collected in *Er-shi-si shi* 二十四史 vol. 16 (Zhong-hua shu-ju 中華書局, Beijing, 1997).

Wang Huizu 汪輝祖, *Xue-zhi yi-shuo* 學治臆說 (Qing publication, undated).

Wang Pinzhen 王聘珍, *Da Dai li-ji jie-gu* 大戴禮記解詁 (Shi-jie shu-ju 世界書局, Taipei, 1974).

Wang Wenliang 王文亮, *Zhong-guo sheng-ren lun* 中國聖人論 (Zhong-guo she-hui-ke-xue chu-ban-she 中國社會科學出版社, Beijing, 1993).

Wang Xianqian 王先謙, *Xuzi Ji-jie* 荀子集解 collected in *Xin-bian zhu-zi ji-cheng* 新編諸子集成 vol. 2 (Shi-jie shu-ju 世界書局, Taipei, 1978).

Wang Xianshen 王先慎, *Han-fei-zi ji-jie* 韓非子集解 collected in *Xin-bian zhu-zi ji-cheng* 新編諸子集成 vol. 5 (Shi-jie shu-ju 世界書局, Taipei, 1978).

Watson, Burton, *Han Fei Tzu, Basic Writings* (Columbia University Press, New York, 1964).

Watson, Burton, *The Complete Works of Chuang Tzu* (Columbia University Press, New York, 1968).

Wei Yuan 魏源, *Laozi ben-yi* 老子本義 collected in *Xin-bian zhu-zi ji-cheng* 新編諸子集成 vol. 3 (Shi-jie shu-ju 世界書局, Taipei, 1978).

Wei Zheng 魏徵, *Sui-shu* 隋書 collected in *Er-shi-si shi* 二十四史 vol. 7 (Zhong-hua shu-ju 中華書局, Beijing, 1997).

Wu, John C. H., *Tao The ching* (Shambhala, Boston, 1989).

Wu Zeyu 吳則虞 *Yanzi chun-qiu ji-shi* 晏子春秋集釋 (Ding-wen shu-ju 鼎文書局, Taipei, 1972).

Xiao Zixian 蕭子顯, *Nan-Qi-shu*, 南齊書 collected in *Er-shi-si shi* 二十四史 v. 8 (Zhong-hua shu-ju 中華書局, Beijing, 1997).

Xu Fuguan 徐復觀, *Liang-Han si-xiang-shi* 兩漢思想史 (Xue-sheng shu-ju 學生書局, Taipei, 1978).

Xu Zi 徐梓 ed., *Jia-xun – fu zu de ding-ning* 家訓- 父祖的叮嚀 (Zhong-yang min-zu da-xue chu-ban-she 中央民族大學出版社, Beijing, 1996).

Xue Juzheng 薛居正, *Jiu Wu-dai-shi* 舊五代史 collected in *Er-shi-si shi* 二十四史 vol. 13 (Zhong-hua shu-ju 中華書局, Beijing, 1997).

Xue Yunsheng 薛允升, *Tang-Ming-lü he-bian* 唐明律合編 (Tui-geng-tang 退耕堂 1922).

Yan Wanli 嚴萬里, *Shang-jun-shu xin-jiao-zheng* 商君書新校正 collected in *Xin-bian zhu-zi ji-cheng* 新編諸子集成 vol. 5 (Shi-jie shu-ju 世界書局, Taipei, 1978).

Yan Yuan 顏元, *Yan Xizhai nian-pu* 顏習齋年譜 (Xin-wen-feng 新文豐, Taipei, 1997).

Yan Yuan, *Xi-zhai ji-yu* 習齋記餘 (Shanghai gu-ji 上海古籍, Shanghai, 2010).

Yang Bojun 楊伯峻, *Mengzi yi-zhu* 孟子譯注 (Zhong-hua shu-ju 中華書局, Beijing, 1960).

Yang Bojun 楊伯峻, *Chun-qiu Zuo-zhuan zhu* 春秋左傳注 (Yuan-liu 源流 Taipei, 1982).

Yang Honglie 楊鴻烈, *Zhong-guo fa-lü fa-da shi* 中國法律發達史 (Shang-wu yin-shu-guan 商務印書館, Taipei, 1967).

Yang Yifan 楊一凡, *Ming da-gao yan-jiu* 明大誥研究 (Jiangsu ren-min Chu-ban-she 江蘇人民出版社, Beijing, 1988).

Zhang Bingnan 張秉楠, *Ji-xia gou-chen* 稷下鉤沉 (Shanghai gu-ji chu-ban-she 上海古籍出版社, Shanghai, 1991).

Zhang Tingyu 張廷玉, *Ming-shi* 明史 collected in *Er-shi-si shi* 二十四史 vols 19–20 (Zhong-hua shu-ju 中華書局, Beijing, 1997).

Zhang Weiren 張偉仁 *Zhong-guo fa-zhi-shi shu-mu* 中國法制史書目 (Zhong-yang yan-jiu-yuan 中央研究院, Taipei, 1976).

Zhang Weiren 張偉仁, *Mo-jing– fa-xue jiao-yu lun-wen ji*" 磨鏡 - 法學教育論文集 (Qing-hua da-xue chu-ban-she 清華大學出版社, Beijing, 2012).

Zhang Yuchu 張宇初, et al, *Zheng-tong dao-zang* 正統道藏 (Xin-wen-feng 新文豐, Taipei, 1985).

Zhangsun Wuji 長孫無忌 et al., ed. *Tang-lü shu-yi* 唐律疏議 (Hong-wen-guan chu-ban-she 弘文館出版社, Taipei, 1986).

Zhao Erxun 趙爾巽, et al., *Qing-shi gao* 清史稿 (Zhong-hua shu-ju 中華書局, Beijing, 1997).

Zhao Shanyi 趙善詒, *Xin-xu shu-zheng* 新序疏證 (Hua-dong shi-fan da-xue chu-ban-she 華東師範大學出版社, Shanghai, 1989).

Zheng Yuan 鄭元 and Jia Gongyan 賈公彥, *Zhou-li zhu-shu* 周禮注疏 collected in *Shi-san jing zhu-shu* 十三經注疏 (Yi-wen yin-shu-guan 藝文印書館, Taipei, 1965).

Zhong Zhaopeng 鍾肇鵬, *Chen-wei lun-lüe* 讖緯論略 (Liao-ning jiao-yu chu-ban she 遼寧教育出版社, Shenyang, 1992).

Index

EU Authorised Representative:
Easy Access System Europe Mustamäe tee 50, 10621 Tallinn, Estonia
gpsr.requests@easproject.com

Printed and bound by CPI Group (UK) Ltd, Croydon, CR0 4YY
17/09/2026
02218450-0002